JAPAN'S SOFTWARE FACTORIES

JAPAN'S
SOFTWARE
FACTORIES

A CHALLENGE TO U.S. MANAGEMENT

MICHAEL A. CUSUMANO
Massachusetts Institute of Technology

New York   Oxford
OXFORD UNIVERSITY PRESS
1991

Oxford University Press

Oxford   New York   Toronto
Delhi   Bombay   Calcutta   Madras   Karachi
Petaling Jaya   Singapore   Hong Kong   Tokyo
Nairobi   Dar es Salaam   Cape Town
Melbourne   Auckland

and associated companies in
Berlin   Ibadan

Published by Oxford University Press, Inc.,
200 Madison Avenue, New York, New York 10016

Oxford is a registered trademark of Oxford University Press

Library of Congress Cataloging-in-Publication Data
Cusumano, Michael A., 1954-
Japan's software factories / Michael A. Cusumano.
p.   cm.   Includes bibliographical references.
ISBN 0-19-506216-7
1. Computer software industry—Japan. I. Title.
HD9696.C63J3134 1991   338.4'70053'0952—dc20   90-7287

3 4 5 6 7 8 9

Printed in the United States of America
on acid-free paper

To the pioneers of software
as a technology and as a business

PREFACE

This book is about the efforts of software producers to organize the design and construction of large-scale computer programs utilizing concepts and tools borrowed from more established disciplines but tailored to the needs of software developers. Their persistence has helped move programming as a technology and as a business beyond the art or craft stage and closer to something resembling engineering and factory production. No firm claimed to have completely mastered all kinds of software development, although management commitments to process improvement, the strategic segmentation of software products and programming jobs, careful process analysis and quality control, as well as extensive investment in tools and methods, personnel training, and systematic reusability of program components, have enabled Japanese firms in particular to make this technology less dependent on a small number of highly skilled engineers and to achieve efficiencies across a series of projects rather than building software from scratch for each customer or job order.

The focus of the discussion is on four leading Japanese computer manufacturers—Hitachi, Toshiba, NEC, and Fujitsu—and their attempts to create and operate software factories between the late 1960s and the late 1980s. To understand the context of their efforts, this book also reviews the general evolution of software engineering and initiatives at several U.S. firms, led by System Development Corporation and International Business Machines (IBM), to introduce factory organizations or practices to software production. In addition, a separate chapter examines government and cooperative initiatives in Japan for standardization, research, and development aimed at improving Japanese capabilities in software production technology for immediate as well as future applications.

Too many people and organizations contributed to this book to thank everyone adequately, but I will try. First and foremost, I must thank the companies that provided the sites for case studies and their managers and engineers who allowed me to visit numerous times during 1985–1989, patiently explained what they were doing (the chapter notes list the names, titles, and dates of those interviewed), and generously provided documentary or technical materials. From the Hitachi group, I must cite Shigeru Takahashi (now of Tokyo Engineering University) and Kazuyuki Sakata as well as Kanji Shibata and Yoichi Yokoyama for innumerable comments. From Fujitsu, I must equally thank Tadashi Yoshida, Noritoshi Murakami, and Hiroshi Narafu; from Toshiba, Yoshihiro Matsumoto (now of Kyoto University); from NEC, Hiromu Kaneda, Yukio Mizuno, Kiichi Fujino, and Motoei Azuma (now of Waseda University); from Unisys/System Development Corporation, Jack Munson, Ronald Atchley, and Terry Court (now of GM-Hughes Aircraft); and James Frame, formerly of IBM and ITT Corp.

The Massachusetts Institute of Technology (M.I.T.) Sloan School of Management under the administration of Dean Lester Thurow and Deputy Deans Arnoldo Hax and Glen Urban created a superb environment for research and writing, making it possible to concentrate large amounts of time on this project. I owe a tremendous debt to them as well as M.I.T. students from the Sloan School and the Management of Technology Program, who both taught me much about software development and assisted directly or indirectly in the research. I especially thank David Finnell and Kent Wallgren for their enthusiastic work on the surveys of manager emphases and project performance as part of their master's theses, as well as John Pilat of Data General and Fred George of IBM for their general advice on the technology and managerial problems while participating in my course on Japanese Technology Management. M.I.T. faculty who commented on working papers or drafts and offered insights as well as encouragement include Mel Horwitch, Chris Kemerer, Ed Roberts, Eric von Hippel, Tom Allen, N. Venkatraman, Michael Scott Morton, Don Lessard, Gabriel Bitran, Wanda Orlikowski, and John Henderson from Sloan, as well as Joel Moses from the Department of Electrical Engineering and Computer Science and Charles Sabel from the Department of Political Science. Other current or former students I need to thank include Wendy McKay (formerly of Digital Equipment Corporation), Varghese George, Nitin Nohria (now of Harvard Business School), Wilson Wong, Bob Arfman (of IBM), Jan Kendrick, and Greg Toole.

Several institutions and programs provided funding for trips to Japan. The research for this book began in 1985–1986, while I was a postdoctoral research fellow at the Harvard Business School, which funded an initial two visits. At M.I.T., in addition to the Sloan School, which provided a reduced teaching load for junior faculty, the M.I.T.-Japan Sci-

ence, Technology, and Management Program, directed by Richard Samuels, the Center for Information Systems Research, directed by Jack Rockart, and the Leaders for Manufacturing Program, directed by Kent Bowen, Tom Magnanti, and Steve Graves, helped fund annual visits to Japan during 1986–1989. The Xerox Corporation and William Spencer also provided support and suggestions for student research on government R&D projects in Japan and Europe.

Among the dozens of Japanese and North American companies to whom I am indebted for participating in the surveys and interviews, several managers provided specific comments on working papers and various information. Most especially, I need to cite Robert Martin and Reva Leung of Bell Communications Research, Jan Norton of AT&T, and Mark Eaton of the Microelectronics and Computer Corporation. Lew Clapp from International Computer Research and Judith Clapp from MITRE, as well as several dozen managers and engineers from Bell Northern Research, AT&T, General Electric, IBM, and Digital Equipment Corporation, in addition to Hitachi, Fujitsu, NEC, Toshiba, NTT, and Mitsubishi Electric, provided helpful data and challenging questions.

I have also presented versions of this research in several forums and need to thank, at M.I.T., participants in the Industrial Relations Seminar, the Strategy and International Management Seminar, the Management of Technology Seminar, the Workshop on Management Information Systems, my course on Japanese Technology Management, and the Management of Research, Development, and Technology-Based Innovation Summer Program, as well as members of the 1988 Conference on Business Strategy and Technological Innovation (especially David Garvin from the Harvard Business School and Ikuyo Kaneko from Hitotsubashi University), sponsored by the Mitsubishi Bank Foundation. Finally, I would like to acknowledge Herbert J. Addison, my editor at Oxford University Press, for his useful suggestions and encouragement, and two anonymous reviewers for their critical but inspiring comments.

Cambridge, Mass.   M.A.C.
April 1990

CONTENTS

JAPAN'S SOFTWARE FACTORIES

INTRODUCTION

The Software Challenge

Writing software—instructions required to operate programmable computers, first introduced commercially during the 1950s—has both intrigued and plagued engineers, managers, and customers since the beginning of the computer era. The development process consists of requirements analysis, system design, detailed program design, coding, testing, and installation, as well as redesign or repairs referred to as maintenance. Yet these phases are usually more iterative than sequential, and often unpredictable in time and costs, because the productivity of individual programmers tends to vary enormously and depend on elements difficult for management to control, such as personal talent and experience with particular applications.

Software producers may thus encounter budget and schedule overruns as the rule rather than the exception, especially when attempting to build large complex systems with many components for the first time. The sheer difficulty of software design and programming, exacerbated by a demand for programs rising faster than the supply of software engineers, led to a situation referred to as the "software crisis" as long ago as 1969.[1] Despite years of advances in tools (specialized programs and databases that aid in the production of other software), design and programming techniques, and products themselves, software has remained a most vexing challenge to all concerned, with many problems that plagued pioneers still persisting through the 1980s:

3

Concurrent with the escalation of customers' expectations, both manufacturers and users have come to feel the impact of what has been called the "software crisis." Software is seldom produced on schedule, it seldom meets its original performance goals, it invariably contains "bugs," and it is extremely hard to modify to meet shifting user requirements. . . . While the complexity of the programs which members of the profession are attempting to develop has grown rapidly in the past 15 years, the spectrum of programming languages used has tended to remain stagnant, primarily because of the difficulty and expense of converting existing programs to new languages. The disparity between the increasing complexity of tasks being attempted and the stagnation of the tools used for their solution are prime reasons for what has been called the "software crisis."[2]

In other industries, years of refinements and innovations have made it possible for producers to make and customers to buy a wide range of sophisticated products at low cost. Without modern engineering and factory systems, for example, few people would ride in cars or use computers so frequently. Continuing difficulties in software, however, have led academic researchers and practitioners alike to claim that frustrations are in part misguided: Writing software is and may forever remain more like an art or a craft rather than evolve into a technology suited to the precise descriptions and predictability of traditional scientific, engineering, or manufacturing disciplines.

Indeed, software appears to have characteristics that make conventional engineering or factory operations difficult to introduce—little product or process standardization to support economies of scale, wide variations in project contents and work flows, cumbersome tasks difficult and sometimes counterproductive to divide, de-skill, or automate. What is more, software producers have struggled to contend with constant evolution in product and process technology as well as in customer requirements, often for programs with unique or tailored features.

To manage such a complex technology in such a dynamic industry, many software producers have resorted to a simple solution: They have tried to remain flexible in structure and processes, hiring as many experienced or talented programmers as possible and relying on small, integrated teams—as in job-shop or craft production in other industries. This approach takes advantage of the greater productivity usually associated with experienced personnel, and reduces coordination or communications problems within the project, as well as the need to divide labor and tasks too rigidly.

In fact, job-shop or craft practices have worked well in software and no doubt proved essential in the early days of the industry, when all products seemed new and changing, and when programs remained small, reflecting hardware limitations. But the software market—demand exceeding the supply of skilled programmers and managers, tight budgets and short schedules, customer requirements for unique features as well as low prices and high reliability, long-term maintenance costs surpassing those of new design work, continual increases in the length and complexity of programs as hardware improves—has created huge incentives for managers to reduce skill requirements and systematically recycle key factors of production (methods, tools, procedures, engineers, components) in as many projects as possible. Thus, as the industry has evolved, loosely structured processes and craft organizations have become inadequate to manage software, at least for many producers.[3]

Small teams working independently, no matter how well they perform or what the individuals learn, will fail to help the firm solve problems systematically unless management finds a way to optimize and improve *organizational* skills—not just in one project but across a stream of projects. To accomplish this, however, and still meet the demands of customers, competitors, and the technology itself, requires firms to balance two seemingly contradictory ends: efficiency and flexibility. This book explores how the leading Japanese computer manufacturers have pursued this balance, not simply through the tools and techniques of software engineering, but through their strategic integration and combination with an equally important element: the skillful management of product, process, and organizational development.

The Japanese Challenge

Japanese firms have competed successfully in industries ranging from automobiles and video recorders to machine tools, semiconductor chips, and computer hardware. They have become well known for high levels of productivity and reliability in manufacturing as well as engineering, and for the rising sophistication of designs. Perhaps their most important contributions have been to exceed the efficiency of conventional mass production firms while introducing increasing levels of product variety and continual improvements in products and manufacturing processes.[4]

If Japanese firms were to transfer the same type of skills they have cultivated in other industries to software, which seemed likely only to grow in importance as a technology because of its critical role in so many industries and organizations, users would probably become better off, with improved products at lower prices. The Japanese, however, would then also confront the United States, where Americans have not only dominated in technological invention and innovation for software but, in contrast to many other industries, seemed to retain a daunting lead over all other nations—including the Japanese.[5]

While Japan had little international market presence in software, industry analysts remain divided over where Japanese firms currently stand in the software field. On the one hand, some reports continue to claim the Japanese are years behind the United States and doubt whether the Japanese will ever duplicate their achievements in a technology like computer programming, which is highly dependent on individual creativity and innovation, and where customers and producers have yet to define product or process standards. Competition in overseas markets also requires fluency in local languages and business practices related to computer usage, as well as a surplus of personnel able to serve foreign customers. On the other hand, there are increasing numbers of reports citing high productivity and quality in Japanese software, as well as arguments that Japanese firms have displayed enormous creativity in other areas of engineering and possessed many abilities that should benefit them in computer programming, especially in large projects: attention to detail, effective production management and quality control techniques, good communication and teamwork skills, strong educational foundations in mathematics and science, and receptivity to extensive in-house training and discipline.[6] The material in this book supports three general observations regarding Japanese capabilities in software.

First, the major Japanese computer manufacturers—Fujitsu, NEC, Hitachi, and Toshiba—which also produce most of Japan's basic systems software (operating systems, language compilers, database management systems) and much of its custom applications, explicitly took up the challenge, first suggested in the United States and Europe during the late 1960s, to apply factory concepts to computer programming in order to bring this technology up to the standards of other engineering and manufacturing disciplines (Table I.1). The evidence suggests strongly that at least these firms have made significant progress in managing the *process* of software development and are now at least comparable and possibly superior to U.S. firms in productivity, defect control, and reusability (recycling software designs or code across more than one project).

Second, in *products*, the Japanese seemed comparable to U.S. firms but not particularly threatening in foreign markets. They made large-scale, complex software, such as IBM-compatible operating systems, telecommunications systems, and customized industrial or business applications, including sophisticated real-time process-control software, such as for manufacturing or power-generation plants. They had, however, only begun to invent international standards or build systems that truly pushed the state-of-the-art in software technology. Nor did the Japanese have a surplus of personnel that allowed them to seek many contract programming jobs overseas or develop standardized programs (called *packages*) specifically for foreign markets. In the early 1990s, meeting domestic demand alone remained a struggle, although the larger Japanese firms excelled in tailored applications software, and they were gradually establishing more software operations overseas, primarily to service Japanese hardware customers. It appeared to be this area—custom pro-

Table I.1 Major Japanese Software Factories*

| | | | 1988–1989 | |
Est.	Company	Facility/Organization	Products	Employees
1969	Hitachi	Hitachi Software Works	BS	5000
1976	NEC	Software Strategy Project		
		Fuchu Works	BS	2500
		Mita Works	RT	2500
		Mita Works	App	1500
		Abiko Works	Tel	1500
		Tamagawa Works	Tel	1500
1977	Toshiba	Fuchu Software Factory	RT	2300
1979	Fujitsu	Systems Engineering Group	App	4000
		(Kamata Software Factory		1500)
1983	Fujitsu	Numazu Software Division	BS	3000
		(Numazu Works est. 1974)		
1985	Hitachi	Systems Design Works	App	6000
		(Systems Engineers		4000)
		(Programming Personnel		2000)

*All facilities develop software for mainframes or minicomputers. Employee figures refer to 1988 or 1989 estimates. BS = operating systems, database management systems, language utilities, and related basic software; App = general business applications; RT = industrial real-time control applications; Tel = telecommunications software (switching, transmission).
Source: Company data, site visits, and manager interviews.

gramming and systems engineering—that Japan might exploit for export competition in the future, especially since Japanese firms were paying increasing attention to product functionality and customer responses.

Third, rather than constituting a radical departure from conventional American or European practices, Japanese software factories represented a refinement of approaches to software engineering introduced primarily in the 1960s and 1970s. Indeed, the very concept of the software factory, despite the greater popularity of this label in Japan compared to the United States or Europe, originated in the United States during the 1960s as a metaphor emphasizing the need to standardize and integrate good practices, tools, and techniques, such as reusability.

American firms, led by International Business Machines (IBM), System Development Corporation (SDC), and TRW Inc., pioneered variations of factory approaches during the 1960s and 1970s, even though only SDC adopted the factory label. Japanese firms not only adopted the word *factory*, but also launched long-term efforts to centralize and systematize software production and quality control, primarily to offset acute shortages of experienced programmers and rising demand for large-scale complex programs, especially of the customized variety. As in other industries, the Japanese emphasized process improvement first, rather than product invention, and this corresponded to Japanese strategies in hardware, which allowed U. S. firms to set product standards. It was also true that these Japanese firms, similar to IBM, all had large revenues from hardware sales and needed to produce software to sell their equipment, whatever the costs of new programs. The Japanese, along with IBM and other U. S. firms, thus had long-term incentives and financial resources to invest in the systematic improvement of their software operations. Nevertheless, acting effectively on these incentives required foresight and perseverance, as well as considerable technical, managerial, and organizational skills—which Japanese firms and managers clearly exhibited, in software as in other industries.

Common Elements in the Factory Approach

The Japanese software facilities discussed in this book differed in some respects, reflecting variations in products, competitive strategies, organizational structures, and management styles. Nonetheless, the approaches of Hitachi, Toshiba, NEC, and Fujitsu had far more elements in common than in contrast, as each firm attempted the *strategic management and integration* of activities required in software production, as well as the achievement of *planned economies of scope*—cost reductions or productivity gains that come from developing a series of products within one firm (or facility) more efficiently than building each product from scratch in a separate project. Planned scope economies thus required the deliberate (rather than accidental) sharing of resources across different projects, such as product specifications and designs, executable code, tools, methods, documentation and manuals, test cases, and personnel experience.[7] It appears that scope economies helped firms combine process efficiency with flexibility, allowing them to deliver seemingly unique or tailored products with higher levels of productivity than if they had not shared resources among multiple projects.

Japanese managers did not adopt factory models and pursue scope economies simply out of faith. Detailed studies concluded that as much as 90 percent of the programs they developed in any given year, especially in business applications, appeared similar to work they had done in the past, with designs of product components falling into a limited number of patterns. Such observations convinced managers of the possibility for greater efficiencies, in scope if not in scale, and set an agenda for process improvement. Companies subsequently established facilities focused on similar products, collected productivity and quality data, standardized tools and techniques, and instituted appropriate goals and controls. Managers found ways to leverage employee skills, systematically reuse components, and incrementally improve process technology and standards as well as products. As the factory discussions demonstrate, Japanese firms managed in this way not simply one or two special projects for a few years. They established permanent software facilities and R&D efforts as well as emphasized several common elements in managing across a series of projects (Table I.2):

Commitment to Process Improvement: The managers who established software factories all believed they could structure and improve software operations and achieve higher, or more predictable, levels of productivity, quality, and scheduling control. They also acted on this conviction, demonstrating a long-term commitment to process improvement—not as a brief experiment but as a fundamental strategy for offsetting shortages of skilled personnel and overcoming problems posed by defects or customer demands for unique products. A serious commitment from top managers proved necessary because of the need to allocate time and engineering resources to study many projects, build tools, train personnel, or develop reusable designs and code. It also consumed time and money to institute policies, controls, and incentives necessary to manage not one project at a time but a stream of projects over years, even at the expense of product innovation or development costs for a given project.

Product-Process Focus and Segmentation: Successful factory approaches focused at the facility or division level on particular types of software products and gradually tailored processes (methods, tools, standards, training) to those product families and particular customer segments, with alternative processes (off-line projects, subsidiaries, subcontractors, laboratories) available for nonroutine projects. This product and process focus proved necessary to overcome a major obstacle: the need for personnel to cultivate functional skills in software engineering, such as good

Table I.2 Common Elements in the Factory Approach

Across a Series of Similar Projects
Objectives
Strategic management and integration
Planned economies of scope
Implementation
Commitment to process improvement
Product-process focus and segmentation
Process-quality analysis and control
Tailored and centralized process R&D
Skills standardization and leverage
Dynamic standardization
Systematic reusability
Computer-aided tools and integration
Incremental product/variety improvement

tools and techniques for design and testing, but, of equal or greater importance, to accumulate knowledge of particular applications—critical to understanding and specifying system requirements prior to building actual programs. Process segmentation supported this as well as allowed managers to channel similar work to specialized groups while sending new or non-specialized jobs, for which the organization had no special accumulation of skills or investment in tools, outside the factory.

Process/Quality Analysis and Control: Accumulating knowledge about products as well as discovering the most appropriate tools, methods, or components required extensive investment in data collection and analysis on the development process for each product family. Achieving greater predictability in cost and scheduling, as well as in quality (defect control proved critical because of the high costs of fixing errors after delivery to customers), necessitated the introduction of performance standards and controls for every phase of engineering, testing, and project management. It remained unnecessary and unwise to dictate the details of each task, since projects had to respond to variations in system requirements and sometimes modify standards, tools, or methods. However, firms could standardize personnel skills and product quality through a product focus and a standard process, as well as training in standard (but evolving) sets of tools, methods, and management procedures.

Tailored and Centralized Process R&D: Many software firms solved the problem of differing product requirements and a rapidly changing technology by making it the responsibility of each project to develop its own tools and methods. The drawback of this approach lay in the lack of a systematic way to exploit scope economies across multiple projects. Projects operating independently might have built nearly identical tools needlessly, for example, or curtailed expensive tool and methodology research to meet short-term budgets. On the other hand, firms that centralized process R&D ran the risk of producing tools and methods unsuited to the needs of diverse projects. Factory approaches in general established organizations for centralized tool and methodology R&D above the level of individual projects; this raised the potential for all projects to have equal access to good tools and techniques. To accommodate the needs of different product types, firms tended to centralize process R&D at the product-division or facility level, rather than at the corporate level, or use other measures, such as joint research between central laboratories and factory engineers, to encourage the introduction of tools and methods that actual developers found useful.

Skills Standardization and Leverage: Too much standardization of tools, methods, and procedures had the potential to constrain an organization and individual projects from meeting the needs of different customers or design efforts. In particular, developers and managers needed some discretion to tailor process technology to unforseen requirements or changes. Yet, even without creating a completely rigid process for software engineering, some standardization at least of skills, primarily through extensive training of all new recruits in a set of standardized methods and tools, proved useful in an industry short of experienced engineers and managers. Training in a standard process based on know-how gained from individual projects or from R&D helped the organization accumulate and leverage skills across many projects systematically. Objectives included the improvement of capabilities for process and quality standardization as well as higher average levels of productivity, especially from new or less experienced personnel.

Dynamic Standardization: All factory organizations discussed in this book, in addition to imposing standards for personnel performance, methods, tools, products, training, and other operations, formalized the process of periodically reviewing and changing standards. Japanese facilities in the early 1990s continued to refine tools and techniques popular in the 1970s, although with modifications such as a stronger emphasis on building new systems around reusable components or designs. The policy of reviewing and revising standards for practice and performance insured that Japanese organizations moved forward with the technology, at least incrementally, and retained the ability to adapt to evolving customer needs. As long as computer hardware and software programming did not change radically, this approach provided an effective balance of efficiency and flexibility. User and producer investments in current hardware and software assets probably precluded radical changes for most segments of the software industry, although R&D organizations provided a mechanism to monitor changes in the industry as well as generate new technologies.

Systematic Reusability: One of the major obstacles to improving productivity and quality, as well as to accumulating knowledge of particular applications, continued to be the unique or customized designs of many software products. This characteristic prevented many software firms from exploiting a strategy commonly used in other engineering and factory processes: the design and mass production of interchangeable components. Craft or factory producers may at any time reuse elements such as requirements specifications, detailed designs, code, tools, or documentation, if individuals remember what software they or other groups had built in the past. Factory approaches, however, took this concept a step further by planning and devising tools, libraries, reward and control systems, and training techniques to maximize the writing of reusable software and the systematic reuse of components across different projects. Design for reuse in particular constituted an investment in an ever-expanding inventory of reusable parts; however, reuse proved especially difficult across different kinds of software, thus making reuse more likely within facilities focused on similar products. Again, the extra time and money often needed to design parts for general applications (rather than for a specific customer or function) required management planning, controls, and incentives above the level of the individual project.

Computer-Aided Tools and Integration: Like many engineering departments and large factories in other industries, all the software facilities described in this book relied heavily on mechanization and automation—specialized programs and databases, sometimes called computer-aided software-engineering (CASE) tools, for product development, project management, data collection or analysis, reuse support, and quality control. These tools captured expertise, reinforced good practices, allowed personnel to spend less time on routine tasks (such as filing reports or coding well-structured designs), and made it possible for relatively unskilled personnel to build complex, and primarily unique or customized, systems. In Japanese factories, however, major tool efforts came relatively late to the factory process and seemed of secondary importance. Companies first strove to establish a standard engineering methodology for each product family, and only then introduced tools to support a methodology. To make tool usage more efficient and coordinated with a standard development process, Japanese facilities also paid considerable attention to integrating tools with each other as well as with standardized methods, reinforcing both through training programs, and pursuing better tools and methods continually through some form of R&D organized above the project level.

Incremental Product and Variety Improvement: As in other industries, Japanese software producers first concentrated on process and quality control and then on process improvement, in response to the challenge of producing software more efficiently and guaranteeing product reliability to customers. Only after demonstrating high levels of productivity and reliability by the mid-1980s did Hitachi, Toshiba, NEC, and Fujitsu turn gradually to upgrading product designs and performance. They also spent increasing amounts of time in design rather than in routine tasks such as coding, and expanded the variety of products they produced in a single facility. This rise in skills and attention to product development, which bode well for the Japanese as future competitors in software, also drew on accumulated capabilities in process engineering and project management. Indeed, building large complex systems quickly and reliably required effective planning, organization, and control, suggesting that the assumption of a fundamental incongruence between efficiency in process and flexibility or quality in products did not necessarily exist.

The Plan of the Book

This book is not a technical manual on how to manage software development, although practitioners and students of management and engineering have already found versions of the material useful examples of good practice. Rather, this study fits within research on the history of technology and organizations that has explored why and how particular firms have tried to evolve beyond craft modes of engineering and production. The methodology follows that of the business historian, utilizing a combination of primary and secondary materials, including in-house technical reports, company records, personal interviews ranging from a few hours to several days (including many trips to Japan during 1985–1989), and formal surveys and questionnaires. These sources made it possible to construct what appears to be the first historical analysis of software production strategies and practices at these firms.

Each chapter also supports a specific argument regarding the rationale underlying a factory approach to software development. While people may debate whether software development should be managed more like an art or craft rather than science, engineering, or manufacturing, the software industry, like other industries, contains different types of products and market segments. Some customers appear sensitive to combinations of price and performance, rather than preferring low-cost standardized products or high-cost customized systems. Furthermore, as software systems increase in size and complexity, ad hoc approaches to managing product development seem to become inadequate, creating opportunities for some producers to become more structured, systematic, or, to use the term metaphorically, factorylike.

Software firms, like producers in any industry, thus face a spectrum of product and process choices. For high-end customers, they may provide leading products, fully customized for each application, such as complex antiballistic missile control systems built for the first time. Customer requirements drive these unique systems, many of which may involve more research and invention than predictable engineering or production tasks. Producers in this market probably need to rely on highly skilled personnel theoretically capable of inventing new designs, as well as methods and tools, as needed by the application and as long as the customer is willing to pay and wait for the result. This is a job-shop or craft approach, suited for unique jobs. It is adequate, however, only if a small group can build the system, if budgets, schedules, and long-term service requirements are not too stringent, and, of course, if there are adequate supplies of skilled personnel. Nor does a job-shop process contribute to fostering organizational capabilities to make new types of products if each project proceeds independently.

On the opposite side of the spectrum are low-end, fully standardized program products or packages. Customers trade off the greater features and tailoring of a customized system for the lower price and immediate availability of a package. Designing a good package might be costly and difficult, but the potential sales are huge for a best seller, such as any one of several popular word-processing or spreadsheet programs for personal computers. Specific applications corresponding to needs in the mass market, rather than of one customer, drive this type of product development. While there is no mass production, in the conventional sense, there is electronic mass-replication of the basic design. Yet this is a simple process and most of the real work is in the research, design, and testing of the product. Companies in the package segment of the software industry, therefore, need to create product-oriented projects as well as cultivate personnel highly familiar with both an application, such as word processing, and the common requirements of users. Again, this approach works well as long as a few people can build a product, skilled people are available, and development costs are relatively unimportant compared to the potential sales of a popular product. Once more, however, this project-centered approach may not contribute in any way to an organization's ability to manage a series of projects effectively.

In between these two extremes exists another option: Producers may choose not to tailor products and processes fully for each customer or package application, nor hire only highly skilled people. Rather, they might seek efficiencies across multiple projects and offer products competing on the basis of a combination of price, performance, delivery, service, and reliability, among other characteristics. Japanese software factories appeared to occupy this middle-ground position. It turns out that producers following this strategy also did not claim to make leading-edge products, at least not through their factories. If customers wanted systems they had never built before, Japanese factory managers created special projects or channeled this work to subsidiaries or subcontractors. Software facilities operating like factories thus focused on familiar but large-scale programs, and tried to offer high reliability, high productivity, and low prices. Most important, to support this strategy, they attempted to cultivate the necessary organizational and technical capabilities (Table I.3).

Part I (Chapters 1 and 2) focuses on the general managerial challenge software poses, examining the strategies available to software producers and the constraints they face as a result of the characteristics of the technology, different products and customer segments, as well as the difficulty of managing complex projects, large organizations, and program developers or engineers. Part II (Chapters 3 through 8) focuses on the factory approach, analyzing efforts, primarily in Japan, to create

Table I.3 Product-Process Strategies for Software Development

Product Type	Process Strategy	Organization Type
High End Unique designs (full custom, "invention") High-priced premium products Small to medium-sized systems	Meet customer requirements & functionality Hire skilled workers to design, build needed tools & methods No organizational skills to perform a series of similar jobs or do large jobs systematically	Craft-oriented job shop
Middle End Partly unique designs (semicustom) Medium-priced products Medium- to large-sized systems	Balance customer needs & functionality with production cost, quality Skilled workers mainly in design, standard development process Organizational skills cultivated to build large systems and reuse parts, methods, tools, and people systematically	Software factory
Low End Unique mass-replicated designs (scale economies from package sales) Low-priced products Small to medium-sized systems	Maximize application functionality for average user needs Hire highly-skilled workers knowledgeable in application No organizational skills to develop large products or a series of similar products systematically	Application-oriented project

software factories or diffuse factory tools and techniques for large-scale commercial software.

Chapter 1 elaborates on the variety of products and process options in software development as well as organizational and behavioral constraints that firms may encounter in attempting factory approaches. While the appearance and appropriateness of standardization and structure in software development are not peculiar to any one national market, as analyses of U.S. firms adopting systematic management practices, even without the factory label, demonstrate, customer preferences in specific markets may make particular techniques more or less suitable; for example, the Japanese and U.S. computer markets clearly exhibit differences that present different problems and opportunities for producers. Most Japanese customers prefer large computer systems (rather than personal computers, although this preference is changing) and products from a single vendor; there is little demand for unique military software; most Japanese companies have let U.S. firms establish product standards, including technical features, performance, and prices. These market characteristics alone create a more stable environment than exists for producers attempting to introduce radically new products or standards, or invent new technologies for unique applications. At the same time, extremely high demand in Japan for custom-built but somewhat repetitive software, rather than for packages, seems to have created huge incentives for Japanese managers to find ways to build nominally customized programs as efficiently as possible, through the systematic reuse of software tools and components, as well as automated support tools to make the customization process less labor-intensive and less dependent on highly skilled (and scarce) software engineers.

Chapter 2 provides technical background for the chapters on individual companies by reviewing difficulties commonly faced in programming since the 1960s and the major tools, techniques, and practices firms have used to make the process more systematic. This review of the technology also supports an argument in favor of factory approaches for many applications: Individuals, on their own or as members of a project, may use any tool, technique, or component as a discrete element to help them design, construct, test, or service a final product. An alternative, however, is to identify good tools, techniques, and components that suit a series of similar projects, and promote their use (or reuse) by adopting formal standards and process strategies, such as to build as much of a new product as possible from a library of existing components, systematically designed and catalogued. Chapter 2 concludes with discussions of major U.S. companies that have also pursued integrated approaches to managing software without necessarily using the factory label: IBM, the world's largest producer of computer hardware and software; ITT Corporation, a diversified conglomerate formerly in the telecommunications hardware and software business; a U.S. consulting firm that is one of the largest vendors of custom-built software and systems-integration services; and Digital Equipment Corporation (DEC), the world's top producer of minicomputers and a major developer of basic software.

The first chapter in Part II does not treat a Japanese firm, but instead focuses on a conceptual and actual pioneer in the factory approach, System Development Corporation (SDC). A former subsidiary of the Rand Corporation established in the 1950s and since the mid-1980s a division of Unisys, SDC's factory effort began in 1972 as an R&D project to develop a standardized set of software tools. After discovering that a factory required more than tools alone, in 1975–1976, the R&D team devised a standardized methodology for all phases and an organizational structure separating systems engineering, done by multiple teams at customer sites, from program construction and testing, done by a centralized group in the newly created software factory, utilizing the factory tool set. While scheduling accuracy, budget control, and quality assurance improved for nearly all the projects that went through the facility, top management allowed the factory to collapse during 1978–1979 after one unsuccessful effort and resistance from project managers to separating systems engineering from program construction, among other problems.

In contrast to SDC, Japanese managers found that a factory approach can succeed—but only if they pay greater attention to balancing product requirements with applications expertise, and allocate the time needed to solve the array of problems that arise in any major instance of process innovation in a dynamic industry. Why Japanese companies persisted in their efforts whereas SDC did not, despite encountering similar obstacles, also reflected differences in corporate traditions, industry and market conditions, as well as managerial strategies.

Chapter 4 describes Hitachi, a company with a 50-year history of independent factories for each major product area, covering both design and production. This traditional structure prompted executives in the computer division to create a separate facility for software when programming became a major activity in the late 1960s. The fact that all Hitachi factories had to adopt corporate accounting and administrative standards then forced software managers to analyze projects in great detail and experiment with work standards, new organizational structures, as well as tools and techniques, aimed primarily at improving process and quality control. The independence of Hitachi factories within the corporation also gave factory managers considerable authority over products and production. While managers underestimated how difficult it would be to implement factory concepts such as reusability and process standardization, Hitachi eventually became a leader in software production technology, especially in quality control. In the late 1980s, Hitachi also boasted the largest software factories in Japan, housing 5,000 personnel at one site for basic software and 6,000 (including both systems engineers and programmers) at another site for applications programs (see Table I.1).

Toshiba, the subject of Chapter 5, created a software factory during 1977 in its industrial equipment division to support a process strategy borrowing directly from engineering and manufacturing practices in other industries: standardization of tools and methods, and reuse of product components. The company achieved these ends with a highly focused facility, devoted mainly to developing real-time control software for industrial applications. Similarities in this type of software from project to project made it possible to build semicustomized programs from reusable designs and code combined with new software tailored to an individual customer's needs. Toshiba did totally new projects outside the factory, but as demand led to repeat projects, new software became part of a growing inventory of reusable components and management added the new products to the factory repertoire. In addition, Toshiba managed to generalize the factory tools and methods for commercial sale as well as transfer to other Toshiba divisions.

Whereas Hitachi and Toshiba efforts centered on one factory in each company, NEC, as discussed in Chapter 6, attempted to structure software production for a wide range of businesses simultaneously—telecommunications, commercial systems software, business applications, and industrial control systems. This presented a more difficult challenge than Hitachi or Toshiba undertook in the 1970s, and while the company faced many difficulties, it also made significant progress. In addition to organizing several large facilities and subsidiaries between the mid-1970s and mid-1980s, NEC launched a series of company-wide programs, directed by top management and a central laboratory, to conduct process R&D as well as standardize software-engineering and management technology, and upgrade quality controls and cross-divisional product and production planning. NEC's broad software needs, and combination of both centralized and divisional management structures, forced software managers to confront tradeoffs between standardization and flexibility almost continually. Only one product division appears to have rejected a major tool set from the central laboratory, although after this experience and the growing tendency of the laboratory toward too basic research, NEC executives began restructuring to encourage a smoother combination of centralized direction and R&D with more divisional discretion.

Chapter 7 shows how Fujitsu began systematizing product handling and inspection procedures for basic software during the early 1970s, after Hitachi but at roughly the same time as NEC and Toshiba. It then developed numerous procedures, planning and reporting systems, tools, and methods, before centralizing basic software in a large facility during 1982–1983. In applications programming, Fujitsu established a laboratory in 1970 but moved gradually toward a more standardized, factory approach, opening an applications factory in 1979. By the mid-1980s, compared to its Japanese competitors, Fujitsu appeared to have the broadest assortment of computer-aided tools supporting design and reusability, as well as the largest number of subsidiaries available to construct designs received from systems-engineering departments.

Chapter 8 examines a series of cooperative efforts from the 1960s through the 1980s, mostly sponsored by the Japanese government and aimed at the design and diffusion of software packages, support tools, standards, and new technology. The focus of this discussion is on Sigma, started in 1985 by Japan's Ministry of International Trade and Industry (MITI) in an attempt to disseminate, through a national communications network and standardization around UNIX as a programming environment, the same type of work stations, support tools, and reusable software techniques that factories such as Toshiba relied on; and the Fifth-Generation Computer Project, started by MITI in 1982 to advance Japanese capabilities in artificial intelligence, logic processing, and parallel computing, as well as their applications. To place the company and project discussions in a broader context, this chapter also includes a brief analysis of Nippon Telegraph and Telephone (NTT) and Mitsubishi Electric, as well as cooperative R&D efforts in software underway in the United States and Europe.

The concluding chapter summarizes the phases Hitachi, Toshiba, NEC, and Fujitsu went through in evolving from craft to factory modes of software production as well as reviews what seem to constitute the key lessons of this study: how Japanese software factories achieved a delicate but effective balance of process efficiency and flexibility in the production of unique and customized software products.

PART I

THE SOFTWARE CHALLENGE

1

PRODUCT-PROCESS STRATEGY
AND JAPAN'S SOFTWARE INDUSTRY

No discussion of the factory approach to software development makes much sense without a consideration of product and process strategies and their suitability given different industry or market characteristics, particularly in Japan. In other industries, all firms are not and need not be in the business of inventing new standards or offering expensive products; many customers prefer a combination of features and prices. Accordingly, producers can offer standardized designs or only partially tailored products, but compete on the basis of high productivity and low cost, or standardized quality (reliability). These approaches may require mastery of the engineering or production process far more than product invention. At the same time, some firms will continue to be product innovators or target niche users, offering unique products at relatively high prices.

If, like other industries, software markets contain multiple customer segments even for similar products, then firms probably have a range of options for managing product development and construction, as well as other operations. As in any industry, however, dysfunctions and waste might occur when the "fit" is poor—for example, when a firm attempts to make products requiring a job-shop or craft approach through an overly structured process, or when a firm continues to build similar products from scratch without adopting factory practices such as reusability or automation. In addition, personnel accustomed to one approach might resist change, such as from an unstructured to a structured process, even if such a transition seems more efficient to management and feasible technically.

Numerous reports indicate differences between the Japanese and U. S. software markets in historical evolution, customer preferences, and process emphases. Several reports have also claimed that the Japanese perform extremely well in quality, productivity, and reusability, but lag behind the United States in product sophistication, invention, and overall competitive capabilities. Survey data cited in this chapter and the appendixes to this book confirm some of these observations but place them in an historical and strategic context. In particular, specific characteristics of Japan's software industry seem to have encouraged Japanese managers, probably more than their American counterparts, to pursue ways to maximize productivity and product reliability, such as by utilizing scarce engineering skills and reusing code or designs across a series of projects. These characteristics include company decisions to allow U.S. firms to lead in hardware and software product invention, as well as Japanese consumer preferences for customized programs and large computers with relatively stable features. Japanese firms do appear to trail U.S. companies in some product areas, although they compete effectively in the largest segments of the Japanese software market and have maintained an overwhelming lead in domestic hardware market shares, which their software skills support.

Product Options

Segments and Standards

Software products fall into two broad categories: basic or system software, and applications.[1] Basic software controls the primary functions of computer hardware, and includes operating systems, database management systems, telecommunications monitors, computer-language translators, and utilities such as program editors. Applications software sits, at least figuratively, on top of basic operating systems, and performs specific user-oriented tasks. These again include prewritten or packaged programs such as for payroll accounting, database manipulations, spreadsheet analysis, word processing, and other standard operations, as well as custom software written for specific tasks and customers, such as in the banking, financial services, manufacturing, government, or defense sectors. Another type of application are programs written as parts of integrated hardware and software systems.

Manufacturers include software packages or program products (an IBM term also used frequently in Japan) with hardware, referred to as bundling in the industry, or sell them separately. International Business Machines' (IBM) decision in 1969 to begin pricing software products and systems-engineering services independently of hardware, except for some basic software programs, created opportunities for other firms—such as Hitachi, Fujitsu, and Amdahl—to design and sell IBM-compatible hardware at lower prices to customers who could still buy or lease IBM software.[2] Bundling still exists in the industry, especially for basic software, though it appears more common in Japan, making it difficult for Japanese firms to recover all their software-development costs.

In addition to function or type, one might further distinguish software by producers and their competitive positioning. Makers of commercially sold software include computer manufacturers as well as independent software houses, systems integrators or consulting firms, telecommunications companies, semiconductor manufacturers, publishing houses, and corporate information systems departments. Any of these producers might focus on high, medium, or low segments of the same product markets, defined by a combination of price and product performance, and provide, for example, more tailored and sophisticated versions of products available as standardized packages.

Market segments also correspond to machine size, since differences in architectures (the defining structure of the basic hardware or software systems) as well as hardware features and memory usually make it necessary for programmers to write software to operate on specific machines. These range from personal computers (a segment that emerged commercially in the 1980s) to large computers or mainframes (which appeared for sale in the late 1950s and early 1960s). The term *compatibility* refers to whether it is possible to use the same basic or applications software on different computers or move data between different machines or programs; this depends on how much producers standardize their internal architectures and interfaces (interconnections) with other machines as well as their modes of data characterization and transfer. For example, while the software a computer "reads" consists of zeros and ones, programmers write programs consisting of lines of code in higher-level languages such as COBOL or FORTRAN that resemble words or expressions from natural languages, primarily English. They also usually write for a particular operating system, such as MVS (IBM), UNIX (AT&T), or VMS (Digital Equipment Corporation), and sometimes for a particular type of hardware.

Since there are different versions of languages for different machines, differences in operating systems or features of the machine hardware may severely constrain portability or reusability of a program (or parts of it) across different machines. Computer vendors such as IBM, Digital, AT&T, and Honeywell/NEC, developed their own operating systems standards in the 1960s; many other hardware manufacturers have followed the IBM and AT&T (UNIX) systems. There are also several different standards for personal computers, and new ones emerging, such as IBM/Microsoft's OS/2 and personal-computer versions of UNIX, although most machines followed either Apple or the older IBM/Microsoft standard, MS-DOS. Numerous efforts around the world are encouraging firms at least to standardize basic internal and external interfaces. IBM's Systems Application Architecture (SAA) specifications, analogues at all the major Japanese firms, and the international Open Systems Interconnection (OSI) protocols, would allow producers and users to move programs and data more easily across different machines as well as link machines and peripheral equipment (printers, external memory drives, facsimile machines, etc.) together more easily.

Progress in architectural and interface standardization across firms has been slow, at least in part because market leaders, such as IBM, have had little to gain from making it easier for competitors to develop similar hardware and software products. Nonetheless, it holds great promise for relieving the shortage of software programmers, in that users could deploy programs written for individual computers more widely. In the 1990s, many companies were also shifting programming operations to languages such as C and Ada, adopting the UNIX operating system, or experimenting with object-oriented programming techniques, all of which make it easier to transfer programs or pieces across different hardware. On the other hand, differences in hardware and software architectures often existed to optimize certain applications, such as transactions processing, database management, scientific calculations, or graphics simulations. Too much standardization of hardware and software, therefore, while desirable for producers, may not meet the needs of different customers.

In the personal-computer industry, programs have been shorter than for larger machines, and thus development times for new products and the apparent rates of product change appear to be faster. New microprocessors have especially spurred hardware and software innovations in this segment of the industry, reflecting the enormous increases in the processing and memory capacities even of small machines. In contrast, while mainframe and minicomputer manufacturers have continued to improve their products, it normally takes several years to design large computer systems and recover investments. Furthermore, mainframe companies that adopted architectural standards in the 1960s have usually promised customers to maintain compatibility with older software. These factors have thus tended to make the life cycles for large-computer systems longer and more stable than software for personal computers.[3] Indeed, many programs written in the 1960s continue to be used in corporations, governments, universities, and other institutions.

Variations in Customer Needs

Not all market segments provide the same opportunities or incentives for process standardization and refinement, or reusability. Some organizations and customers require truly unique systems. These might include companies writing applications software for in-house use rather than for sale, defense contractors writing one-of-a-kind systems for military purposes, or producers of packages in a rapidly changing area, such as for personal computers. On the other hand, the somewhat more stable environment of large computers, with long life cycles and compatible architectures, as well as markets where customers want more tailored features than packages provide but do not always need or cannot always afford fully customized systems, might offer rewards for producers exhibiting an efficient development process that is flexible enough to provide some customization.

Software packages, such as a LOTUS 1-2-3 spreadsheet, represented designs made by just a few people and then mass produced (replicated), not unlike Ford's Model T car. They make a variety of quality products, once developed for individual, high-paying customers, available to millions of people at an affordable price. Packages thus have been a major part of the solution to rising demand for software and will no doubt continue to be important, especially for small computers, where users appear willing to tolerate limited product features, program or machine incompatibilities, design or programming errors, and the issuing of imperfect products followed by updated versions.

Yet even programming for personal computers has become difficult to manage as a result of enormous improvements in processing capabilities achieved with microprocessors that put on one silicon chip what merely a few years ago were mainframes filling entire rooms. Indicative of this new crisis in personal-computer software was the delay of several years in completing operating systems to utilize fully the Intel 80286 and 80386 microprocessors,[4] as well as the long delays in completing a new version of LOTUS 1-2-3. Furthermore, with larger computers, companies often demand programs tailored to individual needs and offering some competitive advantage over software other firms can buy.

Thus, there may always be a limitation on how well standardized or packaged software can meet customer needs and ease the tasks of software producers. This was particularly true in application areas where the degree of direct interaction with customers and the uniqueness of each task often made software development resemble a consulting and engineering service tailored to each order.[5] Nevertheless, any firm in any segment of the industry might choose to go beyond craft modes of operating to compensate for shortages of skilled people, high costs or reliability problems, or simply to create a competitive advantage through process efficiency, especially if customers are sensitive both to price and product functionality. Furthermore, combining the ability to be efficient and to tailor products or services offers potential benefits for customers in the form of shorter waiting times for new products, standardized and improved quality, and perhaps lower prices and wider availability of partially customized programs.

Process Options

The Spectrum of Choices

How to be both efficient and flexible in design or manufacturing is a problem common to any industry where there are differences in customer needs and company offerings, shortages of skilled workers, or competition based on a combination of product features and prices. In other industries, one way managers have dealt with this challenge has been to adopt different processes for different products, sometimes within the same firm: craft-oriented approaches, including special projects, job shops, or laboratories, for unique products, and then more structured engineering and factory organizations for commodity or standardized products. In between exist a variety of process choices and product combinations, which can theoretically accommodate different levels of product variety or tailoring as well as cost competition. Firms may have to accept tradeoffs, such as the difficulty of capturing scale or scope economies in a job-shop environment, or the reduction in potential variety from an infinite number to a few in factory mass production, although advances in production technologies (such as group technology and small-lot production techniques, computer-aided design and manufacturing tools, and flexible manufacturing systems) are continually reducing the need for managers to think in terms of a compromise between process efficiency and flexibility.[6]

For example, a major innovation of mass production—standardized designs and interchangeable components—affected both engineering and manufacturing productivity, since even mass producers reuse components, despite external designs (such as the outer body shell of an automobile) that appear new. Concepts such as group technology (putting together similar parts, problems, or tasks to facilitate scheduling of components production, arranging factory layouts, or rationalizing product design and engineering) have facilitated parts standardization and reuse in a variety of industries, especially with the addition of computer-aided design and engineering tools.[7] Designers can thus respond to different customer segments with different degrees of customization versus reusability (or standardization). Therefore, whether the domain is hardware or software, one might describe process options for product development as existing along a continuum stretching from full customization to full standardization, with a range of choices in between (Table 1.1).[8]

Full customization and full standardization should apply when markets are clearly segmented into completely tailored products on one end and true commodity products on the other. In the latter case, there may be no product features or process elements distinct to an individual customer or project. At either end of the spectrum, a firm might stress a loosely structured environment and the hiring of highly skilled employees to tailor products to customer specifications or make a potential best-seller design. In between, however, even if customers demand different products, firms might still be able to recycle some designs or components for some period of time, as well as recycle procedures, controls, tools, test cases, skilled people, and other factors of production. In other words, unless each product, and the process and know-how required to design and build it are entirely different, then some economies of scope, if not of scale, and thus some combination of efficiency and flexibility, should be possible.

While these types of product and process strategies may be common in other older industries, answering questions such as at what point in time and to what extent have software firms also pursued a spectrum of process options, potentially ranging from job-shop or craft practices to factory approaches, immediately encounters problems of language and sampling. Only a few firms explicitly adopted the term *factory* for their software facilities or management approaches: System Development Corporation (SDC) in the United States during the 1970s, and then Hitachi, Toshiba, NEC, and Fujitsu in Japan between the late 1960s and 1980s (followed by Mitsubishi on a much smaller scale).[9] American and European firms after SDC tended not to use this label except to describe standardized tool sets, although one recent study found as many as 200 enterprises in the United States alone that each had 1,000 or more software personnel in a centralized facility, with all emphasizing, to some degree, standardized designs and reusable components, common tools, formal testing and quality-assurance procedures, productivity measurement and improvement efforts, and process research.[10] IBM, for example, during the 1960s became probably the first company in the world to seek a structured process and organization for software to complete the operating systems for its System/360 family of computers. Yet IBM never used the term *software factory* and has preferred to call its facilities *laboratories* or *programming centers.*

The existence of large software producers, some explicitly using the term factory and others avoiding it though seeming to follow factory practices, merely indicates that adoption of a name, while it may reflect specific management objectives, is not in itself meaningful. If software

Table 1.1 Spectrum of Product-Development Strategies

Craft-Oriented Job-Shops

Strategy	Customize products and processes for individual customers
	Attain high premiums for this service
Implementation	Emphasis on process flexibility for custom requirements
	Unlimited range of products and customer needs
	Little opportunity for process/quality analysis/control
	Project-based process R&D, if any
	Dependence on highly skilled workers
	Minimal reliance on process standardization
	Little opportunity for systematic reuse
	Computer-aided tools individual- or project-oriented
	Emphasis on customized products and customer service
Tradeoff	Customer requirements, product & process flexibility and invention, if necessary, over process efficiency
Assessment	Little strategic management or integration beyond projects
	Few economies of scale or scope
	Best suited for medium-sized, innovative custom projects

Factory Development

Strategy	Efficient production of different products
	High price-performance
	Effective management of large, complex but routine projects
Implementation	Management commitment/investment in process improvement
	Broad but more limited product-process market focus
	Extensive process/quality analysis/control
	Tailored and centalized process R&D
	Standardization & leveraging of worker skills
	Dynamic standardization
	Systematic reuse of product components
	Extensive use of computer-aided tools
	Incremental product improvement
Tradeoff	Effort required to balance process/organizational efficiency with process flexibility & individual creativity
Assessment	High level of strategic integration & management
	Offers systematic economies of scope
	Well-suited for large-scale, complex projects where standards, reuse, and managerial skill are important

Product- or Application-Oriented Projects

Strategy	Design of a best-seller product
	Mass production and sale of low-priced commodity products
Implementation	Emphasis on product appeal (to produce a best seller)
	Focus on particular applications for broad market
	Process efficiency less important than design appeal
	Process R&D to suit particular products
	Emphasis on highly skilled designers
	Little emphasis on process standards
	Reuse less important than best-seller designs
	Tools useful if do not constrain designers
	Innovation more important than incremental improvement
Tradeoff	Product innovation or differentiation over process efficiency in design
Assessment	Little strategic management or integration beyond projects
	High potential economies of scale in package sales
	Not suited for large-scale, complex projects

managers were truly attempting to move software beyond a craft approach, however, then a comparison of facilities on similar dimensions should illustrate a spectrum from something resembling job shops to something resembling factories, whatever their labels.

To explore this proposition, this author surveyed managers at fifty-two large software facilities (twenty-five Japanese, twenty-six U.S., one Canadian) at thirty companies in North America and Japan. These made software products in five major categories: basic systems software, general business applications, real-time process-control software, industrial operating systems, and telecommunications software. The survey remained exploratory in the sense that it came very early in this research and simply asked if managers embraced emphases adopted by the SDC Software Factory, rather than trying to present a definitive model of what constituted a factory approach.

As summarized in Figure 1.1, some of the responses clearly fell into the upper left-hand corner of a matrix counterpoising emphases on process or tool standardization and control with reuse of code (product

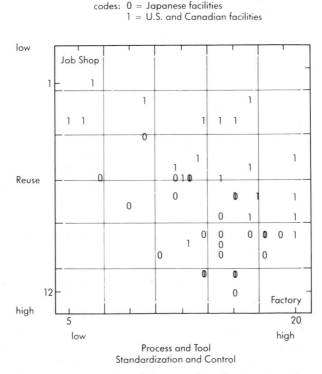

Figure 1.1 Reuse Versus Tool and Process Standardization. (Source: See Appendix A.)

customization). These responses could be characterized as job shops, with little or no emphasis on standardization, control, or reuse, at least in answering the questions posed (see Appendix A for a detailed explanation of these data). Those in the lower right appeared more like factories in the sense that managers strongly emphasized reuse as well as standardization and control in the design and construction of new products, even though these products appeared unique or customized. A test to determine whether product types (as defined in the survey) influenced manager responses proved negative.

The survey thus supports the observation that, whatever terms companies used to describe facilities or approaches to software development, managers have pursued a spectrum in standardization and control among tools, methods, and inputs (reuse). In addition, most responses fell on the right side of the matrix, indicating a general emphasis on standardization and control among managers at large-scale software producers, regardless of the type of product. U.S. responses on tool and process questions did not significantly differ from the Japanese, although most (but not all) the facilities in the lower right turned out to be Japanese. This reflected a higher emphasis on reuse in Japan. The significance of the country of origin as a variable in manager emphases also suggested that national market or industry characteristics may have an impact on the process options companies pursue.

Technical and Organizational Constraints

Apart from whether process options like methodology and tool standardization or reusability are desirable for competitive and technical reasons, managers must consider implementation: whether they can, in practice, introduce standardized procedures, controls, methods, tools, and designs that not only promote goals such as higher productivity and quality but also prove acceptable to project managers and engineers, and other employees. In fact, the debate over the nature of software as a technology and programming as a task dates back at least to the mid-1960s.[11] Several industry experts, reflecting on recurring problems in software development as well as on progress in other industries, recommended that software producers adopt more engineering and manufacturing practices, such as a design and production process divided into distinct phases, with guidelines and controls for each phase, as well as computer-aided support tools and some product construction from an inventory of reusable parts.

Yet firms that attempted to implement these and other ideas associated with modern factories and engineering organizations often encountered resistance from programmers and managers who, like their counterparts in other crafts and professions, preferred minimal controls and a maximum of decentralization to promote the free exchange of information and individual creativity.[12] Organizational theorists, in retrospect, have attributed this resistance to the sheer complexity and still-evolving nature of the technology and the industry—suggesting that factory operations for software were and may still be inappropriate.

A few examples illustrate this argument. At General Electric (GE) during the mid-1960s, an engineer named R.W. Bemer made numerous proposals dealing with problems such as low and variable programmer productivity. His work culminated in a 1968 paper encouraging GE to take the leadership in this new technology and develop a software factory consisting of standardized tools, a computer-based interface, and an historical database for financial and management controls. This appears to be the first published definition of what might constitute a factory approach for software development, although GE management considered Bemer's proposal to be premature and, in the face of continued technical and marketing problems (including strong competition from IBM) exited the computer business in 1970, ending the company's commitment to commercial hardware and software production:

> [A] software factory should be a programming environment residing upon and controlled by a computer. Program construction, checkout and usage should be done entirely within this environment, and by using the tools contained in the environment. . . . A factory . . . has measures and controls for productivity and quality. Financial records are kept for costing and scheduling. Thus management is able to estimate from previous data. . . . Among the tools to be available in the environment should be: compilers for machine-independent languages; simulators, instrumentation devices, and test cases as accumulated; documentation tools—automatic flow-charters, text editors, indexers; accounting function devices; linkage and interface verifiers; code filters (and many others).[13]

While Bemer focused on computerized tools and standardized controls, an acquaintance of his at AT&T, Dr. M.D. McIlroy, emphasized another factory concept: systematic reusability of code when constructing new programs. In an address at a 1968 NATO Science Conference on software engineering, McIlroy argued that the division of software programs into modules offered opportunities for mass-production methods. He then used the term factory in the context of facilities dedicated to producing parameterized families of software parts or routines that would serve as building blocks for tailored programs reusable across different computers.[14] Reception to McIlroy's ideas was mixed, however. It seemed too difficult to create program modules that would be efficient and reliable for all types of systems and not constrain the user. Software was also heavily dependent on the specific characteristics of hardware. Nor did anyone know how to catalog program modules so they could be easily found and reused. These objections proved difficult to overcome, even in the 1980s, when few firms reused large amounts of software systematically.

As will be discussed in Chapter 4, Hitachi in 1969 centralized programming operations in a facility managers formally viewed and labeled as a software factory. While new methods and controls representing good practice in the industry improved productivity, quality, and scheduling accuracy, performance stagnated for the next decade as Hitachi struggled to find the right combination of products, procedures, and tools; for example, because of differences in product requirements, managers were unable to introduce a components-control system (modeled after similar systems in Hitachi's other engineering and manufacturing plants) to promote software reusability. Management also failed to devise a single set of standards and controls for both basic software and customized applications.

As will be examined in Chapter 3, SDC's Software Factory in the mid-1970s incorporated a standardized set of engineering methods, controls, and support tools, as well as a matrix organization separating systems design from program construction. Management planned to make the factory the centerpiece of its engineering and marketing strategies, but abandoned the effort after less than three years of operations. The factory worked well except in one case when systems engineers encountered a new application and had difficulty specifying requirements accurately enough to transfer them smoothly to the factory for program construction. In general, furthermore, project managers preferred to build complete systems in integrated groups, rather than handing off specifications to a centralized organization for detailed design, coding, and testing.

General Telephone and Electric (GTE) attempted to standardize around recognized good practices but found the diversity within the organization to be too great. As a first step, a central steering committee and laboratory issued a set of corporate software-development standards in 1980, based on proven methodologies and ideas from different divisions. These standards specified a hierarchical architecture for all software systems, a formal engineering process based on a common life-cycle model, a method for configuration management (how to design pieces of a system and then put them together), a list of required documents for each phase, and a glossary of terms and symbols for diagramming programs. Creation of a common process and terminology appeared to help engineers and managers communicate, and management encountered little opposition, at first. In a subsequent phase, however, GTE tried to standardize not just terminology but actual practices in different divisions, through the use of required reports to enforce adherence to standards, as well as a common tool set. These measures failed, apparently reflecting the variety within GTE's software activities, the preference of engineers for familiar tools, performance problems users encountered with the standard process and tool set, as well as conflicting perceptions among GTE business units regarding their real needs in software.[15]

Several data-processing companies in Denmark also tried to introduce more standardized procedures, closer employee supervision, and divisions of labor between systems analysis and programming. Workers, however, responded by quitting or ignoring rules, and project managers acquiesced. The researcher who reported on this case in 1987 explained that the company efforts, in addition to being difficult and expensive to enforce, seemed doomed to fail from the beginning because specialists in any field tend to resist management attempts at "the expropriation of craft knowledge":

> By imposing standardization and supervision of the specialists' practice at least two objectives were pursued. One was to reduce costs, another to reduce the dependency on the individual specialist. By making their working methods conform to certain norms, and their products to certain standards, the expropriation of craft knowledge, and the replaceability of the individual specialist were obtained. . . . The division of work between programmers and analysts also falls within this repertoire of control measures.

> However, these efforts that essentially deskill the IT- [Information Technology] specialists were resisted by the specialists in several ways. One was to leave the organizations, if control measures that implied a formalization beyond the specialists' threshold of tolerance were imposed. . . . The second type of resistance was to bypass the rules and regulations imposed. This is a common story from the installations with well-developed methods and standards: that they do exist, but are only utilized to a limited extent. . . . To enforce the rules and methods is time-consuming, difficult, and in most organizations run counter to the efforts to terminate projects with a tolerable exceeding of the time and resource schedule.

> Thirdly, rule enforcement is complicated by the fact that the [data-processing] managers and supervisors in nearly all cases are IT-specialists themselves. Thus they know the problems connected with strict rule adherence, and perhaps share the craft values of the specialists they are supposed to supervise.[16]

The argument underlying this account of the Danish case, borrowing from a framework popularized by Henry Mintzberg and incorporating concepts from several writers, is that a potential incongruence among the nature of the environment, the tasks to be performed, and organizational or process characteristics will lead to failure.[17] One must accept that some industry environments are more stable or dynamic than others, such as in the degree or rate of change in customer preferences, and that some tasks are simpler and others more complex, such as in the number and type of operations that must be performed to design, construct, and test a product. Accordingly, an environment and a technology that are both dynamic and complex should be met with ad hoc organizational responses and constant mutual adjustments—denoting job-shop or craft modes of operation rather than conventional factories, which require standardization and seem far better suited to more stable industries and simpler tasks. A job-shop or craft process, characterized by the ability to adjust easily to change or customer variations, would then appear more appropriate for a complex, unstandardized technology such as software, especially since producers make unique products or customize for individual users (Table 1.2).

Similar stories of failed attempts to introduce factory concepts in software abound, from the United States, Japan, and elsewhere. As will be described in Chapter 6, programmers in NEC's Basic Software Division during the late 1970s rejected a new factory-type tool and methodology set developed in central research, because it proved to be incompatible with existing products and practices. Programmers in a major U.S. producer of custom software, examined in Chapter 2, at least on occasion rejected management regulations that they use a specified "design-factory" process and tool set, requiring detailed specification in flow charts before actual coding.

To many observers, these and other examples evoke potentially dire conclusions. Programmers may be too accustomed to craftlike practices, the technology too unpredictable, and the environment too unstable, for software producers to introduce the type of engineering and factory processes that have dramatically improved efficiency in other industries. Furthermore, becoming more efficient while remaining adaptable to different customer requirements and to evolution itself, in any field, may be too difficult. It may require technical, managerial, and organizational skills that are incompatible or at least difficult to reconcile, especially in a dynamic industry with a complex product and process technology.

All these issues come to a head in the software field, where, in the best

Table 1.2 Environmental and Structural Fit

Environment and Task Characteristics	Stable	Dynamic
Complex	Professional bureaucracy Skills standardization* (eg., hospital)	Adhocracy Mutual adjustment (eg., large job shop or large project)
	Software & the Software Factory?	
Simple	Machine bureaucracy Product-process standardization & mechanization (eg., mass production factory)	Simple structure Direct supervision (eg., small job shop or small project)

*The terms underlined indicate the basic method of coordination for each structural configuration.
Source: Finn Borum, "Beyond Taylorism: The IT Specialists and the Deskilling Hypothesis," Computer History (CHIPS) Working Paper, Copenhagen School of Economics, September 1987, p. 5, adapted from Henry Mintzberg, *The Structuring of Organizations* (Englewood Cliffs, N.J.: Prentice-Hall, 1979), p. 286.

of all possible worlds, one could argue that programs should all be developed on a unique basis by highly skilled craftsman or professionals, who might rightly oppose attempts to de-skill, automate, or routinize their jobs. Customer demands also make mass production, except for the mass replication of software packages, an inappropriate model for a product-development process so heavily preoccupied with the design of unique or tailored systems. But if highly structured engineering and factory production is the wrong organizational paradigm for software development, are factory concepts useful to improve process efficiency at least in some market segments? Or must software producers always manage their facilities as job shops, maximizing flexibility rather than efficiency, even though dramatic improvements in computer hardware, and rising demand for lengthy, complex programs, might stretch their human, organizational, and technical skills to the limit?

Theoretical Interpretations

The de-skilling or routinization of work, high levels of control over production tasks and work flows, division and specialization of labor, mechanization and automation, interchangeable parts, and standardized designs constitute some of the major process innovations associated with factory approaches to production. These usually resulted in cost reductions and lower prices, but sometimes in exchange for decreases in the ability of the organization to offer high degrees of product variety and functionality.[18] Managers and workers alike have found fault with rigid approaches to engineering and manufacturing that constrained employee discretion or creativity and thus hindered a firm's ability to adapt to changes in technology and market needs.[19] Thus, whether factory concepts provide solutions to problems in software production or merely serve to exacerbate them reflects a broad practical and theoretical debate regarding the benefits as well as disadvantages of different types of production strategies, including implementation through specific organizational structures and processes.

One set of positions, represented by various contingency theorists, range from the assertion that there is no one best way to do anything to the belief that optimal selections are contingent on the fit among factors such as the stability of the environment, the characteristics of the technology, the size of the organization, or political processes within the firm.[20] Others argue that managers can shape the structure of their organizations and, therefore, the technology they require—tools, techniques, information, and other elements used to make products or services—by selecting different competitive positions.[21]

In many situations, research has suggested that factors such as the technology or environmental characteristics appear to account for no more than about half of the variability in structure among organiza-

tions.[22] If they exert even this much influence on the options open to managers, or on optimal strategies, then one might indeed argue that all software producers—or all successful software producers—should look like unstructured, highly flexible job shops, not factories. The exception would be if managers can identify segments of their industry where relatively standardized processes and product components are appropriate at least for some customers, and then introduce a more formalized process and organization. This would require not simply an intermediate position between craft and factory production in terms of volume of output or scale of operations. Software factories would also have to reconcile seemingly contradictory elements, such as the ability to standardize procedures, tools, skills, and perhaps product components, but still produce unique or customized systems rather than mass-producing one or two designs per facility. These organizations would also have to standardize the development process yet evolve along with the technology or risk falling hopelessly behind industry leaders.

The characteristics successful software factories need to embrace thus make it difficult to categorize them in terms of conventional production modes, organizational designs, or justifications based on economies of scale.[23] For example, an organization theorist who studied manufacturing firms in the 1960s, Joan Woodward, identified three basic types of production useful to contrast for this study: unit or craft production; mass production; and continuous processing, as in chemical manufacturing. In unit production, which relied on highly skilled workers, little formalization of organizational rules and procedures, and little centralization of decision-making authority, tasks appeared nonroutine and primarily manual. Mass production dealt with more complex but repetitious operations susceptible to standardization, economies of scale, formalization, divisions of labor, and mechanization. Continuous processing, since it proved highly automated, usually did not require extensive centralization, formalization, or divisions of labor.[24]

At first glance, software development, except for electronic replication of finished programs, appears to fall neatly into the realm of unit or craft production—making one product at a time for a specific customer or set of requirements, in contrast to mass-producing components and finished products through a sequential assembly process or continuous automated operation. Yet, as the manager survey in Appendix A and chapter discussions illustrate, some software producers clearly began adopting formal rules and procedures, and divisions of labor, as early as the 1960s. They also managed to mechanize some operations (that is, support them through computer-aided systems) and automate others (that is, design them to be performed automatically, with little or no human intervention). Thus an analysis of actual firms indicates that not all software development has fallen into the category of unit or craft production, except perhaps in the earliest days of the industry.

A classification problem arises with Mintzberg's organizational scheme referred to in the Danish study.[25] In this terminology, software factories probably came closest to a *professional bureaucracy*—with standardized but specialized skills, procedures, and tools controlling the work process rather than a conventional administrative apparatus (see Table 1.2). The notion that a professional work force can serve the same functions as bureaucratic administration in mass production industries, while allowing for more flexibility to adapt to different customer needs or changes in the work flow, dates back at least to the studies of Arthur L. Stinchcombe on the construction industry in the late 1950s.[26] Other examples of professional bureaucracies include engineering consultants and hospitals.

Descriptions of professional bureaucracies claim they rely on decentralized structures—lots of individual or small-group activities—and little formal divisions of labor. As seen in subsequent chapters, software producers nominally adopting factory practices sometimes located teams at customer sites, although they generally did this in the planning and high-level design phases and attempted to centralize detailed design and programming operations in large-scale, capital-intensive facilities. Professional bureaucracies, by definition, also consisted of professionals that had years of education in specific fields. In contrast, software factories in Japan, as well as the American custom software firm discussed in Chapter 2, tended to hire personnel unskilled in software and then train them to use a standardized methodology and tool set as well as reusable designs (built, of course, by more expert people).

In this latter sense, at least some software facilities contained elements characterizing mass production factories in other industries, which some theorists have labeled *machine bureaucracies* (including divisional structures in large organizations): standardized tasks, unskilled employees grouped into functional departments, centralized authority, high levels of rigid mechanization or automation, and formal divisions of labor. Yet software factories did not completely de-skill tasks; most projects required technical knowledge as well as thought and adaptation to build and test products. Functional departments and divisions of labor also seemed adaptable rather than permanently fixed, and managers routinely used *matrices*—project teams consisting of members borrowed temporarily from functional departments—which Mintzberg and many others have associated with a loosely structured *adhocracy*, a term referring primarily to teams of specialists relying on ad hoc structures and procedures.[27] These organizational types contrast to a *simple structure*, characterized by little or no formal procedures or processes, decision making done by one person or a small group, such as in a small family-owned store or entrepreneurial firm. Simple structures appeared common in the early days of the software industry and still seemed to characterize many small software houses. Yet, as companies in various industries have discovered, once organizations, projects, and production operations grow in size, more elaborate structures and controls become essential to operate efficiently, even though too much structure or bureaucracy can also have negative results.[28]

Another classification scheme, suggested by Charles Perrow, gets closer to the nature of software factories and how they are managed by focusing on task variability and the analysis of technical problems. Perrow argued that organizations dealing with *routine technologies* encounter few exceptions and therefore face problems that, over time, become easier to analyze and solve through formal procedures or tools. This standardized process eliminates the need to have large numbers of highly skilled (and usually expensive) professionals capable of reinventing solutions each time problems or projects occur. Firms dealing with *engineering technologies* have more exceptions, but these still seem relatively well defined and manageable systematically. Perrow contrasts routine and engineering technologies with *craft technologies*, defined by a limited range of variability but ill-defined problems difficult to analyze, as well as *nonroutine technologies*, which indicated many exceptional and difficult tasks (Table 1.3).[29]

Japanese software factories, in contrast to the SDC factory or to pure job-shop approaches to software development, appeared to manage what Perrow called "engineering technologies": some exceptions in product requirements but relatively well-defined tasks, perhaps because of similar customer needs but also reflecting management efforts to create permanent groups of people experienced in particular applica-

Table 1.3 Organizational Structure and Technology

Structure	Technology	Tasks & Problems	Characteristics
Machine bureaucracy	Routine, mass production	Few exceptions, well defined	Standardized and de-skilled work, centralization, divisions of labor, high formalization of rules and procedures
Professional bureaucracy	Engineering	Many exceptions, well defined	Standardized and specialized skills, decentralization, low formalization
Adhocracy	Nonroutine	Many exceptions, ill defined	Specialized skills but few or no organization standards, decentralization, low formalization
Simple structure	Unit or craft	Few exceptions, ill defined	Few standardized specialized skills, centralized authority but low formalization

Source: Discussions in Joan Woodward, *Industrial Organization: Theory and Practice* (London: Oxford University Press, 1965); Henry Mintzberg, *The Structuring of Organizations* (Englewood Cliffs, N.J.: Prentice-Hall, 1979); and Charles Perrow, "A Framework for the Comparative Analysis of Organizations," *American Sociology Review*, April 1967.

tions and to channel similar work to these focused facilities. On the other hand, the Japanese factories at times exhibited features of routine mass production—fully standardizing the development of truly common programs, even if they were tailored for different customers—as well as features of craft production. Overall, they standardized many but not all tasks, and only de-skilled tasks in a relative sense; they divided labor only in some kinds of projects and only *relatively* formalized rules and procedures—compared to modes of operations before managers explicitly adopted factory strategies or to implicitly ad hoc approaches with little or no formal structures. These management policies allowed Japanese software factories to combine some of the flexibility of craft or job shops, in that they remained adaptable enough to make unique or customized designs, with some of the efficiencies of engineering and factory production, but based on scope rather than scale economies across a series of projects.

The Japanese Software Industry

Product and Process Characteristics

The survey of managers and other evidence presented in this book suggest that Japanese software producers closely resembled large-scale software firms in the United States, even though they seemed to go further with a particular factory or engineering practice—systematic reusability. Nevertheless, observers of Japan since before World War II have argued that traditions of Confucianism, a centralized educational system, a history of cooperative rice-paddy cultivation, and other elements, have molded a modern work force that is highly disciplined, accustomed to group activities and, as result, more willing to accept the coordination, controls, and teamwork required for efficient and flexible engineering or manufacturing operations, including the approaches used in software factories.[30]

Beliefs the Japanese might have special characteristics that help them in software development date back at least to the 1968 NATO Science Committee Conference on Software Engineering, where several participants insisted the Japanese were already "extremely good at producing software," citing factors such as lifetime employment, which kept workers in one firm; a tradition of self-discipline; a complex native language that appeared to serve as an advantage in programming; and a willingness to work "long hours for low pay."[31] The conference members offered no data on Japanese programmers to support these assertions, and not all subsequent visitors to Japan have been equally impressed with Japanese software skills. Yet several U.S. government and private surveys in the 1980s continued to insist that, as in other industries, Japanese software producers and products exhibited certain strengths as well as weaknesses, compared to their U.S. counterparts.

A review of more than a dozen sources published between 1981 and 1989 revealed a general agreement that Japanese firms performed well in areas related to the *process* of software development: productivity, quality, tool usage, discipline, teamwork, maintenance, project management, and reuse. In the *product* area, many observers agreed the Japanese were at least equal to the United States in custom programming and a variety of specific applications (real-time software, graphics and video programs, supercomputer programs, on-line reservation systems, and embedded software, as in consumer or industrial products). On the negative side, Japanese firms appeared to rely almost entirely on tools and techniques adopted from the United States and Europe, and made some products lacking in sophistication. Japanese software also seemed costly, probably because most programs in Japan were custom built rather than packaged applications, where Japanese firms offered little (but were investing heavily). In particular, the Japanese seemed to trail U.S. vendors in operating systems, office programs, and basic research as well as suffer from a shortage of skilled engineers that made it difficult for them to compete effectively in overseas markets (Table 1.4).

A closer look at some of these reports illustrates the types of claims and evidence. One article that raised considerable interest in Japan came in 1981 (followed by a second in 1984) by two Japanese managers from Hitachi Software Engineering (HSE).[32] Although the authors offered statistics only from their own firm, with no indication of what kind or number of projects or time periods to which the data referred, they claimed that HSE, with extensive investment in process control and employee training, had achieved enormous improvements in project management. In fact, the authors maintained, "The cost and schedule control methods used by HSE today allow the house to complete 98 percent of its projects on time and 99 percent of its projects at an actual cost between 90 and 110 percent of the original estimate" compared to previous delays of months and cost overruns of up to 300 percent at the same firm.

A 1983 article describing a visit to ten Japanese software producers and R&D organizations concluded that, while the Japanese primarily incorporated U.S. and European technology for producing software and lagged in package development, they focused on "practically oriented . . . tangible user products."[33] The Japanese also boasted of facilities, such as Toshiba's Software Factory, that appeared to be "one of the most advanced real-time software engineering organizations in the world," with productivity averaging nearly 3,000 instructions per programmer month. The author concluded that Japanese firms were advanced in real-time software development for process control and in artificial intelligence applications for language translation, and might

Table 1.4 Generalizations about Japanese Software

Positive Comments	Sources*	Quantitative Data
Process		
Good/Ahead in quality (bugs) and product engineering	Zelkowitz 1984	None
	Johnson 1985	None
	U.S. Commerce 1984	None
	Haavind 1986	1 company's data
	OTA 1987	1 company's data
	Gamaota & Frieman 1988	1 company's data
Good/Ahead in tool usage	Kim 1983	None
	Zelkowitz 1984	Site survey
	U.S. Commerce 1984	None
	Johnson 1985	None
	Gamaota & Frieman 1988	None
Good/Ahead in productivity	Kim 1983	1 company's data
	U.S. Commerce 1984	Anecdotal
	Haavind 1936	1 company's data
	Gamaota & Frieman 1988	1 company's data
Ahead in reuse	Standish 1984	Anecdotal
	Haavind 1986	Anecdotal
	Gamaota & Frieman 1988	1 company's data
	Tracz 1988	Anecdotal
	Cusumano 1989	Manager survey
Good/Ahead in maintenance	Kishida 1986	None
	Nikkei/Cusumano 1988	User surveys
Good/Ahead in project management (planning, discipline, teamwork)	Naur and Randall 1969	None
	Tajima & Matsubara 1981	1 company's data
	Zelkowitz 1984	None
	U.S. Commerce 1984	None
	Johnson 1985	None
	Belady 1986	None
Products		
Good/Ahead in custom programming	Nikkei/Cusumano 1988	User surveys
	OTA 1987	None
Good in specific applications (Real-Time, AI, graphics, supercomputer, MIS, on-line reservations, embedded, Jap. language processing)	Kim 1983	None
	Uttal 1984	None
	Sakai 1984	None
	Gamaota & Frieman 1988	None
	Lecht 1989	None
Negative Comments	Sources	Quantitative Data
Process		
Copy/Rely on western tools and techniques	Kim 1983	None
	Zelkowitz 1984	None
	Kishida 1987	None
	Cusumano 1989	Manager's survey
Severe shortage of skilled programmers	Lecht 1989	None
Products		
Lack creativity	Uttal 1984	None
	Rifkin and Savage 1989	None
No product inventions	U.S. Commerce 1984	Historical lists
Less sophisticated products	Uttal 1984	None
Behind in packages	Kim 1983	None
	U.S. Commerce 1984	None
	OTA 1987	Industry data

(continued)

Table 1.4 (*Continued*)

Negative Comments	Sources*	Quantitative Data
Behind in basic research	U.S. Commerce1984	None
	Gamaota & Frieman 1988	Anecdotal
Behind the U.S. overall	U.S. Commerce 1984	None
	Sakai 1984	None
	OTA 1987	Industry data
	Rifkin and Savage 1989	None
	Lecht 1989	None

*Sources are identified in the text notes. AI = artificial intelligence; MIS = management information systems.

even be ahead of the United States in developing and using integrated tool sets for software development.

A 1984 survey of thirty software production facilities at thirteen Japanese and 13 U.S. companies also noted the tendency of the Japanese to make and use tools more widely, perhaps because tool development came out of company overhead rather than project budgets. In addition, the Japanese seemed to focus on small but manageable projects, and to engage in extensive analysis of the causes of software defects.[34] A 1986 article, in addition to describing advanced program-generator and computer-aided software-engineering (CASE) tools, especially at NEC, cited high levels of reuse (65 percent of delivered code) and productivity (2,000 lines per month) at Toshiba, as well as high quality (0.3 defects per 1,000 lines of code).[35] Other reports continued to find high levels of reuse in Japan as well as significant management attention to quality control.[36]

Nonetheless, most observers offered mixed assessments. One 1984 article conceded to Japanese strengths in certain types of software products—video games, super-computer programs, large-scale banking and airline reservation systems—as well as a possible 10 percent to 15 percent edge in productivity; however, the author concluded that the Japanese industry remained too small (one-quarter of U.S. sales) to compete effectively with the United States.[37] Similarly identifying both weaknesses and strengths in Japan, another 1984 writer observed the increase of software factories and their highly systematic approach to software production, as well as Japanese excellence in graphics and embedded software, such as in industrial and consumer products. Yet he also argued that Japanese software "is less sophisticated and more costly to produce than Western software," and that the Japanese have trouble writing packages because their culture suppresses creativity.[38] As late as 1989, two articles asserted that the Japanese software industry remained "small and not very visible," and perhaps two decades behind the United States,[39] and that, while the Japanese might be strong in business-applications software tailored to their home market, they were still too weak in general product development and lacked enough skilled programmers to compete with U.S. firms in the American market.[40]

The U.S. Department of Commerce set the tone for many of these studies in a comparison of the software industries in the United States and Japan (as well as in other countries), also published in 1984. This stated that the Japanese seemed "far behind the U.S. in basic research and advanced development of software," and "have never developed a programming language or an operating system that has become a de facto standard internationally." On the other hand, the government researchers acknowledged Japanese gains in tool usage and product engineering, especially along the factory model, with high productivity and quality: "Japanese programmers average 2000 lines of code per month (versus less than 300 lines per month for U.S. programmers) and have one-tenth the error rate of their U.S. counterparts."[41] Furthermore, the authors felt the Japanese not only emphasized high quality and low cost—strategies that had already proved successful in other industries—but that Japan appeared to be overtaking the United States in the efforts to move software production beyond the craft stage, as well as exhibiting a rising interest in basic research and innovation:

> The Japanese are apparently far ahead of, and increasing their lead over, U.S. firms in making substantial improvements on existing technologies from the United States and Europe, and incorporating these advances into highly marketable products. The Japanese have also made impressive gains in the development of software tools and have encouraged their widespread use within their software factories to boost productivity. . . . By contrast, while the United States is developing software engineering technology, the use of tools in U.S. firms is quite limited. . . . Many U.S. software companies consider programming a craft and believe the future strength of the industry lies in its creativity rather than a disciplined approach to software development as do the Japanese. . . . The Japanese are likely to become the strongest U.S. competitor in the world software market. They may achieve this by following a strategy akin to one they have followed in the equipment area: emphasizing product development in standardized sectors, adding enhancements, stressing quality and offering competitive prices. In the long term, the Japanese will try to emerge as software innovators, as typified by the spirit of the Fifth Generation Computer Project.[42]

Other writers commented on this same theme that the Japanese appeared to manage software differently from U.S. firms and this accounted for superior quality and productivity, even though Japan had yet to catch up in product designs, packages, export skills, or basic research. As seen in a 1985 article, the message also seemed clear that Japanese firms effectively utilized teamwork approaches and tools that helped make software development less dependent on a few highly skilled individuals. This author also criticized U.S. firms as too dependent on craft practices left over from the early days of the industry:

[T]he approach to software technology taken by major developers in Japan, such as NEC, Fujitsu Ltd, and Hitachi Ltd., universally strive to harness that tradition of excellent teamwork. . . . Each of these developers has automated versions of planning and reporting systems that enforce a strict teamwork methodology through the complete life cycle of a computer program—from planning to design to maintenance, and without coding, since high-level language-source codes are automatically produced from the design documents. . . . Until now, the Japanese have been hampered in their software development efforts by a lack of team-oriented tools. The tools borrowed from the United States simply do not fit the Japanese culture because they put too much control in too few hands. In America, industrial software development is generally done in groups that are as small as possible to minimize the communication problems among people. That makes the knowledge of each individual programmer a critical factor to the success of any software-development project. But . . . that is just not tolerable in the Japanese culture. As a consequence, the Japanese have had to perform basic research into software tools that can be wielded by many hands at once. Nobody else was going to develop group-programming tools for them.[43]

The data presented in this book, including the appendixes, tend to confirm many of these generalizations, especially the tendency of the Japanese toward high productivity and quality and more reusability than U.S. firms; tools, techniques, and organizations that try to make software development less dependent on a few highly skilled engineers; and the appearance of both strengths and weaknesses in Japanese software products. More information collected over time from larger samples is necessary to pursue these issues more definitively.

Nonetheless, a particular idea suggested in various reports remains intriguing: that large Japanese companies such as Toshiba, Hitachi, NEC, and Fujitsu, at least in some respects, actually view and manage software development differently from many of their U.S. or European counterparts. While one might explain that Japanese people are unique culturally, some U.S. firms also attempted factory approaches, with or without the factory label. Thus an underlying explanation for differences exhibited by the Japanese might be that software producers in general have different options for managing product development, and that the historical and market context in Japan has encouraged producers to adopt particular approaches that the Japanese and outside observers have categorized as factorylike.[44]

The Historical and Market Context

When Western writers adopted the term *software crisis* during the late 1960s, Japanese software producers faced a challenge of comparable and perhaps greater severity. There existed few centers of even limited programming expertise in Japan at this time—some major universities and government laboratories, Nippon Telegraph and Telephone (NT&T), and the mainframe computer manufacturers, primarily Fujitsu, NEC, Hitachi, and Toshiba. In fact, as discussed in later chapters, contemporary accounts from the 1960s and early 1970s are full of complaints from managers regarding the paucity of people knowledgeable in computer programming and the increasing complexity of the tasks they had to undertake to compete in the computer industry.

To catch up with the West, leading Japanese companies adopted U.S. standards and directly entered into contracts with American firms, through which they acquired both hardware designs and software programs. During the early 1960s, Hitachi, Toshiba, and NEC linked up with RCA, GE, and Honeywell, respectively. Hitachi and NEC also effectively combined learning from U.S. producers with in-house R&D projects, such as for jointly developed machines and large computers sold primarily to Japanese universities.[45] Even Fujitsu, which developed computers independently in the 1960s, in the early 1970s adopted IBM standards for its mainframes and invested in Amdahl, the largest U.S. producer of IBM-compatible machines.[46]

The Japanese government, beginning in the late 1950s, provided an environment conducive to experimentation and gradual improvement through several measures to help local firms get started in the computer industry and then increase their market shares among domestic consumers. The most important consisted of restrictions on hardware imports, including computers sold by IBM's Japanese subsidiary, to machines for which there were no domestic equivalents in production or in the planning stage; subsidies to support the leasing of Japanese-made computers to Japanese users; and subsidies and government contracts to support hardware and semiconductor technology development. The government sponsored several efforts to design software packages and tools during the 1970s, although, as will be discussed in Chapter 8, these had little impact on the practices of individual firms.[47]

The success of company and government efforts in computer hardware became apparent in 1965. This was the first year Japanese computer manufacturers, aided by the production of American-designed machines (except in the case of Fujitsu), captured more than 50 percent of their domestic market. By the late 1970s, Japanese computers had become comparable in performance and price with IBM products, with many machines actually priced below similar IBM models.[48] The Japanese share of the home market increased steadily, reaching 77 percent in 1986 (Table 1.5). To sell hardware in the Japanese market, companies had to offer at least basic programs as well as provide guarantees of quality similar to those provided for hardware products. Thus, during this period from the late 1960s through the 1980s, Japanese computer manufacturers began paying serious attention to the process of software development. Not only did the industry lack skilled engineers, but soft-

Table 1.5 Japanese Computer Industry Revenues (1958–1986)

Year	Revenues*	Japanese Firms' Share† (%)	Year	Revenues*	Japanese Firms' Share† (%)
1958	1	7	1973	528	51
1959	2	22	1974	641	48
1960	7	27	1975	614	56
1961	13	18	1976	732	57
1962	22	33	1977	1,075	66
1963	43	30	1978	1,182	67
1964	42	43	1979	1,308	70
1965	52	52	1980	1,516	73
1966	67	54	1981	1,870	72
1967	109	47	1982	2,268	74
1968	161	57	1983	2,810	74
1969	212	58	1984	3,499	75
1970	331	60	1985	4,104	74
1971	351	59	1986	4,404	77
1972	419	53			

*Billions of yen (annual deliveries including rentals and purchases); †percentage accounted for by Japanese-owned companies, primarily Fujitsu, NEC, Hitachi, and Toshiba.
Source: Marie Anchordoguy, *Computers Inc.: Japan's Challenge to IBM* (Cambridge, Mass.: Council on East Asian Studies/Harvard University Press, 1989), pp. 34–35.

ware costs escalated for Japanese firms because of rapidly expanding demand for labor-intensive customized programs and for complex basic software. In addition, because of bundling with hardware prices, Japanese companies had difficulty recovering their expenses, and they made few applications packages that might sell in large volumes.

A comparison of product segments for the computer industries in Japan and the United States also indicates that producers in the two countries faced different markets and opportunities. In the late 1980s, the U.S. industry remained nearly twice the size of the Japanese in terms of revenues, although software accounted for similar percentages— approximately 38 percent of computer-industry sales in Japan (excluding data-processing services), and approximately 35 percent in the United States (Table 1.6). Japanese firms built a full complement of machines, ranging from personal computers to large systems (generally costing the equivalent of $4 million or more), complete with basic and applications software. Programs included operating systems, language compilers, other basic software, database systems, and applications extending from small word-processing packages to enormous customized and integrated systems for railroad reservations, on-line banking, power-plant control, and manufacturing control systems dating back to the 1960s.

In other respects, however, important differences appear between the two markets. Most notable was the Japanese concentration on large, medium, and small (less than $800,000) mainframes or minicomputers.

Table 1.6 Japan–U.S. Hardware and Software Comparison (1987)*

	Japan		U.S.	
Total market	$34.1		$70.4	
Software revenues/Total market (%)		38		35
Hardware Shipments	$21.0	100%	$45.6	100%
Large systems	8.7	41	9.1	20
Medium systems	3.1	15	8.7	19
Small systems	5.0	24	8.2	18
Personal computers	4.2	20	19.6	43
Software-Vendor Revenues	$13.0	100%	$24.8	100%
Total packages	1.4	11	13.1	53
Types:				
(systems/utilities)	NA	—	(5.0)	(20)
(application tools)	NA	—	(3.7)	(15)
(application packages)	NA	—	(4.5)	(18)
Custom software/system intgegration†	10.1	78	9.6	39
(custom software only)	(7.9)	(61)	NA	—
Facilities management/maintenance	1.4	11	2.1	8
Miscellaneous Data				
1987–1992 compound annual growth estimate for software revenues		17%		20%
Annual growth in supply of programmers		13%		4%
Typical wait for customized programs in months (ca. 1984)		26		40
Computer makers as suppliers				
of basic systems software		70%		45%
of applications software		15%		5%

*$1.00 = 125 yen; †custom software/system integration for Japan includes consulting ($0.67 billion); for the U.S. market, this category refers to contract programming and design. NA = not available. *Source:* International Data Corporation, "Japan Computer Industry: Review and Forecast, 1987–1992," Framingham, Mass., unpublished draft #3900, January 1989; and International Data Corporation, *Computer Industry Report: The Gray Sheet,* Dec. 16, 1988, p. 3. Also, for miscellaneous data, U.S. Department of Commerce, International Trade Administration, *A Competitive Assessment of the U.S. Software Industry*; A. Zavala, *Research on Factors that Influence the Productivity of Software Development Workers,* (Palo Alto, Calif.: SRI International, June 1985); H. Aiso, "Overview of Japanese National Projects in Information Technology," (Tokyo: International Symposium on Computer Architecture, lecture 1, June 1986); Fumihiko Kamijo, "Information Technology Activities in the Japanese Software Industry," *Oxford Surveys in Information Technology* 3, 1986.

These accounted for 80 percent of domestic computer shipments in Japan during 1987. Large computers alone accounted for 41 percent, compared to 20 percent in the United States. Personal computers, in contrast, were only about 20 percent of shipment revenues in Japan, compared to 43 percent in the United States.

One reason for the slow dissemination of personal computers was the technical difficulty of adapting the Japanese language to machines with limited processing capabilities and memories. As the power of microprocessors increased, and larger versions of personal computers overlapped with another category of hardware termed *office computers*, Japanese companies have paid more attention to these small machines and their software needs (usually packaged programs). Nonetheless, the fact that NEC alone accounted for 575,000 or 61 percent of new personal computers shipped from Japan in 1987 reflected the historically small stake in personal computers at most Japanese computer manufacturers.[49]

Japan's bias toward large computers probably left its software market more stable than the U.S. market, particularly because of the way firms competed. On the one hand, large computers constituted the oldest and biggest segment of the industry; producers of these machines built on architectures introduced in the 1960s and 1970s to allow themselves and customers to create software programs and databases compatible with future generations of machines and programs.

Most important, in the major segments of their markets—large, medium, and small mainframes—Japanese companies let U.S. firms lead in architecture development and standardization. Beginning in the mid-1970s, both Fujitsu and Hitachi began producing IBM-compatible machines as well as operating systems and other programs patterned after IBM products. Although Hitachi later allowed the architecture for its domestic machines to depart slightly from IBM, after IBM began placing more features of its architecture onto hardwired chips that were difficult to mimic, Hitachi continued to make IBM-compatible mainframes for export, selling these through Itel in the late 1970s and then through a subsidiary of National Semiconductor until 1989, when Hitachi formed a joint venture with Electronic Data Systems for direct U.S. marketing. Fujitsu, meanwhile, has continued to follow the IBM standard, while NEC in the mid-1960s adopted an architecture initially developed by Honeywell and in 1978 took over a line of mainframes earlier produced by Toshiba that relied on an architecture GE had developed in the 1960s. In addition, all the Japanese manufacturers offered mainframes that ran versions of the UNIX operating system developed originally at AT&T.

The absence in Japan of a large defense sector, which in the United States absorbed significant amounts of unique and innovative software, also fostered stability in the kinds of products Japanese firms had to produce. Many leading U.S. software producers, including SDC's division that once launched a software factory, as well as IBM, TRW, Boeing, Honeywell, Hughes Aircraft, and other parts of Unisys (formerly known as Sperry and Burroughs), competed fiercely in this market and invested heavily in tools, methods, and programming environments (see Appendix A for an analysis of some of these firms). The U.S. Department of Defense also had strict requirements for its contractors, forcing producers to follow a prescribed process (at least nominally) and keep detailed records and documentation. These customer requirements forced companies to create some standards or procedures above the level of individual projects. On the other hand—and this may distinguish even structured U.S. defense contractors from Japanese software factories—U.S. personnel had to be sufficiently skilled and versatile to produce defense systems that might require totally new, highly innovative, and extremely complex functions. For these types of projects, as SDC discovered, attempts to remove programming personnel from individuals knowledgeable in specific applications, or to impose a set of standardized tools over all projects, proved too constraining.

Thus, while custom software and system integration accounted for approximately $10 billion in both the Japanese and U.S. markets in 1987, at least some of the content of this work probably differed. While some jobs might not prove suitable for factory approaches, in Japan, the large amounts of manpower required to develop IBM-like basic software or tailored but relatively similar applications programs seems to have provided strong incentives for Japanese producers to seek process and tool standardization as well as reusability across as many projects as possible.

Perhaps the major difference between Japan and the United States was that custom software and system integration, with only a minimal percentage for defense or aerospace applications, accounted for the vast majority of Japanese software development. In fact, custom software remained the largest single segment (61 percent) of all software sales in Japan in 1987. Combined with system-integration revenues, this accounted for 78 percent of the Japanese software market, compared to 39 percent in the United States. This structural feature of the Japanese market alone suggested that Japanese firms faced different challenges than were common in the United States and had more difficulty relying on packaged software, which accounted for only about 11 percent of the software sold separately from hardware in Japan. (The comparable figure for the U.S. market exceeded 50 percent.)

Recent efforts by Japanese and American-owned firms operating in Japan made packages the most rapidly growing segment of the Japanese software industry in 1987, with annual growth rates of approximately 30 percent expected through 1992. About a third of packages applied to personal computers, the fastest growing hardware segment in Japan, with annual growth rates of 15 percent expected through 1992, compared to 11 percent for hardware in general.[50] In addition, since Japanese customers often opposed paying separately for software when they purchased hardware or integrated systems, Table 1.6 probably understated the overall figures, especially package sales.

Why Japanese producers and customers made such slow progress in packages seemed to reflect a combination of factors. While package sales in the United States increased dramatically with the increase in popularity of personal computers, a segment of the market where custom programming is particularly uneconomical for nonspecialists, personal computers have been the weakest segment in the Japanese industry. In addition, available Japanese-made packages appear to have been of poor quality (in terms of functionality), at least until recently.[51] This perhaps reflects the long-term shortage of programmers in Japan, who would need to be highly skilled both in software engineering and specific applications. Japanese customers also seem to have been slow to accept packaged software imported from the United States without modifications, probably because of differences in requirements as well as preferences for systems using the Japanese language. Furthermore, Japanese customers did not always allow producers to debundle systems software and some other packages from hardware prices.[52]

Yet, despite high relative demand for labor-intensive customized software, the historical backwardness of the package market, and a continuing shortage of personnel (see Appendix C), Japanese producers appeared to be managing their software crisis relatively well. In 1987, the annual rise in software demand was approximately 17 percent, still higher than the 13 percent-annual growth expected in programmers entering the industry but a closer match with supply than in the U.S. market, where growth was about 20 percent and programmer increases merely 4 percent.[53] In addition, perhaps because of an ability to customize software relatively quickly, data indicated that U.S. customers who desired to buy fully customized applications programs typically had a three- to four-year wait, compared to only about two years in Japan.[54] As discussed later, Japanese vendors also priced their packages and systems-engineering or customizing services lower than U.S.-based firms, indicating they were providing software cheaply as well as quickly.

In short, while many products and segments in their industries appeared similar, Japanese software producers operated in a context somewhat different from many of their U.S. counterparts. In Japan's market—characterized by development for large computers with relatively stable architectures and applications, a look to the United States for product standards and innovations, a small defense sector, a tremendous preference for customized programs, and only recent demand for packages and more rapidly changing small computers—it would be logical for producers to focus on process refinements encouraging reusability as well as automation of design, especially in customized applications, the largest single segment of the measurable industry. This would help them tailor programs for customers who might want fully customized systems but could not afford them or for customers who found available packages inadequate but could not afford fully customized products.

Performance Comparisons

No one best way existed to analyze how well firms performed in software development, although various data made it possible to examine the leading Japanese firms and compare them with U.S. companies in a few basic areas. Typical measures in software included labor productivity (output over time, such as in lines of code), reliability (defects or faults per delivered lines of code over time), quality (reliability as well as functionality), product-line and company market shares, or customer (user) satisfaction. Data summarized in this section and in Appendexes B and C indicate that Japanese firms fared well in comparison with U.S. firms and in direct competition with U.S.-based companies operating in Japan. Perhaps most important, the top Japanese firms did extremely well in the segments or qualities most valued by Japanese customers in their home market.

First, with regard to productivity, quality, and other measures of programmer performance, a second survey conducted as part of this research studied approximately forty Japanese and U.S. projects (this is described in more detail in Appendix B and in a separate article).[55] The data is from a relatively large sample for software projects, although not big enough to obtain definitive statistical results. Hence the survey is no more than suggestive. Some measures, such as productivity in lines of code, though the most common method of calculating productivity, also contain numerous problems. An efficient (smaller and fast-running) short program, for example, may take longer to write than a less efficient lengthier program, yet the developer of the shorter and sometimes more desirable program would appear to have a lower productivity rate; there were often differences and inconsistencies within and among firms in how they counted code, especially with regard to whether they included reused or modified code, or how they treated reuse of designs and specifications; or a programmer might write quickly but create numerous errors, which then might require enormous amounts of time to fix later on. Software-engineering literature has widely discussed these and other concerns, and later chapters will return to these issues when considering productivity data from individual firms.[56]

With these limitations, the project survey indicated, at the very least, that Japanese firms were not inferior to U.S. counterparts in productivity or product reliability. To the contrary, as numerous reports suggested, the Japanese numbers seemed superior to those from U.S. firms. Overall, nominal productivity (lines of code produced per work year) was 60 percent to 70 percent higher in the Japanese sample and this seemed to reflect higher levels of reusability. Defects per lines of delivered code in the Japanese sample remained one-half to one-fourth that of the U.S. projects. It also appeared that Japanese firms leveraged their people well by dividing them more frequently across multiple projects for design and spending less time on routine coding tasks. In quality control, Japanese seemed to pay greater attention to statistical methods, quality circles, training, top-management audits of product quality, and companywide activities.

Other ways to measure company and product (including service) performance are market shares and customer satisfaction. While these also remain difficult to analyze precisely, two 1988 surveys of 6,800 Japanese users of mainframes, minicomputers, and office computers, published in Japan's leading computer-industry journal, *Nikkei Computer*, suggested several differences between Japanese firms and U.S. producers operating in the Japanese market (see Appendix C for additional details and reference tables). Japanese producers appeared to have superior applications for large computers, the bulk of the market, in addition to providing cheaper software and systems-engineering services overall. Japanese customers also valued price-performance above all other factors in making decisions regarding purchases of new computers.

The *Nikkei* data on customer satisfaction has the limitation that, since most Japanese customers purchased from one vendor, it is difficult to know to what extent they compared the performance of their hardware and software with products of other manufacturers, or how high their standards were; however, because of IBM's extensive marketing efforts in Japan and attempts to win back customers, especially from Fujitsu (which offered IBM-compatible products) and Hitachi (which offered products comparable to IBM's), it would appear that a large number of customers at least knew what basic features and prices IBM provided. Given these caveats, where it mattered most to their customers, Japanese manufacturers appeared to be equal or even superior to IBM, their main rival in the United States as well as in Japan, and competed effectively with other U.S. firms.

The Japanese mainframe segment remained highly competitive, with seven firms offering comparable products.[57] Whereas IBM accounted for more than 70 percent of worldwide shipments of mainframe computers in the mid-1980s,[58] neither it nor any other one firm reached this level of dominance in the Japanese market. Japan also included vendors of office computers and minicomputers that were not active in the United States, such as Oki Electric, although conversely, many strong U.S. firms, including Digital Equipment Corporation, in the late 1980s had only begun to market their products in Japan.

American-owned computer vendors in Japan primarily sold hardware and basic software designed in the United States, modified systems to handle the Japanese language, and provided systems-engineering and customized applications in direct competition with Japanese firms, mainly in the information, financial, and distribution sectors, with some general systems engineering for office automation and computer-aided manufacturing and design. Employees were mainly Japanese, although in sales of packaged products and in development technology, the U.S.-owned subsidiaries generally followed guidelines their U.S. parents set. This changed slowly in the late 1980s, as subsidiaries of the U.S. firms became more concerned with utilizing the Japanese-language, providing packages tailored to Japanese users, especially for personal or office computers, and offering fully customized systems.[59]

IBM Japan, though it met stiff competition from Japanese firms, remained by far the most successful foreign-owned computer firm, with approximately 21 percent of Japan's 1988 installed base of all computers by value, compared to 10 percent for Unisys (split between Sperry-Univac and Burroughs) and 2 percent for National Cash Register (NCR) (Table 1.7). This company had a history dating back to 1937, and had grown to two or three times the size of other foreign firms in the computer industry. Approximately 20,000 employees worked in areas from R&D to hardware manufacturing and assembly, as well as marketing and programming. As in the United States and Europe, IBM Japan focused on selling very large computer systems while gradually emphasizing smaller office computers and personal computers (tailored to the Japanese market).

Unisys Japan included components of the former Nihon Univac, a joint venture established between Sperry-Rand and Mitsui Trading in 1951, as well as the former Japanese subsidiary of Burroughs International. It also worked closely with Oki Univac, a joint venture with Oki Electric that manufactured disk drives, printers, and terminals designed by Unisys Sperry, as well as maintained a product development center in Tokyo focused on software products. Both Unisys divisions appeared strong in large machines and specialized applications software. The only other major U.S. player, NCR Japan, was founded in 1920 and primarily sold automated teller machines (ATMs), cash dispensers, point-of-sale registers (POS), host computers for these terminals, high-priced office computers, and systems-engineering services.

A first observation one can make from the *Nikkei* data is that Japanese

Table 1.7 Computer Installed-Base Share Comparison in Japan (1988)

Maker	Value (million yen)	%	Units (no. of machines)	%
Fujitsu	538,172	32.7	2,348	36.0
IBM Japan	341,148	20.7	676	10.4
Hitachi	302,084	18.4	894	13.7
NEC	254,367	15.5	1,694	26.0
Unisys Japan	160,267	9.7	500	7.7
(Univac/Sperry)	(117,011)	(7.1)	(209)	(3.2)
(Burroughs)	(43,256)	(2.6)	(291)	(4.5)
NCR Japan	32,328	2.0	291	4.5
Mitsubishi	16,881	1.0	110	1.7
Subtotals				
Japanese		67.6		77.4
U.S.		32.4		22.6
Total	1,645,247	100.0	6,513	100.0

Source: *Nikkei Computer*, Sept. 26, 1988, p. 77.

computer manufacturers were by far the leaders in hardware market shares. They dominated in terms of the value of the installed base (67.6 percent) as well as units in the field (77.4 percent). Fujitsu held the largest share (32.7 percent and 36.0 percent, respectively) as of July 1988 (Table 1.7). IBM had a slight lead over Fujitsu in large mainframes, although Fujitsu remained far ahead in mid-sized systems. NEC, in addition to its overwhelming advantage in personal computers, led in small mainframes (Table 1.8).

Information services, finance, government, and distribution sectors accounted for 61 percent of system placements by value in the Japanese market (Appendix C, Table C.1). Four companies dominated these sectors and the industry overall: Fujitsu, IBM, Hitachi, and NEC. Japanese vendors dominated each individual industry segment, except for financial customers, where IBM remained the market leader and U.S. firms held 53 percent of the installed base by value versus 47 percent for the Japanese. Japanese firms held 95 percent of the government market and this helped their overall shares, although government placements accounted for only 13 percent of the total market. Minus the government sector, therefore, Japanese vendors still accounted for at least 55 percent of the installed base (Tables 1.9 and C.1).

Japanese customers ranked domestic manufacturers considerably above U.S. firms in hardware technology, price-performance (cost per million instructions per second or mips), and hardware maintenance. Hitachi ranked highest in these three categories among all vendors, and was closely followed by Fujitsu (Table 1.10). This combination of empha-

Table 1.8 Installed Base Market Shares by System Size*

	Large (%)	Mid-Size (%)	Small (%)
Fujitsu	28.3	38.2	38.7
IBM Japan	29.8	11.8	1.8
Hitachi	22.0	15.9	7.0
NEC	7.5	21.2	38.9
Unisys Japan	10.9	7.7	10.0
NCR Japan	1.2	2.7	3.6
Mitsubishi	0.3	2.5	—
Subtotals			
Japanese	58.1	77.8	84.6
U.S.	41.9	22.2	15.4
Total	100.0	100.0	100.0
System size	55.8	33.5	10.7

*Systems (including peripherals) were divided as follows: large were those costing 500 million yen and above ($4 million at $1.00 = 125 yen); mid-size from 100 million yen ($800,000) to 500 million; and small below 100 million yen.
Source: *Nikkei Computer*, Sept. 26, 1988, p. 77.

Table 1.9 Percentage of Installed Base by Industry: Manufacturer Market Shares*

Industry	F	I	H	N	S	B	R	M	Japan	U.S.	Total
Info. Services	29	27	25	9	7	3	0	1	64	36	100
Finance	25	29	16	6	14	5	6	0	47	53	100
Government	48	3	20	26	3	0	0	1	95	5	100
Distribution	37	10	17	21	5	6	3	1	76	24	100
Machinery	22	31	23	15	4	1	3	2	62	38	100
Chemicals	32	25	18	13	11	1	1	0	63	37	100
Elec. machines	33	33	11	17	5	0	0	2	63	37	100
Energy	20	22	28	16	14	0	0	1	65	35	100
Institutions	44	9	8	29	4	3	2	1	82	18	100
Construction	43	22	13	16	2	1	1	3	75	15	100
Foodstuffs	26	18	18	28	2	6	2	0	72	18	100
Services	19	8	20	37	7	7	1	2	78	12	100
Others	48	20	9	17	2	2	1	1	75	25	100
Total share	33	21	18	16	7	3	2	1	68	32	100

*Totals may not add up to 100% due to rounding. 100% of total share = 1,645 billion yen. F = Fujitsu; I = IBM; H = Hitachi; N = NEC; S = Unisys/Sperry-Univac; B = Unisys/Burroughs; R = NCR; M = Mitsubishi.
Source: *Nikkei Computer*, Sept. 26, 1988, p. 78.

ses appeared to suit customers extremely well, since Japanese users cited price-performance as the most important factor influencing purchasing decisions (Table 1.11). IBM was actually the price leader, although it achieved this on average by selling mostly very large systems, where prices per processing power tended to decline. Overall, the average price users paid per mip was 58 million yen (about $460,000) for Japanese machines, compared to 73 million yen (about $580,000) for U.S. machines (Table 1.12).

Table 1.10 User Satisfaction Levels by Manufacturer*

	F	I	H	N	S	B	R	M	Weighted Averages Total	Japan	U.S.
System software	6.7	**7.3**	6.6	6.6	**7.3**	**7.6**	6.8	6.3	6.8	6.6	**7.3**
Hardware	**7.3**	**7.3**	**7.6**	6.9	7.0	6.3	6.8	6.8	7.1	**7.2**	7.0
Japanese processing	**7.0**	5.3	6.1	**6.7**	5.9	4.9	5.7	5.5	6.4	**6.7**	5.6
Price-performance	**7.1**	6.4	**7.1**	6.8	6.6	6.3	6.2	6.4	6.8	**7.0**	6.4
Hardware maintenance	**7.8**	7.5	**8.4**	7.4	7.7	6.7	7.3	**7.8**	7.7	**7.8**	7.3
Software maintenance	6.4	**6.7**	**6.8**	6.3	**6.9**	5.7	6.2	6.3	6.4	6.4	6.4
System SE support	6.4	6.3	6.4	6.3	**7.3**	6.1	6.3	**6.6**	6.4	6.4	6.4
Application SE support	**6.0**	5.4	**6.0**	**6.0**	**6.9**	5.7	**6.0**	5.9	5.9	**6.0**	5.8
Salesman relations	6.3	6.2	6.2	6.3	**6.7**	6.2	**6.9**	**6.6**	6.3	6.3	**6.4**
Product information	6.0	**6.5**	**6.5**	5.9	**6.4**	5.5	5.9	5.7	6.1	6.0	**6.2**
General satisfaction	**7.0**	**7.2**	**7.0**	6.8	**7.1**	6.6	6.8	6.5	6.9	6.9	**7.0**

*Scale: satisfied, 9–10 points; somewhat satisfied, 7–8; neither satisfied nor dissatisfied, 4–6; somewhat dissatisfied, 2–3; dissatisfied, 0–1. Bold numbers = above average. SE = systems engineering; company abbreviations as in Table 1.9.
Source: *Nikkei Computer*, Sept. 26, 1988, p. 95.

Table 1.11 Percentage of Factors Influencing System Selection*

	F	I	H	N	S	B	R	M	Weighted Averages Total	Japan	U.S.
Price-performance	**46**	28	**43**	**43**	29	25	21	33	40	**44**	26
Upward compatibility	32	**33**	**37**	27	**36**	**49**	**46**	29	33	31	**39**
Reliability, fault tolerance	**33**	**41**	**38**	27	22	22	29	24	32	32	32
Available software	21	**31**	14	18	**33**	**33**	25	19	21	19	**30**
Company policy, business contacts	14	11	**23**	**19**	7	6	11	**30**	16	**18**	9
Systems engineering support	**13**	7	12	**17**	**23**	13	9	20	14	14	11
Same industry operating results	**13**	9	5	**12**	10	**16**	**14**	10	11	11	**12**
Maintenance service	5	4	6	**7**	**7**	5	**9**	3	6	6	6
Technology excellence	3	**14**	2	4	**6**	**8**	1	3	4	3	**9**
Salesman enthusiasm	2	0	1	**3**	2	**8**	**12**	**4**	3	2	**4**
Installation conditions	**2**	**3**	1	1	1	**2**	**2**	1	2	1	2
Reputation	1	1	0	1	0	0	1	0	1	1	1
Other	5	6	5	**8**	**10**	6	5	**6**	6	6	6

*Users were asked to choose the two most important factors in influencing their purchase decisions. The number of responses citing each factor are given in percentages. Bold numbers = above average. Company abbreviations as in Table 1.9.
Source: *Nikkei Computer*, Sept. 26, 1988, p. 96.

On the other hand, U.S. vendors had an advantage in systems software, marketing, and general satisfaction levels, with Unisys and IBM rated particularly high in systems software (Table 1.10). American firms scored slightly higher in user satisfaction for technical support in system

Table 1.12 Average System Configuration and Software Prices

		Hardware		Software	
	mips	Price (million yen, dicounted)	Price-Performance (million yen/mip, discounted)	Software charges (monthly in units of 10,000 yen)	Ratio (software charges/price-performance)
IBM Japan	9.07	443	49	351	7.2
Hitachi	4.04	208	51	141	2.8
Unisys/Sperry	4.23	399	94	187	2.0
Fujitsu	2.90	157	54	140	2.6
NEC	1.55	105	68	82	1.2
Unisys/Burroughs	1.45	117	81	60	0.7
Mitsubishi	1.45	98	68	181	2.7
NCR Japan	0.85	88	103	96	0.9
Weighted Averages					
Japan	2.62	147	58	122	2.2
U.S.	5.23	301	73	219	3.9

Source: *Nikkei Computer*, Sept. 26, 1988, pp. 79 and 96 (discount rates).
mips = million instructions per second.

systems engineering (design and integration of the basic hardware and software systems) and slightly higher in general satisfaction in system and application systems engineering (development of custom software and, if necessary, integration with or installation on the hardware) (Tables 1.10, C.2, C.3). The U.S. firms also led slightly in salesman relations, product information, and general satisfaction. (Tables 1.8, 1.7, C.2, C.3). These types of factors (specifically, salesman enthusiasm, perception of technology excellence, and reputation), however, had little impact on actual purchasing decisions. Availability of software was another strength of the U.S. vendors and a major reason why Japanese customers chose U.S.-made hardware when they made this decision, but this, too, was not a major factor influencing purchasing decisions, trailing price-performance, upward compatibility, and reliability, where Japanese vendors were either superior, close, or equal to their U.S. counterparts (Table 1.11).

In contrast to systems software, the Japanese firms seemed to have an advantage in applications software and systems engineering. They sustained a clear lead in Japanese-language processing, perhaps as expected, but also proved superior in application systems-engineering support and knowledge of the applications. Unisys/Sperry-Univac and Mitsubishi were best perceived in two surveys of systems engineering in applications, although both had small market shares. Fujitsu, Hitachi, NEC, and NCR had identical scores in applications support, ranking above average, while Fujitsu and NEC were especially strong in Japanese-language processing. In contrast, IBM received somewhat weak scores in both areas. In general systems engineering, software maintenance, and support for new versions of systems software, Japanese and U.S. vendors had almost identical satisfaction scores (Tables 1.10, C.2, C.3).

The survey data also support the observation that Japanese firms followed a low-price strategy, undercutting U.S. vendors in various software charges and services. IBM charged the highest prices for its software, based on average monthly payments for leased programs such as operating systems or standard applications. Even adjusting for the price-performance levels of its hardware, IBM still charged more than twice as much as any other vendor for its software. Overall, the average Japanese monthly charge was 1,220,000 yen (approximately $10,000), compared to 2,190,000 yen ($18,000) for U.S. vendors (Table 1.12). In systems-engineering service charges, the average Japanese price per person-month on a fixed contract was 730,000 yen ($5,800), compared to 930,000 yen ($7,400) for U.S. vendors (although U.S. vendors provided more service without charge) (Table 1.13). In terms of actual charges levied for individual phases, users of Japanese vendors paid less for system consulting, system design, programming, operations, and training (Table 1.14). These differences existed despite a different mix in market shares of the vendors, although the range of systems-engineering

Table 1.13 System SE Service Charges

Company	Service Fee Gratis (%)	Average SE Charges—Fixed Contract (10,000 yen/work-mo)
Toshiba	87	—
IBM	82	107
NEC	71	93
Unisys/Burroughs	68	56
Hitachi	65	60
Unisys/Sperry	64	82
Mitsubishi	62	—
Fujitsu	60	66
Oki	50	—
NCR	41	73
Other	46	—
Weighted Averages		
Japanese	65	73
U.S.	74	93

mo = month; SE = systems engineering.
Source: Nikkei Computer, March 14, 1988, p. 64.

charges varied relatively little by industry segment, except in system consulting (Table C.4).

Summary and Evaluation

A specific set of questions prompted an exploration of manager emphases in software development: Since programs consist of either unique or nominally customized designs, and the industry lacks standards in many areas, each development effort differs, suggesting that software products seem suitable only for a process centering on the customer (job) or a specific application (special project). If so, then software producers might exhibit characteristics resembling job shops or project-oriented craft production. On the other hand, shortages of skilled engineers needed to develop unique or customized products and other factors might encourage managers to organize software development in a more structured or systematic manner. In fact, the evidence presented shows that even producers of comparable software products exhibit different emphasizes and that many managers pursue standardization, control, and reusability in varying degrees. Furthermore, not only do process options appear to exist in software as in other industries, but companies apparently differentiate themselves by prices and features, and by competing in particular segments of the market—again, like firms in other industries.

What product or process strategy appears best for a particular software firm depends on numerous factors, such as management's competi-

Table 1.14 Average SE Charges Reported by Users by Phase
(10,000 yen/work-month)

Company	System Consulting	System Design	Programming	Operations	Training	System Audit
Fujitsu	107	75	56	39	35	73
	(21)*	(84)	(113)	(82)	(3)	(2)
IBM	106	85	63	47	—	30
	(21)	(59)	(69)	(62)		(1)
NEC	95	78	59	45	40	15
	(19)	(52)	(71)	(42)	(3)	(1)
Hitachi	77	73	59	42	48	70
	(29)	(42)	(46)	(42)	(3)	(1)
Unisys/Burroughs	61	90	67	35	—	—
	(4)	(6)	(8)	(7)		
Unisys/Sperry	102	73	54	44	56	110
	(5)	(5)	(20)	(20)	(1)	(2)
NCR	82	48	55	46	—	80
	(1)	(7)	(7)	(4)		(1)
Mitsubishi	160	74	55	47	—	—
	(1)	(4)	(6)	(4)		
Toshiba	20	45	27	—	—	—
	(1)	(2)	(3)			
Oki	—	75	—	27	—	—
		(1)		(1)		
Others	25	65	54	34	—	125
	(1)	(5)	(5)	(4)		(1)
Computing Centers	113	97	89	114	150	15
	(4)	(3)	(4)	(2)	(1)	(1)
Weighted Averages						
Japan	91	75	57	41	41	58
	(71)	(185)	(239)	(171)	(9)	(4)
U.S.	99	81	61	45	56	46
	(31)	(77)	(104)	(93)	(1)	(4)
Total	94	77	58	43	52	84
	(114)	(295)	(376)	(327)	(11)	(10)

*Nos. in parentheses = no. of responses.
Source: *Nikkei Computer*, March 14, 1988, p. 68.

tive positioning, the nature of specific projects and customer requirements, the capabilities of available personnel, or the appropriateness of existing designs, tools, and methods for new work. In any case, firms pursuing a factory approach risk falling behind industry changes or alienating programmers and managers. Yet managers can increase the likelihood that a structured process will match their products as well as prove acceptable to employees and customers by avoiding high-end customization, low-end commodity competition, and the most rapidly changing market segments. They can focus on more stable groups of products, such as commercial software for large computers, as well as on comparable projects, to help them place a boundary on task complexity or the need to accommodate change rapidly.

These considerations appear to have shaped product and process strategies in the Japanese software industry. Customers historically have preferred mainframe computers and programs with relatively stable architectures and features, and exhibited low demand for packages and high demand for tailored applications. Industry or market characteristics thus provided opportunities for Japanese software producers to create a production process to offset a shortage of skilled personnel in various ways, such as by not investing heavily in product invention, adopting U.S. standards, hiring relatively unskilled personnel, and reusing large amounts of software.

The results seemed successful. The Japanese firms studied in this book appear to have found a way to tackle the challenge of software development and manage this technology as effectively as any of their competitors abroad. They made basic software products adequate to dominate the local hardware market and offered applications and systems-engineering services at relatively low prices to more-or-less satisfied customers. And while Japan had yet to make a large impact in overseas software markets, as discussed in later chapters, the leading Japanese computer firms continued to gain experience and invest in research and new product development. Thus it seemed likely Japanese producers would further refine their software skills and compete even more effectively in a wider range of products and markets, within and outside of Japan.

2

THE TECHNOLOGY: RECURRING PROBLEMS AND INTEGRATED SOLUTIONS

Problems often occur in building large software programs in every phase of development and in every aspect of management planning and control because the technology is inherently complex, developers need to understand programming as well as specific applications, customer needs vary widely, and the industry continues to evolve in both products and tools and techniques. Many development tasks also require coordination among numerous people over long periods of time. In addition, new personnel as well as large projects tend to encounter the same types of difficulties year after year, such as inaccurate requirements specifications, overruns on budgets and schedules, huge variations in individual productivity, poor communication among groups working on the same project, quality or reliability difficulties, system changes in the maintenance phase absorbing more manpower than new development, and so forth.

To some people, the recurrence of these problems might confirm that software in general falls short of science, engineering, or manufacturing disciplines and still demands the participation of highly skilled professionals at all levels. Over the past two decades, however, academic researchers and practitioners have produced a wide range of tools, development methods, and management procedures, as well as millions of lines of designs and code; these all represent actual or potential solutions to particular customer needs and development problems. Thus the recurrence of similar difficulties in software projects may result not from the inability of managers and engineers to find solutions but from the inability of software producers to match available process technology and product knowledge with customer problems more systematically.

This chapter argues that the truth probably lies somewhere in between these two extremes. The factory approach, in any case, primarily extends ideas in software engineering dating back to the 1960s and 1970s that called not for purely technical solutions (which seemed improbable) but rather for integrated organizational and technical efforts aimed at bringing together good practices and tools to alleviate fundamental problems and develop or reuse software in a *relatively* systematic manner. Many firms have attempted integrated approaches with various degrees of commitment and success, as selected examples in this chapter dealing with IBM, ITT, a leading U.S. consulting firm, and Digital Equipment Corporation illustrate. As can be seen in the comparison of these firms with Japanese efforts discussed in Part II, however, Japanese factories refined this strategy of an integrated approach to a remarkable degree. They tried to match their best people with their most difficult jobs, and in general limit the variety of problems developers face by building new products patterned after existing ones, with incremental improvements, and by focusing facilities on similar products, with maximum use of standardized methods, automated tools, and reusable software components.

Recurring Problems in Software Development

The Process

One way to view programming is as a process of analysis and translation: analyzing a problem and then breaking it down into a series of smaller tasks expressed in a manner ultimately understandable to a computer. Software developers begin by translating problems into design specifications and then design specifications into *source code* written in a high-level (English-like) computer language. The next step is to translate the high-level program into a lower-level machine language called *object code*, consisting of zeros and ones that serve as instructions for the computer hardware. Special computer programs called *assemblers* and *compilers* usually perform this transformation automatically, although their design, as well as prior steps in program development, frequently require considerable human thought and judgment.[1]

The development cycle continues in that software must still be tested and frequently changed, repaired, or enhanced (maintained), before and after delivery to users. In terms of time and costs, excluding those incurred during operations and maintenance, testing is usually the most labor-intensive phase, followed by implementation (detailed design and coding) and high-level design. For a product that continues in service with periodic modifications, postdelivery maintenance may become by far the most costly activity, consuming nearly 70 percent of total expenditures over its lifetime, according to commonly cited data on life-cycle costs (Table 2.1).[2]

While most software projects go through similar phases that appear sequential, the production process is more iterative; that is, developers go back and forth among requirements analysis, specification, program design, coding, testing, redesign, retesting, and so on. Experienced engineers or managers may give precise estimates of the time and labor each phase requires for particular applications, although numerous uncertainties upset schedules and budgets and thus make software development something less than exactly predictable. This is especially true since project requirements might contain new functions that are difficult to build, customers often change their minds about features they desire, and individuals usually take different amounts of time to perform similar operations. Furthermore, the larger projects become, the more activities, components, and dependent interactions they require, and thus the greater the uncertainty of the final product's cost, schedule, and performance.

Variations in personnel performance appear to stem from differences not simply in native ability, but also in the particular experiences of the individual. An engineer who has written an inventory-control system in the past probably can complete another inventory-control system in less time than it would take a novice. The relationship of experience to productivity reflects the reality that software, though a generic type of product or technology, may vary enormously in content. The number and type of operations programs must perform in each application

Table 2.1 Software Life-Cycle Cost Breakdown (%)

Phase	A	B
Requirements analysis	9	3
Specification	9	3
High-level design	15	5
Implementation (coding)	21	7
Testing	46	15
A Total	100%	
Operations/Maintenance		67
B Total		100%

A = excluding operations/maintenance; B = including operations/maintenance.
Source: Derived from M. Zelkowitz et al., *Principles of Software Engineering and Design* (Englewood Cliffs, N.J.: Prentice-Hall, 1979), p. 9.

greatly affect the amount of thought, time, and experience required to solve problems and write computer code. The need to adjust to each application or situation makes it difficult for producers to establish and maintain standards, controls, and schedules, as well as divide labor, automate tasks, and reuse components—the essence of factory engineering and production. As a result, loosely structured job-shop approaches, with people, tools, methods, procedures, and designs changed, if necessary, for each project, remain highly suitable for many software projects.

On the other hand, there are advantages to pursuing a more structured process, if at all possible. Job-shop or craft-oriented approaches make it difficult for software developers to share experiences in problem solving and apply potentially useful solutions arrived at in one project— such as tools, methods, procedures, and product designs—to other projects. One might even argue that both the difficulty or inappropriateness of product and process standardization across different projects, as well as insufficient efforts toward this end, contribute to the recurrence of similar problems year after year. A major task facing software producers interested in process improvement is thus to identify what problems projects commonly face and then build an infrastructure—tools, methods, reusable components, training systems, and general expertise—to manage more effectively.

Common Problems

Not only do similar difficulties recur in software development with disturbing regularity, but experienced engineers, managers, and academics catalogued basic problems as early as the 1960s—a further indication that remedies in programming have been slow in coming or hard to implement. In fact, one of the most comprehensive discussions on software engineering, and still a most useful treatment, is a 1968 NATO Science Committee conference report. Participants from several countries agreed that difficulties almost always began with the first step— determining system requirements. Because customers often did not know exactly what type of software they would need, designers could not be certain what type of system to build.

This uncertainty led to other difficulties as a project progressed: The initial cost and schedule estimates invariably had to be changed, while programming modifications introduced during system development usually led to configuration, testing, documentation, and maintenance errors. In addition, the NATO committee discussed the special problems of managing large projects, given huge variations in programming productivity, communication problems within projects, few tools, poor measurement standards, rapid growth in demand and size of programs, lack of standardization, few reusable components, and enormous maintenance costs as systems required repairs or changes over time (Table 2.2).

Table 2.2 NATO Report on Software-Engineering Problems (1968)

Lack of understanding in system requirements on the part of customers and designers.

Large gaps between estimates of costs and time with actual expenditures due to poor estimating techniques, failure to allow time for changes in requirements, and division of programming tasks into blocks before the divisions of the system are well-enough understood to do this properly.

Large variations, as much as 26 : 1 in one study, in programmmers' productivity levels.

Difficulty of dividing labor between design and production (coding), since design-type decisions must still be made in coding.

Difficulty in monitoring progress in a software project, since "program construction is not always a simple progression in which each act of assembly represents a distinct forward step."

Rapid growth in size of software systems.

Poor communication among groups working on the same project, exacerbated by too much uncoordinated or unnecessary information, and a lack of automation to handle necessary information.

Large expense of developing on-line production control tools.

Difficulty of measuring key aspects of programmer and system performance.

A tradition among software developers of not writing systems "for practical use," but trying to write new and better systems, so that they are always combining research, development, and production in a single project, which then makes it difficult to predict and manage.

Rapid growth in the need for programmers and insufficient numbers of adequately trained and skilled programmers.

Difficulty of achieving sufficient reliability (reduced errors and error tolerance) in large software systems.

Dependence of software on hardware, which makes standardization of software difficult across different machines.

Lack of inventories of reusable software components to aid in the building of new programs.

Software maintenance costs often exceeding the cost of the original system development.

Source: Peter Naur and Brian Randell (eds.), *Software Engineering: Report on a Conference Sponsored by the NATO Science Committee*, Brussels, Scientific Affairs Division, NATO, January 1969.

A comparison of the NATO report to numerous anecdotal accounts and formal surveys during the 1970s and 1980s confirms the persistance of these same problems. In describing their software factory in 1975, for example, Harvey Bratman and Terry Court cited five recurring difficulties in SDC projects they hoped the factory would solve: (1) lack of discipline and repeatability across different projects; (2) lack of development visibility in project management; (3) difficulty of accommodating changes in specification requirements; (4) lack of good design and program verification tools; and (5) lack of software reusability across different projects.[3]

Richard Thayer of the University of California, who surveyed industry practitioners as well as sixty software projects in the aerospace industry, compiled a similar list in the late 1970s. Thayer concluded that managers were most concerned with seven issues, all related to planning or control:

(1) incomplete, ambiguous, inconsistent, or unmeasurable requirements specifications; (2) poor project planning; (3) poor cost estimation techniques; (4) poor scheduling estimation techniques; (5) lack of decision rules to help in selecting the correct design techniques, equipment, and other design aids; (6) lack of decision rules to help in selecting the correct procedures, strategies, and tools for software testing; and (7) lack of standards and techniques for measuring the quality of performance and the quantity of production expected from individuals.[4]

But perhaps the most famous account of problems in software development has been *The Mythical Man-Month*, published in 1975 by Frederick P. Brooks, Jr. In recounting his experiences managing production of the primary operating system for IBM's System/360 family of mainframes in the mid-1960s, Brooks concluded, as did others before and after, that difficulties in software development were interrelated, nearly impossible to isolate, and thus inherently systemic. Most vexing in his work at IBM were planning, project control, quality management, and maintenance.

Brooks was particularly eloquent in arguing that poorly developed estimating techniques and methods to monitor schedule progress made projections based on "man-months" so inaccurate as to be practically "mythical" in content. He also claimed that the difficulty of achieving "efficiency and conceptual integrity" in a large project with many participants could be described by an "n-square law" effect, where n objects had $n(n-1)$ possible interactions. Brooks left readers with frightening imagery, comparing the task of large-scale software development to prehistoric animals struggling futilely to escape an unforgiving tar pit and sinking deeper with each movement:

> No scene from prehistory is quite so vivid as that of the mortal struggles of great beasts in the tar pits. In the mind's eye one sees dinosaurs, mammoths, and sabertoothed tigers struggling against the grip of the tar. The fiercer the struggle, the more entangling the tar, and no beast is so strong or so skillful but that he ultimately sinks.
>
> Large-system programming has over the past decade been such a tar pit, and many great and powerful beasts have thrashed violently in it. Most have emerged with running systems—few have met goals, schedules, and budgets. Large and small, massive or wiry, team after team has become entangled in the tar. No one thing seems to cause the difficulty—any particular paw can be pulled away. But the accumulation of simultaneous and interacting factors brings slower and slower motion. Everyone seems to have been surprised by the stickiness of the problem, and it is hard to discern the nature of it. But we must try to understand it if we are to solve it.[5]

A study from 1980 told much the same story while probing backwards in time into the origins of the software crisis. The report, funded by the

National Research Council and named the Computer Science and Engineering Research Study (COSERS), reinforced the notion that problems recurred because they were multifaceted in nature: affected, for better or worse, by characteristics of the industry, the technology, specific applications, organizations, and people such as managers, developers, and customers.[6] The report went on to describe how, before the appearance of FORTRAN and other high-level languages beginning in the late 1950s, programming took place in the machine languages unique to each computer; processing and memory capacities were small until the mid-1960s, which meant that programs were relatively short and simple, compared to those of later years. With high-level languages it became possible to train a programmer in a few weeks, at least to an elementary level. As a result, in the early years, managers and programming personnel did not have to pay much attention to readability, program documentation, or even formal correctness. The loose approach that followed then became part of the craft or culture of software programming—at least in the United States.

The COSERS authors believed that the lack of systematic thinking about design techniques, tools, work environments, and managerial control was not a major problem until computers became more powerful, customers began demanding more programs, and developers had to take on larger and more complex design problems. Increases in product demand led to personnel shortages so severe that it became common for managers with no first-hand knowledge of programming to be managing large projects, and personnel with only a few weeks training to be maintaining highly complex programs. With so little experience, it became commonplace for managers to underestimate the difficulty of programming, and this exacerbated the inadequate training of programming personnel and widespread tolerance of what the COSERS called "sloppy and wasteful practices."

In addition, the duplication of similar but incompatible products even within the same firm, and increasing amounts of manpower spent on maintaining old programs, brought the industry close to the state where "maintenance eventually precludes all possible future development." Many large software programs had even reached the point where it was impossible to correct one error without introducing another. Finally, it seemed that, while users welcomed and promoted innovations in hardware, every advance—even extremely useful features such as interrupts, virtual memory, and better addressing schemes—created "a whole new set of problems for the software developer."

> Systems which people felt would be easy, but tedious to build—the command control system, the information management system, the airline reservation system, the operating system, the world champion chess player— turned out to be extremely difficult or even impossible. Major undertakings

often took 2 to 10 times their expected effort, or had to be abandoned . . . What happened was complexity growing out of scale.[7]

Underlying Causes

Why complexity grew "out of scale" appeared to be the result of numerous factors. Many problems seem linked to the *inherent difficulty of designing, building, and testing software products*, especially the unpredictability of component interactions as programs become large in size; the different ways of designing or coding similar functions; and the near impossibility of fully checking all possible interactions of components and operating conditions. Software producers employed countermeasures, such as high-level languages, structured programming and design techniques, and a variety of support tools and documentation procedures. It also proved possible to reduce variability or the uncertainty of estimates of human performance by standardizing skills through training programs, providing everyone with the same tools and methods, keeping detailed data on the performance of specific individuals in different types of projects as well as data on the average performance of individuals with certain years of experience or training. Reuse of designs and code might have further lessened both complexity and variability by cutting the amount of new software developers had to write.

These kinds of solutions—systematic collection and utilization of individual performance data; standardized training, tools, and methods; and reusability—appear frequently in engineering and manufacturing operations in other industries. Managers, however, still could not predict what the process would be without some form of control or enforcement of standards and procedures that might not have suited all projects and development personnel. In this sense, to what degree a particular firm might be able to structure its process for software development was not simply a technological problem. It depended on the kind and variability of projects as well as the appropriateness of tools and methods given market needs, technological changes, and the preferences of individual managers, engineers, and customers. These factors remained difficult to predict and control since they were both external and internal to the firm.

The need to acquire both *technical expertise in computer programming as well as applications expertise in the area of each program* created hurdles for software developers as well as managers. While various tools and techniques continued to make program design, construction, and testing easier in many respects, in order to utilize fully their knowledge of computer languages, tools, and hardware features, developers had to comprehend the details of user requirements. The time needed to learn how to write software for different applications also varied widely, with some domains relatively simple, such as common business applications, and others extremely complex, such as certain types of process-control software. Therefore, the importance of combining functional know-how in programming with domain-specific know-how presented a general dilemma. This touched managers as well in that personnel with such broad knowledge were usually scarce and took years to cultivate. In addition, de-skilling or automating software development completely remained an elusive goal for all but the simplest of programs, at least given the state of the technology circa 1990.

Diversity in user requirements and applications presented another problem that put practical limits on reusability and repeatability of procedures, tools, or code from project to project, and raised the potential risks of standardizing designs, tools, methods, or training. Variability appeared necessary to accommodate different user needs and technological innovation. When this reflected a lack of standards, poor planning and control, or insufficient product and market focus, managers probably could have done more to limit the diversity they needed to manage, both in external market requirements and internal organizational practices.

At the same time, the *still-evolving state of both hardware and software technology*, especially the frequency of product and process innovations, made it difficult and risky for managers to attempt to focus, standardize, and de-skill operations too much. Especially in segments changing particularly rapidly, such as personal computers or engineering work stations, a prudent strategy might have been to avoid investing in standardization of methods, tools, or program libraries of reusable code that might soon become outdated. Again, however, despite limits to what managers could do, they clearly had some options. They might have concentrated on the more stable segments of the industry, such as software for commercial mainframes, and standardized around good practices and tools that worked in this segment. Companies also could have designed tools to be updated, and encouraged reuse and modification of design skeletons rather than compiled code. Indeed, as the cases in Part II describe, periodic reevaluations of standard procedures, tools, and reuse libraries made it possible to evolve along with technology and markets while still achieving scale or scope economies and other benefits of standardization.

Software developers themselves, however, contributed to managerial and organizational constraints. They sometimes insisted on using their own methods and tools, despite company standards, or disliked filling out detailed reports needed for project control or process and quality analysis. In addition, they often preferred to build ever more sophisticated and innovative systems, rather than reusing specifications, designs, and code to make products similar to previous ones. In fact, one of the major difficulties cited in the 1968 NATO conference proceedings dealt with this last item, that is, that software developers too frequently wanted to write novel programs, and thus they constantly immersed themselves (and the firm) in "research" and thereby reduced their (and the firm's) ability to benefit from previous experience:

> Instead of trying to write a system which is just like last year's, only better implemented, one invariably tries to write an entirely new and more sophisticated system. Therefore you are in fact continually embarking on research, yet your salesmen disguise this to the customer as being just a production job. . . . This practice leads to slipped schedules, extensive rewriting, much lost effort, large numbers of bugs, and an inflexible and unwieldy product. It is unlikely that such a product can ever be brought to a satisfactory state of reliability or that it can be maintained and modified. . . . [T]his mixing of research, development, and production is a root cause of the "software gap". . . [8]

This scenario prevailed at many firms in the 1980s, as seen in an example from Bell Communications Research (Bellcore), which developed data-processing and communications software for Bell telephone operating companies. According to a manager responsible for one of the largest software projects undertaken in the company, a tradition dating back to Bellcore's origins as part of AT&T Bell Laboratories consisted of hiring the best people managers could find. On the positive side of this tradition, Bellcore's software engineers tended to be creative and talented. On the negative side, the company had what might be described as "too many chiefs and not enough Indians"—too many software developers who wanted to work only on projects interesting to them, and with extensive independence. He found it difficult to assign manpower where the company needed it, collect productivity and quality data systematically, analyze where costs came from, and reuse software across different projects by focusing less on innovation and more on building simple, practical, and reliable systems.[9]

AT&T Bell Laboratories, known for innovations ranging from the transistor to the UNIX operating system and the C programming language, continued to face similar problems. The degree of discretion and variation in how individual project managers and engineers conducted their work made it extremely difficult for management to standardize tools or practices that appeared standardizable, or to obtain accurate measures of costs, quality levels, or productivity. Managers did not view their plight as serious when Bell Labs remained part of a government-sanctioned telecommunications monopoly. After becoming a private company in 1984, however, achieving greater control over software productivity and quality became a major competitive issue. At least one AT&T manager had reached a conclusion similar to his contemporaries at Bellcore: that hiring only well-trained people and letting them solve problems individually no longer worked. Even extensive investments in personnel courses seemed useful only as "general education," because divisions had no sets of practices and tools they could teach to employees as "the AT&T process."[10]

Discrete Versus Integrated Tools and Techniques

Kinds of Solutions

TRW Inc. provides another example of a U.S. firm that discovered it required more than talented engineers to guarantee successful outcomes to software-development efforts. A 1977 study had recommended that projects hire better and fewer people, and then manage through a sequential life-cycle plan, use a structured top-down approach to program design (determining the overall tasks of a program first, then breaking down the program into independent parts or modules in a hierarchical fashion that can be divided into smaller parts for coding), perform continuous validations, maintain disciplined product control, and institute clear accountability for results.[11] Yet, in practice, managers eventually concluded that reliance on outstanding project personnel, or on techniques such as structured design and programming, proved inadequate substitutes for an organized system that would insure continued improvements and consistent application of software-engineering principles across successive projects.[12]

Another interpretation of the experiences of Bellcore, AT&T, and TRW is to make a distinction between *discrete* solutions for problems in software development—tools, techniques, or practices that can serve individuals and stand alone—versus *integrated* solutions—more comprehensive approaches that strategically combine tools, techniques, product and component designs, training, and other elements to complement and reinforce each another as well as allow management to guide the development process at levels above the individual programmer and the individual project. Indeed, while this book appears to be the first historical inquiry into the factory model, academic and industry experts have clearly come to recognize the advantages of moving toward more integrated processes for managing at least large-scale or repetitive software development.

A particularly elegant testimony to this trend was a 1986 article surveying the evolution of software engineering by R. Goldberg, a consultant at the IBM Software Engineering Institute. In the early years of programming during the 1960s, Goldberg claimed that managers at IBM and other firms focused on improving the performance of individuals, not on devising a comprehensive process. Technological research, accordingly, centered on experimental techniques, such as structured programming and design, primarily for use by individuals. As product requirements became more demanding during the 1970s, however, companies introduced formal, standardized methodologies, based on refinements of individual tools and techniques, and began paying more attention to refining the overall development process, from basic design through maintenance. Still, in Goldberg's view, not until the 1980s did companies become openly committed to integrating tools and methods with better programming environments, and pay adequate attention to process management. It also seemed to Goldberg that many software engineers had yet to grasp the need to make choices among tradeoffs, not simply in terms of costs in production versus testing, but also in the size of programs versus performance, or performance and function versus costs—decisions made as a matter of course in other industries.[13]

Structured Design and Programming

Among the tools and techniques that many firms used to create a standardized approach to design and coding, structured programming has been especially important. Academics advanced the underlying concepts during the 1960s and then companies adopted these for commercial programming in the early and mid-1970s. While each firm might define its practices somewhat differently, structured design generally included some sort of top-down approach, hiding the details of the lower-level components from higher levels, as well as modularization of system parts, formalized program verification (mathematical testing of logical correctness), and standard procedures for phase control and project management. Structured programming encouraged top-down coding (writing the code for higher-level modules before lower-level components, as opposed to writing code for lower-level modules or subsystems and then integrating them in at higher levels, in an ad hoc or bottom-up fashion) and rules such as avoidance of "GO TO" statements, which make programs difficult to follow and test.[14]

Companies considered structured techniques more an academic topic until a 1972 article by F.T. Baker in the *IBM Systems Journal*. Baker explained the basic principles of structured design and coding, as well as the opportunity this created for a division of labor in project teams by functional assignments, with a chief programmer designated to do high-level design, and then recounted IBM's use of these techniques to develop a large-scale on-line information system for the *New York Times*. A 1974 article in *IBM Systems Journal* by W.P. Stevens, G.J. Myers, and L.L. Constantine told in more detail how to break down a program into smaller parts, or what have come to be known as modules. Brooks drew further attention to structured design, coding, and rationalized or functional management concepts in his 1975 book.[15]

In practice, these techniques had disadvantages as well as advantages. Firms have had difficulty finding enough skilled people to serve as chief programmers. Top-down coding has proved cumbersome, as opposed to top-down design and more bottom-up or iterative coding, because of the inability of designers and programmers to foresee all the necessary requirements of a system prior to attempting to build it. Top-down design and coding also provided little room for personnel to reuse code or to accommodate changes, such as customer suggestions, during the development process. As Stevens et al. pointed out, structured design helped eliminate redundancies within a program by identifying common functions and allowing developers to cite or reuse particular modules. On the other hand, the hierarchical "tree-structured" programs that resulted, with interdependent modules, sometimes made it difficult to reuse or change portions of the system easily.[16] In addition, as programs grew in size and functions, the number of possible combinations of data manipulation and procedures usually increased to the point where it turned out to be impossible to test their logical correctness, making initial goals of structured design and programming less than fully attainable. Nonetheless, structured techniques facilitated testing, divisions of labor, occasional reusability, project management, and maintenance, at least compared to unstructured approaches.

The Emergence of Software Engineering

In addition to structured techniques, several ideas provided important guidelines for helping companies turn software development into more of an engineering discipline as well as a business activity where it became possible to keep closer track of methods standardization, costs, quality, and schedules. One of the most important authors of the field, and a major contributor of concepts highly relevant to factory approaches, has been Barry Boehm, a Harvard-trained mathematician who worked for Honeywell and then TRW. His 1976 article, "Software Engineering," reinforced the association of engineering practice with software development by defining the discipline as "the practical application of scientific knowledge in the design and construction of computer programs and the associated documentation required to develop, operate, and maintain them." Following the lead of the 1968 NATO conference, Boehm recommended analyzing and controlling development by viewing it as a life cycle consisting of distinct phases: system requirements, software requirements, preliminary design, detailed design, code and debug, test and preoperations, and operations and maintenance. Defining a life cycle itself became an important step for many firms, because it provided managers and software personnel with a common language to describe the phases and milestones necessary to structure, measure, and assign work.

Boehm also stressed the importance of preventing costs from program changes or maintenance from becoming unmanageably large. A survey of several firms indicated that the cost to fix defects in a software program became 100 times greater in the operating stage than in earlier phases, because of program interactions; this explained why corrections, modifications, or updates consumed up to 70 percent of total costs over the life cycle of a typical program. Boehm decried as well the "ad hoc manual blend of systems analysis principles and common sense. (These are the good [programs]; the poor ones are based on ad hoc manual blends of politics, preconceptions, and pure salesmanship.)"[17] To solve these problems and reduce costs, he argued that firms needed to (1) understand existing software through improved documentation, traceability between requirements and code, and more structured code; (2) design more easily modifiable software; and (3) find better ways to revalidate modified software, such as through design structures that facilitated selective retesting. Although no one had studied these problems systematically as of 1976, Boehm advocated the use of top-down design and structured programming, automated formatting and documentation tools, modularization, program support libraries, and new testing tools.

Boehm's review of problems and "frontier" solutions constituted a useful glimpse of the state of practice circa 1976, as well as future directions—at least from his vantage point (Table 2.3). For requirements specifications, in contrast to what he felt were ad hoc techniques normally used, Boehm thought the frontier consisted of problem-statement languages and analyzers, system-design support tools, and automatic programming. For software design, he described 1976 practice as primarily manual, bottom-up, and error-prone, whereas he believed the future lay in top-down design techniques, modularization, and structured design representations such as flow charts. In programming, much of then-current practice consisted of unstructured code, while Boehm's frontier called for greater use of new computer languages that facilitated structured coding, such as PASCAL. For software testing and reliability, Boehm saw 1976 practice as consisting of enormous amounts of wasted

Table 2.3 Software Problems and Solutions (1976)

Problems	Current Practices	"Frontier" Solutions
Requirements specifications	Ambiguous, errors, ad hoc	Problem statement languages and analyzers; system-design support tools; automatic programming
Design	Manual, bottom-up, error-prone	Top-down, modularization, flow charts and other representations
Implementation	Unstructured code	Structured programming
Testing	Unplanned, much wasted effort	Reliability models, automated tools
Maintenance	Unsystematic, costly	Structured programming, automated formatting and documentation tools, modularization, program libraries, testing tools
Project management	Poor planning, control, resource estimation, accountability, and success criteria	Management guidelines; integrated development or "factory" approaches combining design, process, and tool standards

Source: Barry W. Boehm, "Software Engineering," *IEEE Transactions on Computers* C-25, 12, December 1976.

effort resulting from the lack of advance testing plans. The frontier he saw as reliability models and error-data analysis, automated tools for static code analysis, test-case preparation, and test monitoring. As Part II of this book details, Boehm's recommendations in fact became widely used in the industry, especially in Japanese software factories with centralized management and process-R&D efforts.

Boehm also provided a list of common difficulties in current practice: poor planning, resulting in large amounts of wasted or redundant effort; poor control; poor resource estimation; poorly trained management personnel; poor accountability (too diffuse delineation of responsibilities); inappropriate success criteria (for example, minimizing development costs with the result that programs are hard to maintain); and procrastination in key areas of project development. He concluded that, rather than continued refinement of discrete tools and methods, management initiatives were key to improving software development: "There are more opportunities for improving software productivity and quality in the area of management than anywhere else."

To accomplish this improvement, Boehm recommended what he saw as the frontier solution for software project management: integrated development approaches combining specific management guidelines and objectives with design and process standards, automated tools, reporting systems, budgeting procedures, documentation guides, and other elements. Although he felt it too early to tell if it would be successful, Boehm cited the SDC Software Factory as an example of a truly integrated approach, noting it had "an interface control component . . . which provides users access to various tools and data bases . . . a project planning and monitoring system, a software development data base and module management system, top-down development support system, a set of test tools, etc."[18]

Recent Developments

Almost a decade after Boehm, a group from the University of California at Berkeley, led by C.V. Ramamoorthy, offered another glimpse of the industry and new solutions for the usual problems in a 1984 article (Table 2.4). As Boehm had hoped, they noted advances in formal specification languages and methodologies to write requirements specifications, replacing ambiguous natural languages, as well as "multiple representations" and "executable specifications."[19] New specification methodologies such as the Structured Analysis and Design Technique (SADT) simplified the writing of specifications and permitted developers to analyze these for internal consistency and accuracy more easily. Since specifications consisted of functional (input/output behavior) as well as nonfunctional characteristics (any other system features), and usually showed either the control or data flow, software engineers were also

Table 2.4 Software Problems and Solutions (1984)

Problems	"Frontier" Solutions
Requirement specifications	Executable specifications; multiple representations; report generation
Design	Knowledge-based automatic design (program generators)
Testing	Automatic test input generators and verifiers; testing at requirement and design levels
Maintenance	Configuration management systems; system upgrading
Quality assurance	Alternate test strategies; metrics for design and quality control
Project management	Cost estimation based on requirement complexity
Prototyping	Enhanced methods; executable specifications
Reusability	Software libraries; design methodologies; program generators

Source: C. V. Ramamoorthy et al., "Software Engineering: Problems and Perspectives," *Computer*, October 1984, p. 205.

moving toward representing specifications in multiple ways. Reports including text and graphs, for example, helped potential users and software developers visualize the overall functions of a program before writing detailed designs and code. Executable specifications allowed developers to take an initial input/output design and run it on a computer, to simulate the performance of the system before completing the design and coding.

The design process, including breaking down specifications into parts for coding, remained difficult to rationalize. One continuing problem Ramamoorthy and colleagues observed was that designers used one set of criteria (such as functionality, dataflow, or data structures) but then, in partitioning the resulting procedures into modules, they had to take into account whatever nonfunctional requirements the user specified, such as maximizing maintenance, reliability, speed, reusability, or memory constraints. The final step required design of actual data structures and algorithms, and transcription into text or graphic forms; however, no design methodologies in the mid-1980s proved totally satisfactory for complex control structures and real-time computer applications (programs with a computation speed fast enough so that data and instructions put into a computer can guide a physical process while it is transpiring), or new distributed processing requirements. Nonetheless, they felt research was moving forward quickly, improving the new specification languages as well as program generators that automatically produced code from requirements.

A key challenge in testing continued to be how to select the fewest number of cases that would verify a program is logically correct and meets user specifications. Minimizing test items remained critical to reducing the huge amounts of time and labor normally required to evaluate large, complex software systems. Ramamoorthy and colleagues cited advances in tools that automated aspects of test-data generation, error location, and results verification, using static analysis (examination of the program structure), dynamic analysis (examination of a program while in operation), and checks of intermodule interfaces (common boundaries or linkages between parts of a program).

These researchers again pointed to maintenance as the most costly phase of software development, for familiar reasons: insufficient documentation; inconsistency between documents and code; designs difficult to understand, modify, and test; and absence of good records on past maintenance. They recognized some progress in tools that analyzed source code and generated information such as the control flow or dataflow. In general, however, they urged managers to enforce more precise development methodologies, plan for maintenance in the development stage, and better document work, such as through configuration management databases to store programs and project management information.

For quality assurance and project management, various metrics under development attempted to measure phase productivity, cost, and quality. Quality measures tracked factors like correctness, modifiability, reliability (defects per lines of code, or mean time between failures), testability, performance, complexity, and maintainability, with varying degrees of precision. For productivity, companies had improved estimation models derived from empirical data for different phases in the development cycle, although none seemed particularly accurate in the earlier stages.[20]

Performance of individuals remained difficult to measure precisely, as the following example illustrates. A highly skilled and highly paid engineer might require 1,000 lines of source code and 1 month to write a particular program. If the same set of functions, using the same computer language, takes a less experienced, lower-paid programmer 1,500 lines and 1.2 months to implement, perhaps even incorporating some reused code, then the nominal productivity of the second programmer is higher, 1,250 lines per person-month, and costs per line of code would probably be much lower. The first programmer's code is shorter and should run faster on a computer—common measures of higher product quality for software. On the other hand, if the hardware is powerful, the program's length might not matter to the user at all. In this case, the longer, less costly program might be totally adequate and preferable for the customer and perhaps for the producer as well, especially if the producer is short of experienced personnel.[21] This latter approach—use of less-skilled programmers, reusability, some compromises in product performance in exchange for lower prices to the customer—very much categorizes the strategies followed in Japanese software factories as well as other firms that seek a compromise of process efficiency and product differentiation.

Prototyping involved creating executable partial specifications that outlined the major functions and interfaces of a software system in a computer language, running this preliminary system on a computer, and then using this to test the program's feasibility or suitability for the customer before completion, adding or modifying the software as needed. Engineers also could construct prototypes by linking together reusable modules or using program generators that automatically produced code from specifications. Some critics argued prototypes were too expensive to build, while supporters claimed they provided a more useful preview of a program, from the user's point of view, than simply reading conventional requirements specifications. This debate went back at least to Brooks, who in 1975 insisted that software developers should *always* plan to write a pilot system and then "throw one away," because no one was likely to get requirements right on the first try:

> In most projects, the first system built is barely usable. It may be too slow, too big, awkward to use, or all three. There is no alternative but to start again, smarting but smarter, and build a redesigned version in which these problems are solved. The discard and redesign may be done in one lump, or it may be done piece-by-piece. But all large-system experience shows that it will be done. Where a new system concept or new technology is used, one has to build a system to throw away, for even the best planning is not so omniscient as to get it right the first time.[22]

Reusability and Supporting Techniques

Reusability of software presented another bold but old concept, dating back at least to the informal recycling of mathematical subroutines in programming during in the 1950s. Commercial packages for technical FORTRAN subroutines also became available in the 1960s.[23] Yet more grandiose schemes for large-scale, systematic reuse, such as M.D. McIlroy of AT&T proposed at the 1968 NATO Science Committee Conference, did not meet with much acceptance; however, since his notion of reusability came to play a larger role in the industry and in software-factory management, McIlroy's proposal, as well as reasons why reuse remains both attractive and difficult, are worth exploring in more detail.

McIlroy had suggested that governments and companies establish components factories that would create mass-producible modules to serve as "black boxes" for new programs. While he expected it would take time and money for firms to accumulate large inventories of reusable components, in the long term, he expected producers to benefit by building new programs from existing components that represented efficient designs. Users would benefit from products that producers, though using some standardized parts, could tailor to their individual needs. Reusability and customization thus would lessen the need for customers and producers to accept tradeoffs in software development. No one would have to settle for final products that were too standardized, unreliable, or inefficient:

The most important characteristic of a software components industry is that it will offer families of routines for any given job. No user of a particular member of a family should pay a penalty, in unwanted generality, for the fact that he is employing a standard model routine. In other words, the purchaser of a component from a family will choose one tailored to his exact needs. He will consult a catalogue offering routines in varying degrees of precision, robustness, time-space performance, and generality. He will be confident that each routine in the family is of high quality—reliable and efficient. He will expect the routine to be intelligible, doubtless expressed in a higher level language appropriate to the purpose of the component, though not necessarily instantly compilable in any processor he has for his machine. He will expect families of routines to be constructed on rational principles so that families fit together as building blocks. In short, he should be able safely to regard components as black boxes.[24]

Benefits of software reusability can be seen in the following example. Assuming the cost breakdown for software development follows Table 2.1, reusing requirement and then detailed design specifications (even without the actual code) had the potential of saving a great deal of effort since these accounted for about 35 percent of development costs prior to maintenance, compared to about 20 percent for coding. A firm could also achieve large savings in testing, nearly 50 percent of costs prior to maintenance, if it built reusable modules as independent subsystems and then thoroughly tested these before recycling. In addition, reuse had the potential of allowing firms to leverage the skills of their best designers across more than one project, and thus build at least parts of systems with less experienced or skilled people. Other industry experts, including one of the founders of the SDC Software Factory, John B. Munson, even argued that, since research on software tools and methodologies had brought only limited gains, reusability remained the only way to achieve dramatic advances in productivity:

> [S]oftware development tools and methodologies have not continued to dramatically improve our ability to develop software. Although in the field of computer hardware fabrication, new methods continue to raise productivity, in software we have not experienced even an order of magnitude improvement over the past decade. . . . [O]ne concept which we believe has the potential for increasing software productivity by an order of magnitude or more . . . has come to be known by the phrase "reusable software."[25]

On a small scale, during the 1970s, firms met McIlroy's goal with the increasing use of subroutines and modifiable packaged software, as well as with the gradual introduction of operating systems such as UNIX and programming languages such as C that supported reuse or portability of code and tools across different hardware architectures.[26] Despite some progress at Raytheon in the late 1970s, however, extensive reuse appeared not to catch on as a major objective of software-engineering practice in the United States until a revival in the early 1980s in academic circles and at firms such as ITT Corporation. In the meantime, Japanese applications software producers, led by Toshiba, began pursuing reusability as a primary production strategy in the mid-1970s, although they, too, did not seem to achieve high levels of reuse until the accumulation of better component libraries and support tools in the 1980s.[27]

Thus, while the design and reuse of standardized components in different products had become common in other industries by the early part of the twentieth century, it remained rare on a large scale in software, for a variety of reasons. First, structured techniques taught developers to conceptualize software systems anew in a top-down manner, from large functions to smaller tasks, and to write programs for specific applications. Reusing designs and code, on the other hand, required conceptualization and construction around pieces of software already existing and therefore, as often as not, acceptance of compromises in features or performance of the system; for example, programs containing reused code might be longer or not as functional as software newly conceived and optimized.

Reusability across projects also presented overhead costs for an individual project. Systematic reuse of designs or code required standardization of module interfaces to fit components together, whether or not these standards proved useful or necessary for a given system. Developers also needed common tools, such as libraries to store programs and documents, and reusable-parts retrieval techniques, to make it easier to find and understand pieces of software someone else had written. Furthermore, designing software for potential reuse probably consumed more time and expense, because designers had to think of more possible applications and carefully document their work. Reuse thus involved potential tradeoffs in product uniqueness and production costs in the short term for any individual project, despite the promise of higher productivity and perhaps quality in the long term, for a series of projects.

Proponents of software as an art or craft might therefore argue that all programs should be uniquely designed to operate in an optimal manner. Indeed, companies that faced totally different applications with each project, by definition, had to make software products in batches of one to serve their customers properly. Yet many studies, as well as data collected as part of the research for this book, indicated that somewhere between 40 percent and 85 percent of all the code many established firms delivered in a given year consisted of similar or redundant functions.[28] With some foresight, as a former IBM manager noted, these functions "could be standardized into a fairly small set" of reusable modules—McIlroy's goal in 1968.[29] As seen in the Japanese factory cases, systematic reuse of designs, code, and other elements grew with the refinement of an infrastructure of techniques, tools, and incentives above the level of the individual project, especially since reusability as a concept applied to various kinds of software components: designs, data, system architectures, and documentation, in addition to executable code, which often provided most difficult to reuse across different applications or computer systems.[30]

Reusable data, for example, referred to the standardization of data-interchange formats to facilitate recycling of program parts and data sharing. There was, as in other areas of software, no universally accepted way to exchange data, so standards depended on project or intracompany efforts. Reusable architectures consisted of a set of generic functions that could be assembled to create any type of program. Most came in well-defined applications software and involved designing all data descriptions, constants, and input/output controls to be external to the modules intended for reuse. Estimates of the number of generic functions needed to build all potential applications from standardized parts ranged from less than 100 to more than 1,500.

Reusable designs involved standard patterns that served as references or skeletons for new programs. Some common forms, as identified in a 1983 survey, covered assemblers and compilers, databases, operating systems, data-sorting routines, and graphics processing. Reusable designs were becoming more popular in the later 1980s, since they allowed projects to circumvent constraints of incompatible hardware or operating-system architectures. Reusing a design still required coding, although tools such as code generators, which automatically produced code from structured designs, eliminated much of this additional step.

Reusable programs referred to the idea of utilizing standardized packages in place of fully customized software. This also appeared to be an increasingly common alternative, based on growth rates of packages. A 1983 study of eleven *Fortune* 500 companies, for example, indicated that standardized programs supported approximately 70 percent of functions in the areas of finance, personnel, and sales reporting. Machine and data incompatibility, and lack of standardized data interchange and function formats, restricted package use in many other areas, although the gradual introduction of various industry standards promised to make the reuse of whole programs more common even across different machines and operating systems.

Reusable modules consisted of parts of programs suitable for recycling. These included common subroutines, such as square root extractions, date conversions, statistical functions or other procedures that could be linked into a program without having to be coded more than once. High-level languages in general, especially C and Ada, as well as the UNIX operating systems, facilitated this type of reuse. In addition, developers could draw on commercially available collections such as the 350 reusable functions in the UNIX Programmers Workbench, or standardized COBOL routines available through Raytheon's ReadyCode Service, which generally allowed users to create semicustomized programs writing only about half the code from scratch. For internal company use, or for internal production operations for outside customers, the Bank of Montreal and ITT's Hartford Insurance subsidiary, as well as Toshiba, Hitachi, NEC, and Fujitsu, provided examples of firms with extensive and continually expanding libraries of reusable modules.[31]

Also facilitating reuse, as well as testing and maintenance, were techniques such as data and procedural abstraction, and object-oriented programming. Abstraction presented a simple idea: Design modules hierarchically so that they operate with generically defined data types or procedures. Hide specific data types from higher-level modules and place them in a program only at lower levels, contained in "objects" with distinct names. An example is a generic program for entering any type of data for a series of objects. At lower levels, one might define the objects as students in a particular class, and define the data to be entered as grades for a particular term. This type of program could be used for a variety of data-entry applications. In contrast, one could write a shorter program simply entering grades along with the names of Mary, John, and Joan. This latter program should be faster and simpler to write, but would not be useful except for this one application. Yet a drawback remained in that abstraction for complex programs generally required considerable skill. In addition, while a skilled engineer might create neat abstractions in a variety of computer languages, most did not support this concept directly, in contrast to new languages such as Ada, completed in 1980 and supported by the U.S. Department of Defense, which specifically facilitated data·abstraction.[32]

Object-oriented programming techniques and specially adapted languages such as Smalltalk and C++ represented a major step toward simplifying abstraction techniques. Object orientation required software developers to go beyond simply defining abstract procedures or data types and formally identify objects, representing numbers, text, subprograms, or anything desired. The objects needed to be isolated modules in the sense of including both instructions for manipulating the data as well as the actual data. Thus a developer could change the software simply by redefining, adding, or subtracting objects, rather than rewriting complex procedures or redefining individual sets of data, as conventional techniques and languages required, including Ada.[33] Even though most firms used languages that did not have specific features to support object-oriented programming, languages and tools based on this concept were becoming more available.[34]

Computer-Aided Tools

Both Boehm and Ramamoorthy et al. envisioned a future making greater use of code generators and other programs that supported the development and testing of software as well as project management. The term in vogue during the later 1980s to describe these was *computer-aided software-engineering* or CASE tools. Some restricted their use of the term to automated or semiautomated support of program design and implementation (code generation and testing or debugging). Taking the term literally, however, CASE included any of a wide range of tools that assisted developers and managers in nearly every activity required to develop software (summarized in Table 2.5).[35]

Some tools appeared far more common and useful than others. Code or program generators had become particularly important in software factories and applications development in general because they reduced the effort required for coding, as well as testing. A simple code generator, for example, read flow charts and then turned out code in standard languages, such as COBOL. IBM users introduced such a tool for generating programs in the APL language as early as 1973.[36] Other tools aided the developer by locating reusable software parts from libraries of subroutines as well as executable code and designs. Still others generated new code from structured design formats or menus, and combined two or more of these functions, sometimes with project-management capabilities.

Examples of advanced tools used in Japanese software factories and sold to customers in Japan for reuse support and program generation consisted of Hitachi's EAGLE-II, NEC's SEA/1, Fujitsu's PARADIGM, and a series of related tools. Notable U.S. vendors of design-automation tools included Index Technology, Nastec, KnowledgeWare, Cadre, Texas Instruments, Cortex, and Tarkenton Software. The Texas Instruments product appeared to be one of the first to tackle the entire systems-development life cycle, including business objective analysis and database generation. Cortex's system, called the Application Factory, ran on Digital Equipment Corporation's VAX minicomputers and automatically generated code from specifications set by computer professionals.[37] The technology remained imperfect, however, in that most program generators worked only with highly structured designs and a few languages, and often required manual coding of module interfaces. Other generators that assisted in design primarily facilitated development for well-understood applications, though companies continually introduced improved versions.[38]

In addition to CASE tools available for sale, firms also developed systems for in-house use. In the United States, two of the first systems were ARGUS, designed by TRW as an advanced software engineering workbench and integrated methodology;[39] and the Automated Interactive Design and Evaluation System (AIDES), developed at the Hughes Aircraft Company to automate many of the manual procedures accompanying IBM's structured-design methodology.[40] The next step in automation linked CASE tools with artificial intelligence (AI) or expert systems technology, to automate the steps from initial design through code gen-

Table 2.5 Computer-Aided Software-Engineering (CASE) Tools

Tool	Function	Comments
Planning Phase		
Requirements analyzer	Lists system functions and models data structures	Hard to automate and integrate; few available
Configuration management tool	Tracks versions and status of programs and modules	More common for engineering than for data processing
Project management tool	Breaks down work into tasks; tracks schedules and timing; reports on progress	Functions frequently not automated; rising integration with tools for other phases
Design Phase		
Diagrammer	Draws pictures, flow charts of system and modules	Widely available
Screen painter	Writes code to produce standard screen layouts	Common; usually integrated with code generator
Data normalizer	Assists designer in defining and using data consistently	Not common; applies only to large data processing
Data dictionary	Lists data elements; cross references and ensures consistency among modules	One of the most common tools but useful only if integrated with other tools
Control-flow analyzer	Maps program and module interactions; ensures all elements are referenced	Cannot be used unless integrated with control-flow design tools
Subsystem and interface modeler	Tracks individual data elements; ensures that modules pass data correctly	More common for engineering than data processing
Dataflow modeler and analyzer	Models data paths; shows connections between modules; checks all data references	Very common
Tasking analyzer	Insures parallel tasks in real-time systems are synchronized	Not common; analysis hard; usually used in military or aerospace fields
Implementation Phase		
Code generator	Creates programs in standard languages from design specs	Most produce usable code
Subroutine library	Contains code for common functions programmers use	Common, even if not a computer-aided tool
Syntax editor	Checks format and syntax of text; finds coding errors	Common; often "stand-alone"
Test-data generator	Develops data sets to test modules and interactions	Primitive and not comprehensive, though improving
On-line code debugger	Shows data during running; highlights errors	Common; an "old" tool
Maintenance-Support Phase		
Backfill dictionary	Documents logic and cross references for existing code	Useful but tracking single data fields difficult
Code restructuring tool	Cleans up existing source code to make it easier to understand and maintain	Useful, but cannot compensate for poor designs

Source: John Voelcker, "Automating Software: Proceed with Caution," *IEEE Spectrum*, July 1988, p. 27.

eration. Research efforts at Hitachi, Toshiba, NEC, Fujitsu, and most other major U.S. and European computer or software firms, as well as many smaller companies, focused on making these linkages.[41]

It was easy, however, to overestimate the state and current importance of CASE tools, as pointed out in a 1988 survey of 152 managers of information systems conducted by *Computerworld*. Managers generally found CASE tools expensive to develop or buy, therefore they required some economies of scale or scope to justify. Secondarily, the benefits of many tools seemed unclear or even unproven. Other problems managers cited included the abundance of tools and the paucity of standards to guarantee their usefulness, resistance from software developers to using the tools, shortages of linked computers or work stations, and the costs involved in training personnel.[42]

Integrated Approaches

This review of problems and solutions in software engineering suggests several observations. Individual engineers and managers know what difficulties they are likely to face, and they have a variety of tools, techniques, and concepts to help them. Phases of the development process are interrelated, however, and large projects require many individuals and groups to complete and maintain. Meanwhile, companies continue to face shortages of experienced software personnel and managers, while programming tasks continue to grow in size, complexity, and cost. The result is that discrete solutions, such as in the form of stand-alone tools and techniques, are inadequate to address all the problems *organizations* face in managing software development.

Boehm and a colleague reinforced this argument in a 1983 article. Their studies of software cost and productivity at TRW, as well as of project performance at other firms, all pointed to the need for comprehensive, strategic efforts on the part of management. They noted that, "Significant productivity gains require an integrated program of initiatives in several areas, including tools, methods, work environments, education, management, personal incentives, and reusability." As for the benefits of such an approach, their studies indicated that, "An integrated software productivity program can produce productivity gains of factors of two in five years and factors of four in ten years, with proper planning and investment." Yet they did not suggest firms could achieve such gains easily, and warned that, "Improving software productivity involves a long, sustained effort and commitment."[43] As comparative material for the factory cases, the following discussion illustrates how several U.S.-based firms not explicitly adopting a factory label for their facilities encountered numerous problems and then introduced elements of an integrated process for software development that either influenced the Japanese or serve as useful comparisons for their efforts.

Examples from U.S.-Based Firms

International Business Machines (IBM)

IBM in 1987 had total sales of $54 billion, including software revenues of nearly $7 billion ($4 billion in basic system software, $2 billion in tools, and the rest in applications packages),[44] which made it by far the largest commercial software producer in the world. In addition to a large lead in market share, historically, IBM also pioneered the introduction of highly complex, innovative programs, especially in basic software, that required the development of a relatively standardized and integrated approach to design, programming, testing, and management control over multiple sites. Many of its practices have been discussed in publicly available articles beginning in the 1960s, including Japanese-language journals.[45] These had a direct impact on the tools, methods, and concepts adopted in Japanese software factories and other firms around the world. At the same time, reflecting its size, diversity, and product strategies, IBM continued to face numerous difficulties managing software development across the firm with equal degrees of effectiveness.

According to James H. Frame, a former IBM executive who entered the company in 1956, IBM managers first decided in 1960 to adopt a companywide strategy for basic software production and elevate system programming (though not applications development) to a level more comparable to hardware engineering, or at least to raise it above the status of a support activity. The critical juncture was a conference held in New Hampshire, where top executives reviewed several powerful computers either due for delivery or in development. Programming until this time had been a relatively simple matter for IBM and customers in terms of personnel requirements and organization, since machines remained small and companies only needed a few people to write programs. Discussions focused on the need to organize a better corporatewide system for producing basic programs to run the new machines. In addition to the challenges of the new hardware, two major reasons why software got this attention in IBM at such an early date were a growing consensus that IBM should correct the "terrible" quality of its early programs as well as the personal leadership of T. Vincent Learson, then a vice-president and head of the Data Systems Division, and a future president of IBM, who made certain that the company took initiatives to improve the management of programming operations.[46]

Over the next few years, IBM set up a worldwide development organization for the System/360 operating system (OS/360), probably the most difficult and expensive commercial software project undertaken up to that time. Though some U.S. vendors, such as Burroughs, appear to have offered products with some more advanced features, OS/360 probably contained the broadest assortment of multiterminal, on-line, real-time processing capabilities and other functions. In fact, OS/360 set new standards for IBM's subsequent operating systems as well as for the software of many other producers, including RCA, Hitachi, and Fujitsu.[47]

The basic software for System/360 hardware included four different but "upward-compatible" versions of the operating system, each for machines of different sizes. OS/360 stood at the top of the line. Other less complex systems, providing basic programming capabilities through management of external disk and tape memory drives, were Basic Programming Support (BPS), Basic Operating System (BOS), Disk Operating System (DOS), and Tape Operating System (TOS).

IBM completed the smaller operating systems close to the schedule, and they worked relatively well. OS/360, however, presented major difficulties. While IBM announced the System/360 family in 1964 and planned the first shipments for mid-1965, OS/360 was not ready, forcing IBM to ship the hardware with the simpler operating systems. After 5,000 man-years expended in design, construction, and documentation over a period of three years, including as many as 1,000 employees working on the system simultaneously, IBM finally delivered a first version of OS/360 in 1966, containing huge numbers of defects that would require years to correct.[48]

The organization IBM used to produce System/360 software and later programs consisted of multiple development laboratories, each with hardware-engineering, programming, and marketing divisions or centers. Each laboratory took responsibility for different sizes of computers aimed at different customer markets, although each programming center had a formal mission or product-development assignment that contributed to a larger effort. A vice-president responsible for programming operations oversaw the different centers, and corporate IBM provided whatever financial resources managers needed for product development, tool and method R&D, and training. IBM distributed the development work among New York City (languages), Sweden (sort routines), Rochester, Minn. (processor control), San Jose (access methods), Raleigh, N.C. (communications), Poughkeepsie, N.Y. (large operating system), and Endicott, N.Y. (mid-range operating system). Other centers in Kingston, N.Y., Germany, and additional locations also aided the effort.

This organizational structure reflected a strategy to create centers of experienced software developers around the world, specialized both in functions, such as sorts or communications software, and in machine types or sizes, such as midrange versus large machines. Managers considered this dispersion necessary because of the logistical difficulty and expense of centralizing thousands of programmers. IBM, in the past, had already distributed hardware design, and management wanted to locate software personnel nearby hardware engineering for specific machines.[49]

Dispersion and independence for each programming site contributed to organizational as well as technical problems in completing System/360 software and subsequent products. For example, directors of each programming center, as well as project managers and individual engineers, retained considerable autonomy and thus had the authority to decide what specific tools or methods they would use. Even as late as 1970, IBM had yet to establish a coordinated system for quality assurance and maintenance, and the lack of centralized control allowed the release of many important products with large numbers of defects, including OS/360 as well as a highly popular database management system, IMS. Simply correcting old problems, according to Frame, consumed enormous expenses and manpower resources that directly detracted from new product development.

IBM also applied what managers later decided was the wrong organizational structure for software maintenance, a critical area in general and especially since released IBM software had so many errors. The company first patterned maintenance after hardware divisions, where mechanics individually went to customer sites and fixed problems as they occurred. In software, where thousands of customers might use a single package such as an operating system or database management program, decentralized or individual maintenance proved to be far too labor intensive, costly, and unnecessary.

Perhaps the major challenge IBM faced became the growing difficulty of coordinating large software projects dispersed around the world and then expecting groups to complete components on time that would work together according to technical specifications. IBM failed to do this not only with OS/360 but also with planned new versions of DOS/360, which IBM canceled even before a public announcement. In addition, specifications for OS/370, announced along with the hardware in 1970, called for adding virtual memory capabilities to the basic operating system, and this required major technological changes in programming concepts that made new projects even more complicated. Poor planning in another huge project to produce a successor to System/370, dubbed the FS for Future System, added to IBM's costs and manpower shortages. IBM management decided in 1974 to cancel this effort after spending $5 billion and using approximately half of all basic software personnel on the project, because FS would not run programs written for the 360 and 370 architectures and it seemed unlikely customers would accept the new system.[50]

In an attempt to streamline and systematize its operations, IBM changed several practices, at least for basic software development. One move, which some executives had demanded directly after the OS/360 experience, set up a system of strict individual accountability for new products, committing project managers to guarantee specific dates when their components would be ready. IBM also established an organization for what it called *remote maintenance*, with specialists in a centralized location fixing software before rereleasing it to customers. In addition, IBM began more centralization of development, though in the mid-1970s there remained as many as eight sites making interdependent language compilers, database management systems, and access programs. This situation persisted until Chairman Frank Carey and President John Opel decided to concentrate these programming activities in one location in California and assign the consolidation task to Frame.

Research in software engineering had gradually moved away from mainly basic testing and coding to include design and issues of process management, primarily a more integrated view of people, tools, and methods, and how performance related to the physical layout of work areas.[51] IBM itself, based on an analysis of the *IBM Systems Journal* from its first year, 1962, through 1986, clearly seemed to be evolving in these directions (Tables 2.6 and 2.7). Work on general-purpose (rather than product-specific) tools in the 1960s and 1970s centered on testing, simulation and other forms of product evaluation. Articles on generic tools in the 1980s were more varied but dealt heavily with design. In the methods area, most articles in the 1960s treated design, coding, and testing, with shifts away from coding in the 1970s and 1980s toward project management and programming environments, but still with considerable attention to design and testing. Along with new concerns, by the mid-1970s, IBM also had adopted an implicit lifetime employment policy, as well as the practice of putting all new employees through a twelve-week training program and then two-year apprenticeships, accompanied by education courses in the second year and training for twenty to twenty-five days per year thereafter, in addition to a separate management-development program.

With an extensive and continually growing base of software-engineering know-how, training programs, and support from its highest executives, IBM in the late 1970s appeared ready to take a further step in organizational and technological integration by creating a new software facility combining the latest tools, techniques, and concepts regarding programming environments: the Santa Teresa Laboratory. This facility, opened in 1977 and headed by Frame, brought together 2,000 software personnel organized along functional product lines (languages, database systems, access methods) and provided a new physical setting, designed by the head of Harvard University's School of Design, Gerald McCue.[52] IBM executives, according to Frame, did not view Santa Teresa as a factory, and labeled it as a laboratory. In practice, however, they created a highly centralized, functionally organized facility, with a standardized process and physical layout designed to facilitate program-

Table 2.6 IBM Systems Journal Topical Analysis (1962–1986)*

Software-Engineering Tools
Design
   1967 modeling program
   1981 software simulation as a tool for usable product design
   1982 DB/DC data dictionary for business systems planning
   1983 abstract design and program translator
Coding
   1968 FORTRAN subroutine package
   1975 program generator
   1979 automatic programming for energy mangement
   1985 tools for building advanced user interfaces
Testing/product evaluation
   1962 general purpose systems simulator
   1963 generation of input data
   1963 laboratory data-taking system
   1964 systems simulation
   1965 expanded general purpose simulator
   1969 simulating operating systems
   1970 automatic generation of test cases
   1971 FORTRAN extended-precision library
   1972 management business simulation in APL
   1975 performance measurement tools for VM/370
   1984 automatic generation of random self-checking tests
   1984 design and use of a program execution analyzer
Phase/project management
   1985 automating the software development process
Documentation
   1985 project automated librarian

Software-Engineering Methods
Design
   1963 construction of minimal project networks
   1963 requirements generation
   1963 programming notation in systems design
   1969 three-value design verfication system
   1972 techniques for developing analytic models
   1974 structured design
   1974 elements of probability for system design
   1976 top-down development using a program design language
   1976 HIPO and integrated program design
   1982 strategies for information requirements determination
   1982 technique for assessing external design of software
   1983 simple architecture for consistent application program design
   1983 software reliability analysis
   1984 architecture prototyping in the software engineering environment
   1985 a process-integrated approach to defect prevention
   1985 strategies for problem prevention
Coding
   1965 tables, flow charts, and program logic
   1968 system for implementing interactive applications
   1969 data management
   1969 coding for error control
   1971 formal description of programming languages
Testing/product evaluation
   1965 testing real-time system programs
   1965 reliability of polymorphic systems
   1969 synthetic job for measuring system performance

Table 2.6 (*Continued*)

1971 time-sharing performance criteria and measurement
1972 scientific computing service evaluation
1972 a perspective on system evaluation
1973 user program performance in virtual storage system
1973 experimental evaluation of system performance
1974 performance analysis of the Skylab terminal system
1975 performance analysis of virtual memory time-sharing systems
1975 testing in a complex systems environment
1976 design and code inspections to reduce errors
1982 cost-benefit analysis and the data-managed system
1983 testing of interactive applications
1983 performance/availability measurement for IBM information network
1985 quality emphasis at IBM's Software Engineering Institute
Maintenance
1985 requirements methodology for software system enhancements
Phase/project management
1963 project evaluation and selection
1972 chief programmer team
1973 forecasting techniques
1975 productivity of computer-dependent workers
1976 model of large program development
1977 method of programming measurement and estimation
1978 measuring programming quality and productivity
1979 managing VM/CMS systems for user effectiveness
1980 management of software engineering
1980 systems management
1982 use of data flow to improve application development productivity
1985 programming productivity measurement system for system/370
1985 worldwide systems engineering
1985 the system planning grid
1985 programming process architecture
1985 programming process study
1986 software engineering
Programming environment
1978 IBM's Santa Teresa Laboratory
1981 Human Factors Center at San Jose
1982 towards an integrated development environment

*Each year and topic refers to one article. The list excludes articles describing individual products and refers to generic tools and methods. CMS = Code Management System; HIPO = hierarchical input/output.
Source: This is based on a study of indexes, tables of contents, and actual articles in the *IBM Systems Journal.* My thanks to Wilson Wong, a former student in Electrical Engineering and Computer Science at Massachussetts Institute of Technology, for his assistance in reviewing the journal articles for an undergraduate thesis project under my supervision.

mer performance, comfort, and communication. This consolidation, moreover, saved on overhead costs by eliminating duplication in many staff positions and gave management more immediate control over product development and testing, of new and existing products.

IBM in the 1980s operated other sites with several hundred and even

Table 2.7 IBM Systems Journal Generic Articles Summary (1962–1986)

	Tools			Methods			Total		
	1960s	1970s	1980s	1960s	1970s	1980s	1960s	1970s	1980s
Design	1		3	4	5	7	5	5	10
Coding	1	2	1	4		1	5	3	1
Testing	6	4	2	3	9	4	9	13	6
Process management			1	1	7	9	1	7	10
Documentation		1					0	0	1
Maintenance						1	0	0	1
Programming environment					1	2	0	1	2

Source: Table 2.6.

more than 1,000 software personnel in a single location, although management did not appear to duplicate the degree of consolidation at Santa Teresa (except for an applications facility in Tokyo with several thousand personnel on one site, although IBM tended to manage this as a collection of independent projects, albeit with strict quality controls, rather than as an integrated software factory). On the one hand, moving more than 1,000 developers and their families from eight different areas to Santa Teresa became extremely expensive. Top executives in the United States decided not to invest in a similar effort unless it seemed absolutely necessary. In addition, because of the sheer size of IBM's hardware development and programming operations, it seemed unlikely management would ever try to centralize development operations completely and risk losing the ability to tap expertise around the world, even though dispersed operations made it difficult to coordinate and standardize methods, tools, and controls.[53]

Equally important, IBM encountered practical limits to large-scale integration and consolidation of personnel in functional departments; for example, Santa Teresa first attempted a relatively strict functional organization, with large departments handling all coding or all design. Ultimately, however, IBM managers that succeeded Frame concluded this structure did not help them serve individual customers effectively when new products required closer coordination between design and product construction. Santa Teresa thus shifted toward a mixture of functional and product-centered departments in the late 1970s and 1980s, with specialized design, coding, and testing groups within product-oriented divisions—a structure similar to Japanese software factories. Glenn Bacon, the IBM executive who presided over this transition, explained his reasoning:

> I had reorganized the Santa Teresa Lab from a functional organization to a
> product manager organization. There were two principal reasons for this

change. First, the product manager organization was likely to be much more responsive in making major strategy changes that we intended. Second, the separation between design and implementation impeded the kind of teamwork and customer orientation that the marketplace required at that point.

The functional separation had been in place several years and had made significant accomplishments in establishing a programming process discipline and architecture. These were measurable as consistent gains in both quality and productivity. These processes and measurements were not changed when we went to a product manager organization. Further, the product management groups were still large enough to maintain specialists in all aspects of design and production, thus I saw no loss in economies of scale. We also kept a group dedicated to exploring process improvements.[54]

In addition to finding a better compromise between organizational efficiency and flexibility, IBM in the late 1980s also worked toward solving another issue: increasing its ability to standardize hardware and software internal architectures and interfaces. An example of this effort, IBM's SAA initiative, when completed, would provide a uniform interface to make it easier to reuse portions of systems and tools as well as whole programs across previously incompatible machines. At one time, incompatible lines supported an effective marketing strategy aimed at meeting different market segments with different products and dissuading competitors from introducing an equally broad range of computers. IBM in the past also tended to view applications software as an extension of sales and did not subject this area to the same discipline and structuring as basic software.[55] By the mid-1980s, however, intensified competition from firms such as Digital, which offered compatible small and large machines that could use the same software and databases, had forced IBM to reevaluate its strategy and attempt tighter controls and integration, even in applications development.

Articles in a 1985 special issue of the *IBM Systems Journal* on process technology reflected IBM's awareness of organizational and technological differences within the company and a desire to move further toward a "consistently repeatable discipline for developing software." One piece of evidence attesting to these concerns consisted of metrics to compare sites on various attributes and their overall level of integration. The metrics, called a "process grid," began with a craft-oriented or traditional approach and ended with an "integrated management system" (Figure 2.1). Although IBM researchers admitted that not all development centers had reached the most advanced stage (they released no specific data), the practical value of this exercise came from identifying good tools and techniques and then encouraging their transfer among different sites. Watts Humphrey, formerly director of Programming Quality and Process, in an introduction to this issue, explained the optimal process IBM defined for software development, focusing on four elements closely resembling factory approaches adopted in Japan:

	TRADITIONAL 5	AWARENESS 4	KNOWLEDGE 3	SKILL & WISDOM 2	INTEGRATED MANAGEMENT SYSTEM 1
PROCESS	NOT DEFINED OR USED	DEFINED BUT INCONSISTENTLY USED	DEFINED BUT STATIC	DEFINED AND IMPROVING	LEADING EDGE AND INTEGRATED INTO BUSINESS
METHODOLOGIES	NOT AWARE OF STATE OF THE ART	AWARE BUT NO USE	AWARE BUT CASUAL USE	MORE USE THAN NOT	FULLY EXPLOITS STATE OF THE ART
ADHERENCE TO PRACTICES	NONE TO LITTLE	SOME BUT NOT CONSISTENT	MORE CONSISTENT THAN NOT	CONSISTENT	CONSISTENT AND TOTAL ACROSS PROCESS
TOOLS	NOT AWARE OF STATE OF THE ART	AWARE BUT NO USE	AWARE BUT CASUAL USE	MORE USE THAN NOT	FULLY EXPLOITS STATE OF THE ART
CHANGE CONTROL	NONE TO LITTLE	INCONSISTENT. LACKS ENFORCEMENT	FOLLOWS A PROCESS BUT DIFFERENT FROM MAINLINE	TENDS TO FOLLOW PROCESS, BUT IS COMPROMISED	FOLLOWS MAINLINE PROCESS, IS NOT COMPROMISED
DATA GATHERING	NONE TO MINIMAL PRIMITIVE DATA BASES	INCONSISTENT. NON-STATE-OF-THE-ART DATA BASES	ACTIVE ACROSS PARTS OF PROCESS. BEGINNING STATE-OF-THE-ART DATA BASE USE. MORE TRUE THAN NOT	ACTIVE ACROSS PROCESS. STATE-OF-THE-ART DATA BASES	COMPLETELY INTEGRATED AND EVOLVING ACROSS BUSINESS
COMMUNICATION AND USE OF DATA	NONE TO LITTLE	SOME BUT NOT CONSISTENT	CONSISTENTLY USING FEEDBACK	ACTIVELY PURSUING IMPROVEMENT THROUGH INFORMATION FLOW	FULLY INTEGRATED INFORMATION FLOW AS A WAY OF DOING BUSINESS
GOAL SETTING	NONE TO LITTLE	BEGINNING: NO FEEDBACK	ESTABLISHED: LITTLE FEEDBACK	ACTIVE AT ALL LEVELS: SOME FEEDBACK	ACTIVE AND EVOLVING WITH FULL FEEDBACK THROUGH PROCESS
QUALITY FOCUS	NONE TO LITTLE	SOME BUT NOT CONSISTENT	KNOWS HOW TO IMPROVE	ACTIVELY PURSUING IMPROVEMENT	FULLY INTEGRATED AS A WAY OF DOING BUSINESS
CUSTOMER FOCUS	NONE	SOME FOCUS: NO FEEDBACK	SOME FOCUS: SOME FEEDBACK	MAJOR FOCUS WITH SOME FEEDBACK	MAJOR AND INTEGRATED FOCUS: FULL FEEDBACK
TECHNICAL AWARENESS	MINIMAL	AWARE OF OPPORTUNITIES: MINIMAL USE OR PURSUIT	PURSUING OPPORTUNITIES	VIGOROUSLY PURSUING OPPORTUNITIES	FULLY PURSUING INTERNAL AND EXTERNAL PROFESSIONAL AND TECHNICAL OPPORTUNITIES

Figure 2.1 IBM Process Grid. (*Source*: R. A. Radice et al., "A Programming Process Study," *IBM Systems Journal* 24, 2, 1985, p. 94. Copyright © 1985 International Business Machines Corporation. Reproduced with permission.)

People Management:
— Professionals are the key to the programming process, and they must be ultimately involved in its improvement.
— Management must focus on defects not as personal issues but as process problems.

Process Methodology:
— The process is formally defined.
— Goals and measurements are established.
— Statistical data are gathered and analyzed to identify problems and determine causes.

Process Control:
— Management practices are established to control change.
— Periodic process assessments are planned to monitor effectiveness and identify needed improvements.

— Procedures are established to certify product quality and implement corrective actions.

Process Support:
— Special process groups are established.
— Needed management and professional education is provided.
— The best tools and methods are obtained and used.[56]

A fundamental belief that structure and discipline in software development remained both possible and desirable underlay this philosophy and investment in process analysis, methodologies, tools, training, and control systems. Humphrey's position, which appeared consistent with the actions of IBM managers dating back to 1960, also held that structure and process analysis improved rather than constrained employee performance as well as product quality—again, much like managers believed at the major Japanese firms, who often claimed to have received much of their inspiration from IBM:

> An orderly and structured process addresses programming quality by providing an environment that fosters predictable results and eliminates mistakes. To use the analogy of advanced medical research, for example, it is understood that a controlled environment is essential for competent work. A similar environmental discipline is now recognized as an important element in good programming. Without change control, test-case tracking, statistical data bases, and structured requirements, the programmers often repeat past mistakes or resolve the same problems. Process discipline reduces such waste, permits more orderly learning, and allows the professionals to build on the experiences of others. That discipline also provides the essential foundation for increased mechanization of the programming job itself.

ITT Corporation

ITT Corporation (formerly International Telephone and Telegraph) was another firm with varied software needs and development operations that, by the mid-1970s, had become both essential to the company and extremely difficult to manage consistently. Problems stemmed from size, diversity, and geographical dispersion, as well as the absence of a coordinated infrastructure for software development. ITT ended most of its efforts in software when it sold its telecommunications operations to a European company, Alcatel, in the mid-1980s (while retaining a minority interest in this business as a joint-venture partner). Nonetheless, between 1978 and 1985, ITT launched an extensive initiative to structure software development along the lines of IBM's basic software divisions that yielded considerable insights into how managers might better organize and promote software production in a firm with widely varied programming operations.[57] The task proved particularly daunting since ITT, by the late 1970s, had become one of the world's biggest conglomerates. In 1978, it had 300,000 employees around the globe, $15 billion in sales, and 200 diverse subsidiary companies, mainly acquired through acquisitions. Approximately 110 of these firms and 6,000 employees were involved extensively in software development for ITT's primary business, telecommunications, as well as defense contracting, internal business applications, and other areas.

ITT's chairman, Harold Geneen, initiated a revamping of the company's software operations after expressing concern with their disorganization and recruiting James Frame, then head of IBM's Santa Teresa Laboratory, as a vice-president in charge of programming in 1978. Geneen charged Frame with making ITT a "world leader in software-engineering technology" by lowering software costs, shortening development times, and improving quality for all ITT programming facilities. Frame began by collecting a staff, mainly from IBM, and determining specific action plans. These included surveying and measuring ITT's current programming operations; changing the "corporate culture" of ITT programming groups; improving software-development technology by acquiring proven tools and methods as well as by producing new ones through R&D; and building a capability to generate new revenues by selling software-engineering tools, methods, and work stations. To support and coordinate these efforts, Frame set up a new R&D facility in Connecticut, called the Programming Technology Center (PTC). At its peak in 1983, the PTC had a staff of 150 software professionals, recruited from within and outside ITT, serving 8,000 developers mainly through education programs and development of tools and methods for measuring as well as improving software quality and productivity (Table 2.8).[58]

An obstacle Frame's group immediately encountered reflected ITT's lack of previous organization for software operations. The corporation had no central records identifying software managers and staff, most of

Table 2.8 ITT Programming Technology Center (1983)

Department	Staff	Functions
Education	40	Worldwide training of ITT staff
Advanced Technology	30	Development of new tools and methods
Applied Technology	25	Tool and method study and acquisition
Business Support	15	Unbundling, software pricing
Communications	15	ITT conferences, journals, news
Measurements	10	Productivity and quality metrics
Administration	10	Personnel and administration
Network Development	5	ITT internal network development
Total	150	

Source: Capers Jones, "A 10-Year Retrospective of Software Engineering within ITT," Cambridge, Mass., Software Productivity Research, Inc., May 15, 1988, p. 5.

whom the company simply classified as engineers. Therefore, to communicate with these personnel, such as to survey them or provide them with information on new procedures, tools, or training, required a census and compilation of a mailing list. ITT also had 800 different managers with software-development responsibilities and no central coordination. To correct this, Frame introduced IBM's concept of programming directors by appointing senior executives responsible for large groups (100 or more) of software professionals. To improve skills and redirect the culture of programming in ITT toward a more structured and standardized approach, Frame also set the policy of providing each manager and developer with ten days of training a year, as well as instituting formal conferences and workshops for software personnel, a software newsletter and journal, executive briefings, and software-engineering awards for excellence. Among other measures, ITT adopted a dual salary plan, which allowed software technical personnel who did not move into a management track to achieve salaries equivalent to high-level managers.

In terms of programming technologies, ITT researchers focused on introducing object-oriented and other new design languages, on-line work stations, and automated documentation-support tools, including common data dictionaries and databases. Another effort, termed *defect removal support*, stressed the improvement of reviews, inspections, and testing procedures, to eliminate bugs in newly written code. A number of areas, however, combined what Capers Jones, a member of Frame's staff both at IBM and ITT, called "improvements with both a technical and cultural component." Overcoming resistance here required a resocialization of managers and engineers through extensive presentations and technical forums, as well as solicitation of support from Chairman Geneen and other top executives.

These technical and cultural challenges included the establishment of standardized measurement techniques for software quality and productivity, which software personnel tended to resist, as well as overcoming opposition from project managers and developers accustomed to independent operations to having outside groups inspect their software. Programmers also reacted negatively to standardizing tools and management procedures based around a common database and data dictionary, which Frame wanted "so that all financial information, communication, plans, progress reports, and many technical deliverables could be developed and monitored easily."[59] In addition, reusability became a technical and cultural issue because, while many projects had common functions that did not need customized code written from scratch each time, ITT had developers spread out around the world, hindering communication across projects, and developers preferred to view all software as unique. With time, however, some ITT divisions overcame these obstacles, as Jones recalled:

The concept of reusability is that software projects have many common functions that do not need customized code or customized design, and where a library of reusable components can improve quality and productivity at the same time. This concept is counter to the standard software engineering education, where the uniqueness of software is stressed. The success of ITT's reusability work was also made difficult by the international nature of the corporation. Nonetheless, reusability quickly became a recognized area of software research and some ITT units such as Hartford Insurance were soon achieving more than 50% reusable code by volume in their new applications.[60]

Improving estimating techniques proved equally essential for management planning and control. Since this "had previously been a manual task carried out by trial and error," it required extensive effort to convince project managers and software developers to adopt new automated tools and procedures. The PTC also built a tool for project estimating and long-term forecasting of personnel requirements. Although the PTC completed only a prototype, the projections indicated that, unless ITT improved quality control, within a few years programming staff would have to double to about 25,000. ITT projected that increased maintenance needs alone would consume 65 percent of these expanded ranks of software personnel, leaving only 35 percent for new development. On the other hand, it appeared that more effective quality controls would keep maintenance personnel at less than 50 percent of the programmer population, as well as keep the total programming staff at about 12,000.

Software-inventory surveys and project studies revealed other information that helped managers devise a strategy for improving both productivity and quality. First, they discovered that purchased packages accounted for the largest source of new software, measured by lines of code per work-year, followed by applications and tools developed for internal use (primarily for management information systems or MIS), and externally sold products, mainly for telecommunications. Custom military software, usually embedded in hardware systems, consumed a relatively small portion of existing software, though it received a great deal of attention. Second, they noticed wide differences in productivity for different types of software, with rates for in-house MIS applications programming more than twice as high as for military systems (Table 2.9).

In searching for reasons behind productivity differences, and possible countermeasures, Frame's group reached several conclusions. For in-house MIS applications, productivity measured by lines of code per work-year appeared better than for other areas, in part because of much less paperwork than for products sold externally; however, rather than maximize productivity, with this type of software, ITT most needed to satisfy the requirements of in-house users, and this demanded more

Table 2.9 ITT Software Volume and Productivity (ca. 1980)

Software Type	Volume* (1970–1980)	Source Statements (per work-yr)
Purchased		
Packages	17,000,000	12,000
In-House Developed		
Internal MIS applications	15,000,000	4,000
Internal support software	13,000,000	3,500
Telecommunications	12,000,000	2,200
Military projects	4,000,000	1,800
Miscellaneous/systems software	4,000,000	3,000

*Amount of software developed or purchased at ITT. MIS = management information systems; yr = year.
Source: Capers Jones, "A 10-Year Retrospective of Software Engineering with ITT," pp. 16–17.

intimate user participation in development. Automated design tools, program generators, reusable code, and new higher-level languages seemed useful to facilitate efficient design and production. In addition, Frame's group concluded that, compared to writing equivalent code from scratch, packages produced the highest levels of productivity and could be more useful if managers used them more widely. Their survey, however, also indicated that departments needed to find packages that did not require much modification after purchase, because modifications could consume as much labor as building new software from scratch.

ITT also demonstrated high productivity for in-house tool development, though practices remained unsystematic and ad hoc, suggesting room for improvement. To increase management control here, Frame's group recommended tighter reviews and inspections, and more rigorous planning. In the telecommunications area, unstable hardware—specifically, changes in the switching systems introduced while software was under development—seemed to constrain productivity. The most important factor ITT identified to improve performance here was more extensive reviews and inspections of all specifications and code, to minimize the need for changes, although hardware problems continued to plague this area of ITT's business. For military projects, ITT displayed the lowest productivity, apparently because approximately 50 percent of total budgets went toward paperwork rather than software production. This suggested automated support for documentation and other indirect tasks would significantly improve employee performance.

According to Jones, their efforts resulted in significant progress in defect removal and prevention, measurements and estimation, executive briefings, and management and staff education. Yet they had less success in reusability and creating an integrated development environment. How much further ITT might have improved became a moot point after problems with telecommunications hardware continued and Alcatel bought this business from the company. Frame and Jones left to become independent consultants while, to avoid duplication with its European laboratories, Alcatel in 1987 closed the ITT Programming Technology Center.

A U.S. Consulting Firm

One of the world's largest accounting and consulting firms (whose name remains anonymous here, despite its listing in the Appendix A survey, because of a confidentiality agreement between the company and the researcher on whom this description is based) provided perhaps the most extreme case of a factory approach in the United States, closely resembling Japanese applications facilities described in Part II of this book.[61] The firm, while better known for accounting services, had expanded into custom applications software and system integration as part of management consulting for the financial services, manufacturing, retail, telecommunications, transportation, and government markets. In 1988, systems-integration revenues alone reached approximately $350 million (about 40 percent of total sales), placing the company in the top four U.S. firms competing in this segment of the software industry (behind IBM, Electronic Data Systems, and Computer Sciences).[62] Products included software packages (standard applications programs and software support tools), custom-built software systems, and related services, including system installation and modification of packages for specific customers.

Most distinctive about the firm appeared to be its high level of standardization in development methodology and tools, as well as designs that could be modified for different customers. This approach reflected a deliberate strategy, dating back to the 1970s, when software and system-integration revenues began increasing rapidly. Top managers decided to hire operations-research specialists and create an infrastructure emphasizing "production efficiency type of skills."[63] The firm also chose to invest in standardization and training rather than hiring large numbers of highly paid experts. The company generally recruited college graduates unskilled in software engineering and then educated them for six weeks in the standardized methodology and tool set, before sending them to work in project teams at client sites. To maintain these employees, the firm created a formal career path, from staff analyst to senior manager and then partner, although high personnel turnover encouraged the continued reliance on computer-aided tools as well as standardized methods and designs.

The development process, which employees referred to as the *Modus* methodology, filled ten thick volumes in paper or fourteen personal-computer diskettes. Managers claimed that Modus reflected "over 30 years of experience . . . in developing and maintaining information systems," with frequent updates to incorporate advances in both hardware and software. One senior partner described the rationale behind Modus as an attempt to institutionalize good practice and create economies of scope: "We used to be very case oriented, but as we started encountering bigger jobs about twenty years ago, we realized we had to pull out some general procedures, so we could share knowledge about projects across offices as well as interchange personnel. So we developed a standard development life cycle for all our offices." While more detailed examination of the origins of Modus indicates that it evolved from refinements of standards devised for a particular project, divisionwide standards were consistent with the culture and traditions of the firm, which, as auditing specialists originally, utilized formal standards and controls for other operations.[64]

Modus included both a project-management system and a "philosophy of design." Project management followed accepted software-engineering practices and relied on a sequential life cycle (system requirements, system design, programming, testing, conversion, and installation), with work divided into a series of tasks, milestones to monitor project progress, standards for documentation and evaluation, and procedures for estimating schedules, budget, and manpower requirements. Projects could adopt a more iterative approach, utilizing prototyping and more interaction with customers to refine designs before completion, although they followed this type of process infrequently.

While the philosophy of design borrowed from practices commonly described in software-engineering literature, some methods seemed outdated or tedious. Analysts utilized data-structure diagrams (Warnier charts) to outline the logic of each program so that separate groups (and tools) could turn the detailed charts into executable code. New alternatives being explored included logic-oriented as well as object-oriented design approaches. Design consisted primarily of customizing generic program skeletons (shells) and macros (subroutines, or sets of computer instructions, that can be referred to repeatedly within a program without rewriting the instructions) as well as elements defined in a data dictionary. Program generators eliminated the most routine coding tasks, with as much as 80 percent of the code on some projects automatically produced.[65]

Most of the automated tools dated from around 1980, when management adopted the strategy of deliberately introducing more computer-aided systems to support the Modus process. As with the standardized methodology, most tools originally came from specific projects rather than through a central R&D organization, although company engineers modified them to link the tools integrally with software-development methods and project-management procedures. Personnel referred to the tools collectively as the *Design Factory*.[66] Like Japanese factories, the firm also sold the following as an integrated workbench package, running on IBM hardware:

— Utilities for creating a data dictionary that defined most of a system under development (data items, records, files, databases, screens, reports, programs, etc.) as well as checked for cross-reference errors or inconsistencies.
— A project-estimating tool based on LOTUS 1-2-3 that allowed analysts to estimate project requirements based on standard estimating factors.
— A project-control system that measured project status and performance.
— Screen and report design aids that generated code for actual screens and reports used in new systems.
— Data and program design aids that assisted in database structural design and in drawing dataflow and structure charts.
— Installation tools for programming and testing, including compilers, macros, linkage editors (special programs that convert the output of assemblers and compilers into modules that can be loaded and run on a computer), loaders (special programs that transfer users' programs along with the needed basic system software to the central processor of the computer for execution), file-maintenance programs (software that allows users to modify the contents of computer files, units of related instructions, data, and other information), source-code editors, documentation generators, and libraries of various types to test-support tools, database development tools, and application-program shells in COBOL, as well as COBOL code generators.
— Prototyping support facilities.

The de-skilling nature of automated tools, as well as of standardized methods, designs, and training programs, became somewhat controversial within the company—as in other firms moving toward a highly structured or explicit factory approach to software development. Management aimed at using its most experienced (and expensive) people only for high-level system design or tool development, with less experienced people completing program construction and, in general, taking on more activities in routine projects. Company consultants and managers openly described the strategy behind this process as leveraging the skills of a few across more than one project:

> We use tools to leverage people's skills. One person who is more skilled than everyone else does the program shells, and then you can take people who are less skilled and they can use those shells. So we don't reinvent the wheel. And instead of everyone having to get the same level of skills, we only need a few people with the higher skills. . . . With tools we can make money leveraging people, that is, having many bodies even at lower rates can be

profitable with tools. Tools allow us to do what we are always trying to do in the Firm, to push work down to the lowest skill level possible. They allow a factory mode of operating.

. . . the Firm takes a high risk by investing knowledge in individuals who may leave soon. We need to leverage that risk. We have to be able to divorce knowledge from programmers; that's why we invest in tools. . . .

Productivity tools allow us to leverage inexperienced people. . . . So we can take a kid out of school, let's say with a major in English, and in a very short time he can achieve high productivity, that is achieve the productivity level of a client programmer with ten years experience. It's not that we are making him more effective at his job, but we are dumping him into a production environment that has ten years of programming experience built into it.[67]

Yet automation and standardization posed their own constraints, and in many ways opposed common views of custom-software development as requiring more adaptability or responsiveness to individual customers, as well as high levels of individual skill. The firm's process (like that in Japanese factories) seemed particularly restrictive because tools supported the Modus methodology and developers had to follow the methodology to use the tools. Hence, since tools and methods mutually reinforced each other, tools served as a form of technical control over project members, making sure they followed the prescribed methods. Whether this degree and manner of control appeared positive or negative depended on one's point of view.

From management's perspective, building expertise into tools and methods, and dividing labor among skilled and less-skilled personnel, allowed the company to utilize the best people in critical areas and increase the number and size of projects it undertook, thereby raising potential profits and sales.[68] This benefit existed despite limitations and tradeoffs, including overhead costs. First, the approach worked best for familiar applications that fit standardized designs and procedures, thus restricting the type of projects the company could effectively undertake without modifying its process and personnel policies or risking disappointed customers. In addition, tools involved time and money to develop and then to train people in their use; tools required more precision in areas such as program specification; tools also seemed to encourage project members to do more redesign, which could add unnecessarily to company expenses.

As another, potentially more serious consequence of reliance on Modus and the Design Factory tools, current personnel appeared to have a less detailed knowledge of software technology than their predecessors, who had not had the benefits of so many automated tools or standardized methods and procedures. In fact, in the opinion of Wanda Orlikowski (this discussion is based mainly on her research), much of the firm's system development had become exercises in "filling in forms." Apart from the intended objective of de-skilling software design and coding, tools had become a crutch at least for some designers, who used them to generate standardized programs rather than thinking about how to produce a better product for the customer. In this sense, the standardization of tools and methods both facilitated and constrained product development as well as cast into doubt how well the firm would be able to sustain its strategy of offering customers innovative customized systems.

This issue became controversial in the company precisely because some managers argued that basic skills and knowledge remained essential for effective systems development, particularly when consultants encountered new situations that went beyond the limited options available in their tool kits or manuals. On nonroutine projects, a lack of widespread technical expertise could hinder progress—the very opposite of management's goal to increase productivity and profits. Despite these concerns, however, many senior managers minimized the importance of understanding technical details, as long as they felt consultants knew enough to use the standard tools and perform adequately in most projects.[69]

The factory cases in Part II suggest that whether this position was wise depended very much on the type and variety of work a firm accepted as well as how it competed and priced products and services. There also seemed a strong consensus among managers at IBM, SDC, and Japanese firms adopting factory approaches that facilities had to tailor methodologies and tools to·different product families for them to be effective and acceptable to developers and customers, because no one development process and tool set appeared suitable for all applications.

In contrast, the U.S. consulting firm did not limit "the number of client types to which it applies formalized, canned solutions." Instead, management claimed the "'Modus methodology' *applies to any systems project, regardless of the equipment, industry, application, complexity or size* [emphasis added]."[70] The Design Factory tools also seemed difficult to modify for new tasks, perhaps reflecting the ad hoc nature of tool development. In addition, the Modus standards, though updated periodically, in the interim did not make it easy for project members to move to new techniques, such as a more interactive design methodology based around prototyping for customers before finishing the actual systems.

Project members retained some flexibility to make adjustments to different situations. Management did not directly enforce the Modus methodology and allowed personnel to "employ some discretion over which 'Modus' procedures to follow" to solve the problems of individual clients. In this respect, the firm used both factory and ad hoc procedures. Yet a potential problem persisted in that adjustments required expertise, while overreliance on automated tools and standardized procedures, as well as the hiring of unskilled personnel, meant a gradual reduction in the technical knowledge managers could expect individuals to possess. Furthermore, the tools and standards themselves enforced fairly strict controls at least indirectly, and restricted the ability of projects to operate in a truly decentralized or independent manner.[71]

In the short term, the firm continued to generate business and profits as well as rank as a leader among U.S. companies in custom software and systems integration. Some managers and employees complained of the constraints a standard process imposed, although few individuals or groups mounted any serious resistance. A minor incident occurred at least once, when a few designers decided not to follow the standard procedure of doing high-level design in detailed flow charts and instead substituted pseudo-code (because it saved time), which a separate group of programmers then translated into executable code. Orlikowski concluded that opposition to the structured approach was "dampened by the collective culture of the Firm which generates a sense of community . . . the *'project as a team'* is a concept the Firm uses to attempt to evoke bonding and commitment."[72] Withal, from the customer's point of view, the firm provided nominally customized programs more tailored to user needs than packaged software and potentially cheaper or easier to obtain than fully customized systems written from scratch by highly paid software experts.

Digital Equipment Corporation

Digital, the second largest U.S. computer producer in 1988, had sales of nearly $11.5 billion, mainly in minicomputers and peripheral hardware but also in basic systems software and a smaller portion in applications.[73] Digital widely dispersed applications projects geographically, such as at regional sales offices or at customer sites. As a result, applications development, much like at IBM, remained decentralized and unstandardized in content or process, focusing instead on serving a variety of customer needs with versatile and skilled developers. On the other hand, Digital needed to control basic software development since this remained critical to selling its proprietary hardware. As a result, management centralized development projects in a large facility in Spitbrook, New Hampshire, with only a few dispersed groups connected to Spitbrook through an on-line network. As in many other companies, including IBM, Digital organized systems-software groups by product, with each software product linked to specific hardware systems such as the VAX and PDP minicomputers.[74]

But Digital provides another case of conflict between efficiency and flexibility, as well as between technological aims and in-house or craft-based cultural constraints. Management historically embraced a strategy and organization emphasizing not standardization and control but individual creativity, innovation, and independence. Yet the rise of highly efficient competitors, the growing complexity of software, continued shortages of skilled personnel, and customer demands for higher quality, lower prices, and faster delivery, made it imperative for Digital to exert greater control over product development, particularly in basic software.

Anne Smith Duncan and Thomas J. Harris, managers in Digital's Commercial Languages and Tools (CLT) Group, offered in a 1988 in-house report a remarkably candid account of software practices at Digital, both before and after efforts to introduce more tools and systematic methods. The picture they painted of Digital before the mid-1980s revealed a true project-centered organization relying entirely on highly skilled people with great amounts of autonomy. Members of each software project determined their own standards and conventions. The company offered no centrally supported tools, so tool development depended on uncoordinated efforts at the project level. Few activities or operations benefited significantly from automation. Nor did Digital create a system for collecting and analyzing information on critical areas such as defects. In addition, projects often invested hundreds of man-hours writing similar code, with no mutual knowledge or sharing. As a result of these craftlike practices, each group tended to view its problems, and its solutions, as unique. Its culture and structure left Digital with no organizational capability to identify and transfer good practices and technologies, redeploy existing investments in designs, code or tools, or even compare current levels of performance with the past, as Duncan and Harris described:

> The Digital engineering culture allows each software project team substantial freedom to determine its own conventions, standards, and infrastructure. In this culture, moving a successful "process" from one completed project to a new one depended on the people who moved between them. In the 1970s and 1980s few supported tools were available, and tool development was done at the project level, if at all. Some processes were automated, most were not. Regression testing (regression tests reveal whether something that previously worked still does) was done by hand, bug lists were compiled on blackboards, and debugging major integrations at base levels was difficult and time consuming. The project members paid minimal attention to tracing how and when things happened, and they documented this activity on paper, if at all.
>
> Another aspect of this culture was the sense that each project team had to write all the code needed for that project. This attitude meant that code to do common routines was duplicated from project to project. Each team believed that its problem was unique, that it could not share code with any other team. The belief was pervasive that each problem was different and that each project team had found the only appropriate techniques.[75]

To a large extent, Digital management made a strategic and organizational choice, compared to producers that emphasized process efficiency. Management organized software development in highly independent

groups in an attempt to inspire innovative software products that demonstrated the unique capabilities of Digital hardware. In particular, management promoted the design of compatible hardware and software architectures for the entire range of Digital machines, to support a greater
interconnection (networking) capability than other vendors offered. Integrating hardware and software products required creative product development as well as careful coordination of specifications among groups
working on different systems. Yet, managers tended to focus not on *how*
people wrote programs, but on *what* the programs did, as well as *when*
they completed the work.[76] Digital projects thus operated with far less
standardization and control than in companies such as IBM and the U.S.
consulting firm discussed earlier, or in Japanese software factories. Individual product managers had ultimate responsibility for each phase of
development, and no staff group supervised the development process.
Only by imposing controls on what final products looked like did Digital
management exert influence, indirectly, over development.

Most important in this indirect form of control proved to be a set of
corporate guidelines or checklists for software development outlined in a
manual, the *Phase Review Process* (Table 2.10). This listed each phase for
review, based on a life-cycle model, and specific milestones a product had
to pass through before project mangers could move it on to the next
phase. The manual also required reports or documents attesting to completed work and satisfactory reviews at each phase. Yet only at Phase 0
did the product managers hold open meetings, and these mainly sought
agreements on the functional specifications among parties interested in
the product.[77] After Phase 0, project managers submitted budget requests, based on individual estimates of how many work-years would be
required to develop the system. Project managers retained individual
responsibility for reviews as well as costs and schedules, which appeared
useful even in factory approaches, although Digital did not require a
central database of production-management or quality data, or formal
measurements of productivity and reuse rates.

While few outside or direct controls may have maximized creativity
within individual projects, and company executives placed a high value
on introducing innovative products to market quickly, Digital's approach
had negative consequences. It seemed common, for example, for managers to overspend budgets rather than delivering late or incomplete
products.[78] This was perhaps expected, since Digital did not base com-
pensation for project managers primarily on meeting schedule or budget
deadlines.[79] Yet loose controls over spending tended to raise costs for
new product development. Furthermore, without formal monitoring
during development, phase reviews often turned out to be loose and
overly subjective, causing both managers and customers to complain of
budget and schedule overruns as well as high maintenance costs stemming from programming or design errors.[80] These problems suggested

Table 2.10 Digital's Phase Review Process

Life-Cycle Management

Phase	Title
0	Strategy and requirements
1	Planning
2	Design and implementation
3	Qualification
4A	Engineering, manufacturing, transition
4B	Manufacturing volume production
5	Retirement

Required Milestones Documentation

Phase 0
1. Business plan draft
2. Market requirements
3. Product requirements
4. Alternatives/feasibility
5. Manufacturing impact

Phase 1
1. Final business plan
2. Functional specifications
3. Project plan
4. Manufacturing plan draft
5. Customer services plan

Phase 2
1. Revised business plan
2. Marketing/sales plan
3. Detailed design/code freeze
4. Verification test plans
5. Manufacturing plan
6. Customer services plan
7. Final prototype
8. Prototype test results

Phase 3
1. Final business plan
2. Product announcement criteria
3. Verification tests results
4. First shippable product available
5. Field customer service criteria met

Phase 4
1. Post partum review
2. Manufacturing process certification
3. Market performance review

Phase 5
1. Retirement business plan
2. Production stopped
3. Marketing stopped
4. Support services stopped

Source: Cynthia Schuyler, "The Software Development Process: A Comparison—Toshiba vs. Digital Equipment," Dec. 11, 1987, exhibits 5 and 6.

that the Phase Review system fell short of providing adequate process control, at least since this objective had become more important to Digital customers.

With regard to quality, formal procedures appeared stricter than the phase-review system, though Digital still did not enforce these directly during the development process. An independent group for Software Quality Management (SQM) reporting to a vice president in charge of software engineering took responsibility for final product testing as well as dealing with customer complaints. Yet product managers, as with project control, remained solely responsible for testing during the development phases. Digital's final SQM tests seemed more standardized and rigorous than the phase reviews, according to a former employee, and they provided a "strong incentive to avoid any risk of errors. . . ."[81] In particular, knowledge of the SQM group's testing procedures appeared to influence the early stages of product development. Nonetheless, without formal monitoring during development by the SQM group or another outside party, project groups tolerated wide variations in procedures and effectiveness. Some tested modules primarily by functionality, some wrote executable specifications or prototypes to test whole programs early in the requirements definition stage, and some used code reviews by outside parties while others did not.

Overall, Duncan and Harris admitted that Digital's process for quality control fell short of meeting the rising complexity of new software and the increasing demands of customers for more reliable products. Digital also seemed at a disadvantage compared to some other firms because it did not emphasize central support for tool and methodology development. In the mid-1980s, management had established a Software Technology Group, but this provided only limited assistance to project groups, and did not introduce a standardized set of tools or methods required for all software projects.

On the other hand, centralization at Spitbrook, and electronic integration through on-line networks, provided Digital with enormous potential for disseminating a wide range of tools and reusable software, as well as for improving its methods for control and data gathering.[82] In particular, Digital's electronic mail system allowed employees to circulate various languages, tools, and programs to other employees throughout the world. The two Digital operating systems, VMS for the VAX machines and RSX for the PDP-11s, contained uniform, compatible user interfaces, facilitating portability of tools and code. Digital also had a Code Management System (CMS) available to serve as a program library and project-management tool by storing and sorting code. This could work along with another tool, Datatrieve, which provided database management capabilities, such as for project-control information. Nonetheless, managers did not require the use of these or other tools, and preferred to let individual product groups choose their own process technology.[83]

Digital's personnel policies and related management practices also contrasted with those of the U.S. consulting firm or Japanese software factories. Most software employees came to the company with college degrees in computers or related areas of engineering, math, and science or with outstanding personal skills in programming. Managers encouraged software personnel to become involved with each product and each step of development, despite some allocation of tasks according to ability. The accepted process thus called not for divisions of labor by levels of skill, but for software development by multiskilled engineers who did their own design and coding, as a former employee noted: "The corporate culture is one of entrepreneurial independence and therefore encourages each software employee to 'take ownership' (a favorite Digital term) of his piece of the project. . . . The prevalent attitude at Digital is that design and coding are two parts of a single process; hence, the concept of improving 'manufacturing' productivity is absent."[84]

Yet, by the mid-1980s, Duncan and Harris admitted that Digital customers and, finally, company engineers and managers had "started to pay much more attention to software costs, as the costs of software development and maintenance began to exceed the cost of hardware."[85] The market demanded more reliable software while technical requirements had become more complex, requiring better coordination and control among disparate groups: "Communications between teams became increasingly difficult as the normal communications paths became clogged." What is more, advances in computer hardware placed increasing strains on software developers at the same time that maintenance of old software products had come to consume "human and hardware resources that should be used to build new products."

Faced with these changes in its competitive environment, and estimates of shortages of software engineers for the next twenty years, top management resolved to improve quality and dependability of software products while finding ways to reduce costs. Part of the new strategy focused on leveraging the skills of its engineers by creatively eliminating redundant work "to solve new problems in creative ways, and . . . solve each problem only once." This objective led, first, to systematic studies of programmer productivity within the company, beginning in 1985, as Duncan and Harris recalled: "[W]e needed to understand how we were doing at a point in time compared with how we had done in the past." Between 1985 and 1988, Digital then attempted to introduce or increase the use of several basic tools and methodologies that would add more structure and standardization, as well as automated support, to the development process.

One tool set, the VAX DEC/CMS and VAX DEC/MMS (Module Management System), automated the maintenance of difference versions of source code, the identification of modules that belonged to particular versions, and the building processes. Previously, "the procedures for building and controlling source code were usually listed on a blackboard, in a notebook, or in someone's head." In addition, the VAX DEC/Test Manager simplified statistical regression techniques for use in testing, defect analysis, or code optimization, relying on the assumption that a simplified process would encourage developers to run these tests more often. The VAX Notes System served as a "distributed conference tool," to assist "in automating and tracking project design discussions and decisions." The VAX Common Run-Time Library provided approximately 1,000 commonly used software routines. While this system first became available in 1977, according to Duncan and Harris, Digital management now encouraged "software engineers . . . [to] search for code, designs, additional tools, and documentation that can be reused. Both managers and engineers consider reused code as an investment in design, programming, and testing that has already been paid for. Moreover, the support for that code has been planned and is in place."

Experimental results from the new emphasis on process improvement, reuse, and tool support appeared excellent for a selected group of projects in Digital's Commercial Languages and Tools Group. These projects developed tools for broad dissemination and thus had to achieve high levels of reliability. While the data were not necessarily representative of other Digital groups, they provided some indication of the gains possible using a more structured approach to production and quality control. In lines of code productivity, for example, for fourteen products, mean output per work-month increased from 792 lines during 1980–1984 to 2,169 lines after January 1985. This represented nearly a threefold improvement, primarily reflecting reuse rates ranging from 22 to 56 percent of the delivered code across the later projects. Duncan and Harris also claimed that defect rates per 1,000 lines of code dropped from between 0.07 and 1.51 prior to 1985 to between 0 and 0.066 afterwards. Other data confirmed the benefits of productivity and quality gains by indicating Digital delivered these products at lower costs than it did prior to 1985.

Summary and Evaluation

Producers may never solve all the difficulties in many kinds of software development because many new products and large-scale systems in general are inherently complex, contain applications that differ widely, and involve a technology that continues to change. As a result, existing tools, techniques, and knowhow always prove inadequate at least for some projects. Furthermore, while phases in software development may seem straightforward and linear, projects in operation follow an iterative process with many interdependent activities. Problems in one phase (such as inaccurate specifications or changes in designs) may create difficulties in other phases as well as throughout the lifetime of a product. Software managers and developers thus have no easy solutions, but they clearly have choices: tools and methods to use in particular circumstances, people to match with suitable tasks, jobs to accept or reject and channel elsewhere. Yet even good tools, methods, or reuse libraries provide little benefit if management cannot get an organization to utilize them systematically.

Several general points can be made from the brief discussions of IBM, ITT, the U.S. consulting firm, and Digital; all will be treated further in the factory cases in Part II. First, software products exhibit variations in average levels of productivity; these differences may reflect varying levels of difficulty but also different project approaches as well as optimal processes for development. This means that managers and engineers, if they want to improve software operations, probably need to begin by identifying different product, process, and customer needs, and then comparing the abilities of personnel to find an appropriate mix of tools, methods, skills, and objectives for each project. Complete standardization alone may prove counterproductive, especially if customers require unique or tailored systems, and if the firm encounters too much variety in demand. While some kinds of software appear less amenable to a standardized or automated approach than others, accumulations of experience, process R&D, and proper matching of methods, tools, and personnel probably will lead to steady improvements in productivity and quality. It also seems possible for firms to reuse software or recycle packages more systematically.

IBM, beginning in the early 1960s, organized an international network of facilities to build basic software and emphasized a combination of initiatives. These integrated personnel training, methods, controls, and process support in a way that closely resembled Japanese software factories, with some exceptions such as less apparent concern with reusability or structuring applications development (until recently). ITT strove to impose greater structure on widely diverse software operations and turn these into a more orderly business. While the company sold most software operations before making major advances, a new technical staff documented the wide range of productivity found in different programming areas as well as proposed numerous countermeasures to offset both technical and cultural obstacles to improving management of software development, such as through standardization of metrics, tools, and methods, or systematic reusability.

The U.S. consulting firm, like Japanese producers, imposed strict standardization in methods, tools, and training, and appeared to de-skill much of the software-development process. This approach allowed management to leverage the skills of a few experienced employees in design while providing customers with at least some customized product features. While the company proved extremely successful in the marketplace, at least one researcher displayed concerns that too much structure and standardization brought on negative consequences, such as constraining the inventive or learning capabilities of employees and thus their long-term ability to accommodate different or evolving customer needs.

Yet even Digital managers had come to recognize the need for structure and standardization in software operations. This company, historically, competed on the basis of product innovation and allowed programming personnel and managers considerable freedom to define their own methods and tools. The results: innovative products but uneven quality, unpredictable schedules, and high development and maintenance costs, as well as duplication in tool and program development. Consequently, by the mid-1980s, Digital managers concerned with improving the company's capabilities in software had begun to pay more attention to process issues, achieving remarkable improvements in quality and productivity at least in selected projects.

Managers of software development thus face a classical dilemma. On the one hand, too much emphasis on individual creativity and independence might create problems in controlling development costs, quality, and long-term maintenance. On the other hand, too much structure and control might stifle creativity, innovation, and the ability to change—as well as prompt rebellions from managers, developers, and perhaps customers. Managers of any new, complex technology, where products, processes, and customer needs continue to evolve, need to find a balance between these two extremes. In software, integrated approaches combining good tools and methods for each phase of development with personnel training and other elements appear to provide some help to managers. As the SDC case reveals, however, a factory strategy and structure may be far easier to conceive in theory or in an R&D environment than to implement and sustain within a real organization facing the competitive demands of a dynamic industry.

PART II

THE FACTORY APPROACH

3

SYSTEM DEVELOPMENT CORPORATION: A U.S. FACTORY EXPERIMENT[1]

System Development Corporation's (SDC) attempt in the mid-1970s to establish a software factory proved significant for several reasons. First, this provided the first case in the United States of a company explicitly adopting a factory label and strategy for a software facility. Second, SDC committed several years of research and experimentation in search of tools, methods, and organizational concepts aimed at achieving in software the kind of efficiencies found in factory assembly lines, systematically moving products through design, construction, and testing. The factory process worked remarkably well for most projects that went through the facility, bringing noticeable improvements in scheduling, cost control, quality, and customer satisfaction, although SDC encountered several difficulties. Yet, rather than solving them, management disbanded the factory after approximately three years. As the discussion in this chapter illustrates, nonetheless, the SDC case offers numerous lessons regarding the problems inherent in moving a loosely organized group of engineers toward a more structured mode of operations.

Most important, SDC managers and factory architects discovered that standardized tools, initially seen as the crux of a factory process, proved much less useful and transportable than a standardized methodology. SDC's factory also demonstrated how too much specialization or division of labor does not work as well in software development as in conventional engineering and manufacturing, because knowledge of particular applications, such as how a radar system or a bank works, remains as

119

important to writing specifications and computer code as understanding the tools and techniques of software programming. SDC showed as well how creating a factory process requires not merely tools and a standardized methodology but a reorganization and socialization of people as well as work. Finally, it became clear that a sustained effort, which SDC failed to achieve, depended first on support from top management, to absorb the expenses and time needed to get the factory working smoothly, and then on leadership and cooperation from middle management, who had to implement the new approach.

The Corporate Setting

Company Origins and Products

SDC originated as a nonprofit, government-sponsored corporation on the model of M.I.T.'s Lincoln Laboratories and MITRE Corporation. In the mid-1950s, the U.S. Air Force gave a contract to the Rand Corporation to build what would become the world's first real-time command and control system for air defense, SAGE (Semi-Automatic Ground Environment). Rand management then decided to spin off its System Development Division as an independent entity, named System Development Corporation.[2] The new company required increasing numbers of programmers to build SAGE and then a variety of other projects, and expanded from 450 employees in 1956 to 3,500 by 1959.[3] After completing SAGE by the late 1950s, for example, SDC designed a command-control system for the U.S. Strategic Air Command, SACCS (SAC Command and Control System). The operating system alone, which ran on an IBM mainframe, exceeded 1 million lines of code, an astounding length for a program at that time. SDC continued during the 1960s to build other complex software systems for the U.S. government to handle air defense and communications, satellite control, various types of simulations, and the Apollo space missions. Projects for the private sector included information management systems for hospitals, the National Science Foundation, state governments, airports, libraries, and other customers.

The reputation SDC gained from these projects was as a product innovator: "pioneering . . . timesharing technology, user-oriented data management and display systems, and tools and languages enabling programmers to interact readily with computing machines."[4] Yet the need to attract new business and hold talented employees with higher salaries led SDC's board of directors to abandon the nonprofit status in 1969 and compete aggressively for contracts across the United States and abroad.

This transition proved difficult. Years of decline in government procurement for air defense systems, vertical integration by hardware man-ufacturers such as Boeing and TRW into software programming, and entrance into the software contracts business of about 2,000 new firms after 1960, greatly increased competition for the type of work SDC did. Furthermore, after 1969, the U.S. government no longer guaranteed SDC a steady stream of contracts as one of the Department of Defense's special nonprofit suppliers. To survive in a more competitive setting, SDC now had to submit low-priced bids for a wider range of software and hardware systems and for different types of customers, not only the Department of Defense. In particular, the need to write software for a variety of mainframes, minicomputers, and smaller machines made by Digital, Gould, Burroughs, IBM, Amdahl, Univac, and other computer vendors complicated SDC's system design and programming tasks.

Under these conditions, SDC management retrenched and reduced its employees whenever contract orders fell; employees thus dropped from a peak of 4,300 in 1963 to 3,200 in 1969 and to merely 2,000 by 1971. After continued financial losses, the board of directors launched a na-tionwide search and in 1971 selected Dr. George Mueller, who had gained in NASA and TRW a reputation for "cost reductions, technology development, and marketing," as the new chief executive officer (CEO). Mueller had started his career as a system designer for Ramo-Woolridge Corporation in the 1950s and then worked as a vice-president for R&D in TRW's Space Technology Laboratory. He went on to serve as an associate administrator for NASA during the Gemini and Apollo flights during 1963–1969, and as a senior vice-president in General Dynamics.

Mueller quickly set out to change SDC's marketing strategy and meth-ods of operations. One issue for the company was how to get more orders from customers not dependent on U.S. defense spending. An-other was to learn more about integrating hardware products with soft-ware. Procurement officials in the government and private industry had gradually come to prefer total systems suppliers—companies that could design and install computer hardware and communications devices as well as software. Many hardware vendors, such as Boeing, developed this capability by setting up in-house software divisions and contracting out less software to firms like SDC. A third issue was how to achieve an advantage over its competitors. As recounted by the company history, Mueller saw the software industry as maturing and it did not appear to him that SDC, plagued with unpredictable demand for costly, custom job orders, could offer significantly better product or process technology than other firms:

> The problem facing SDC in 1971 was that we were building custom soft-ware on a "one-by-each" basis, in a fast-maturing industry where SDC's competitive edge had all but eroded, predominantly for a single customer—the Department of Defense—with unpredictable demand for our services and at a price that covered our labor plus a small government allowed

markup. The answer to growth in revenues and profits was clearly not in doing more of the same.[5]

Taking advantage of the crisis atmosphere, Mueller launched a review and streamlining of all operations—planning, finance, administration, personnel, reporting and control systems—and created profit centers to make managers directly responsible for their margins above costs. He brought in professional managers from Ford, General Dynamics, RCA, Rockwell, Computer Sciences Corporation, and Singer. Along with these efforts, Mueller pushed SDC into nondefense areas such as air-traffic control systems; command, control and intelligence systems for local governments and police departments; custom work stations; communications networks; and management information systems. By 1974, defense contracts had fallen to just 30 percent of SDC's business. Meanwhile, SDC doubled revenues from $45 million in 1971 to $90 million in 1974, and employees to 3,900. Profits recovered, but Mueller still sought a way for SDC to capitalize on its accumulated technical skills. He personally took charge of the R&D department and set out to create "a methodical 'factory' approach to developing software."[6]

The Factory Initiative

SDC's factory initiative thus grew out of a particular setting: a CEO who believed the computer industry had stabilized to become more focused on cost reductions and that loosely organized production operations had become too expensive. The company history even explained the factory as an attempt to "embody Mueller's concept of a streamlined approach to the manufacturing of software" and thereby make SDC "the first company to develop custom software more scientifically, economically, and reliably."[7] While SDC projects tended to be highly advanced in terms of product technology, management usually accepted fixed-price contracts, which meant SDC lost money every time a project went over budget. This often occurred because of the difficult jobs SDC accepted: "All were pushing the state of the art in real-time command-control information systems. All had fixed prices or cost ceilings. All called for major software developments to be performed away from SDC's Santa Monica headquarters, near the customer. And all suffered from early schedule and, consequently, cost difficulties."[8]

SDC managers did not usually insist on careful project control or reuse of software to reduce development time and costs. In fact, when Mueller joined the firm, SDC had no "standard policy or engineering procedure for company-wide software development. . . . [E]ach programming project was thought to be so unique as to defy a common policy. The entire domain of software development was deemed more an art than a science by its practitioners." Jim Skaggs, SDC president after the merger with Burroughs and the manager who headed the Systems Group at the time of the Software Factory, described the usual state of SDC operations in the early 1970s: "We were engaged in creating a 'one-time miracle' in three places at once."[9]

Mueller set up a Software Development Department within the R&D Division in fall 1972 to identify the best tools around and make them available for use consistently on different projects. To head this effort he selected a senior project manager in SDC's Government Systems Division named Terry Court, a B.A. in mathematics from the University of California at Los Angeles (UCLA) with a master's degree in systems management from the University of Southern California. Mueller gave him the goal of achieving "a methodical, standardized engineering approach to software development" and called the effort *The Software Factory*, registering the name as an SDC trademark. Court hand-picked his team, which included Harvey Bratman, another B.A. in mathematics from UCLA.

Bratman and Court described their efforts in a 1975 article in the journal *Computer*.[10] They discussed how studies of software development had found a poor correlation between programmer productivity and experience, and suggested this indicated "the lack of a methodological and well founded body of knowledge on the software development process."[11] Despite the continued refinement of tools and programming concepts, Bratman and Court also complained these "are either not used at all in system development or, when they are used, they are not used in an integrated manner, but are put together ad hoc each time a large system programming project is begun." The SDC researchers hoped their factory approach would solve five categories of recurring problems:

1. *Lack of Discipline and Repeatability*: Bratman and Court referred to the absence of "standardized approaches to the development process. Each time a software system is developed, the process is partially reinvented, with the consequence that we never become very proficient at this process, nor are we able to accurately predict the time and resources required."
2. *Lack of Development Visibility*: Managers often used code production to indicate progress in completing a software project, but this did not measure "completeness of performance requirements, the design itself, or how well the code implements the design." Not until system testing did it become clear how well a project had progressed; and fixing problems at this stage "is exceedingly expensive and time consuming. . . . Managers have difficulty in tracking the progression of the system from phase to phase, and as a result they have problems in planning and controlling the developing system."
3. *Changing Performance Requirements*: The problem here was that "performance requirements are subjected to interpretation and change as soon as the system design and implementation process

begin the translation of requirements to computer programs." Not only did it seem nearly impossible to specify completely performance requirements before detailed design and coding, but projects often experienced disagreements on the meaning of certain requirements and changes demanded by the customer.

4. *Lack of Design and Verification Tools*: Several tools—such as high-level languages, database management systems, subroutine libraries, and debugging tools—facilitated coding and debugging; however, Bratman and Court asserted that these activities accounted for only about 20 percent of development costs: "There are few widely used tools and techniques which provide significant support to other components of the development process such as requirement and design specification, verification and validation, project management and control, documentation, etc."

5. *Lack of Software Reusability*: Bratman and Court complained that, while firms remained short of skilled personnel and many applications contained similar logic or designs, SDC and other firms exhibited little capability to reuse software components. On the other hand, "extensive use of off-the-shelf software modules would significantly lessen the risk and shorten the time required for software development."[12]

To improve SDC's capabilities to manage these areas, Bratman and Court described a software factory consisting (in their 1975 formulation) of "an integrated set of tools that supports the concepts of structured programming, top-down program development, and program production libraries, and incorporates hierarchically structured program modules as the basic unit of production." Reusability they hoped to attack through "the careful system component structuring, the specific relationship with performance requirements, and the improved documentation inherent in software developed in the factory."[13]

None of the procedures and tools under development seemed new or revolutionary. Nevertheless, Bratman and Court insisted that, when integrated and applied consistently, these procedures and tools should result in a process with the potential to introduce significant improvements in developing software systems "regardless of size, complexity, application, or programming language." With the factory, they therefore hoped to achieve "a disciplined, repeatable process terminating in specified results within budgeted costs and on a predefined schedule." A specific goal was to eliminate or reduce the need to retool for each new project, thereby allowing the organization to get underway quickly and improve, through capturing the benefits of experience, specific functions such as program design, code production, testing, and project management.[14]

Court headed the factory project until 1975, by which time Mueller had become impatient with the R&D effort and wanted someone to form a task force to transfer the tools already developed to an operating division. To accomplish this, Mueller asked John B. "Jack" Munson, then a divisional vice-president.[15] Munson had joined SDC in the 1950s, after graduating with a degree in mathematics from Knox College. Initially, he had worked as a mathematical programmer on SAGE and then moved up into management during the 1960s. At the time of his interviews with this author, Munson was a Unisys vice president based in Houston, Texas.

A major problem with the R&D effort was that, until 1975, it had concentrated on tools, which remained difficult to use on different computer systems. Mueller, a physicist by training and a hardware systems specialist, did not fully understand these issues at first, although Munson quickly shifted the emphasis of the R&D group to methods and organizational concepts.[16] This shift in thinking is evident in Bratman and Court's 1977 update on the Software Factory, compared to the 1975 account, which did not even mention what Munson later considered the most important part of the factory, the *Software Development Manual* (the "*SDM* handbook"). Munson explained in a 1987 interview with this author how they came to realize that tools were probably the least valuable element in a software factory:

> Court and Bratman both came to work for me over in the Defense Division. And we spent about a year or so, prior to the time we set up the factory, thinking through the implications of what they had, and what the real problems are. One of the major conclusions we came to at this point in time was that tools can't drive the technology. Tools have to support the technology. And that while the tools seemed like a great deal, without a methodology that the people were using, and that the tools were supporting, it was the wrong way to go. So what we did was stop the tool development at that point for a bit and spend about a year working on the methodology, which was the *Software Development Manual*. We got that produced, and then we essentially fitted the tools that they had to the methodology and then defined some new tools that we wanted.

By 1976, Munson's team had come to view the factory as composed of three interrelated elements: (1) standardized procedures for all phases of program development and project management; (2) an organizational structure separating systems engineering from program production and testing; and (3) a set of advanced design-support and project-management tools. This order ultimately reflected how they viewed these elements in terms of importance in that the tool set had to support the standardized methodology as well as the new structure. The major organizational innovation necessary to make the factory work turned out to be a matrix system where program managers held responsibility for systems engineering at customer sites and for the overall project, while other functional managers took charge of building and testing the software in a centralized factory. Bratman and Court, in their 1977 article, described this broader view of the factory in the following terms: "The Software Factory Concept [is] a software development facility consisting of an integrated set of standards, procedures, and tools that supports a disciplined and repeatable approach to software development and re-places *ad hoc* conglomerations of developmental techniques and tools with standard engineering practices."[17]

Factory Components: Methodology, Organization, Tools

Element 1: Standards and Procedures

It took one and a half years during 1975–1976 for Munson's team to identify a set of standards and procedures—general rules and specific guidelines—that they felt might be applied to a variety of software pro-jects. They based the process around a life-cycle model of software devel-opment covering the major activities, events, and product components common to all projects. The methodology defined in the *SDM* remained consistent with, and in instances borrowed from, existing "U.S. military standards, U.S. Air Force Manual 375 requirements, and the better com-mercial practices."[18] The required programming techniques included structured design and coding, top-down development, and program production libraries. In addition, *SDM* outlined a management and con-trol process that provided guidelines for planning, project control, re-view and evaluation procedures, and quality assurance. After Munson's group finished writing the manual in 1976, Mueller encouraged all line organizations to adopt it for current and future projects.[19]

Deciding on the standards and procedures for the factory was essen-tially a matter of examining previous projects SDC had done, reviewing records and interviewing personnel, determining what had worked well, and codifying what appeared to be "best practice." This process ap-peared necessary, according to the factory architects, to provide a com-mon language and methodology to make the factory more than just a building housing a large number of programmers working from a single pile of tools. Bratman and Court explained this reasoning in 1977:

> The procedures hold the disparate portions of the Factory together: the standards are the means of making the Factory efficient and easy to use and learn. Without the standards that establish the Software Factory methodol-ogy and the procedures that establish the precise way of doing a task, the Factory is little more than an agglomeration of software development tools. Standardization, initially established and faithfully maintained to reflect changing conditions and continual improvement, is essential to the success of the Factory. The . . . standards . . . establish a working environment where the creative design solutions of key technical personnel can be imple-

mented in high-quality products, on schedule, and within budget. More specifically they:

— promote repeatability in the software development process;
— allow rapid transfer of expertise from one project to another;
— establish a consistent framework for cost estimating;
— make it possible for people to interact efficiently and with a common understanding of goals;
— provide the capability to measure project progress in a realistic manner;
— enforce technical and management techniques;
— establish a basis for assuring and measuring software quality.[20]

Munson, in his interview, offered a similar explanation, describing the compilation of the *SDM* as an exercise to avoid having to "reinvent the basic process" with every new project. He also wanted to provide a "transition vehicle" for projects to move into the factory mode of production by standardizing around good practices that existed within the firm in some groups but that were not commonly used:

> The reason for it [*SDM*] was really one that said we need engineering handbooks for our people to use. We shouldn't reinvent the basic process. How do you build a building? You don't reinvent it every time. We know these things, and we know what good practices are, so lets put them in a handbook that we require our engineers to use. And that was really the reason for the detailed handbook. . . . It wasn't that it was any big original concept at that point in time. A lot of people recognized it and were trying to do something, and were doing good things. . . . Once we got that handbook done, we worked on the organizational concepts. That was when we implemented the Software Factory by collecting up all the software projects that were being done in Santa Monica at that time. We had already picked some of the better people around and had them working with us on the handbook for a year. . . . We had some of the best people out of the line engineering organization working with the R&D people in developing that handbook. We as a team became the transition vehicle.

The first standards in the *SDM* defined a "time-phased software development life-cycle" composed of six phases: planning, requirements and performance, design, development, test and acceptance, operations and maintenance (Figure 3.1).[21] Each phase contained specific "objectives, inputs, outputs, functions . . . and criteria for corporate review of successful completion. . . . Each phase can, in turn, be broken down into smaller activities, each of which yields a product; each product requires a standard, each activity a procedure."

The Planning Phase required a strategy for program development and a schedule of measures to carry out the plan. This activity accomplished three things: (1) It identified the specific tasks required to deliver the product; (2) it identified and allocated resources needed to complete the tasks; and (3) it set up procedures for monitoring and controlling project performance. Managers were responsible for drawing up a detailed

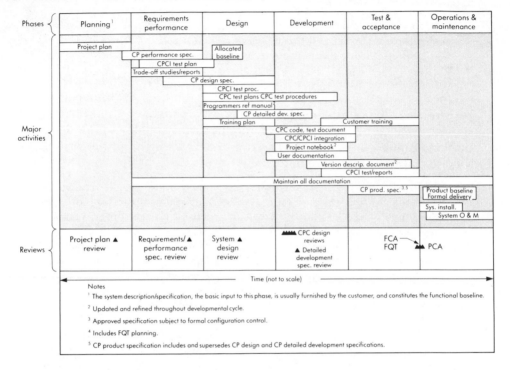

Figure 3.1 Software Systems Development Life Cycle. CP = Computer Program; CPC = Computer Program Configuration; CPCI = Computer Program Configuration Index; FCA = Functional Configuration Audit; FQA = Functional Qualification Audit; FQT = Functional Qualification Test; PCA = Physical Configuration Audit; System O&M = System Operation and Maintenance. (*Source*: Harvey Bratman and Terry Court, "Elements of the Software Factory: Standards, Procedures, and Tools," in Infotech International Ltd., *Software Engineering Techniques* [Berkshire, England: Infotech International Ltd., 1977.] p. 122. Copyright © 1977 System Development Corporation [Unisys Corporation]. Reproduced with permission.)

"master project plan," which included eight elements: (1) software development plan; (2) project work plan; (3) project organization and staffing plan; (4) project budget; (5) documentation plan; (6) configuration management plan; (7) quality assurance plan; and (8) project monitoring and control procedures.

In the Requirements/Performance Phase, managers had to "delineate and describe the software system's functional characteristics and performance parameters, and the means for verifying that the system meets these requirements." This included deciding on computer languages and design standards, selecting production tools, and "investigat[ing] available software modules that could potentially perform the required functions."

The Design Phase called for determination of the details of the software system structure in a top-down fashion—"continual functional decomposition of the higher-level modules into more and more detail—and continued until completion of all the modules decided on in the requirements phase." Managers also had to decide how to develop the product "by multiple teams without excessive coordination," as Bratman and Court described: "The end result of the design phase is a system representation which consists of descriptions of all system components (modules, data elements, and control logic); their dependencies and relationships, both to each other and back to the performance specification; and the accompanying schedules and resource allocations."

In the Development Phase, programmers completed detailed designs of the components identified in the computer program's design specifications, coded the modules, and verified their correctness. A Program Production Library (PPL) tool tracked each version of the system as it evolved. The *SDM* provided extensive examples and guidelines on how to complete and document a detailed modular design in a top-down, hierarchical manner, culminating in a "system representation . . . consisting of operational code."

The Test and Acceptance Phase began "with delivery of the program package to the PPL for testing and ends with acceptance of the program system by the customer." The basic objective was to determine if the coded modules worked reliably in conjunction with each other and the system hardware, as well as performed according to the customer's requirements.

The Operations and Maintenance Phase consisted of installing the system, training support personnel, correcting errors or inefficiencies, and then adding improvements as necessary.

Element 2: Organization

Mueller and the R&D team did not conceive of the factory initially as being more than a set of tools (and, later, standard methods), which they hoped SDC facilities around the country might use; in other words, they did not think of the Software Factory as a physical, centralized facility, similar to factories in other industries. One reason was that the Department of Defense and other customers frequently required software contractors to locate development teams at the computer sites. Other factors also had made a large, centralized facility impractical, although circumstances were changing.

The incompatibility of many computers for which SDC wrote programs, and the wide variety of applications in the jobs SDC accepted to keep its employees active, had made it logical for SDC and most other software producers to organize work in projects, with integrated teams building their own tools and deciding on practices suitable for each job. This project- or job-centered approach made it difficult to standardize practices or eliminate redundancies across projects in areas such as tool development, design, and coding, but it brought customers, systems engineers, and software developers together and seemed to increase the likelihood that a system would meet customer requirements. A growing shortage of skilled programmers, however, made it harder for managers to find the proper set of experts on components such as operating systems, compilers, interfaces, and telecommunications in different locations or to locate engineers willing to move frequently. By 1976, this shortage of people had prompted SDC management to consider an alternative organization.

After working with the R&D team for one year on tools and methodologies, Munson recommended that SDC create a single facility—an actual factory—to build software for SDC's Systems Group. This facility would locate specialists in one site while management would bring programming jobs to them. Engineers in the facility would use the tools and methods developed in R&D as well as remote-terminal and computer technologies that allowed "a single set of personnel to monitor and control a large number of software projects concurrently, taking advantage of economies of scale and providing for cross-utilization of scarce skills."[22] Ronald Atchley, who joined the factory in 1977 and in 1987 served as director of SDC's Software Engineering Systems Group, the staff successor to the Software Factory, saw the facility not as a totally new approach but as a formalization of the organization SDC had used for SAGE and some other projects:

> We implemented [the Factory] with the idea that we would have three separate groups of people. We would have the requirements analysts, designers, or what now is possibly called systems engineering. We would have the program production, which is now software engineering. And we would have the test and evaluation. Those three would be disciplines whereby the work would be done, and the work would flow through the Factory. . . . In the SAGE environment we had a group called Requirements Design

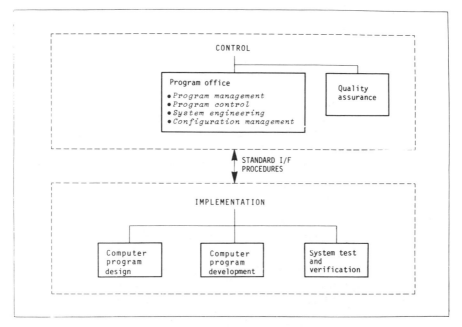

Figure 3.2 Software Factory Organizational Principles. I/F = Interface. (*Source*: Bratman and Court, "Elements of the Software Factory," p. 127. Copyright © 1977 System Development Corporation [Unisys Corporation]. Reproduced with permission.)

> Branch, and they did the specification. We had the Programming Development Branch, and they did the coding and the preliminary testing; and we had the System Test Group in Phoenix, which did the final testing. So we just kind of moved that concept into place and made it more formal.[23]

As in the past, the factory structure required program offices at each customer site (Figure 3.2). Program managers maintained responsibility throughout the life cycle for project management, customer relations, requirements and performance specifications, systems engineering, and quality control and assurance. To build the actual software and test it, however, program managers had to transfer system specifications to what was essentially an assembly line of three groups within the factory: Computer Program Design, Computer Program Development, and System Test and Verification. Bratman and Court expected this division of labor to facilitate continuity and pooling of skilled personnel, the use of a centralized program library, familiarity with a set of tools, and control over product development through the review procedures at the end of each development phase:

The basic tenet of this philosophy is that increased benefits accrue over time if essentially the same people are responsible for production activities in the Software Factory. Familiarity and facility with tools is gained with repeated use; general purpose libraries are built up which simplify new production efforts and centers of technological expertise can be maintained which allow the best talent to be applied to multiple activities. Within this production organization several further divisions seem to make practical sense in accomplishing the management objective of maximum visibility. This involves organizationally separating design, production, and test. Since the end result of each group's activities is a tangible product, the requirement for turnover forces top-level visibility and represents a natural point for review and quality control.[24]

The SDC authors, at least in 1977, recognized that separating system design from program production offered both an advantage in maintaining closeness between systems engineering and customers as well as a potential disadvantage in removing the program developers and testers from the customers and systems engineers; however, they hoped that informal communication and methodological standards—"a normal, well-understood interface procedure"—could overcome any problems:

One of the major advantages of this allocation of responsibilities is that the program office is not tied to the computer location. In fact, it is highly desirable for the program office to be co-located with the customer/user to assure the rapid unambiguous coordination of program activities. On the other hand, remoteness of the program office from the development facilities does present a set of potential advantages and challenges. The problems of separation must be mitigated by a normal, well-understood interface procedure.[25]

Element 3: The Tool Set

SDC gave the name Factory Support System to the "basic structural and control components" designed to facilitate the factory methodology.[26] This tool set, written in a high-level language to ease portability, ran on an IBM 370 mainframe computer and used the facilities of IBM's operating system to automate procedures for keeping track of program development and collecting data (Figures 3.3 and 3.4). The tools supported top-down development, automated several management activities, maintained requirements through implementation, provided a library history for programs, allowed for symbolic system-data control, and automated aspects of program inspection and qualification.

The tools relied on three subsystems: The Factory Access and Control Executive (FACE) performed control and status gathering services for all processors, supported the factory command language, integrated the processors with the system development database, and provided PPL services. Integrated Management, Project Analysis, and Control Tech-

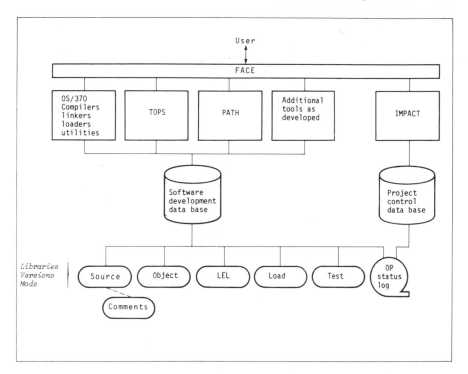

Figure 3.3 Software Factory Architecture. FACE = Factory Access and Control Executive; IMPACT = Integrated Management, Project Analysis, and Control Techniques; LEL = Link Editor Language; OP = Operational Program; PATH = Program Analysis and Test Host; TOPS = Top-Down System Developer. (*Source*: Bratman and Court, "Elements of the Software Factory," p. 129. Copyright © 1977 System Development Corporation [Unisys Corporation]. Reproduced with permission.)

niques (IMPACT) utilized production database information on milestones, tasks, resources, system components, and their relationships to provide schedule, resource computation, and status reports at the individual components level or summarized at any module or task hierarchy level. The Project Development Data Base facilitated the automation of program development, project management, configuration control, and documentation, by establishing databases for each project in the factory and keeping track of schedules, tasks, specification components, and test cases. This tool actually consisted of two databases, one for software development and another for project control. The Software Development Data Base extended the concept of a program library and kept copies of modules from their first functional definition through their completion. The Project Control Data Base maintained the system and program descriptions as well as management data, which SDC oriented

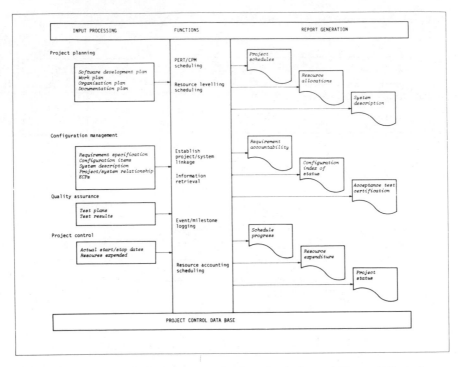

Figure 3.4 Integrated Management, Project Analysis, and Control Techniques (IMPACT) Capabilities. CPM = Critical Path Method; ECPs = Error Correction Procedures; PERT = Program Evaluation and Review Technique. (*Source*: Bratman and Court, "Elements of the Software Factory," p. 132. Copyright © 1977 System Development Corporation [Unisys Corporation]. Reproduced with permission.)

toward the software system structure and the activities performed to develop the software.

As the integrating tool in the factory, IMPACT assisted project managers in planning and monitoring the production of various items, such as specification documents, program modules, and user manuals, for which they were responsible. "It helps . . . plan, monitor, and control the work; define and control the software configuration; and ensure the observance of quality assurance measures. It assists . . . in the preparation of management reports, in the evaluation of project progress, and in spotting potential difficulties and developmental trends." IMPACT also supported structured programming and modular design by fostering the creation and integration of a hierarchical structure of program components. In preparing input data, IMPACT then forced another discipline on project planners by requiring them to know and define all the elements of the project and the relationships among them. Elements included requirements and deliverable items; requirements and program functions; program functions and program modules; high-level program modules and lower-level program modules; program modules and equipment; deliverable items and the activities that produce them; and activities and the resources necessary to support them.

IMPACT's project-management functions covered three areas: database generation and maintenance, project planning and control, and report generation. It built databases with information such as descriptions of program items and activities. Data could be inserted and processed interactively during the development cycle. Project planning and control involved three major functional modules: the Scheduler, which derived and optimized critical path schedules and resource allocations; the Trender, which tracked trends and anomalies in project performance; and the Threader, which interpreted the hierarchical structure of the software system and the organization of project work. For example, a manager or engineer could direct the Threader to "pull a thread," that is, call for a trace on the development status of elements at various levels of abstraction. The report generation function of IMPACT provided access to the information stored in the development and control databases. Reports that personnel could request included the management summary, resource allocation, configuration index and status, configuration summary, modification index, modification summary, and the module run summary reports. These capabilities not only assisted in project planning; according to Bratman and Court, they also "constituted a powerful modeling capability designed to significantly increase the project manager's efficiency and effectiveness."

Other tools provided a variety of additional support functions. The Automatic Documentation Processor (AUTODOC) produced program and system documentation, using comments inserted into the program modules by the programmer. Program Analysis and Test Host (PATH) analyzed a source program and inserted calls to a recording program at appropriate locations.[27] Bratman and Court claimed this helped to provide information about the structure of the program, to aid in thoroughness of testing. The Data Definition Processor (DATADEF) provided a central means of defining data for system programs written in several common programming languages to assure that all program modules of the system would have compatible data references. The Test Case Generator (TCG) automated aspects of designing testing data, while the Top-Down System Developer (TOPS), a modeling tool, helped outline and verify designs as well as describe much of the control and data interface logic in the actual coding language.

Bratman and Court interpreted the Factory Support System as flexible in the sense that it allowed for the addition of new tools as they became available. This versatility proved necessary because the R&D group had not yet completed all the tools they had planned to develop when the factory went into operation. In fact, Atchley admitted in a 1987 interview that some of the planned tools never materialized: "We still don't have a good editor. . . . We had to do the traceability by hand." Yet Bratman and Court felt totally confident they could build a fully automated software factory and concluded their 1975 and 1977 articles with identical words of optimism: "Our long term plan is that the Software Factory will be augmented by the continued development of more sophisticated tools and techniques such as application-oriented process design languages, re-usability technology, correctness verifiers, and cross compilers and will therefore evolve into a truly automated software development facility."[28]

The Factory Opening and Closing

SDC opened its Software Factory in December 1976 with approximately 200 programmers operating out of a single building in Santa Monica, California. Atchley recalled the site: "That's the only large open office we had at that time. We were in a building about a block long, two stories high, three long corridors with cross corridors and patios in the center. Everyone had an outside window. That building still stands, but we've moved out." Jack Munson served as the first manager of the factory, which formally belonged to the new Software Engineering Organization established within the SDC Systems Group.

Approximately ten projects went through the factory between 1976 and 1978. Four of the largest were TIROS-N, a $7 million data-processing system completed in 1978 for the TIROS-N weather satellite; the Mobile Sea Range Scoring system for navy battle training; the Morocco Air Defense System (MADS), a $12 million contract for systems engineering, software development, and training, with Westinghouse as the prime contractor, based on the SAGE and BUIC (Back-up Interceptor Central) design and described by SDC's company history as "the first airspace system to use a standard commercial computer (the Burroughs B7700) and to be implemented in a standard higher-order language (ALGOL). . . . "[29] ; and the Emergency Command Control Communication System (ECCCS), a $28.5 million project for the Los Angeles Police Department. The police system, referred to in the company history as "the largest and most complex police command-control system ever conceived," handled 3 million calls per year and 1 call every 4 seconds at peak loads, as well as 1.2 million vehicle dispatches per year, linking 850 mobile digital terminals in patrol cars as well as 5,000 portable two-way communication devices.[30]

SDC managers claim all the projects that went through the factory, with the exception of the system for the Los Angeles Police Department, came in on time and within budget, and with fewer defects and problems than SDC usually experienced with large projects. The company history also described the major projects as "accurate, timely, and on budget," and as models of "optimum software development."[31] Terry Court, who headed the Development Group within the factory after leading the R&D effort in the early 1970s, confirmed this performance in a 1989 interview:

> We noted that as we started to use the methodology and the organizational concept, things seemed to go more smoothly. On most of the projects that we did, we seemed to get through on schedule, we seemed to meet each of our milestones adequately, and the products seemed to be far more error free than previous products. . . . [C]ustomer satisfaction is always a function of did you deliver on schedule and did the system work operationally with a minimum of problems? Again, there tended to be much more of that sort of satisfaction with those systems.[32]

The factory process worked well enough for Mueller to adopt the methodology as a corporate standard, with Munson promoted in 1978 to oversee its dissemination while his assistant, Robert Hamer, took over the factory.[33] It turned out, however, that Munson's personal advancement contributed to the end of the factory, because it fell gradually into disuse as the number of new projects going through the facility declined. In this respect, Munson recalls, the Software Factory ended "not with a bang, but a whimper":

> It just sort of disintegrated. . . . New stuff didn't come in. They started letting stuff go out. The Software Factory stayed and eventually it became like a one-project thing, then it became a functional staff organization. And it just kind of disappeared by dissolution, evolution. It became a resource for staffing other programs and got dissolved that way. Good people went here to this program, good people went there to that program. And, in fact, Atchley's title is still Director of Software Engineering, back in that old division, and so, essentially, he's currently the Software Factory. . . . It devolved. But, for all intents and purposes it never was officially stopped. . . . Nobody ever really put a bullet in it's head. You couldn't point to the day it died.

The general lack of tool portability provided one reason why Mueller began to lose interest in the factory concept; however, problems with a particular project led Mueller to end his support and provided ammunition for program (project) managers who did not want to use the factory structure to build their software.[34] This was the ECCCS system for the Los Angeles police.

According to Court, who headed the software-development effort for this project, ECCCS broke down mainly from SDC's lack of experience in systems engineering for this type of application. In terms of writing and testing code, the job of personnel in the Software Factory, ECCCS resembled other systems SDC had built. It was a real-time command and control application, with strict time and space constraints, and lots of communications and data-management requirements; however, the functionality of the application differed from anything SDC had done before: a police-department information system. Thus, in Court's words, "Our systems engineering could not dominate the process, because they knew very little about police work and police operations. So the police tended to dominate the process, and as a result, the requirements kept on expanding and expanding." This led to a nearly "endless discussion and analysis of requirements" that consumed two years, throwing off the entire schedule and budget. The specifications SDC eventually agreed to also turned out to be more complex and to take longer to code than managers had anticipated, particularly since they tended to exceed the capabilities of the hardware (four Digital PDP 11/70 minicomputers) and this made it necessary to refine the software to make it run as efficiently as possible. SDC lost a large sum of money since it had agreed initially to a fixed-price contract.

To complete ECCCS, SDC reverted to its former structure and created a dedicated project team of the best people available, including Terry Court, and this group finished the specifications as well as built and tested the software. Future jobs also went back to the project system, rather than using the factory developers.[35] As Atchley described, however, the factory methodology, embodied in the *SDM* , remained: "You would not see a sign in this building that said 'Software Factory'. . . . We've moved on. . . . We still have the disciplines, standards, and concept, but the work does not flow through the factory. The factory workers go to the work."[36] SDC also updated the manual every few years and continued to use it through the late 1980s.

In addition, the factory methodology became institutionalized outside SDC when the U.S. Department of Defense contracted with SDC in 1976 to devise guidelines for military-use software procurement. Munson directed the effort and SDC completed the first set in 1979, with the help of the Department of Defense and an offshoot of M.I.T.'s Lincoln Laboratories, MITRE Corporation. The government subsequently published these procedures as a sixteen-volume set of guidebooks.[37]

Regarding the dispersion of programmers, Clarence Starkey, another SDC manager, claimed that assignments to different customer sites allowed personnel to specialize in particular applications.[38] Some former factory workers also served in new staff roles, working at customer sites to help with proposals, new business development, customer relations, strategic planning, and other tasks. Dissolution of the factory tool set also seemed a natural outcome, in Atchley's view, because of the dynamic nature of tool development for software and the incomplete state of what the factory had to offer. SDC never completed all the tools and had expected them to evolve. Meanwhile, old tools simply fell into disuse. On the other hand, ten years after the end of the factory, at least some SDC divisions were still trying to build a common tool set and programming environment:

All the tools weren't there; some were, some weren't. The concepts were there, the ideas were there, but it wasn't all there. . . . They weren't really dismantled. They were in disuse because new ones came along, and we just no longer used them. The only thing we're still using, and we won't use it much longer, is PDL [Program Development Language, a Pascal-based system SDC developed for in-house use]. . . . Within the next six months, we're going to be all converted over to BYRON [a commercial product]. . . . We're moving to ARGUS, we're using a new editor. Times change. . . . What we're trying to do now is establish a common software environment where we provide tools and the environment to develop software from the beginning up to the coding stage.[39]

In the 1980s, SDC management also appeared to be moving some facilities back toward centralization, but without separating systems engineering from program construction so rigidly, and letting facilities focus on specialized lines of business. This seemed a better way to gain some scope (or scale) economies despite the lack of a more rationalized structure, like the original factory had attempted. For example, Atchley claimed that SDC's facility in Paoli, Pennsylvania, which had roughly 500 programmers, already brought work to a permanent group of programmers in one location. According to Munson, Paoli did not use the term factory nor did it introduce the same factory organization as in Santa Monica, although Paoli's program managers seemed to accept the intermediate approach better: "They are not anywhere near as structured as our Software Factory. They are kind of a hybrid, they've got some functional and some matrix organizations. It's kind of a compromise. But not bad. Maybe that is what we should have tried."

Initial Problems Revisited

SDC did not publish or collect data on projects that went through the Software Factory nor report in detail on the effort after 1977. Accounts of the factory's performance, therefore, are subjective, as well as retrospective. Nevertheless, interviews and existing materials present enough information to revisit the five problems that motivated the factory's inception and provide some gauge of how well the factory operated, given the initial goals of management and the R&D team.

Problem #1:

Absence of a standardized, predictable approach to the development process stemming from a "lack of discipline and repeatability."
Did the Factory solution work in practice? Yes, and no.

On the yes side, division of the development process into distinct phases, standardization of the process as outlined in the *SDM*, and the tracking capabilities of the Factory Support System databases, improved predictability and control for budgets and time schedules—as long as systems engineers (and factory personnel) understood the application, and this was most of the time. Additional evidence for the general useful-ness of the factory concept as a mechanism for project and quality con-trol, in Munson's view, was the decision of the U.S. Department of De-fense to model its standards for military contractors after the SDC procedures. SDC also continued to use and refine the manual.

One must qualify this success, however, because the factory effort failed to develop metrics to measure performance or introduce systems that institutionalized discipline and repeatability once Munson left. Munson recalled that, although he kept statistics and used these for management purposes, after 1978, other managers did not collect data systematically. Atchley confirmed this, claiming that, when he joined the factory in 1977, no one kept accurate numbers on reuse rates, productiv-ity improvements, schedule completion, or program quality, and that this made it difficult to identify improvements in efficiency or productiv-ity, and determine how the factory performed.[40]

Munson ascribed these events to losing the "advocate" for the process innovation the factory represented. Once he moved into higher levels of administration, no other manager in SDC proved to be as successful in promoting the factory idea among skeptical program managers. Fur-thermore, to learn from the data and make the factory work to its full potential would have required more than the few years top management allocated. For these reasons, Munson concluded that, while the factory represented "a great start," SDC proved unable to sustain the effort:

> We did keep statistics but, unfortunately, after the organization ceased to exist, people didn't keep them very clearly. I was the advocate, if you will, for the factory, and when I moved out of that specific organization, which was what was intended—I was going to spend a couple of years there setting it up and then the agreement was that I could move on to something else—the problems with the factory occurred after I left. For the couple of years I was there, everything was going well and it was on an upswing. And I think when you take an advocate out of something that is as fragile as this was conceptually in our organization, then it kind of lost the heart. And the people just didn't have the will to make it succeed. . . . [W]hen I passed the baton, the advocacy, the evangelism went out of it. It tried to become some-thing routine, and lost something. It needed a lot of effort to make it work, and a lot of force, drive, and selling . . . . Did the factory solution work in practice? My attitude towards this is one that I would summarize by saying that we made a great start and what happened is we lacked the will and skill to keep it going. . . . One of my problems is that these kinds of experiments are not two- to three-year experiments. They are five-, six-, seven-year experiments, in order to get good data, and so we just didn't go long enough. . . . We had a bright beginning that was never fulfilled.

Problem #2:

Project management difficulties stemming from a "lack of development visibility."
Did the factory solution work in practice? Yes.

The same positive factors discussed under Problem #1 affected this issue. The clear division of product development and other operations into distinct phases ending with design reviews, and the tools of the Factory Support System, all provided a means for managers to visualize better the process flow. In particular, the IMPACT tool served as a control mechanism for tracking costs and schedules, completion status, and monitoring lines of authority and responsibility for a project. During the planning and system definition phases, managers used IMPACT data to allocate resources, check functional designs against performance requirements to assess their completeness and accuracy, and to generate reports. IMPACT as well as TOPS provided visible assessments of design completeness, while the PATH tool provided a more quantitative assessment of testing completeness. These tools evolved over time into different and no doubt better versions, but some indication of their effectiveness is that similar tools soon became common in nearly all software organizations faced with managing large, complex projects.

Problem #3:

Inability to define accurately a customer's performance requirements at the beginning of development or to deal easily with changes made during the development process.
Did the factory solution work in practice? No, and yes.

Rather than a simple no, it should be said that this continues to be a critical problem in software development that no one seems to have solved, especially when engineers face a new application or have to accommodate many changes in a design that affect, sometimes in unpredictable ways, other parts of a system. The SDC approach actually worked well, given the variety of programs SDC made and the technical challenges projects faced. Management realized too late, however, the dangers inherent in separating systems engineering from development for new and unfamiliar applications or that following a strictly sequential process of waiting to define all requirements before writing code could lead to disaster—systems engineers might never complete the requirements, leaving valuable personnel sitting idle! For new, unfamiliar work, small, integrated teams seemed the superior approach, until the application became known to company engineers.

There is a second part to the question: Did the factory better manage changes in requirements made during the development process? Modifications in requirements resemble engineering change orders frequently cited by manufacturing managers in other industries as the bane of their existence. Only design efforts for truly common or standardized products could probably eliminate these completely—but did the factory process help?

The answer seems to be that it did, a bit. For familiar projects, the factory approach appeared useful to the extent that the *SDM* captured some of the knowledge of experienced systems engineers on how to define customer requirements. It codified these "best practices" in writing and they became procedures available for everyone to use, even novices, subject to improvement over time. Division of the development process into distinct phases with design reviews, but with some interaction between systems engineering and development, rather than a rigid separation, also made it easier to identify if detailed design and coding actually implemented the customer's requirements, at least as written in the design documents. Tools such as IMPACT helped personnel keep track of the interrelationships among system components, and this should have facilitated analysis of the effects of changes on the product's architecture. Munson also felt the factory process of handing off specifications to an implementation group highlighted discrepancies between design requirements and actual products:

> One of the things that we were trying to do, by breaking it like we did between the requirements and the implementation, was to create a very, very visible interface as to what the status was of the requirements when they were turned over to implementation. In most projects, requirements are just a flow in the implementation. It is very easy for that to merge and never be seen by top management. . . . We didn't do much better in making requirements more thoroughly determined ahead of time. But, on the other hand, we were clearly able, because of the interface on the hand-over between the requirements people and the production people, to make it very, very visible as to what the status was. And we were able to put into our plans, then, the fact that we didn't have yet a good set of requirements. So, we didn't solve the basic problem. But we sure made the characteristics of the problem more visible. And we made the impacts of the problem more manageable in the production process, because we at least recognized it.

Problem #4:

Lack of tools for design and verification.
Did the factory solution work in practice? No, and yes.

The Software Factory began as an effort in tool development and the R&D team clearly did a lot of work in this area. TOPS and DATADEF improved the levels of automation and verification (tests for logical correctness) in the design process and smoothed the transition between design and program coding. In general, however, the most effective and lasting tools assisted project management; tools that interacted directly with the product, such as to test design correctness, usually had to run on the same hardware and perhaps even be written in the same computer language to work. Thus, as a result of the variety of projects it accepted, SDC never succeeded in producing standardized design-support and verification tools, and this remains a problem in software engineering.

Complicating SDC's task, top management did not continue allocating corporate money for tool development once the factory went into operation. Mueller wanted Munson to charge tool costs to the expenses of individual projects, which meant that SDC funded R&D for general-purpose tools only during the few years preceding the factory's opening in 1976, as Munson recalled: "Of course one of the motives of Mueller at the time was to stop spending company money on this thing and get contract money to support it. So, we basically were put on a shoe-string budget, and told to go make it real."

Yet the difficulties inherent in tool development required a constant well-funded effort. As another manager, David Deaver, noted with regard to the goal of portable tools, SDC clearly appeared to be "ahead of its time."[41] This seemed to be the case; true tool portability remained an elusive goal even in the late 1980s, because of machine and language incompatibilities. Munson, still frustrated with this issue, envied the Japanese as well as U.S. companies who could develop general-purpose tools since they worked primarily on compatible hardware:

> We never did solve the problem of heterogeneous hardware, and the fact that tools weren't very portable. . . . They were able to run on one system [but] were not easily ported to other systems. And many times we were working on government supplied equipment, which meant we had to use their equipment, we couldn't afford to pay for an overhead facility. . . . And the technology, in fact, isn't yet here today, where a common set of tools are really portable around a whole bunch of different environments. And that was what SDC was faced with—a whole bunch of different environments. Now you take a Hitachi or a NEC, or even the commercial part of the Unisys Corporation, where the bulk of the work that they're doing is done on their own set of equipment, that are constant and homogenous. They yield a better chance even today, and certainly in those days, of making a success of these available tools. . . . But, in any event, I think we pioneered and, if we failed, it was because we were ahead of our time. . . .

Problem #5:

Lack of reusability of code.
Did the factory solution work in practice? No, and yes.

SDC did not design its Software Factory tools and procedures specifically to encourage reusability. Bratman and Court believed that practices such as careful structuring of modules, and improved documentation, would help programmers reuse code. Atchley confirmed that the factory architects viewed reusability in this way: "They felt that if we used this technique (top-down program design) and if we used modules, that the reusability would fall out of it. . . . [Y]ou would decompose your requirements into functions and come up with code that was modular and reusable by following the techniques in the *SDM*. And then, as a fallout of that, you could go back and find it and reuse it."

These practices in themselves remained insufficient, however; the same frustrations SDC encountered in tool portability applied to reuse. SDC achieved reuse only with similar or identical applications and computers. Reusability in the Software Factory, then, primarily came as a function of similarity in applications and hardware, and thus from chance as much or more than from a deliberate strategy. Managers could take advantage of similarities across different projects by submitting low bids for projects similar to what they had done before. In this sense, centralizing people and program libraries in the factory helped achieve and exploit reusability. Yet managers could not really plan for similarity in projects unless they had a surplus of work, and SDC did not in this division. Furthermore, because it proved difficult to reuse code or designs, and because managers did not require it, programmers generally did not try to reuse components from the program library. Modules also seemed difficult to find in a library without an effective coding or indexing scheme, which SDC apparently failed to develop. In fact, Atchley explained it often appeared easier to write code from scratch than to find parts of old programs:

> [W]e changed machines from project to project, and it was very difficult to reuse the code. We had an electronic funds transfer program that was done on DEC's PDP-11. And then we went to the Emergency Command and Control System for the Los Angeles Police Department which was also done on the PDP-11. And we tried to find some of that software that we could reuse, and some of the modules. We had not done a good job in EFTS [Electronic Funds Transfer System] of providing a road map to get it, even using some of the same programmers. They would say, "I know I did it and I think we saved it; I'll go look for it. . . ." They expressed a willingness verbally to do it, and it sounded like a good idea, but at that time we were unable to capture much. It was easier to do it than to go find it. If you did find it you had to re-code it. Basically, it offered you a detailed design. Not bad, but you had a different database, a different language, different applications, and it was hard to find the building blocks that remained the same. We were at that time doing the police system, an air defense system, a ground telemetry system, and an intelligence classifying system. They were on four different machines, they had four different sets of requirements, and it was very hard to find any reusability or savings among the four of them. We did set up a library, where we collected all the software produced, filed it, and documented it. Usage of that library was very minimal.

When asked how he felt about the low incidence of code reuse in the early days of the factory, Atchley commented, "it's been ten years, and we're now coming up with an ability to do that. . . . The idea is good but the fact that it's taken us so long . . . is kind of sad." Even in 1987, only one programming project in SDC Atchley knew of reused large amounts of code, and he admitted that, again, this proved possible because, "It's the same machine and the same application. That's really simple. . . . No fights, no arguments about it; we just do it. And we're not getting any static at all. But when the applications aren't the same, it's hard." SDC actually bid on this project assuming it could reuse 80 percent of the program code from existing SDC systems (the real figure turned out to be more like 50 percent).[42]

Munson also believed code portability across different types of computers provided the major obstacle to wide reuse of code, and that, with the same or similar hardware, reuse levels rose dramatically. For example, Munson tracked reuse rates and costs for four functionally equivalent air defense systems built after SAGE. The first was SAGE's immediate successor, the BUIC system, the second an air defense system for Spain contracted to Hughes Aircraft, the third a system for Morocco (contracted to Westinghouse), and the fourth a similar system for Thailand:

> The first time we didn't use a lot of the code but we used an awful lot of the design . . . and we came in on cost. And then the second time we were able to get a competitive advantage because we didn't have to create almost any new code for the Thailand system. . . . We had commonality of equipment. They were both on compatible Burroughs computers. SAGE cost in excess of 100 million dollars for the computer programs. BUIC cost about 30 million dollars for the computer programs. The Hughes system cost about 12 million dollars. Morocco cost about 3.5 million dollars. And the new one we are building today for Thailand is zero million dollars, because we are basically using all the existing code. The reason Morocco was cheapest, for instance, in our line to BUIC, is because we used a lot of design and knowledge. . . . We didn't have to spend all the time working out what the dynamics were for interceptors and what the equations of motions were and all the database functions and structures. . . . [D]esign is about 40% of the cost of a system and the test is about 40% of the cost of the system. If you reuse the design you can reuse a lot of your test, so it cuts a lot of that 80% of the cost of the system out . . . [I]t talks to the fact that . . . when the programmers really do understand the problem, they have a much better chance of doing it right and cheaper, as opposed to bringing in a new pro to do it. . . .

This type of reuse involved redeploying an entire software and hardware system in another location, rather than utilizing modules of code as building blocks for truly different programs, whereas some Japanese software factories stressed reuse of large and small chunks of code and designs. In comparing SDC to the Japanese, as he did with tool portability, Munson attributed the greater apparent emphasis of the Japanese on reuse to more commonality in machines and applications—what SDC needed more of in the Software Factory:

At the macro level we are talking about with air defense systems we really didn't do anything specific other than use the good programming practices that we had built up for the factory anyway. And when we reused the total system, we aren't talking about modular reuse. . . . Where Japan is getting a lot of their productivity out of reusability are in things that are multiple uses of common products able to move across homogeneous product lines. And a lot of it is not in the applications software, it's in the overhead software— utilities, operating systems, macro libraries. A Fujitsu, NEC, or Hitachi can do that because they're not programming for IBM, DEC, or Burroughs. And their architectures tend to be instruction compatible. . . .

Munson also pointed out that SDC's factory architects viewed re-usability in terms of "reuse of people"—allowing designers and pro-grammers to apply the learning they acquired on one project to new projects. In this sense, the facility, while it existed, seemed far more effective than a job-oriented system, where project managers formed new groups with each customer order, with little guarantee of repeated experiences among the team members:

People reusability is almost as important as code reusability. It's clearly true in our business that the second time the same guy solves the same problem, he does it better. That goes back to Wolverton's studies in the early 1970s that talk about delivering the second version of your system, and throw away the first version. You clearly learn something the first time through it so you can apply productivity and quality on the second time through . . . assuming you use the same people. . . . [W]hat the factory did was keep the people together in one organization. The same people were there the second time it came through, as opposed to doing it here one time, then reconstructing a team somewhere else another time—which is what normally happens with pro-jects. So, in that sense [the factory] created a focus where all the software resources were in place and therefore the managers managing at that point in time had the ability to reapply the people. They weren't dispersed, off working on somebody else's contract in some other location.

Yet SDC failed to anticipate or solve another issue relating to reuse: Writing designs or code for reusability, rather than for a specific project, generally requires more time and effort to consider various potential applications and to document the software thoroughly so that anyone could find it and reuse it. Writing for reuse appeared economical for groups that repeatedly built similar systems and rewarded personnel for creating reusable designs and code. SDC, in contrast, took on a variety of jobs because its defense business declined after 1970. Furthermore, man-agement did not institute mechanisms for funding or rewarding individ-uals that would have promoted the systematic design of software for use across more than one project. Court recalled this problem:

[Reuse] was a serious objective in the sense that we were structuring compo-nents in our database to allow enough description of software modules so that a future designer could bring those descriptions up and understand what that module did and therefore whether or not it was appropriate to his applications. So there was serious intent there. It just turned out that, again, in order to structure a module for reusability, you probably would have to do some additional work to it. Therefore, it becomes more costly, and going back to program managers and customers, nobody is willing to fund the additional effort so that the next guy can get the benefit. That was sort of a problem that we ran into. . . . unless you have a product line where you are going to do the same thing over and over again, and then it makes sense.[43]

Other Problems the Factory Exposed

SDC's Software Factory exposed other problems that contributed to declining support for the factory from top management and to resistance from project managers. These other difficulties, which managers of software factories elsewhere had to solve to operate effectively, arose in three general areas: (1) Imbalances in managing the work supposedly flowing into the factory from systems engineering in a predictable, sequential manner. Imbalances made sustenance of the factory—a relatively large group of software developers—difficult for management to justify when the level of programming work fell. This situation resulted, in the case of the ECCCS system, from underestimations of how long systems engineering would take and, in general, from the reluctance of project managers to use the factory to build software, as opposed to organizing their own teams of developers. (2) Challenges, both political and technical in nature, of managing within a matrix system. The matrix attempted to spread among more than one project at a time functional expertise in systems engineering, software development, and testing, at the expense of applications expertise (such as in business-information systems, or defense command-control systems). Knowledge of particular applications, however, turned out to be as important as knowledge of software engineering. (3) Failure of top management to control and carry out the changes in process and organization the factory required to work in the face of resistance primarily from program managers.

Work-Flow Management

SDC intended the factory to operate in much the same way as factories in other industries, where producers separated product design and engineering from production, and separate groups cultivated expertise in functional specialties as well as benefitted from economies of scale (or scope), where applicable, such as in tool investment. In fact, Bratman and Court compared the Development Data Base to a conveyor and control system that brought work and materials (documents, code modules) through different phases, with workers using standardized tools and methods to build finished software products: "In the Factory, the

Development Data Base serves as the assembly line—carrying the evolving system through the production phases in which factory tools and techniques are used to steadily add more and more detail to the system framework."[44]

A serious work-flow imbalance occurred that made it difficult to sustain a permanent group of programming and testing specialists. In part this reflected the fluctuating nature of the division's business—customized programs, mainly for the federal government or local governments. Other factors proved to be SDC's strategy as well as its planning and control systems. Because projects came about on a contract basis, SDC had no guaranteed flow of work, and management generally hired programmers for individual projects as it needed them. If the company did not require manpower immediately for another project, managers let programmers go, as reflected in the wide variations in the number of SDC employees (Table 3.1). The organization always tried to be, in Munson's words, "lean and mean. A project would build up and when you got finished you answered to people and fired them. And that is essentially the same attitude they took towards us [the Software Factory]. . . . [W]e did not have the work to sustain it, and work wasn't coming through and we had our ups and downs."

The Systems Group's business seemed sufficiently cyclical to make a factory of thousands of personnel (as in Japanese facilities in the 1980s) impractical. According to Munson, the division specialized in large-scale projects requiring two or three years to complete, and SDC had few of these. Those it acquired came primarily from Department of Defense contracts, and these SDC could not easily "inventory," that is, create a backlog of them, because the government generally wanted projects completed by a certain date. Nonetheless, SDC made no provisions to

Table 3.1 System Development
Corporation Employees (selected years)

Year	No. of Employees
1956	450
1957	1,270
1959	3,500
1963	4,300
1969	3,200
1971	2,000
1974	3,900
1978	4,200
1980	3,800

Source: Claude Baum, *The System Builders: The Story of SDC* (Santa Monica, Calif.: System Development Corporation, 1981), and SDC annual reports.

keep software personnel on the payroll in between projects, even though Munson saw this as a bad policy because the key asset of the factory, and of SDC in general, was the supply of experienced engineers:

> I always recognized this as a potential problem and I kept trying to convince [top management]. . . . We needed to charge more for the work in the factory, so that we could essentially set up a "fly wheel" capability. We knew the work was going to fluctuate. Although everybody wanted to make the assumption that all it would do is grow, grow, grow, we knew it wouldn't. We wanted to make a way to build up a pool so that we had our own money, if you will, to cover us during the time work was lean, so that we would have the people around when the work was back. And we looked at it two ways. First, we needed a capital investment from the company. The second was to charge more for any given job and have the excess go into, if you will, a pad, or a cushion. But we could never get the company to step up and do either. But that is what you have to do. You have to recognize that, like any factory, there will be times of 65% capacity and 85% capacity. But the problem is our factory was basically people and people are very expensive and nobody wanted to consider people as important tools in the factory as if they were machine tools. But they are very similar if you think about it in an analogy sense. When you are not using them you still need to keep them there. You don't go sell them.

SDC's commercial software area had more customers and a far easier time creating a backlog of work to keep a permanent group of programmers employed. In fact, SDC's Business-Applications Group at times overloaded, and this led top management to move Munson, after the Software Factory opened, to another division:

> The reason I left this organization was really to concentrate on our commercial area, which was in chaos, a disaster at that point in time, and try to bring more discipline to that. And they had big backlogs. It worked fine. But those are generally not the job-shop kinds of jobs you get with the military. DoD [Department of Defense] wants a weapon system and they want it delivered in 48 months. It is hard to put a competitive procurement into backlog, whereas an MIS department that has a whole bunch of changes they want in their MIS system might be willing to put that kind of stuff in a backlog.[45]

Yet, despite the nature of their work, Court maintained that SDC had enough jobs to sustain the factory. Many projects were small and some required work away from Santa Monica and would have been difficult to do in the factory; however, even the local area probably would have generated a sufficient number of contracts if program managers had cooperated and brought their work to the factory, as management initially envisioned:

> There was enough work but that work wasn't a lot of big programs. Some were remote—they were in Colorado and in the East, and other places. And indeed there was enough work in Santa Monica, but . . . there were project managers and program managers in other parts of the organization that

had their own integrated, dedicated teams that truly refused to participate. So we had this one big organization that was kind of starving.[46]

The Matrix: Functional Versus Application Expertise

The matrix organization, creating functional specialists that had to work with program managers, presented political, or organizational, as well as technological hurdles. Munson found the political issues the most vexing, because too many people seemed "dedicated to seeing that it didn't work." Program managers wanted complete control, and engineers wanted to "flow with the job":

> One of the basic problems was, from my point of view, a political problem. Why it didn't really become as successful as it could have was a lack of management commitment to make it work. In our organization, there has always been a "defined right of kings" syndrome where people want to own the resources that are doing their work. . . . So there was a fair share of the population that was dedicated to seeing that it didn't work, because they wanted to have control of their own resources, as opposed to having a matrix organization that did the work for them. . . . Also, we were fighting social history. There were just a lot of professional people, the engineers, that didn't like the concept because they wanted to flow with the job, rather than work on pieces of the job.

As the ECCCS project demonstrated, technical issues also provided arguments for managers that opposed the factory's separation of systems engineering from program development. Developers needed functional expertise in software engineering, but they required familiarity with particular applications to specify requirements and write accurate, structured, and maintainable code. When the same group of people wrote the system requirements, the actual programs, and even test cases, then understanding of the customer's needs, and the written requirements, seemed easier. In the organization SDC had in place, however, some projects were likely to encounter difficulties, as Munson admitted:

> [The factory] really failed to take into account the fact that experience in understanding the application you are working on is almost as important as understanding the technology you're applying to it. . . . For instance, if you're working with a banking system, understanding intuitively how a bank works is almost as important as understanding how to program computer systems. Or, say, with programming a radar system, you just don't take any programmer and say, "Program a radar system." There is no management or technical substitute for your people understanding the problem. . . . This really turns out to be at the lowest level, . . . the guys that are making the implicit and derived functional-requirements implementation. The intuitive understanding of the problem helps you in the production process. . . . The fact is that we had, on the one hand, managers who were fighting the matrix-functional problem, and we had people, technical

people in the organization, that were fighting that problem. So we were kind of getting it from both sides.

Court held the opinion that SDC may have pushed the matrix and factory analogy too far in trying to develop software in neatly sequential rather than iterative phases—that is, completing all the requirements before programmers began writing any code. Following the sequential approach too rigidly contributed to dissatisfaction from program managers and engineers, as well as exacerbated the work-flow imbalance. A lack of work for developers in the factory clearly resulted when systems engineers encountered an unfamiliar application and, as in the ECCCS project, took longer than planned to write the requirements. It also became impossible to meet customer requirements when neither customers nor systems engineers knew what functions a system needed to contain. Court explained, however, that SDC adopted the matrix and sequential process to correct an earlier problem, where programmers often coded before they fully understood an application and eventually produced poorly structured and unmaintainable software:

> We started out with this very purest view in the Software Factory, that you ought to do all of your requirements and, at some very clean point in time, hand over this requirement spec to the development organization. . . . And as we went along we found that doesn't work very well. You need to get your chief software designers involved early, make them privy to the requirements-analysis process, let them start structuring the system before you quite finish with the requirements. And to a certain extent that was also true of the test organization. . . . In the early days, software had a few people that did everything. Of course, one of the problems was they had a tendency to start coding before they had done any design or requirements analysis or anything. And that was wrong. And then the pendulum swung completely the other way and I think that it went too far. It swung to where you had totally different people doing requirements and totally different people doing development and you have to do them in sequence and you have got to finish one completely before you start the next. . . . As we went through that a couple of times . . . we started to mellow on that concept. A key point in that mellowing was a beginning of that L.A.P.D. [Los Angeles Police Department] contract, when we had a whole development organization that was sitting around not doing anything and the program was getting farther and farther behind and the requirements people were sitting around day by day further developing their requirements. And there was this great impatience that progress wasn't being made.

Management Control and Organizational Change

Even had SDC generated enough work of a similar nature to sustain a software-development facility with a staff of 200, another aspect of the work-flow imbalance and matrix problems was that top management did not require program managers to use the factory to build their software.

Managers of large projects had considerable responsibility and Mueller gave them the authority to determine how they used their resources. The head of the Software Factory, organizationally, held no more authority than program managers. As long as Jack Munson, who commanded a great deal of respect in the company, remained head of the factory, at least some managers put their development work into the facility. But, as Court described it, when Munson moved on to another job, the matrix broke down:

> Jack's a very eloquent, very convincing guy. He got along well with most people and he knew everyone. . . . He was very capable of jawboning and getting his point of view to carry with people who were his peers and people who were his superiors, while the fellow who followed him was on paper equal in stature but had no where near the respect of the other managers and the program managers. It was obstacle after obstacle for him. So I think that is a key point for almost everything. Things only succeed if you've got somebody who knows how to deal with people in charge. No matter how good your systems are and your methodology and your tools, if you've got somebody running it that doesn't get along with other people and they don't respect, then it is not going to work. So it worked really well at first with Jack there because he was able to convince people to bring their projects to the Software Factory. They trusted Jack. . . . When Jack left, they weren't so comfortable with the guy that followed him.

Munson blamed the decline of the factory on a lack of commitment to the factory idea from his superiors, as well as on SDC's strong tradition of managing software development in integrated projects. When program managers insisted they wanted their own teams of developers, top executives relented and let the factory wane:

> In my opinion, they [top management] were hedging their bets. They weren't willing to make a commitment. . . . All these guys out here [the program managers] would just say, "A factory can't do this, I've got to do it out here for some reason. My customer wants me to be in his facility." And management never fought very hard. It didn't say, "No, there is one way we are going to do it and this is the way.". . . And that goes back to the cultural, the projectized versus the functional kind of organizational aspects. SDC historically has built into its genes, even built into the software business genes, this projectize mentality—the only way you can build software is to projectize it.[47]

Atchley added that program managers seemed disturbed by the additional overhead associated with the matrix, which came from having to pay for two sets of management—one inside the factory and one outside. Since program managers could not influence what happened to expenses once a project got inside the factory, the issue of control became more important than simply being unable to manage programmers directly. It became a matter of economics:

What happens is that you've got a program manager who's come to you with his program and he's given you the task to do, but really he doesn't have any control over you. And if you overspend, what's he going to do? He has to have the job done. So there was not enough incentive on the part of the factory to produce at an economical cost . . . [These] were the complaints of the other managers. It was costing them money. . . . There were some complaints about the fact that now they had two managers, that they had doubled the overhead . . . since you had the management of the Software Factory but you still had the management of the program.[48]

Given the hurdles they faced, Deaver believed that only a "drastic change in culture and philosophy" would have made the factory work as intended.[49] This seemed true with regard to matrix management and shared responsibility, where, for example, Court became convinced that only program managers who had experience as managers both of functional departments and of projects would be able to appreciate the factory concept and cooperate sufficiently for it to work. This "cross breeding," as Court termed it, was uncommon in firms such as SDC, which tended to have separate career lines for technical and management specialists.

Even use of the mere word *factory* provoked resistance to the organizational concepts underlying it. Munson viewed the factory analogy positively, as both an engineering and marketing tool: ". . . it has a connotation to the general population of organized, methodical, chunk-it-out, make schedules, do it on time. I have always thought, and we of course have a copyright on the expression Software Factory, that was a very valuable concept to the world that is afraid of software, that it would tend to give it a more engineering concept." But no one seemed to like the term, and after 1978 SDC stopped using it. Atchley even claimed the word became an "anathema" to managers and programmers alike. Munson attributed this to the fact that software programmers preferred to think of themselves as professionals, not as factory workers:

Again, it has to do with the culture, the image. These people that are computer programmers think they are professionals and the concept that they'd be associated with a factory kind of grated them instead of seeing it as a great sales tool. You know, they tended to take it as being a slur on their professionalism and that's why it really became an anathema. . . . I always thought the factory was a good metaphor for what we were trying to do. A lot of people didn't like it. They made a lot of fun out of it.[50]

Ironically, the company history reveals that the matrix organization SDC had tried during the 1950s to maximize scarce personnel resources did not work well either. SAGE began with a project system, where all the necessary personnel, from different functions, came together in a single group responsible to one program manager. In 1958, however, SDC created functional offices for personnel, production, engineering, and programming, while still maintaining program management offices responsible for specific subprojects but sharing functions such as engineering and programming. Yet this structure encouraged conflicts between the program managers and functional managers over budgets, schedules, and worker performance, and in 1959 top management decided to return full authority to the program managers.[51] Had the planners of the Software Factory been aware of this experience, they might have anticipated resistance and better prepared themselves, as well as program managers and engineers, for the changes and cooperation required to make the factory work. Or, they might not have attempted the factory effort at all.

Other Retrospective Assessments

More than ten years after the Software Factory disbanded, Court remained convinced that SDC had been correct in its attempts and had learned how to manage software development better. He felt most projects succeeded admirably in budget, schedule, and quality control, although SDC did not collect statistics to verify this. Overall, Court attributed the end of the factory not merely to the ECCCS debacle but also to a general lack of patience among key executives, the loss of Munson, and the frustrations of poor tool portability:

> I think at the time we did what we felt was right and we were on the right track. Again, I think that the problems we encountered were sort of a lack of patience and perseverance with the concept. Top management sort of lost interest because it wasn't providing immediate feedback and immediate results and they tended to lose patience and it lost some of its sponsorship. The loss of Jack at a crucial point was one of the problems. I think early on our great mistake was our interest in tools. We should have realized the portability problem was going to come back and haunt us and it surely did. But I think that everybody that was involved learned a great deal and there was a lot of improvement in the process because of that, so I think that the company was well compensated for its contribution. . . . I feel that it was a good experiment.

Atchley's impressions appeared more mixed. The lack of data made it impossible to tell if the factory improved efficiency or if gains came from other factors, such as accumulated experience. Nevertheless, Atchley maintained that the factory increased awareness among software engineers of the product life cycle and greatly improved quality through a more structured approach to design and more formalized testing procedures. Yet he also believed the factory did not work up to its potential for improving reusability and productivity, and he regretted SDC did not do much beyond standardizing procedures and centralizing some programming, such as at Paoli. Atchley concluded that SDC now lagged behind the most advanced firms or universities, rather than being in the forefront of software engineering, as the Software Factory had once brought the company:

> I think that, while we may not be organized the way we were, our people are more aware of the software life cycle now. I seriously doubt that it [the factory] reduced cost. Were the people more efficient? It's hard to say they were more efficient because of the factory or that they became more efficient because we became more efficient. I presume there was a fallout there on efficiency and productivity. I think the structured approach helped quality immensely. I think the fact that we became very formal with the independent test organization improved the quality of the product we delivered. Whether that was the Software Factory or not, I don't know. . . . I think it's a good concept. I think discipline can be applied to the software development process. I think that reusability and productivity should be the main factors out of it. We're not doing as good a job today as we were ten years ago in keeping it alive. We've made a lot of progress, but we could be better if we had really actively pursued the concept and grown the concept as new ideas came out of the schools and papers were written. If we'd kept the factory concept more prominent, I think we would have been able to put more of those ideas in sooner. As it is now, there's a lag. Instead of being at the forefront, we're kind of dragging.

Munson felt slightly more positive. While acknowledging that the tools remained incomplete and that SDC had to replace nearly all those developed for the factory, he insisted this constituted progress. The major gains he saw from the factory came in increased attention to problems and needs of software development as a business. Furthermore, while SDC did not fulfill all its goals with the Software Factory experiment, he insisted SDC served a valuable role as pioneers who laid a groundwork for the future:

> [I]f you thought about it in the context of the factory, that's called growth— the evolution, the fact that we are not using the same PDL today as we did ten years ago. We never expected to. We weren't building something to last 100 years. We were building something to grow. . . . It shouldn't be an indictment of the factory; that was what we were trying to do. We just wished we could have done it in the context of the factory. . . . The factory identified software as a major management issue. It got high visibility for software, got it up to the top level where management would see it. We got a lot of synergy out of the factory, getting people together . . . but we were the pioneers in this, and you know what happens to pioneers. They get arrows in the back, and eventually some settlers come along later and build on those ideas that the pioneers had. . . . I tend to be a typical impatient American as opposed to the Japanese that can look at 20-year plans. . . . And I was impatient because I knew it was the right thing to do and people still think it's the right thing to do. People are moving towards it. I think it was just a little early. . . . We may have suffered the fate of General Custer, but we were out there in the frontier.

Nor did Munson see himself as involved in a "noble experiment," trying to manage delicate tradeoffs between, say, maximizing cost reduction as opposed to raising product functionality or customer satisfaction. SDC did not attempt to make better products; that seemed too ambitious a goal. His primary concern, Munson claimed, was merely to make the development process more predictable and manageable:

> My first goal was to get control of an uncontrolled process. In my mind, software development in general was out of control. It was not predictable, it was not manageable. . . . At that point in time, the two terms, software engineering and computer science, were contradictions in terms. There was no engineering in software and no science in computers. I considered it survival and more than a noble experiment. We were just really, really trying to get some terrible problems under control. And we thought this would be a way to approach it. . . . Some of those other things were second order. We were just trying to do it good. Better was later. If we could just get it controlled and bring in a project on time with some relationship to the cost we had bid for the job, we would have been satisfied. At that point, really, it wasn't a productivity issue, as such, although we saw it as leading to that. Once we had it under control, then we could get to the issue of how can we make it cheaper. But once it's out of control . . . garbage for whatever price is still garbage. And that was the situation.

In contrast to the impatience of these American managers, several Japanese firms carried on where SDC's Software Factory left off. Munson recalled that he had first became aware of their factory attempts during the late 1970s and early 1980s, through Japanese participation in international conferences on software engineering. On a visit to Japan in 1981, he even visited the Toshiba facility, among others. Munson also had to contend with frequent visitors from Japan who wanted to learn about SDC's Software Factory. While Munson felt U.S. companies maintained a lead over their Japanese counterparts in software skills, and believed creativity remained critical in software and that U.S. practices appeared better suited to foster this, he believed the Japanese would catch up with the U.S., as they have done with other technologies. He also saw important benefits in Japan's more homogeneous hardware and less "cultural" resistance. Moreover, Japanese software factories did not depend on projects to exist but were truly long-term efforts:

> It must have been 1980–81. Hitachi came over to visit us in Santa Monica to find out about the Software Factory. . . . [W]e had a delegation in from one of the Japan companies about every 3 months, it seemed like, wanting to hear what we had to say on the subject. . . . I think [the Japanese] are doing very much what we tried to do. I think they have a little advantage, and that's the homogenous equipment. I think I could make homogenous equipment a spectacular success. I think we were trying to fight too many problems all at the same time—personnel problems, social problems, cul-

tural problems, customer problems, work-flow problems. With the Japanese factories, most of them are on budgets. They are not on contracts. And that makes a huge difference, because they have continuity, year to year to year. More power to them. . . . [But] we are still sufficiently ahead of the Japanese in software and that is because of exactly the reasons why a software factory is more possible in Japan than here. We allow more creativity, make more of the advances. I really think that it is going to take the Japanese a while yet to catch up to us. But they will.[52]

Summary and Evaluation

SDC ceased to exist as a separate company in 1981, after a merger with the Burroughs Corporation, which later joined with Sperry to form the Unisys Corporation in 1986. Even though SDC no longer operated independently, it still survived in the mid-1980s as a major source of software and systems-integration services, with the Unisys divisions that formerly constituted SDC generating approximately $2.5 billion in revenues, primarily from defense contracting, with 6,000 employees across the United States.[53] More important, in addition to the Software Factory, SDC left a long legacy of contributions to the industry, beginning with the SAGE project in the 1950s and continuing through to the U.S. space shuttle in the 1980s, where a group of 850 Unisys/SDC employees, based in Houston and directed by Jack Munson, helped maintain 14 million lines of code.[54]

SDC's experiment with a software factory presented many lessons, both negative and positive. On the negative side, the facility made progress in methods standardization and project management, but fell short of solving other problems that motivated its establishment—how to manage requirements specification and changes, build general-purpose design and verification tools, and reuse software more systematically. Nor did it function well in other areas the Introduction to this book associated with factory efforts, as summarized in Table 3.2.

Part of the explanation seems to have been SDC's position as a pioneer; some companies had to lead the way and fall short of ambitious goals, especially given the complexities of software as a technology and as a business. The factory approach also seemed somewhat of a mismatch with SDC's corporate strategy and the state of software technology in the mid-1970s. SDC had built a reputation for producing innovative software systems for a variety of customers; this strategy required a flexible, job-shop type of organization, at least for unfamiliar and dissimilar projects.

Nevertheless, SDC had repetitions in its work and these, in fact, helped inspire the factory initiative. In addition, key managers as well as the factory architects believe they could have managed the factory better, in several areas: They underestimated the degree to which little por-

Table 3.2 SDC Software Factory Summary

Concept	Implementation
Process improvement	The factory initiated as an effort in process improvement, focusing first on tools, and then on methodology and organization. A history in SDC of project-support tools, but the corporate strategy and culture emphasized product innovation and customized systems, for a variety of applications, making factory standardization and labor specialization difficult. The factory also suffered from insufficient support for the concept from top management and program managers.
Product-process focus & segmentation	The division in which the factory operated focused on real-time applications, mainly for defense, but with much variety in hardware. The factory worked well except for projects outside the traditional focus, because it then became difficult to specify requirements precisely and maintain schedules. Projects were done on a matrix system, with a centralized factory for product construction and testing, and systems engineering separate at customer sites.
Process/quality analysis & control	No systematic collection of data on process or quality; no systematic analysis or control, except through a standardized methodology and some tool usage. But recollections of ten or so projects from the factory report major improvements in budget, scheduling, and quality control, with one exception when systems engineers had difficulty specifying requirements for an unfamiliar application.
Tailored/centralized process R&D	Process R&D initially centralized and focused on tools. This effort ended with portability problems. Process R&D then shifted to methods and organization, but without tailoring to applications or operating environments, since SDC handled many different jobs and hardware. Management also discontinued corporate funds for process R&D after establishment of the factory, and made continuance of this effort dependent on support from projects, which was insufficient.
Skills standardization & leverage	Adoption of a standardized methodology and some tools but no formalized training or controls to ensure all personnel and projects utilized these methods and tools.
Dynamic standardization	No funding or operational mechanism to modify performance standards, methods, and tools; not enough time allocated to refine the factory system, although SDC gradually refined the methodological standards.
Systematic reusability	No set of procedures, tools, or incentives to support systematic reuse, except for better documentation and a program library. Resistance from program managers to building reusable software, which was more costly, if only other projects benefited. Some "accidental" reuse when there were similar applications and hardware platforms.

(*continued*)

Table 3.2 (*Continued*)

Concept	Implementation
Computer-aided tools	Successful project-management and testing tools, but limited portability. No centralized, sustained tool effort after 1976.
Incremental product/ variety improvement	Improvement in product quality but not enough time allocated to the factory for SDC to incorporate systematic improvements in product development or variety within the factory context.
Assessment	
Strategic management & integration	After initial planning focused on tools, the actual factory integrated tools with methods and an organization in a single facility, but with a decline in support from top management, lack of cooperation from program managers, lack of control over the work flow and job variety, insufficient concern for the need to balance applications expertise with functional specialization, and no structure for training or incentives to promote factory goals.
Scope economies	Some scope (and scale) economies probably achieved through central development of tools and procedures, standardized methods, and accidental reuse. But the factory's short life and small size limited the benefits.

tability of software among different computers and operating systems would make it difficult to standardize tools and reuse code. They misjudged the importance of applications expertise, especially in systems engineering, as opposed to functional expertise in software programming. They did not provide a mechanism to keep work flowing into the factory in the event requirements took longer than planned to specify. Management also failed to reorient program managers to the new system and introduce sufficient controls so that the factory would have enough work to keep it operating. Finally, rather than focusing on the benefits of the new process and allowing enough time and resources for refinements, SDC executives exhibited insufficient patience and allowed a fragile but innovative organization to become overly dependent on the enthusiasm and leadership of one individual. The effort thus fell short of laudable goals and ended prematurely.

At the same time, the factory experiment had many positive sides. Within the company, the factory initiative highlighted software production as a critical area deserving top-management attention and resources. Managers and engineers discovered much about what was possible and impractical in software development, given the constraints imposed by the technology, customers, and producers themselves. The factory procedures, which represented best practice as well as SDC's R&D team could define it, also became the basis for new standards throughout the company for design, quality assurance, and project management. Outside the company, the factory became a model for practices in the U.S. defense industry as well as provided at least some inspiration to a generation of Japanese managers, who gave factory concepts the time and attention needed to make SDC's experiment a smoothly operating reality.

4

HITACHI: ORGANIZING FOR PROCESS AND QUALITY CONTROL

Among all the companies in the world, Hitachi in 1969 first established a software facility labeled and managed as a factory, calling the facility the Software Works or, more literally, the Software Factory.[1] SDC's early models in project management during the 1960s helped inspire some of the practices Hitachi adopted. Hitachi's factory, however, came not as the result of a deliberate effort in process R&D. Nor did Hitachi managers have as clear an idea as their counterparts in SDC what a factory system might look like for software production.

Hitachi's motivations to establish a software factory stemmed primarily from shortages of skilled programmers and quality problems with existing software, and the conviction of several managers, as well as the company president, that centralizing engineers with responsibilities for software development in one facility operating as a profit center independent of hardware development would be a first step toward achieving levels of process and quality control comparable to Hitachi's engineering or manufacturing operations in other product areas. After 1969, the need to accommodate corporate practices, such as for cost and quality controls, as well as work standardization, allowed Hitachi managers and engineers to experiment with different standards, methods, and tools. Again unlike SDC, however, the factory approach Hitachi eventually defined became the primary system for software development in the company and its major subsidiaries, rather than a temporary organization dependent on the support of project managers.

While Hitachi experienced immediate benefits from extensive data collection and analysis, formulation of process standards, centralized tool development, and employee training, it took a decade or more to find a suitable mixture of standards, methods, and tools for different product areas. Hitachi then displayed gradual but steady improvements in productivity, quality, and scheduling accuracy. In computer-related sales, Hitachi continued to trail Fujitsu and NEC, as well as IBM Japan. By the late 1980s, however, it had acquired a reputation as the industry leader in several key areas. As seen in the *Nikkei Computer* surveys, Hitachi in 1988 ranked highest among Japan's computer vendors in customer satisfaction with hardware, overall price-performance, and maintenance services for both hardware and software (Table 1.10), as well as in fixing software defects promptly (Table C.2). Hitachi also offered, compared to other U.S. and Japanese firms, relatively low prices for its hardware and systems-engineering services (Tables 1.12 and 1.13).

The Corporate Setting

Company Origins and Products

Hitachi originated in 1908 as the machinery repair section of a mining company in the town of Hitachi, Japan, about two hours by train north of Tokyo. In fiscal 1987 it had approximately 80,000 employees and nonconsolidated sales of $23 billion (nearly $40 billion including subsidiaries). Hitachi's major area of business was communications and electronics equipment, including computers and software (42 percent of 1987 nonconsolidated sales). Hitachi divided the remainder of its business among heavy machinery (21 percent), consumer electronics (18 percent), transportation equipment (10), and industrial machinery (9 percent). In information systems sales among Japanese companies during the mid-1980s, Hitachi generally ranked behind Fujitsu and NEC, as well as IBM Japan, which were more focused on computers and communications products, although Hitachi usually led Japanese firms in large mainframes (Table 4.1).[2]

For most of its history, Hitachi's organization has centered around factories, of which the company operated more than twenty-four domestically in the late 1980s. These belonged to six operating groups (also referred to as divisions): Computers, Electronic Devices, Consumer Products, Industrial Components and Equipment, Industrial Processes, Power Generation and Transmission. Group headquarters retained responsibility for sales, while factories managed both product engineering and manufacturing, and operated as independent profit centers, with financial management based on six-month budgets for each factory.

Table 4.1 Comparison of Japanese Computer Manufacturers (1987)

Company	Sales* (consolidated sales)	Information Systems Sales*† (export %)	Nonconsolidated Sales Breakdown (%)
Hitachi	$23.4 (39.8)	$6.4 (18)	Communications and electronic equipment (42), heavy machinery (21), consumer electronics (18), transportation equipment (10), industrial machinery (9)
Toshiba	21.5 (28.6)	3.1 (22)	Data-communications systems and electronic devices (46), heavy machinery (26), consumer electronics (28)
NEC	18.4 (21.7)	8.6 (17)	Computers (44), communications equipment (32), electronic devices (19), home electronics (5)
Mitsubishi	15.6 (18.9)	1.3 (19)	Data-communications systems and electronic devices (31), heavy machinery (27), consumer electronics (24), industrial machinery and autos (18)
Fujitsu	13.7 (16.4)	10.1 (17)	Data-processing equipment (72), communications equipment (16), electronic devices (12)
Oki	3.3 (3.6)	1.5 (NA)	Data-processing systems (45), telecommunications systems (30), electronic parts (23), other (2)
NTT	45.3	—	Telephone services (80), data-communications services (8), other (12)

*Billion dollars with $1.00 = 125 yen; †estimates that exclude electronic devices and some communications systems. NA = not available.
Sources: Toyo Keizai Shimposha, *Japan Company Handbook,* Winter 1987; and International Data Corporation, *EDP Japan Report,* April 8, 1988, p. 11 (Information Systems sales data).

Plant managers were thus responsible for engineering and production costs, the setting of production amounts, and any related expenses; and company policy required factory managers to institute standardized controls and procedures for administration as well as engineering and manufacturing management.[3] There were no exceptions, even for a relatively new technology such as software, once a product moved into the factory system.

The Computer Group

Hitachi engineers began experimenting with computers in the mid-1950s and completed their first computer in 1957, using parametrons (a solid-state device used primarily in Japan during the 1950s). Hitachi next finished a transistorized business computer in 1959, based on a model made at the Ministry of International Trade and Industry's (MITI) Electrotechnical Laboratory during 1956—two years before the commercial introduction of transistorized computers in the United

States.[4] Management then set up a division for computers in 1962 by consolidating departments for hardware design and manufacturing in a communications equipment factory, the Totsuka Works. This was in preparation for more aggressive computer sales through a licensing agreement Hitachi signed with RCA in 1961 and which lasted until 1970. Through this agreement, Hitachi manufactured RCA-designed computers, as well as sold RCA software, for resale under the Hitachi label in Japan.

The RCA technology allowed Hitachi to compete more directly with IBM models during the 1960s. Combined with its own in-house research skills, by the late 1970s, Hitachi was exporting machines fully compatible with IBM software. The 1982 incident in which U.S. agents from the Federal Bureau of Investigation caught several Hitachi engineers attempting to buy information on IBM's 3081 operating system, particularly new features that IBM decided to include in the microchip designs, reflected Hitachi's active pursuit of information on IBM to help its hardware and software engineers design compatible products.[5] While legal or illegal information gathering no doubt aided the performance of Hitachi products at least by providing design and performance objectives, it was also the case that Hitachi had accumulated considerable technical expertise in computer technology since the 1950s, as seen in recent products.

One example was the AS/9000, a large-scale mainframe made by Hitachi and sold in the United States by National Semiconductor during the early 1980s. Hitachi introduced this around 1982 to compete with IBM's 3081 family, utilizing denser semiconductor circuitry and a shorter dataflow path than the equivalent IBM machine to provide considerably more computing power for the dollar. The Hitachi model, according to *Datamation*, was "a more expandable and more cost-effective mainframe, with expanded performance levels when compared to a similar IBM system."[6] Other examples include the AS/XL 60 and 80, which Hitachi introduced in 1985 to compete with IBM's new 3090 Sierra series. These also used more advanced semiconductor technology as well as innovative architectural features, such as a buffer-cache memory, to achieve computing speeds equivalent to the IBM machines with half the number of processors and at a lower price.[7]

Hitachi's Computer Group in the mid-1980s consisted of six main facilities, two for software and four for hardware (Table 4.2). The Software Works, located in Totsuka, Yokohama, started with 348 employees in 1969 and had more than 2,000 (excluding personnel from subsidiaries and other software houses) when management split this into two separate factories in 1985. The original facility continued to grow and had 5,000 employees in 1989, including 3,000 on assignment from Hitachi subsidiaries or software subcontractors, and continued to produce operating systems for mainframes, minicomputers, and office computers, related systems software, such as language processors, and on-line

Table 4.2 Hitachi Computer Group (ca. 1988–1989)

Facility	No. of Employees	Products/Functions
Hardware		
Kanagawa Works	3,000	Mainframe computers
Odawara Works	2,500	Peripherals
Asahi Works	1,500	Small-scale computers
Device Development Center	100	Semiconductor devices
Software		
Software Works	2,000 (plus 3,000 employees from subsidiaries and subcontractors)	Systems software
Systems Design Works	2,000 (plus 4,000 employees from subsidiaries and subcontractors)	Applications software

Source: Estimates based on company publications in Japanese and personal interviews cited in the text.

database programs. The second facility, the Systems Design Works (formerly the Omori Software Works), located in Shin-Kawasaki, nearby Yokohama and Tokyo, had approximately 6,000 employees in 1989, including 4,000 from subsidiaries and other subcontractors. This factory specialized in large-scale custom applications programs such as real-time banking systems. Approximately 500 of the more experienced engineers also made business-applications packages for general sale.[8]

It should be noted that neither Hitachi software factory was a blue-collar facility. The workers were engineers and the setting consisted of offices. The new Systems Design Works, for example, boasted elegant furnishings and housed personnel in twin thirty-one-story towers, with one terminal or work station (also referred to as a workbench—powerful desk-top computers with more processing capacity and memory than personal computers, and advanced graphics capabilities) for every three engineers. In addition, of the 6,000 personnel, approximately two-thirds were college graduates and 4,000 were engaged in systems engineering (design) rather than routine jobs such as coding.

Research and development on new hardware technologies as well as on software tools and design concepts took place in two corporate facilities. In addition, Hitachi had numerous subsidiaries producing computer-related products and services, including approximately twenty-four producing software. Hitachi classified these subsidiaries into ten areas, with several overlapping (Table 4.3). The largest were Nippon Business Consultants (approximately 3,350 employees in 1988 and recently renamed Hitachi Information Systems), established in 1959; Hitachi Software Engineering (approximately 3,600 employees), established in 1969; and Hitachi Micro-Computer Engineering (approximately 2,000 employees), established in 1982.

Hitachi also relied on other company factories for specialized software integrated with hardware. The Omika Works, for example, which pro-

Table 4.3 Hitachi's Software-Producing Subsidiaries (1986)

General Systems and Applications Software Houses
　Nippon Business Consultants, Hitachi Software Engineering, Hitachi Information Networks, Hitachi Computer Consultants, Hitachi Computer Engineering; FACOM-HITAC; regional companies Hitachi Chugoku Software, Hitachi Tohoku Software, Hitachi Chubu Software, Hitachi Nishibu Software

Industrial-Use Control Systems
　Hitachi Industrial Engineering, Hitachi Process Computer Engineering, Hitachi Control Systems

Semiconductor and Micro-Computer Software
　Hitachi VLSI Engineering, Hitachi Micro-Computer Engineering

Information-Processing and Telecommunications Systems
　Hitachi Electronic Service, Hitachi Communications

Video and Audio Equipment, Personal Computer Video Systems
　Hitachi Video

Semiconductors and Electronic Devices
　Hitachi Electronic Devices

Precision Instruments Software
　Hitachi Instruments Engineering

Automotive Electronics
　Hitachi Automotive Engineering

Robotics, Control Equipment, Business Personal Computers
　Hitachi Kyoba Engineering

Personal Computers
　Hitachi Micro-Software Systems

VLSI = very large-scale integration.
Source: Hitachi Seisakusho, "86 shisutemu/sofutouea no Hitachi gurupu" [The '86 Hitachi group for systems and software] (Yokohama: Hitachi Computer Division, 1986).

duced control computers and terminals in Hitachi's Power Generation and Transmission Group, employed another 1,000 programmers writing real-time industrial control software. There were also several hundred programmers each at the Totsuka Works, writing switching systems software, and at the Kanagawa Works, writing design automation software. The Omika, Totsuka, and Kanagawa factories, as well as Hitachi subsidiaries, worked in close cooperation with Hitachi's Computer Group and R&D facilities, and many used versions of the tools and methods Hitachi developed for its in-house software factories.[9]

Origins of the Factory Strategy and Structure

Early Software Development

Like other computer manufacturers, Hitachi did little software development during the late 1950s and early 1960s because of the simplicity of its computers. During the mid-1960s, it also depended on RCA for hardware designs and software for its business computers. Nevertheless, an in-house scientific computer project, begun in the early 1960s, as well as the analysis and modification of RCA software, provided important opportunities for Hitachi engineers to learn about software product and process technology.

The first Hitachi computers introduced during the late 1950s and early 1960s used magnetic drums for main memory and paper tape for entering programs and data as well as receiving output. As a result, software requirements consisted of relatively simple language processors, input/output programs, and a few subroutines for scientific calculations. Members of the Engineering Service Section in the Totsuka Works, relying on their knowledge of digital technology for telephone equipment, learned how to do this basic programming on their own.[10] With the inclusion of core memory and card readers during 1963–1965, it became feasible to use higher-level languages such as FORTRAN and to write more sophisticated programs, although the hardware still had no interrupt features, and so control or monitor programs (the predecessors of operating systems) remained small. In 1965, however, RCA provided Hitachi with a FORTRAN monitor that had numerous functions and resembled a modern operating system. Hitachi introduced this with the HITAC 4010, a Japanese version of RCA's model 401, which Hitachi produced from imported parts and subassemblies.[11] Since both the hardware and software were RCA products, Hitachi required little product engineering or software knowledge, except to service the machine.[12] The Hardware Design Section in the new Kanagawa plant took charge of writing or revising software for the new RCA machines.

An R&D project provided Hitachi with direct experience in hardware and software development but placed a strain on engineering resources. Hitachi's Central Research Laboratory took on contracts with Tokyo University, the Japanese Meteorological Agency, and the main laboratory of NTT to build a very-large scale computer capable of time sharing (using a computer to perform more than one job or serve more than one user simultaneously, rather than sequentially) which was dubbed the HITAC 5020. The Central Research Laboratory completed one unit for its own use in 1964 and then assigned twenty-five engineers to produce a simple operating system that would allow the 5020 to perform input, output, and computation functions simultaneously. The central labs had prior experience developing an assembler and FORTRAN compiler for early Hitachi computers, and along with Totsuka was one of two sources of computer expertise in Hitachi at the time.[13]

The major source of ideas for the operating system came from the Massachusetts Institute of Technology (M.I.T.), where a Hitachi team visited in 1965 through an introduction from a Tokyo University professor. M.I.T. researchers were then developing their own time-sharing system, *Multics*, using a GE mainframe. The Hitachi group received a copy of the manual, which, the team leader recalled, "made our mouths water" by discussing new ideas for storing and accessing data. As soon as the group returned to the Central Research Laboratory, they began working on a comparable operating system in cooperation with Tokyo University's Computing Center. The first outside delivery of the 5020 hardware came in 1965, to Tokyo University. Hitachi then finished a Japanese version of *Multics* in 1968, a few years before M.I.T. completed its system.[14]

The 5020 was not suited for the much larger business market, however, and the project team became short-handed as Hitachi management gave priority to developing system software for new commercial computers, the HITAC 8000.[15] These models, introduced during 1967–1969, were Japanese versions of RCA's Spectra series, which was partially compatible with the IBM System/360. The 8000 family also provided a major incentive to create a formal strategy and organization for programming, because RCA was not developing adequate system software. Hitachi management had wanted to use the RCA operating system, TDOS, but this required at least two magnetic-tape stations for compilers and the program library. In contrast, a major feature of the IBM System/360 was that all functions were available on a faster and larger disk-drive system. While RCA hesitated over whether or not to develop a disk system, and Japanese customers continued to insist on this feature, Hitachi started modifying RCA's TDOS around 1966 and created a proprietary disk-operating system, referred to as DOS.[16]

Yet designing a disk system capable of on-line processing exacerbated the strain on software-engineering resources in Hitachi. The manager of the project, Kazuyuki Sakata, found several dozen engineers to work on the effort, gathered from Hitachi's Central Research Laboratory, the Totsuka Works, two subsidiaries, Hitachi Electronics Service and Hitachi Electronics Engineering, and a subcontractor, Yoshizawa Business Machines. (The teams from Hitachi Electronics Engineering and Yoshizawa remained together and formed the basis of Hitachi's largest software subsidiary, Hitachi Software Engineering, in 1969.)[17] Both TDOS and DOS provided the basic structure of EDOS, completed in 1969, which allowed for greater volume in on-line and large-scale batch processing; EDOS then became the foundation for Hitachi's current operating system for large-scale computers.[18]

Yet another software effort Hitachi tackled in the 1960s was an operating system for an initiative sponsored by MITI and NTT to build a very-large scale computer, called the HITAC 8700/8800 within Hitachi (the NTT version, the 8800, was used for telecommunications data processing). Development work for the software started in 1968 at the Kanagawa Works and was then taken over by the new Software Works in 1969. The commercial operating system that resulted from this project, OS7, compared favorably to other operating systems of the time, such as IBM's, offering multiprocessor, multivirtual memory capabilities, as well as supporting large-scale batch processing, time sharing, and on-line real-time computing.[19] The first commercial deliveries came in 1972–1973, primarily to universities and research institutes.[20] The computer fell short of sales objectives, however, reflecting Hitachi's limited marketing effort and a shortage of business-application software, compared to the more powerful IBM System/370 series, which IBM introduced while the 8700/8800 was in development. Nonetheless, the project provided Hitachi engineers with independent design experience for IBM-compatible hardware, integrated-circuit logic chips, and large-scale systems software. Furthermore, the 8700 successfully targeted a relatively large domestic market for IBM-compatible machines, which Hitachi was able to switch during the late 1970s to its M-series, the models that competed directly against the IBM System/370 and successor mainframes.[21]

In addition to operating systems and other basic software, Hitachi had to learn how to make complicated applications programs, since few companies in Japan outside of the computer manufacturers had in-house programming experts. According to Hitachi sources, demand in Japan for on-line information processing systems increased from 5 in 1964 to 186 in 1970.[22] Hitachi's orders included a series of real-time reservation systems for the Japan National Railways (the first programmable system Hitachi delivered in 1964, with 1,100 terminals throughout Japan); on-line currency exchange and deposit systems for the Tokai Bank (1965) and Sanwa Bank (1967); and real-time production control systems for Toyo Kogyo (Mazda) and Nissan (1968).[23]

The banking systems were especially important for the experience they provided and the visibility they gave to Japanese software producers. Most Japanese banks in the 1960s were buying software from IBM; Hitachi's system marked the beginning of a shift to domestic suppliers and, therefore, even more applications orders.[24] Developing the Tokai software, which connected 200 remote terminals around Japan to a central processing center in Nagoya, proved to be extremely difficult and costly for Hitachi, however. Before taking on the job, Sakata and other Hitachi engineers spent nearly two months in the United States during 1963–1964 studying U.S. airline reservation and banking systems, including Howard Savings in New Jersey and Continental Illinois in Chicago. They were thoroughly dismayed at how complex the programming looked, but returned to Japan and completed an initial system for the Tokai Bank. After delivery, however, Hitachi took a full year to get the software working properly. The contract terms contained the worst part of this story: Tokai did not have to pay for unplanned debugging time and thus Hitachi had to absorb the expenses itself.[25] The cost and frustrations of this project convinced Sakata and other managers that Hitachi had to improve its ability to control schedules and time estimates, as well as defects.

The Factory Strategy: From "Service" to "Product"

Hitachi managers also worried that continued dispersion within the company of a scarce resource—software engineers—would make it difficult to write programs for the 8000 series. This situation prompted the creation of a centralized System Program Department in the Kanagawa plant in 1965, headed by Sakata and modeled after a similar department in RCA.[26] The new department formally brought together the team in the Central Research Laboratory that had been developing software for the 5020, the software engineers already in the Kanagawa Works, and a program section at the division level (although physically located in the Kanagawa Works) that had been studying RCA programs for pre-Spectra computers Hitachi also sold in Japan. The core group consisted of about 80 persons.[27] Underlying the formation of this department, according to the head of the design section and Sakata's successor as department manager in 1969, Satoshi Fujinaka, was also "the anticipation that we would develop software as a factory product." With the 8000 series going on sale and software for the 5020 yet to be delivered, noted Fujinaka, "Work was increasing so rapidly that the new structure couldn't catch up with it. Every day was a struggle with time."[28]

In retrospect, creation of a software factory merely accompanied a rapid and hectic expansion of Hitachi's operations in the computer business in general. In fact, growth of the Computer Division had caused severe shortages of space and personnel in both hardware and software areas. Hitachi expanded the building housing the Kanagawa Works, but this still proved insufficient. It then built another facility for peripherals at Odawara in 1966 and constructed a new mainframe plant nearby (the current Kanagawa Works). The mainframe design and production departments moved to the Kanagawa Works in 1968, leaving most of Hitachi's software departments at the old Totsuka building; a few others, for systems engineering and small-scale computers, remained within the division's staff organization until later in the 1970s. In February 1969, Hitachi management officially upgraded the Totsuka building to the status of a separate factory—the world's first for software.[29]

Managers who set up the new facility cited two reasons for their decision. One was the acute shortage of software personnel, despite a nationwide search, and the hope that centralizing software development in a single facility would bring about an increase in productivity, as had been the case when Hitachi established factories for other products. The second was a corporate decision to stop treating programs simply as an engineering "service" that Hitachi performed to sell hardware but to view them as separate "products" that Hitachi would produce in a disciplined setting comparable to Hitachi's other engineering and manufacturing facilities so that the company could inspect systematically as well as guarantee product quality to customers. Hitachi managers were thus searching for simultaneous improvements in productivity and quality through a factory production system.[30] Japanese customers also pressured Hitachi to move in this direction by complaining bitterly about the large number of defects in RCA programs.[31]

Yet Hitachi managers seemed unclear about how they would produce software in a "factory" manner. Japanese university professors criticized Hitachi, arguing that software was not sufficiently understood to be produced through factory methods. Executives at the highest levels of the company also debated the name and nature of the new facility, with opponents of the factory concept preferring a "software center," presumably to be managed more like an R&D laboratory. Hitachi President Kenichiro Komai finally settled the debate by deciding they would organize a regular factory and make it an independent profit center, in keeping with Hitachi's traditional organizational structure and control system for major product areas.[32] The task of devising process and quality control systems for the new factory fell initially to Sakata, who had served as manager of several key projects as well as the System Program Department. He thus brought to the Software Works a long history in production management and inspection for conventional (nonsoftware) products, and a determination to transfer this discipline to a new technology.

Sakata had entered Hitachi in 1941 from a technical high school and gone to work as a machine operator in the Totsuka Works. After additional training at Hitachi's in-house engineering school and a two-year stint in the army, he joined Totsuka's Production Engineering Department in 1945 and began studying job tasks, scheduling, and conveyor systems in machining departments to improve productivity and develop standard times (the average times management expected particular operations to take). In 1957, Sakata moved to the Accounting Department and got his first glimpse of a computer—an IBM 421 tabulating machine. In 1960, he took over as manager of the new Computer Inspection Section and then in 1962 moved to the Computer Division as head of the Engineering Service Department, which did systems engineering for Hitachi customers as well as system inspection. In 1965, with the formation of the System Program Department, Sakata became responsible for software production and quality control.

The two major frustrations Sakata recalled in his new job were the many defects in RCA software and Hitachi's lack of programmers, which the company needed for the RCA programs, the 5020 project, and applications development. Sakata converted some hardware engineers by having them study and translate RCA's COBOL, FORTRAN, and Assembler manuals; he also put more than half a dozen to work reviewing RCA software and correcting defects before shipment to Hitachi customers. Continuing quality problems in software, such as with the Tokai system, as well as Hitachi's high standards for other product areas, challenged Sakata and others in Hitachi to make the factory approach work.

One of the younger engineers working under Sakata who became responsible for refining many of the factory procedures was Kanji Shibata, in 1989 the head of the Engineering Department in the Software Works. Shibata had joined the Engineering Service Section of Hitachi's Computer Division in 1964 after majoring in electrical engineering at Shinshu University, and later moved to the System Program Department and then the Production Administration Section of the Software Works. Why he became Hitachi's in-house expert on software-engineering management—a very novel subject in the mid-1960s—reflected how Hitachi encouraged new graduates to pursue subjects they felt were important to the company.

Hitachi's training program for college-educated engineers required them to take several months during their second year in the company to write a paper on a theme related to their work and then give a presentation. Shibata, who had noticed how difficult it was to estimate and monitor software development, chose to collect data on programmers working on software for the RCA machines and the 5020—how much time they spent each day on different activities and different types of programs. Programmers did not like being watched closely or keeping records, Shibata noted, so they stopped doing this in 1966, after he wrote his paper. Nevertheless, Sakata read Shibata's report and decided these data were too valuable not to collect. Sakata then hired several clerks to keep the records, and this database became the foundation for production planning and control in the Software Works.[33]

Factory Organization and Management Systems

Structure and Processes

With the decision to open a software factory, Hitachi relinquished the luxury of treating software development as an art or craft. The experience of Sakata and other managers in producing computers and other conventional products had led them to believe that improvements in productivity and reductions in defects were most likely to come from process analysis and then standardization of procedures, design methods, and components; formalized management systems; and better tools and techniques. Creating these factory systems, however, required years of trial and error, since the inputs for software products and the development process in general differed significantly from operations in Hitachi's other divisions. Nonetheless, within a decade, Hitachi had devised an integrated set of managerial controls and databases; standards for design methods, program construction, documentation and manual compilation, product inspection, and worker training; as well as a variety of general-purpose tools to support these activities. In combination, they constituted the factory infrastructure for software.

In terms of organization, from the inception of the Software Works in 1969, Hitachi mixed functional with product-oriented departments, and gradually accommodated different types of programs. The factory began with three design departments for three products: custom business applications, system (user) programs (basic software), and on-line programs (large-scale real-time database and other applications software for the National Railways, NTT, banks, and other industrial or institutional customers). Over time, Hitachi consolidated some functional departments, added other product-design and functional departments, such as for AI and computer graphics, and moved large-scale custom applications development to a second facility, the Omori Software Works, which Hitachi relocated, expanded, and renamed the Systems Design Works in 1989 (Table 4.4).

The eight design departments contained in the Software Works in 1986 covered mainframe operating systems (Nos. 1 and 2 systems programming), database programs, language processors, AI graphics, and small-scale operating systems. Each design department had several hundred people. The NTT Systems Department was the largest, with approximately 900 persons. Hitachi organized work in projects, generally with members from a particular department and broken down into groups of approximately 100 and then again into more manageable teams of no more than 30 or so members. Typical projects had several hundred people, although teams served as the primary operating units.[34]

The process flow for systems software (outlined in Table 4.5) followed a standard life-cycle model, from basic design through debugging. Data from 1985 indicated that Hitachi devoted roughly 50 to 55 percent of work-hours to planning and design, 5 percent to coding, 30 to 35 percent to debugging, and 10 percent to inspection. Hitachi managed these phases through a matrix, with project managers sharing tasks and responsibilities with managers of functional departments. Hitachi did not separate system design from program construction (module design, coding, and testing) in basic software; the design departments managed all phases of product development. The only division of labor between design and program construction was informal in that managers generally asked younger programmers to do most of the coding. In contrast to project-centered organizations, however, an independent department for quality assurance conducted final inspections and this department, rather than project managers, had the final authority to release products.

In applications development, Hitachi used more of a factory division of labor, separating systems engineering from program construction, as

Table 4.4 Hitachi Software Factories' Organizational Evolution

Hitachi Software Works (1969)	
Design Departments	*Functional Sections*
System Development	Administration
Design Groups (6)	Inspection
System Programs	Engineering
Planning Group	Accounting and Control
Design Groups (2)	General Affairs
On-Line Programs	Computer Technology School
National Railways (2 groups)	
NTT (4 groups)	
Banking (2 groups)	
Government (1 group)	

Hitachi Software Works (1986)	
Design Departments	*Functional Departments*
No. 1 systems programming	Product Planning
No. 2 systems programming	Engineering
Database programming	Documentation/Manual Devel-
Data communications program-	opment
ming	NTT Systems
Language processors	Quality Assurance (Inspection)
Artificial intelligence	Computer Center Service
Computer graphics	Software Education Center
Small-scale systems programming	General Administration
	Purchasing
	Accounting and Control
	Software Technology Center

Omori Software Works (1987)	
Systems Engineering Departments	*Programming Departments*
Banking	Analysis, Planning, Design
Media	Implementation
Hospitals	Inspection & Quality Assurance
Local government	*Functional Departments*
Industrial	Program Support
Distribution	Contract Service Program
Accounting	Technical Support Center
Payroll	System Design Automation
Networks	Computer Center
Tool development	System Simulation Test

NTT = Nippon Telegraph and Telephone.
Sources: Hitachi Seisakusho, *Sofutouea Kojo 10 nen no ayumi* [A 10-year history of
the Software Works] (Yokohama: Hitachi Ltd, 1979), pp. 192, 200; Hitachi Software Works memorandum, July 1986; Hitachi Seisakusho, "Omori Sofutouea
Kojo annai" [Guide to Omori Software Works], pp. 6–7, 11.

SDC had attempted (see Chapter 3). Yet there were several differences
between Hitachi and SDC that, in retrospect, seemed to help Hitachi
avoid some of the problems SDC encountered. First, Hitachi located the
systems-engineering departments (which did high-level design, including system proposals, demonstrations, and estimates) and the programming departments (which did program analysis, detailed planning and
design, as well as coding and module testing) in the same buildings,

Table 4.5 Software Process Flows: Systems and Applications

	Systems Software
Design Departments	*Inspection Department*
Basic Design	Initial Inspection Planning
Functional Design	
Structural Design	
Coding	Documentation Planning
Stand-Alone Debugging	
Combination Debugging	
Comprehensive Debugging	Inspection Program Compilation

Final Product Inspection

	Applications Software
Systems Engineering Departments	*Programming Departments*
System Proposal Compilation	System Construction/Consultation
Demonstration	System Design
Estimate	Program Implementation
	Conversion
	System Test
	Inspection and Quality Assurance
	Final Inspection

Follow-Up Service

Sources: Hitachi, *Sofutouea Kojo*; Kanji Shibata interview, Sept. 1, 1987; Hitachi, "Omori Sofutouea Kojo annai."

along with separate departments for inspection (quality assurance) and other staff functions. A few team members worked some of the time at customer sites, although there was no formal geographic separation. Second, Hitachi organized systems engineers by different industries or applications—such as for banking, media (newspaper database systems), hospitals, local governments, distribution, accounting, and payroll systems, among others. This structure allowed designers to specialize in particular applications, rather than building a broad range of products that might extend beyond their expertise. Hitachi did allow movements of personnel among projects, such as when an important project began falling behind schedule, although movements were generally within a department.

The evolution of the functional departments illustrates how Hitachi managed this delicate sharing of work and responsibility, within the Software Works and within the Computer Division. One of the most important, the Product Planning Department, Hitachi set up in 1970 to centralize planning activities then dispersed among the System Program Department and the Administration Section in the Software Works and other large-scale programming groups in the Computer Division. An initial task for the department was to formulate strategies for new products and exports.

In 1974, for example, the department set up conferences to discuss plans for Hitachi's M series, which Hitachi was designing to compete directly with the IBM System/370 family. These activities included preparing for exports to the Itel Corporation (a computer leasing company) in the United States and studying how to make the Hitachi hardware fully compatible with IBM machines. To assist in this effort, the Computer Division established a Liaison Office in Mountain View, California in 1972, to serve as a source of information on IBM products and the U.S. market (replacing RCA), and charged the Product Planning Department in the Software Works with administering this directly, before the San Francisco office of Hitachi America absorbed the Liaison Office in 1978. In the late 1970s, the Product Planning Department also became involved in pricing decisions, once Hitachi separated software from hardware, as well as administration of overseas technical contracts.

The Engineering Department, which originated in the 1960s as the Software Section in the Engineering Department at the Kanagawa Works, handled production scheduling and control. The first Engineering Department in the Software Works had two sections, Engineering and Administration, with a total of thirty-six members. The Engineering Section served as a liaison group for the Computer Division, other Hitachi factories, and subcontractors, providing explanations and documentation on product pricing and progress in new product development. The Administration Section took on a broad range of responsibilities in work scheduling, managing the computer and software centers attached to the factory, setting standard times for software-development tasks, and overseeing measures for cost control and productivity. The section also assisted in developing control systems to monitor design and inspection as well as a variety of tools, often in conjunction with Hitachi's Systems Development Laboratory and the Software Work's Software Technology Center. Two other sections in the Engineering Department Hitachi later made into independent departments: Procurement, which purchased software from overseas and local subcontractors, and Documentation/Manuals.

The Quality Assurance Department in the Software Works (the literal translation of the Japanese name is the "Inspection Department") had a long history in other forms prior to the factory opening. It also took on numerous responsibilities in addition to inspecting and approving finished goods. The department began in the 1960s as a group that supervised testing and debugging, and then in the mid-1970s started design-review task forces that included reviewers from several different departments as well as evaluations of programs at customer locations. Department personnel also took charge of maintenance for basic software, compiled information on defects from historical field data, and devised methods of testing and forecasting potential defects, such as the "needle probe," which tested parts of programs in development to identify problems and provided data to revise estimates and formulate countermeasures. From 1977, it began operating the System Simulation and Test (SST) Center, a facility (and set of procedures) that simulated user conditions to detect program errors. In addition, the department instructed new programmers and managers in quality control procedures.

The Accounting and Control Department set up and maintained the Software Work's cost-accounting system. While a major problem in the beginning was how to treat orders, sales, and income, the department eventually adopted the practice of calculating total development expenses for basic software after a project's completion and then charging these costs back to the Kanagawa Works. Charges for custom-built applications programs Hitachi included with the hardware; the Software Works, and later the applications factory, then received payments from the Computer Division by submitting in-house order tickets. The system for determining costs rested on the standard times the Engineering Department set for all activities, from design through maintenance.

Product Engineering

Managers at Hitachi Software Works outlined their approach to product engineering during the first decade of operation under the categories of standardization, design and inspection, and center operations (Figure 4.1). The main objective—to develop standards for all activities—resulted in procedures for documentation, design reviews, design and coding methods, defect analysis, components (module-configuration) control, manuals and support tools registration, and project proposals. During the late 1970s and 1980s, Hitachi gradually refined and integrated these techniques as well as invested in support tools called the Computer-Aided Software Development (CASD) system.

Work Standardization: A primary concern in the Software Works and other Hitachi software facilities, as in well-run conventional factories, was "work standardization," so that employees made products in similar and consistent ways. The degree of emphasis Hitachi managers placed on discipline and standardization can be seen in a comment by two managers who led in the transfer of software production technology from Hitachi to its subsidiaries: "To meet our production criteria, project procedures have been standardized and imposed on employees. If any modules deviate from the coding standard, they are returned to the production line."[35]

Hitachi management institutionalized this concern with standardization through corporate policies that required formal procedures for every step in planning, design, production, and testing for every product made in the company. Nonetheless, as acknowledged even in the official history of the Software Works, establishing work standards for software

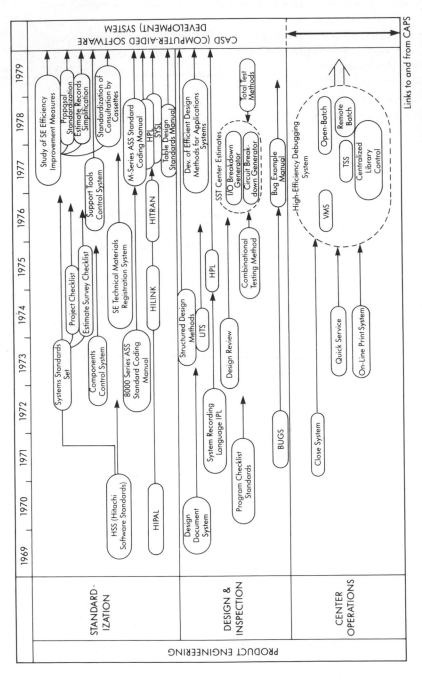

Figure 4.1 Product Engineering at Hitachi Software Works, 1969–1979. CAPS = Computer-Aided Production Control System; HILINK = Hitachi Users' Program Library Network; HIPAL = Hitachi Program Application Library; HITRAN = Hitachi Translation Program Library; HPL = Hitachi Programming Language; I/O = input/output; IPL = initial program load; SE = systems engineering; SST = Systems Stimulation Test; SYSL = System Language; TSS = Time-Sharing Terminals; UTS = Universal Translator System; VMS = Virtual Memory System. (*Source*: Hitachi Seisakusho, *Sofutouea Kojo 10 nen no ayumi* [A10-year history of the Software Works] [Yokohama: Hitachi Ltd., 1979], p. 122.)

proved to be far more difficult than anyone had anticipated, and initial efforts were less than successful.[36]

For example, Sakata and Shibata set out in 1969 to introduce standards for development tasks as well as for product components. Shibata's goal was to get programmers to design general-purpose modules that would serve as the equivalent of standardized hardware parts: "Around 1970 we believed we had to introduce a components control system similar to what you find for hardware, and in the Software Works we established a committee to take this up as a special project." The committee members, however, soon realized that "software is not sufficiently standardized to be treated the same as in hardware components control." They changed their priorities and decided to find a way to standardize product designs, and then worry about components.

A survey of research in the software field suggested that structured design and programming techniques would help standardize design and coding. The committee thus renamed itself the Structured Programming Methods Committee and spent several years studying these techniques (as they were evolving) and analyzing programs Hitachi had already written. This was truly a pioneering move, because it would be several years before articles in industry journals began discussing structured design and programming widely and companies such as IBM adopted these practices for their internal standards.[37]

Another committee for work standards took on the task of establishing procedures for other activities, based on the life-cycle model of development. This committee met almost weekly, studying available materials on software development and examining practices within Hitachi. It completed a first-cut set of standards by the end of 1970, referred to as the Hitachi Software Standards (HSS), covering product planning, design and coding methodology, documentation and manuals, testing, and any other activities necessary to complete a software product (see Figure 4.1). Although Hitachi managers clearly recognized these would evolve as personnel and technology changed, and they made provisions to revise some standards annually, they were significant mainly as an attempt to uncover "best practices" within the company and the field and then make sure these became generally followed in Hitachi projects.

Struggling with work standards also helped the committee recognize the need to distinguish between basic systems and applications software, rather than trying to impose similar controls and expectations on all types of software development. It started developing separate standards for applications during 1971–1972 and published system-consultation standard times in 1973. By 1975, the Software Works had completed an initial set of procedures now termed HIPACE (Hitachi Phased Approach for High Productive Computer System Engineering) to standardize formats for proposals, designs, and program construction, as well as to aid in developing tools for design automation. The evolution of different standards and tools then made it relatively easy to establish a separate applications software factory in the 1980s.[38]

Another important juncture came in 1973, when management at the Software Works began training programmers in structured design and requiring new projects to follow structured concepts, to facilitate design standardization as well as maintenance and portability. Somewhat longer programs appear to have resulted, but managers such as Sakata considered the benefits to be significant.[39] At this point, the factory finally instituted an initial version of the components-control system Shibata had wanted several years earlier to standardize procedures for module construction and configuration. This system also helped simplify design and maintenance, and increased the potential portability of code, though reusability was not yet a major goal in Hitachi.[40]

Design Methodology: The design standards Hitachi adopted in the early and mid-1970s, and refined in subsequent years, called for "phased development" with engineers following the top-down structured design and programming methodologies then popular at least in the academic literature. A 1980 article in Hitachi's in-house technical journal described these as well as the factory's underlying design strategy, which covered five distinct phases: (1) determination of product or user requirements; (2) determination of external specifications (the program's logic structure); (3) determination of internal specifications (the program's physical structure); (4) manufacturing (coding); and (5) testing, debugging, and inspection.

The logic structure represented the functional layers of a program and the interconnections (inputs and outputs) between those layers. Hitachi required programmers first to write specifications in natural language and then use an in-house tool, cause-effect graphs (CEG), and decision tables to identify logical inconsistencies. The next step broke down the desired layers into partial functions to develop algorithms to implement each specification. The physical structure represented the actual modules making up the program (their hierarchical arrangement as well as interconnections) and data (data hierarchies, data and module interconnections, and data-point relationships).

Structured design and programming as Hitachi defined it centered around three major objectives: (1) match the physical structure as closely as possible to the logic structure; (2) standardize the physical structure; and (3) make the elements of the physical structure as independent as possible. The third objective required each module to have only one input and one output, making each module in effect a "closed subroutine." Documentation also followed a standardized format, while several support tools relied directly on the standardized design structures; for example, Automated Generator of External Test (AGENT) automatically generated test items from the cause-effect diagrams and served as a logic-design support tool. Automated Design and Documentation System (ADDS) served as a design-support tool for the physical structure by analyzing design information and generating documents in graphic form.[41]

Inspection: Figure 4.1 (and Figure 4.2) illustrate how Hitachi viewed inspection as part of the design process and quality control as a separate activity linked conceptually to production management. In practice, inspection procedures were part of a quality assurance system, as discussed in the next section. Inspection at the Software Works began with a set of procedures derived from practices used in the Kanagawa Works for hardware products. Managers in the new software factory added a checklist system in 1969 and then formal design reviews in 1972–1973, to inspect programs in development at the end of each phase and review programming practices, documentation, and error levels. Other parts of the inspection process were testing procedures and simulation and debugging practices introduced during the latter half of the 1970s. These put software through "combinational testing" (testing of modules in combination with others), system simulation, and total system test (software and hardware).

Production Management

As indicated in Figure 4.2, Hitachi managers visualized software production management in terms of four areas of control: manpower, process, quality, and products. Manpower control focused on standard times, cost accounting, and production planning; process control on project management; quality control on defect forecasting and analysis; and product control on finished-program registration and storage.[42] Since each area related closely to others, accurate scheduling and budgeting depended on accurate planning, data comparability, and data sharing. To facilitate the data tracking and analysis, Hitachi began automating many of these functions during the late 1970s and early 1980s, and integrating various tools and databases into its Computer-Aided Production Control System for Software (CAPS), primarily used for basic software, and other systems for applications development.

Manpower Control: Standard times for all phases of development, beginning with basic design, constituted the primary mechanism for manpower control in Hitachi's software factories and major subsidiaries. For coding, standard times listed the number of debugged lines of source code expected per individual per day or month, taking into account factors such as the type of program, languages used, and the class of programmer, distinguished by experience and training as well as formal

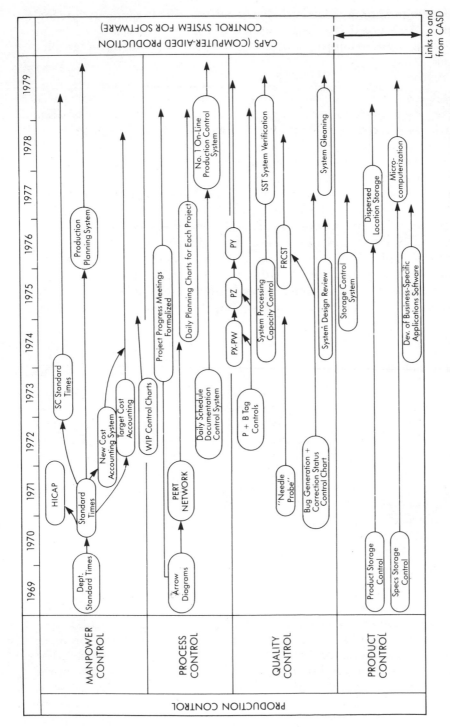

Figure 4.2 Production Control at Hitachi Software Works, 1969–1979. FRCST, see text; HICAP = Hitachi Computer-Aided Planning; PERT = Program Evaluation and Review Technique; SC = System Consultation (see Figure 4.1. for other definitions). (*Source:* Hitachi, *Sofutouea Kojo,* p. 122.)

test scores. Other phases used other measures, such as pages of requirements or documentation.

Collection of data on projects began in the mid-1960s, when Shibata first tracked programmer productivity and computer time. Articles SDC published during 1967–1968 on standard times for software also provided basic guidelines for Shibata.[43] By 1967, Hitachi had enough data to derive rough standards and establish formal procedures for estimating both labor-productivity and machine (computer-time) hours. Initially, employees placed the standards and estimates on job tickets that accompanied documentation for each program in process, indicating the schedule and progress to date. When the inauguration of the Software Works in 1969 made it necessary to adhere to Hitachi's companywide budgeting and cost-accounting procedures, which used standard times as basic accounting units for all engineering and production activities, the Software Works at least had a rudimentary system in place.

Several corporate policies in Hitachi also encouraged managers in the Software Works to standardize and seek other ways to improve productivity and quality. For example, a companywide effort launched in all Hitachi factories in 1968 and continued through the present, the Management Improvement (MI) program, required the factory to establish specific goals and implementation plans not only for standardization but also for quality and productivity.[44] During 1969–1971, MI initiatives took the form of reviewing standards for design, programming, and testing activities, introducing a document-control system and a zero-defect program, and beginning a study of how to reduce personnel costs and increase programmer output. In 1973, employees submitted 1,437 suggestions on how to improve productivity, including many that helped convince management to adopt structured programming techniques and better debugging methods. In the later 1970s, again participating in the MI program, the Software Works launched studies of design productivity, reliability, profit generation, and market-share improvement strategies, and established a Rationalization Promotion Center, headed by the factory manager, to encourage adoption of new measures.[45]

Hitachi did not publish figures on how manpower performance changed over time, although it released figures on employees and sales for the Software Works (Table 4.6). These numbers, however, did not provide a direct measure of productivity. The employee data excluded a large number of staff assigned from subsidiaries and other subcontractors, while the sales data probably reflected increasing revenues from packages as much as higher output per person. The best that can be inferred from these data is that the Software Works appeared to grow steadily between 1969 and 1985 (at which time applications became a separate factory), with substantial increases in sales per Hitachi employee (excluding subcontracting), especially just after establishing the factory and then again in the 1980s.

Table 4.6 Hitachi Software Works Sales per Employee (1969–1984)

Year	No. of Employees*	Nominal Sales Per Employee†
1969	348	100
1970	675	200
1971	926	176
1972	1,107	188
1973	1,169	202
1974	1,079	328
1975	1,093	310
1976	1,141	356
1977	1,288	382
1978	1,395	464
1979	1,398	500
1980	1,398	588
1981	1,419	672
1982	1,437	784
1983	1,666	934
1984	1,833	1,244

*Average number of full-time Hitachi employees working in the facility. These numbers exclude employees assigned from subsidiaries and other subcontractors, which probably numbered more than 2,000 in 1985; †reflects the value of software products (basic software and applications programs) sold by Hitachi Software Works to other Hitachi profit centers as well as to outside customers. Outside sales represented approximately 90% of revenues; Hitachi appeared to charge in-house customers prices slightly below market rates.
Sources: Calculated from data in Hitachi, *Sofutouea Kojo*, p. 203, updated by Kanji Shibata.

Nor has Hitachi published formal analyses of factors contributing to productivity improvements, although interviews with Shibata indicated that the initial standardization of procedures and methods appeared most important. Other factors that later seemed significant included the increasing use of high-level languages, new production-management and design-support tools, and savings in labor generated from declines in defect rates as well as from standardized documentation, which made inspection easier.

Process Control: Sakata claimed that refining the factory's capabilities in process planning and control constituted his most enduring problems. The Sales Department in Hitachi's Computer Division announced new systems-software products and specifications before the Software Works completed development, and customers often wrote applications programs based on the advance specifications. This situation placed a tremendous burden on product managers to meet scheduled targets with as few changes as possible.

Standard-time estimates, relying on accumulated data from past projects, provided a basis for control, especially as they became more accurate during the 1970s with better data and annual revisions. Rather than simply measuring coding, however, standard times covered all phases of development. From around 1973, for example, the Software Works began monitoring project status by estimating the number of documents required for design and then tracking their completion. Scheduling program construction then required an estimate, from the functional specifications, of how many lines of code these represented, although this type of estimate was the most difficult and, according to Shibata, error-prone part of scheduling. Managers again used standard times for coding and debugging, adjusted for the skill levels and particular programming experiences of the employees available.

To monitor the progress of a project, at the inception of the factory, Hitachi began using simple arrow diagrams. As an experiment in adopting computer-aided tools, the factory introduced a new tool in 1971 to diagram significant events or milestones in a construction project, the PERT Network System or PNET (PERT stands for Program Evaluation and Review Technique).[46] Hitachi then linked this to a planning simulation program, Hitachi Computer-Aided Planning (HICAP) (see Figure 4.2). HICAP proved to be inaccurate, however, and managers found they had to rely on meetings to coordinate work. Hitachi during 1973–1974 then formalized the practice of holding regular meetings, at least once a month to discuss scheduling and other issues. Managers also found it more convenient to use arrow diagrams on paper rather than computer-generated reports, the HICAP printouts, because of the many schedule changes usually necessary. Hitachi thus went back to manually written arrow diagrams for schedule planning and control, although the introduction in 1978 of the CAPS successfully automated many functions necessary for project management.

The arrow diagrams from 1973 until the late 1970s tracked job or work tickets that accompanied software documentation (see Figure 4.2). These tickets indicated progress and status: PW tickets reflected the schedule for planning, design, and coding; PX tickets debugging status; PY tickets the inspection (design review) status; and PZ tickets specific types of defects that needed further analysis. Other tickets indicated the state of work-in-process and progress in correcting defects. Hitachi later incorporated the ticket system into CAPS.

The ticket system, combined with design and coding standards, appeared to be a useful control system at least for kinds of software familiar to developers and managers. It allowed Hitachi in the 1970s (as well as in the present) to utilize a simple method to determine the percentage of a project that was complete. Personnel learned to develop software in modules roughly equal in size and difficulty; as they finished a module, they noted this on the work tickets. If a program design called for 100 modules and a project had 80 completed, then managers considered the project 80 percent finished.

Hitachi data indicated that this formalized approach to project planning and control brought significant improvements in scheduling accuracy. As seen in Table 4.7, the percentage of late projects in the Software Works (projects that went over the initial scheduled target for submission to final inspection) dropped dramatically, from more than 72 percent in 1970 to 13 percent in 1973 and to a remarkably low 7 percent in 1974 and 1979. These improvements occurred despite a tripling of employees and significant increases in sales per employee.

There was a rising tendency for projects to exceed schedules in the 1980s, although part of this appeared to result from the increasing size and complexity of operating systems and applications programs, as well as delays in completing hardware that remained compatible with IBM machines. Variations in the figures for project lateness also reflected the level of activity within the factory, with more late projects when Hitachi worked on large new projects, for example, a new mainframe operating system. Overall, Hitachi managers attributed the improvements that occurred to more careful compilation of data for each phase of the development process and continual refinement of planning techniques that came with the efforts to integrate controls over manpower, the process flow, and quality.

Another benefit of the factory system was that, if projects were falling behind schedule, Hitachi managers claimed they could add people and finish closer to the target than they would have without having added personnel. Hitachi tried to find the best people available to join a project midway, rather than just adding anyone available. Nonetheless, the fac-

Table 4.7 Hitachi Software Works
Project Lateness (1969–1985)

Year	Projects Late (%)*	Year	Projects Late (%)*
1970	72.4	1978	9.8
1971	56.6	1979	7.4
1972	36.3	1980	10.7
1973	13.0	1981	14.0
1974	6.9	1982	12.9
1975	9.8	1983	18.8
1976	16.8	1984	16.3
1977	16.1	1985	18.0

*Late submission to the Quality Assurance (Inspection) Department for final inspection, based on the original schedule target. The percentage does not reflect *how* late projects were, however.
Source: Hitachi, *Sofutouea Kojo*, p. 114 (updated by Kanji Shibata).

tory environment—a focus on similar families of software products, adoption of a standardized approach to structured design and coding, standard times for all phases, a formal system of planning and monitoring, as well as standardization of tools and methods, with these elements reinforced by a common training program—appeared to facilitate rapid understanding and communication among project members.[47] In contrast, IBM managers developing the System/360 basic software found that adding people tended to make projects later, as a result of the time lost when personnel on a project had to show new members what they had done so far, what tools and methods they were using, and the like.[48]

Quality Control: Quality improvement was probably more of a direct concern in the Software Works than costs or productivity, although Hitachi managers seemed to operate on the assumption that extra effort expended in detecting or, better yet, preventing defects early in development would improve productivity and thus lower costs in the long term by facilitating testing and inspection and reducing rework during debugging or maintenance. Some Hitachi managers even saw the essence of the factory approach as the ability to control quality.[49]

Hitachi managers and engineers defined software quality control in two ways: preventing the creation of defects in the design stage, and meeting performance specifications, which included the elimination of defects. Since these two factors directly affected the customer, managers claimed to give them primary concern, although Hitachi tracked two other features of quality that directly affected the manufacturer: maintainability and portability.

Defect reduction relied on three elements: (1) careful design reviews, instituted from 1974, beginning with functional specification and detailed design phases to catch defects early in development; (2) elimination of tedious tasks such as coding through automatic code generation from structured problem-analysis diagram (PAD) charts, which Hitachi used for both systems and applications software, or through reusable software modules; and (3) utilization, since 1975–1976, of a time-series statistical program (FRCST) to predict defect levels and then test, with the aid of various tools, until identification of the predicted number of defects. Defect prevention relied initially on structured design methods, high-level languages, and formal monitoring and analysis systems, all introduced in the mid-1970s. Refinements in the 1980s focused on analysis of defects and providing information to design, so as to prevent the repetition of similar mistakes, and to inspection, so as to improve testing—practices characteristic of Japanese quality control efforts in a variety of industries.

Figure 4.2 outlines briefly the evolution of Hitachi's quality control practices in the Software Works. In 1971, the factory instituted control charts (borrowed from other divisions) showing the generation of defects and status of corrections, as well as the "needle probe" technique, developed by Sakata, to test a program when it was approximately 60 percent completed and then revise overall defect estimates.[50] In 1972, Hitachi added P tickets to designate program changes and B tickets to indicate defect (bug) corrections. In 1974, management linked these to the PX-PW-PZ ticket system, to improve scheduling estimates and project management. In 1975, the needle probe technique and data on actual defect generation for different types of programs became the basis of the FRCST program, which also provided programmers with examples of defects in different types of software to help them avoid making similar errors. Hitachi supplemented these other measures with design reviews from the initial phase of requirements definition.[51]

Another companywide practice Hitachi incorporated into its quality control system for software, called *system gleaning*, originated with the founding of the firm in the early 1900s. The Software Works adopted this practice in 1977, with the particular objective of reducing the recurrence of product or system problems customers identified. Management asked workers to pick out product-design or system-design errors, analyze them, and then make formal presentations on their findings while recommending countermeasures. Factories had case reports once a month; divisions had reports approximately once every other month.[52] (Hitachi also used small-group sessions [quality circles] for software personnel to discuss problems and quality improvement measures, although management appeared to place less emphasis on this technique than on its other practices.)

The focus of the Software Works in quality assurance during the 1980s, with assistance from the Systems Development Laboratory, emphasized continued refinement and automation of various practices as well as integration into a single system. The result of their efforts, the Software Quality Evaluation (SQE) system, still treated quality as reliability (defect detection or prevention) but, unlike with previous practices, it did not evaluate quality simply through statistical measures of finished programs. SQE formalized the process of systematic error analysis, feeding information back into design and testing, and creating new standards or monitoring guidelines for future projects.[53]

Specifically, SQE procedures required projects to (1) report on defects customers identified to estimate how many latent defects existed; (2) combine this information with in-house data on defects uncovered; (3) predict the number of defects in new, similar products; and (4) attempt to locate these "built-in errors" through testing. Hitachi used simple statistics to estimate and analyze errors: program size (lines of code); program content and structure; program configuration; percent of the program written in high-level languages; number of design and testing work-hours, adjusted for program size; number of checklist items, given the size of the program; comparison of the estimated and actual sizes of the program; and patterns formed by detected defects.

The SQE tool set, which supported this analysis process, had three subsystems: design quality evaluation, test quality evaluation, and total quality evaluation (Figure 4.3). Each covered different phases of development and provided information—feedback as well as "feed for-

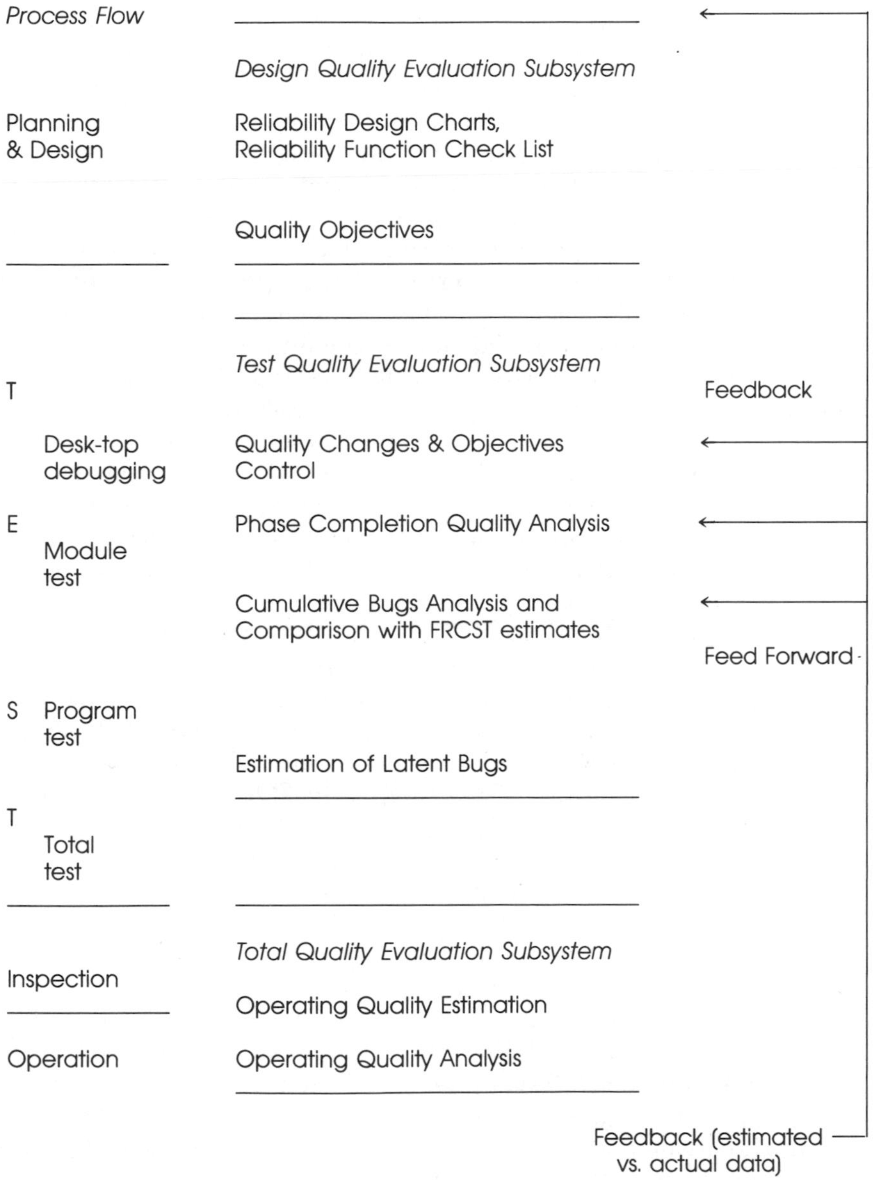

Process Flow

Design Quality Evaluation Subsystem

Planning   Reliability Design Charts,
& Design   Reliability Function Check List

                 Quality Objectives

Test Quality Evaluation Subsystem

T   Feedback

    Desk-top   Quality Changes & Objectives
    debugging   Control

E   Phase Completion Quality Analysis
    Module
    test
                  Cumulative Bugs Analysis and
                  Comparison with FRCST estimates

                                                          Feed Forward

S   Program
    test
                  Estimation of Latent Bugs

T
    Total
    test

Inspection   *Total Quality Evaluation Subsystem*

               Operating Quality Estimation

Operation   Operating Quality Analysis

                                        Feedback (estimated
                                        vs. actual data)

Figure 4.3 Software Quality Estimation (SQE) System. (*Source*: Hashimoto Yaichiro et al., "Sofutouea hinshitsu hyoka shisutema 'SQE'" [Software Quality Estimation System 'SQE'], *Hitachi hyoron* 68, 5, May 1986, p. 56.)

ward"—so that other phases of design, test, or inspection could adjust practices and estimates while a program was being developed.

The design-quality estimation subsystem applied to the planning stage. To analyze design reliability, first, the system compiled tables for each new program listing the number of errors expected in the software and the number detected as development progressed. Second, a reliability checklist made sure the software performed the basic functions required in the design specifications. Third, as part of error analysis, SQE contained a "quality objectives establishment" program to model the occurrence of defects, relying on coefficients drawn from historical data on factors such as program size, processing content and structure, percent written in high-level languages, and number of work-hours spent on design and testing. The test-quality estimation subsystem evaluated quality during the different testing steps. A graph charted actual defects detected on one axis against estimated defects likely to occur in different stages; this made it possible to monitor visually progress in error detection as well as provide immediate information to design and testing—before a product was completed. To track the data on actual defects versus estimates at the completion of each development phase, and to generate estimates on how many defects were likely to remain undetected, Hitachi used the FRCST program. The total-quality evaluation subsystem assisted in final inspection, drawing on data the other two subsystems generated and evaluating programs on the basis of eight criteria covering product design, product quality, and operating quality.

As long as there was not too much change in product types and user environments, Hitachi managers felt confident they could use historical data to predict latent defects in new programs, particularly since the data made it possible to revise estimates continually. Hitachi also claimed the SQE measures, tools, and analysis techniques were sufficiently flexible to adapt to changes in programming environments over time. One adaptation, for example, consisted of a version of the SQE system for personal computers.

These various efforts in quality control appeared to be highly successful. Hitachi had a reputation among Japanese customers as the leading firm in the industry for maintenance and defect repair (see Tables 1.10 and C.2). Managers from other Japanese firms also cited Hitachi as having the most stringent quality control procedures and probably the fewest defects in the industry.[54] Confidential Hitachi data tended to confirm this reputation and showed a consistent record of improvement, although the numbers Hitachi publicly released (see Table 4.8), similar to its sales and employee data, did not directly reflect performance. Using 1978 as an index, Hitachi reported that defects identified by users divided by the number of machine placements fell 87 percent between 1978 and 1983. While some of this decrease came from the expanding number of machines in the field, rather than declines in defects, the level

Table 4.8 Hitachi Software Works Quality
Index (1978–1985)

Year	Defects/Machine Index*
1978	100
1979	79
1980	48
1981	30
1982	19
1983	13
1984	13
1985	14

*Average number of system faults in delivered software reported by outside customers per machine per month.
Source: Kanji Shibata interview, July 23, 1986.

of defects Hitachi reported for its applications and systems projects in surveys conducted by this author were considerably lower than the averages both for other Japanese and U.S. firms (see Appendix B).

Reusability: Reusability, an objective early in the history of the Software Works, did not become practical until the adoption and integration of specific tools and techniques in the 1980s designed to support reuse of designs and coded subroutines, mainly in applications programs. Hitachi managers were becoming more interested in promoting reusability and planning for this at the beginning of design because reuse could help meet or surpass standard times and allow projects to meet their cost and schedule targets with less effort.

The tradeoffs, according to Shibata, involved performance and enhancements: Structured programs designed to contain reusable modules did not always perform as well as newly written programs. A general rule Hitachi used was that, if programmers had to revise 30 percent of the code in a module, then, in terms of functional performance, they should write a new module from scratch. Hitachi did not have much historical data on reuse and only in 1985 did management begin requiring projects to keep records on reuse.[55]

The Systems Design Works and Hitachi's main software subsidiary, Hitachi Software Engineering, especially emphasized reusability since they built large numbers of custom applications programs that contained similar functions that need not be written from scratch for each customer. Both relied on parts libraries dedicated to particular applications that contained reusable design skeletons (called patterns) and subroutines for common functions such as message reception, message format and contents checking, database management system processing, message editing and switching, screen mapping, line overflow, error displays, program-function key code analysis, screen editing, and table lookup. Hitachi policy encouraged programmers to peruse the reuse library during design to determine if there were parts they could reuse. Some managers even assigned programmers exercises on a monthly basis to make them familiar with subroutines stored in the program libraries.[56] Specific groups of engineers also screened new modules recommended by project managers for registration in the parts libraries. To reinforce these practices, management gave out awards to programmers who registered modules with particularly high potential levels of reuse, based on an analysis of the specifications. Through these and other measures, including extensive application of a reuse-support tool described later, EAGLE (Effective Approach to Achieving High-Level Software Productivity), some departments reported an increase in reuse rates from a level of 10 percent to 20 percent in the early 1980s to approximately 40 percent in 1987.[57]

Other tools or libraries supported another aspect of reuse, portability (the transfer of programs among different machines). Hitachi launched the Hitachi Program Application Library (HIPAL), an on-line database of applications programs and utilities, within the Computer Division in 1968 and then expanded this at the Software Works. Hitachi separated a tool for translating programs for different machines, HITRAN (Hitachi Translation Program Library), from the HIPAL system in 1977. Hitachi retained both of these for in-house use, although HILINK (Hitachi Users' Program Library Network), a separate system begun in 1975, allowed Hitachi customers to exchange their programs (see Figure 4.1).[58]

Training and Career Paths

As a corollary to the factory's systems for product development, beginning in the early 1970s, Hitachi created an elaborate training system for all new and continuing personnel, including managers. This taught valuable skills in software engineering as well as made sure everyone understood Hitachi practices and tools. Moreover, management considered the accurate classification of programmers by ability essential to factory planning and control. Consequently, Hitachi in the mid-1970s began introducing programmer evaluation and qualification procedures, and then tied these into its production-management system.

Evaluating programmers actually dated back to the earliest years of the Software Works and grew out of necessity. The initial 348 employees at the factory in 1969 had widely different skill levels, since they consisted of experienced personnel transferred from other areas of the Computer Division, newly hired Japanese who had studied computers in the United States, and high school graduates with no prior knowledge of computers. Tripling software personnel to more than 900 by 1971 created a severe strain on in-house instructors. Hitachi managers thus decided to hold large classes to train these people in basic techniques and give formal tests to determine their strengths and weaknesses.[59] Next, Hitachi instituted standardized curriculums for different levels of programmers and continued to refine courses as well as methods of evaluation.

The Computer Division's Education and Training Division coordinated the education of software personnel and managers at Hitachi's two software factories as well as major software subsidiaries, allied software houses, dealers, and customer locations. Hitachi also tailored this instruction to different product areas and allowed departments in its two software factories to operate the actual classes. In general, introductory training for new personnel (college and high school graduates) consisted of three months of classroom instruction and another three months of additional education in the first year. Hitachi then offered a variety of short courses and home-study materials for continuing education.[60]

Hitachi tailored education by clearly separating new and experienced employees according to skill levels and had them focus either on applications or systems software. In applications divisions, for example, Hitachi divided college graduates into four classes: Primary (first year), Intermediate I (second year), Intermediate II (third to fifth years), and Senior Systems Engineers (sixth year and beyond).[61] Primary training concentrated on features of Hitachi's operating systems and programming in different languages (COBOL, PL/I, FORTRAN, ASS, BASIC, C, LISP, and PROLOG). Subsequent training mixed courses in the use of the factory tool sets (EAGLE and SEWB, the Software-Engineering Work Bench, discussed later), as well as more detailed examination of operating systems and then databases and data-control techniques, system proposal and consultation, system construction and design (using EAGLE), presentation techniques, and industry areas (production, distribution, finance, and public utilities). The industry material began with general introductions to each line of business (for Intermediate I personnel) and then (for Intermediate II personnel) focused on functional requirements of these different fields, such as production planning, purchase control, and process control for production; retail, wholesale, shop, and merchandise management for distribution; and deposit, security, loan, exchange and finance systems for financial industries (mainly banking).

Employees in the Software Works and related subsidiaries and software houses fell into four parallel categories, although instruction in this area focused on topics appropriate to development tasks in basic systems software (also called user programs in training literature). In the Introductory classes, material covered programming, module design, compiler construction, test/debugging, basic computer mathematics, and manual development. Intermediate I courses taught more advanced versions of these subjects as well as material on hardware design, operating systems, databases and data control, and language processing. In Intermediate II, employees learned system-test methods, logic-structure design methods, reliability design, and other topics in software engineering. Advanced courses covered material such as product planning as well as AI.

Although Hitachi did not publish precise numbers for average class hours after the first year of employment, company records indicated that a large number of employees attended courses. In 1988, for example, Hitachi training courses for applications development throughout Japan listed 8,774 students, approximately 60 percent of which were new employees or young engineers aged 26 years or younger. More than one third of these students (3,223) were from software subsidiaries or software houses working with Hitachi. Training in basic systems software covered approximately 10,000 employees during the same year.

Perhaps the most distinctive feature of Hitachi's factory approach to personnel management, even compared to other Japanese firms, was its qualification system and linkage of this to production management. Hitachi formally evaluated all college graduates in software development not only at company factories but also at subsidiaries and affiliated software houses. The five classifications began with assistant programmer and ended with chief systems engineer or senior analyst, with rising job levels or responsibilities defined for each classification (Table 4.9).

Promotions depended on a point system, where ten points qualified an individual for a higher classification. An individual received five points according to his or her technical level (apparently based on years of experience and a special series of tests given twice annually to individuals and teams, and based on Hitachi standards and products). Five other categories represented one point each: talent (apparently based on eval-

Table 4.9 Qualification and Test System for Software Engineers

Class (yrs)	Applications (SE)		Systems (user programs)	
	Type	Job Level	Type	Job Level
S5 (1–2)	Assistant programmer	Auxiliary work based on direct instructions	Assistant programmer	Coding & testing
S4 (2–3)	Assistant SE	Auxiliary work for part of a project	Programmer	Coding & testing Module design
S3 (3–6)	SE	Management of part of a project	Senior programmer	Module design
S2 (6–10)	Senior SE	Project management	Analyst	Functional design
S1 (10+)	Chief SE	Management of multiple projects or large projects	Senior analyst	Basic design

SE = systems engineering or systems engineer; (yrs) = years of employment in Hitachi.
Source: Hitachi, Ltd., "Computer Training System and Activities," Computer Department, Education and Training Division, May 1988, p. 47.

uations from superiors), attendance at training courses, design-test results (given once a year using a national test for software engineers), English test results, and other qualifications related to information-processing technology. The Hitachi tests varied with the level of the employees, covering material such as job knowledge (standards, products), programming (program readability tests, mathematics, basic theories, algorithms), basic software design (system analysis, layer separation, reliability, patents, cost control), and systems engineering (ease of operation, system design, compatibility, project management, legal issues).

Management connected its qualification system to production management by recording individual test results and overall classifications in a database and using this information as a reference for project planning, scheduling, and budgeting. In general, seniority alone was a fairly accurate indicator of performance, according to Hitachi managers, and it usually took about three years to reach standard times for coding and longer (about six years) for design.[62] Nonetheless, wide variations in performance still existed between the best individuals and the average programmer, and the evaluation system exposed and quantified these differences, as well as made the information available to management for control and training purposes.

While Hitachi designed parallel training, evaluation, and career-path systems for applications and basic software personnel, some differences remained. In basic software, where there was no organizational separation of program design from program construction, young employees who started out doing coding eventually could move up to become designers. In applications, however, Hitachi separated systems engineers from specialists in implementation (program construction), even though they had the same titles. Within the implementation departments, a young employee might move up from doing simple coding to detailed design and planning, but would not normally switch to systems engineering. The reason was that Hitachi managers felt implementation and systems engineering for outside customers required specific and different sets of skills, in which engineers should specialize after approximately two years of experience in general programming.[63]

Computer-Aided Tools and Supporting Techniques

Hitachi initially attempted to organize its software factory around a combination of manual techniques that managers felt represented "good practice" in the industry—structured design and coding coordinated with data collection and standard times for each activity, detailed documentation, design reviews independent of project personnel, rigorous defect analysis, and other elements. Only after spending years studying and standardizing the development process did Hitachi invest heavily in computer-aided tools, relying on engineers mainly from the Software Works and the Systems Development Laboratory.

The tools Hitachi adopted for its software factories were comprehensive, covering each function and activity in software development. For basic software, during the late 1970s, Hitachi introduced CASD to facilitate design, coding, documentation, and testing, and CAPS to manage manpower estimation, process flow control, and quality control. Both CASD and CAPS were continually evolving, as seen in Hitachi's gradual adoption in the late 1980s of a new system for project control, Project Diagnostic Check (PDOCK) system.

For custom applications, in the mid-1970s, Hitachi also began developing a set of tools and methodologies under the label ICAS (Integrated Computer-Aided Software Engineering system).[64] The most important tools consisted of the SEWB, which supported both system design and programming on advanced work stations, and EAGLE, which ran on Hitachi mainframes and helped programmers build software from reusable modules as well as structure new designs and code for reuse. HIPACE, a formalization of structured design and coding methods Hitachi adopted in the mid-1970s, served as the basic methodology used with these and other tools.[65]

CASD

CASD grew out of various design and debugging tools and techniques the Software Works integrated during 1975–1977 to standardize the design process. This mandated the use of structured design and programming as well as high-level languages for system construction, and deployed an on-line network of terminals (for centralized or distributed development) and a program library. As programs continued to grow in size and complexity, Hitachi added to CASD systems for reliability improvement and linkages with the production-management system, CAPS.[66]

Two assumptions motivated Hitachi's continued investment in CASD. One was that management could raise labor productivity by standardizing the tasks for each activity. A second was that performance would improve further by adding automated support tools and integrating these into a single system. In the words of CASD's chief engineers, the system tried to "modernize" as much as possible what had formerly been "manual" activities.

The version of CASD used in the late 1980s contained three subsystems for design, coding, and testing (Figure 4.4). The design-support subsystem assisted in constructing design documentation and analyzing design specifications, relying on the structured-programming tool ADDS and Hitachi's Module Design Language (MDL) (Figure 4.5A). MDL made it possible to standardize and formalize design specifications at the

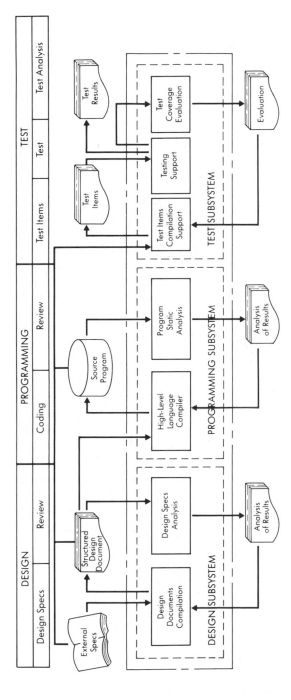

Figure 4.4 Computer-Aided Software Development System (CASD). (*Source*: Kataoka Masanori, Hagi Yoichi, and Nogi Kenroku, "Sofutouea kaihatsu shien shisutema (CASD shisutema)" [Computer-Aided Software Development System], *Hitachi hyoron* 62, 12, December 1980, p. 34.)

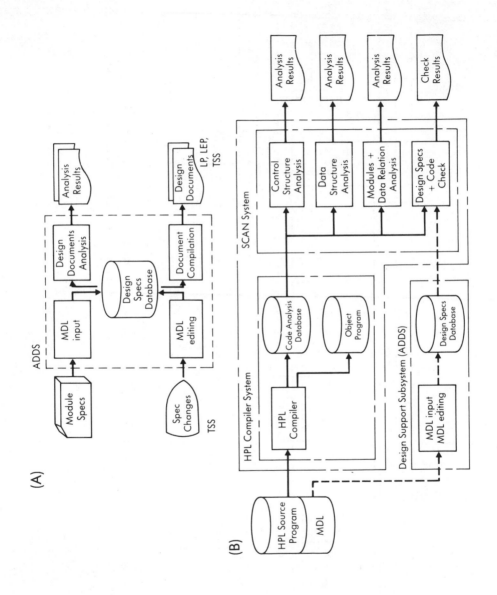

(A)

ADDS

Module Specs → MDL input → Design Documents Analysis → Analysis Results

MDL input → Design Specs Database → Document Compilation → Design Documents → LP, LEP, TSS

Spec Changes → MDL editing → Design Specs Database

TSS

(B)

HPL Source Program / MDL

HPL Compiler System

HPL Compiler → Code Analysis Database
HPL Compiler → Object Program

SCAN System

Control Structure Analysis → Analysis Results
Data Structure Analysis → Analysis Results
Modules + Data Relation Analysis → Analysis Results
Design Specs + Code Check → Check Results

Design Support Subsystem (ADDS)

MDL input MDL editing → Design Specs Database

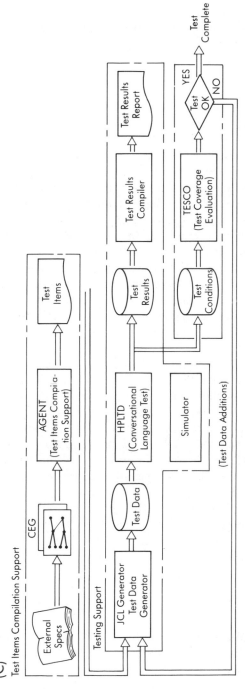

Figure 4.5 Computer-Aided Software Development (CASD) Subsystems. **(A)** Design Support Subsystem; **(B)** Programming Support Subsystem; **(C)** Test Support Subsystem. ADDS = Automated Design and Documentation System; AGENT = Automated Generator of Test Case; CEG = cause–effect graphs; HPL = Hitachi Programming Language; HPLTD = HPL Test & Debugging; JCL = Job Control Language; LBP = Laser-Beam Printer; LP = Line Printer; MDL = Module Design Language; SCAN = Static Code Analysis; TESCO = Test Coverage Manager; TSS = Time-Sharing Terminals. (*Source*: Kataoka, Hagi, and Nogi, "Sofutouea kaihatsu shien shisutema [CASD shisutema]," pp. 34–35.)

module level; ADDS placed this documentation, as well as corrections or changes, into a central database, and checked for obvious errors, thereby assisting in design reviews. Printers and terminals provided the capability to "visualize" the design documentation. Tables and charts outlined the functional layers of a program, module specifications, the dataflow path, module connections, and summaries of the modules, functions, and any changes made.

The programming-support subsystem made it possible to write a program using a high-level language and analyze the results, relying on a language similar to PL/1 for coding, the Hitachi Programming Language (HPL). It also contained several functions that facilitated design reviews (Figure 4.5B). HPL's main components consisted of a compiler and what Hitachi called the Static Code Analysis (SCAN) system. While coding reviews supposedly caught defects as early as possible and provided a way to examine the program logic, Hitachi managers and engineers apparently became frustrated because design reviews, mainly a manual process, depended too much on the varying skills of individuals. To address this problem, the SCAN system received static-code analysis data from the HPL compiler and put out various reports in graphic form for use in the coding review. These reports analyzed the program control structure, the program's data structure, and the module-control structure and relationship between modules and data. SCAN then checked the results of these analyses with design information from ADDS.

The testing-support subsystem helped devise test items, test the programs, and evaluate the results (Figure 4.5C). Hitachi engineers believed this tackled problems of quality control and productivity simultaneously by identifying defects and, correspondingly, reducing work-hours devoted to testing. There were several specific objectives for the testing subsystem. One was to clarify in detail the design specifications, on the assumption that the test items had to determine the conformity of the program to its specifications. Another was to establish testing standards for a given program, recognizing that it was impossible to test all potential operating conditions. In addition, the subsystem automated large portions of the testing process as well as evaluated the comprehensiveness of the tests, relying on several dedicated tools—CEG, AGENT, HPL Test and Debugging (HPLTD) system, and Test Coverage Manager (TESCO).

CAPS

The Software Works launched CAPS during 1977–1980 to support project estimating, scheduling, and quality control by requiring (as did CASD) the use of structured methods and providing an interconnected network of databases, tools, monitors, and printers (Figure 4.6).[67]

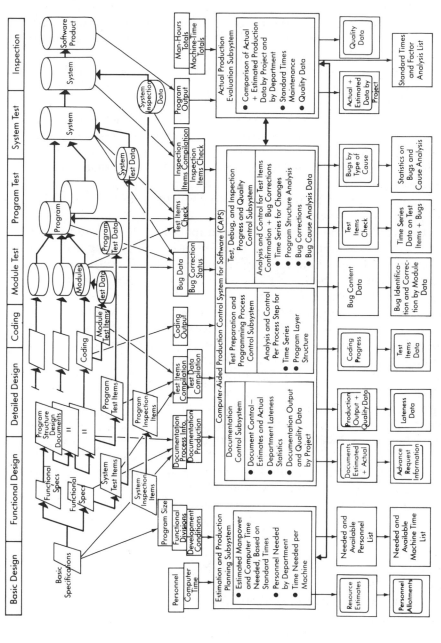

Figure 4.6 Computer-Aided Software Production System (CAPS). (*Source*: Shibata Kanji and Yokoyama Yoichi, "Sogo sofutouea seisan kanri shisutemu 'CAPS'" [Computer-Aided Production Control System for Software 'CAPS'], *Hitach hyoron* 62, 12, December 1980, p. 38.)

Hitachi utilized the system mainly for large basic software projects developed through on-line terminals, although a version of CAPS for personal computers facilitated its use in smaller projects and distributed efforts. Most apparent in analyzing the history of CAPS was its gradual evolution, integrating and automating several techniques introduced between the late 1960s and the mid-1970s, as well as its dependence on structured methods. Figure 4.2 and Table 4.10 outline the milestones Hitachi managers considered most essential as preparation for the successful development of CAPS.

The specific motivation for CAPS, according to Hitachi managers, came from a desire to build a system that would feed estimated and actual times into a central production database directly from on-line terminals and allow managers to compare actual cost and progress to the estimates and revise schedules while a project was still underway. Reducing management work hours and compensating for a shortage of skilled managers comprised two major objectives. Other goals, common to similar systems at SDC and elsewhere, were to make the production process for software more visible; better manage systems of increasing scale and complexity; and expose ways of improving developer productivity.[68]

The structured methods CAPS enforced built on CASD and defined eight phases: basic design, functional design, detailed design, coding, module test, program test, system test, and inspection. A common approach to modularization made it possible to estimate and track schedule progress more accurately as well as outline programs using graphics on computer monitors and in detailed printouts. In addition to schedule progress, CAPS tracked and stored product and project information that facilitated productivity and cost analysis, such as type of object machine (large, medium, small, peripheral); type of program (control program, on-line user control, generator, simulator, etc.); process phase (basic design, functional design, etc.); degree of difficulty (newness of the program type); production volume (lines of code); language being used (assembler, COBOL, FORTRAN, etc.); and machine type used. By 1980, CAPS had grown to five subsystems, for estimation and production planning; documentation; test preparations and programming control; test, debug, and inspection; and production evaluation. Working in combination, these assisted managers and project-team members in several ways.

The estimation and production planning subsystem took data from the basic specifications on program size, functional divisions of the program, and other specific considerations, compared these with historical standard times for personnel and computer time needed to build similar programs, and generated estimates for manpower and computer time for each phase of development. Computer monitors presented resource estimates and personnel allotments. Printers printed out lists of needed and available personnel and computer time.

Table 4.10 Chronology of CAPS Development

1967	Completion of a system for computing labor and machine hours for software development (Kanagawa Works).
1969	Establishment of standard times for software development (Software Works).
1971	Establishment of programmer ability coefficients and amendments of standard times.
	Completion of an estimation and budget system using standard times and a simulation system for resource planning.
	Completion of a PERT Network System (PNET), an automatic diagramming system for schedule control.
	Implementation of a manual system for time-series analysis of test processing and quality control.
1972	Completion of a system for budget-vs.-actual expenditure control for work-hours and machine-hours for each project and department.
	Implementation of manual system for document schedule control.
1973	Implementation of a manual system for job process control.
	Implementation of a manual system for productivity analysis and control.
1974	Completion of a productivity analysis system for each project and department.
1975	Implementation of a manual system for defect factor analysis and quality control.
1976	Development of a time-series statistical program for forecasting defects (FRCST).
	Establishment of a standard scheduling system.
	Introduction of structured design methods.

Source: Hitachi Ltd. memorandum, "Table 1.2 Background and Conditions Affecting CAPS Development," ca. 1986.

The documentation-control and programming process-control subsystems automatically compared estimated and actual times as project personnel completed documentation and coding for each module. Another database for testing, debugging and inspection kept track of the schedules for these functions as well as monitored quality information such as errors in the specifications, design documents, or manuals; defects found in test items and coding; and analysis of the causes of defects and countermeasures taken. Separate databases stored finished modules and documentation as well as test items and test data as they were compiled.

The production and evaluation subsystem compared actual times and other production data for each project and phase of development with the original estimates, and then channeled the appropriate statistics into specialized databases for analysis of project schedules, quality, and standard times. After certifying completion of inspection activities, the system registered a program as a finished software product and stored it in a product-control database, ready for delivery to customers.

One of the constraints Hitachi faced in creating and expanding CAPS consisted of the need for better hardware. First, CAPS required high-performance computing power so that 100 or more programmers could comfortably use terminals connected to the centralized databases. Hitachi solved this problem by using its largest mainframes, beginning with the M-180 and M-200H (first delivered in the late 1970s), as the central processing units. Automated production control also demanded increased storage capacity for the databases recording past and current statistics on project management, and for comparing these data with standard times; this capability came through another Hitachi product, Mass Storage System (MSS). To use MSS efficiently required a large-scale database management system; Hitachi filled this gap with the development of several systems, most notably Adaptable Data Manager (ADM). Hitachi managers also wanted simple visual graphic output, to make it easier to follow the process flow; this they achieved through the use of nonimpact laser beam printers that printed Japanese characters as well as English.

Hitachi managers felt that monitoring and reducing programmer work-hours and computer machine time were critical because these accounted for more than 90 percent of software production costs. Experience suggested that cost overruns and late deliveries resulted from inaccurate daily scheduling and planning, which could be improved through better collection and analysis of data, and the use of various tools. To raise scheduling accuracy, for example, Hitachi engineers wrote an algorithm that calculated manpower needs and schedules automatically, taking into consideration the actual working hours of the committed programmers and the minimum necessary times required for different phases for each type of software program, based on standard times. This approach assumed a strong correlation between the progress of a software project and its quality; an ideal process-control system would thus integrate production management and quality control data. Therefore, successive additions to CAPS allowed it to estimate automatically the number of defects likely for each phase of development, according to the type of program, lines of code, items tested, and other factors, based on historical data.

As a continuing area of research and development, Hitachi attempted to automate further the information flows from terminals or engineering workbenches and among databases, and to improve the degree of integration between CASD and CAPS, which had evolved in parallel but separately, as well as with successor systems supporting product engineering and project management. These goals required both standardization and flexibility in data structures, databases, and tools, as well as software to connect the different systems. Between 1980 and 1983, Hitachi succeeded in creating links that made it possible to register program modules in the CAPS program library automatically from CASD and feed data on defects automatically from CASD to CAPS. As of the late 1980s, however, Hitachi still had not fully connected CAPS and CASD; for example, CASD did not automatically send its output files or corrected modules to the CAPS production database source file.

As suggested previously in Table 4.7, CAPS apparently helped Hitachi manage the development of large systems, reducing the percentage of late projects to as few as 7.4 percent in 1979. As projects continued to grow in size and complexity, however, lateness increased gradually, prompting management to study the sources of continuing difficulties. A survey of projects indicated that 37 percent of problems fell into the category of project planning, while 21 percent related to quality control and 18 percent to project control. Since more than half stemmed from project planning and control, Hitachi management in 1985 decided to invest in another system, PDOCK, that would evaluate and optimize project plans and improve information analysis, helping transfer know-how obtained in successful projects to other projects. Hitachi had the first prototype ready for trial use in 1987, running on a Hitachi work station.

PDOCK focused on nine areas: measuring and limiting program size, with controls at each phase of development; optimizing the project team organizational structure; checking manpower allocation rates; checking on schedule progress; checking available methods and tools, as well as computer resources; creating and evaluating quality targets; assessing various risk factors, such as not meeting performance or delivery targets, and planning countermeasures; targeting and evaluating development or maintenance productivity; and checking management control, utilizing another 200 items. Two databases kept track of manager estimates and actual figures, and the system automatically provided comparative analyses in graph form. The system relied on CAPS procedures and databases, but further integrated data collection and analysis, and, most importantly, combined the CAPS approach with more formalized procedures for project evaluation, carried out in mandatory project-review sessions. These sessions were analogous to design reviews and brought together managers from different departments involved in a given project. It was their responsibility to quantify and discuss project estimates, review actual progress and performance, as well as examine past cases of successful and unsuccessful projects, thereby mixing quantitative analysis with qualitative insights from individuals. Because it required extra time to conduct these sessions, Hitachi continued to use CAPS most of the time, but utilized PDOCK for particularly important projects.[69]

ICAS

The researchers and factory engineers who worked on ICAS systems, which Hitachi used mainly for custom applications, continued to follow a distinct factory approach, but aimed at increasing the applicability or versatility of tools. The tools contained constraints: ICAS systems did not let users decide which design methodology to employ. Instead, they provided a "fixed development methodology of multi-purpose use," helping users complete software quickly with advanced tool support but "without having to worry about which methodology to apply."[70]

Similar to CASD and CAPS, ICAS consisted of several subsystems, most of which Hitachi had completed and transferred to operating facilities as of 1989. These subsystems fell into four areas: (1) a structured methodology for applications development that Hitachi had been using since the mid-1970s (HIPACE), but refined with abstraction techniques and incorporation of a special design language and graphic notations; (2) interactive tools for each phase of the development life cycle, from requirements analysis through operation and maintenance, as well as for software reuse support (EAGLE); (3) an "intelligent" software-engineering workbench (SEWB), consisting of powerful desk-top computers with graphics interfaces and linkages for distributed development as well as access to central mainframes and databases, that allowed programmers to connect tools and have "dialogues" with various computers; and (4) an information-management system for all development phases, called the integrated Software Engineering Database (SEDB), which made it possible to use the various tools together, store and analyze data generated by each tool through a relational database, and edit documentation (Figure 4.7 and Table 4.11).

HIPACE standardized procedures for system analysis and planning, system and program design, program construction, testing, installation, and evaluation, beginning with a stepwise refinement of procedural, functional, and logical requirements. From a conceptual model of the object program, engineers determined the control structure, abstracted data and formed data modules, and defined functional algorithms limited to three control elements—sequence, repetition, and selection. Several tools that ran on the SEWB helped refine the requirements and convert the functional algorithms into executable statements in COBOL, PL/1, C, or FORTRAN.

Formalized Requirements Analysis Method (FRAME) provided standard forms for initial requirements definition. Planning Procedure to Develop Systems (PPDS) and Standard Procedure to Develop Systems (SPDS) served as documentation and project-management procedures for subsequent activities in the development process, while a set of work sheets referred to as Work Breakdown Structure (WBS) offered a format for planning the actual design, programming, and testing tasks. On the SEWB system, for detailed design, Structured Data Flow (SDF) diagrams allowed users to map out the dataflows for new programs, such as for inventory control, using graphical symbols and tables, and then automatically generate system-flow diagrams. (Hitachi also referred to these tools and techniques as HIPACE-SA, for structured analysis, HIPACE-SD, for structured design, and HIPACE-SP, for structured programming).[71]

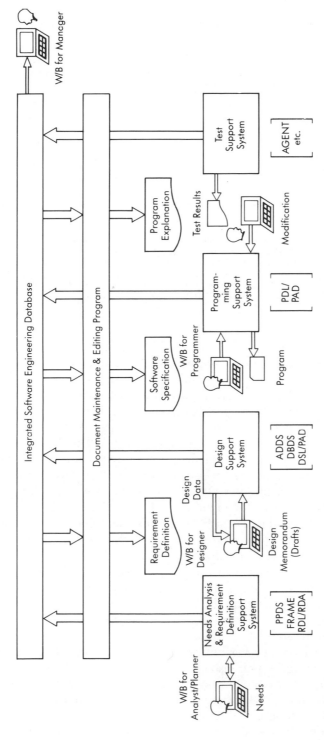

Figure 4.7 Integrated Computer-Aided Software Engineering (ICAS) System. DBDS = Database Design System; DSL = Design Support Language; FRAME = Formalized Requirements Analysis Method; PDL/PAD = Problem Design Language/Problem Analysis Diagram; PPDS = Planning Procedure to Develop Systems; RDA = Requirements Definition Analysis; RDL = Requirements Definition Language; W/B = Workbench (see Figure 4.5 for other definitions). (*Source:* Kobayashi et al., "ICAS: An Integrated Computer-Aided Software Engineering System," *IEEE Digest of Papers-Spring '83 COMPCON* [IEEE Computer Society Press], p. 243. Copyright © 1983 IEEE. Reproduced with permission.)

Table 4.11 Support Range of HIPACE, SEWB, and EAGLE

	Phases Supported By		
	HIPACE	SEWB	EAGLE
Requirements analysis (basic specifications)	X		
System planning (development cost & schedule)	X	X	
System design (database/data-control specification)	X	X	X
Program design (structured design)	X	X	X
Program product (programming, unit test)	X	X	X
System test	X		X
Operation	X		X

EAGLE = Effective Approach to Achieving High-Level Software Productivity; HIPACE = Hitachi Phased Approach for High Productive Computer System Engineering; SEWB = Software Engineering Work Bench.
Source: Adapted from Hitachi Ltd., "System Development Support System EAGLE/SEWB," unpublished company document, Feb. 6, 1989, p. 2.

The SEWB work stations incorporated Database Design System (DBDS) and testing tools such as AGENT, TESCO, and CEG, also used with CASD, as well as other design- and programming-support tools—ADDS, MDL, developed originally as part of CASD, and, perhaps most important, PDL/PAD (Problem Design Language/Problem Analysis Diagram). PDL/PAD helped automate coding and integrate design documentation with source programs. The tool also aided program logic design and automatically converted design documents into high-level language source programs, or vice versa. On average, according to Hitachi data, projects writing in COBOL automated as much as 30 percent of coding tasks usually done manually.[72]

Hitachi first introduced PAD diagrams into its facilities during the late 1970s as substitutes for flow charts. The diagrams consisted of two-dimensional tree structures, modeled after Warnier diagrams but allowing more complete descriptions of the program logic and control structures, in addition to automating many coding tasks. Hitachi also modeled the PAD diagrams after the PASCAL language, forcing programmers to follow a highly structured, "step-by-step" approach to defining the problems they wanted to code, and to use a standardized notation (Figure 4.8).[73] PDL was a language version of the PAD diagrams. The SEWB tools for programming support also included an editor to refine the PAD diagrams, a code generator, and an "auto documentation subsystem" that automatically edited PAD diagrams or PDL to create documentation to go with high-level language source programs (Table 4.12).

EAGLE provided four main functions: (1) conversational language

		PAD	FORTRAN	PL/1	COBOL
R E P E T I T I O N	UNTIL	(L) until Q — H	L CONTINUE H IF (Q̄) GO TO L	L H; IF Q, GO TO L,	PERFORM H PERFORM H UNTIL Q (H is a paragraph name)
	WHILE	(L1) while Q — H (L2)	L1 CONTINUE IF (Q̄) GO TO L2 H GO TO L1 L2 CONTINUE	DO WHILE Q; H; END;	PERFORM H UNTIL (NOT Q)
	DO	i = M to N — H (L)	DO L I = M, N H L CONTINUE	DO I = M TO N BY 1; H; END;	PERFORM H VARYING: FROM M BY 1 UNTIL I > N
	DOWN TO	I: = M down to N — H (L)	DO L II = N, M I = N + M − II H L CONTINUE	DO I = M TO N BY −1; H; END;	PERFORM H VARYING: FROM M BY −1 UNTIL I < N
S E L E C T I O N	IF THEN ELSE	Q — H1 (L1) — H2 (L2)	IF (Q̄) GO TO L1 H1 GO TO L2 L1 CONTINUE H2 L2 CONTINUE	IF Q THEN H1, ELSE H2;	IF Q H1. ELSE H2.
	IF THEN	Q — H (L)	IF (Q̄) GO TO L H L CONTINUE	IF Q THEN H;	IF Q THEN H.
	ARITHMETIC IF	(L1) — H1 < 0 (L2) — H2 e = 0 > 0 (L3) — H3 (L4)	IF (e) L1, L2, L3 L1 CONTINUE H1 GO TO L4 L2 CONTINUE H2 GO TO L4 L3 CONTINUE H3 L4 CONTINUE		
	COMPUTED GO TO	(L1) — H1 L1 (L2) — H2 L2 I = : Ln (Ln) — Hn (L)	GO TO (L1, L2, ..., Ln), I L1 CONTINUE H1 GO TO L Ln CONTINUE Hn L CONTINUE	GO TO I; L1: H1; GO TO L; Ln: Hn; L:	GO TO L1, L2, ..., Ln DEPENDING ON I L1, H1. GO TO L. Ln, Hn L.

Figure 4.8 Problem Analysis Diagram (PAD) Comparison. Q̄ = negation of Q. O is written in the coding phase if necessary. (*Source*: Y. Futamura et al., "Development of Computer Programs by Problem Analysis Diagram [PAD] [Paper delivered at the Fifth IEEE International Conference on Software Engineering, San Diego, Calif., March 1981], p. 327. Copyright © 1981 IEEE. Reproduced with permission.)

Table 4.12 Software Engineering Work Bench (SEWB) Tool Configuration

SEWB Tool	Function
Analysis & Design	
SDF editor	Application design support with system design flow diagrams
SFD editor	System flow diagram (batch-job process) support
Screen/Form design	Design of screen form definition
Screen transition simulator	Simulation of screen transition for on-line applications
File/Record design	Design of file/record definitions and generation of record layout documents
Build & Test	
Source editor	Editing of source code
Decision table to COBOL source code generator	Decision-table definitions and generation of COBOL source code
COBOL source code to PAD generator	Generation of PAD charts from COBOL code
PAD editor	Program design support with PAD
PAD to COBOL source code generator	Generation of COBOL source code from PAD
COBOL source code execution tester	Unit testing of COBOL programs, with supported language specification limited to frequently used functions
COBOL PAD tester	COBOL program execution tests with PAD

PAD = Program Analysis Diagram; SDF = Structured Data Flow; SFD = System Flow Diagram.
Source: Hitachi Ltd., "Demonstration of SEWB and EAGLE2," unpublished company document, May 23, 1989.

processing from system design through testing; (2) construction of a central database for design specifications and program implementation, as well as for project management (tracking information from the standardized work sheets defined in the *SPDS* manual) and maintenance; (3) automated construction of new source programs from standardized patterns (also called "skeletons" or simply designs) and parts (executable, and thus coded, subroutines); and (4) automatic compilation of maintenance documentation.[74]

Program development with EAGLE followed the HIPACE methodology but emphasized the automatic generation of programs from reusable designs. In fact, Hitachi claimed that its personnel could develop 60 percent of the applications programs customers demanded from twenty-two patterns, all accessible in the EAGLE database, modified only slightly for individual customers.[75] Hitachi also provided its pattern library to customers along with the EAGLE tool package. In addition, EAGLE worked with PAD diagrams, making it possible to write new designs and combine these with existing modules retrieved from the parts database.[76]

Users of EAGLE first had to analyze data items and interrelationships and then catalog these in a data dictionary database. Next came registration of the system-design and program specifications in another database. At this point, EAGLE searched a central pattern and parts library for existing components the system might reuse. This made it possible to assemble some programs almost entirely from the library, although most programs written with the tool contained reused patterns and parts as well as new designs and routines. (Hitachi personnel found, however, that data modules were easier to use than processing algorithms, which tended to be more difficult to standardize.) EAGLE next generated an outline of the program from the detailed (module-level) specifications and then produced a source program. Programmers could then edit the source program to add particular functions wanted by individual users. Finally, EAGLE automatically generated test commands and carried them out in conversational Japanese (Figure 4.9).

Hitachi's efforts during 1984–1986 to refine EAGLE focused on making it more flexible for meeting the needs of both customers and software developers. First, Hitachi upgraded the conversational interface, allowing the system to handle PL/1 and CORAL (Customer-Oriented Application Program Development System—a Hitachi prototyping language for writing specifications in Japanese) in addition to COBOL. The new version of the tool also let customers design their own menus (within certain limits), rather than relying only on the ones Hitachi provided. With these improvements, Hitachi itself began using EAGLE to construct database and data-communications programs, in addition to common business-applications programs. Another modification made EAGLE accessible from the SEWB workbenches, which, by the late 1980s, had become the standard development environment for applications in Hitachi, rather than time-sharing terminals. Although EAGLE continued to require a mainframe computer to operate, Hitachi modified its systems so that SEWB workbenches could serve as terminals and access the EAGLE libraries and databases.

In terms of performance, according to Hitachi's internal audits, programs designed with EAGLE generally showed a 2.2-fold improvement in productivity (measured by lines of code per programmer or manpower costs in a given time period). As indicated in Table 4.13, EAGLE also shifted more effort into system design and substantially reduced time necessary for testing. For a hypothetical program taking a year to develop without EAGLE, this would mean a reduction in development time to 5.4 months, with testing being reduced from 4.8 to 1.4 months and program implementation from 4.8 to 1.9 months.

The Systems Design Works as well as Hitachi subsidiaries modified EAGLE and created specialized libraries to suit their particular needs. An illustration of this is Applicable Program Products (APP), a set of design-support libraries developed at FACOM-HITAC, Ltd., a subsidiary that refined the basic EAGLE system. As of 1987, APP libraries existed for banks (on-line banking, credit evaluation, customer information); broadcasters; hospitals (accounting); local governments (residents information, library information); finance (accounting); personnel man-

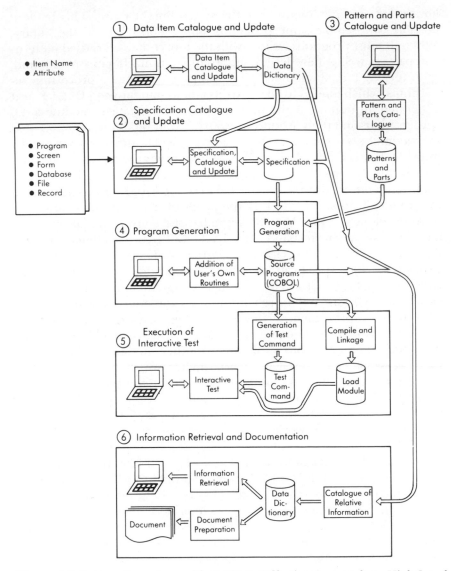

Figure 4.9 System Procedure with EAGLE (Effective Approach to High-Level Software Productivity). (*Source*: Hitachi Ltd., "System Development Support System EAGLE/SEWB," February 1989, p. 4. Copyright © 1989 Hitachi Ltd. Reproduced with permission.)

agement and payroll calculation; videotext; and computer-room operations and control. The Systems Design Works utilized similar libraries. Hitachi and it subsidiaries also combined EAGLE with design-support tools incorporating AI techniques to automate some of the systems-engineering tasks, such as documentation construction, data retrieval for

Table 4.13 EAGLE Productivity Comparison

	Without EAGLE		With EAGLE	
Development	100%	(12 mo)	45%	(5.4 mo)
System design	20	(2.4)	38	(2.1)
Program implementation	40	(4.8)	36	(1.9)
Test	40	(4.8)	26	(1.4)

EAGLE = Effective Approach to Achieving High-Level Software Productivity; mo = months.
Source: Hagi Yoichi et al., "Shisutemu kaihatsu shien sofutouea 'Eagle,'" [Integrated Software Development and Maintenance System 'EAGLE'], *Hitachi hyoron* 68, 5, May 1986, p. 34.

hardware and software configurations, and system simulation. The reported benefits of these advanced versions of EAGLE and supporting tools, according to development engineers, included not only reduced costs and shorter lead times, but also guarantees of at least "stable quality in operations."[77]

Centralized (and Tailored) Process R&D

For software process R&D—exploration, development, and refinement of new tools and methods—Hitachi relied both on a centralized laboratory, mainly but not exclusively for basic technology, and on engineering departments within its factories and major subsidiaries, for more applied technology. For example, CAPS, CASD, EAGLE, SEWB, and other tools were products not of a single facility but joint efforts by the Systems Development Laboratory, the Software Works, and the Omori Software Works/Systems Design Works.[78] This structure, common in other industries as a way of managing product and process R&D, allowed Hitachi to concentrate researchers and other resources in the hopes they would generate useful technologies the company could later make available to different projects, reducing redundancies that might exist if every software-development project independently produced its own tools and methods. On the other hand, as in systems design or programming, knowledge of particular applications or customers was probably as important in tool and method research as knowledge of software engineering. For this reason, Hitachi also allowed engineering departments within its factories and subsidiaries to participate or even lead in process research, with attempts by management to coordinate efforts throughout the Hitachi group, where possible.

Compared to other Japanese software producers, Hitachi made the earliest and largest commitment to a central facility dedicated to researching software-engineering tools and methods as well as various communications technologies. Its Systems Development Laboratory, created in 1973 as one of nine corporate laboratories, in 1989 had approximately 400 researchers in a main facility and another 400 people employed at subsidiaries. These researchers worked in three broad areas: systems development, systems software techniques, and computer software.[79] Table 4.14, which provides more specific examples of recent research efforts, illustrates the breath of topics, extending from still-experimental work on "fuzzy" control systems, neural networks, and knowledge processing (AI systems) to applied areas such as software-engineering workbenches and reuse technology (culminating in SEWB and EAGLE) as well as communications network standards.

Not all the tools and methods that came out of the Systems Development Laboratory proved to be acceptable to software developers in Hitachi factories, although laboratory managers appeared to focus most of their efforts on tools or techniques that development engineers needed. Hitachi followed two approaches to increase the applicability and acceptance of its R&D. First, the Systems Development Laboratory tended to operate in joint projects that combined researchers from the laboratory with engineers from factories and subsidiaries, and sometimes with other researchers from Hitachi's Central Research Laboratories. In this way, the mixed teams directly addressed concerns or suggestions from the operating divisions. Second, in the early 1980s, Hitachi established a Software Technology Promotion Center, within a corporate Production Engineering Department, specifically charged with promoting technology transfer from the laboratory and other Hitachi facilities to different divisions and subsidiaries.[80]

Summary and Evaluation

Because the state of software as a technology and as a business during the late 1960s and 1970s continued to evolve, creating a factory system for software development very much resembled an exercise in process and organizational innovation—with a great deal of trial and error. Hitachi managers made initial miscalculations, such as overestimating their ability to impose a components-control system and underestimating the need for tailored sets of standards, methods, and tools for basic as opposed to applications software. Nonetheless, the approaches they eventually adopted, following years of studying internal and industry practices, incorporated good concepts and tools for all phases of development and project management, enabling Hitachi to improve significantly in process and quality control as well as accumulate sufficient skills to become a major producer of computer hardware and software.

Perhaps most striking in Hitachi's history is the company's foresight and persistence. Managers sanctioned detailed studies of programmer performance and the development process in the mid-1960s, years before this became fashionable in the industry, and personnel painstakingly con-

Table 4.14 Major Research Areas at Systems Development Laboratory

Systems Planning Techniques
  Systems planning methodologies
  Autonomous decentralized systems
  Reliable design, operation, and control systems
  Fuzzy control systems
  Knowledge-based control systems
  Real-time decision-support systems
  Simulation techniques
Software Engineering
  Integrated software production system
  Workbench for software development
  Reusable software techniques
Communication Networks
  Satellite communcation systems
  Open systems interconnections (OSI)/Hitachi network architecture (HNA)
  Integrated services digital network (ISDN)-equivalent communcation techniques
  Network management/security techniques
  Local area networks (LAN)
Office Information Systems
  Work station/office production/terminal systems/document image processing (optical
    disk file/document system)
  Integrated office-automation software
  Decision support systems
Knowledge, Natural Language, and Image Processing
  Knowledge processing language/knowledge-system building tools
  Expert systems (control, business applications)
  Machine translation systems
  Japanese interface techniques
  Image processing (remote sensing, medical electron microscope)
  Neural networks
Basic Software and Design Automation
  Virtual machine systems
  Extended architectures
  Operating systems
  Databases (distributed, relational)
  High-level languages, compilers
  Design automation
  Superparallel computer systems

Source: Hitachi, Ltd., "Systems Development Laboratory," undated company brochure.

tinued to collect data on every project built. The result: an enormous and growing store of knowledge about software development and manpower requirements available to all Hitachi managers. Moreover, at a time when engineering and factory systems appeared far removed from craft practices dominating software, Hitachi's Software Works began building an organization that subjected all products to a uniform (and high) set of standards for process and quality control.

  Most of Hitachi's factory tools and methods evolved from structured design and programming concepts, and these still provided the foundation for its process technology in the late 1980s. In this sense, Hitachi's development technology seemed both effective and relatively old. Struc-

Table 4.15 Hitachi Summary

Concept	Implementation
Process improvement	Division-level management determination in the late 1960s to create a factorylike facility to centralize programmers. Initial focus on debugging basic software inherited from RCA and building large customized applications. Strong emphasis on process and quality control, influenced by company traditions and programs, such as for quality analysis and management improvement.
Product-process focus & segmentation	Product focus on IBM-like basic and applications software. Systems and applications first combined and then separated. Other facilities and subsidiaries handle miscellaneous or specialized software and provide regional service.
Process/quality analysis & control	Project data collection begun in mid-1960s. Methodology and performance standards first adopted in 1970. Use of control charts for quality as early as 1970. Emphasis on testing until all predicted defects are found. Use of data analysis and feedback from customers and developers to prevent new defects. Quality assurance and product release done by staff departments separate from project management.
Tailored/centralized process R&D	Process R&D first centered in the software factory and then done with a division laboratory. Major subsidiaries also develop tools and methods. Clear distinction made between tools, methods, standards, and training for basic as opposed to applications software. Historical emphasis on project management and quality control systems. Shifting emphasis to design support tools and integration of tools and management databases.
Skills standardization & leverage	Tendency to hire unskilled people and then train them with an extensive set of courses for new programmers and managers in the Hitachi approach, coordinated with career paths for systems and applications personnel to provide advancement. Specialization in application domains for designers, with implementation in separate departments. Basic software done in integrated teams.
Dynamic standardization	Performance standard times reevaluated annually. Gradual evolution of tools and methods, some of which were old but extremely well refined.
Systematic reusability	Components control a goal ca. 1970 but not successful, due to lack of product focus and other problems. More support in the 1980s through application-specific libraries of reusable designs and code, including packages, and computer-aided tools.
Computer-aided tools	Extensive tool support for all phases of development, wisely introduced after standardization of methodologies and integrated with methods and training. Initial focus on discrete project-management, design-support, and testing tools still not fully integrated. Current focus on integration of tools and databases through on-line workbenches for applications development.
Incremental product/ variety improvement	Product improvement historically seen mainly as reducing defects, both through inspection and better engineering (prevention), as well as lowering costs and lateness, and raising conformance to specifications. New tools allowing more time for design relative to coding.

Table 4.15 (*Continued*)

Concept	Implementation
Assessment	
Strategic management & integration	Factory initially established to centralize and standardize software product engineering according to corporate practices, as well as to improve productivity and product reliability. Gradual coordination of product focus with tailored methods, tools, and training that were mutually reinforcing. Long-term allocation of R&D to support the factory systems.
Scope economies	One factory handled or managed most unique and custom software development for the entire computer division from 1969–1985. Applications and systems separated in 1985. Huge scale of facilities and apparent scope economies through standardized or shared tools, methods, designs, personnel experience, and R&D. Subsidiaries and software houses closely coordinated.

tured flow charts provide an especially good example of a useful but, in the opinion of some, an outdated technique. On the other hand, Hitachi, and other Japanese firms, refined their structured diagrams as well as other basic tools and techniques to a remarkable degree, incorporating new design concepts and computer-aided tools that automatically generated code in a variety of languages and on customized menus or tables. Some of Hitachi's integrated tool and methodology systems, such as EAGLE and other ICAS technologies, were as advanced as any in the industry. Thus, Hitachi, and other Japanese software factories described in subsequent chapters, while not always using the latest tools and methods in the field, clearly stood near the forefront of software process technology. Most important, their organization and management systems insured that all projects and project members had access at least to proven tools and methods.

One problem Hitachi continued to face resulted from the independent evolution of its systems for design support and project management (CASD and CAPS). Hitachi had yet to link all the databases and tools associated with these and newer systems, even through the SEWB workbench. Nonetheless, it seemed likely Hitachi would make further progress in tool integration as well as in other areas of software engineering and management, such as design technology and reusability. Overall, as Table 4.15 summarizes, by the late 1970s Hitachi had clearly gone beyond SDC to create a comprehensive factory infrastructure for basic and applications software development. This built not only on current practice in software engineering but on historical, companywide traditions emphasizing the rigorous management of process and quality control in all product sectors and in both engineering and manufacturing operations.

5

TOSHIBA: LINKING PRODUCTIVITY AND REUSABILITY

Unlike Hitachi, the initiative within Toshiba to establish a factory for software development came not from a commercial computer division, which made a variety of basic software and customized business-applications programs, but from a division making large-scale, real-time industrial control systems with high reliability requirements, much like SDC produced. Unlike SDC, however, Toshiba wrote for Toshiba hardware, which facilitated tool and software portability; and Toshiba, at least initially, had more focused product lines. Toshiba also succeeded in introducing a delicate matrix organization that allowed systems engineers (called analysts in Toshiba) as well as the actual software designers and testers (but not necessarily the programmers who wrote code from designs) to specialize in particular applications areas, thus solving another difficulty SDC encountered in finding a balance between expertise in customer applications and in software engineering.

More focus in applications and hardware, in addition to a remarkably integrated set of tools, techniques, management procedures, controls, incentives, and training programs, facilitated Toshiba's efforts to systematize reusability of designs, code, specifications, and other elements, which it did probably as much or more than any other software facility in the world. Not all its product departments utilized available process technology to the same degree, reflecting the need to tailor practices to different application domains. Nonetheless, Toshiba's factory of 2,300 personnel in the mid-1980s delivered systems containing, on average, nearly 50 percent reused code. This degree of reuse, along with a supporting technical infrastructure and organization, helped Toshiba achieve high levels of productivity and quality simultaneously, despite building sophisticated customized software with many relatively unskilled employees. Furthermore, Toshiba management claimed that the factory infrastructure in place by the late 1970s allowed it to build huge plant-control systems unprecedented, at least in Japan, in their size and degree of automation.

Information remained scarce on customer satisfaction, since Toshiba mainly sold embedded software and not separate programs. Nonetheless, Toshiba appeared to offer an effective combination of product features and low prices. The *Nikkei Computer* surveys of the Japanese market indicated that Toshiba provided both the most systems-engineering services free of charge and the lowest average prices for these services (Tables 1.13 and 1.14). In addition, a sister facility to its software factory that used a version of the factory tools and methods for office-computer systems ranked above other Japanese producers and the same or higher than U.S.-based firms in Japan in areas such as system-configuration support, problem solving, technical support for software development and communications, defect repair, and application-system development methodology (Tables C.5 and C.6).

The Corporate Setting

Company Origins and Products

Toshiba's origins date back to the establishment of two firms: one set up in 1875 to manufacture telegraph equipment and another founded in 1890 to produce incandescent lamps. By the time these two enterprises merged in 1939, they had expanded, respectively, into heavy electrical equipment and consumer appliances. Between the 1950s and 1970s, Toshiba diversified further into commercial and industrial-oriented computers, including software, as well as a variety of related products and components such as semiconductors. In 1987 it was Japan's second-largest electrical equipment and appliance manufacturer, with nearly 71,000 employees (121,000, including subsidiaries) and worldwide sales of $17 billion (nearly $23 billion, including subsidiaries) divided among data-communications systems and electronic devices (46 percent of unconsolidated sales), heavy machinery (26 percent), and consumer electronics (28 percent).[1] Toshiba organized these products into ten operating groups, with support from numerous staff and divisional departments and laboratories (Figure 5.1).

Toshiba competed during the 1960s and 1970s as a comprehensive

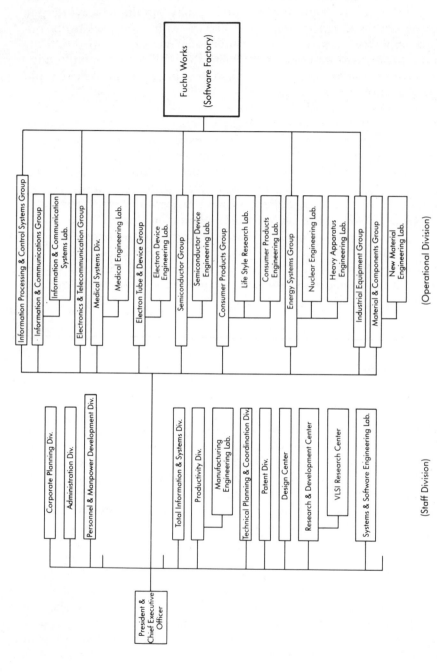

Figure 5.1 Toshiba Management Organization, 1987. VLSI = very large-scale integration. (*Sources*: Toshiba Corporation, "Toshiba Systems and Software Engineering Laboratory," company publication, 1987, p. 1; Toshiba Corporation, "Toshiba Fuchu Works," 1987, p. 5.)

manufacturer of hardware and software for computers of various sizes, based on designs licensed from GE. Following GE's exit from the computer industry in 1970, Toshiba withdrew from mainframes in 1978 and sold this business to NEC, with which it had developed some machines in the 1970s. Toshiba maintained a large business in minicomputers, however, used primarily for control applications, and by the 1980s had built a position as Japan's leading producer in this segment of the industry. Toshiba also became, in the 1980s, a major producer of lap-top and office computers, and among Japan's domestic computer manufacturers in the mid-1980s ranked fourth in information-systems revenues, behind Fujitsu, NEC, and Hitachi.[2]

Evidence of the importance of software for Toshiba can be seen in that more than one out of seven employees in 1987, or approximately 11,000, were involved in software development. The largest concentration appeared in a single facility within the Industrial Equipment Group, the Fuchu Works, which produced a variety of heavy industrial machinery and control systems, many requiring large-scale, complex software. To meet these programming needs, the Fuchu Works organized a software factory in 1977 that grew to 2,300 personnel by the mid-1980s, including employees assigned from approximately eight subsidiaries as well as from independent subcontractors. The Fuchu Works also employed 1,000 engineers producing microcomputer software. Other software development within Toshiba occurred at six smaller factories, in various information systems areas throughout the corporation, and in a series of R&D laboratories (see Figure 5.1 and Table 5.1).

Origins of the Factory Strategy and Structure

Toshiba's decision to establish a software factory stemmed from rapid increases in actual and projected demand, beginning around 1975, for industrial control systems relying on a new generation of relatively inex-

Table 5.1 Toshiba Software Facilities

Facility	Main Software Product Area
Fuchu	Real-time industrial applications
Ome	Office automation
Hino	Telecommunications
Komukai	Defense systems (radar, satellites)
Yanagimachi	Automatic dispensing machines (banks, railway tickets)
Nasu	Medical systems
Isogo	Nuclear energy equipment

Source: Yoshihiro Matsumoto interview, Sept. 4, 1987.

pensive minicomputers. Prior to the mid-1960s, Toshiba had "hard-wired" controls with electromagnetic relays that did not involve programming. The introduction of transistors in the mid-1960s started the transition to programmable controls, although not until Toshiba introduced a new microprocessor-based control computer in 1974 did management begin to view its shortage of software engineers as a true crisis in the making.[3]

Typical of the changing demands Toshiba faced as sales of its control minicomputers increased were orders from Japanese power-utility companies to develop automated thermal-power generating stations. These used enormous and growing amounts of software; the typical power-generation control system increased from a few hundred thousand lines of code in the mid-1970s to two million by the early 1980s, necessitating years of development and hundreds of new programmers. Furthermore, to achieve safe and untended operation, the hardware and software for these and many other control systems had to be nearly free of defects or at least highly tolerant of system faults.[4]

As at SDC and Hitachi, large, centralized software factories remained uncommon in the mid-1970s and depended on the enthusiasm of a few managers willing to champion the concept. The individual who headed the research effort behind Toshiba's software factory, Yoshihiro Matsumoto, was one of the few people in the company (and in Japan) to have accumulated significant expertise in real-time computer systems. A graduate of the Electrical Engineering Department of the University of Tokyo (he also received a doctorate from the same department in 1974), Matsumoto had entered Toshiba in 1954 and specialized in process-control system design, initially for power utilities. He also learned much about control computers from frequent visits to GE facilities in the 1960s. He became increasingly interested in software engineering and, in the 1970s, headed efforts in this area at the Fuchu Works.

The specific impetus for the factory came from a market study Matsumoto completed in 1975 that projected large increases in software demand and system size. This convinced him and other managers that Toshiba had to achieve substantial improvements in programmer productivity and product reliability to meet the needs of its industrial-equipment business. A software factory emphasizing reuse and automation seemed plausible after he read about SDC's efforts as well as AT&T's Programmers' Workbench (PWB) system, a set of tools for assisting in software development relying on functions offered by the UNIX operating system. The name and architecture of the tools Matsumoto's group set out to build, dubbed the "SWB" (Software Workbench), Matsumoto patterned directly after the AT&T system.[5] Toshiba also added a UNIX interface to its operating system for industrial computers, making it possible to use tools or applications software written for UNIX on Toshiba machines.

To improve both process efficiency and product reliability, Matsumoto introduced four policies for all projects except those that were completely new in content. These he borrowed from concepts or practices used to manage engineering and manufacturing in other industries. The first policy was to standardize the development process, rather than allowing project personnel to design products in any manner they pleased as long as products met specifications. Matsumoto's thoughts on this can be seen in a 1987 article, where he stated that the primary objective of a software factory should be to offer "an environment which allows software manufacturing organizations to design, program, test, ship, install, and maintain commercial software products in a unified manner . . . [and] attain specified quality and productivity levels."[6]

The second policy was to reuse standardized inputs (code as well as designs, documentation, and test cases), rather than producing programs from scratch with each order. It was systematic reusability that, to Matsumoto, most distinguished "factory production" from traditional software programming. Matsumoto openly advertised this strategy, such as in a 1984 article where he insisted a factory should have a strategic commitment, supported by tools, methods, and an entire organization, to producing software by reusing as many existing components as possible: "Software production is distinct from software development in that production management is directed toward the use of existing software and enforces the idea that designers should build new software from existing codes."[7]

The third policy was to create standardized and integrated tools and methods to raise the average level of worker performance. The notion that standardization and economies of scale might compensate for uneven worker skills or reduce the need for highly skilled employees was essential to investments in factories in other industries since the industrial revolution began. Similar efforts based more on economies of scope and aimed at improving the performance of workers with average skills were apparent even in product engineering and small-scale production operations such as machine tools, where a variety of methods and tools, including Computer-Aided Design and Manufacturing (CAD/CAM) systems, in a sense served to "capture" the expertise of a few individuals and facilitate required activities to raise productivity, shorten lead times, and improve quality simultaneously. Matsumoto stated in a 1986 article that the objective of the software factory's tool set was precisely one of "leveling off the engineers' ability"—assisting the average programmer to design higher quality products more easily. "The path from requirements definition to conceptual design primarily requires the intellectual ability of the engineer. Supporting this part is believed to produce the greatest achievements in quality improvement by leveling off the engineers' ability. Support for this part, however, was considered technically difficult. Fortunately, the recent progress in work stations and knowledge engineering helped to solve this problem. As a result . . . support elements are added to the SWB system."[8]

A fourth policy was to provide continual training for new employees as well as hold personnel reviews and plan for individual career advancement. This approach, to Matsumoto, merely recognized that software development constituted a process requiring extensive human involvement and investment in people, to improve their skills and reduce mistakes, as he noted in a 1984 article: "[H]uman factors in software management are becoming increasingly important; therefore human-oriented reviews and inspections are being applied to increase software reliability."[9]

According to Matsumoto, Toshiba managers and customers perceived different but complementary benefits in the factory approach. Customers were extremely sensitive to software failures, and therefore found the factory attractive for potential improvements in product reliability. The factory thus served Toshiba as a tool for product marketing as well as production management, similar to how SDC managers had wanted to use their factory. Matsumoto made this observation in a 1981 article, where he asserted that, since his main customers wanted real-time systems for facilities such as nuclear power plants, electric utilities networks, chemical-processing factories, air terminals, and steel-rolling mills, major breakdowns could be "disastrous," making it imperative for Toshiba to have a software capability that maximized product reliability.[10]

The potential productivity benefits of the factory were less obvious to customers, because the total system price (hardware and software) Toshiba quoted usually did not include an estimate of software as a separate item. This situation remained common in Japan—software bundled with hardware, especially in custom applications—making software development a cost to an integrated hardware-software system, rather than a source of direct profit. Accordingly, Toshiba operated the factory—its staff, equipment, and facilities—as a "cost center," with projects responsible for expenses but not an added margin for the factory. Toshiba then measured final profits at the project level, as well as at the product department and division levels.[11] The profitability of a project and product department, however, often depended on how efficiently they managed software development. Thus the factory's potential for higher software productivity, such as through better programming techniques, tools, quality control, and maintenance, in addition to reuse of code or designs, appeared to Matsumoto the most important reason why Toshiba's top management supported his efforts even when the software factory remained a very tenuous concept in the mid-1970s.

Factory Organization and Management Systems

Toshiba pursued its factory much in the same manner as SDC, starting with an R&D project in 1976. Unlike SDC's first efforts, however,

Toshiba did not concentrate solely on tools, even though they formed a key part of the infrastructure for the factory system. Toshiba attempted to integrate tools with methods or procedures for project management, cost control, productivity management, quality assurance, design review and inspection, reuse support, standardization, documentation, and training and career development (Table 5.2). Although software factories at Hitachi, NEC, and Fujitsu contained similar elements, Toshiba appeared to place more emphasis on productivity through reusability, and managed through a particularly intricate system of product departments, independent projects, functional staff at several organizational levels, and, of course, the factory infrastructure of tools, methods, libraries, and databases, used by software personnel.

The physical structure of the software factory as of 1989 consisted of four interconnected buildings housing individual and group work areas, an SWB service center, a documentation service center, a file storage room, lounges, and facilities for testing completed software with hardware. Each work area came with an SWB terminal or a Toshiba lap-top computer serving as a work station and terminal connected to central databases and libraries as well as a hard-copy printer. The factory had approximately one terminal or work station for every three software developers, a low number compared to many U.S. firms but up from one per four employees in 1987 and comparable to Hitachi, Fujitsu, and NEC.[12] (Japanese software developers still wrote basic outlines of systems and many reports by hand, creating the situation where every em-

Table 5.2 Elements of the Toshiba Software Factory

Combined Tool, Methodology, and Management Systems
  Project progress management system
  Cost management system
  Productivity management system
  Quality assurance system with standardized quality metrics
  Standardized, baseline management system for design review,
    inspection and configuration management
  Software tools, user interfaces and tool maintenance facilities
  Existing software library and maintenance support
  Technical data library
  Standardized technical methodologies and disciplines
  Documentation support system

Personnel Systems
  Quality circle activities
  Education programs
  Career development system

Physical Infrastructure
  Specially designed work spaces

Source: Yoshihiro Matsumoto, "A Software Factory: An Overall Approach to Software Production," in Peter Freeman (ed.), *Tutorial: Software Reusability* (Washington, D.C.: IEEE Computer Society Press, 1987), p. 155.

ployee did not need to use a computer all the time, although Toshiba managers recognized that more computers might improve productivity further and were introducing more gradually.)

Engineering Matrix Management

Perhaps the most delicate feature of the Toshiba Software Factory was its organizational structure, a matrix imposed over product departments from several operating groups and divisions, all located in the Fuchu Works. Toshiba referred to vertically linked staff activities as its "product engineering system," horizontally linked industrial-sector activities as its "production engineering system," and the overall arrangement as "engineering matrix management."[13]

Established in 1940 and set on 198 acres in the western outskirts of Tokyo, the Fuchu Works in 1987 had 7,500 employees working primarily in four areas: Information Processing and Control Systems, Energy Systems, Industrial Equipment, and Semiconductors (Printed Circuit Board Division) (see Figure 5.1).[14] Operating departments within the divisions corresponded roughly to nineteen product lines (Table 5.3). Each department contained sections for hardware and software design as well as for manufacturing (in the case of software, detailed design, coding, and module test), testing, quality assurance, and product control. Approximately half the Fuchu Works' employees were software developers, with a third working in the software factory at any given time, assigned from product departments for particular projects.[15]

The recognition that some application areas required specialized systems analysis and design skills, and that all departments could benefit from sharing scarce software-development resources, led to the adoption of this organization. Alternative structures would have been to carry out software development in each product department, or to establish one centralized factory with a permanent staff. SDC attempted the latter but, as discussed in Chapter 3, experienced a reluctance on the part of project managers to hand over designs to a centralized facility. Toshiba, as well as Hitachi and Fujitsu, introduced modified versions of this matrix arrangement, sharing design and coding expertise across different projects while allowing systems analysts to specialize in applications and limiting most of a facility's programming activities to a related product family. Toshiba, however, remained the only Japanese software factory existing as a matrix imposed over product departments that built both software and hardware components.

Following the matrix structure, Toshiba had no single manager of its software factory, although the facility contained a permanent staff spread over five sections. Four provided administrative support for software production, relying on systems analysts as well as programming and testing personnel from product departments. The fifth maintained

Table 5.3 Major Divisions and Products of the Fuchu Works

Information Processing and Control Systems Division
    Information systems for public facilities
    Industrial automation systems
    Industrial-use computers
    Information-processing and control systems equipment

Energy Systems Division
    Digital control systems for power generating stations
    Automated power supply and distribution systems
    Computer-aided business operations systems for electric
      power utilities
    Control equipment for power plants
    Electronics equipment for power transmission systems
    Protection equipment for electric power systems
    Advanced technology-applied power systems

Industrial Equipment Division
    Switch gear
    Factory automation components
    Power electronics equipment
    Mechatronics equipment
    Elevators/escalators
    Rolling stock systems
    Transportation/carrying systems
    Electronic modules

Printed Wiring Boards Division
    Printed wiring boards
    High-density hybrid functional circuits

Source: Toshiba Corporation, "Toshiba Fuchu Works," 1987, p. 5.

the SWB tools, helped R&D teams develop new tools, and operated the SWB Service Center, the file-storage room, and other related SWB facilities. It also coordinated software quality assurance plans for the entire factory and provided assistance to keep these plans on track, in addition to collecting data to evaluate productivity and software reliability.

Compared to the total number of personnel in the factory, the amount of staff appeared small. Functional departments generally had twelve or twenty-four people. The group responsible for maintenance of the factory environment had merely twenty, while tool development involved fifteen to twenty engineers. The latter were included in the factory personnel numbers but functioned as part of the Fuchu Works's R&D staff, located in the Heavy Apparatus Engineering Laboratory. The Fuchu Works' also had an Engineering Administration and Information Systems Department that provided staff-level guidance to the groups from different applications departments on methods development, equipment, and programming technique, as well as staff departments for customer-site installation, customer claims, and overall quality assurance and control.

Project managers came from product departments; unlike systems analysts and other software development personnel, the factory employee totals did not include them. Systems analysts worked directly with customers (mainly at the customers' locations) to define requirements and basic designs. Toshiba management encouraged them, as well as designers, to specialize in industry-specific applications and did not move them among different product departments. The analysts usually visited the factory several times a week during the building of a system and handed specifications as they completed them to designers in the factory, who then passed on detailed designs to programmers for module coding and testing. The designers and programmers worked both in the factory buildings and sometimes at customer sites, depending on the project and the particular tasks. Toshiba also assigned personnel to customer sites, such as for long-term maintenance, where they used a version of the SWB tool set for distributed operations, tying into the factory databases and libraries through telephone lines.

In contrast to the systems analysts and designers, Toshiba treated programmers as a nonspecialized resource and, particularly during their first three years in the factory, might move them around to different projects as needed; this appeared possible without extensive retraining because of the standardization of methods and tools. Toshiba also, on occasion, transferred programmers from plants in other divisions that experienced decreases in sales. For example, while the software factory in 1987 operated at 100 percent capacity for power-systems development (that is, all the designers and programmers from this area, which accounted for approximately 60 percent of the factory's revenues and personnel, were busy all the time), other areas, such as for nuclear power stations, railway systems, and factory automation, were not as busy, so Toshiba managers drew on these for software manpower.

Production Management

The systems Toshiba sold to customers from the Fuchu Works usually included computer and peripherals hardware, the applications software (including fully customized and packaged programs), software utilities (such as database management systems, user interfaces, or input/output interfaces), as well as an operating system and language compilers, as needed. Hardware sections in the product departments made the minicomputers, which, in the mid-1980s, contained from 4 to 32 megabytes of main memory and operated at speeds of 5.6 to 16 million instructions per second (mips). Software sections made the applications programs as well as the systems software, using the facilities of the software factory.

Individual software systems were huge. The average applications program consisted of about 4 million equivalent-assembler source lines (EASL) of code; the range was 1 to 21 million EASL. Projects (including hardware and software components) generally took three years to complete. Four or five systems analysts normally did high-level design and worked full-time on one project until completion. Another ten to fifteen engineers did detailed design, while seventy to eighty programmers completed the coding and debugging.[16]

To divide and then coordinate the activities of so many people over such long periods of time, Toshiba broke down the software production process into distinct phases, following a life-cycle model common to both hardware and software products—requirements specification and design, manufacturing, testing, installation and alignment, and maintenance. Prescribed procedures and specific tools from the SWB system provided support for each phase, as listed in Table 5.4. Since the software accompanied hardware systems produced in parallel at the Fuchu Works, Toshiba tended to conceptualize and manage the development cycles of the two components—hardware and software—in similar ways (Figure 5.2). This appeared to work well for applications programs Toshiba had made before, so that design, programming, and testing

Table 5.4 Software Development Phases and Tool Support

Requirements Specification and Design Phase
1. Definition of user requirements and preparation of functional diagrams and documentation describing module and data structures, with support from SWB-III (design support tool); definition of requirements for computer hardware and peripherals

Software Manufacturing Phase
2. Application to the SWB service center for an SWB file assignment, used to build the actual program
3. Inputing of data or program components through SWB-I (programming-support tool) terminals
4. Assembly or compilation of the program using SWB-I; correction of errors using the workbench editor

Software Testing Phase
5. Down-loading of object code into the target computer through the SWB terminal
6. Use of the simulation language, setting up of a test scenario and pseudo real-world conditions
7. Use of SWB-II (testing support tool) to start test execution. Correction of errors by moving back to step 3; quality assurance procedures executed using SWB-Q (quality assurance tool)
8. Delivery of system to user

System Installation and Alignment Phase
9. At the customer site, modification of programs, if necessary, using portable workbenches accessing the central SWB system through telephone lines

Maintenance Phase
10. Maintenance of customer software, using SWB-IV (program maintenance tool)

SWB = software workbench.
Sources: Yoshihiro Matsumoto et al., "SWB System. A Software Factory," in Horst Hunke (ed.), *Software Engineering Environments* (Amsterdam: North Holland, 1981), p. 315, and "Management of Industrial Software Production," *Computer*, February 1984, p. 60.

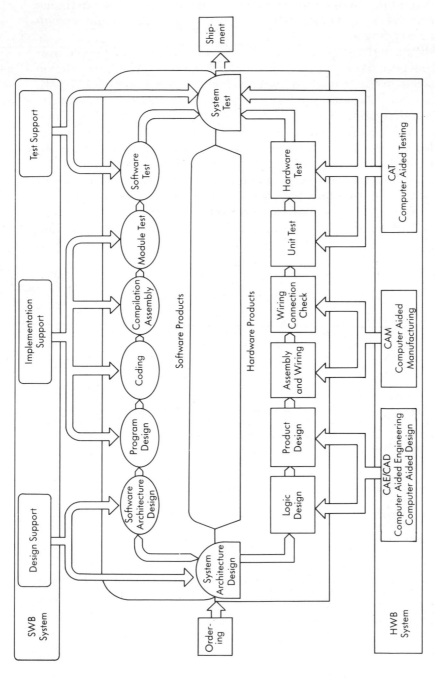

Figure 5.2 System Products Development. HWB = hardware workbench; SWB = software workbench. (*Source:* Yoshihiro Matsumoto and S. Yamamoto, "The SWB System Supports Industrial Software Production," *Proceedings of the International Workshop on Software Engineering Environments* [Beijing, China: China Academic Publishers, August 18–20, 1986], p. 79.)

could proceed more or less according to a predictable schedule, in tandem with hardware design, assembly, and testing.

Matsumoto thus claimed that the software factory served Toshiba as a device to make sure software products flowed through a standardized development process: "Each project . . . follows the same disciplines and management procedures of the software factory once it becomes part of the factory." The only exceptions were for totally new projects—types of software done for the first time, such as manufacturing automation programs in the late 1970s. Rather than putting them through the normal factory work flow, Toshiba organized separate projects on more of a job-shop basis. Work of this type—done in off-line projects outside the factory—comprised from 10 percent to 20 percent of orders in any given year.[17] If demand for a new product became large enough, then Toshiba created another department in the Fuchu Works and moved software development to the standard process, tailored, as necessary, to the particular application.

Factories in other industries, as opposed to job shops that combined design and production operations, generally had manufacturing departments that made products designed in separate engineering departments, using blueprints or specifications of some kind to transfer design ideas into material objects. As seen at SDC, separating design from program construction could prove extremely difficult or even impossible in situations with imprecise or totally new requirements and necessitating direct dialogue between customers and systems analysts (who wrote down the requirements) and between analysts and the designers and programmers (who turned the written specifications into detailed designs and then code). While a job-shop approach might ease this transformation by having the same individuals handle requirements and coding, Japanese applications software factories tended to enforce a division of labor. Hitachi managed this by combining systems engineers (including designers) and programmers in the same factory, allowing the former to specialize in particular areas. Toshiba operated differently from Hitachi in that the Fuchu Works consisted of integrated hardware and software product departments (which facilitated integration as well as area specialization by industry or application) containing analysts, designers, and programmers, with software developers resident in the software factory (to facilitate functional specialization in software engineering and have access to the tools and methods of the factory). Having analysts, designers, and programmers in the same departments also encouraged communication between the different groups, although Toshiba relied on a highly formalized process for requirements specifications and design, which it broke down into two parts.

Part I included the customer's specific objectives as well as constraints such as cost and time, and particular methodologies the customer wanted Toshiba to follow. Systems analysts drew up these system designs.

Part II, a more precisely structured document done after analysis of the Part I requirements, outlined the overall functions of the program and simulated its operation to generate performance parameters that Toshiba used to negotiate prices and other contract elements with the customer. Designers already assigned to the project and physically located in the software factory drew up these Part II specifications. On some occasions, such as when they did not want to share too much proprietary knowledge with Toshiba, customers wrote their own Part I specifications and then the software factory turned these into code.

Matsumoto provided an example of program development in a 1984 article describing the design and coding of control software for part of a steel-rolling mill.[18] The requirements stage, which he referred to as the first level of abstraction, defined a model of what the mill was supposed to accomplish. In one set of operations, four roller tables, holding iron slabs or ingots, moved the slabs from one side to another, while a roller squeezed them to produce sheets of steel plate (Figure 5.3). To write the specifications, systems analysts used a graphic grammar resembling a commercial product, SADT, made and copyrighted by a U.S. company,

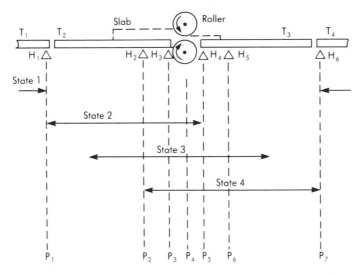

Figure 5.3 Steel-rolling mill model with four roller tables (T_1 through T_4) and one roller, hot metal detectors (H_1 through H_6), which close contact when a hot slab approaches, load cell (LC), which closes contact when the slab is under the roller, seven processes (P_1 through P_7). Not shown is a manual switch (STP) which closes contact when depressed by the operator. The four program STATEs in this model are (1) no slab; (2) slab approaching roller; (3) slab between rollers; and (4) steel plate leaving rollers. (*Source*: Yoshihiro Matsumoto, "Management of Industrial Software Production," *Computer*, February 1984, p. 62. Copyright © 1984 IEEE. Reproduced with permission.)

Softech. This had an interface section and a body section. Figure 5.4 shows what a portion of this specification might look like. The full specification would include a requirements model diagram and contain information on constraints, the static, dynamic, and kinetic behavior of the external objects, and other data. Even at this early point in development, Toshiba procedures called for requirements written in a capsulated for-

```
01   Requirements description for MILL-SPEED-CONTROL IS
02   with
03   object: SLAB: EXTERNAL __ ENTITY:
         A pair of iron to be rolled by the mill
04   object: ROLLER: EXTERNAL __ ENTITY:
         A pair of rolls rotating uni-directionally
05   object: TABLE 1, TABLE 2, TABLE 4:
         EXTERNAL __ ENTITY:
         —Moving tables to convey slabs. Tables are
         —located on both sides of the roller
         —numbered in the order of 1..4 from left to
         —right. TABLE 1 and TABLE 2 exist in the left.
06   object: P1, P2, P3, P4, P5, P6, P7: EXTERNAL __ ENTITY:
         __Check points positioned along the lines.
07   Object: PROCESS __ INPUT __ CONTROLLER: INPUT
         __ INTERFACE:
08   object: MILL __ SPEED __ CONTROLLER:
09   Object: REAL __ TIME __ KEEPER: INPUT __ INTERFACE:
10   end with:
11   requirement MILL-SPEED-CONTROL is
12   interface relationship is
13   triggered by REAL __ TIME __ KEEPER
         with REAL __ TIME __ INTERVAL: event
14   —use PROCESS __ INPUT __ CONTROLLER
         to GET (SENSOR __ VALUE: MILL __ DATA):
15   -type MILL __ DATA is
         record
         H1, H2, H3: analog:
         LC: digital:
         H4, H5, H6: analog:
         STP: digital:
         end record:
         end type:
16   acknowledge MILL __ SPEED __ CONTROLLER
         with READY: event:
17   used by MILL __ SPEED __ CONTROLLER which wishes
         to OBTAIN (MILL __ SPEED: SPEED __ DATA):
         type SPEED __ DATA is;
         (IDLE, LOW, HIGHS):
         end type:
18   end interface relationship.
```

Figure 5.4 Requirements Description Example. (*Source*: Matsumoto, "Management of Industrial Software Production," p. 62.)

mat specifically to simplify reuse of the modules and to facilitate understanding of how a module related to other parts of the program. The
interface section defined these relationships.

The second level of abstraction, data/function design, used a specification language consisting of graphic diagrams to define the user requirements more precisely in terms of data structures, functions, dataflows,
and control flows. This step also allowed designers to view the control
and data flows on one sheet of paper. Each of the functions shown in the
example in Figure 5.5 can be refined further with subsidiary data-
function diagrams. Figure 5.6 shows part of the documentation specifying data, function, and control for the function "INPUT_HANDLER."
Matsumoto described the design process based on a simplified model of
how the mill operated:

> The mill-control system software synchronizes the operation speeds of the
> four roller tables and the roller in the following way: the program remains
> in state 1 (no slab) and stays there until input I2 (slab transferred from table
> 1 [T1] to table 2 [T2]). The program continues in state 2 (slab approaching
> roller) during inputs I3, I4, and I5. When the slab passes between the roller
> and the load cell [LC] . . . a transition occurs, and the program is trans-
> ferred into state 3 (slab under roller). The program continues in state 3 until
> the slab is transferred from table 2 (T2) to table 3 (T3) and is then trans-
> ferred into state 4 (steel plate leaving roller). No transitions occur until the
> steel plate is completely off table 4 (T4). The system then returns to state 1

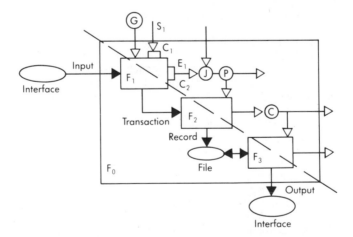

Figure 5.5 Data Functional Diagram. C = conditional select; G = generate control periodic; J = join; p = parallel begin (fork); *open arrows* = control; *solid
arrows* = data (input, output, record, transaction); *squares* = function; *ovals* =
data set (interface, file); *circles* = control node. (*Source*: Matsumoto, "Management of Industrial Software Production," p. 63. Copyright © 1984 IEEE. Reproduced with permission.)

```
data/function description for INPUT __ HANDLER is
with object: PROCESS __ INPUT __ DRIVER: INTERFACE __
FUNCTION:
object: SPEED __ SELECTION: FUNCTION:
     —select mill speed using NEW __ INPUT
     —generated by INPUT __ HANDLER.
Object: ERROR __ HANDLER: FUNCTION
Object: ALARM __ HANDLER: FUNCTION:
end with:

data/function for INPUT __ HANDLER is
interface relationship is
activated by REAL __ TIME __ KEEPER
with REAL __ TIME INTERVAL: SIGNAL:
converse with PROCESS __ INPUT __ DRIVER
to READ (H(1), H(2), H(3), H(4), H(5), H(6):analog).
     to READ (LC, STP: digital):
call ERROR __ HANDLER to EHANDLE (ERROR:integer):
call ALARM __ HANDLER to AHANDLE (ALARM:integer):
activate SPEED __ SELECTION
with READY (NEW __ INPUT:FRAME): SIGNAL:
     type IN is
     (h(1), h(2), h(3), 1c, h(4), h(5), h(6), stp):end:
     type FRAME is array (IN) of boolean:
end interface relationship:
```

Figure 5.6 Data/Function Description Example. (*Source*: Matsumoto, "Management of Industrial Software Production," pp. 63–64.)

(no slab). . . . The requirement of MILL_SPEED_CONTROL_ is transformed into seven functions: (1) PROCESS_INPUT_DRIVER, (2) INPUT_HANDLER, (3) SPEED_SELECTION, (4) SPEED_CONTROL, (5) ERROR_HANDLER, (6) ALARM_HANDLER, and (7) PROCESS_OUTPUT_DRIVER.[19]

The third level of abstraction transformed the data-functional diagrams into an actual program, following three steps: (1) planning of the large program structure, resulting from (a) determination of tasks, (b) determination of packages and subprograms, and (c) identification of data structures; (2) writing of package specifications; and (3) design of the internal structure of packages and data structures. What Matsumoto referred to as "packages" were subprograms completing a particular set of tasks or functions, such as speed control for the mill's rollers. Figure 5.7 contains an example of the main features of this type of package, with Ada used to describe the program structure. Toshiba also required designers to map out the interrelationships among modules in different levels of the program, as defined in the speed control example, and compare the final code with documentation from the early development phases. This insured that the documentation was complete.

```
package MILL __ SPEED __ CONTROL is
    type IN is (H1, H2, H3, LC, H4, H5, H6, STP):
    type FRAME is array (IN) of boolean:
    type SPEED is (IDLE, LOW, HIGH):
    task INPUT __ HANDLER is
    entry REAL __ TIME __ INTERVAL:
    end:
    task SPEED __ SELECTION is

    entry CALC __ SPEED (NEW __ INPUT:FRAME):
    end:
    task SPEED __ CONTROL is
    entry SET __ SPEED(MILL __ SPEED:SPEED):
    end:
    end MILL __ SPEED . . CONTROL:

package body MILL __ SPEED __ CONTROL is
    task body INPUT __ HANDLER is
    NEW __ INPUT:FRAME:

end INPUT __ HANDLER:
```

Figure 5.7 Program Design Package Example. (*Source*: Matsumoto, "Management of Industrial Software Production," pp. 64–65.)

Matsumoto characterized the approach to production management that accompanied this development process as "look-forward." Before Toshiba opened the factory in 1977, managers were able to attempt corrective actions regarding project schedules or expenditures only if (and after) they asked for reports on specific items. The factory, in contrast, introduced general procedures that each project had to follow, constituting a series of daily and weekly reports that made it possible to act while a project was still in progress.

First, managers settled on a schedule and target cost at the start of a project. Then at the beginning of each development phase, they divided the project activities into unit workloads, with each unit consisting of tasks that one person could complete in one or two months. At these times, managers also defined target costs (and reusability goals) for each unit workload, derived from the total estimate. Specific planning followed the definition of each unit workload, covering who would be responsible for each unit workload, how many specification sheets or source lines should be completed, what the cost or hours might total, and how much software should be reused. Toshiba managers also adjusted these estimates according to the skill or experience levels of the personnel available and the difficulty of the software being developed (on a subjective five-point scale). While projects were underway, a database tool tracked the status of each project and expenditures, based on information each person in charge of a unit workload entered daily or weekly through the workbench terminals. The system also displayed deviations between current status and targets, as well as sent printed reports (called unit workload order sheets or UWOS) to each individual with an assignment.

Controlling projects mainly through definition of small unit workloads (as did Hitachi and other software factories, as well as IBM[20]) came out of Toshiba's experience that project management focusing mainly on a single large budget for the entire effort made it difficult to identify and reduce potential cost overruns. Managers also claimed that Toshiba's target-cost and unit-workload system (also called SofPit, for Software Profit Improvement Tactics) helped the Fuchu Works reverse a history of losses on software development and maintain profit margins on projects of about 4 percent; for example, approximately half the projects in one major department met their cost targets in 1988–1989, with the remainder two or even three times over budget in the worst cases. Cost overruns came primarily from overtime (135 percent of regular pay) to complete projects. In terms of scheduling, however, only about 2 percent or 3 percent of projects came in beyond the scheduled completion time, with the worst projects about 10 percent late.[21] In addition to using overtime to complete projects within the schedule, Matsumoto (similar to Hitachi managers) claimed the factory system made it possible for Toshiba to add people in the programming and testing phases to speed up progress on projects running late. Adding manpower at the design level, however, did not reduce lateness, because of the difficulty involved in dividing design tasks among more than a few people.[22]

Productivity and Cost Accounting

Similar to factories in other industries, Toshiba managers considered better productivity and cost control to be major benefits of the factory process, and they believed that these required systematic efforts at collecting and analyzing data on project performance. Initially, Toshiba tracked productivity as well as demand for new programs to determine how much and how fast to expand the size of the software factory. Over time, accurate measurements, as long as they did not require too much administrative overhead to compile, allowed managers and engineers to study the factory's operations and identify areas for improvement.[23]

Attaining consistent measurements proved to be a major problem for many software producers, including Toshiba, because programmers wrote programs of varying degrees of complexity in a variety of languages, making productivity or quality comparisons difficult. In addition to the expansion in the size and variety of software coming from Toshiba, in the mid-1970s, the factory most frequently used assembler, a low-level language that requires many lines of code to execute functions written more concisely in higher-level languages. In contrast, during

1986, approximately 60 percent of the code the factory delivered was in FORTRAN, 20 percent in high-level problem-oriented languages, and only 20 percent in assembler, with future plans calling for greater use of C.[24]

Despite numerous arguments against interpreting productivity as lines of code, in 1977, Matsumoto and other managers at the Fuchu Works decided to use EASL as the primary output measure of the factory. This involved converting lines written in different languages to the approximate number of lines required to implement the same function in assembly language (which corresponds more directly to actual machine instructions that run a computer). Toshiba managers made this decision primarily because of its simplicity, as Matsumoto explained in a 1987 article: "Our aim in measuring productivity is improvement. What we need are easily understandable indices with which we can compare current and past productivity data in some consistent manner. . . . Measurements must be extended to every detail of all software products. The amount to be measured is so large that the measuring must be as simple as possible. Expending significant overhead cost for the measurement should be avoided."[25]

Toshiba thus counted the number of source lines delivered from all projects in a given year, including both data declaration lines and executable lines of code (but not comments), for new programs and maintenance work, and then converted these numbers to EASL using standard conversion coefficients; for example, one line of code in FORTRAN might equal three lines in assembler, depending on the efficiency of the compiler.[26] While this method could be imprecise, especially when comparing numbers from different individuals and projects, used consistently among similar projects, EASL provided Toshiba with relatively comparable output numbers for the combined efforts of factory personnel.

For total code delivered from the factory, Toshiba used the term *gross production rate* (GPR). Newly produced source code (the original high-level statements of a program not yet in executable form) was called GPR-0. Toshiba then broke down gross production into GPR-1 (new source code plus reused source code) and GPR-2 (total delivered object or executable code) (Figure 5.8). Managers looked to GPR-1 as the most accurate reflection of the factory's production, since this represented actual delivered software (excluding basic software such as operating systems, system utilities or language compilers that Toshiba also sold with its custom applications software).[27]

To calculate a general measure of productivity, Toshiba totaled up the number of personnel working on projects in the software factory in each year, including systems analysts and design personnel, programmers and testers, maintenance engineers, and subcontractors (which accounted for as much as 80% of the work done on projects in the factory), and divided

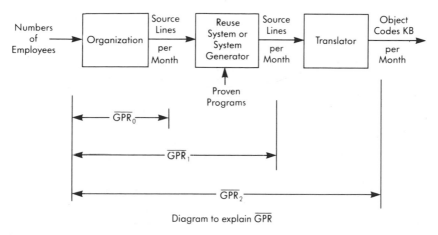

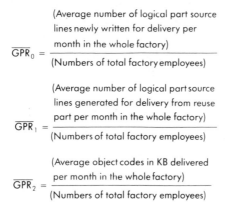

Diagram to explain $\overline{\text{GPR}}$

$\overline{\text{GPR}}_0$, $\overline{\text{GPR}}_1$, $\overline{\text{GPR}}_2$ are defined as:

$$\overline{\text{GPR}}_0 = \frac{\text{(Average number of logical part source lines newly written for delivery per month in the whole factory)}}{\text{(Numbers of total factory employees)}}$$

$$\overline{\text{GPR}}_1 = \frac{\text{(Average number of logical part source lines generated for delivery from reuse part per month in the whole factory)}}{\text{(Numbers of total factory employees)}}$$

$$\overline{\text{GPR}}_2 = \frac{\text{(Average object codes in KB delivered per month in the whole factory)}}{\text{(Numbers of total factory employees)}}$$

Figure 5.8 Productivity Accounting. GPR = gross production rate. (*Source*: Yoshihiro Matsumoto et al., "SWB System. A Software Factory," in Horst Hunke, ed., *Software Engineering Environments* [Amsterdam: North Holland, 1981], pp. 307–8. Copyright © 1981 Gesellschaft für Mathematik und Datenverarbeitung mbH. Reproduced with permission.)

this into the annual production amounts (but with no adjustments for overtime, which managers estimated at sixty to eighty hours per month per employee).[28] Toshiba also kept separate statistics of output and quality productivity for each class of personnel. Managers measured systems analysts by the number of requirements-specification pages they created per month or week as well as the number of defects per page found in design reviews and test inspections, including tests at the customer's site; designers by the number of design-description pages they wrote and the number of defects per page; programmers by EASL produced per month or per week and defects detected per 1,000 lines; and test engineers by the number of test items they completed per month or week as well as the number of incorrect reports per test item.[29]

Table 5.5 shows gross software productivity for the Fuchu Works and the Toshiba Software Factory from 1972 to 1985 (the last year for which Toshiba had made data public), and reuse rates in the programming or coding phase as well as new code estimates from 1977 (the year the factory opened). Particularly striking is the rise in productivity (delivered EASL or GPR-1 per person per month, excluding operating systems, utilities, and other basic software) and the obvious impact of increasing reuse (measured at the code level). Productivity increased from 1,390 lines per person per month in 1976 to more than 3,100 in 1985, while reuse levels (lines of delivered code taken from existing software) increased from 13 percent in 1979 to 48 percent in 1985.

In terms of improvement rates, in the five years prior to the start of the factory, productivity gains appeared erratic, even decreasing 12 percent in 1975. Fuchu software developers improved output 13 percent between 1972 and 1973, but nominal productivity in 1976 was still no

Table 5.5 Productivity and Reuse at Toshiba Software Factory

Year	Total EASL* Delivered (per person per mo)	Index†/ (100)	Change‡ (%)	Reuse§ (%)	New Code‖ (EASL)	Defects# (per 1,000 EASL)	No. of Employees (all phases)
Pre-Factory Estimates							
1972	1,230	100	—	Data not available			
1973	1,390	113	+13				
1974	1,370	111	− 2				
1975	1,210	98	−12				
1976	1,390	113	+15				
Post-Factory Estimates							
1977	Data not available						
1978	1,684	137	—	—	—	7–20	1,200
1979	1,988	162	+18	13	1,730		1,500
1980	2,072	168	+ 4	16	1,740		1,700
1981	2,443	199	+18	29	1,735		2,050
1982	2,595	210	+ 6	26	1,920		2,100
1983	2,763	225	+ 7	41	1,630		2,150
1984	2,931	238	+ 6	45	1,612		2,250
1985	3,130	254	+ 7	48	1,612	0.2–0.05	2,300

*Debugged and delivered equivalent assembler source lines per programmer per month, averaging all projects in the factory and including all phases and manpower (requirements analysis through maintenance); †based on 1972 equivalent assembler source lines (EASL) productivity estimate (1,230); ‡percent increase or decrease over previous year; §percent of delivered lines of code taken from existing software with little or no modifications (usually no more than 20% of a given module); ‖EASL × [(100 − Reuse %)/100]; #defects per 1,000 lines of delivered code converted to EASL. mo = month.

Source: The prefatory figures are from K. H. Kim, "A Look at Japan's Development of Software Engineering Technology," *Computer*, May 1983, p. 33. The 1978–1985 figures are estimated from index data presented in graph form in an internal Toshiba memorandum, "The Factory History Data Based on the Values of 1978," received by M. Cusumano from Dr. Yoshihiro Matsumoto, September 1988, using actual 1985 values published in Matsumoto, "A Software Factory: An Overall Approach to Software Production," p. 5.

higher than the 1973 level. In contrast, output per worker increased dramatically in 1978, the first full year of factory operations, while productivity doubled the 1975 level by 1981. Productivity improvements slowed considerably after 1981, but still averaged 6 percent or 7 percent annually. Production of new code actually followed a declining trend, since reusing more code required more time to read and modify the recycled parts, as well as more time to write code (and designs) for reuse. Toshiba's ability to recycle code also showed a declining trend, stopping at just under 50 percent. Thus the general leveling off of gross productivity improvements appeared to relate directly to the ceiling Toshiba hit for reusability.[30]

Despite slowing gains in productivity and reusability, output per employee at the software factory already appeared high by the mid-1980s. The 3,130 lines of EASL source code per month per employee in 1985 translate into approximately 1,000 lines of FORTRAN[31]—considerably more than the 200 to 300 lines of new code per month cited in various sources for U.S. programmers making similar real-time applications.[32] This monthly productivity estimated in FORTRAN equaled the annual average for Japanese projects reported in Appendix B, also adjusted for language differences, and exceeded by a large margin the U.S. adjusted monthly average of approximately 600 lines.

Other adjustments to the Toshiba numbers produce figures that, while still laudable, are not quite as good as nominal productivity suggested to many observers. Subtracting reused code (which is not completely fair, since reusing code systematically requires time to write for reuse and to implement reuse) from the 1985 data, Toshiba employees averaged a still impressive 1,612 EASL or approximately 500 lines of new FORTRAN code per month. Adjusting for estimated overtime, however, of, say, 70 hours per month by recalculating for a 160-hour month (a recalculation that some Japanese firms, such as Hitachi and Fujitsu, did for their productivity measurements, but which most American firms did not),[33] Toshiba personnel in 1985 delivered approximately 2,200 EASL (730 FORTRAN-equivalent), including reused code, and approximately 1,100 EASL (370 FORTRAN-equivalent), subtracting reused code. This latter number did not suggest that Toshiba had a huge advantage over other firms, although it still amounted to a fine performance, given the size and complexity of the systems Toshiba delivered, the low level of defects (discussed later), and the fact that half the factory employees were high school graduates (albeit *Japanese* high school graduates, with basic calculus, statistics, and a variety of science courses and other college-level material behind them).[34]

Before placing too much significance on the meaning of any of these numbers, however (as discussed in Chapter 2), productivity and reusability, as well as quality, were difficult to compare accurately across firms. Products, applications, tools, and methods of counting differed widely in the industry (and, too frequently, within the same firm). Even if Toshiba were consistent in counting, its numbers also probably suffered from a variety of common defects. There were always potential errors in conversion, since the figures for annual gross production were in various languages that Toshiba converted to EASL. Production did not correspond precisely to annual software development but reflected deliveries of code to customers. And, although one could subtract reused code, the new code numbers included reworked (changed) code, which still consumed large amounts of time. It was also difficult to measure reuse of designs, which was often more important than reuse of executable code, since designs could be modified more easily for different applications and machines. Matsumoto reported for 1985 that the factory reused approximately one-third of the design documentation, although it was not clear how this reuse affected EASL numbers.[35]

Another element difficult to adjust for was the cost of designing highly modular and potentially reusable code. This strategy required programmers to write standardized interfaces for each module, a practice that might take longer to do as well as make programs longer than they need be for one application, thus detracting from productivity. Toshiba partially compensated for this by not encouraging projects to reexamine designs or code to make them shorter, except for segments of programs where speed and timing were critical; in these areas, programmers usually wrote in assembler, which took more time and skill than high-level languages. As a general rule, managers appeared to encourage personnel to maximize long-term productivity by developing programs from reused software and writing new software for easy reuse and maintenance, as long as new software met the basic requirements and reliability levels customers demanded.

While performance data should be compared across firms and projects with great care, Toshiba appears to have collected its numbers consistently. The data thus provide some sense of changes in productivity and reuse over time at the factory, and suggest strongly that: (1) the factory system brought improvements in productivity and reusability (as well as quality); (2) the factory emphasis on reusability doubled nominal productivity levels; and (3) reusability seemed to involve some costs, such as in overhead as well as in a decline in new code output. On this last point, Toshiba's internal studies of reuse rates, number of lines in modules changed when reused, and overall output per person, indicated that productivity was significantly improved only if about 80 percent of a module was reused without changes. If only 20 percent was used unchanged, the impact on overall productivity was negative. There was no noticeable impact on productivity between 20 percent and 80 percent.[36]

Apart from productivity analysis, it became important for Toshiba to collect numbers consistently because the factory's control procedures required project managers and analysts to use the production figures for planning and pricing decisions. Project managers estimated how much code they would need to generate or reuse to reach profit goals, and then attempted to deliver this code without exceeding a separate budget for hiring new programmers. According to Matsumoto, profit goals forced managers to limit hiring of software employees to a maximum of 4 percent per year after 1981. This meant they had to attain certain improvements in GPR-1 productivity to meet new demand, which the factory achieved.

Toshiba also used the gross output figures to calculate other productivity measures used for planning and control. Cost-based productivity centered on estimates for each project's development cost. This target cost, plus the factory's desired profit margin for a total system (hardware and software), determined the price Toshiba charged a customer. Toshiba thus calculated cost per person per month, profit per person per month, and cost per EASL, for six-month financial periods, for the entire factory and for each project. Capability-based productivity was more subjective, although managers used the data for progress control, work assignments, and education planning and career development. Again, Toshiba collected measures for the factory as a whole, for each project, and for each analyst, designer, programmer, or test engineer, adjusting EASL or documentation productivity according to the type of function or purpose of the software being developed; correctness versus speed of the employee, including the number and type of defects identified in design reviews, testing, or by the customer; and type of product, in terms of EASL size as well as specifications and test items.[37]

Detailed collection and analysis of performance data also led Toshiba managers to refine their strategy for productivity improvement to embrace four broad areas: (1) standardization of inputs, through promotion of program or module registration and reuse; (2) automation of design and programming, through the introduction of system-generator tools; (3) other tool support, for all phases of development and maintenance; and (4) quality improvement, through minimizing rework on delivered products by strict control of software quality (detection and prevention of errors) before shipment, as well as by improving the specification process for customer requirements.[38]

As the data in Table 5.5 suggest, these efforts appear to have worked. Not only did output measures show a correspondence between reuse and productivity, but a 1985 survey asking employees in the software factory to rank the impact of various factors on meeting their individual productivity and quality targets also cited reusability as the major factor.[39] Another in-house study concluded that the SWB tools probably accounted for approximately one-third of the productivity gains for writing new code in the decade since the factory opened in 1977. One-third increase seemed to come from better management methods, and the remainder from the greater use of high-level languages. It also appeared that, similar to what Hitachi experienced with the EAGLE tool, reuse procedures and factory support systems allowed personnel to spend more time on design and less on tedious tasks such as coding and testing.[40]

Quality Control

The factory's performance in quality improvement surpassed the doubling of productivity between 1978 and 1985. As indicated in Table 5.5, residual defects (called *faults* in Toshiba) per 1,000 source lines (that is, errors remaining after final testing) averaged between 0.20 and 0.05. To reach this level usually required more than one year of testing for large systems.[41] These figures, again, compared extremely well to averages reported for Japanese and U.S. projects (in Appendix B), although, as with lines of code productivity or reusability, firms often count defects inconsistently and numbers may not be comparable for other reasons as well, such as differences in product types.[42] Toshiba also varied testing times and thus final quality according to customer specifications for fault tolerance, hence averages for the factory (rather than a range, as in Table 5.5) made little sense to calculate or compare. Be that as it may, apparently consistent measures of quality over time suggest a sevenfold improvement in the decade after the factory opened since, in the mid-1970s, a typical program had seven to twenty faults per 1,000 lines of source code at the end of final test.[43]

Toshiba closely allied its approach to quality control with measures to improve productivity, costs, and reusability. Since Toshiba based its prices on estimated total costs plus a profit margin, defect avoidance and efficient detection could have a major impact on earnings by reducing the large expenditures of time and manpower often required to fix defects. Furthermore, constructing software with 50 percent of the modules taken from debugged program libraries offered potential savings in testing and maintenance. Toshiba also tried not to produce software that had fewer defects or more functions than customers wanted. Project managers and analysts negotiated with each customer to arrive at a particular level of product reliability (estimated number of residual faults remaining after testing) at a given price for a delivered system. As a result of these negotiations, and the types of products Toshiba made, factory policies tended to treat software quality more in terms of "fault avoidance and tolerance" rather than as the elimination of defects or high functionality.[44]

For example, most software the factory developed had to meet the following requirement: . . . "any fault of Product 2 which causes Product 1 to deviate from the specified performance is not allowed within 8000 continuous hours of real-time operation." Testing then became an iterative process of detecting and correcting errors, with the objective of making sure the software met all specifications under conditions agreed on in the contract with the customer. Toshiba estimated the number of residual faults in software products before shipment, using a method developed by Matsumoto's group in cooperation with the Tokyo Institute of Technology. Counting faults started with integrated test and continued through the end of the plant test. The cumulative number of faults and the calendar time elapsed during the test period served as a basis for estimating the number of residual faults at the end of the tests. Personnel corrected defects before proceeding to subsequent tests, making it possible to evaluate software quality in terms of error frequency in final testing done at the software factory and in an endurance run at the customer site. Toshiba engineers also negotiated and wrote the final quality assurance tests with each customer and allowed customer representatives to witness each test.

While most of these efforts revolved around testing, the factory procedures included subjective inspections of requirements, designs, and code, primarily through eight design reviews at the completion of each phase (called a *baseline*) in the development cycle (Table 5.6). The section responsible for each phase carried out the review, although reviewers (Engineering Section, Design Section, etc.) invited in other groups to these sessions as they deemed necessary, and an independent Quality Assurance Section conducted the design review at the end of factory test.[45]

Factory procedures defined eleven quality factors and twenty-three individual items for reviewers to check. These represented the perspectives of both the producer (Toshiba) and the customer: correctness, reliability, maintainability, testability, flexibility, reusability, portability, interoperability, efficiency, integrity, and usability (Table 5.7). Development personnel checked similar items, making entries on copies of the checklists, as they finished work at each baseline. In the design review meetings, managers then compared the responses with the checklists reviewers filled out.

Table 5.6 Toshiba Software Factory Design Review (DR) System

DR	Promoter	Purpose
A	Engineering Section	Review of specifications
B	Design Section	Review of overall design
C	Design Section	Review of detailed design
D	Manufacturing Section	Review at start of manufacturing
E	Manufacturing Section	Review at end of manufacturing
F	Quality Assurance Section	Review at end of factory test
G	Plant Engineering Section	Review at end of site test
H	Engineering Section	Review of performance

Source: "Design Review System," transparency copy received form Yoshihiro Matsumoto, Sept. 4, 1987.

Table 5.7 Toshiba Software Quality Evaluation

Criteria	Related Factors
Traceability	Correctness
Completeness	Correctness
Consistency	Correctness, reliability, maintainability
Accuracy	Reliability
Error tolerance	Reliability
Simplicity	Correctness, maintainability, testability
Modularity	Maintainability, testability, flexibility, re-usability, portability, interoperability
Execution efficiency	Efficiency
Storage efficiency	Efficiency
Access control	Integrity
Access audit	Integrity
Operability	Usability
Training	Usability
Communicativeness	Usability
Software system independence	Portability, reusability
Machine independence	Portability, reusability
Communications commonality	Interoperability
Data commonality	Interoperability
Conciseness	Maintainability
Generality	Flexibility, reusability
Expandability	Flexibility
Instrumentation	Testability
Self-descriptiveness	Maintainability, testability, flexibility, reusability, portability

Source: "Software Quality," transparency copy received from Yoshihiro Matsumoto, Sept. 4, 1987.

In addition, like other Japanese facilities, the Toshiba Software Factory ran small group meetings or quality circles (approximately 700). The most common theme discussed in 1986 was quality improvement (45 percent of topics), followed by productivity problems (20 percent), methodology improvement (15 percent), and the education system (10 percent). The Fuchu Works also held factorywide quality control conferences twice a year and groups with particularly excellent presentations participated in companywide quality control conventions. Toshiba management encouraged participation by giving out awards for excellence in quality-related activities.[46]

Training and Career Development

As Chapter 2 suggested, many common problems in scheduling or controlling software development seemed to stem from huge differences in performance capabilities among individuals, especially between the most and the least talented or experienced. Some firms tried to leverage their best people by dividing tasks, such as putting their best people in systems engineering and newcomers in coding. This factorylike division of labor, however, introduced communication or translation problems, such as those seen at SDC—translating requirements written by one person into design and then code written by others. Other firms recruited primarily highly skilled people and asked them to write requirements, designs, and code—what this book has called a craft or job-shop mode of production.

Toshiba's approach, like Hitachi's, resembled factories in other industries. Management tended to hire individuals with low levels of training in software or computer engineering, educate them in the technology and the factory's tools, procedures, and products, ask them to work initially at relatively simple tasks such as coding, and then help them advance with additional training. New Toshiba employees spent 150 to 200 hours in classes (1 to 1.5 months) learning the factory's approach to software development, and then another several months in their product departments observing different types of systems in operation. This sequence provided them with a fundamental understanding both of the applications areas they would work in and of software engineering as practiced in the factory. Toshiba also offered a succession of courses to continue training beyond the first year and did not give long-term assignments to individuals for specific jobs until after their third year in the factory.[47]

While half of the employees doing programming at the end of 1986 had only graduated from high school, the Toshiba Software Factory was not an attempt to turn software development into an unskilled "blue-collar" process completely. The high school graduates had excellent backgrounds in mathematics and science, even if they were not from technical schools, and quickly advanced their skills in company training programs. In addition, approximately 30 percent of the factory personnel had bachelor's degrees and 20 percent had doctorates or master's of science degrees. Furthermore, of new employees in recent years, approximately 60 percent were college graduates and only 20 percent were coming directly from high school, as fewer Japanese decided not to attend college. Thus the factory was moving even farther away from less-educated employees as the pool of high school graduates available to employ declined.

Toshiba's training program within the factory consisted of three sequences containing a total of twenty-two separate courses plus five optional courses (Table 5.8). The Fuchu Works' departments for personnel and engineering administration, as well as the Heavy Industrial Engineering Laboratory, administered these courses jointly. Factory guidelines required each new employee to become familiar with the basic operations of the factory, regardless of their educational background, before choosing a specialization. This meant, in practice, that everyone—Ph.D.s and high school graduates—started out doing programming and learned other tasks thereafter.

The length of time an assignment lasted depended on the individual.

Table 5.8 Toshiba Software Factory Education Program*

Basic Courses (required course of study for all new employees)
1. Introduction to computer control systems
2. Computer system architecture
3. Programming languages
4. Test and debugging techniques
5. Structured design
6. Data structure/databases
7. Programming styles

Application Courses (for employees entering design)
1. Requirements definition
2. Documentation techniques
3. Test and inspection techniques
4. Control theory
5. Simulation techniques
6. Evaluation techniques

Advanced Courses (for employees entering systems analysis)
1. Contracts/negotiation
2. System theory
3. Quality control
4. Project control
5. Cost estimation
6. Software engineering
7. Management techniques
8. Human relations
9. Decision making

Optional Courses
1. Industrial engineering
2. Operations research
3. Patents
4. Value analysis
5. Integrated circuits

---

*Courses ranged in length from a few days to approximately one month.
Source: Yoshihiro Matsumoto, "Software Education in an Industry," *Proceedings of Computer Software and Applications Conference—COMPSAC '82* (Los Angeles, IEEE Computer Society Press, November 1982), pp. 93–94; interviews with Shuichi Yamamoto, Yoshio Ebata, and Yoshio Ikeda, July 17, 1989.

A minimum three-year assignment to do design work followed programming on the career ladder. After this, individuals chose specific career paths that best fit their interests and skills, as illustrated in Figure 5.9, where the letters *a* through *d* indicate points of entrance for new graduates into the factory. The average high school graduate programmed for six years, then moved into software design for three years and systems analysis for five years, before reaching the position of software engineering manager or software engineering specialist. Employees determined their career goals and drew up formal training plans through a series of discussions with their superiors and staff devoted to career consultation and planning. Managers also strongly encouraged high school graduates

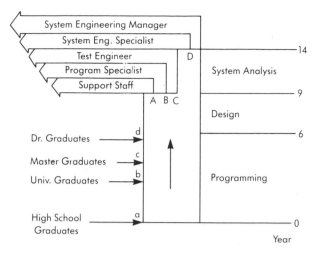

Figure 5.9 Career Patterns for Software Engineers. (*Source*: Yoshihiro Matsumoto, "Software Education in an Industry," *Proceedings of Computer Software and Applications Conference—COMPSAC '82* [IEEE Computer Society Press, November 1982], p. 93. Copyright © 1982 IEEE. Reproduced with permission.)

to take the equivalent of two years of full-time advanced courses in the company college, so they could more easily advance up the career ladder.[48]

Computer-Aided Tools and Supporting Techniques

The Software Workbench

Toshiba's SWB, developed by the research staff at the Fuchu Works under Matsumoto's direction (until 1989, when he joined the faculty in information science at Kyoto University), provided a common infrastructure of tools and techniques for systems analysts, designers, programmers, test engineers, and managers working at the factory and at customer sites. The new version of the SWB supported requirements definition and basic system design, program construction (detailed module design and coding), project control (productivity, costs, schedules), configuration management (how to integrate pieces of a system developed separately), documentation, testing, quality assurance, program maintenance, reusability, and prototyping (Figure 5.10).

   Not every product department utilized the full or identical set of tools. Some required modification for particular application areas, and individual product departments had the responsibility to make these changes as well as add specialized tools or methods that appeared useful for their

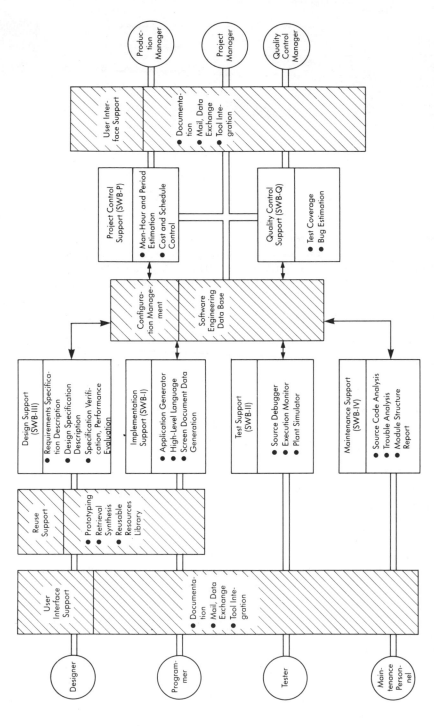

Figure 5.10 Configuration of the Software Workbench (SWB) System. (*Source:* Yoshihiro Matsumoto, "A Software Factory: An Overall Approach to Software Production," in Peter Freeman, ed., *Tutorial: Software Reusability* [Washington, D.C., IEEE Computer Society Press, 1987], p. 167. Copyright © 1987 IEEE. Reproduced with permission.)

domains.[49] Nonetheless, the SWB presented a common environment and support infrastructure for developing software in diverse product departments. Its creation and refinement reflected both long-standing commitment and considerable foresight on the part of Matsumoto and other Toshiba managers and engineers.

As early as the mid-1970s, management recognized the importance of software to its future businesses, especially in industrial systems, and allocated manpower and other financial resources needed to improve company skills in this area. The initial research staff for the software factory remained modest, consisting merely of ten to fifteen members. Toshiba provided continued support, however, for tool and methodology development—not by taxing individual projects with limited lifespans and budgets, as at SDC, nor a line profit center such as the Fuchu Works, whose sales and earnings might be cyclical as well as relatively limited. Toshiba funded the SWB system and other process research for the factory mainly from the corporate R&D budget.[50]

Toshiba also managed this development well, as the history of the SWB illustrates. Before 1977, most programming at Toshiba was on punched cards. Project groups, spread across a half dozen locations, determined their own methods and tools, with little or no coordination or central support. Managers thus sought to standardize program production across different sites and find a way to allow several dozen or more programmers to work effectively on single large projects.

The initial step came in 1977 with the first SWB tool, then called the Software Production System (SPS). This provided a uniform interface and network linkages (based on the UNIX operating system) to software developers at six different locations in the Tokyo-Kawasaki area (thirty to forty kilometers apart), all making minicomputers and microcomputers. The software people were not together in one site because, like IBM, Toshiba had not centralized hardware development and company managers wanted programmers located in each facility, close to the sources of hardware expertise. By 1978–1979, SPS supported 600 programmers at these different sites and 150 on-line terminals.[51]

Despite the goal of standardizing program development, Toshiba did not try to complete a set of tools and techniques at one time but introduced them gradually, working up from simpler to more difficult technologies. While this approach resembled Hitachi, it contrasted markedly with SDC, where impatient managers attempted to create a comprehensive infrastructure of tools even before they had standardized methods or refined their organizational structure. Toshiba took eight years to build up the SWB system to cover all phases of software development, from requirements specifications through maintenance (Table 5.9). Only after completing tools for relatively simple tasks, such as programming and testing, did the factory introduce more sophisticated tools for project management, quality assurance, requirements specification and

Table 5.9 Evolution of the Software Workbench (SWB) System

Initial Development	Support Tool	Improvement/Automation Focus
1976–1977	SWB-I	Programming environment (programming, assembly, compiling, debugging in the source level, project files, program generation, program reusing and link edit)
1978–1980	SWB-II	Test environment
1980–1985	SWB-P	Project management
1980–1985	SWB-Q	Quality assurance
1981–1983	SWB-III	Design support (requirements specification, software design description, and documentation)
1981–1984	SWB-IV	Program maintenance
1986–1988	Various	Document preparation
		Expert system (for design)
		Reusable software
		Integrated database

Source: Matsumoto, "A Software Factory: An Overall Approach to Software Production," p. 12; "Development of SWB for Toshiba Fuchu Software Factory," transparency copy received from Y. Matsumoto, Sept. 4, 1987; Yoshihiro Matsumoto interview, Aug. 24, 1988.

design, and maintenance. In the mid-1980s, the SWB system increasingly incorporated advanced computer-aided capabilities, facilitating documentation, design automation, reusability, and construction of integrated databases. The latest changes moved the tools to Toshiba minicomputers from mainframes, improved the way the system worked at remote sites, simplified interfaces for the tool users, and introduced more terminals or work stations, mainly in the form of lap-top computers.[52]

SWB-I, or rather, an initial version introduced during 1976–1978 to run on a mainframe computer, served as the base around which Toshiba built other tools. It supported structured coding from hierarchical flow charts (HIPO), automated code generation, and debugging through a command-control facility, a text editor, language processors, and debugging facilities for all the computers Toshiba manufactured (in the late 1980s, these consisted of at least four types of compatible minicomputers and five or more microcomputers). On-line terminals provided access to project files and on-line libraries; other libraries were accessible through separate facilities or magnetic tape. Assemblers and compilers for TPL (a high-level real-time control language for minicomputers, developed in 1977), FORTRAN, and PL/7 (a machine-oriented, high-level system description language for Toshiba's minicomputer series, similar to PL/360) produced object code for the target computers (the machines the factory wrote code for and sold to customers). A librarian tool managed the object code and added, deleted, or replaced modules in a series of object-code libraries created for different applications.[53] The Software Engineering Database (SDB) and the Program Information Management and

Service System (PROMISS) maintained libraries storing registered program parts and related information such as changes and release histories. Management information covered program-registration locations; system, program, or module names and configurations; a list of documentation; and the function of the code, target-computer names, languages described, version status, modification notes, and released job or customer names (Figure 5.11).

Matsumoto openly noted that they designed the SWB system to "level out the engineers' ability" and reduce product variability resulting from the different skills of individuals. Two instances of how SWB-I accomplished this can be seen in coding support and program generation. For coding, SWB-I's "lexical editor" used simple commands to display, automatically, constructions such as "do while" for different languages. Programmers merely filled in blank spaces, without having to study the grammar of different languages and risk making coding errors. SYSGEN (System Generator) facilitated the creation of semicustomized programs from reused software through tables and menus that helped analyze requirements described in a specific format and select standardized packages from a reuse database.[54]

Automated program generation, a major goal of Toshiba in general, remained possible mainly for well-defined applications where Toshiba had a lot of experience and customer requirements were not rapidly changing. To build electric power-plant control software, for example, the product department responsible for this area modified SYSGEN and introduced a specialized version, COPOS, consisting of three separate generators. The action-list generator presented a series of menus that helped designers name all the automatic controls in a plant, before translating the inputs into a programming language. The input/output list generator noted the various inputs and outputs, and translated these into the data format of the desired programming language. The program generator contained a master file with all the options for different types of power-plant control systems and thus helped engineers select specific functions. It then combined all the generated code, completing the software system.

SWB-II provided facilities to control test execution, collect and analyze test data, simulate real conditions, and generate test records. Software for this tool resided in a test-support computer, which Toshiba connected to computers being tested for customers through high-speed dataways. Toshiba initially based SWB-III on the SADT tool purchased from Softech that supported various approaches (contextual, functional, dynamic) to analyzing user requirements. It relied primarily on three subsystems. The first, CASAD (Computer-Aided Specification Analysis and Documentation), analyzed different views of requirements, defined relationships, generated documents and tried to match desired specifications with modules in a reusable parts database as well as link them

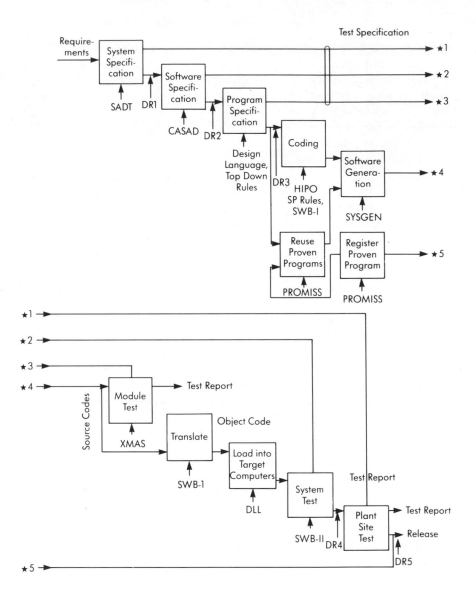

Figure 5.11 Software Production Life Cycle, Milestones, and Tools and Methodologies. CASAD = Computer-Aided Specification Analysis and Documentation; DLL = Down-Loading Line; DR = Design Review; HIPO = hierarchical input/output; PROMISS = Program Information Management and Service System; SADT = Structural Analysis and Design Technique; SP = Software Production; SWB = Software Workbench; SYSGEN = System Generator; XMAS = Executive Model Analyzing System. (*Source*: Matsumoto et al., "SWB System. A Software Factory," p. 310. Copyright © 1981 Gesellschaft für Mathematik und Datenverarbeitung mbH. Reproduced with permission.)

together automatically. FCL/FCD (Functional Connection Language/ Functional Connection Diagram) described functional dependencies, data structures, and external interfaces, while PDL (Program Description Language) described module structures and internal interdependencies. SWB-P supported project management by monitoring schedules and progress toward milestones and generating reports.

Since target computers differed, Toshiba had to centralize text editing, components assembly, compiling, and debugging through a group of general-purpose mainframes with a single interface to users. The factory personnel did large-scale data processing, using various compilers or assemblers, in a batch mode, and program design, editing, and debugging on-line from remote terminals. A host disk centrally controlled the source programs, allowing designers to build programs in working files utilizing various layers of the SWB system. As Matsumoto explained, the first layer served as a centralized program library, the second as a centralized production-management database, and the second and third together as project-development databases:

> In the top layer: a large general purpose computer (ACOS 1000) serves as a storage of all completed software products which are already in operation at each customer site. The software products include all documents such as specifications, manuals, notes, program source lists and operational instructions. In the second layer: several clusters are connected to the ACOS 1000 mentioned above through a local area network. A cluster consists of a large minicomputer (GX) with 32–64 MB [megabytes] main memory, a second level local area network and plural work-stations connected to the second level local area network. The GX mentioned above has a storage of documents, data, programs and others which are needed to execute project management, configuration management and quality management. The above mentioned second layer file connected to the mini-computer (GX) also stores standardized templates for the specifications, formats, texts and illustrations. Reusable specifications, reusable program modules and reusable documents are stored in the same file and can be retrieved through personal work-stations. In the third layer: A file server is connected to the second level local area network. Designers can personally store under-developed documents, programs and data in the memory of each work-station. If they want to store any information or software resources which are commonly usable among project members, they can store them in the file server.[55]

When a project met a particular milestone, the design reviews, code inspections, and tests utilized the documentation and data generated directly from the tools and activities of developers at each phase (see Figure 5.12). Plant-site tests, for example, used system-specification documents from the initial requirements analysis to make sure performance followed requirements. These specifications were also critical to system

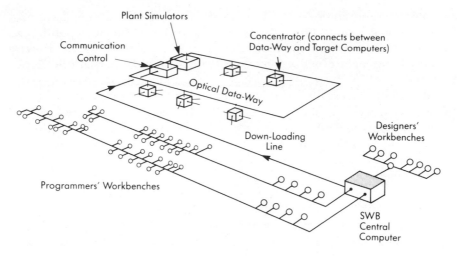

Hardware Configuration of the Centralized SWB System

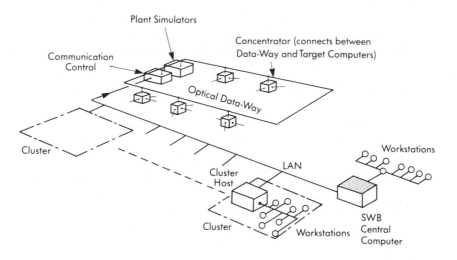

Hardware Configuration of the Dispersed SWB System

Figure 5.12 Centralized and Dispersed Software Workbench (SWB) Configurations. LAN = local area network. (*Source*: Matsumoto, "A Software factory," pp. 168–69. Copyright © 1987 IEEE. Reproduced with permission.)

test. Program specifications (the detailed top-down, modular structure of the code) and automatically generated code formed the input data for the module tests. Specifications from registered programs used in a new system were checked as part of the final test and program release process. In addition, the software factory sent data to other sections in the Fuchu Works, to link software with hardware development.

The SWB system worked both in a centralized mode and in distributed clusters of work stations. In the 1980s, Toshiba primarily used the centralized layout, with approximately 750 workbenches or on-line terminals connected to a central computer and a data highway transmitting new programs to target computers for testing within the factory (Figure 5.12). The distributed mode consisted of groups of SWB clusters with work stations connected to a minicomputer and the clusters connected to the factory computers, databases, and libraries through local area networks (LAN).[56] The trend in Toshiba was to make greater use of distributed clusters, to add capacity to the factory's limited space and to work more at customer sites around Japan. Toshiba also had plans to use the Sigma network (see Chapter 8) to connect remote sites with the factory.[57]

The SWB, along with standardization of techniques and procedures to support structured design and programming, of necessity limited the factory from moving to new process or product technology quickly. In fact, Toshiba continued to rely on a model of software development and tool support that Matsumoto's group defined in the mid-1970s. Nonetheless, Toshiba made considerable efforts to refine and incorporate good software-engineering technologies as they appeared. All new employees, for example, learned modularization and abstraction techniques and how to apply these to maximize reuse of designs, code, and documentation. In the late 1970s and early 1980s, Toshiba also introduced automated program generation and prototyping, even though these techniques tended to deviate from the sequential approach to development normally used in the factory:

> The software life-cycle model and various software engineering techniques based on the model are . . . worthwhile from the viewpoint of production management. However, other development systems deviate from the life-cycle approach, such as prototyping and program generating, that are equally important and vital to the development of new software. The concept of "levels of abstraction" is applied to both early design and manufacturing phases in order to incorporate these techniques. In order to manage traces between different abstract levels, modularity or encapsulation in the requirements and design levels is considered. Modularity in the early stages of software development aids in the reuse of existing modules and prototyping.[58]

Program generating involved the use of software programs designed to automate assembly and construction of new programs, usually for specific applications, through the selection of existing modules from a database and then the generation or construction of appropriate interfaces. Prototyping required developing a partial system that interacted with external equipment driven by the software in order to forecast, during early stages of design, the final performance results of a completed program. Prototypes consisted of skeleton versions of what final programs might look like, written in languages such as PROLOG, APL, or BASIC; or programs derived from existing designs or code, modified to fit new requirements.[59] In addition, for certain well-understood applications, such as control software for steel processing and nuclear power-plant operations, Toshiba mandated the use of what management called *paradigms*—tailored models of development for particular applications that helped engineers build parts of the software more quickly in parallel fashion rather than in a more time-consuming sequential manner. These relied on past experience to outline system components, identify areas where simultaneous coding and design were possible, and suggest plans for testing and maintenance.[60]

Reusability

Toshiba engineers, in a 1987 conference paper, explained their reuse strategy in a way that reflected the same logic found in mass production engineering and manufacturing as well as newer flexible design and production concepts in a variety of industries. The basic idea was to accommodate rising demand and insure a high level of productivity and quality, despite variations in individual skills and diverse customer requirements, by building products from standardized components reassembled or combined with new components:

> Recently, the demand for software is increasing at a rate of 40% per year, and the fields of its demand are diversifying at a rapid pace. . . . The key solution technique of this problem is to apply reusable software components. That is, differences in personal capabilities should be minimized by using pre-produced standard components at the design stage. Different combinations of components should be used for diversified applications, and the quality of individual components should be systematically assured. In actual practice, mostly the know how for producing resembling software and the produced program codes are being reused.[61]

This approach—systematic creation and reuse of reusable software parts, as opposed to development from scratch or "accidental" reuse— lay at the heart of Toshiba's concept of *factory* production of software; but how the factory carried out reuse in the face of long-standing organizational as well as technological problems provides a superb example of integrated management: of product planning, development techniques, computer-aided tools, and controls and incentives.[62]

On the organizational side, as discussed in Chapter 2 and elsewhere, writing and documenting components for reuse generally required extra time that individual customers might not or should not want to pay for. Project managers, and project members, also have good reason to resent this extra time, unless they see opportunities to save time in the future. On the technical side, many factors influence whether a particular project can recycle existing components. These factors included the match in application or function of the existing software with the new design requirements; the particular language(s) used and the characteristics of the target computers; and the program structure and degree of modularity—how independent modules were of other modules or subsystems in the original program, based on the construction of the interfaces between various layers in a complete system (the new application software, subsidiary applications packages, utilities, the operating system, and the hardware).

Toshiba did not solve all problems related to reusability. Rather, the factory presented a system that simplified or restricted problems to manageable areas, and that provided incentives both for project managers and personnel to write reusable software and reuse it frequently. Table 5.5 reflected the success of these efforts, indicating that approximately half the software Toshiba's factory delivered in 1985 consisted of reused code, including some with modifications (usually no more than 20 percent of the contents of an individual module). The other half of delivered software consisted of new code, mainly written for an individual plant or application, as well as some applications packages product departments developed to serve as major components of customized systems.

Toshiba actually reused a number of items in addition to whole subsystems or packages, including documents (contracts and manuals) and requirements specifications, as well as detailed (module-level) designs, executable code in the form of subroutines or utilities (programs performing a range of standard functions, such as handling data or searching databases), tools, and even test cases. The SWB system collected data on these various reusable elements, although management paid particular attention to a simple measure: the number of reused lines converted to EASL code in a delivered system.

Table 5.10 provides a breakdown of the three categories into which the 50 percent reused software fell in a typical year. One category consisted of packages of design skeletons, called *white-box* parts, kept in department program libraries. These described functions common to applications within a particular domain, such as nuclear power-plant control systems, or steel-mill process control systems, and ranged in size from 1,000 to 10,000 EASL. Software developers in the factory often merely had to choose the right package and fill in blank slots for different customers; they could also modify the designs. Another portion consisted of relatively large utilities that worked in between operating systems and industry-specific applications packages to control communications, database management, and other basic functions; or tools and other imbedded subprograms generally usable in a variety of systems. Toshiba appeared to depos-

Table 5.10 Approximate Breakdown of Reused Software in Toshiba

	Breakdown	Comments
100%	*Total System*	Delivered lines of custom applications software for an indiviual project, excluding basic systems software.
		size: 1,000,000–21,000,000 EASL
50%	*Reused Software* White-box designs	Applications-specific packages or subsystems of design skeletons. Written, documented, and registered for reuse in product-department application libraries.
		size: usually 1,000–10,000 EASL
	Utilities, tools	Applications-specific utilities, tools, or other special programs imbedded in delivered software. Written, documented, and registered for reuse in product-department libraries mainly but also in a central factory library.
		size: usually 10,000–100,000 EASL
	Black-box modules	Coded subroutines common to most software made in the factory. Written, documented, and registered for reuse from a central factory library. Approximately 10% of reuse.
		size: usually up to 3,000 EASL
50%	*New Software*	Plant- or customer-specific software, not considered reusable but written, documented, and registered in a similar manner for maintenance. Often written with advanced fourth-generation languages that generate code from menus or tables of application functions or specifications.

EASL = equivalent-assembler source lines.
Source: Based on interviews with Yoshio Ikeda and Shuichi Yamamoto, July 17, 1989, and data in Matsumoto, "A Software Factory: An Overall Approach to Software Production," pp. 171–174.

it these components, which ranged in size from 10,000 to 100,000 EASL, mainly in department libraries but also in the factory library system. The final category (approximately 10 percent of reused code) consisted of *black-box* modules, usually no more than 3,000 EASL in size. These common subroutines, also accessible from across product departments through a central factory library, covered functions demanded in most systems the factory built, such as for managing general-purpose displays or converting temperature data.[63]

For the other 50 percent of delivered software that Toshiba wrote from scratch for individual customers, in addition to SWB tools and conventional languages such as FORTRAN, factory departments were beginning to deploy very high level (fourth-generation) applications-specific languages for systems design that eliminated coding as a separate task. An example is POL (Problem-Oriented Language), which the nuclear power-plant department used extensively to design components specific to individual customers. Unlike conventional computer languages, POL relied on menus and tables with blank spaces representing control logic for various functions (found primarily in nuclear power plants, however, limiting the use of this language to one application domain). Engineers filled in the blanks and a compiler produced executable code. Another tool that worked with POL, RRDD (Reverse Requirements Definition and Documentation) system, generated updated documentation automatically, in the event personnel changed parts of an existing program.[64]

In order to build programs around existing components as much as possible, Toshiba required projects to draw up plans, called *repeat maps*, at the requirements-analysis and module-design phases. Systems analysts produced the first map by comparing the main subsystems they wanted to build with existing packages in the department and factory libraries. After inserting the appropriate packages into the system under construction, designers in the factory drew up another set of repeat maps, identifying specific modules to reuse or modify and new components needed to implement requirements.[65]

The organization Toshiba created to promote reuse and overcome short-term concerns of project managers and development personnel relied on Software Reusing Parts Steering Committees and a Software Reusing Parts Manufacturing Department and Software Reusing Parts Center (Figure 5.13). The factory formed a steering committee for different areas (with different members, depending on the application) to determine if customers had a common set of needs suitable for a package, and then allocated funds from the Fuchu Works' budget for these special projects. Some packages were utilities usable in different departments, although most served specific applications. For example, PODIA (Plant Operation by Displayed Information and Automation), a package created in the department building nuclear power plants, covered all the basic functions common to these systems and accounted for about half the software the department delivered.[66]

The Reusing Parts Manufacturing Department and Parts Center evaluated new software (and documentation) to make certain it met factory standards; after certification, engineers registered the software in department or factory reuse databases (libraries). Registered items required a keyword phrase to represent the functionality of the part or correspond to a specific object, as well as a brief "Description for Reusers" (DFR) that explained the part's basic characteristics. Figure 5.14, part of a DFR for a steel-rolling mill speed-control package, shows how these descriptions came in a codelike format, with specific names such as *slab* or *roller* converted to generalized notations like *MOVING_OBJECT*. The cataloguing procedures also required engineers to identify parts

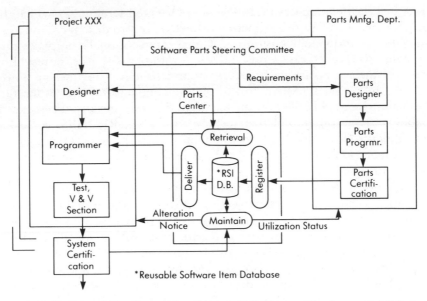

Figure 5.13 Reusability Promotion System. V & V = verification and validation. (*Source*: Matsumoto, "A Software Factory," p. 173. Copyright © 1987 IEEE. Reproduced with permission.)

they expected to reuse frequently, such as common subroutines, and those they did not, such as job-oriented applications packages they might retrieve once at the beginning of development rather than daily. The factory kept the frequently reused software (source code and functional abstracts) on easily accessible disk files and the less frequently reused software on magnetic tape.

Evaluation criteria to determine which software parts were good enough for reuse focused on measures such as fitness, quality, clarity, abstractness, simplicity, coupling level (with other modules), completeness, "human interface" (module identification and algorithm descriptions), software interface, performance (response time), and internal configuration of the module. These criteria supported more specific, factory-oriented guidelines. One, the contents of a module (objects, relationships between objects, algorithms) had to be easily understandable to users who did not develop the code. Two, the interfaces and requirements to execute the software (other code needed, language being used, operating system, automatic interrupts, memory needed, input/output devices, etc.) had to be clearly specified. Three, the software had to be portable (executable on various types of computers). Four, it had to be transferable (modifiable to run on different computers, if not designed to be portable). Five, the software had to be retrievable in a program library by people who did not originally write it.

DFR of package MILL __ SPEED __ CONTROL
in the requirement level is
   with
    object:MOVING __ OBJECT:EXTERNAL __ ENTITY;
    object:PROCESS __ INPUT __ CONTROLLER:
    INPUT __ INTERFACE;
  object:REAL __ TIME __ KEEPER:INPUT __ INTERFACE;
  object:OUTPUT __ CONTROLLER:OUTPUT __ INTERFACE;
end with;

requirement STATE __ BASED __ CONTROLLER is
  interface relationship is
    triggered by REAL __ TIME __ KEEPER
      with REAL __ TIME __ INTERVAL:event;
    use PROCESS __ INPUT __ CONTROLLER
      to GET(SENSOR __ VALUE:analog and digital);
    acknowledge OUTPUT __ CONTROLLER
      with READY:event;
    used by OUTPUT __ CONTROLLER
      to OBTAIN (RESULT:STEPPED __ VALUE);
        type STEPPED __ VALUE is
            (VERY __ LOW,LOW,HIGH);
end interface relationship;

requirement body STATE __ BASED __ CONTROLLER is
  object:OBTAIN(RESULT:STEPPED __ VALUE)PROCESS is
    object:SENSOR __ VALUE:analog and digital;
    object:STATE:INTERNAL __ ENTITY 1;
      type INTERNAL __ ENTITY is
        (STATE1,STATE2,STATE3,STATE4):
  begin
    estimate STATE of MOVING __ OBJECT
      using SENSOR __ VALUE:
    if MOVING __ OBJECT is in STATE1 then

           RESULT:= VERY __ LOW;
      elseif MOVING __ OBJECT is in STATE2 or STATE4 then
        RESULT:=LOW;
      elseif MOVING __ OBJECT is in STATE3 then
        RESULT:=HIGH;
      end if;
      acknowledge OUTPUT __ CONTROLLER
        with READY;
    end;
  end requirement body;
end requirement STATE __ BASED __ CONTROLLER;

constraints description: . . . end constraints;

required resources: . . . end required resources;

end presentation;

Figure 5.14 Reusers (DFR) Example. (*Source*: Matsumoto, "Management of Industrial Software Production," pp. 68–69.)

Toshiba's R&D group introduced a tool to facilitate the labeling and retrieving of reusable modules that relied on a special language, OKBL (Object-Oriented Knowledge-Based Language), and asked users a series of questions to define precisely what type of part they needed. If engineers wanted to see what functional modules were in the system for a particular application, for example, they would enter the library for that application and then type "function" when the system asked for "Super-class." If the desired function was to scan analog data from a measuring instrument, they would type "scan" when the system asked for the subclass and "analog" when it asked for the kind of data. The system would then go on to specify the method of scanning, providing choices under another subclass, and so on.

Yet, while the OKBL tool appeared relatively easy to use and would probably become more useful as Toshiba refined it, factory personnel, especially those having worked several years in the factory, seemed to rely mainly on manual techniques and experience—printed catalogues of reusable software and knowledge gained from prior efforts—to find software in libraries appropriate for new situations. Since Toshiba organized most reusable software as large packages in department libraries, and many departments used only a few packages to build most of their systems, engineers quickly became familiar with the contents of different packages and did not seem to require much tool support.[67] On the other hand, Toshiba reused only about 10 percent of reusable software *across* product departments. Thus better tool support to index and retrieve software components in a more generic fashion seemed important to increase reuse further because this would make more designs, code, or packages accessible to members of different product departments who did not have a personal familiarity with either the application or existing software.

But even though Toshiba still had room to improve interdepartmental reuse, within the departments, management relied on an integrated set of incentives and controls to encourage project managers and personnel to take the time to write reusable software parts and reuse them frequently. At the start of each project, managers agreed to productivity targets that they could not meet without reusing a certain percentage of specifications, designs, or code. Design review meetings held at the end of each phase in the development cycle then checked how well projects met reuse targets, in addition to schedules and customer requirements. At the programmer level, when building new software, management *required* project members to register a certain number of components in the reuse databases, for other projects. Personnel also received awards for registering particularly valuable or frequently reused modules, and they received formal evaluations from superiors on whether they met their reuse targets. The SWB system, meanwhile, monitored reuse levels as well as deviations from targets both at the project and individual levels, and sent regular reports to managers. Matsumoto described the system in detail:

> Factory members are enforced [sic] to register a designated number of reusable modules in every fiscal term. The registration is received by the reusability promotion group which is a permanent organization in the factory. A standardized formalism is enforced for describing specification, logic representation and semantics of each module to be registered. The reusability evaluation committee examines the quality of each registration, and decides if it is acceptable or not. The accepted registration is taken by the reusability promotion group and transformed to the form which is included in the second layer (GX) database. . . . Persons who registered valuable reusable modules or frequently reused modules are rewarded.
>
> At the beginning of each project, each project manager is given several objective parameters with which to steer his/her project. Project productivity is one of the given objectives. Without reusable modules, given objective productivity is not attainable. Reusing is autonomously promoted by each project member to attain the given objective. . . . (1) At the end of the requirements definition phase, the semantics of the implementation model is created. Then existing reusable modules which seem to fit the model are selected at the design review meeting. (2) Objective parameters which are given to the project are refined so that each . . . parameter represents an objective for implementing each workload unit. (3) An accumulation of personal accomplishment is entered to the SWB system by each designer or programmer daily or weekly. The SWB system is capable to display deviation between accumulated effort and corresponding objective quantum. Each individual corrects activities by checking the deviation.[68]

To implement reuse objectives at the level of module design and coding, as opposed to the level of system design, Toshiba relied on another methodology, called "50SM" (50 Steps/Module). As suggested by the name, the basic concept involved limiting the number of lines of code (steps) in one module to fifty or less (about one page), making the parts easier to understand and redeploy. The 50SM method covered three kinds of modules—procedural (subroutines, functions, macros, etc.), data (files, variables or constants in memory, interface data, etc.), and packages (abstract data types, library programs, etc.). The factory also required a technical description formula to outline the external and internal module specifications as well as intermodule relationships. The 50SM presented a constraint in that the technique primarily supported structured design and reuse in procedural languages such as C, FORTRAN, COBOL, PASCAL, and Ada, rather than the use of newer object-oriented or logic-programming languages, which, for some applications, had specific advantages (see Chapter 2).[69] Furthermore, in practice, only about half the new modules projects produced tended to meet the 50-line limit, although the remainder were close, usually within 100 to 150 lines.[70] Nonetheless, it helped make reusable code and designs understandable, and worked well with tools such as code generators and editors.

Toshiba management also reinforced its reusability strategy through training of new personnel in program development and in maintenance. Toshiba courses showed employees how to build software starting at higher levels of abstraction (requirements and design) and then working downward, a practice Matsumoto claimed "increases extraordinarily the number of reused modules and the reuse frequency of a reused module." At the same time, in program design, Toshiba trained personnel to abstract data, define standardized interfaces and parameters, and follow the factory procedures for cataloging and documenting. Furthermore, even if projects did not reuse particular programs, managers felt the same techniques for design, testing, documentation, and library registration that aided reuse simplified software maintenance, perhaps the most costly part of software development for programs with long lifespans and frequent changes.[71] It might even be the case that savings in maintenance alone made the extra effort required for reusability worthwhile.

Process-Technology Transfer and Development

Two key problems faced at SDC and other firms attempting to improve scope or scale economies through centralized development of tools and methods, or systematic reuse, were suitability and portability to different applications, hardware platforms, or computer operating systems. Toshiba encountered less difficulty than SDC simply because most of the computers it wrote for were compatible Toshiba machines; UNIX interfaces also aided portability. In addition, Toshiba focused increasingly on reuse of designs rather than executable code dependent on machine architectures and particular operating systems. Yet Toshiba managers struggled with two related challenges: how to transfer the process technology developed for the Fuchu factory, embodied mainly in the SWB tools and supporting techniques, to Toshiba facilities making other types of software; and how to insure that software engineering continued to advance in Toshiba beyond the limitations of current technology.

First, it seems that Toshiba succeeded in transferring at least the basic structure of the factory tools and methods to the Ome Works, a Toshiba facility in another western suburb of Tokyo that produced software for office computers (not compatible with Toshiba's minicomputers) as part of the company's Information and Communications Group. Ome began writing software in 1968, even before the establishment of the Toshiba Software Factory. Although its venture into commercial computers proved unsuccessful and management divested the mainframe business in 1978, Toshiba continued to produce smaller computers. In 1980, to support a new effort in office equipment, Ome imported the SWB and accompanying techniques, which its engineers customized for business-applications software. Ome then introduced its own version of the tool and methodology set in 1984, the Automated System Technology and Revolutionary Organization (ASTRO).

In contrast to the Fuchu Works, where product departments corresponded directly to customer applications, Ome divided its several hundred software personnel into groups for systems software, minicomputer applications software, office-computer applications software, and systems administration. The last department handled software project management within Ome and at a dozen subcontracting firms and subsidiaries (housing at least another 1,000 software personnel). Most personnel working at Ome or in linked clusters of work stations used the ASTRO system, which accommodated up to 1,800 software developers, assuming three assigned to each station.

Like the original SWB system, ASTRO incorporated several subsystems: ASTRO-M—project management, cost and process control, productivity evaluation; ASTRO-V—documentation and project support; ASTRO-Q—quality control and maintenance; and ASTRO-D—requirements definition, test evaluation, and maintainability improvement.[72] Another tool developed at the Ome Works specifically for business applications, MYSTAR, supported systems analysis and design control as well as program generation and prototyping. In addition to incorporating a central database linking work stations through a local area network and tracking development progress, MYSTAR offered standardized forms (menus) for system specification and program specification. An on-line design-data dictionary served as a database for program components and information on their interrelationships; these fell into categories defined as nodes (points of convergence on a diagram or chart, designating states, events, time, or flows of some kind), tasks and functions, files, graphics, charts, and subprograms. The design-data dictionary, in combination with the on-line workbench, served as a prototyping tool in that developers could construct program outlines from the registered design data, in either static or dynamic modes. Program generation was possible in COBOL directly from the design specifications.[73]

To pursue advanced research as well as create a more general-purpose version of the SWB system, and to promote technology transfer among other Toshiba divisions, Toshiba also established a new corporate R&D facility in 1983, the Systems and Software Engineering Laboratory (see Figure 5.1).[74] The staff, approximately 100 in 1988, worked in several areas, including software production engineering, system technology, and AI. As listed in Table 5.11, major topics in software production were refinement of prototyping tools for requirements definition, computer-aided design, and knowledge-engineering techniques for reusable-components storage and retrieval. Toshiba was also developing a common support system for microcomputer users and network technology

Table 5.11 Advanced Software-Engineering Research Topics

Software Production Engineering	
Design and Testing	*Engineering Environment*
Requirement definition	Distributed network architecture
Design	Automatic management data gathering
Reusability	Network security
Problem-oriented language generator	Distributed database
Software verification	Man-machine interface
Microcomputer Environment	*Development Management and Quality*
Real-time testing	Systematic development methodology
Multitarget language processing	Software auditing and rights protection
Optimizing memory/performance	Quality management
	Development management
	Time study/productivity/quality metrics
	Software engineering education

System Technology	
Distributed Architecture	*Simulation and Modeling*
Distributed scheduling	Objected-oriented modeling
Distributed inference	Modeling language
Communication systems	Numerical analysis
Distributed OS/data base	Fluid and heat transfer simulation
System Control Technology	*System Evaluation*
Fuzzy control	Decision support system
Multivariable control	Structural modeling
Learning control	System performance analysis
Rule-based control	System evaluation language and OS
Cognitive science	

Artificial Intelligence (AI)	
Intelligent Interface	*Expert Systems*
Cognitive science	Knowledge acquisition
Natural language interface	Advanced inference
Man-machine interface	Large-scale knowledge bases
Knowledge engineering	Expert shells
AI Languages	*Intelligent Programming*
Object-oriented language	Program transformation
Knowledge-processing language	Theorem proving
Specification description language	Prototyping
Logic programming language	Software module synthesis
Concurrent programming language	Specification acquisition

OS = operating system.
Source: Toshiba Corporation, "Toshiba Systems and Software Engineering Laboratory," Kawasaki, 1987, pp. 3–9.

for distributed software development as well as experimenting with management techniques that applied conventional time studies to software development (similar to Hitachi practices). In system technology, along with distributed architectures, the laboratory researched control technology using a variety of techniques to capture the expertise of experienced plant operators and incorporate this into rule-based systems, decision-support systems, and other modeling approaches. In the area of AI, Toshiba conducted extensive work on intelligent interfaces between human operators and computers, language technology, expert systems, and automatic ("intelligent") programming.

Laboratory engineers called the generalized version of the SWB system the Integrated Software Management and Production (IMAP) support system.[75] Similar to the new SWB at the Fuchu Works and to AS-TRO, in contrast to the old SWB based on mainframe computers and on-line terminals, the IMAP workbenches and network seemed to offer more integration among key databases, such as for project-management and planning data, completed products (at the factory and project levels), and reusable components. It also seemed to provide faster and easier links among databases for distributed groups of developers using the system.[76]

Toshiba presented no data on how many projects had adopted IMAP, although performance claims closely resembled those from the SWB. One project reported that reuse through IMAP tools brought an estimated 85 percent reduction in work-hours (compared to building from scratch) usually needed to finish a large software system containing more than 100 subprograms, each with about 500 modules and requiring approximately 1.3 work-days per module to complete.[77] Other comments and evaluations summarizing IMAP's features and underlying philosophy suggested that Toshiba engineers and managers remained convinced IMAP would fulfill Toshiba's broader goal of moving software production throughout the company closer toward a factory approach:

> In order to cope with the increasing demand for software, the industrialization of software production has become a problem of great urgency. Division of labor through clarification of production phases and visualization of management are the conditions necessary for the industrialization. IMAP has realized (1) the development of tools for consistent production; (2) building the database for software configuration management; (3) the automatic collection of management data; (4) building the supporting tools corresponding to the purposes of management; (5) building the production environment based on distributed environment utilizing EWS (engineering work station). Thus it has established the industrialization that unites software production and management.[78]

Summary and Evaluation

Like any successful endeavor in management, the Toshiba Software Factory represented the culmination of years of planning, research, experimentation and development. Toshiba still had progress to make, such as in bringing all product departments to the same level of tool support. Yet the factory clearly brought together many of the elements needed to move a new, complex technology toward a more strategically managed and integrated mode of operations. To a large extent this proved feasible because the factory concentrated on related products; focus facilitated standardization of tools, techniques, and training, as well as reusability, across a range of projects, rather than building one system at a time (Table 5.12). The factory thus achieved high average reuse and output

Table 5.12 Toshiba Summary

Concept	Implementation
Process improvement	Factory established through the initiative of a R&D manager to improve productivity, cost, and defect control, and accommodate projected increases in demand for large-scale, complex, customized software. Emphasis on standard methods and tools, reusability, automation, divisions of labor, and training of relatively unskilled workers.
Product-process focus & segmentation	Production of software mainly for real-time industrial control applications accompanying Toshiba hardware made in parallel. Personnel taken from application-oriented product departments through a matrix structure. Gradual expansion into other types of similar software. Customer segmentation by negotiations over system features, reliability, and price. Experimentation with new applications in off-line projects. Other facilities handled other types of software.
Process/quality analysis & control	Systematic analysis and rigorous controls since the mid-1970s through standardized methods and training, tools, management systems, and design reviews from specifications phase. Much data collection and control automated through on-line workbench system. Quality control defined as reliability, subject to customer requirements, and closely integrated with productivity-cost management and reusability but independent of project management.
Tailored/centralized process R&D	Tool and method development first at the factory in a division laboratory and tailored to real-time process control software. Departments also tailored tools and methods. Corporate laboratory recently added for advanced R&D and technology transfer.
Skills standardization & leverage	Extensive set of courses, supporting the factory tools and methods, required of new employees and offered along with a career path for promotion. Standardization of methods and division of labor in all phases, but with specialization of systems engineers and designers by application. Systematic reuse of designs, code, and documentation part of an integrated strategy to leverage limited skills across multiple projects.
Dynamic standardization	Periodic revision or upgrading of standards, methods, and tools, though mainly a long-term, incremental approach to tool and methodology development, adding more complex functions over time.
Systematic reusability	Product planning, as well as factory tools, methods, controls, incentives, and training, all promoted reuse of designs, code, test items, and requirements. For example, reuse planning from requirements analysis; reuse targets built into project schedules and budgets; programmers required to develop and register reusable parts, as well as reuse them.
Computer-aided tools	Integrated support through the Software Engineering Workbench, for all phases of development and in centralized or distributed modes. Increasing automation, such as in program generation, reuse support, or project-control data collection.

Table 5.12 (*Continued*)

Concept	Implementation
Incremental product/ variety improvement	Focus on balancing costs with customer needs. Rigorous emphasis on reuse meant Toshiba delivered nominally customized systems containing 50% "old" components, hence only incremental product improvement was possible. Factory infrastructure, however, also allowed Toshiba to build very large, complex systems relatively cheaply, use skilled people effectively, and put more effort into design. Management also continually added new product areas to the factory process.
Assessment Strategic management & integration	Management objectives, product focus and marketing tightly coordinated with the factory process, training, management controls and incentives, as well as long-term tool and methodology development. Organization and management through product departments allowed some differences in practices.
Scope economies	Scope economies achieved in production of customized products through centralization of program development, standardized methods and tools, and high levels of reuse, as well as through connecting distributed clusters using the factory tools and databases. More sharing of software across product departments a potential area for additional scope economies.

per employee as well as high quality, especially given the sophistication, size, and variety of customized software that it built, and the limited educational level of its work force.

Did Toshiba's factory present a challenging place to work for software engineers and project managers? This remains difficult to answer with this research. To an extent, Toshiba appeared to redefine creativity, for example, by rewarding people who wrote reusable software rather than elegant programs. Toshiba also appeared to be a leader in producing large-scale automated systems, even though the company did not stress product innovation and delivered software containing on average about 50 percent "old code." The factory also required high levels of standardization and control, building reuse targets into factory budgets and schedules as well as reinforcing them in design reviews, training programs, and personnel evaluations. The structured mode of operations in the factory by design limited experimentation and innovation, especially since, like Hitachi and other Japanese software factories, Toshiba based its production system on incrementally refined tools and techniques dating back to the 1970s.

While goals such as process standardization, components reusability, and other factory practices placed constraints on individual behavior and project management in general, Toshiba tolerated some diversity in development processes and systematically invested in the factory's evolution. Product departments tailored tools and methods to suit their application areas. The Fuchu Works also accepted new jobs and did these, initially, outside the normal factory routines. Product and process technology progressed, albeit somewhat slowly, and benefitted from an R&D infrastructure at the division and corporate levels that explored new software-engineering technologies as well as promoted technology transfer from the factory and the laboratory to other Toshiba divisions. Management also made continued training and career advancement available, especially to high school graduates.

Overall, Toshiba, despite a complex matrix setting, succeeded in moving software development closer to an engineering and manufacturing discipline, with an infrastructure to support productivity, cost control, and quality regardless of the level of an employee's skills or experience. Toshiba also marketed the factory's products strategically, offering low prices, at least some customized features, good service, high reliability, and a range of quality levels. This approach appeared to meet the needs of its Japanese customers, who seemed especially sensitive to a combination of cost, functionality, and quality —precisely the benefits that a software factory should be able to provide.

NEC: A MULTIPRODUCT, MULTIPROCESS FACTORY NETWORK

One of the difficulties inherent in moving any large diversified corporation toward more standardized methods and tools, or more centralized and coordinated management, is the need to accommodate variety in products and customer requirements. In contrast to SDC, Hitachi, and Toshiba, where managers centered their initial factory efforts on one facility before considering extensions, NEC attempted to structure as well as tailor process technology across several product divisions and subsidiaries almost simultaneously by promoting common goals such as standardization and quality improvement, automation, and reusability. The result—in effect, a multiprocess, multiproduct factory network— presented NEC with a managerial challenge more ambitious in scope than its Japanese competitors faced, even though all attempted to move software development beyond craft practices.

While NEC managers and engineers struggled to balance standardization and centralization with the sometimes incompatible needs and practices of individual product areas, the material in this chapter, as well as market and customer-satisfaction data, suggest that the company made significant progress and effectively supported a variety of hardware operations. In the late 1980s, for example, NEC led its Japanese competitors in total software revenues and produced an impressive number of systems for large industrial and business computers, telephone switching and data transmission equipment, office and personal computers, in addition to microprocessors. At the same time, however, NEC continued

273

to trail Japanese and U.S. competitors in specific areas, indicating a need to continue improving its software operations.

According to the 1988 *Nikkei Computer* surveys, Japanese customers ranked NEC below Fujitsu and Hitachi in hardware and price-performance as well as in maintenance for hardware and software. Nor did customers perceive NEC so well in providing support for office computers (Tables C.5 and C.6)—a market that, given its experience as the leading Japanese producer of personal computers, might have been a source of strength, although NEC tended to allow software houses and outside firms to produce many of the programs for this segment. On the other hand, users in Japan scored NEC comparable to its competitors in systems-engineering support and applications, as well as systems software, and behind only Fujitsu in Japanese-language processing (Table 1.10). In applications systems engineering, Japanese customers ranked NEC near the top in system planning and design, knowledge of specific applications and industry trends, communication abilities in sales, and technical support in communications (Table C.3). Japanese users also rated NEC above average in new system configuration support and technical support for software development, as well as in communications areas for basic software (Table C.2).

The Corporate Setting

Company Origins and Products

NEC originated in 1899 when two Japanese businessmen and AT&T's Western Electric subsidiary formed a joint venture to manufacture and import telephone equipment. It later became an independent company affiliated with Japan's Sumitomo group and, over time, expanded into a variety of electrical or electronic components and finished products. An $18 billion multinational corporation in 1987 (including consolidated subsidiaries), NEC revenues came mainly from two groups: information processing, which consisted of computer hardware and software systems and services (44 percent of 1987 sales); and communications products and services (32 percent), which consisted mainly of switching and transmission systems. Other product groups included semiconductors and electron devices (19 percent) as well as home electronics (5 percent) (See Table 4.1 and Table 6.1).[1]

The Computer Business

Like Hitachi and Toshiba (as well as Fujitsu), NEC had a long history of computer hardware and software development. NEC produced what company historians have claimed was the first commercially sold transistorized computer in the world, introduced for scientific applications in

Table 6.1 NEC Operating and Marketing Groups (1987)

Operating Groups	Marketing Groups
Research and development	NTT sales
Production engineering development	Government sales
Switching	Domestic sales
Transmission and terminals	International operations
Radio	Advertising
Information processing	
Electron devices	
Home electronics	
Special projects	

Source: NEC Corporation, "Guide to NEC," Tokyo, 1987.

1958. To advance its skills in making computers for businesses, NEC entered into a licensing arrangement with Honeywell in 1962 through which it manufactured Honeywell machines for sale under the NEC label in Japan and upgraded its hardware and software design technology. While this technical relationship continued until 1979 and the two companies still cooperated in marketing, technology transfer reversed in the 1970s as NEC started supplying mainframe hardware to its American partner and to Bull in France.[2] This reversal of fortunes reflected NEC's consistent growth into one of the world's premier computer (as well as semiconductor) manufacturers, ranking, among Japanese firms, first in software, microcomputers, and data-communications sales, and second in mainframe revenues, trailing only Fujitsu (1987 data).[3]

Similar to Hitachi, NEC built its computer business through a combination of in-house initiatives, beginning in the mid-1950s, and technology transfer from abroad, primarily the acquisition of hardware designs and some software programs from Honeywell in the 1960s. The key figure in software development from the 1950s was Yukio Mizuno, who entered NEC in 1953 after graduating from the Tokyo Institute of Technology, from which he also received an engineering doctorate in 1960. In the 1980s Mizuno served as the senior vice-president in charge of software operations for the entire NEC group.

NEC built its first programs in 1955–1956, when Mizuno and several other engineers constructed an analog computer and then a message and accounting data sorter for a nonstored program machine—a computer that was, essentially, hard-wired. Their next project required programs for storage in memory—the NEAC 2201, a transistorized computer NEC completed in 1958, and the 2203, an enlarged version introduced for commercial sale in 1959. The NEAC 2201 and 2203 prompted NEC managers to establish a Programming Section in 1959, with approximately twenty-four engineers, besides Mizuno. As one of their major accomplishments, they completed Japan's first language compiler.[4] The technology changed quickly, however, and several Honeywell machines supplanted the NEAC models in 1962–1963. These gave way after 1965 to the NEAC 2200 series, which contained re-packaged versions of three small and medium mainframes Honeywell had designed to compete with the IBM 1400, as well as several larger machines NEC designed independently to compete more directly with the IBM System/360 family. The 2200 series remained as NEC's basic product line until the ACOS series, which NEC introduced in 1974 to compete with the IBM System/370 mainframes.[5]

Despite the technical arrangement with Honeywell, a decision in 1965 to build a large-scale computer for the Japanese market, the NEAC 2200–500, led NEC to use integrated circuits, printed circuit boards, and large-capacity core memory for the first time. It also developed independently an advanced operating system capable of on-line processing and time sharing similar to M.I.T.'s *Multics* system. The hardware and software presented major technical and organizational challenges to NEC engineers, who had never tackled such extensive projects, but did much to advance the company's skills in technology and management.

NEC based the 2200–500 machine on a design completed in 1964 at NEC's Central Research Laboratories. To turn the central processing unit into a commercial model, in 1964 NEC established a computer factory at Fuchu, Tokyo, with a development group of approximately thirty engineers, including Mizuno as head of the Programming Section. It appears that Honeywell personnel tried to dissuade NEC from taking on this project, arguing that the U.S. models were adequate and that the proposed software would be too difficult to write. Much to Honeywell's surprise, however, NEC completed the machine and operating system on time in 1968, delivering the 2200–500 to Osaka University and receiving an award from the *Nikkan* industrial newspaper for Japan's first computer utilizing integrated circuits. Honeywell thereafter brought NEC formally into its process for product planning and began cooperating with NEC to design future machines.[6]

NEC patterned the operating system for the 2200–500, named MODE IV, after IBM's OS/360. NEC provided approximately 90 percent of the engineers who built the system; the 10 percent Honeywell contributed came to Japan and worked under Mizuno in Tokyo. Honeywell was quite helpful in teaching NEC managers how to plan and manage a large software project, although Honeywell's systems for estimating defects, costs, and software productivity seemed extremely poor to the Japanese managers. The need to improve estimation techniques prompted NEC to begin collecting its own project data and devising new planning models, which became the basis for software production control at NEC in the later 1970s and 1980s.[7]

Organization of Software Development

The decision to build a new operating system for the ACOS series presented major opportunities for standardizing control methods, tools, and development procedures. These decisions led, first, to the separation of basic software from hardware development and establishment as an independent division in 1974, headquartered at the Fuchu plant, which also designed and manufactured NEC mainframes.[8] From 1974, the Fuchu Works (which NEC personnel informally referred to as a "software factory") also became the center of software process-technology R&D until NEC established a separate laboratory for this purpose in 1980. NEC later organized an Information Processing Group containing separate divisions for basic software as well as large-scale custom software (systems engineering projects) and business applications software, with main facilities located in the Mita section of Tokyo, close to NEC headquarters. In addition, divisions for transmission and switching systems created their own programming departments nearby at NEC's Tamagawa and Abiko plants.

Unlike Hitachi and Fujitsu, NEC did not try to produce machines compatible with IBM's, since it continued to support and refine the Honeywell operating system as its main architecture for large computers. According to Mizuno, NEC managers chose this strategy after observing RCA in the United States and Unidata in Europe, which had built machines compatible with the System/360 and then failed to match IBM's subsequent 370 models. Yet, despite achieving some independence from IBM, NEC still had to offer competitive features and prices to attract new customers that NEC had not yet "locked" into its architecture and to prevent existing customers from switching to other vendors. To accomplish this, as head of software product planning in 1974, Mizuno moved from NEC headquarters to the Fuchu Works and spent three years directing the design of the new operating system. Because the System/370's basic software did not have strong time-sharing features and seemed ill suited for large databases, NEC added these functions and a task-level virtual machine capability to its new design by using a high-level language, HPL (a PL/1 subset), in contrast to IBM, which had used assembler.[9]

For future product development, two decisions in 1975 had long-term significance. One was to train programmers in structured programming methods and to design standards and tools based on this methodology for newly written application and system programs.[10] Another was to create subsidiaries to provide regional programming services in addition to specialized products, beginning with NEC Software, Ltd., and to encourage managers to recruit software houses to serve as subcontractors to subsidiaries and NEC divisions (Table 6.2).[11] NEC's divisional facilities, led by the Fuchu Works, and subsidiaries, led by NEC Software, thus became the basis of a distributed software-factory network making multiple products with tailored as well as some standardized tools and techniques.[12] By the end of the 1980s, software personnel accessible to the NEC group totaled more than 18,000, divided approximately evenly between in-house divisions and twenty-five subsidiaries.

Table 6.2 NEC Software Organization and Subsidiaries (1988)

NEC Organization	Main Facilities	No. of Employees
Information Processing Group		
Basic Software	Fuchu	2,500
Systems Engineering	Mita	2,500
User Applications	Mita	1,250
Communications Divisions		
Transmission	Tamagawa	1,500
Switching	Abiko	1,500
Specialized Subsidiaries		
NEC Software		2,300
NEC Information Service		950
Nippon Electronics Development		1,300
Nihon Computer Systems		800
NEC Communication Systems		800
NEC Technical Information Systems		350
NEC Management Information Systems		300
NEC Microcomputer Technology		NA
NEC Engineering		NA
NEC IC-Microcomputer Systems		NA
NEC Telecom Systems		NA
NEC Aerospace Systems		NA
NEC Robot Engineering		NA
NEC Ocean Engineering		NA
Regional Subsidiaries		
Kansai NEC Software		500
Chubu NEC Software		300
Kyushu NEC Software		200
Tohoku NEC Software		100
Hokuriku NEC Software		NA
Chugoku NEC Software		NA
Hokkaido NEC Software		NA
Shikoku NEC Software		NA
NEC Security Systems		NA
Shizuoka NEC Software		NA
Okinawa NEC Software		NA

NA = not available.
Source: Company interviews and public information.

Origins of the Factory Strategy and Structure

Product-Market Segmentation

The chairman and CEO of NEC, Koji Kobayashi, in discussing the general strategy NEC followed for software development in a 1985 publication, clearly reflected assumptions fundamental to product-market segmentation and factory systems in a variety of industries: Not all customers desire state-of-the-art products, therefore, firms can modify their development process for customers who will accept products made through standardized methods and tools. Restating the conclusions of his engineers (discussed in more detail later), Kobayashi insisted that a process based on standardization and automation, rigorous production-management and quality-control systems, and employees of average skills, was sufficient to produce 90 percent of business-applications programs in demand. Only for the other 10%—new applications not yet well understood—did a firm need to rely on highly skilled personnel and manual techniques:

> I personally believe that as in the case of hardware production, software production is not difficult and that more than 90 percent of software can be produced by rationalizing work processes and utilizing modern facilities supported by computers. I compare the development of software with climbing Mt. Fuji, the highest mountain in Japan. By volume, 90 percent of the mountain lies below the fifth station, which anyone can easily reach by car or bus. However, the remaining 10 percent, from the fifth station up, must be climbed on foot. This is true mountaineering, where physical strength and vigor are required. I believe that it is possible to produce effectively the majority of software by adopting new methods . . . and by using good tools. . . . As in other fields it will be possible to standardize and modularize software in producing that 90 percent of the volume that corresponds to the part of the mountain below the fifth station, and it will also be possible to apply production and management techniques. . . . In contrast, the software above the fifth station is small in quantity, yet it includes advanced and innovative software, namely knowledge information processing systems and software for automatic language translation. These are fields that have yet to be explored, and we will need to exert our full intellectual powers to develop these new types of software.[13]

Movement Beyond Craft Production

Mizuno, and other NEC managers, took up the challenge of taking NEC beyond the craft stage in software production—not simply one facility or one division, but the entire NEC group, subsidiaries and subcontractors included. The ideas and plans they followed evolved gradually over at least a decade, as reflected in a series of articles dating back to the mid-1970s.

Mizuno began publicly discussing a factory approach to software development in an October 1975 article in a leading Japanese journal on information processing. Then the manager of NEC's Basic Software Development Division, he stressed that the software industry had already evolved to where cost and quality mattered to customers. Therefore, he argued, producers had to move beyond individual or craft approaches to production and find ways to apply modern engineering or manufacturing practices and tools to software:

> As the use of computers has become more diverse and at higher levels, software—quantitatively and qualitatively—has become increasingly im-

portant. . . . Thus, software is no longer the individualistic, craft-like product it once was; there is evidence that it has become a modern product with a market value and market distribution. Accordingly, we have reached the point where the development process for software must move beyond the individual or craft stage to a more rational, modern production system. Namely, we have reached the age where there is a strong demand for high quality, maintainable software as well as for software cost reduction and productivity improvement. . . .

In general, consciousness of software as a highly modern and major product is still extremely low among both software producers and users. The result is a tendency to pay too little attention to software inspection or quality assurance and not to invest enough time and resources in the software development and production process. . . . It seems we have reached the stage where current methods for software production, which resemble a cottage industry, may be moving toward "manufacture" (factory-method industry). . . . [But] the tools used at the present for software development—paper, pencils, machines, basic language processors—are extremely primitive. . . . To improve productivity in software development, to produce software of higher quality, it is necessary to go beyond cottage-industry type production methods. This higher level of technology for the software production process can be referred to by the term "software engineering."[14]

This article, published shortly after SDC released information on its Software Factory and IBM reported on structured design and project-management techniques, elaborated on the concept of a distributed software-factory network, with programmers utilizing standardized procedures, tools, and components. Mizuno predicted productivity gains of two to fivefold with such a system, if firms could introduce the appropriate methods, tools, and management systems.

First, Mizuno believed that a software-factory approach needed more expandable and versatile high-level languages suitable for system description through structured programming methods. Second, he advocated the use of structured techniques such as top-down design, data and procedural abstraction, segmented and layered program structures, reduction of GO TO statements in coding, listing of program modules, and standardization of subroutine input/output interfaces. Third, to improve productivity and quality systematically, he felt firms had to analyze and standardize their software-production process, very much like Frederick Taylor, the American pioneer in applying scientific methods (statistical time and motion studies) to the analysis of production operations, had advocated for other industries in the early 1900s: "In the average production process, through Taylor's methods, standardization of tasks led to dramatic increases in productivity. In the same way, standardization in the software development process of the construction flow and documentation should make it possible to improve productivity. In addition, standardization should help reduce careless mistakes and increase reliability." Fourth, Mizuno proposed a formal plan for software process control, which he called a *phase-plan* system, to add visibility to the development process through checkpoints and reviews of standardized documentation for each step. Fifth, Mizuno believed a software factory should have a comprehensive system for quality assurance (Tables 6.3 and 6.4).[15]

As NEC made progress in standardizing its development processes, Mizuno gradually shifted his concerns to quality control and reusability. This change, discussed retrospectively in a published 1986 interview, reflected a broader strategy for achieving continuous increases in productivity. One element was a rigorous quality control initiative to prevent errors, since they became more difficult and expensive to fix after a company released a program to customers. A second was to invest in technology fostering the "accumulation of knowledge" about software engineering and pass this on to others through reusable software modules or designs, defect analysis data, and formal testing rules and process check points. Building on process standardization and control as the foundation of a factory approach, as well as automatic program generation tools that would grow in capabilities with each program written, Mizuno explained how, in the 1980s, the software factory had become a "concept" rather than a material thing:

> The term "software factory" does not indicate a physical building. It is a method of producing software, or the tools used in this method, for example a control system. The software factory refers to the integration of these types of things. It must be understood as a concept. Another point that should be emphasized is that it is important for a software factory to be a

Table 6.3 1975 Software Factory Concept

Methodology and Management
1. High-level structured programming language for system description
2. Disciplined structured programming and top-down modularization techniques
3. Standardization of the development process
4. System for process control
5. System for quality assurance

Specific Tools and Techniques
1. (High-level) language processing
2. Program and data commonality
3. On-line memory and control of program components and information units
4. Simple system for integrating parts of programs being developed separately
5. High-reliability file system
6. High-level virtual memory
7. Suitable development language and program control function
8. "Boot-strap" function (capability of testing software developed in the factory in the actual mode or on the actual machine it will run on, to ease transfer)
9. Tools for debugging, dynamic link functions, project control, and continuous operation

Source: Yukio Mizuno, "Sofutouea enjiniaringu no hitsuyosei," *Joho shori* 16, 10, October 1975, pp. 837–38.

Table 6.4 1975 Phase-Plan System

Phase 0: Planning	
Definition	Determination of product based on market needs, development costs, and technical capabilities
Documentation	Planning specifications
Review	Schedule, cost
Phase I: Basic Design	
Definition	Analysis of the objective of the planned project and establishment of programming objectives
Documentation	Basic design specifications
Review	Performance, cost
Phase II: Detailed Design	
Definition	Design of detailed functions and structure based on the programming objectives
Documentation	Functional and logic specifications
	Manual draft
Review	Cost, functions
Phase III: Implementation	
Definition	Coding and debugging of each component based on the detailed design
Documentation	Programming completion document
	User manual
Review	Schedule, cost, functions
Phase IV: System Integration	
Definition	Test of debugged modules in combination
Documentation	System integration test document
Review	Performance
Phase V: Inspection	
Definition	Examination of whether the completed system meets the planned specifications
Documentation	Inspection completion document, release announcement
Phase VI: Maintenance	
Definition	Support and improvement of completed system
Documentation	Program lists and internal documents

Source: Mizuno, "Sofutouea enjiniaringu no hitsuyosei," p. 838.

place where systems are introduced that incorporate the experience of people who have made software in the past with new methods or particularly effective techniques. It is an accumulation of knowledge. Even if it doesn't go as far as a knowledge database, it should be something where there is an accumulation of knowledge. For example, in coding inspection, a particular group keeps making mistakes in register manipulation. Or they forget to close a table. In a software factory, it would be important to have a system for development-process control that, relying on a history of these mistakes, would prevent them from recurring.[16]

A Tailored Factory Network with Centralized R&D

Kiichi Fujino, a manager working directly under Mizuno who also played a major role in strategy formulation and implementation, stressed similar ideas but placed more emphasis on the need to centralize process R&D while tailoring tools and techniques to the different types of software products. These two objectives, centralizing and tailoring, posed somewhat conflicting aims, as NEC and many other firms have discovered. Not surprisingly, NEC encountered its share of conflicts and mistakes, although managers also proved able to overcome many hurdles by using or experimenting with a variety of organizational mechanisms to foster common goals as well as encourage better communication between central R&D and product divisions.

Fujino's personal background leaned heavily toward central research as well as an academic perspective. He entered NEC in 1968 after working for eleven years in the Production Engineering Laboratory of Waseda University, and had been one of Waseda's first graduates in computer science, receiving a bachelor of science degree in 1955, a master's in 1957, and a doctorate in 1973.[17] In NEC he joined and later headed the Computer Science Research Laboratory, founded under NEC's Central Research Laboratories to study software engineering, and subsequently managed the Basic Software Development Division, before becoming director of the Software Product Engineering Laboratory in 1981.

In a 1984 article, Fujino revealed that, in reviewing its communications and computer businesses in the mid-1970s, NEC managers had come to the conclusion that they had to master five types of software development to serve the needs of NEC customers effectively: "basic software for host computers; distributed systems application software; on-line real-time control software; industry-oriented application software; and built-in microcomputer software."[18] They also concluded— backtracking slightly from an earlier attempt to promote standardization—that, "NEC must meet different customer needs, so it is difficult and not really desirable to standardize completely."[19] At the same time, Fujino and other NEC managers apparently affirmed their commitment to some type of factory rationalization for software production, because they saw this as equally essential "to accommodate the expanding use of computers." After reflecting on what they and other firms had done in software since the beginning of the industry, they went on to refine ideas such as Mizuno had discussed in 1975 and revise the factory concepts NEC would attempt to introduce.[20]

Until around 1970, Fujino noted that most firms wrote software with individuals or small groups of skilled engineers using computer languages tailored to particular machines, with some primitive time sharing among project members but mainly individual work and batch processing, that is, writing programs that at a later time ran as separate jobs on the computer. There was not much integration of tools, techniques, or management. By the mid-1970s, however, firms had begun to introduce more conversational languages as well as utilize techniques such as structured design and coding, top-down design, and chief-programmer teams, in addition to UNIX and other environments that facilitated distributed software development and the sharing of tools, files, and program components, as well as coordinated project management. These tools and techniques represented first steps toward a factory or engineering process. In the 1980s, many companies introduced even more integrated and conversational modes of programming, and more closely linked tools, control systems, methods, and databases that made up the programming environment, in order to promote coordination within large projects and across different teams and functions, such as development and maintenance, since software programs had become very long and complex. Yet the technology was still evolving, as seen in the trend beginning in the late 1980s toward more "intelligence oriented" programming, that is, applying AI technology to tools in even more highly integrated programming environments (Figure 6.1).[21]

Fujino not only saw NEC as participating in these trends but as leading the way in some areas, such as with its own system for a "modern software factory." This consisted of a centralized laboratory directing tool and method development for closely linked operating divisions and "sat-

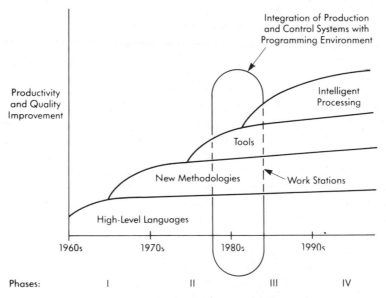

Figure 6.1 Evolution of Software Production Systems. Phase I = source-oriented (batch or large time-sharing systems); II = on-line conversational mode (UNIX, work stations, specific techniques); III = integrated conversational-mode (integration of tools, methods, controls); IV = intelligence-oriented (applications of artificial intelligence). (*Source*: Fujino Kiichi, "Sofutouea seisan gijutsu no genjo" [The Trends of Software Engineering], *NEC gijutsu* 40, 1, 1987, pp. 3, 8.)

ellite offices," including subsidiaries. The objective—a distributed and centralized "factory network"—would allow NEC to accommodate software demand well into the future by taking advantage of programmers in different locations, rather than relying solely on the limited and expensive supply of manpower in Tokyo (Table 6.5).[22]

Permanent But Flexible Factory Environments

Motoei Azuma, an engineering graduate of Waseda University who entered NEC in 1963, played a major role in conceptualizing and constructing software-factory environments—tools, methods, and physical layouts—as head of the Software Management Engineering Department in the Software Product Engineering Laboratory. Before leaving NEC in 1987 to join the faculty of industrial engineering at Tokyo's Waseda University, which cooperated closely with NEC in various areas, Azuma had supervised NEC's research on software-engineering management and, at Waseda, continued working with NEC on factory environments.

Azuma believed that, while producing new types of programs resembled R&D, treating all software development as a form of R&D—that is, as an activity that a firm cannot closely control or systematize—would not bring the degree of improvements in productivity or quality he and other NEC managers wanted. They recognized that aspects of software development made it inappropriate to transfer manufacturing practices too directly from hardware plants, so they sought to devise specific standards, methods, tools, and programming environments—in essence, different factory infrastructures—to optimize the software production process for the different types of programs NEC's businesses required.

Developing large operating systems, for example, appeared more like R&D to Azuma than manufacturing, since they required experimentation in design and thus more process flexibility. Smaller software products like facsimile or PBX software, however, closely resembled hardware design projects and thus, he thought, lent themselves to more precise

Table 6.5 1986 Software Factory Concept

Central research laboratory for developing
    tools and methods
Software work stations
Communications utilities for satellite offices
Appropriate physical environment
Management engineering techniques
    Productivity metrics
    Quality metrics
    Cost control system
    Management visibility

Source: Kiichi Fujino interview, July 28, 1986.

control. Business applications programs were often very similar across different projects and contained modules that could be reused. This kind of software also offered possibilities for an automated production process. In fact, building on the standardization and structured methodology efforts of the 1970s, and the quality control program of the early 1980s, the Software Product Engineering Laboratory during the mid-1980s studied both automation and reusability, and produced program-generator tools such as SEA/I (System Engineering Architecture/1) for applications software, which Mizuno considered a "first step" in the development of an automatic programming tool that truly accumulated knowledge in the sense of offering a continually expanding database of new programs and components.[23]

Another reason Azuma and other NEC managers pursued factory concepts was to introduce more of a permanent "department management" structure for software development rather than simply relying on ad hoc groups and procedures established for each customer or project. Azuma felt strongly that organizations utilizing ad hoc projects alone focused too much on short-term schedules, specification changes, and quality problems while neglecting the long-term allocation of resources to develop employees, facilities and tools, and programming environments.[24]

This last point reflected another of Azuma's interests—designing optimal "software factory environments." He began research in this area during 1980, with the assistance of Katsumi Honda and other researchers from NEC and Waseda University, applying industrial-engineering and ergonomic techniques borrowed from conventional manufacturing but taking into account the greater "mental effort" required in software development. Their objective was to provide guidelines for constructing software facilities without presenting a fixed design, so that facilities could adapt to different types of projects and evolve along with the technology:

> Software productivity can be improved by a well-designed work environment, as holds true in the case of hardware production. Environmental requirements depend on how work is to be carried out in the environment. However, since software projects are changing every day, and since software development methodology, tools and other technologies are always evolving, the best work environment should not be considered as being firmly fixed. Instead, a software work environment should be designed so that it can be modified in accordance with software project changes and software development technology evolution. Therefore, it is necessary to provide guidelines, which set forth the environment design methodology and environment database.[25]

The project team NEC organized to study factory layouts consisted of software engineers, architects, and other potential users of the facility, as well as experts on software-engineering environments. The team identified seven elements that seemed to define an optimal facility, that is, one providing enough flexibility for different products and promising improved process and quality control. Their factory thus offered a more integrated development environment specially designed for software engineers and complete with more tools, methods, and staff support than ad hoc projects could provide, as Honda and Azuma described in a 1988 paper:

1. A software factory is a total system entity which consists of work environment, development environment, software tools, manufacturing technologies, organizations, and management system, specially designed for software products manufacturing.
2. A software factory manufactures software products, which are to be sold to customers as is or as a part of a system product. Software products include computer programs, appropriate documents, such as users' manuals, and customer support activities.
3. The work environment, such as building or floor space and accommodations, have been designed, selected and arranged specifically for software production work, considering the work behavior and communication between engineers.
4. The development environment, such as work stations or computer terminals, operating systems and a local area network, was installed so that the maximum range of software tools can be most effectively utilized.
5. A set of standardized software tools is provided along with standard utilization methods. Each tool and method has been selected or developed carefully so that they may be coordinated with other tools and methods, and so that they may constitute an effective software manufacturing system.
6. The organizational structure for a software factory could be either functional or matrix, instead of making sole use of a project team. At the very least, a quality assurance function, a software engineering function and a cost and schedule management function are independent from the manufacturing function.
7. The management system supports ways to manage personnel, resources, processing, quality control and work schedules to enable manufacturing software products having the required quality within a specific budget by the set delivery date.[26]

Factory Organization and Management Systems

In retrospect, NEC's first step toward a factory structure for software development consisted of founding the Basic Software Development Division at the Fuchu Works in 1974, thereby separating organizationally operating-systems development from hardware development. NEC subsequently established other organizations at Mita, Tamagawa, and Abiko, all within the Tokyo metropolis or suburbs, for its other software needs, as well as dispersed programming work throughout Japan and, on a smaller scale, abroad, to Korea and Singapore. NEC introduced companywide standards and linked some sites through communication networks.[27] The separation and separate histories of these facilities, however, gradually presented greater problems for managers pursuing standardization and common goals such as quality improvement throughout the NEC group. Table 6.6 and the following discussions summarize the key initiatives NEC managers adopted to create a more effective multi-product, multiprocess factory network.

Software Strategy Project, 1976–1979

After establishing a separate division for basic software, NEC's next major step consisted of the Software Strategy Project, started in 1976 as a three-year effort to integrate programming operations on a groupwide

Table 6.6 Software Factory Implementation

Year	Initiative	Focus/Outcomes
1974	Basic Software Development Division	Organizational separation of software from hardware development
1976–1979	Software Strategy Project	Standardization of data collection, tool and structured-programming methodology for basic and applications software throughout the NEC group, with the objectives of raising productivity and quality
1980	Software Product Engineering Laboratory	Centralization of process and tool R&D for dissemination to divisions and subsidiaries
1981	Software Quality Control (SWQC)	Establishment of a groupwide methodology, training program, and control measures for improving software quality, including quality circle activities
1982–1985	Software Problem Strategy Project	1) "Mapping" of software development activities 2) Subcontracting management 3) Software productivity improvement
1986	Software-Factory Design Project	Establishment of Hokuriku Software Development Center, based on ergonomic principles and other software-factory concepts
1987	C&C Software Development Group	Reorganization of the Software Product Engineering Laboratory and expansion of applied research

Source: Kiichi Fujino and Motoei Azuma interviews, July 28, 1986; Yukio Mizuno interview, Aug. 25, 1988.

basis (including all in-house divisions and subsidiaries, rather than just the Computer Division). Mizuno chaired the committee, which oversaw two subprojects: one for applications software (headed by Mizuno) and one for systems software (headed by Fujino).

The project, while unique at the time in Japan's software industry for its scope and prescience, resembled efforts firms in other industries had pursued to eliminate waste in engineering and production operations. Elimination of waste in software, to NEC managers, meant reducing redundancies among projects by introducing standards for tools, procedures, and methodologies for all phases of development and all aspects of management. Yet a key difficulty remained: how to accomplish this while allowing individuals, projects, and divisions sufficient flexibility to tailor standards to the needs of their products and customers.

Fujino, as he proclaimed in a 1983 article, clearly saw more efforts at standardization as the key to better productivity and quality: "The one way to improve software productivity and quality is standardization. Not only standardization of the components and functions used to write software products, but also the development and production process, the maintenance and operations process, work tasks, system interfaces, system utilization procedures, system operating methods—the standardization of all these facets touching software will become increasingly important in the future."[28] He thus pushed divisions in the late 1970s to reexamine development procedures, methods, documentation, product requirements, components, data collection, and tools, and seek opportunities for standards and improvement. Divisions also reexamined control and management systems, where Fujino suggested there were opportunities to improve planning and estimation techniques, technology accumulation and sharing, programming environments, quality, standards promotion, and inspection.

Perhaps the project's most important achievement centered on the introduction of a set of tools and techniques based around structured design and programming. In particular, NEC created STEPS (Standardized Technology and Engineering for Programming Support) to guide applications software development, from requirements specification through maintenance. This proved useful not only because it promoted standardization around good techniques; STEPS (described later) also facilitated communication and divisions of labor among project personnel.[29]

Software Product Engineering Laboratory, 1980–1987

When the Software Strategy Project ended, managers who worked on the effort noticed another weakness in NEC's structure for managing software development: the lack of permanent staff to explore and follow through on key issues or technologies. Project members had worked on assignments only in their spare time, and the infrequency of meetings had limited progress. Mizuno in particular concluded that "we had to be more systematic" if NEC were truly going to continue improving productivity, quality, and management control.[30] Thus, to insure continuity and proceed beyond the Software Strategy Project, NEC in 1980 established the Software Product Engineering Laboratory to lead the company's efforts in software engineering R&D, making this organization part of NEC's Central Research Laboratories.

Mizuno launched the new laboratory and then delegated the post of director to Fujino in 1981. At this time the laboratory contained approximately 30 full-time researchers and another 30 affiliated members. By 1986, the number of researchers had grown to 170 full-time members (out of 900 total staff assigned to the Central Research Laboratories), including those in a newly separated laboratory for microcomputer software development. The mission of the laboratory, under Fujino's direction, retained an emphasis on general productivity, quality, and management issues as well as support technologies, but, as seen in the list of objectives below, researchers also pursued specific themes, including the refinement of automated tools, reusability techniques, and factory concepts:

1. Improvement of the production process and environment through work standardization and introduction of software CAD/CAM and other computer-aided tools.
2. Systematic reuse of existing software and knowhow through the standardization of software design structures, techniques to display the contents of software components, and standardization of component interface technology.
3. Prevention and elimination of waste by establishment of a process that minimizes bugs and mistakes, R&D on inspection and quality-assurance tools and techniques, and prevention of duplicate development by horizontal product planning.
4. Improvement of upstream phases and tools through expansion of tools and techniques for requirements analysis and specification, prevention of waste by strengthening reviews early in development, and extension of reuse for specifications and design information and knowhow.
5. Improvement of individual skills and knowledge through increasing training of engineers and managers.
6. Establishment and application of the software-factory concept through construction of a software production line and integrated factory control and information system.[31]

Fujino organized the facility into three departments covering software-engineering technology (methodologies and tools for software design, production, and maintenance), software-management engineering (methodologies and tools for software production and product management), and interface architectures (networks and information portability).[32] Funding came mainly but not entirely from corporate R&D funds. If a division wanted to sell a particular tool the laboratory developed, NEC could choose to treat the tool expenses as part of product-development expenses, and request at least some divisional revenues to cover the costs. Tools that NEC would not sell outside the company as products, but which had specific in-house applications, NEC funded primarily by R&D expenses but also might charge some to in-house divisions that eventually used the tools. In either case, like Hitachi and Toshiba, from 1980 on NEC did not tie process R&D to specific projects or divisions, but carried this out as a permanent, staff activity with multiple sources of funding.

This mode of financing also helped forge necessary, though not always successful, linkages between divisions and the central laboratory. Two issues—how to make sure the researchers worked on tools and methods appropriate for developers in the product divisions, and how to transfer technology from the laboratory to other parts of NEC—continued to preoccupy NEC managers and encourage them to experiment with various organizational alternatives. One solution to both problems was for research staff to plan and develop tools or methods in conjunction with engineers from the product divisions. Another was for researchers to develop tools and then teach divisions how to use them. A staff-level Software Education Department also assisted laboratory personnel in education planning and training, especially in areas such as quality control methods, although, perhaps reflecting Fujino's background, the laboratory tended toward academic research, prompting another series of organizational changes in the late 1980s.

Software Quality Control (SWQC) Program, 1981–

The SWQC Program dates back to 1978, when a handful of NEC managers established a software quality control study group. There was not at this time much knowledge available about software quality control within Japan, and Japanese managers feared they were falling far behind the United States. NEC Chairman Kobayashi proposed they initiate a formal review of software quality techniques and enlisted the help of a Japanese professor as well as quality experts from NEC's hardware divisions. Mizuno led the study group, which included Fujino and Azuma and remained active for three years. Similar to the original Software Strategy Project, however, this was not a full-time activity for the committee members. They had no regular staff, and meetings lasted a few hours once or twice a month. Nonetheless, they covered a wide variety of quality-related problems and began drawing up guidelines for quality control procedures that would have a major impact on NEC operations in the future.[33]

Several specific conclusions came out of the review. First, research in software development indicated a strong correlation between quality and productivity, reflecting the manpower required to fix defects. Hence, they concluded that any revolution in software productivity would require correspondingly dramatic improvements in quality control practices. The best strategy, Fujino recalled, seemed to be to "pursue quality in software, and productivity will follow." They also thought it impossible to "inspect out bugs," and this meant that quality had to be "built in at each phase of development," with department-level managers, as well as developers, fully involved in any quality control effort.[34] Taking the position, however, that software differed from hardware development because it required more "intellectual activity" and "desk work," they decided not to copy hardware quality control practices and rely on hardware quality experts. Instead, NEC hired several U.S. software quality specialists, including Gerald Weinberg, to help them develop a unique system for software quality evaluation and design reviews. Surveys of NEC projects also supported the observation that "human factors," that is, differences in programmer skills and experience, seemed to be the most important elements influencing individual performance, and that NEC had to address training more seriously if it were to make major advances in productivity or quality.[35]

NEC management acted quickly on these observations. Mizuno decided that, while the laboratory and some division personnel should continue to work on new tools and techniques, NEC had to set up a broad quality control program that focused on motivation, teamwork methodologies, training, and other factors affecting individual performance.[36] Since evidence from manufacturing departments indicated that bringing employees together in small groups helped solve quality problems, NEC imported the concept of quality circles. In a six-month trial during 1980, NEC also experimented with applying other techniques used in hardware quality control, including statistical quality control and studies of worker behavior, modified for software.

Next, in 1981, NEC created a formal, companywide organization covering all aspects of software production, management, services, sales, and training, named the SWQC Program (Table 6.7). Mizuno headed the SWQC Group Activity Steering Committee and Fujino the Administration Committee. NEC first managed the effort as part of an existing zero-defect program, but later made it independent, placing it under the Planning Office of a new Computers and Communications (C&C) Software Development Group established in 1987.[37]

NEC departments then formed quality circles under the guidance of another new organization, the SWQC Information Center.[38] Initially,

Table 6.7 NEC's Software Quality Control (SWQC) Organizational Structure (1986)

Structure	Focus
Zero-Defect Steering Committee	General hardware and software quality policy formation, corporate-director level
Companywide SWQC Group Activity Steering Committee	Software QC policy formation, division-manager level
Administration Committee	Planning for training and education
SWQC Information Center	Training and education
Study Group	Research and recommendations
SWQC Group Activity Management Committee	Policy and implementation, department-level and suppliers
SWQC groups	Quality circle activities for all employees

Source: Yukio Mizuno, "Software Quality Improvement," *Computer*, March 1983, p. 71; Kiichi Fujino interview, July 28, 1986.

staff members from the center estimated where and how many sections should form these groups and then they asked managers to allow employees to devote some time, usually once a week for two hours, to circle activities. Once formed, the groups analyzed data on errors, reported on their results, and participated in the establishment of measures to prevent similar errors from recurring (Table 6.8). SWQC groups also performed internal reviews of programs in development, in order to catch mistakes early; these supplemented formal third-party technical reviews conducted in later stages of development. To guide group activities, the center held training workshops for group leaders and published handbooks and manuals, such as *The Seven Tools of SWQC*. These manuals presented quality control techniques based on those used in other Japanese industries and outlined how to deploy data sorting, control charts, and Pareto charts for data analysis, and then brainstorming, cause-effect

Table 6.8 Software Quality Control (SWQC) Process

1. SWQC grouping
2. Target setting
3. Orientation
4. Data collection
5. Cause analysis
6. Consideration of radical measures
7. Filling in the SWQC report
8. Proposal and implementation
9. Reporting
10. Publication of excellent results
11. Management evaluation and awards
12. Repetitive enforcement

Source: Mizuno, "Software Quality Improvement," p. 70.

diagrams, and other methods to find the sources of errors in software products.

According to Mizuno, despite the popularity of quality circles in other NEC divisions since the 1960s, NEC programmers at first resisted the idea of joining them. "Every programmer was against me," he recalled. "They're white-collar workers and they protested that quality control was a blue-collar problem." Eventually, however, Mizuno and other NEC managers persuaded 95 percent of NEC's software developers to join the groups.[39] As of 1985, NEC had approximately 1,700 software quality circles involving 10,000 software personnel.[40]

Managers devoted so much attention to the SWQC Program and quality circles, according to Mizuno, because they proved to be essential not only for quality control but also for individual and team motivation. Circle activities helped people communicate and cooperate in teams, while SWQC conferences held twice a year, an awards conference held annually, and prizes given to teams, provided recognition to both individuals and groups. As an example of their impact, in a 1983 article, Mizuno reported major reductions in debugging time, defect rates, program sizes, and specifications changes achieved through specific efforts made through the SWQC activities (Table 6.9).

In addition, as Azuma noted, NEC managers came to use quality circles as effective supplements to the two or three months of formal training required of all new software personnel. The practice of individuals coming together regularly to study various problems and techniques also seemed to reduce differences in skill levels by helping new or weaker personnel improve more quickly.[41] Structuring the development process to encourage teamwork and lessen variability in individual performance reflected another factory goal, as Mizuno discussed in a 1983 article:

> Software projects tend to overemphasize technical aspects. After all, people organized into teams do the work. For projects to proceed smoothly, the human factor must receive adequate consideration. The capability of those

Table 6.9 Software Quality Control (SWQC) Program Results

Division	Target	Results
Switching	Machine time for debugging	Down 1/3
Transmission Control	Defect ratio	1.37–0.41/ks
Minicomputer Operating System	Defect ratio	0.35–0.20/ks
Mainframe Operating System	Defect ratio	6–0.9/mo
	Source size	20–8ks
	Object size	72–26kb
Large Applications	Specification changes	Down 40%

mo = month. ks = kilo-steps (1,000 lines of code). kb = kilo-bytes.
Source: Mizuno, "Software Quality Improvement," p. 71.

involved in software work varies remarkably. Many claim that the relative abilities of programmers can vary by as much as 30 to one. . . . It will become ever more vital to structure projects so that software quality and productivity do not directly reflect these differences. Training can develop skills, and we can produce tools that yield quality and productivity within given ranges regardless of the worker. We can also assemble teams and assign work in ways that compensate for individual differences.

We need to develop better techniques for software production, but we must also carefully study our organizational frameworks for software development and maintenance. We must devise control methods that match the frameworks.

People are at the heart of software work; obviously, human error cannot be allowed to lead to major bugs or malfunctions. Here, teamwork will be the key. Team members working together are, in their collective wisdom, far more effective than individuals working alone.[42]

Software Problem Strategy Project, 1982–1985

Unlike the SWQC Program, which remained an ongoing effort within NEC, the Software Problem Strategy Project launched in 1982 was another temporary, three-year effort. The previous (1976–1979) strategy project had developed new methods and tools relying heavily on structured techniques, and began introducing these for different product families. The follow-up attempted to encourage more standardization in development and quality control practices, explore various productivity-improvement measures, and establish or formally designate a series of software factories to serve NEC's different product divisions. NEC President Sekimoto formally headed the project, with Mizuno acting as the subleader.[43]

In particular, the new project dealt with two emerging trends managers believed NEC had to confront to remain competitive in the software business: decentralization—the growing geographical distribution of groups developing and supporting programs; and "asynchronism"—the reality that groups developed parts of programs at different times, as well as in different places.[44] The cost of physical space and the shortage of programmers living or willing to live in Tokyo, and the need to service customers from all parts of the country, had forced NEC to spread its software operations around Japan, and this complicated the tasks of managers who wanted to achieve greater levels of standardization, control, and performance.[45] In applications development, for example, while NEC did not emphasize the separation of systems engineering or design from program construction as formally as other Japanese facilities, it was still common to divide work among NEC divisions, subsidiaries, and affiliated software houses, depending on manpower availability and expertise.[46] As the scale of these operations grew, NEC needed a better way to insure that groups used similar methods and tools, as well as met other management objectives, such as for cost or quality.

NEC executives decided to act in three areas. First, they carried out a "software production mapping." This consisted of constructing a logistical and organizational layout of programming operations within NEC by product (basic software, industrial systems, business applications, transmission systems, switching software, and microcomputer software), to determine which software houses divisions were using to assist in development and whether divisions needed more help, such as new subsidiaries that might serve as additional software factories. Second, they decided to formalize and systematize procedures for managing software subcontractors. And third, they launched another effort to improve and link software productivity and quality assurance measures by establishing a Software Productivity Committee to study documentation control, quality control, software productivity and quality measurements, cost estimation, personnel education, project management, support tools, and production environments.[47]

Software Factory Design Project, 1986–

Since the mid-1970s, NEC executives, led by Kobayashi, Mizuno, and Fujino, had stressed the importance of moving software development beyond the craft stage to a level of discipline and productivity comparable to modern engineering and factory operations. They did not attach the words *software factory* to specific buildings but instead emphasized concepts such as process standardization, quality control, reusability, or automated tools. One of the next steps in the research on programming environments at the Software Product Engineering Laboratory was to develop guidelines for designing actual software factories, from higher-level concepts, such as tool and methodology standardization, to smaller details, such as how to arrange programmers' work spaces or recreation areas.

The first beneficiary of this effort turned out to be a new subsidiary in Ishikawa Prefecture, NEC Hokuriku Software. In 1986, NEC funded the construction of a new software center, modeled to some extent after IBM's Santa Teresa Laboratory but with a specific difference. NEC's objective was to make and operate the facility more like a factory than a collection of private offices in a laboratory atmosphere, as the authors of a 1987 paper explained: "A characteristic feature of the NEC Hokuriku Software Center is that it was not primarily designed as an office. Instead, it was designed as a software factory, based on the software factory concept."[48] NEC researchers also described the elements they felt created a total factory system, linking methods, tools, control procedures, organizational structure, and product objectives.

For the development environment, Hokuriku and other facilities received work spaces and equipment intended to maximize programmer productivity. While the NEC researchers acknowledged that individual activities were "the most significant productivity work in software development," they also viewed meetings and other "communication efforts" as essential. In addition to allocating space for meeting rooms and recreation areas, the project thus designed both individual work cells and clusters of cells for group work in a "team oriented work style." In the tradition of job studies in other industries, they also examined programmer motions and equipment layout, such as the arrangement of desks, chairs, filing cabinets, or terminals, which might require unnecessary movements; physical factors, including furniture and lighting, which contributed to fatigue; and elements affecting concentration and motivation, such as noise or color coordination in the surroundings. The researchers also discovered that, in contrast to U.S. firms, where programmers appeared to prefer separate work areas, NEC personnel preferred to work in open clusters, in a more team-oriented fashion.[49]

C&C Software Development Group, 1987

The centralized laboratory for software-engineering R&D did not work quite as well as NEC managers had hoped. According to Mizuno, a split had emerged. Older laboratory researchers were becoming more academic in orientation while engineers and SWQC teams in the product divisions seemed to be doing more valuable applied studies. To encourage more practical research that better met the needs of product divisions, but without eliminating fundamental research, a 1987 reorganization moved the basic researchers to NEC's Central Research Laboratories. This involved no organizational change, since the Software Product Engineering Laboratory had been a part of the central labs; however, physically removing the more academic researchers left a group more concerned with applied work. Management then expanded the number of applied researchers and divided them into four areas under the umbrella of a newly created C&C Software Development Group, headed again by Fujino.[50]

As seen in Table 6.10, the Software Planning Office took charge of running the companywide software quality control effort. The Software Engineering Development Laboratory conducted research on tools and integrated development environments, as well as software-engineering management, and established a consulting department to help transfer technology or assist operating divisions and subsidiaries. The C&C Common Software Development Laboratory developed packages and other "common" software for microcomputers, including programs written for the TRON operating system and hardware architecture (see Chapter 8).

Table 6.10 Computers and Communications (C&C) Software
Development Group Organization (1988)

Software Planning Office (SWQC)
Software Engineering Development Laboratory
   Development Technology
   Engineering Management
   Consultation
C&C Common Software Development Laboratory (microcomputers)
C&C System Interface Laboratory

SWQC = Software Quality Control.
Source: Yukio Mizuno interview, July 25, 1988.

Finally, the C&C Systems Interface Laboratory worked on compatibility
and network technology.

Development Techniques and Computer-Aided Tools

Product-Process Segmentation

NEC's efforts during the 1970s and early 1980s in strategic planning,
standardization and quality control, as well as process R&D, all reflected
a common goal: improve software productivity. Management primarily
focused on data collection and analysis for incremental improvement of
manual techniques. In the 1980s, however, along with continuing pressures for standardization, NEC added other areas of emphasis: (1) application of CAD/CAM for software; (2) reuse of existing software to build
new programs; (3) more cross-product planning and better requirements definition, to reduce duplication and waste in development; and
(4) extension of standardization, quality metrics, quality assurance methods and tools, and education programs to raise the quality of NEC products and the performance of software personnel throughout the NEC
group.[51] For any of these emphases to succeed, managers also concluded
they had to establish a distinct process strategy for each of the different
products NEC produced.

As Azuma and Mizuno explained in a 1981 article, experience indicated that general-purpose basic software, like control programs for operating systems, usually had to be compact, use as little memory as possible, and offer a variety of functions for different users. Therefore,
writing this type of software "required . . . a high degree of skill" as well
as new designs, so reuse of standardized modules or patterns seemed
inappropriate. Nevertheless, to improve productivity, they still thought
it possible to standardize methods for development, quality assurance,
and project management. On the other hand, language processors and

certain kinds of applications software contained many similarities and less functional constraints, and offered more opportunities for modularization, structured techniques, and even assembly of new programs from standardized components.[52]

Within applications programming, Azuma and Mizuno identified several specific types, each with very different characteristics. One they called "large-scale and/or complex software used repeatedly." This included train-seat reservation systems, process-control programs for steel mills, factory-production control systems, and on-line banking programs. All had a common primary requirement, "to operate accurately." Yet, rather than focusing on tools to verify logical correctness or to reuse code, as some other producers did, they promoted accuracy in development through "techniques, documentation, nomenclature, etc. important for harmonizing work by many programmers." For the most part, NEC relied on the STEPS methodology for this type of software development, unless customers specified other standards.

Medium-scale software for scientific and engineering calculations demanded even more accuracy and reliability. Since the algorithms code implemented remained complex, the NEC managers chose verification technology as the main area of research. Azuma and Mizuno further concluded that, "Programs of this type have a character close to the arts, and standardization is not a significant factor." In contrast, another application type, "small-scale, simple software used only once," such as for management reports from databases or simple engineering calculations, seemed easy and inexpensive to write. Therefore, for this type, they did not stress highly standardized methods or tools.

NEC originally developed the STEPS methodology for a fourth type of applications software, "small-scale, simple software used repeatedly." This included batch-processing programs such as for inventory updates and common business applications averaging 500 lines of code in COBOL and ranging to no more than about 3,000. Research in this area provided the data Chairman Kobayashi later drew on to claim that factory methods suited 90 percent of common software applications, as Azuma and Mizuno noted: "When these programs are classified according to process patterns such as updating and inquiries, about 90% of them belong to any one of about 20 types of patterns. Programs involving entirely new patterns are few." Since there was so much similarity, NEC found it relatively easy to develop standardized techniques, nomenclature, and documents, as well as standardized reusable components.

Management Systems and Tools for Basic Software

Product-Line Incompatibilities: An historical artifact complicated standardization efforts during the 1970s and 1980s: NEC supported four incompatible operating systems, including one inherited from GE via Toshiba. On the one hand, groups developing and maintaining these incompatible systems had become accustomed to their own sets of tools and techniques, which made switching psychologically difficult. In addition, many of the tools and techniques relied on particular features of the hardware architectures and operating systems, presenting technical obstacles to switching or to reusing tools and code across systems. Rather than be defeated by diversity and inertia, NEC managers claimed their situation forced them to plan even more deliberately than their counterparts in other divisions to gain any economies across different product lines.

Even though the architectures differed (despite converging gradually), NEC found ways to reuse software parts at least for language utilities and database programs.[53] By creating a system description language (CPL) independent of hardware architectures, developers were able to reuse modules for common functions such as file input/output, library access, display management, and system information acquisition. In one study of fourteen compiler development projects for small and medium mainframes as well as "intelligent" terminals (terminals that contained their own data-processing or computing capabilities, in addition to linking the user with a central computer located elsewhere), NEC reported that, after building the first version from scratch using CPL, subsequent compilers averaged approximately 90 percent reuse of the original design.[54]

In general, however, the incompatibility of different machines and the presence of old software and documentation made it difficult to standardize tools and reuse code in basic software. This prompted NEC managers to delay the full introduction of integrated design-support and process-control tools, such as in use at Hitachi and Toshiba, and instead emphasize the refinement of existing tools as well as generic techniques for project management and quality control, as the examples discussed later will illustrate.

Early Project Management: NEC began experimenting with different techniques for project management and cost modeling in the late 1960s, relying heavily on Honeywell as well as SDC. First, after Honeywell successfully completed an operating system for its mainframe computers, NEC's Computer Division, to develop its own MODE IV operating system, decided to copy Honeywell's project-management process, which relied on a PERT model diagramming the path for critical events in an overall program-development process. "We were very influenced by Honeywell," Mizuno admitted. Yet the Japanese soon realized that the PERT diagrams were only as accurate as their planning parameters, and these proved so inaccurate that none of the actual projects came out close to the scheduled time or cost estimates.

Next, NEC adopted a planning and forecasting model SDC had designed for the U.S. Navy during the 1960s. This estimated schedules and costs in more detail, breaking them down for specific development phases, defined as specifications design, detailed design, coding, and component test. NEC managers felt this was superior to Honeywell's PERT charts and vague guidelines, although Mizuno found serious deficiencies in the SDC system as well. The main weakness stemmed from SDC's decision to fix the parameters and coefficients in the model, and base them on the average performance levels of its engineers, who, compared to the Japanese, were relatively skilled and experienced. The model could not take into account different skill or experience levels, or changes in productivity over time. NEC managers thus determined that they needed a more dynamic model that could accommodate various performance levels as well as any additional factors that might affect software costs and productivity.

At this point, around 1967, NEC engineers took matters into their own hands. They had accumulated enough project data from MODE IV to calculate standard times for different development activities according to the type of basic software and to begin devising a new planning model, completed in rough form during 1969–1970. Mizuno admitted that the new standard times and model were primitive, primarily because they lacked a good metric for measuring productivity and relied simply on lines of code in a given period of time. Recognition of this inadequacy led NEC managers to collect and analyze more data as well as do more work on cost modeling, project management, and documentation: "We came to the conclusion that we had to introduce more scientific measures for software productivity."

NEC continued to refine its cost-estimation model over the next several years and finished a completely new version in 1977, based on multifactor regressions derived from the research of J.W. Bailey and V.R. Basili at the University of Maryland. Bailey and Basili provided several standard expressions that allowed users to select from their own data different factors that appeared to affect costs. To make it easier to use, the expression of the NEC model followed the popular COCOMO format that Barry Boehm and his staff at TRW had earlier proposed, thus taking into account elements such as program size, tools and methodologies, operating system and hardware interface, years of experience for the project members, dependence on outside work, frequency of change in specifications, user characteristics, product flexibility, novelty or complexity of the product, quality requirements, and overall team ability.[55]

NEC revised standard times annually and used comparisons of estimates and actual project data to continue improving the model.[56] This constant updating and refinement eventually made the model useful as a tool for detailed productivity analysis. By establishing a productivity range and mean productivity coefficient value for each factor, for example, the model determined the effect of particular factors on productivity and estimated where and how much improvement was feasible in each area. Recent data suggested development tools, quality requirements, outside procurement, product flexibility, and frequency of specification changes offered the most room for improvement.[57]

Integration of Tools and Techniques: As part of the SWQC activities at the Fuchu Works during the early 1980s, managers in the Basic Software Division's Quality Assurance Department decided to compile a manual detailing the use of this model and other techniques and integrate them into a more comprehensive "scientific" production and quality control system. The name they chose for the system, reflecting its experimental nature, was HEART (Hopeful Engineering for Advanced Reliability Engineering). The Quality Assurance Department took on the role of promoter and assisted NEC subsidiaries and affiliated software houses in adopting the HEART techniques.[58]

In proposing HEART, NEC managers followed the assumption that better quality leads to higher productivity, and that they should link data collection and analysis efforts for both process and quality control. To implement this strategy, HEART techniques covered several areas: project management, including performance standards and team-oriented methods; standardization of design and programming methods and tools; modularization techniques to promote reuse (as well as maintenance); and formalization of testing tools and procedures.

For project management, HEART required detailed process-data collection, mainly tracking scheduling and productivity, for seven phases: requirements analysis and definition; functional design; detailed design (in SPD charts); coding (mainly in a PL/1 subset, HPL, with some in C and assembler); unit and function test; system integration; and system test. As in Hitachi's factory for basic software, NEC did not divide labor among these phases except to the extent that less-experienced programmers tended to do detailed design and coding while more experienced personnel handled requirements analysis and high-level design.[59] Primarily, NEC used the phase breakdowns for managerial control, relying on data collection and reports at specific points, including development-item histories from requirements analysis through coding and quality-accounting reports from unit/function test through system test.

Also similar to Hitachi's CAPS and Toshiba's SWB, new HEART tools automated some of the data input and kept project and testing information in a central database accessible to managers through on-line terminals (Figure 6.2 and Table 6.11). In addition, HEART procedures called for periodic "process management meetings" to discuss two issues: adherence to promised delivery (release) dates; and quality of the final product. Managers considered data from several models, but primarily

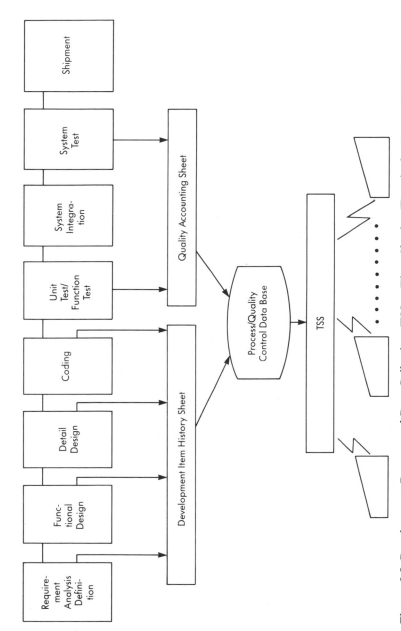

Figure 6.2 Development Process and Data Collection. TSS = Time-Sharing Terminals. (*Source*: NEC Corporation, "QA System in NEC: Scientific Control of Production and Quality in NEC—Basic Software," unpublished internal document, Sept. 8, 1987.)

Table 6.11 Process-Control Data Items

Requirements Analysis/Definition Process
  Estimated date of completion of each process
  Estimated program size
  Estimated manpower
  Person in charge of development and years of experience
  Language in use
  Development form (new development/modification/division trans-
    plant)
  Difficulty level of development (type of program)

Functional Design Process
  Completion date
  Actual manpower used and breakdown by persons in charge
  Difference between the standard times and the manpower used
  Quantity of functional specifications and revision history
  Scale of design review (number of workers/time) and the number of
    corrections

Detailed Design Process
  Completion data
  Actual manpower used and breakdown by persons in charge
  Difference between the standard times and the manpower used
  Quantity of design specifications and revision history
  Scale of logic inspection (number of workers/time) and the number
    of corrections

Coding Process
  Completion data
  Actual manpower used and breakdown by persons in charge
  Difference between the standard times and the manpower used
  The development size
  Detailed information for each program to realize functions
  Scale of code inspection (number of workers/time) and the number
    of corrections

Unit Test/Function Test Process
  Number of test cases to be executed
  Target bugs to be detected
  Required manpower
  Number of test cases executed previously in a certain period of time
  Number of bugs detected previously in a certain period of time
  Manpower used in the past

System Test Process
  Number of test cases to be executed
  Target bugs to be detected
  Required manpower
  Number of test cases executed previously in a certain period of time
  Number of bugs detected previously in a certain period of time
  Manpower used in the past

Source: NEC Corporation, "QA System in NEC: Scientific Control of Production and Quality in NEC—Basic Software," unpublished internal document, Sept. 8, 1987, pp. 3–9.

relied on the twelve-factor cost model discussed earlier. Differences between estimated and actual manpower figures required a review of the managers in charge.[60]

For design and programming, with the exception of special projects following different customer specifications, all NEC software facilities—both for applications and basic software—used versions of SPD (Structured Programming Diagrams) and DECA (Detailed Design and Coding Assistant).[61] The SPD diagrams, which resembled Hitachi's PAD, Fujitsu's YAC-II, and NTT's HCP charts, represented program modules hierarchically and showed interrelationships in the flow of control, with text in Japanese or any other language (Figure 6.3). NEC introduced its first version of the diagrams in 1974, but encountered considerable resistance from software personnel, who had no experience in structured design. The early versions of SPD also constrained programmers because they had only simple lines and notations and lacked symbols such as for node control (input/output paths) or module names. Continual modifications and a new version introduced in 1981 along with tools such as logic tables to describe process specifications and better editors, as well as the DECA code generator, significantly increased the acceptance of SPD diagrams as well as structured methodologies within NEC.[62]

DECA translated SPD diagrams automatically into source code (C, FORTRAN, HPL, and COBOL) or source code into SPD diagrams.[63] The combination of these two tools eliminated much of the tedium (and potential errors) of coding in a variety of languages, although, compared to other CASE tools available for routine business applications (described later), DECA remained only "semi-automated." Users still had to write code to create interfaces between different modules, limiting the degree to which NEC could simplify or de-skill basic software development.[64]

Although NEC did not publish specific details of HEART tools, techniques, or performance data, according to Yozo Hirai, in 1987 the manager of the Quality Assurance Department in the Basic Software Division, HEART brought improvements in several areas. NEC generally delivered basic software products within a month of planned release dates; while these schedules included some "buffer time" to allow for slippage, Hirai claimed his division experienced an improvement of approximately 20 to 30 percent in scheduling accuracy over the past five years, and cost estimation and budget control closely followed scheduling accuracy. In addition, similar to the experiences of Hitachi and Toshiba, Hirai maintained that the HEART standards and common training allowed NEC to add people to the development process and reduce rather than increase lateness.[65]

As another indication of the usefulness of the HEART techniques, the Software Product Engineering Laboratory borrowed the project-

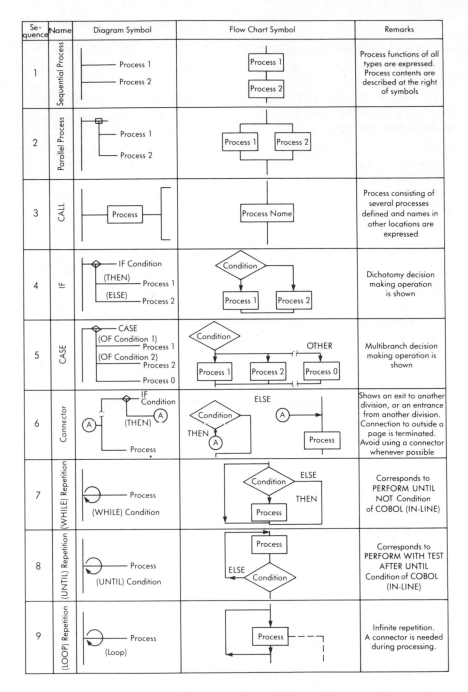

Figure 6.3 Symbols Used in Structured Programming Diagrams (SPD). (*Source*: Motoei Azuma and Yukio Mizuno, "STEPS: Integrated Software Standards and Its Productivity Impact," *Proceedings of IEEE Computer Society Conference—COMPCON '81* [IEEE Computer Society Press, 1981], p. 92. Copyright © 1981 IEEE. Reproduced with permission.)

management model and produced a version suitable for personal computers, called Table-Oriented Manager's Tool (TOMATO). This used a relational database format like LOTUS 1-2-3 to allow managers to track schedule progress, compare actual times to estimates, and do simple productivity-factor analyses.[66] A companion tool, Planning Manager (PLAM), generated graphic representations (charts) of schedule progress from TOMATO's database.[67]

Quality Control: For quality control, a particularly important technique, also devised by Basic Software's Quality Assurance Department but then transferred to other NEC facilities, was a "quality accounting system."[68] Department literature explained this as a "system in which defects generated into a program are regarded as a debt, this debt is repaid through bugs detected with a test and the shipment is performed when the debt becomes 0." The specifics of the system reveal that it closely resembled Hitachi's approach, calling for predictions of the number of potential defects, establishment of a defect control curve, and execution of tests and quality evaluations.

A simple reliability-prediction model estimated the number of defects likely to be in a certain type of software based on past data regarding the number of defects generated in similar programs (Figure 6.4). The model adjusted for eight factors: program size; degree of inspection and design review (number of corrections in functional specification, detailed design, and coding, divided by the number of documentation pages or program size); development form (new, modified, or transplanted code); language of development and degree of difficulty; type of operating system/hardware interface; years of experience of project team members; frequency of specification changes; and sufficiency of manpower. As test data accumulated for a current program, NEC substituted these in the model for the estimated figures. A control curve determined whether or not the detection of defects through testing was going according to predicted levels, based on a Gompertz curve reliability growth

$$B = a \cdot \prod_{i=1}^{n} \alpha_i \cdot S^{b_0}$$

$$\alpha_i = 10^{b_i x_i} \qquad (i = 1, 2, \ldots, n)$$

Figure 6.4 Basic Form of Reliability Prediction Model. B = number of potential bugs when the test starts (this is substituted by the number of detected bugs during the test); S = development/modification size (KL) of program; X_i = various development factors; a, b_i = proportional coefficient; b_0 = exponential coefficient. (*Source*: NEC Corporation, Basic Software Division, unpublished internal document.)

model. Test results differing significantly from predicted defect levels prompted a required investigation into the causes of the discrepancy. As at Hitachi, NEC managers considered testing completed only "[w]hen all predicted bugs are detected."

In addition, under the direction of the Quality Assurance Task Group NEC management organized in 1982 as part of its productivity improvement effort, NEC adopted another quantitative set of metrics, methods, and tools called Software Quality Measurement and Assessment Technology (SQMAT).[69] Based on the Software Quality Metrics (SQM) system developed by Gerald Murine, a U.S. consultant, the SQMAT procedures called for the determination of quality targets before each phase of development; planning meetings to discuss quality criteria; checkpoints for measuring quality; and action plans for corrective measures before proceeding on to the next phase. Factors analyzed included an interrelated set of Software Quality Design Criteria (SQDC) and Soft-

Table 6.12 Relationship between Software Quality Requirement Criteria (SQRC) and Software Quality Design Criteria (SQDC)

SQDC	SQRC	C	R	M	F	U	E	S	I
Traceability		0							
Completeness		0							
Consistency		0	0	0					
Simplicity			0	0					
Accuracy			0						
Error tolerance			0						
Modularity				0	0				
Self-descriptiveness				0	0				
Conciseness				0					
Instrumentation				0					
Generality					0				
Expandability					0				
Training						0			
Communicativeness						0			
Operability						0			
Machine independence					0				
Software system independence					0				
Execution efficiency							0		
Storage efficiency							0		
Access control								0	
Access audit								0	
Data commonality									0
Communication commonality									0

C = correctness; R = reliability; M = maintainability; F = flexibility; U = usability; E = efficiency; S = security; I = interdependability.
Source: Toshihiko Sunazuka, Motoei Azuma, and Noriko Yamagishi, "Software Quality Assessment Technology," *Proceedings ICSE* (IEEE Computer Society Press, 1985), p. 5.

ware Quality Requirements Criteria (SQRC), ranked in order of importance and measured statistically (Table 6.12).[70]

Integrated Tool Set for Communications Software

A more advanced set of tools and techniques that NEC began working on in the mid-1970s, Software Development and Maintenance System (SDMS), supported development of basic software and communications programs.[71] NEC started planning for this in 1975 and finished a first version for in-house use in 1980. A 1979 article NEC personnel published in Japan's leading journal on information processing directly compared SDMS to the SDC Software Factory as well as to other integrated tool sets at MITRE Corporation (called Simon), Softech (Software Engineering Facility), TRW (SREP), Fujitsu (SDSS), and Toshiba (SWB). According to the authors, however, while these other tools concentrated either on design support or project management, SDMS integrated both functions.[72]

The initial version of SDMS consisted of a software-development database and three subsystems. The design subsystem used state-transition diagrams for system analysis, a standardized design language (SDL) that relied on graphical representations for structural design, and tables with Japanese text for detailed (module) design. The methodology emphasized modularization and sophisticated dataflow and abstraction techniques, with editing facilities for modifications, automated error checking, and automated document generation, as well as code generation. A product-management subsystem supported module configuration as well as updating and retrieval for maintenance. The project-management subsystem tracked progress control and productivity.[73]

Several new projects using SDMS reported significant improvements in productivity and quality. In the design of a comptroller system and database, teams employing SDMS showed twice the output rates of teams not using the tool on comparable projects, with productivity aided by the discovery of 90 percent of the design errors before the programming phase and automatic generation of more than 90 percent of the design documents, which other teams hand wrote. In maintenance of a switching system, SDMS helped reduce man-hours in producing upgrades and revisions by 90 percent.[74]

Yet, aside from a few projects done within divisions and the Software Engineering Development Laboratory (and its predecessor), a lack of acceptance from engineers and project managers prevented SDMS from becoming the standard tool and methodology set for systems software development within NEC. As a result, despite years of effort in R&D, SDMS became relegated to service primarily as a CAD tool for new communications programs or the communications portions of operating systems.[75] Why SDMS failed to live up to early expectations reflected some poor planning as well as the many hurdles firms encounter when attempting to introduce new process technology into an existing engineering and production organization.

First, the time required to learn the structured design methodology and language that came with SDMS constituted an initial problem. Devoting hours to studying tended to delay the start of actual work and slow down progress, because personnel had to become familiar with the new tools and techniques. In some cases, opposition on these grounds alone from project managers, who also faced schedule deadlines and cost pressures, led to the suspension of plans to experiment with SDMS more widely.

A second problem related to compatibility. The SDMS methodology did not work well with existing code written with less emphasis on data flows and abstraction. Yet NEC's Basic Software Division needed to continue upgrading previous systems since replacing old software entirely would be inordinately expensive. Hence, many managers could not justify switching to SDMS as their primary tool and methodology set.

A third difficulty stemmed from the design of SDMS itself. The tools and databases (at least, in the versions prior to 1989) ran only on NEC's large-scale ACOS mainframe hardware and operating system, whereas NEC, as noted earlier, had to write basic software for several incompatible lines of computers. Developers writing software for one machine usually found it far more convenient to use that machine as part of their development and testing environment. Using more than one machine and operating system presented unnecessary complications.

Another issue was inertia, or familiarity. Especially for project management and development practices, NEC divisions had devised their own tools and standards over the years, such as HEART for basic software. Projects engaged in joint development with other firms also had to accommodate different requirements. Thus a complete changeover to SDMS tools and techniques seemed unnecessary and perhaps impossible. In any event, NEC managers eventually acknowledged that switching would take time.[76]

Rather than discarding SDMS or the broader goal of offering more advanced and integrated tool support to developers of systems software, NEC researchers spent more than a decade modifying the tools and features to make them more compatible with division needs. In particular, the 1987 version ran on the UNIX operating system, which was becoming a new standard development environment for mainframes and minicomputers, and on NEC personal computers, in addition to NEC's existing mainframes and operating systems. The new version also contained simplified graphics and conversational Japanese interfaces. The tool and methodology set still met limited acceptance in NEC, but, by the late 1980s, projects making complex switching systems and communications-control portions of operating systems reportedly were using SDMS consistently, with apparently positive results.[77]

General Business Applications

Methodological Standardization: NEC encountered obstacles again but eventually found more success in standardizing methods and tools for general business-applications software, especially data-processing programs written in COBOL, as well as large-scale industrial systems. To produce these kinds of software, NEC facilities and subsidiaries increasingly relied on the STEPS procedures accompanied by a library of reusable design patterns and common subroutines. In content as well as philosophy, STEPS closely resembled Hitachi's HIPACE and the development methodology and management systems Toshiba used with its SWB tool set, openly borrowing concepts from other engineering and manufacturing industries in an attempt to move software development beyond the craft stage.[78]

Explanations of STEPS' evolution from NEC managers invariably pointed to conventional manufacturing and engineering industries where companies had found ways to improve productivity through standardization, divisions of labor, and process rationalizations focused on analyses of raw materials, intermediate products, final products, work methods, and product utilization. In a 1981 paper, for example, even while acknowledging that programming differed from making other products, Azuma and Mizuno insisted conventional process inputs had conceptual counterparts in software, which STEPS used to structure the development process:

> The productivity of industry has greatly increased after the Industrial Revolution. The basic concept of the Industrial Revolution was to achieve high volume production of standardized products . . . drastically reducing the manufacturing cost . . . by thoroughly incorporating standardization not only of the final products but also their parts. . . . In spite of essential differences between software and hardware, a number of similarities can be found where standardization is concerned.
> 1. Program language, macros, subroutines, etc. which correspond to raw materials in producing software. . . .
> 2. Documents and specification documents corresponding to intermediate products. Their standardization facilitates division of labor and automation.
> 3. Programs and documents correspond to products. Mass production of standard products are similar to general purpose applications of computer manufacturers and software houses. The needs and circumstances of users are identical to other examples where production of orders are tailored to the customer. Products should perfectly be made with parts in units which are as large as possible, that is, by combining standard modules.

4. Tools correspond to the software used for software production. Compilers, test data generators, etc. are examples of these.
5. Work methods represent standardization of methods such as application system designs, software designs, and coding.
6. The product utilization method concerns which data is processed by the software. To efficiently design individual items of software and to eliminate contradictions among them, standardization of data will be important. In other words, this concerns standards of languages, modules, program structures, tools, methods, documentation, and data, and standardization must be conducted systematically under a consistent philosophy.[79]

Like other structured approaches, STEPS divided systems development into analysis, general system design, detailed system design, manufacture (coding), system test, and installation, and called for the use of standard patterns or skeletons for general design, structured programming diagrams for detailed design, and standard structured coding methods for program manufacture (Table 6.13). Subsets of activities and work sets for each activity prescribed specific procedures and basic work elements, which managers monitored as part of scheduling and progress control. Process standardization came from standardizing each work set and accompanying documents, using form sheets or simple headings for "work of a more creative type." Azuma and Mizuno considered this degree of standardization essential for personnel to work more effectively in teams, with minimal problems from incompatible tools and methods or poor communication among members: "Regardless of how excellent these [software-engineering] technologies are, the desired objective cannot be accomplished if each member of a team or an organization developing software adopts them at his own will. This problem occurs because some technologies conflict with each other and communication between engineers is restricted. Hence there is necessity for standardization of software." STEPS also promoted division of labor to the extent that standardized methods and documentation helped NEC divisions hand requirements to subsidiaries for detailed design, coding, and testing, when NEC needed extra programmer capacity.[80]

Table 6.13 STEPS Programming Standards

Standards	Work	Outputs
Design patterns	General system design	Processing flow
Structured specifications (SPD diagrams)	Detailed system design	Program specifications
Structured programming	Manufacture	COBOL source code

SPD = Structured Programming Diagrams.
Source: Motoei Azuma and Yukio Mizuno, "STEPS: Integrated Software Standards and Its Productivity Impact," *Proceedings of COMPCON '81* (IEEE Computer Society Press, 1981), p. 88.

Reusability: As they refined the STEPS methodologies, NEC researchers considered various ways to promote reusability. One approach—to locate and utilize similar programs for new applications—they rejected, according to Azuma and Mizuno, because this method lacked versatility, and modifying existing programs consumed time and led to errors. Another—having developers memorize specific recurring patterns— experienced personnel already did as a matter of course, although this practice seemed difficult to systematize into a set of engineering techniques. A third way—to prefabricate programs for common applications, with parameters entered in place of specific data—they found useful for simple jobs but not for complex functions. A fourth— generating programs from parameters or from special language descriptions—encountered similar problems with complex functions. In fact, the descriptions needed to specify the patterns came so near the complexity of COBOL that it made little sense to create a new language. A fifth avenue—to place frequently used modules in macros—they found too rigid and cumbersome to cover all types of functions. NEC persisted, however, and eventually researchers determined they could construct a wide variety of business-applications programs not from existing programs or routines but from a limited set of modifiable designs or patterns (Figure 6.5):

> It should be possible to modify standard patterns to suit every user, and modification of standard divisions for every program should be easy in order to be able to apply standard patterns to a larger number of programs. . . . A program developer first writes a process flow to match a standard pattern in general system design phase. There is a standard program specification corresponding to each standard pattern. Program Designer compares it with a requirement specification in detailed system design phase. This eliminates unnecessary functions, and defines processing intrinsic to business that is to be added and inserted. Next, in the programming phase, standard programs are modified if necessary, and additions and insertions of processes intrinsic to application are performed.

STEPS guidelines thus required developers to break down a customer's system into five types of procedures (Table 6.14). Three corresponded to "black boxes" in the sense that developers tried to identify and insert existing patterns for various data-processing procedures. Another level corresponded to common subroutines that, again, developers identified and inserted. The final level was one in which customers defined procedures unique to their needs. At this point, NEC personnel would write new specifications and then detailed designs, although they still did little actual coding, since STEPS patterns and new designs used SPD diagrams that could be compiled directly into one of several languages.

To achieve systematic design for reuse as well as reusability when developing new programs, NEC managers encouraged other standard

(Patterns for Batch Processing)

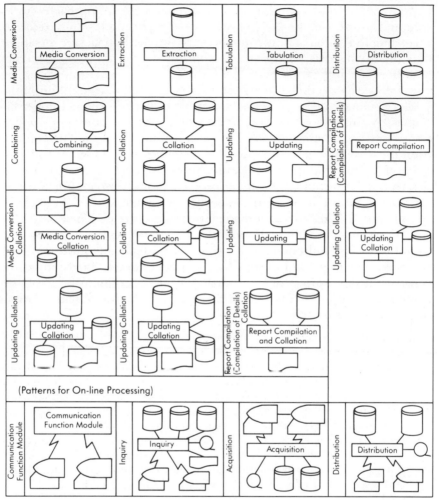

Figure 6.5 Standard Technology and Engineering for Programming Support (STEPS) Standard Patterns. (*Source*: Motoei Azuma and Yukio Mizuno, "STEPS: Integrated Software Standards and Its Productivity Impact," *Proceedings of IEEE Computer Society Conference—COMPCON '81* [IEEE Computer Society Press, 1981], p. 90. Copyright © 1981 IEEE. Reproduced with permission.)

activities prescribed in the STEPS guidelines: (1) the classification of standard source codings intrinsic to common patterns; (2) compilation of easily understandable lists of program patterns; (3) creation of short, easily readable documentation to accompany the lists; (4) designs emphasizing clarity in structure for easy maintenance and modification; (5) use of COBOL as the standard coding language; (6) use of structured

Table 6.14 STEPS Standard Codings

Identification Division
Environment Division
Data Division
   File Selection
   Working Storage Section
Procedure Division
   Level 1 (Process Division)
   Level 2 (Primary Process Function)
   Level 3 (Specific Processing of the Primary
      Process Function)
   Subroutines
   Users Level

Source: Azuma and Mizuno, "STEPS," p. 91.

design and programming techniques modified for greater versatility; and (7) adoption of precise standards for design, documentation, coding, module nomenclature, and other elements basic to system development.

Unlike Toshiba, NEC did not usually enforce reuse objectives through project schedules and budgets, nor did it formally require personnel to register a certain number of reusable modules per month. Nonetheless, through the SWQC program of awards for suggestions that improved productivity and quality, NEC was able to provide bonuses to personnel who produced modules or programs that turned out to be frequently reused.[81] In addition, NEC and its subsidiaries, like other major software producers in Japan and elsewhere, circulated reusable patterns, as well as executable program parts, documents, packages, and software tools, through library networks (Table 6.15).

Yet, as in the case of SDMS, acceptance of STEPS within NEC took years and met early resistance. After beginning a study of current practices in applications development in 1971, NEC released an initial version of STEPS for in-house use in 1972. Azuma and Mizuno recalled that, "The first version was intended to be comprehensive, foolproof and was compiled in the form of a manual 30 cm thick. Therefore it was never used." This rejection led them to simplify and shorten the STEPS manual in 1974, and then make annual revisions. By 1984, STEPS had become the standard practice at approximately 1,200 NEC and NEC-customer sites, and managers considered the methodology a major success.[82]

Among programmers surveyed at 800 in-house and customer sites in 1980, for example, approximately 88 percent found STEPS very easy or easy to learn; 55 percent found it made coding and debugging very easy; and 81 percent felt it had a positive effect on productivity. Productivity improvements measured by work-days required for similar programs developed with and without STEPS ranged from a 26 percent reduction in the specification phase and 91 percent in coding to 35 percent in

Table 6.15 NEC Software Library Samples

Packages
    Automatic translation system for accounting information
    Entry system for accounting chits
    Accounting information database program
    Management information system
    Sales control system
    Procurement control system
    Payments control system
    Hotel customer information system

Tools
    POS log data analysis
    Voice ID code editing program
    IBM SNA interface tool
    Circuit trace analysis program
    List output program
    Automatic report editor
    Library control list output
    Data check program
    Job status report tool
    Back-up data transfer
    Program source transmission
    Program copy generator

Parts
    Bar code reader subroutine
    Graph editor subroutine
    Standardized-format pattern editor
    Binary data conversion subroutine (transmission use)
    Digital and character code conversion
    Assembler debugging macroroutine
    Local area network file directory access routine
    Personal computer operating system interface module
    Common routines for COBOL program generation
    Floppy disk drive logic input/output routine

Patterns
    Master file maintenance pattern
    Database on-line job support system
    STEPS patterns
    Floppy disc control system
    Data entry pattern program

ID = identification; POS = point-of-sale; SNA = System Network
Architecture; STEPS = Standardized Technology and Engineering
for Programming Support.
Source: NEC Software, Ltd., *NEC Sofutouea ryutsu seido: toroku
sofutouea sogo katorogu* [NEC Software distribution system: general
catalog of registered software](Tokyo, 1987).

compile time for debugging and 53 percent overall.[83] According to 1984
data from 1,200 sites, users of STEPS experienced a 20 to 50 percent cost
reduction in analysis and design phases, and a 50 to 80 percent savings in
program construction expenses.[84]

Advanced Tool Support: NEC also had a counterpart to Hitachi's EAGLE
tool for program generation, reuse support, and project management in

the domain of business-applications programs written primarily in COBOL: SEA/1. Like EAGLE, which worked with the structured HIPACE methodologies, SEA/1 used a version of the STEPS procedures and reuse guidelines, as well as incorporated several tool subsystems and databases, including a library of reusable specifications, design patterns, and subroutines. The tools fell into five groups: computer-aided prototyping, design, manufacturing, system launching, and engineering, labeled respectively as CAP, CAD, CAM, CAL, and CASE (Table 6.16).[85]

Researchers at the Software Product Engineering Laboratory began working on SEA/1 around 1980 and released a version for in-house use as well as commercial sale in 1984. The commercial product, which ran on an NEC minicomputer and supported up to ten work stations, NEC priced at the equivalent of around $10,000. The three subsystems consisted of an empirical information base (EIB), the tool set, and the work methodology covering system proposals, design, implementation, testing, and installation. The EIB provided set formats and ready access to previously written system definitions, layout designs, system and program structures, program modules ("source parts"), tested programs,

Table 6.16 SEA/1 Tools and Functions

Function	Computer-aided Tools
Prototyping	PROTOS (Prototyping Tool): defines system's external specifications visually
Design	SYSDES (System Structural Design Tool): simplifies breaking down of system layers into "form-based" description
	FOMDES (Form Design Tool): supports system design by forms or graphic symbols
	PRGDES (Program Structural Design Tool): support for design at the module level
Manufacturing	FMPGEN (Format Parameter Generation Tool): generates graphics and printed reports on format parameters
	CODGEN (Data/Procedures Definitions Source Generator): generates graphics, files, and documentation from form (graphic) designs
	METMNG (Parts Construction Support Tool): construction and maintenance of source-code parts
	COBSYN (Program Synthesizer): combines program components based on program structure data
System Launching	SYSTES (Test Support Tool): automates aspects of system test and installation
	ENVGEN (Environment and Operations Automated Set-Up Tool): automates calculation of needed file space and allocation for system start up
Engineering	EIBMNG (Experience Information Control): centralized database for "experience" information and control
	DOCGEN (Automated Document Generator): automated generator and modification of documentation from the experience information database

Source: Matsumoto Masao et al., "Joho shisutemu-kei sofutouea togo seisan shisutemu" [Integrated software life-cycle system for information systems], *NEC gijutsu* 40, 1, 1987, p. 21.

and test data. Managers viewed this portion of SEA/1 as a major technical advance because it "learned" in the sense that the number of reusable parts in the database increased every time developers designed and registered new software with the system.

Rather than requiring one development methodology for all customers, SEA/1 specified five approaches (resembling Toshiba's "paradigms"), depending on the process and product objectives, and the library contents. First, SEA/1 users could adopt a conventional life-cycle model and move, sequentially with the usual iterations, from requirements definition through implementation and testing. A second model relied on SEA/1's software CAD capabilities for prototyping, design, and then semiautomated generation of program components (automation except for some special coding). A third model called for building new software from the reusable design specifications and coded modules, with minimal modifications but customization in the sense that NEC could offer different configurations of the components for different customers. This approach minimized testing, since the program components came from a library of fully tested items. A fourth model addressed the development of customized systems where NEC could build a prototype and finished program without changing individual modules but by offering the customer a combination of existing applications packages. In this case, personnel needed to do little if any new coding or testing. The fifth model called for the use of SEA/1 tools to analyze, restructure, and redocument existing programs built before the introduction of SEA/I, to facilitate enhancements, reuse, or maintenance of these older software systems.

Within the limited domain of data-processing applications using COBOL, SEA/1 directly addressed many problems commonly encountered in software projects. As summarized in Table 6.17, to simplify requirements specification and design, design reviews, and maintenance, SEA/I provided facilities for prototyping, image-based (graphics) design, and automatic document generation. To improve productivity and quality in implementation, SEA/I supported modularization through structured techniques in addition to automating aspects of program configuration and installation. The tools and techniques facilitated modularization by automatically generating data definitions and various functions for program evaluation, parameterization, testing, module registration, and search. Configuration support came from a tool that combined modules based on a tree-structure of program definitions and a structural design of the software system. The synthesizer function checked syntax validity, data name consistency, and attribute consistency, to make sure modules would work together. SEA/1 also automated set up to the extent that it could analyze a system design and source code from test and operating data. Finally, SEA/1 encouraged software reuse not only through a database of designs and code but through a facility

Table 6.17 SEA/1 Solutions to Software-Development Problems

Problems	Solutions	Implementation
Difficulty of specification and design, design reviews, maintenance	Visualization	Prototyping Image-based design Automatic document generation based on program analysis
Improving productivity and quality in system development and operation Implementation productivity and software quality improvement	Modularization	Materials construction (autogeneration of definition sources, program evaluation, parameterization, parts registration)
	Automated configuration	Program configuration from design definitions, system structural design
	Automated set up	Use of testing and operations data with design and source code
Reuse of existing software	Reverse development	Automated extraction of design information from source code

Source: Matsumoto Masao et al., "Joho shisutemu-kei sofutouea togo seisan shisutemu," p. 20.

NEC termed *reverse development*, which was the automated extraction of design information from source code.

Since SEA/1 mechanized or automated a development methodology already standardized through STEPS, it appears that NEC divisions easily accepted the tool set, especially after trial use indicated dramatic increases in productivity. For example, in three business-application projects for sales, personnel, and inventory control systems, including time spent in system design and inspection, NEC personnel averaged more than 16,000 lines of code per person per month (Table 6.18)! While these numbers clearly included the reuse of large amounts of designs and whole packages, NEC data from a sample of fifteen projects using SEA/1 also noted substantial improvements specifically in the areas of reducing time required for design, coding, correcting documentation errors, and inspection.[86] It thus seemed difficult to deny that, at least when projects achieved high degrees of reuse or programming automation, SEA/1 raised productivity to very high levels.

Process R&D

NEC researchers took SEA/1 and reuse objectives a step further by introducing an integrated system for software houses serving NEC's hard-

Table 6.18 Manpower Efforts Comparison with SEA/1

	Requirements	System Design	Program Design	Coding	Module Test	Integrated Test	Total
Manual Process (Old Management-Information System)							
	108	108	163	245	244	217	1,085
	(10%)	(10%)	(15%)	(23%)	(22%)	(20%)	(100%)

1,085 work-hours, 39.45 work-hours/1,000 lines of code,
4,300 lines of code/work-mo
System size: 27,503 lines of code

	Requirements	System Design	Program Design	Coding	Module Test	Integrated Test	Total
SEA/1 Process (average of new projects A, B, C)							
	40	36	37	23	7	18	161
	(25%)	(22%)	(23%)	(14%)	(4%)	(11%)	(100%)

161 work-hours, 10.4 work-hours/1,000 lines of code,
16,346 lines of code/work-mo
Average system size: 15,481 lines of code

Project Comparison
A Shoe-Wholesaler Sales-Control System

	Requirements	System Design	Program Design	Coding	Module Test	Integrated Test	Total
	12	41	30	21	8	15	127
	(9%)	(32%)	(24%)	(17%)	(6%)	(12%)	(100%)

B Golf-Course Personnel Management System

	Requirements	System Design	Program Design	Coding	Module Test	Integrated Test	Total
	50	21	40	15	5	26	157
	(32%)	(13%)	(25%)	(10%)	(3%)	(17%)	(100%)

C Foodstuffs Company Stock-Control System

	Requirements	System Design	Program Design	Coding	Module Test	Integrated Test	Total
	59	46	41	34	7	12	199
	(30%)	(23%)	(21%)	(17%)	(4%)	(6%)	(100%)

Source: Calculated from Matsumoto Masao et al., "Joho shisutemu-kei sofutouea togo seisan shisutemu," data on p. 24.

ware customers, called Integrated Application Support System (IASS).[87] In addition to the software comprising the SEA/1 tool set, IASS provided manuals detailing the procedures for system development and program generation (based originally on STEPS and called Application Developer's Interactive Combination Equipment or ADVICE); a library of software parts that ran on SEA/1 and used the ADVICE methodology (called SEA/1 Application Library or SEA/1-APLIKA); a menu-based tool to help users with no knowledge of programming create simple data-processing and report-generation programs from the reuse database (called Manager Easy Reporting Interactive Tools or MERIT); a library for registering and reusing parts across different projects and firms (called Application Library by Office-Automation Channels and Software Houses or APLOACH); and access to a network (referred to as SEA/1 Network Service) that distributed software and reusable parts among different NEC facilities, software houses, or customers.

As in Hitachi's EAGLE and Toshiba's SWB, these tools, in particular SEA/1-APLIKA, formalized the notion that some reusable software components could be recycled across different kinds of programs (general-purpose parts) while others related to specific types of applications (business parts), such as for sales, accounting, or payroll management. Within each type, parts performing common functions could be "fixed," that is, reused as executable code in the form of subroutines or macros, while others performed common functions slightly different with each customer and therefore should be stored in the form of modifiable design patterns (Table 6.19). Like STEPS before it, the ADVICE procedures provided detailed guidelines for analyzing customer requirements and general system designs to determine what portions of a new system developers might build from different kinds of reusable components.

NEC researchers were also using their experience with SEA/1 to devise more advanced tools. PGEN (Program Generator), an experimental code generator, automatically produced executable COBOL from module specifications written in conversational Japanese as well as in figures and tables, as long as the system dictionary included the necessary specification elements and grammatical expressions. The dictionary as of 1987 was small, though expandable.[88] ISMOS (Information Semantic Model Oriented System), a system similar to PGEN but dedicated to automatic generation of database programs, used graphical symbols to define a system's components and ran both on personal computers (UNIX and non-UNIX) as well as on NEC minicomputers.[89] SPECDOQ (System Requirements Specification-Documentation) supported both requirements definition and documentation through use of graphics, menus, and diagramming functions linked to a relational database. This allowed users designing programs on STEPS specifications documents to change the documents for different applications without having to revise

Table 6.19 Classification of Software Parts in SEA/1-APLIKA

I. *Classification By Customization*	
Fixed parts	Parts that cannot be customized
Customizing parts	Parts that can be customized
II. *Classification By Control and Function*	
Control parts	ADVICE pattern program parts controlling function parts of an individual program
Function parts	Parts that express the application function of an individual program, with customization of 3 part types: addition, replacement, adjustment
III. *Classification By Compatibility*	
General parts	General parts that are widely used
Business parts	Parts that can be used depending on the type of industry or business application
Program parts	Parts that can be used within only one program

ADVICE = Application Developer's Interactive Combination Equipment; SEA/1-APLIKA = Systems Engineering Architecture/1 Application Library.
Source: Hideo Yoshida, "Integrated Application Support System," *NEC Research and Development* 91, October 1988, p. 121.

the documentation manually. The initial version of the tool ran only on the UNIX operating system, however, limiting its use within NEC.[90]

Summary and Evaluation

NEC's approach to software development clearly resembled those of its competitors in Japan and abroad, although top executives and R&D engineers articulated their thoughts and strategies with unusual clarity. NEC managers in particular exhibited a clear understanding of what firms in other industries had encountered in their struggles with process improvement, and they offered compelling historical reasons why NEC should endeavor to move software, like other technologies before it, from the craft to the factory age. Kobayashi, Mizuno, Fujino, and Azuma also argued openly that most software products were more alike than different, and that most software NEC could produce with standardized tools, methods, designs, and components. This conviction, along with a recognition that software still came in many different forms, inspired managers to view the software factory not as a building or tool set, nor as the systematization of development operations in one particular area. As Mizuno emphasized from the mid-1970s, they saw the software factory as a concept representing broad goals such as standardization, re-usability, quality control, and automation.

NEC made too many different kinds of software products to impose one mode of production on all projects. In this sense, business strategies and market needs forced NEC to tailor processes to the peculiarities of individual applications even while encouraging greater standardization and other common objectives for all company divisions and subsidiaries. As summarized in Table 6.20, by the late 1980s, NEC had already bene-fitted from more than a decade of high-level attention to software and made significant progress in productivity, quality, automation, and other areas, relying heavily on executive committees, projects, and central R&D to formulate and implement strategy across a diverse corporation.

Like its Japanese and U.S. competitors, NEC encountered difficulties in meeting goals and even wrote papers trying to learn from past mis-takes.[91] In particular, the central laboratory for process R&D became too academic in focus, producing tools and methods seemingly more for discussion in journals or conferences than for practical use in NEC divisions. Accordingly, major tool and methodology initiatives met resistance on the division and project levels—sometimes for excellent reasons, including incompatibility with existing products, time required to learn new approaches, and the lack of compelling reasons to abandon familiar practices and tools.

NEC managers persisted, however, and the company as a whole displayed organizational, technological, and strategic flexibility. The labo-

Table 6.20 NEC Summary

Concept	Implementation
Process improvement	Strong commitment from top management and high-level division management to move software development beyond the craft stage to more engineering and manufacturinglike processes. Treatment of the software factory as a concept representing standardization, quality control, reusability, automation, etc.
Product-process focus & segmentation	Separate facilities as well as tools and methods for different software areas, such as basic systems, business applications, and telecommunications. Large network of subsidiaries for specialized applications and regional services.
Process/quality analysis & control	First efforts in process control in late 1960s. More systematic attempts from 1976 with Software Strategy Project. Major effort in quality begun in 1978, followed by Software Quality Control (SWQC) program in 1981, emphasizing data collection and analysis, quality circles, training, and companywide standards. Extensive integration of quality control procedures with project management.
Tailored/centralized process R&D	Tools and related methods developed at divisions and a central research laboratory (established 1980); mixture of central R&D and division autonomy, although a tendency of the central lab to be too academic. The more successful tools and methods developed jointly with divisions and tailored to different product families.
Skills standardization & leverage	Common training for all software personnel but special emphasis on quality control techniques. In business applications, specific strategy of recycling "knowledge" through tools supporting reuse of designs and code.
Dynamic standardization	Annual revision of performance standards and continued refinement of methods and tools. Process standardization for systems software around HEART and business applications around STEPS methodologies, with various tailored tools.
Systematic reusability	Emphasis on reuse of program patterns (designs) for applications programs defined by STEPS, and supported by libraries and computer-aided tools. Most applications built with SEA/1, which supports design reuse. A general system description language facilitated reuse in systems software.
Computer-aided tools	Wide range of tools integrated through SEA/1 for business applications in COBOL. DECA standardized program generation for various types of software. SDMS available for communications and control software. Other discrete computer-aided tools available, such as SPECDOQ for requirements analysis and documentation.
Incremental product/ variety improvement	Basic software products derived initially from Honeywell and GE (through Toshiba), with increasing levels of independent development after 1970. Historical emphasis on process standardization without overlooking the differences among product types, although main strengths in quality control (reliability). Support tools allowing more time to be spent on design.

(continued

Table 6.20 (*Continued*)

Concept	Implementation
Assessment	
Strategic management & integration	Very strong direction from top management. Centralized resource allocation, planning, and coordination to achieve management goals, with standards and quality procedures strongly encouraged across all company divisions. Too much centralization of R&D led to some wasted efforts and eventual compromises with product divisions, giving them more autonomy in defining standards and tools.
Scope economies	Programming concentrated in division facilities and in specialized and regional subsidiaries, all making unique or customized products by utilizing similar tools and methods from central R&D as well as program libraries. Some limitations on sharing due to wide variety of products and customer requirements.

DECA = Detailed Design and Coding Assistant; HEART = Hopeful Engineering for Advanced Reliability Engineering; SDMS = Software Development and Maintenance System; SEA = Systems Engineering Architecture; SPECDOQ = System Requirements Specification-Documentation system; STEPS = Standardized Technology and Engineering for Programming Support.

ratory revised its mission as well as the tools and methods it produced. Top managers experimented continually, establishing companywide strategy and quality control projects, setting common goals for diverse divisions, strengthening applied process R&D, and forming a consulting group to help transfer new technology and provide assistance for ongoing problems, among other measures. Top managers also gave product divisions with good ideas, such as the Basic Software Division, autonomy and opportunities to lead the company in areas of their expertise, for example, techniques for quality assurance and project management. Thus, while the multiproduct, multiprocess factory structure remained imperfect, in the late 1980s it worked well enough to help NEC sell more software than its Japanese competitors. Top executives, laboratory engineers, and division managers and other personnel also seemed thoroughly committed to making the factory concept evolve even further.

7

FUJITSU: PROCESS CONTROL TO AUTOMATED CUSTOMIZATION

The products Fujitsu made, as well as the concepts, tools, techniques, and organizations it used for software development, closely paralleled those at its Japanese competitors, but with somewhat different timing and emphases. Like Hitachi, NEC, and Toshiba, Fujitsu built on its knowledge of telephone-switching and electromechanical equipment to enter the computer industry in the mid-1950s. It adopted transistors and introduced commercial models a few years later than its leading Japanese competitors. Yet Fujitsu also proceeded without foreign assistance, at least until investing in Amdahl in the early 1970s, and instead relied heavily on its own talented designers as well as careful studies of U.S. technology.

In basic software, Fujitsu did not formally promote the concept of a software factory, but operated as if it did—centralizing most programming operations at a single facility and adopting rigorous standards and controls during the mid-1970s, in addition to quantifying management variables and de-skilling testing. In applications, Fujitsu began centralizing programming operations in 1970 and then standardized methods before establishing a software factory in 1979 to perform detailed design, coding, and testing, initially for specifications done in systems-engineering departments outside the factory. Like its Japanese competitors but apparently to a greater degree, the applications factory also invested in a wide assortment of automated tools and software packages to facilitate rapid product customization.

This cultivation of in-house engineering skills, gradual development of tools, techniques, and management systems, as well as the creation of probably the largest network of software subsidiaries and subcontractors in Japan, all helped Fujitsu become Japan's top computer producer in 1968 and remain in this position through the 1980s. The *Nikkei Computer* surveys provided data on just how effectively Fujitsu competed in nearly all segments of the Japanese market. In 1988, it led Japanese and U.S.-based competitors in the value of placements for small, medium, and large computer systems (Tables 1.7 and 1.8). Fujitsu seemed especially strong in sales to institutions and government agencies but also held a major position in industries ranging from information services, distribution, chemicals, electrical machinery, and construction to foodstuffs (Table 1.9). Japanese customers in 1988 ranked Fujitsu first in Japanese-language processing software among all major firms competing in Japan.[1] They also rated it ahead of or equal to the best of its competitors in basic systems software, hardware price-performance, applications systems-engineering support, and general satisfaction (Table 1.10).

The Corporate Setting

Company Origins and Products

Fuji Electric, an electrical-machinery producer affiliated with Siemens of Germany and dating back to 1923, established Fujitsu in 1935 by incorporating its telephone equipment division as a separate company. The new firm commercialized Japan's first digital calculator in 1935 and expanded into switching systems and other electric and electromechanical equipment, before introducing a primitive nonprogrammable computer in 1954. Fujitsu gradually expanded product development and marketing for communications and office equipment, computers and computer peripherals, and data processing services. In the year ending March 1988, Fujitsu had more than 52,000 employees in the parent corporation, with more than one out of five personnel involved in software production or staff support. Nonconsolidated sales totaled more than $13.7 billion (more than $16 billion including some 70 subsidiaries). Fujitsu led all Japanese firms in data-processing sales, which accounted for more than $10 billion (72 percent) of its total revenues. Other major revenue sectors for Fujitsu, both closely linked to its computer businesses, were communications systems (16 percent) and electron (including semiconductor) devices (12 percent) (see Table 4.1).

Fujitsu organized its product divisions into more than a dozen operating and marketing groups (Table 7.1).[2] Several produced computer programs for internal or commercial sale, while a Systems Development Engineering Department established in 1982 (formerly the Software De-

Table 7.1 Fujitsu Operating Groups (1986)

Group	Comments
Computer Systems	Mainframe and minicomputer hardware and software, factory automation
Printed-circuit board products	Office equipment and personal computers, work stations, terminals, software
Information Equipment	Disk drives, printers, facsimile machines, other peripherals
Transmission Systems	
Switching Systems	
Telecommunications Systems	
Semiconductors	
Electronic Devices	
Electronic Devices Exports	
Systems Engineering	Large-scale custom applications, applications packages
Field Service Engineering	Maintenance
Systems Sales	
Office Automation Sales	
Nippon Telegraph and Telephone Sales	

Source: *Nikkei Computer*, Oct. 13, 1986, pp. 70, 79.

velopment Planning Group and in 1989 part of the SE Technical Support Center in the Systems Engineering Group) assisted in planning for tool and methodology research as well as technology transfer for Fujitsu facilities, subsidiaries, and subcontractors. Factory concepts and practices were most prominent at Fujitsu's two largest software facilities: Numazu, the main site in the Computer Group, located near Mt. Fuji in Shizuoka prefecture, which made large computers as well as their basic systems software (operating systems, control programs, network software, database systems, language processors), Japanese word-processing packages, and automatic translation programs;[3] and the Software Factory Department at the Information Processing System Laboratory in Kamata, Tokyo. The laboratory served as the main facility in the Systems Engineering Group, which made customized applications software and applications packages.

Evolution of the Computer Business

Fujitsu historians mark the company's entrance into the computer business with the 1954 introduction of a dedicated accounting machine, the FACOM 100. This was not a programmable computer but was hardwired, using electromagnetic relay switches adapted from telephone switchboards. Fujitsu introduced several other relay computers before adopting parametron circuits in 1958, following the lead of Hitachi and NEC, although these computers also functioned as dedicated calculating machines. Again following Hitachi and NEC, Fujitsu began working on a transistor-based, programmable computer in 1958 and introduced its first commercial models in 1961, for business applications. Management then signaled a major commitment to the new industry by establishing a computer division in 1963.

Fujitsu approached IBM for assistance in computer development, but when this initiative failed management pursued the business independently, investing in in-house research as well as frequently sending company engineers to the United States to learn from American firms and university researchers. Prospects for Fujitsu seemed dim, since it was already behind Hitachi, NEC, and Toshiba, reflecting a late switch to transistors and the assistance U.S. firms were providing Japanese competitors. When the flow of new models from the United States all but stopped during the later 1960s, as GE and RCA prepared to exit the computer business, and as Honeywell reduced its product development efforts, Fujitsu engineers were able to offer hardware superior to that available from Hitachi, NEC, or Toshiba.[4]

Fujitsu's most competitive machines proved to be the 230 series of small, medium, and large mainframes, initially introduced in 1965 with transistors but upgraded in 1968 with more advanced integrated circuits. These models attracted many Japanese customers, especially in the banking industry and at universities, as a result of their low prices and powerful processing capabilities. The Japanese government also aided these sales by placing restrictions on purchases of non-Japanese computers, including models from IBM Japan (which remained in effect until the late 1970s). The popularity of the 230 models made Fujitsu Japan's largest computer manufacturer in 1968 and helped computer revenues exceed 50 percent of Fujitsu's sales, for the first time, in 1970.[5]

Independent development would clearly have failed without the contribution of talented engineers led by Toshio Ikeda (1923–1974), a graduate of the Tokyo Institute of Technology who had entered Fujitsu in 1946. After designing telephone switching equipment, he moved into computers and quickly gained recognition as Japan's best computer designer. Ikeda's fame and interests led him in 1969 to meet Gene Amdahl, his counterpart at IBM who had designed the System/360 and then left IBM in 1970 to found the Amdahl Corporation, to produce larger IBM-compatible mainframes. Their meeting began a relationship that continued through the 1990s, with Fujitsu owning 45 percent of Amdahl's outstanding shares. In the mid-1970s, Amdahl assisted Fujitsu in implementing a key change in its product strategy: adoption of IBM compatibility.

Amdahl and Fujitsu were logical partners since Amdahl needed financing and Fujitsu managers believed they could expand their market share with computers that competed directly for IBM customers. Hitachi managers had reached a similar conclusion, and, with MITI's encouragement, Fujitsu and Hitachi agreed to standardize their mainframe architectures but without jointly developing hardware or software. Together they introduced a series of models (some overlapping and competing) that matched segments IBM's System/370 covered.

Fujitsu also became Amdahl's largest shareholder after the premature death of Ikeda in 1974 and the recognition of Fujitsu executives that they could use some assistance in hardware design.[6] With help from Amdahl to produce IBM-compatible logic circuits, utilizing the most advanced semiconductor technology available, Fujitsu by the late-1970s was able to deliver hardware comparable to IBM in performance at given price ranges (although Amdahl, with the exception of a version of the UNIX operating system, did not cooperate with Fujitsu in software development).[7] Fujitsu's machines proved attractive inside and outside Japan: It manufactured central-processing units not only for Amdahl but also for ICL in Great Britain, modified to their specifications, and sold complete mainframes (as well as its large-scale operating system) to Siemens for marketing in Europe under the Siemens label.[8]

Product Strategy: Compatibility and Comparability

Fujitsu's computer products in the late 1980s included personal computers (running MS-DOS as well as OS/2), work stations (running a proprietary Fujitsu operating system as well as the Sigma version of UNIX), mid-size business computers (running another proprietary operating system), and commercial mainframes (compatible with IBM machines) as well as a supercomputer line that ran some IBM programs. Fujitsu studied the products of various vendors and occasionally introduced creative innovations, such as to accommodate two central-processing units in its largest 230-series model computer during the late 1960s, as well as to compete with IBM products during the 1980s. Since the bulk of Fujitsu's hardware revenues and profits appeared to come from mainframes that could operate with software written for IBM machines, preserving compatibility with IBM remained a critical element in Fujitsu's product strategy.

All producers of IBM-compatible hardware and software followed at least the external specifications (descriptions of what products do, rather than how they operate internally) and the interface specifications (instructions for handling data and other commands needed to operate programs or peripheral equipment) that IBM set with the System/360 and then refined with subsequent models. Since IBM allowed detailed information on the System/360 architecture to enter the public domain, presumably to encourage customers and other software producers to write programs, some manufacturers proceeded on the assumption that they could also follow IBM specifications and produce hardware and software compatible with IBM's next mainframe family, the System/370, as well as its successors.[9] Firms designing hardware and software to operate with IBM machines did not necessarily lack the ability to innovate—to create their own standards and specifications. Rather, one could argue that these companies—led by Amdahl, Fujitsu, and Hitachi (for its export models, sold prior to 1989 through National Semiconductor)—treated IBM compatibility as an industry standard. This made sense, given IBM's historical market shares in large computers of well over 50 percent.

Other studies have examined the competition between IBM and compatible producers from several perspectives, covering technical and marketing issues, as well as legal actions by and against IBM stemming from IBM's attempts to protect its standards.[10] This study focuses on a different topic—evolution of the factory approach for software development. Yet, since IBM compatibility also had a large potential impact on software as well as hardware product development, this subject needs some treatment in any discussion of Fujitsu, as well as Hitachi and other compatible vendors.

Product development for systems software, for example, requires a detailed knowledge of the hardware platform, or at least interface specifications, in order to write an operating system and other basic software that will work with IBM hardware and applications software written for IBM machines. Writing the basic software requires a definition of the overall design or specifications for the software system, before proceeding to functional and structural designs at the subsystem level, and then the detailed designs at the module level, followed by coding. IBM compatibility requires considerable adherence to the external and interface specifications IBM has established, and this places constraints on hardware and software design.

IBM has argued that firms designing machines able to run its software have at times delved into proprietary details of IBM products through illegal means. This need not be the case, since compatible machines primarily have to emulate or simulate characteristics, using rewiring or programming, that define the interface between the hardware and the operating system. Proprietary information on the internal specifications of IBM products helps, of course, and Japanese firms, led by Fujitsu and Hitachi, have employed various measures to learn as much about IBM products as possible, as early as possible in their product-development cycles.

Commentators on the Japanese computer industry have echoed these concerns, claiming that most mainframe and basic software development at Fujitsu (and to a lesser extent at Hitachi) between the mid-1970s and early 1980s consisted of working backward from IBM manuals and product information, often illegally and without inventing new functions or standards. While one can argue IBM has set technical norms so popular the inventor should no longer be allowed to constrain competitors, the issues are complex, and arbitration proceedings have supported positions both Fujitsu and IBM have maintained. The 1988 settlement between these two firms guaranteed Fujitsu the right to review licensed IBM manuals and source code released through 1997, primarily to understand the interface specifications so that users of Fujitsu hardware could run software written for IBM machines or other IBM-compatible computers. Fujitsu also had to pay IBM a lump sum of several hundred million dollars in licensing fees, plus an annual fee, for this privilege.[11]

To what extent producers of compatible hardware and software have violated IBM property is a matter outside the scope of this study. Producers of compatible hardware may also choose not to write software, since their machines should be able to run programs written for IBM equipment. Nevertheless, relevant to the factory approach is the bias IBM compatibility may create in an organization, leading it to adopt a technological position as a follower rather than as a first-mover innovator. This seems particularly true in the case of firms that tried to offer not only compatible hardware but also software with features comparable to IBM products. Pursuing both compatibility and comparability may allow firms to avoid some of the more uncertain aspects of new product development, such as defining new functions or standards customers might reject, and shorten time needed for original research and development.

Yet compatibility as a product strategy presented disadvantages as well as advantages. IBM, as the leader in the IBM-compatible market in most segments, was able to set or modify hardware and software standards (although it had to maintain compatibility with previous products or risk alienating customers). It best understood how to utilize or disguise the underlying features of its systems, and had more leverage than competitors over schedules (and prices) for new product introductions.

Producers of compatible hardware and software thus faced a nontrivial challenge, especially since simulating the operations of new IBM hardware proved increasingly difficult after the late 1970s, when IBM began to embed more functions in hard-wired chips difficult to duplicate. Mainframe producers committed to IBM compatibility had to devote more time to working backwards from often incomplete specifications, and risked falling seriously behind in new product introductions as they waited for IBM to deliver or explain the details of its new systems. Applications producers needed to know the future specifications of IBM and compatible products to write software that would work. At the same time, producers of basic software compatible with and comparable to IBM needed to offer systems that could run on old and new machines, especially if they wanted to attract more customers.

The technical challenges of compatibility, therefore, proved formidable to maintain as well as to achieve initially. In hardware, as discussed in Chapter 1, Japanese firms (and Amdahl) competed primarily with machines that, even if later in delivery than IBM products, seemed to offer superior price-performance. Those firms making hardware as well as basic and applications software, such as Fujitsu and Hitachi, usually tried to offer technical compatibility and functional comparability. They were also adopting other existing or emerging standards, such as UNIX, OSI, Sigma, and TRON, at least for some products. But for their major lines of large computers, historically and still in the early 1990s, the best competitive scenario was for their hardware and software together to provide a superior combination of price and performance. This product strategy, for hardware as well as software, demanded creative engineering to maintain compatibility. For the most part, however, comparability and superior price-performance required careful pricing and integrated management of design, engineering, production, marketing, service, and quality assurance.

Software Production Strategy

In the early 1970s, similar to what occurred at other Japanese firms and at roughly the same time, Fujitsu managers in both basic and applications software began promoting measures for process standardization and control aimed at the "accumulation and improvement of technology." According to internal Fujitsu materials used in training employees, these measures centered on three broad areas, as outlined in Table 7.2: development technology (for software engineering), specialization (of production facilities and equipment), and mechanization or automation (of software development processes and management).

The drive to improve development technology focused on making greater use of fundamental advances in software engineering coming

Table 7.2 Software Productivity-Improvement Strategies

Development Technology	Specialization	Mechanization/Automation
Common development	Organizational	Software tools and other computer-
Modularization	structure	aided systems for planning, devel-
High-level languages		opment, testing, maintenance
Reuse	Subsidiaries	
Review procedures		
Structured design	Software pack-	
Structured	ages	
programming		

Support and Control Technology	
Project management	Standardization
Development planning and phase	Quality control activities
completion reporting system	(high-reliability program)
Management by objectives	Training

Source: Fujitsu Ltd., Information Processing Group, No. 1 Software Division, "Sofutouea kaihatsu: hinshitsu-seisahsei kojo ni tsuite" [Software development: quality and productivity improvement], unpublished company document, received Sept. 24, 1985, pp. 40–41.

mainly from the United States and Europe: higher-level languages (though modified for in-house use and for the Japanese language), modularization and structured methods for design and programming, quantified controls for product inspection, and process reviews to insure product reliability and reduce time spent on fixing or altering programs. A related objective aimed at minimizing the volume of unique systems personnel had to produce by emphasizing what Fujitsu called *common development*—writing designs in a computer language or flow-chart form that could be compiled into different languages and stored in a reusable library; and designing basic programs, such as compilers or specific system components, for use with more than one of Fujitsu's operating systems.[12]

Specialization included the establishment of development organizations dedicated to different types of software. Management began by establishing the Numazu Works in 1974 to produce the FACOM-M series hardware and basic software. The Software Division, housed in a separate building (connected to the hardware building) constructed in 1981, consisted of two departments for software engineering, eight for product development, and another for quality assurance. A separate group, the Field Support Center, provided maintenance services.[13] The approximately 3,000 software personnel working at Numazu in the late 1980s included about 1,000 from software houses and subsidiaries.[14] Despite the large scale and focus of operations, Fujitsu managers did not label or publicize Numazu as a software factory.[15] Nevertheless, the level of standardization, control, and integration, especially after 1974–1975, the centralization of most basic software development at this facility by 1984, and the general style of management, made Numazu by the late 1980s indistinguishable from facilities making similar products and referred to as software factories at Hitachi and NEC.

In 1970, Fujitsu also established the Information Processing Systems Laboratory in Kamata, Tokyo, to house the Systems Engineering Group, which had approximately 4,000 engineers during 1988–1989. This laboratory began a decade-long effort to centralize custom programming for banks, securities firms, government departments, and manufacturing as well as distribution companies. Continuing this trend toward centralization, management created a software factory in 1979 as a department within the laboratory. Experienced systems engineers continued to cultivate specialized knowledge to develop unique designs, and, in the late 1980s, also began to write more software packages for sale as individual products and for integration with new software to produce semi-customized systems. The factory itself, with approximately 1,500 personnel during 1988–1989, generally performed programming and module test operations based on specifications received from systems engineers, and did increasing amounts of systems design as Fujitsu introduced more automated support tools and reusable designs.

The Kamata factory also relied heavily on personnel from subcontractors—more so than its Japanese competitors. In addition, whereas Hitachi and other Japanese firms tended to bring personnel physically to their main facilities, Kamata served more as a hub for a network of distributed development, taking place mainly at subcontractors. In fact, merely 200 or so of the engineers in the Kamata factory came from Fujitsu proper, and only 10 to 30 from subsidiaries. The remainder, nearly 1,300, were employees of independent software houses. Most remained at their parent firms, usually linked by networks to computers and databases in the software factory.[16]

Like Hitachi, Toshiba, and NEC, Fujitsu supplemented in-house facilities with a large number of subsidiaries, totaling 56 in 1989 and employing more than 14,000 personnel in systems engineering, applications programming, basic software development, and microcomputer software development (Table 7.3). This extensive network provided specialized skills as well as regional services throughout Japan, and helped Fujitsu accommodate variety and variations in demand, even though software engineers remained relatively scarce (and expensive) in Tokyo. Including in-house facilities, subsidiaries, and affiliated subcontractors, available software personnel in the Fujitsu group in 1988 came to approximately 20,000—probably the largest total for any firm operating in Japan.[17]

Mechanization or automation referred to the use of computer-aided tools to support design, coding, testing, maintenance, and management, including reuse-support systems. Fujitsu in particular emphasized automated tools for custom applications development, although managers also viewed the application of automation and mechanization to control technology in the form of tools for planning, project management, testing, and quality evaluation, integrated with standards, manual procedures, and practices such as quality circles, as another way to support development technology and specialization. While they invested in these types of tools initially for basic software production and later for applica-

Table 7.3 Fujitsu Software Subsidiaries and Employees (1988)

Software Area	Companies	No. of Employees
Systems engineering and custom applications	37	7,800
Basic software	9	3,000
Communications	7	2,400
Microprocessors and personal computers	3	900
Total	56	14,100

Source: Nikkei Computer, Oct. 13, 1986, p. 75 (updated to 1988).

tions, another characteristic of Fujitsu was the occasional exchange of tools and techniques between Numazu and Kamata, as well as among other Fujitsu facilities.

Basic Software

Fujitsu's decision in the 1960s to develop computer products independently challenged company engineers to master not only hardware design but also software programming. A sampling of packages Fujitsu's basic software personnel produced between 1960 and 1984, listed in Table 7.4, provides some indication of the scope and scale of their efforts. From 1960 onward, Fujitsu offered an increasingly wide range of compilers, operating systems, database-management systems, and tools (in addition to customized programs for banking, government, manufacturing, distribution, and telecommunications applications). By the late 1980s, Numazu's major software products had become lengthy and complex, totaling as much as 2 million lines of C and LDL (Logic design language) source code (without comments) per operating system, with major subcomponents running from 100,000 to 800,000 lines.[18] As at Fujitsu's competitors, systematically managing efforts of this scale required a series of initiatives to coordinate product and process standardization, control measures, and development technology.

Early Efforts

Fujitsu's experience with software development began in the early 1960s with the introduction of several transistorized computers, since the relay and parametron computers of the 1950s were either hard-wired or required only minimal programming. Even Fujitsu's first transistorized machines did not have modern operating systems but performed simple batch-processing operations and only required specialized routines and language compilers. Following the lead of IBM and other U.S. companies pioneering in the computer industry, Fujitsu, as well as its Japanese competitors, gradually introduced more sophisticated software and hardware.

In 1964 Fujitsu delivered a particularly important computer system, the FONTAC, to the Electronics Industry Promotion Association of Japan. MITI had sponsored this cooperative project among Fujitsu, NEC, and Oki Electric to encourage domestic firms to build a large-scale computer roughly equivalent to IBM's 7090 machine, introduced in 1960. By 1964, IBM had moved on to another generation of computers, the System/360 family, with far greater capabilities. Nonetheless, the FONTAC effort exposed Japanese engineers to computer programs and languages many had not seen before. Fujitsu designed the main processor and the

Table 7.4 Basic Packages Offered with Fujitsu Mainframes (1960–1984)

1960	ALGOL compiler
1961	assembler compiler
	FORTRAN compiler
1963	Data-communications software
1965	FORTRAN IV compiler
	MCP (control program for the FACOM 230-20/30 maniframes)
	MONITOR II (proto-operating system for the FACOM 230-50)
1966	KEMPF (econometrics modeling and analysis system)
1968	MONITOR V (large-scale mainframe operating system)
	STAT (statistical package)
1969	BOS (medium mainframe batch operating system)
	ROS (medium mainframe real-time processing operating system)
	PL/1 compiler
	EPOCS (medium mainframe data-control program)
	ADSL (continuous simulation system)
1970	RAPID (database system)
1971	MONITOR V TSS (time-sharing function added to MONITOR V)
	BOS II (successor to BOS and ROS operating systems)
	OS II (operating system for FACOM 230-45/S and /55 mainframes)
	ASTRA (structural analysis program)
1972	UMOS (minicomputer operating system)
	TIMS (time series analysis program)
1973	MDS (management decision-making support tool)
	MPS (mathematical planning tool)
1974	BOS/VS and OS II/VS (medium operating systems with virtual memory control function)
	MONITOR VI/VII (large-scale mainframe operating system)
1975	OS IV/F4 (operating system for largest M-series mainframe)
	FEM (finite element analysis program)
1977	AIM (on-line database system)
	FNA (Fujitsu Network Architecture)
	OS IV/X8 (medium operating system for FACOM M series)
	OS IV/F2 (small operating system for FACOM M series)
	PDL/PDA (performance measurement and analysis tool)
1978	OS/UAS (minicomputer operating system)
	FAIRS-I (information retrieval system)
	KING (Japanese-language line printer support program)
1979	JEF (Japanese-processing Extended Feature)
	INTERACT (end-user support system)
	FAIRS-II (management information search system)
	FDMS (document control system)
	GEM (library control program)
	SSOPTRAN (FORTRAN source program optimizer)
1980	FORTRAN77 compiler
	AOF (computer center operations support tool)
	ARIS (resident information system)
	HOPE (hospital administration system)
1981	OS IV/F2 ESP (small-scale operating system for FACOM M-series)
	ICAD (computer design support system)
	HYPER COBOL (high-productivity version of COBOL)
	DOCK/FORTRAN77 (FORTRAN debugger for system displays)
	ANALYST (statistical data processing package)
	PLANNER (Planning and control information system)
	AXEL (conversational language data analysis system)
1982	OS IV/F4 MSP (large-scale operating system for FACOM M-series)
	AIM/RDB (relational database system)
	DRESSY/P (simplified graphic system)

Table 7.4 (*Continued*)

1983	ADAMS (Application Development and Management System)
	FOS (Fujitsu Office System Concept)
	OS IV/X8 FSP (medium operating system for FACOM M-series)
	UNICUS (minicomputer operating system)
	JEF II (Japanese-processing Extended Feature II)
	MACCS/REACCS (information analysis and search system)
	ODM (documents-processing system)
	ELF (electronic file system)
1984	OS IV/ESP III (small-scale operating system for FACOM M-series)
	IMPRESS (image information system)
	IPS (small-scale printing control system)
	UPLINK III/PS (personal computer network system)
	FCAD-11 (personal computer CAD system)
	ATLAS (automatic language translation system)

Source: Fujitsu Kabushiki Kaisha, "FACOM no ayumi" [FACOM development], *FACOM janaru* 11, 1, 1985, pp. 20–47; and Fujitsu Kabushiki Kaisha, "FACOM seino ichiran" [Overview of FACOM performance] in *Ikeda kinen ronbun shu* [Anthology of articles in memory of Ikeda] (Tokyo, Fujitsu Ltd., 1978), pp. 254–67.

card punch equipment, while NEC and Oki Electric made the subprocessors and input/output devices. Fujitsu also took charge of programming, with assistance from NEC and Oki engineers, several Japanese professors, and a few American consultants. The software Fujitsu provided consisted of a monitor, based on earlier control programs available in Japan, as well as ALGOL, COBOL, FORTRAN, and assembler compilers; a library editor; a sort generator; an executable coded tape editor; utility programs; and several applications programs. Fujitsu later modified the FONTAC monitor and introduced this in 1965 as MONITOR II with its 230–50 mainframe, Fujitsu's commercial version of the FONTAC processor.[19]

A more serious challenge came in the 1960s to develop an operating system comparable, at least in essential functions, to IBM's OS/360, which had set new standards for the entire industry. Fujitsu needed this software for the upgraded 230-series models, especially the dual-processor 230–60, which incorporated integrated circuits and offered, for the time, extensive processing capabilities. The demands of this programming led Fujitsu to establish a separate department for the 100 or so employees needed to build the operating system, MONITOR V. Fujitsu completed this in 1968, after two years of development and numerous difficulties.

According to several Fujitsu engineers, MONITOR V proved extremely hard to design and build because of the dual-processor architecture, then available only in U.S. military computers. Fujitsu had not yet designed a sophisticated operating system even for one processor, let alone two; and while Fujitsu used OS/360 as a conceptual model, the 360 architecture differed radically. Fujitsu engineers, including Ikeda and the head of the project as well as the new Software Department, Takuma Yamamoto (Fujitsu president and CEO in 1990), made several trips to the United States to seek assistance from American software houses and computer manufacturers. This was typical of Fujitsu. Rather than entering into a licensing arrangement with a U.S. producer, as did Hitachi, NEC, and Toshiba, management encouraged personnel to travel abroad frequently, especially to the United States, to visit and learn from consultants, suppliers, and competitors, even without formal contracts. Fujitsu also received assistance to complete and debug the system from Kyoto University, which received an initial version for its computer center in 1969.

While delivery came months behind schedule, in retrospect, MONITOR V and the 230-series overall proved major successes commercially and provided invaluable lessons in computer technology as well as in engineering management and organization. Perhaps most important, MONITOR V demonstrated to company officials, at an early period in the evolution of this industry, that Fujitsu needed executive leadership as well as a comprehensive system to manage large-scale software development. In recognition of his success in producing MONITOR V, top management in 1968 promoted Yamamoto to director of programming for both systems and applications. A 1949 graduate of Tokyo University's Electrical Engineering Department, Yamamoto, like Ikeda, had started in hardware, designing telephone switching equipment and then relay computers before moving to data-processing equipment design and then MONITOR V. As he rose in the executive ranks to corporate director in 1975 and company president in 1981, Yamamoto made certain that Fujitsu allocated sufficient management attention and resources to continue improving its technology and organization for software development.

MONITOR V also helped prepare Fujitsu for the major task of the 1970s: to produce a more advanced operating system comparable to OS/370 that would serve the FACOM-M hardware. Fujitsu managers in the early 1970s had introduced a succession of procedures and control systems for successor products, beginning with MONITOR VII (completed in 1974); however, to minimize the development effort for the M-series software, management decided to produce three operating systems to cover the small, medium, and large mainframes, in contrast to the five separate programs IBM offered for its 370-series models. Fujitsu promptly delivered the first version of the operating system for its largest mainframes, OS IV/F4, in 1975, and followed with versions for medium and small mainframes in 1977. These came in more-or-less on time and turned out to be commercial successes, although the scale and complexity of the M-series programs again convinced Fujitsu management to take steps to upgrade and standardize procedures, methods, tools, and management systems for basic and applications software.[20]

Another manager who rose to prominence during this period, Mamoru Mitsugi, later a senior executive director and head of Fujitsu's Systems Engineering Group, moved from NTT contract software to commercial basic software and then to applications, promoting the creation of the Kamata Software Factory in 1979 and a predecessor facility for program conversion. Like Ikeda and Yamamoto, and many other Fujitsu engineers in the computer area, Mitsugi had first worked as a hardware designer for telephone exchange systems supplied to NTT. But he was one of the first managers to acquire a background in software inspection, initially for programs supplied to NTT along with switching equipment, before joining the basic software group in 1973 to head operating-systems inspection.

While Japanese firms separated commercial software development from NTT contracts, working for NTT in the early 1970s clearly shaped the thinking of Mitsugi and his counterparts at NEC and Hitachi. Implementing specifications received from NTT for its domestic telephone network (Distributed Information Processing System or DIPS), and producing the hardware and software in conjunction with other firms, required all contractors to follow strict standards. Since these were even more rigorous than in commercial departments, because of the telephone company's exacting requirements, managers who moved from NTT work to commercial systems tended to bring with them higher management standards. After joining the basic software group, for example, Mitsugi compared its product and process control operations and decided he had to strengthen the Quality Assurance Department as well as expand its role to improving process standardization rather than just inspecting finished products.[21] He also realized Fujitsu had to make these long-term improvements while meeting short-term development targets—an intractable problem for commercial divisions during the 1970s as a result of rapid growth in demand:

> At the time, NTT was very advanced in its thinking. The DIPS software was really a large system. Since three companies, including us, had to develop the software, standardization was essential. My impression was that NTT was able to devote more effort to software phase divisions and carrying out work standardization than we were able to do in the private sector. Of course, we influenced that thinking, too, since there was an interchange among us, an exchange of information. . . . This was a period of rapid growth, and demand for software was increasing rapidly too. We had to write programs quickly to meet this demand, and worried about preparing documentation later. In other words, we gave top priority to writing programs. This tended to defeat documentation and program conformance. In the long run this is self-defeating, and, like NTT, it is better to review and inspect every phase, and get rid of as many bugs as possible in each phase. But, in the private sector, since software development must have more constraints on time and costs, even though we were aware of this problem, there was not much we could do.[22]

Upgrading Standards and Controls

An important characteristic of Fujitsu's development approach and organization for basic software was the gradual integration of controls for product, process, and quality. Direction of Fujitsu's efforts in these areas, as at NEC, came from the Quality Assurance Department in the Numazu Works's Software Division, which Mitsugi headed before becoming division manager in 1974.

According to a chronology the department prepared, these efforts fell into three main phases: prior to 1970, when Fujitsu had no set procedures and managers allowed programmers to test software at their own discretion; 1970–1978, when Fujitsu set up its first product and process standards and formal systems for inspection and quality control; and the period after 1978, when Fujitsu began placing more emphasis on structured design and programming techniques and established the procedures that formed the basis of its current practices. Distinguishing the last phase was a broadening of the Quality Assurance Department's concerns to include not simply testing and documentation conformance, or product evaluation, but analysis of the development process itself (Table 7.5).

While measures outlined in this chronology closely resembled actions taken at other Japanese and U.S. firms, Fujitsu managers had their own set of emphases. First, they appeared to view inspection and quality more from the perspective of the customer than in an absolute sense, such as zero defects, which Hitachi tended to do. This orientation emerged during the development of MONITOR V, when Fujitsu established a Program-Testing Section in 1968 to evaluate software by comparing specifications stated in manuals to product performance. Previously, assisting designers in debugging had been the group's primary function. The next step came in 1971, with the creation of formal product-inspection procedures, such as requiring completed software and manuals to pass a formal inspection process before release to the customer. To manage this, Fujitsu instituted systems for product handling, evaluation, and registration. The product-handling procedures required that the source code, manuals, and other documentation not only agree but that development groups bring these product components to the Quality Assurance Department together. In the past, groups had often completed and released programs without proper documentation or testing. After 1971, however, no product received a registration number, necessary for release to customers, without meeting these requirements and gaining the formal approval of the Quality Assurance Department.

After making progress in product control, Fujitsu managers turned to defects, launching three interrelated efforts during 1973–1978: standardization of software-development practices, collection of quality and performance data, and application of quality control techniques used in

Table 7.5 Chronology of Basic Software Process Development (1966–1984)

1966	Programming Department established.
1968	Program Testing Section established.
1970	"Strengthen Inspection" effort begun (1970–1973), extending testing from debugging to evaluating software from the user's perspective, such as comparing performance to specifications stated in manuals.
1971	Software Product Registration System established, requiring new software to undergo inspection and receive product numbers before being released. Product handling regulations formalized procedures for software products, manuals, and documentation, requiring all product components to be brought in simultaneously, not one-by-one, to the Inspection (later renamed the Quality Assurance) Department for testing and evaluation.
1972	Planning Section established.
1973	Preliminary version of Development Planning and Report System.
	"Application of QC (quality control] Techniques" effort begun (1973–1978), aimed at forecasting and then eliminating bugs.
	MTS (Multi-Terminal Simulator) tool developed for testing.
1974	Software Division established.
	"Product and Process Standardization" effort begun. Involved estimating what the phases would be for the life cycle of individual software products, and then determining what to design in a given period of time, as well as what programming techniques to use.
	Bar charts instituted for project control, replacing PERT (Program Evaluation and Review Technique) charts.
	Inspection procedures and forms standardized (main factor analysis).
	HTS (Hardware Trouble Simulator) tool developed for testing.
1975	Phase divisions formalized and SWN (Software *Normen*) Standards effort launched.
	BSMS (Basic Software Project Management Support System) started.
	Procedures for bug analysis and data gathering formalized. "Quality Control Data Accumulation" effort formally begun.
	Estimates handbook drawn up, with actual data on past projects to aid managers in estimating project requirements.
1976	Software Administration Department established.
	BSMS database started for project control and estimation.
	Current Development Planning and Report System instituted, software product delivery procedures formalized, and BSMS required for in-house use.
1977	"Inspection of Quality and Evaluation Indicators" (1977–1978) begun.
1978	Structured design and programming emphasized.
1979	"Consolidation of Inspection Ideology." Concept of software inspection formally promoted as extending beyond testing, to evaluation of final products and the development process.
	"Quality Assurance through Organization" effort launched. Formalization of quality assurance as an organizational function not restricted to inspection but extending to design and planning.
	Phase Completion Reporting System instituted.
1980	Development Planning and Report System (version no. 2) instituted, adding productivity data and review data reporting.
	Campaign to increase quality threefold and productivity 30% by 1982.
	Software Division actively promotes small-group activities as part of the companywide High-Reliability Program.
	Software Division quality objectives established—formalization of procedures for establishing project estimates and standard times.
	"Diffusion of Inspection Ideology through Horizontal Development." Effort to spread knowledge and "good practices" horizontally, i.e. beyond one's own department.

(continued)

Table 7.5 (*Continued*)

1981	"Advancement of Quality Concepts" movement begun, including ease of use evaluations (ESP) and Quality Assurance Liaison (QAL) initiated to facilitate interdepartmental sharing of data on bugs.
1982	"Performance checking" begun directed by Quality Assurance Department. Quality objectives control system instituted and Software Quality Subcommittee established. Six program development departments established at Numazu Works and located in new software building.
1983	New Software Division centralizes basic software development in Numazu Works.
1984	Software Division extends quality assurance and quality-circle activities to software subcontractors, as part of the second companywide High-Reliability Program.

Source: Fujitsu Ltd., Quality Assurance Department, "Kensa-bu no rekishi" [History of the Quality Assurance Department], undated internal company memorandum, received Sept. 24, 1985.

other divisions to software. A planning section organized in 1972 oversaw these initiatives for the first few years. In addition, recognizing the growing scale and importance of its operations, Fujitsu elevated basic software to divisional status in 1974.

Increasing product size and complexity persuaded Fujitsu managers to pay more attention to project management as well as process standardization. During 1973–1975, the division started a Development Planning and Report System that set up formal work-estimation procedures for project managers to use in estimating manpower needs, quality objectives, product objects, and schedules. As an outline from 1984 shows (Table 7.6), the system did not simply divide authority or tasks functionally but required different groups to share responsibility for quality, planning, and control in all development and testing phases.

The chronology in Table 7.5 also charts the application of computer-aided tools to process control and their integration with standardized methods. In 1975–1976, for example, to automate data collection for quality and budget measurements, Fujitsu introduced Basic Software Project Management Support System (BSMS), after two years of research and trials. BSMS supported new project-management and development procedures and gradually became valuable as a tool for estimating schedules and monitoring the development process, as well as for aiding testing and inspection.

BSMS and the Development Planning and Report System continued to be the centerpieces of Fujitsu's production-management system for basic software in the 1980s. The systems worked as follows: First, project managers had to apply for a product number to begin a project. If their superiors approved, they submitted a budget. The development and planning documents also required a market survey and basic design specifications listing functional, performance, and reliability objectives,

Table 7.6 Development Planning Items and Responsibilities

Items	Check Points	C	P	E	D	T	Q
Quality Objectives							
Development objectives	Program positioning, development results, marketability	o	X	o	o	o	o
Desired functions	User needs and program functionality		X		X	o	X
Performance	Objectives, measures, comparative analyses, appropriateness		o	o	o	X	X
Compatibility	Objectives, appropriateness and completeness		X	o	o	o	X
Reliability	Appropriateness of objectives, likelihood of implementation		o	o		o	X
Planning Implementation							
Development size, language	Appropriateness of size given functions, modularization/reuse	X		X		o	o
Development process	Appropriateness of delivery time to user, easibility	X	o		X	X	X
Manpower & machine time	Match of productivity and budget, manpower allocations, subcontracting %, progress	X					o
Review & test plans	Review/test amount, appropriateness of bug detection				X		X
Work objectives	Sufficiency of measures for raising quality, efficiency	o		X	o		o
Development structure	Organization, work distribution	o				o	o

C = control; P = planning; E = engineering; D = development; T = integration testing; Q = quality assurance; o = included in activities; X = major responsibility.
Source: Morita Shoken and Serita Shigeru, "Sofutouea hinshitsu no toraekata" [Understanding software quality], *Hinshitsu kanri*, 14, 2, April 1984, p. 91.

as well as estimates of manpower and machine time. The control system then centered on the development and planning documents and monthly reports of actual work hours, computer time, and phase completions, which BSMS tracked and compared to the initial estimates.[23]

The development process and controls followed a conventional life-cycle model: basic design, functional and structural design, detailed design and coding, unit and combined test, component and system test, product inspection, delivery and maintenance. Like Hitachi and NEC, Fujitsu had used PERT charts to manage these phases for MONITOR

VII, but found they did not work well and switched to bar charts in the mid-1970s, generated manually at first and then automatically through the on-line BSMS system. The introduction of BSMS also helped the Software Division compile and maintain an estimation handbook containing actual data on past projects to guide managers.

Completion of functional and structural design required documents detailing the function of each system component, module structure, and interfaces between each module, plus a testing plan. Detailed design required flow-chart and tabular documentation on the internal structure of each module, as well as inputs and outputs. At the completion of unit and combined test, Fujitsu required a programming report, which included the detailed design documentation, review data, test specifications and results, as well as the source modules. After system test, the testing report documentation included the inspection specifications, test specifications and results, and the test set. Final inspection generated another set of data.

The most important quality measures Fujitsu used in the 1970s consisted of reliability in component test, conformance to documentation, number of defects detected, and mean time between failures. Mainfactor analysis techniques, introduced in 1974 (and influenced by practices at Hitachi), required testers to sort through intermediate test data to identify sources of errors, before final testing. Standardizing testing and review procedures was an important milestone, because Fujitsu had not yet created a consistent approach for predicting and eliminating defects. Individual programmers had decided which tests to run and when to stop them, without formal planning or supervision. Better control in this area then allowed Fujitsu in the later 1970s to track other measures, such as productivity, software functionality, and portability.

In the period after 1979, Fujitsu management stressed three themes: quality assurance through organization, diffusion of inspection ideas through horizontal development, and advancement of quality concepts. The notion underlying quality assurance through organization was to make quality control part of the formal organizational and job structure for every employee and especially those in design and planning, rather than relegating this function to the Quality Assurance Department. Fujitsu implemented this new emphasis by instituting in 1979–1980 a Phase Completion Reporting System, resembling the design-review systems used at other firms, and then a new version of its Development Planning and Report System. The new reporting system required, for the first time, programmers and managers to collect productivity data. Standardized productivity data then allowed Fujitsu to introduce standard times for worker performance in 1980, based on actual previous data for different types of software, and incorporating quality objectives. Although Fujitsu was several years behind Hitachi and NEC, standard times quickly became the basis of project management.

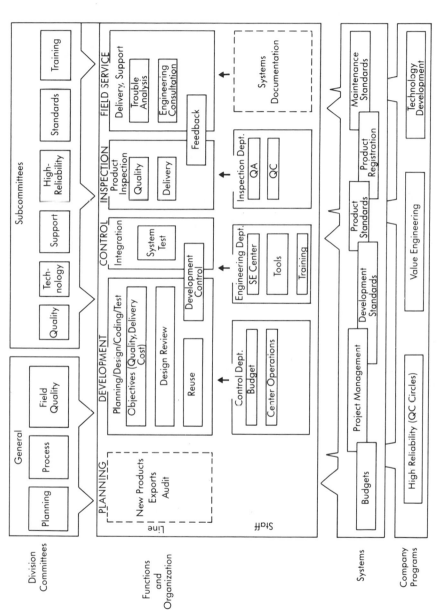

Figure 7.1 Software Development Total Quality Control (TQC) Organizations. QA = quality assurance; QC = quality control. (*Source*: Nihon Noritsu Kyokai [Japan Management Association], *Fujitsu no koshinraisei undo* [Fujitsu's High-Reliability Movement] [Tokyo: Nihon Noritsu Kyokai, 1985], p. 149.)

Diffusion of inspection ideas through horizontal development referred to deliberate efforts to spread good thinking and practices regarding quality control beyond one's small group. The mechanism Fujitsu used was to create a Quality Assurance Liaison (QAL) system—regular meetings where different departments and projects shared data on defects and other information affecting quality. Advancement of quality concepts centered on lectures, workshops, and measures dealing with interpretations of product quality that extended beyond zero defects to characteristics such as product design, function, performance, ease of use, and maintainability, as U.S. experts like Barry Boehm encouraged.

Fujitsu managers interpreted these efforts as constituting a transition from emphasizing process control in the 1970s to Total Quality Control (TQC) in the 1980s. TQC, a term coined during the 1950s in the United States but more popular among Japanese firms since the 1960s, represented comprehensive quality assurance measures that covered product planning, design, manufacturing, and service, rather than simply inspection after production. The origins of the TQC movement in Fujitsu date back to 1966, after management had launched a High-Reliability Program, primarily to improve quality in hardware engineering and manufacturing divisions. Fujitsu's efforts in basic software gradually came to include procedures for project and budget control, work and product standards, product evaluation, registration, and maintenance, set by a series of committees (Figure 7.1).[24] Another element, especially after 1980, became the use of small groups (called quality circles in other firms) that met once or more a month to discuss a range of issues related to productivity and quality as well as work conditions. Managers also used the small groups to supplement formal training required of new company employees. In addition, as part of a second High-Reliability Program, initiated in 1984, the Software Division began working extensively with subsidiaries and subcontractors to establish TQC systems similar to what existed at Numazu.[25]

Quantified Management System

Managers at the Numazu Works also attempted to quantify basic measures of performance and then introduce standardized procedures and tools, much as conventional factory organizations did. They hoped to reduce individual variability and dependency on high levels of experience or skill, and help developers build in quality at each phase, rather than relying on inspection at the end of the development process.[26] To achieve these ends, Fujitsu staff in quality assurance followed four approaches. First, they tried to quantify and then analyze systematically information on project progress and product quality. Second, they introduced methods to predict error occurrence in the programming phase and instituted a management-by-objectives system aimed at insuring error correction. Third, to determine test items, they introduced statistical Design of Experiment techniques (often referred to in the United States as the "Taguchi method" for its leading proponent, Gene Taguchi), previously applied primarily in product development and manufacturing of conventional products like automobiles. Fourth, they tried to evaluate quantitatively the concept of user friendliness.

Measuring design progress remained problematic because the most common way to evaluate schedules was to compare actual progress, such as the number of completed modules, or in Fujitsu's case, completed "design sheets" and "work items," with estimates made prior to starting work. Accuracy of the measure thus depended on the accuracy of the prediction, which managers could not fully determine until completion of a project. Thus, to evaluate projects more precisely, Fujitsu eventually adopted two indexes: one measured quality, based on how many points reviewers gave, and another measured quantity, based on how well predicted amounts of work fit actual results. These procedures and data helped managers define tasks in small, realistic segments, and minimize estimation errors.

The system worked as followed: In the planning stage, managers determined work items (segments of design or other activities that individuals or small teams could finish in about two weeks), recorded these on work-item sheets, and then entered this information into the BSMS database. The Software Division organized projects in groups, and each group leader was responsible for one work item at a time. Each project member had to fill out a "review trust sheet," as well as undergo reviews from several other people, including a chief reviewer. Reviewers used a checklist to evaluate work, and members had to make changes until they satisfied the chief reviewer. At weekly progress meetings, managers and group leaders checked the progress of each work item. The quality index compared the number of quality points received in reviews with the number of predicted quality points, assigned through a simple scheme. Projects received 50 points for completion of materials for reviews, 100 points for completion of required changes, and 50 or more additional points depending on the review evaluations.

Using these formulas, Fujitsu quantified measures for each project member and project, including product quality. In addition, Fujitsu regularly used statistical regressions and factor analysis to identify probable causes of errors, estimate numbers of defects and manpower requirements, and test the accuracy of estimates. Progress evaluations still depended on the accuracy of the predicted values, which sometimes strayed well beyond actual values. Overall, however, Fujitsu managers claimed to have solved major problems with the system and reported significant improvements in progress control as well as quality (see the discussion on performance later).

To quantify ease of use, Fujitsu employed manual reviews and inspections, and validated their accuracy by surveying users through question-naires. Users evaluated products on specific items, which numbered as many as 113 in some surveys, using simple yes or no responses and giving more points for major as opposed to minor items. These items evaluated basic product characteristics (product performance, reliability, operability, compatibility, coordination, ease of maintenance, quality of information, price and delivery), design quality and consistency (defined as the "degree to which software targets and specifications meet user needs," and the "degree to which the finished software meets the design targets and specifications"), and sufficiency and attractiveness ("the extent to which products are acceptable to users"). The surveys indicated that users grouped these features into three categories: major (such as friendliness, efficiency, understandability), intermediate (such as productivity, ease of learning, maintainability), and minor (such as syntax flexibility, speed of operation).

De-skilling and Standardizing Testing

In testing, managers claimed they wanted to detect 65 percent of the errors in a new program by the end of the coding phase review, 95 percent by the end of system test, and nearly all the remainder by the end of the inspection process.[27] Meeting these goals consistently proved difficult because, as in any complex product or process, large programs contained too many combinations of factors and conditions to test completely. Furthermore, company data showed that significant improvement in the ability of personnel to detect errors in software came only with experience and gains tended to level off after about six years. As a result of these observations, Fujitsu managers decided to experiment with a method for selecting test cases that less experienced personnel could utilize, as an engineer in the Quality Assurance Department explained in a 1987 article:

> In tests involving many inspectors, a means is essential to standardize the quality of testing conducted by each inspector, but there is a limit as to the extent to which one can share the knowledge and skill through training. . . . The omission of test cases during test factor analysis is often associated with problems relating to the scope of knowledge and insight of the testing personnel. . . . The omission of test cases during test case generation is often caused by omissions or careless errors. . . . [T]he number of test factors increases in proportion to employed years up to 6 years and stays constant after that. Therefore, to improve the quality of test factor analysis as a whole, it is . . . significant . . . to transfer knowledge to less experienced testing personnel.[28]

Two avenues appeared most useful in standardizing and transferring testing knowledge. One was to develop tools that automated as much of the testing process as possible, particularly the generation of initial tests based on a program's external specifications or input characteristics. Such tools often could identify critical factors that proved to be the source of most errors in a program. Yet the conventional way to generate initial test cases, through often subjective constructions of CEGs, required too much knowledge for most personnel to use effectively. A second approach consisted of creating a database on test-factor analysis methods and conditions, complete with an editing support function to help personnel utilize the database to create test cases for new programs. Fujitsu adopted this latter technique and, around 1980, added to it the Design of Experiments methodology.

The new methods still required experienced personnel since they relied on educated guesses of where problems were likely to exist. To simplify the process, however, Fujitsu compiled lists of possible causes for easy reference, and then coordinated these with procedures recommending specific tests for different situations. The test selection and analysis process relied on tables of orthogonal arrays (statistically independent groups of factors) to indicate the probable causes of most problems, based on how the factors within independent groups interacted. Engineers claimed the Design of Experiments approach made it possible to control the number of combinations that existed between any two factors, minimize measurement errors and other conditions, and identify correctable defects more quickly than cause-effect graphs. Fujitsu data indicated that these methods actually detected at least five to ten times the number of errors usually found with conventional methods, and with fewer test cases.[29]

Computer-Aided Tools

Again similar to Hitachi, Toshiba, and NEC, in the mid-1970s, Fujitsu began introducing numerous computer-aided tools to support the development and maintenance of basic software. Numazu remained the center of this tool R&D until the mid-1980s, when Kamata and the central research facility, Fujitsu Laboratories, began studying how to automate system design and program construction. Perhaps because management had no specific factory plan for Numazu, the Basic Software Division tended to introduce tools for discrete use rather than as parts of an integrated system. Nevertheless, by the mid-1980s, Numazu had created linkages among major tools for project management, programming, and maintenance (see Table 7.7).[30]

The operation of these tools closely resembled comparable systems at Hitachi, Toshiba, and NEC, as well as other firms such as IBM. BSMS, for example, performed functions similar to Hitachi's CAPS and Toshiba's SWB systems. Fujitsu also utilized another tool for project management, in addition to BSMS, called Generalized Program Editing and Management Facilities (GEM), a library-management and data-

Table 7.7 Major Systems Software Development Tools (1985)

Design

YAC II (new version 1983) (Yet Another Control chart). Detailed design language, combining aspects of conventional flow charts and pseudo code.

Program Editing/Code Generation

GEM (1979) (Generalized Program Editing and Management Facilities). Automatically maintains a development history of a program. Linked to PRISM.

PRISM (1982) (Problem and Repair Interrelated System Management Extended). Maintains a database of the program source and automatically tracks maintenance changes. Linked to GEM.

COMPACT (1982) (Compact Print-out Utility). Compacts and prints out compiled and assembled code.

TOOL 2 (1983) Allows on-line search, from time-sharing terminals, of program source code and lists.

YPS (1983) (YACII Programming System). Allows the user to edit YACII diagrams and then automatically generates code in several languages.

Testing

SAT/ART (1980) (Systematic and Automatic Testing/Automatic Regression Testing). Automates regression testing tool for operating system development.

TDQS (1977) (Test Tool for DQS). Automated regression testing tool for on-line display operations.

INDS (1983). (Interactive NCP Debugging System). Allows checking and analysis of NCP test results from time-sharing terminals.

MTS (1971, 1977) (Multiterminal Simulator). Simulates remote terminals for host load testing.

TIOS (1977) (Time-Sharing System Input/Output Simulator). Simulates remote terminals for host load testing.

HTS (1977) (Hardware Trouble Simulator). Simulates hardware bugs for functional test evaluations of software responses.

DOCK/FORTRAN77 (1981). Debugging system for FORTRAN, using a "slow video display."

PIC (1984) (Program Information Control system). Allows inspection and analysis of memory-dump lists from time-sharing terminals. Linked to the Kamata-Numazu Dump Transfer system.

ATOS (1982) (AIM Test Oriented System). Automatically records on computer database results from testing and inspection.

Documentation

ODM (1983) (Office Document Manager). Document handling system for Japanese lanaguage.

Manual Compilation Automation System (1979). Automated editing of electronic documentation files.

EGRET-4 (1983) (Easy Graphic Report Generator).

ATLAS (1982). Automatic translation of Japanese documents into English. English to Japanese system added in 1986.

Maintenance

TDP II (1980) (Total System for Difficulties Information Processing). Database for software report information.

ITS (1981) (Incident Tracking System). Control system for questions from customers.

Table 7.7 (*Continued*)

Kamata-Numazu Dump Transfer (1982). On-line transfer of data and reports on bugs. Linked to PIC testing tool.

PDE (1983) (PTF Document Editor). Automatically edits documents on program corrections, based on TDP II data.

Control

BSMS (1976) (Basic Software Project Management Support System). Database and control tool for software project management.

NOA (1978) (Numazu Office Automation). Employment data control system.

In-House Training Database System (1982). Relational database system for in-house training administration.

Source: Fujitsu Ltd., "Sofutouea kaihatsu: hinshitsu-seisansei kojo ni tsuite," unpublished company document, received Sept. 24, 1985, pp. 37, 44.

collection system that automatically generated graphic reports, for groups and individuals, on productivity (lines of code developed), progress status (by month and week), and quality (defects per module). The library functions included version control for modules and completed programs, as well as compressed data to reduce the volume of stored files.[31]

Similarly, for detailed program (module-level) design, Fujitsu introduced a structured flow-chart methodology in 1980 that closely resembled Hitachi's PAD and NEC's SPD diagrams, called Yet Another Control (YAC) chart. In 1983, Fujitsu completed a new version (YACII) that worked with a computer-aided tool, YACII Programming System (YPS), to generate code automatically from the structured diagrams. (The Systems Engineering Group actually developed these and then transferred them to Numazu and other Fujitsu facilities and subsidiaries.) YPS contained an editor, compiler, debugger, and documentation generator, and received inputs in structured conversational Japanese on work stations or terminals. A special program translated the inputs into machine-readable YACII charts and then executable code in C, FORTRAN, COBOL, or LDL, a language based on C for basic software design that Fujitsu developed to use with YACII charts.[32]

Again, similar to Hitachi, Toshiba, and NEC, the combination of tools such as YACII and YPS seemed to enhance productivity in nearly all phases of development after systems design. They helped eliminate poorly structured programs by supporting top-down, structured design through graphical and text representations. They practically eliminated coding errors, since the designs were executable. They facilitated reuse of whole programs, program parts, or edited portions of a program at the design-specification level and thus across different computer languages or architectures. They included executors, test-coverage evaluators, and debuggers that executed the charts, and helped developers evaluate the comprehensiveness of test cases, collect and analyze data, and debug programs. The tools also facilitated maintenance, both fixing problems and adding enhancements, first by minimizing coding errors and then by presenting designs in standard formats that were relatively simple for third parties to understand, while the document generator produced detailed specifications automatically from the design charts. In addition, YPS and other systems included reverse generators that produced design charts from source code; developers could then edit the charts more easily than source code as well as store the charts in a database for later retrieval.[33]

Performance Improvement

Fujitsu did not publish or publicize much performance data for basic software or for applications. Part of the reason is that only within the last few years, in contrast to Hitachi and Toshiba, have Fujitsu projects begun to collect data in a standardized fashion. Nonetheless, data available for this study (including confidential statistics reviewed by this author) indicated steady gains in the decade after 1975 in quality (program reliability), schedule control (project lateness), and productivity (lines of delivered code per month).

For all code in the field (new code plus maintained software), between 1977 and 1979, defects reported by users dropped by one-third, and then another one-third between 1979 and 1982 (Table 7.8). By 1985, defect levels for outstanding code had fallen to practically zero (0.01 and below). Fujitsu would not allow the publication of data on errors in newly

Table 7.8 Systems Software Quality Performance (1977–1985)

Year	Defects/1,000 Lines of All Maintained Code*	Bug Detection Method (estimates)		
		Test (%)	Source Code Review (%)	Design Sheet Review (%)
1977	0.19	85	15	—
1978	0.13	80	15	5
1979	0.06	70	20	10
1980	0.05	60	25	15
1981	0.04	40	30	30
1982	0.02	30	30	40
1983	0.02	—	—	—
1984	0.02	—	—	—
1985	0.01	—	—	—

*All defects reported by users per 1,000 lines of code over 6-month periods in the field (i.e., newly delivered code plus supported outstanding code).
Source: Based on Yoshida Tadashi, "Sofutouea no keiryo-ka [Quantifying software]," *Joho shori* 26, 1, January 1985, p. 49; and Tadashi Yoshida interviews, July 31, 1986, Sept. 7, 1987, and Aug. 22, 1989.

written code, but this showed a nearly identical downward trend. Defects per 1,000 lines of new code reported by users (generally about ten times the level for all code) fell fourfold between 1980 and 1981 alone. Improvement since 1981 leveled off, as defects dropped to approximately 0.1 and below, although this level was already excellent by most standards (see the averages reported from Japanese and U.S. projects discussed in Appendix B). Fujitsu data also suggested that the review procedures instituted after the late 1970s helped create these low defect levels and, especially, cut down the number of design errors. In 1977, for example, Numazu personnel detected approximately 85 percent of defects found through testing and 15 percent through reviews of source code (coding-phase review). Design-sheet reviews, instituted in 1978, found more errors and gradually became the major method for defect detection, increasing from 5 to approximately 40 percent by 1982.

In addition to apparent increases in quality, Fujitsu's emphasis since the early 1970s on product handling and project control gradually led to progress in scheduling accuracy. Most projects came in late in the early days of programming, with "late" defined as reaching the Quality Assurance Department after the scheduled time. Even during the latter half of the 1970s, approximately 40 percent of projects fell behind schedule and thus over-budget. By the early 1980s, however, Numazu had reduced this to approximately 15 percent (a level comparable to Hitachi, Toshiba, and NEC). Most delays that remained came in the transition from functional design to coding, phases that continued to be difficult to estimate accurately because of variations in skill levels as well as changes in product specifications or designs[34] (including changes in IBM designs).

Current measures of productivity, in addition to the standard lines of code (steps) per person per month (adjusted for overtime), covered number of documents per month, total development costs per 1,000 lines, machine time, and pages of documentation per 1,000 lines of code.[35] According to in-house data, Numazu appeared to experience major improvements in lines-of-code productivity between 1975 and 1978, corresponding to new procedures for project management, and somewhat less dramatic but still significant gains during the mid-1980s, following new efforts in quality control and centralization of development efforts at Numazu.

Applications Software

Formation of the Systems Engineering Group

Fujitsu's decision to create a specific organization for custom programming stemmed from the same need Hitachi, Toshiba, and NEC encountered: to produce a variety of nominally different programs more efficiently, primarily for the company's own hardware and basic software. In the early 1960s, Fujitsu's few computer customers had performed most of their own programming, with assistance from service personnel in the new Computer Division. Several large orders for on-line banking, securities, and data-processing systems inspired management to create a larger Systems Department in 1964 to build programs for and with customers.

By 1970, however, this organization had become unable to meet demand generated by the popular 230 series, prompting Fujitsu to establish the Information Processing System Laboratory in Kamata, Tokyo. This laboratory, with an initial staff of 700, allowed Fujitsu to centralize training operations as well as customized programming for business, engineering, and scientific applications. The M-series then brought new orders for even larger and more complex programs, inspiring managers to organize a Systems Engineering Group in the mid-1970s as well as to establish a software factory (Table 7.9).[36]

Table 7.9 Chronology of Applications Software Process Development (1964–1987)

1964	Establishment of Systems Department.
1970	Centralization of applications development at Information Processing System Laboratory in Kamata, Tokyo.
1976	Establishment of software-engineering team within Systems Department to develop SDEM (Software Development Engineering Methodology).
1977	Establishment of the Software Conversion Factory and SDEM standards. EPG (Executive Planning Guide) and C-NAP (Customer Needs Analysis Procedure) commercialized for in-house use and sale.
1978	Introduction of SDSS (Software Development Support System).
1979	Establishment of the Software Factory Department in Kamata.
1980	SDEM standards commercialized for sale.
1981	YAC (Yet Another Control chart) developed for design notation. Commercialization of PARADIGM (methodology and tool for developing reusable programs).
1982	Commercialization of BAGLES (Banking Application Generator's Library for Extensive Support).
	Commercialization of ADAM (Applications Development and Management System)
1983	SIMPLE tool-set introduced for commercial sales, beginning with LINDA (Logical Information Support Tool of Dataset) and DBSP (Database Support Program).
	YACII and YPS (YAC II Programming System) developed.
	SDT (SDEM Design Technique) developed.
1984	On-line SDEM developed.
1985	ACS-APG (ACS Application Program Generator) from the SIMPLE series commercialized.
1987	DRAGON (Driver and Stub Generator for On-line and Batch Test) from the SIMPLE series commercialized.
	SDAS (Systems Development Architecture and Support Facilities) commercialized.
	EPGII/CNAPII commercialized, adding to 1977 version design concept and data-analysis capabilities.

Source: Fujitsu internal data.

   As of 1988, the Systems Engineering Group consisted of three main areas, subsidiaries, and a research institute (Table 7.10). The Common Technology Area included the SE (Systems-Engineering) Technical Support Center, the Applications Software Planning Division, and the Office Computer Systems Support Service Division. The SE Technical Support Center housed the Software Factory Department and a portion of its 1,500 programmers, as well as other departments for Systems Development Engineering (technology planning and transfer), Information Support (product information for customers), Systems Engineering Support Services (tools and methods), and the Sigma project (see Chapter 8). The factory built approximately 20 percent of the new applications done in the Systems Engineering Group as well as handled approximately 75 percent of all program conversion work (modifying software to run on new Fujitsu machines). Most of the remaining jobs, approximately 800 small projects per year in the late 1980s, went to thirty-seven subsidiaries (see Table 7.3) as well as subcontractors outside the factory.

Table 7.10 Systems Engineering (SE) Group Organization (1989)

Common Technology Area
SE Technical Support Center
   Systems Development Engineering Department
   Software Factory Department
   Information Support Center Department
   Systems Engineering Support Services Department
   Sigma Project Systems Promotion Office
Office Computer Systems Support Service Division
Applications Software Planning Division
   Applications Software Planning Department
   Software Distribution Department

Industry-Related Departments
Finance
Insurance/Securities
Manufacturing/Distribution
Scientific/Technical
Nippon Telegraph and Telephone
Government/Mass Communication

Functional Departments
Management Information Systems
VAN (Value-Added Network) Systems Engineering
Information Network Systems Engineering
Personal-Computer Systems Engineering
NCC (new common carriers) Systems Engineering

Systems-Engineering Subsidiaries
Industry-related
Functional
Regional

*Fujitsu Research Institute for Advanced Information Systems
and Economics*

Source: Nikkei Computer, Oct. 13, 1986, p. 79 (updated to 1989)

A second area consisted of departments with systems engineers specializing in particular industry applications (finance, insurance, securities, manufacturing, distribution, NTT, scientific, technical, government, and mass communication), so that they had adequate knowledge to specify customer requirements and write accurate system designs. The third area, functionally specialized departments of systems engineers, designed management information systems, "value-added networks" for different on-line services, personal-computer systems, and software for new telecommunication firms (the new common carriers or NCCs).

Factory Evolution: Conversion to New Development

Fujitsu managers cited several reasons behind their decision to create a software factory in the late 1970s. Primarily, they saw this structure as a mechanism to separate high-level design (systems engineering) from product construction, and then centralize and standardize similar, relatively routine tasks, in an attempt to improve productivity, quality, and scheduling control. They expected improvement because centralization would allow more projects to benefit from knowledge accumulated within Fujitsu regarding support tools, structured methods, and techniques for project management. In particular, managers hoped the factory would improve their ability to control large projects, especially those involving numerous subcontractors, who required better coordination to meet budgets, schedules, and quality objectives.[37]

Fujitsu began cautiously. First, it experimented with a centralized organization by setting up a Software Conversion Factory Department in 1977, with approximately 100 personnel. This modified the huge number of programs customers wanted to run on the new M-series machines, which were not compatible with Fujitsu's previous architectures, as well as software originally written for other companies' machines for operation on Fujitsu hardware. Managers believed conversion work was more straightforward than new development and that centralization of personnel and equipment would foster standardization and thus dissemination of good methods and tools, making tasks easier to manage while raising productivity and quality. This seemed feasible especially since, in coordination with the factory establishment, a team of Fujitsu engineers defined a set of structured design and programming techniques as well as detailed procedures for project management, called Software Development Engineering Methodology (SDEM), and introduced support tools for programming in FORTRAN, called Software Development Support System (SDSS), which Fujitsu quickly replaced with tools for COBOL programming.[38]

The conversion factory worked well enough so that Mitsugi, after he became head of the Systems Engineering Group, decided to expand the facility to include program construction. He added another 200 personnel and charged them with turning requirements specifications received from systems engineers into code. Prior to this, Fujitsu had managed systems engineering and program construction in integrated projects, with no separation of these two functions. Nevertheless, the new factory did not work smoothly for all projects. In fact, Mitsugi admitted that "the original factory idea, because of our inexperience, went too far," in the sense that it proved difficult and unnecessary to separate program construction from systems engineering too rigidly. Much like SDC had experienced a few years earlier, Fujitsu managers found that many projects depended on close interactions with customers and knowledge of very different requirements, or that writing the application program required access to proprietary information that customers, for security reasons, preferred not to give Fujitsu personnel unless they worked at the customers' own sites. On other occasions, Fujitsu needed to provide programming services at locations around Japan, again departing from the centralized factory model. In addition, as Fujitsu improved the tools and reuse databases available in the factory, less-experienced programmers became better able to build complete systems on their own, making separation of work and use of the more skilled systems engineers unnecessary. Rather than abandoning the factory, which SDC did, Fujitsu managers improved the system gradually, recognizing that different projects had different optimal processes. The major change consisted of expanding the scope of work in the factory departments to let factory personnel do detailed design and eventually systems design for projects where it was difficult or unnecessary to separate these tasks, either for logistical reasons or because factory engineers had the expertise to design and build systems on their own (Figure 7.2).

Fujitsu introduced other changes. One encouraged systems engineers outside the factory, who initially did surveys and project planning, systems design, and a program's structural design, to leverage their expertise more widely not only by letting the factory personnel do more work but by writing software packages to cover the needs of many users with a single design effort. Any packages or pieces of them that Fujitsu could deploy for custom jobs, as is or modified, reduced the need to write new software. In addition, to spread the burden of programming more widely, Fujitsu management established or engaged more subsidiaries and subcontractors, as well as leased methods, tools, and training services to customers of Fujitsu hardware, beginning with SDEM in 1980 (see Table 7.9).[39] Fujitsu also continued to refine the factory's methods and tools, as the nature of demand changed. In particular, orders Fujitsu received in the mid-1980s from Japanese banks for huge on-line systems requiring several million lines of code provided an important stimulus to find ways to manage large projects more effectively and automate, or mechanize, aspects of design, programming, and testing.

System Engineering Departments

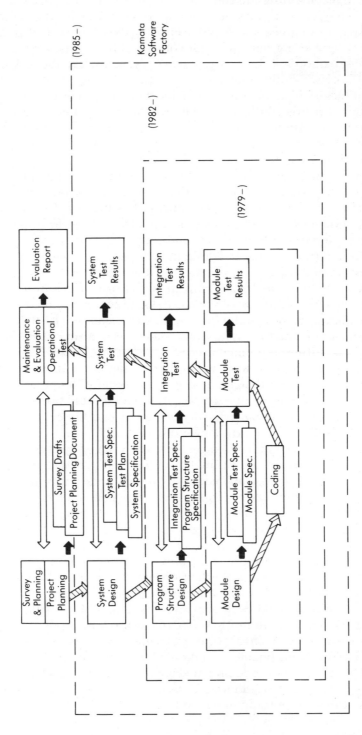

Figure 7.2 Fujitsu Applications Factory Process Flows. (*Source*: Hiroshi Narafu and Noritoshi Murakami interviews, Aug. 28, 1988, and May 4, 1988.)

Methodological Standardization

The Systems Engineering Group had guidelines for product development and project management prior to 1977, but management vaguely defined them and weakly enforced them. Development proceeded very much in a craft mode, with programs more the property of individuals than the product of an organization. Documentation and standardization were so lacking that, as the engineers who developed SDEM and SDSS recalled, it was difficult to understand programs other personnel wrote:

> We had software development standards before SDEM and SDSS were developed but the standards had no clear definition of the development phases. This lack of definition resulted in so much freedom that software systems often became the products of individuals. It was not easy for a person who had not designed a program to understand how it worked. To improve on this situation, we concluded that clear, reasonable definitions of the developing phases and activities were required. The kinds of tasks performed during each activity also needed standardization.[40]

A team Fujitsu established in 1976 to study these problems considered two options: improve and standardize procedures, techniques, and other elements that made up the programming environment; and automate program generation, relying on standardized formats for specifying user requirements and advanced tools. Since program generation remained an uncertain technology, they decided to begin with standardization. The team also realized they had to establish a formal methodology before pursuing more automation:

> There are two approaches to software engineering. One approach is to upgrade current development methods by standardizing development procedures and by improving both programming techniques and the development environment. In the other approach, programs are directly generated using formal specifications of user requirements, and this approach involves the application program generator or automatic programming. The latter approach is one way of accomplishing our ultimate goal of software engineering, and if we narrow the applied field this approach is feasible. However, it is very difficult to realize these latter technologies at the present state of the art, if we apply them generally. . . . Therefore, we addressed the following items based on the evolutionary approach: 1) clarification of software development methods and standardization for development activities, 2) utilization of tools to computerize development activities.
>
> We developed SDEM around the first item. For the second, we developed SDSS as a set of tools to support the phases after system design. . . . Our basic attitude toward software development is that it is more desirable to first clarify software development methods and a software development system, then to approach these problems and solutions rationally and systematically, depending heavily on feedback from the actual system developers.[41]

After studying current practices in the industry, the team wrote four manuals to set down what they called the SDEM methodology. The *SDEM Concept Manual* outlined basic standards and development techniques, with a life cycle divided into six stages and twelve specific phases, from survey and planning through maintenance and evaluation (Figure 7.3). The *SDEM Introduction and Application Manual* explained project-management procedures and guidelines. The *SDEM Standards Reference Card* listed specific procedures and work items for each development phase and software developer. The *Detailed SDEM Standards Manual* elaborated on work items and documentation requirements, with examples. SDEM also called for the use of standard times for coding (primarily in COBOL and FORTRAN) and other activities, to help managers estimate schedules and budgets, although project managers remained free to tailor standards, methods, and tools, as well as performance expectations, to accommodate programs of different types and sizes.

While the SDEM procedures also covered quality control, it took until 1987 for the Systems Engineering Group to establish a department for inspection or quality assurance independent of individual projects, primarily to coordinate and check work done at subcontractors. Applications projects thus had more autonomy than basic software projects, although SDEM established a formal process that seemed effective for checking work in progress and providing feedback to engineers, project managers, and staff responsible for quality and work standards. The software factory, like Numazu, also automated aspects of quality control, such as with tools that checked programs against specified coding or design rules, and collected various data automatically for later analysis.

Another difference from Numazu was that, rather than having management set quality objectives, project managers in applications tended to negotiate with customers to determine quality targets—the "maximum allowable number of errors per 1000 statements." In other areas, both in basic software and applications, quality procedures required project members to propose solutions to problems they uncovered and then to solve them. If early tests indicated defect levels were above target, the developers had to validate the target levels and then describe the countermeasures they planned to use. Common countermeasures to decrease building in defects included standardization controls, reuse of program parts or designs, automation of code generation, and data dictionaries. To increase the detection of defects, SDEM procedures encouraged the use of design reviews, source code checks, test-coverage tools, and verification tools.[42]

Process and Work-Flow Management

The team that developed SDEM expected the same kinds of benefits other factories sought from methodological standardization. They

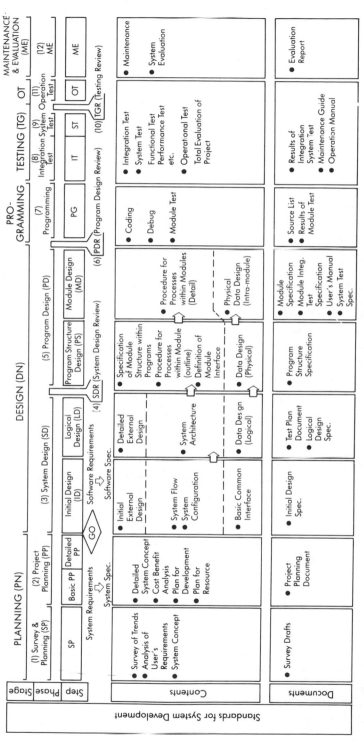

Figure 7.3 Outline of Software Development Engineering Methodology (SDEM). (*Source*: Noritoshi Murakami, Isao Miyanari, and Karuo Yabuta, "SDEM and SDSS: Overall Approach to Improvement of the Software Development Process," in Horst Hunke, ed., *Software Engineering Environments* [Amsterdam: North Holland, 1981], p. 285. Copyright © 1981 Gesellschaft für Mathematik und Datenverarbeitung mbH. Reproduced with permission.)

claimed the new standards would even out the quality of products, help in maintenance, reduce the dependency of the development process on individual experience, ease tool introduction, and simplify management control.[43] Fujitsu, however, had another major objective for SDEM: to facilitate the separation of requirements specification and program construction, as well as the transformation of the former into the latter.

Most custom applications projects in the Systems Engineering Group during the first few years of the factory ran from approximately 10,000 to a few hundred thousand lines of code, and took a few months to one year to complete. They included both a chief systems engineer, from a department outside the factory (as in Toshiba), and a chief programmer, from within the software factory (or a subsidiary or subcontractor). The chief systems engineer remained primarily responsible for dealing with the customer as well as delivering a system that correctly met the contracted requirements.[44]

The original work flow for a typical project at Kamata in 1979 called for a team of four or five systems engineers to take charge of planning, system design, and program-structure design, transfer the program designs to the factory for implementation, and then oversee integration and system testing. The systems engineers also wrote designs in a standard format using conversational language (Japanese mainly), and provided input/output diagrams and mathematical equations, as necessary, to clarify the design and minimize the degree of skill required in subsequent stages. Personnel in the software factory (or a subsidiary) wrote module designs in flow charts and then generated or wrote code as well as tested each module, working in teams of seven or eight programmers for each systems engineer.

System designs consisted of external specifications that did not rely on specific hardware, languages, or operating systems. Program designs consisted of finer but still functional descriptions of how parts of the system were to operate, depending to some extent on characteristics of the particular hardware, languages, and basic software. Module designs in structured diagrams were constrained by the availability of compilers for specific coding languages, and also might reflect or take advantage of features in the hardware and basic software.[45] Therefore, developing system and program designs separately from the module designs and code might hinder an entire implementation effort, especially in new or particularly complex applications where engineers required frequent communication and experimentation to find the proper designs and code to meet customer specifications.

Most software producers, since the beginning of the industry, have encountered problems transforming requirements into designs and code. Separating these phases may force engineers to clarify the design, and thus simplify the process for implementation into code. On the other hand, poorly specified designs, or changing requirements, will complicate the transformation, especially if the tasks are separated. As noted in earlier cases, for basic software development, where company engineers produced their own designs rather than writing specifications for outside customers, and where, presumably, competition for new products required a high level of communication and experimentation, none of the Japanese firms studied in this book physically or organizationally separated systems designers from coders. In applications software, however, all the Japanese software factories made some separation, as well as relied heavily on computer-aided design and reuse-support tools, at least for relatively routine applications they had done before.

Fujitsu's applications factory was no exception. To tackle this problem of specializing and dividing tasks, as well as minimizing communications problems, managers adopted two approaches. First, they promoted close interactions between customers and systems engineers and then between systems engineers and factory personnel during the entire development process, as well as conducted a series of design reviews, to clarify the accuracy and meaning of design documents as early as possible. Second, they gradually expanded the activities of factory personnel to include more design work.

While standardized training in the SDEM methodology and support tools alone helped communication, if the factory personnel did not understand part of a design document, SDEM procedures encouraged them to contact the responsible systems engineer and discuss the problem directly. When factory personnel finished turning part of a design into code and testing their portion, they would send it back to the systems engineers, who would then check and examine the software with the customer. After building and testing all components, some of the systems engineers and factory developers also moved to the customer's site to conduct system tests. (Service engineers in the field performed operational tests with customers and Fujitsu provided some assistance in maintenance, although Fujitsu customers frequently did their own maintenance).[46]

When systems engineers understood the customer's requirements relatively well, and factory personnel understood the program designs, dividing tasks proceeded smoothly, allowing systems engineers to cultivate their applications expertise and factory personnel to cultivate their functional expertise in module design, coding, and testing. Yet Fujitsu managers soon discovered that this divided process was not optimal for all projects. Some systems proved difficult to specify clearly enough for module design to proceed smoothly, necessitating frequent discussions during the various levels of design and programming. For this reason alone, it seemed logical to move program design closer to module design while upgrading the skills of factory personnel and expanding their role in the development process.

As managers gradually gave factory projects more design work, the factory personnel acquired broader skills and experience, as well as libraries of reusable designs and code, in addition to new tools—for particular applications areas, even though factory departments did not specialize as narrowly as systems-engineering departments. Thus, by the mid-1980s, the Kamata factory had become capable of doing program design at least for familiar applications. This freed senior systems engineers outside the factory to leverage their expertise better by working with more customers in systems planning, without taking the additional time to specify program structures, or by writing packages for many users. Fujitsu managers thus instituted a second pattern around 1982 for some projects, forming teams within the factory to do program structure design and integration test, in addition to the usual module design, coding, and module testing (see Figure 7.2).

The continued accumulation of experience, tools, and reuse libraries prompted managers to adopt a third pattern around 1985, again, where appropriate. This process called for factory personnel to specify, design, build, and test complete systems—including the initial customer consultations and project planning, as well as operational test, evaluation, and some maintenance. Many of these projects consisted of huge banking and value-added tax calculation systems that exceeded 1 million lines of code and took two or three years to finish.[47] These were not simple systems to build. Nonetheless, after experienced engineers built a few of them, it became unnecessary to complicate the development process by separating design and programming tasks, and feasible for factory personnel to develop comparable but still tailored systems for new customers.

During the 1980s, managers in Fujitsu's Systems Engineering Group, like managers of engineering and factory production in other industries, thus had to devise guidelines for deciding how, when, and why to divide and apportion work. They still organized projects and small teams, as did other Japanese software factories; however, they had moved beyond craft or job-shop structures, with a new organization that required decisions on whether to send out specifications for implementation and then to where—the software factory, a subsidiary, or an outside subcontractor.

It followed that, first, managers had to make a *capability* decision. They had to determine if particular factory departments or other organizations could handle a specific job. Then they had to make a *capacity* decision, to determine if people were available to do the required work. For products that demanded special experience in an application even to do coding, such as scientific, space, and nuclear power-plant software, or for software packages in nearly any area (since developers needed an intimate knowledge of user needs to write a program fulfilling common functions), systems engineers usually built the entire systems themselves, without handing off specifications. These types of specialized jobs accounted for 10 to 20 percent of the Systems Engineering Group's work in the late 1980s. The software factory, as well as subsidiaries and subcontractors outside the factory, handled the remaining jobs, depending on where there existed adequate capacity and capabilities for a given project.

In general, Fujitsu managers tried to steer to the factory projects similar to previous work done by its personnel but large enough so that the jobs could fully utilize the factory's special capabilities. In 1984, for example, the Kamata factory introduced an on-line SDEM system that allowed up to 1,000 people to participate in a single project simultaneously, with 200 to 300 terminals and workbenches connected to a single mainframe, and with up to six mainframes holding files and data for the one project. In addition, the factory had direct access to the latest set of tools, packages, and reuse libraries.

Managers also tried to give small, one-time projects to subsidiaries or subcontractors outside the factory. This practice allowed the factory to continue accumulating experience with similar work and let the Fujitsu group accommodate different jobs without overtaxing in-house personnel or adding too many full-time (and usually higher-paid) employees to the ranks of its permanent work force. On other occasions, Fujitsu simply used subsidiaries and subcontractors as sources of extra manpower to meet demand peaks or help with large projects running late within the factory. (As at other Japanese software factories, Fujitsu managers claimed they were able to add people to phases such as coding without delaying projects further because of standardized methods, tools, and training even for subcontractors' personnel, who tended to work on a long-term basis with Fujitsu.)[48]

Training and Career Paths

Kamata, like other Japanese software factories, contained a mixture of high school and college graduates (more from college than high school), and few employees with backgrounds in computers or software engineering.[49] Also like its Japanese competitors, Fujitsu offered full-time classes and on-the-job training to turn new graduates into software engineers, teach them a common set of methods and tools, and prepare employees for advancement.

Fujitsu began limited general education with the establishment of the Information Processing System Laboratory in 1970, though several years passed before the Systems Engineering Group settled on standards for applications development and coordinated these with training. One milestone was the completion of the SDEM standards and the creation of seminars in 1977 to teach these to managers and engineers. Fujitsu followed these seminars with periodic workshops for project managers and a lengthier education program for new employees, in addition to courses for customers and personnel from subsidiaries and other firms interested in writing or maintaining software for Fujitsu machines. As an example of the scale and breakdown of this effort, in 1987, Fujitsu offered courses on computers and software education to more than 89,000 people. The largest group, approximately 57,000, were Fujitsu customers. Of the remaining, 12,000 were Fujitsu employees, 13,000 came from systems-engineering subsidiaries or affiliated subcontractors, and 4,000 worked at dealers or independent software houses.

Fujitsu coordinated its formal education program with career paths that also resembled those at Hitachi, Toshiba, and NEC. New employees remained trainees for their first year and attended full-time classes for three months, learning assembler, COBOL, machine input/output routines, and other areas of basic programming and computer architecture. They next received training on the job after the initial classroom lectures. After the first year, Fujitsu classified employees as junior systems engineers, and training continued on the job through coding simple programs. These personnel also received continuing education in classes and workshops consisting of two or three days every month or two months, in addition to independent study and quality circle activities. This training covered topics such as writing and speaking, system design, project management, contracts and law, network design and requirements analysis, and product-specific information (Table 7.11).

The junior systems engineers usually did coding for two or three years, before moving on to module or structural design. For education planning, rather than for project management (as at Hitachi), Fujitsu also assigned skill levels to personnel on a scale of one to five, based on self-evaluations as well as testing from course work. After three years of experience, depending on an individual's ability, junior systems engineers might receive the title of systems engineer and actually do systems engineering within the factory. Thereafter, they might become more senior in the factory or move into the systems engineering departments or into project management and support. Project management and support functions included revising standard times, carrying out quality assurance measures, proposing means for quality and productivity improvement, or developing and evaluating new tools and methods.

The Systems Engineering Group granted the rank of senior systems engineer to personnel with from nine to thirteen years experience, depending on whether they were high school or college graduates. These engineers specialized in application areas, in contrast to factory programmers (although managers tended to assign programmers to projects similar to what they had done in the past). To improve its training of systems engineers as well as utilize experienced people to help service customers, in 1986 Fujitsu also established the Fujitsu Research Institute for Advanced Information Systems and Economics. Staffed with thirty

Table 7.11 Systems Engineering Group Training and Career Paths

Year 1	*Education Dept.*	*Assignment to Factory Divisions*	
	New entrant education →	Training in divisions →	Project work introduction →
Training	Joint sessions: Languages OS System design SDEM methods	Factory work standards On-the-job instruction	Project standards: Process Tool use Documentation ·Coding
Time	3 mo	1–2 mo	7–8 mo
Title	Trainee		

Year 2–4	*Project Work*		
	Coding → Module test	Module design → Test specifica- tions	Programming → Structural design
Training	Junior: writing and speaking, information and communications, system design, product-specific skills and information Regular: project management, contracts and law, network structure de- sign and requirements analysis		
Titles	Junior systems engineer (1.5–3 yrs experience) Systems engineer (3–13 yrs for high school graduates; 3–9 yrs for college graduates)		

Year 5+	*System Design Work* Logic design → Initial design Integrated test System test *Project Management and Support Work* Scheduling, quality, budget control and risk management Development process and project-management methods Tool planning and development
Training	Continues regular curriculum for systems engineers
Title	Senior systems engineer (from 9–13 yrs experience)

Source: Hiroshi Narafu correspondence; Fujitsu Ltd., "Kyoiku jigyo no gaiyo" [Overview of education], in-house customer materials, August 1988.

managers and seventy systems engineers, this facility trained Fujitsu personnel in systems consultation as well as assisted customers in planning and problem solving.[50]

Computer-Aided Tools

Like Numazu, the Systems Engineering Group invested in computer-aided support tools for all phases of applications development and project management, with special attention to automating aspects of design and coding as well as reuse support. Staff engineers in the SE Technical Support Center conducted much of this R&D, with some assistance from Fujitsu's central research laboratories. Kamata also imported some tools from Numazu (as Numazu sometimes did from Kamata).

Noritoshi Murakami, a manager in the Systems Development Engineering Department who earlier had worked on the SDEM refinements, presented an overview of automatic programming that helped locate Fujitsu's efforts within the broader spectrum of computer-aided tools assisting developers through the four phases of planning, system design, program design, and coding and testing (Figure 7.4). In this scheme, "classical automatic programming" consisted of compilers that turned computer code into machine-readable object languages, and thus assisted only in the fourth stage. Software producers developed compilers during the late 1950s and early 1960s to avoid having to write programs in machine language, and they continued to be essential for use with high-level languages. Nonetheless, the degree of automation was minimal since software developers still had to do planning as well as system and program design manually.

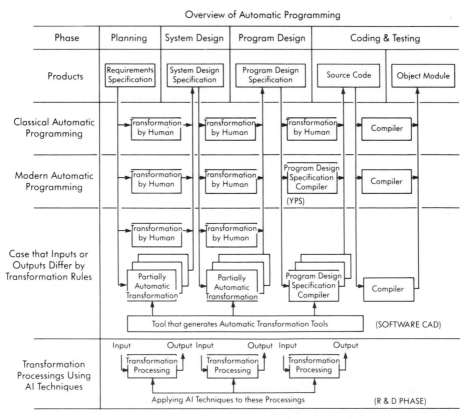

Figure 7.4 Overview of Automatic Programming. AI = artificial intelligence; CAD = computer-aided design; YPS = Yet Another Control Chart (YAC)II Programming System. (*Source*: Murakami interviews.)

The technology Murakami referred to as "modern"—represented by YPS in Fujitsu as well as comparable systems in Hitachi, NEC, Toshiba, and other firms—automated the transformation step from program-design specification to machine-readable code. These "program design specification compilers" read structured designs or diagrams like PAD, SPD, or YACII, and then generated code more or less automatically (module interfaces might have to be written manually), usually in COBOL, FORTRAN, PL/1, or C. More advanced tools helped automate earlier steps in the development cycle; that is, system planning and design. Tools such as Fujitsu's Software CAD (discussed later) attempted this through transformation rules the tool user defined, and fell into the category Murakami called a "partially automatic transformation tool." At the R&D level in Fujitsu (and in many other firms) were tools that tried to automate the transformation of system requirements into executable code, utilizing AI techniques.[51]

Automated design-support and programming tools also served two constituencies: software experts and nonexperts. Fujitsu literature, for example, maintained that its more advanced tools could "free software engineers from the tedious and cumbersome job of writing run-of-the-mill computer programs and turn their talent to more creative work." This occurred because engineers no longer had to compose in computer languages but could focus on business problems and write programs "more finely attuned to the requirements of the end-user." In addition, Fujitsu claimed its design-support tools could "enable computer users to develop their own application software without the help of expert programmers."[52] While many software producers were developing or using tools with similar capabilities and objectives, Fujitsu offered what seemed to be the broadest collection in the Japanese software industry.

Kamata's first integrated tool set, the SDSS, introduced in 1978, relied on a project library for FORTRAN source programs, designs, test data, and documentation; a module description language and analyzer containing information such as the name and module function, interfaces with other modules, and syntax; and subsystems for module test, results analysis, module path tracing, and test-case selection. Although Fujitsu soon replaced these with tools to support business-applications development, SDSS helped managers identify needs and set an agenda for future tool development.

One of the first tasks was to build a system that handled languages other than FORTRAN, since most business applications required COBOL. Improving the module-description language to represent more complicated data structures and support the beginning of program design, rather than only module definition, constituted another challenge. Other objectives established in the late 1970s for tool research included the automation of program generation and reuse support, as well as the generation of maintenance documents from source code.[53] Fujitsu accomplished these goals and more, introducing numerous tools during the 1980s that, from 1987, the Systems Engineering Group began offering as an integrated tool and methodology set (the methodology was a refinement of SDEM), referred to as Systems Development Architecture and Support (SDAS) facilities.

To supplement its own tools, the factory used systems deployed at Numazu, in particular YACII and YPS, the primary tools in Fujitsu for designing and editing new software as well as for generating code from detailed designs. Kamata also utilized GEM, Numazu's tool for program-library and project-management support,[54] in addition to ADAMS (Application Development and Management System), introduced in 1982. ADAMS resembled GEM but Fujitsu engineers tailored it to work with programs written in a Japanese version of COBOL or the macro-based HYPER COBOL. One of ADAMS' most important functions was to store design documentation in the form of tables or YACII charts that could be retrieved for modification and reuse, with menus in Japanese eliminating the need for specialized programming commands. The management database also kept track of schedules and manpower.[55]

In the area of system planning, Fujitsu in the late 1970s began working on approaches to standardizing and simplifying requirements specification and design. Two tools that came out of this effort, also included in the SDAS package, were EPGII (Executive Planning Guide II) and C-NAPII (Customer Needs Analysis Procedures II). EPGII outlined planning and analysis procedures as well as presented work sheets for designing corporate information-management systems; these helped systems engineers map out a customer's needs against systems already existing in the company. C-NAPII set forth another series of procedures and work sheets to define the specifications necessary to write the software.[56] The original versions of the tools, which came out in 1977, merely put onto a computer database and screen guidelines and work sheets that engineers could use without a computer. The second versions, introduced in 1987, provided assistance, such as in data analysis or making choices among design concepts (see Table 7.9). Neither automated the transformation of plans or designs into executable code, although this remained a subject of R&D within Fujitsu and many other firms (including government-sponsored cooperative projects discussed in Chapter 8).

Fujitsu did offer tools that effectively automated parts of system design as well as program design, code generation, and reuse support. An early system, PARADIGM, issued around 1980 for in-house use and available to Fujitsu customers since 1981, supported module design and coding, testing and maintenance, as well as reuse, for batch-processing and relatively simple transactions-processing applications. This and other Fujitsu tools in the same genre closely resembled Hitachi's EAGLE and NEC's SEA/1. The PARADIGM library stored functional and structural program specifications, standard design patterns written as YACII charts (which could be compiled automatically using YPS), as well as executable subroutines for common functions. These were indexed by functional key words, such as input/output check. Users of the tool first accessed the specifications from a terminal or work station and used these as well as standard patterns and subroutines to write as much of a program as possible. In addition, users could create new parts and then register them in PARADIGM's library, causing the capabilities of the tool to grow with each new piece of software. The library also contained utility programs for use on multiple operating systems, referred to as *black box* components. To assist managers, PARADIGM (and related tools) tracked how many lines of source code programmers reused and thus supported reuse planning in the design phase (although Fujitsu did not include reuse objectives in project schedules and budgets or incorporate them in design reviews, as Toshiba did.)[57]

ACS-APG (Application Control Support-Application Program Generator), a refinement of PARADIGM for developing more complex on-line transactions-processing systems through modifiable logic tables, offered users more functions on preset screens (menus) as well as allowed more flexibility in describing input/output logic in outline form. Engineers could also use the ACS functions to produce a prototype system before completing the design and coding. The program generator read logic tables and design work sheets for specific applications (these contained blank slots engineers filled in for different customers), and then produced COBOL code or inserted existing patterns or subroutines. ACS also stored the logic tables, work sheets, patterns, and subroutines in a parts library to facilitate reuse, testing, and maintenance.[58]

BAGLES (Banking Application Generator Library for Extensive Support), a specialized version of PARADIGM, served as the primary tool in the software factory and other Fujitsu facilities (and many customer sites) for producing standard banking software, such as to control automated teller machines or move funds among different bank locations through on-line transfers.[59] The large size, complexity, high demand, and similarity in functions of these programs for different customers led Fujitsu to begin developing a support tool specifically for the banking industry in 1980. Fujitsu introduced a prototype in 1981 and thereafter produced versions for in-house use and commercial leasing.

The original tool, available only on large computers, contained 2 million lines of code and required a huge amount of memory to generate programs that covered from 500 to 1,400 terminals and from 50,000 to 150,000 transactions per hour. Logic-design representations, in the form of simplified decision tables (menus) using conversational Japanese, outlined common banking functions and allowed users of the tool to customize programs. The library database again stored design documents, patterns, and subroutines for reuse as well as testing and maintenance,

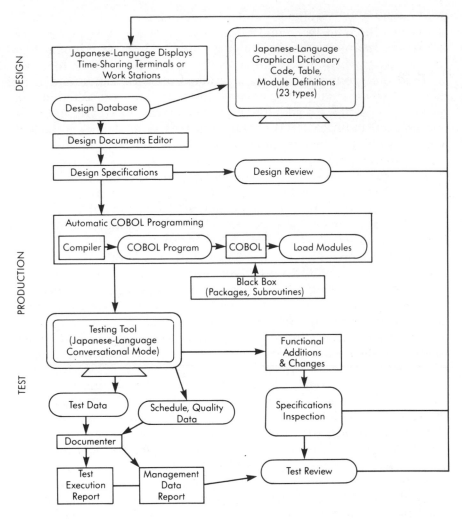

Figure 7.5 Banking Application Generator Library for Extensive Support (BAGLES) Process-Flow Outline. (*Source*: Tsubuhari Yukio, "Tosha no kinyu shisutemu kaihatsu ni okeru seisansei kojo" [Productivity improvement in the company's financial systems development] in Kindai Serususha, ed., *Jitsurei konpyuta bankingu* 13, Jan. 20, 1987, p. 228.)

while automatic COBOL generation made it unnecessary to write code (eliminating most coding errors). BAGLES also generated documentation automatically (Figure 7.5).

BAGLES' ability to reproduce common banking functions and lessen tedious tasks such as coding proved useful, but the tool still required considerable knowledge of software programming. Users had to define data types and procedures, specify modules and the logic flow of the program, and determine other elements in almost as much detail as writing COBOL code. To simplify banking-applications development further, Fujitsu introduced BAGLES/CAD in 1984. According to both in-house personnel and customers, users of this tool, even with little knowledge of programming, could produce complete programs in half the time experts writing in COBOL would normally require. BAGLES/CAD (as well as the latest versions of YPS and comparable tools at Hitachi, NEC, and Toshiba) provided windows that expanded or contracted the graphical representation of a program in order to view the whole system (or a large part of it) or focus on the structure of individual modules. The improved format, including revised decision tables, helped users define banking operations and integrate packaged subsystems and reusable patterns with new designs. As with the original BAGLES, all the graphical design representations were executable as COBOL code. Unlike the original, BAGLES/CAD also ran on personal computers or work stations, making it more accessible to potential users.

From 1983, Fujitsu offered other menu-based design tools for commercial leasing, referred to as the SIMPLE series and connected with ADAM. These included LINDA (Logical Information Support Tool of Data Set) for general applications development, DBSP (Data Base Support Program) for creating database management systems, and DRAG-ON (Driver and Stub Generator for On-Line and Batch Test), among many. Yet another tool frequently used in the software factory, CASET (Computer-Aided Software Engineering Tool), supported development of common business applications such as inventory or sales control systems written in COBOL, relying on preset lists or tables in conversational Japanese to help users define common functions.[60]

Advanced Tool and Interface Development

PARADIGM, as well as the family of tools that followed it (ACS-APG, BAGLES, CASET, et al.), proved useful for well-defined applications described in preset tables, menus, work sheets, patterns, or subroutines. Yet they still fell a step or two below automating system planning and design for new applications. Software CAD, developed initially in the mid-1980s,[61] was the most advanced tool for new applications regularly used in Fujitsu's Systems Engineering Group in 1989.

Company engineers described Software CAD as "a general tool for the drawing, verification, and transformation activities of software development . . . independent of any particular methods or development phases. . . . [D]evelopers can customize [Software CAD] to fit particular methods for their own circumstances."[62] Fujitsu completed a version and introduced it into Kamata in 1987, primarily for writing tools such as YPS and PARADIGM that converted design diagrams to code. The initial system ran on a Fujitsu mainframe and did not receive much use until Fujitsu moved it to work stations and modified Software CAD for utilization with YPS and APG. During 1988–1989, projects were gradually extending their use of Software CAD to develop a variety of special programs for operating systems, switching systems, communications software, and microcode embedded in semiconductor chips.

The latest version of Software CAD contained general purpose notations combining text, tables, and diagrams, as well as an editor and compilers that transformed standardized notations into modifiable design documents and then different types of code. The notation system contained six types of objects for describing program structures: forms (graphic models of the program), tables, nodes (graphic symbols specifying particular attributes of the program), edges (symbols representing connections between nodes), inclusions (symbols representing relationships between nodes and edges), and text fields (inputs of data into any of the objects). The Notation Specification (NS) compiler took specifications written by program developers in the specified format and produced machine-readable notations. These became inputs to the Software CAD Editor for modification, which the tool deposited in the Software CAD Document Database when finished (Figure 7.6).

The editor allowed the user to access the Document Database and modify any of the objects, relying on templates as well as a mouse interface and a multiwindow environment (both originally introduced by Xerox and then used by Apple with personal computers, but now common with the latest versions of many Japanese tools, in Fujitsu and other firms). The Software CAD Transformer relied on rules the user specified to transform the documents stored in the database into either executable code or textual documentation. The notation system, according to Fujitsu, was relatively easy to learn, requiring a few hours for an experienced programmer and a few days for a new employee. Describing the transformation rules was not simple, although Fujitsu claimed that tools and other programs developed with Software CAD still came out faster than comparable systems done manually.

Ongoing R&D in Fujitsu attempted to integrate AI techniques with Software CAD and apply AI in other support tools. Fujitsu's approach was to use AI to process design documents using a knowledge database for specific applications, a model of the desired design, and a knowledge-transformation algorithm. Based on inferences made in processing the documentation, for example, a tool would produce documents for a subsequent phase—planning inputs would produce a detailed system design, which would be processed into a program design, which would be transformed (compiled) into source code. Fujitsu engineers were especially interested in applications to requirements specification and lexical (design-language) editors, since AI appeared useful to help designers understand constraints in hardware, operating systems, computer languages, or specific applications, as well as to verify designs. For example,

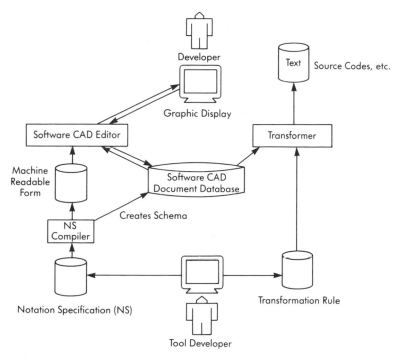

Figure 7.6 Software Computer-Aided Design (CAD). (*Source*: Kazuo Yabuta, Akihiro Yoshioka, and Noritoshi Murakami," 'Software CAD': A Generalized Environment for Graphical Software Development Techniques," *Proceedings of the International Computer Software and Applications Conference—COMPSAC '87* [IEEE Computer Society Press, 1987], p. 3.)

a LISP-based expert system available in prototype form helped inexperienced personnel consult with customers and produce customized systems for a variety of applications.[63] Fujitsu also applied inference search methods to identifying software components for reuse, and was studying testing support and maintenance applications, such as problem diagnosis.

In the telecommunications area, a tool employing AI became available for switching systems development in 1984, the Specification and Description Language (SDL) support system. Fujitsu Laboratories began working on this in the late 1970s, writing in UtiLISP. SDL resembled NEC's SDMS and contained graphic symbols to represent different states, tasks, or signal input and output; graphics as well as text editors; a document database; automatic document compilation and inspection subsystems; a knowledge database of different functions or tasks performed in a switching system; and subsystems to translate the graphically represented requirements into state-transition diagrams and then these into executable code. This was also an intelligent system, however, in the sense that it withdrew information from the graphical designs and deposited this information in a database in the form of general and detailed state-transition diagram elements. Subsystems then used inference rules to produce input/output transformations automatically and generate computer code.[64]

Systems Integration Architecture (SIA), which Fujitsu announced in 1987 along with the SDAS tool set, aimed at creating a standard interface

Table 7.12 Systems Development Architecture and Support (SDAS) Facilities

Systems Planning Techniques	
EPGII (corporate systems planning)	C-NAPII (systems requirements analysis)

Productivity Tools	Industry Application Packages
Systems Development YPS YPS/APG CASET BAGLES BAGLES/CAD ADAMS SIMPLE	*Finance* APFS, BANK-ACE (on-line banking) BDSB (banking and securities) LONGS (loan management) FNIS (foreign network information system)
End-Users INTERACT DSM/EPOC OAP/BASE	*Manufacturing* PROFIT (production control) ICAD (design, manufacturing support) MOLD (design, manufacturing support)
Specialized ESHELL/X	*Distribution* CIRCL-ACE (customer information) FRENS (communications & sales)
	Local Government ARIS (resident information) FARMS (farming information)
	Medical HOPEIII (hospital administration) LAMBDA (clinical examination)
Tool Standards (SDEM)	Package Standards (SDEM)
SIA (Systems Integration Architecture)	

ADAMS = Application Development and Management System; APG = Application Program Generator; BAGLES = Banking Application Generator Library for Extensive Support; CAD = computer-aided design; CASET = Computer-Aided Software Engineering Tools; C-NAPII = Customer-Needs Analysis Procedures II; DSM = Distributed System Manager; EPG II = Executive Planning Guide II; Interact = Interactive System; OAP/BASE = Office Automation Products/BASE; SDEM = Software Development Engineering Methodology; YPS = YAC II Programming System.
Source: Based on Fukuda Zenichi, Yoshihara Tadao, and Maruyama Takeshi, "SDAS sogo kaihatsu shisutemu no teisho" [SDAS Systems Development Architecture and Support Facilities], *Fujitsu* 39, 1, 1988, p. 5; and Fujitsu Ltd., "SDAS: Application Software Development Made Easy," *Electronics News From Fujitsu* 9, 7, July 1987, p. 1.

for programming in COBOL, FORTRAN, C, LISP, or PROLOG and for using the different SDAS tools and applications packages on Fujitsu mainframes, office computers, and work stations (Table 7.12). The interface remained incomplete in 1990 since Fujitsu still had to define all its elements. It was also open to question how compatible or competitive SIA would be with existing or emerging industry standards, including those from other vendors such as IBM. In any case, Fujitsu expected SIA to be available for all its machines by the early 1990s. Management also viewed the standardization of interfaces and architecture as complementary to its production strategy, since this would make it easier to break large programs into distinct units that personnel could develop on different work stations and then combine later.[65]

Package Utilization

Increasing package utilization, especially across different machines (which would become more feasible after the implementation of SIA), constituted another key area of activity at Fujitsu.[66] The reasons were clear and well established. Packages facilitated almost instantaneous reuse and thus provided an easy way to meet the needs of a large number of customers with no new effort in development beyond the original project. Reusing packages to cover portions of customer requirements in custom jobs also represented an effective mode of reuse.

Problems with packages remained, as reviewed in Chapter 2, in that corporate or institutional customers usually had some or many unique requirements, and modifying packages (or any reusable code) could take as much or more time as writing new code from scratch for a specific application. Thus a major challenge was to produce packages that could fit as is into larger systems, or build them so that users could tailor them without too much difficulty.[67] Technical avenues Fujitsu (and the other Japanese firms discussed in this book) pursued included the reuse of generic design descriptions rather than code, programming in C (a more portable language than COBOL), object-oriented design techniques (useful for modularizing and identifying software components), and even tools that automated the transformation of requirements into code, thus making reuse unnecessary.

In addition, the Fujitsu group relied on two registration and library systems to promote package use within its family of applications facilities, subsidiaries, subcontractors, and customers. The largest catalogue of original Fujitsu packages totalled approximately 1,000 in 1986 and had increased 40 to 50 percent per year in the mid-1980s. Another library registered software that users or computer dealers developed; in 1986, these totaled about 300.[68] These packages appeared to cover a wide range of user needs, as indicated in Figure 7.7. Manufacturing systems extended over the broadest range, with larger ones requiring

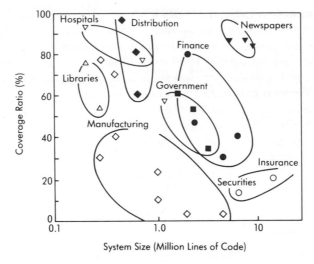

Figure 7.7 Package Coverage Ratio. Symbols: ▼ = newspapers; ● = financial; ■ = government; ◇ = manufacturing; △ = libraries; ▽ = hospitals; ◆ = distribution (chain stores). (*Source*: Masayuki Akiyama and Shuji Nishimura, "SDAS ni okeru pakeji kaihatsu to sono tekiyo gijutsu" [SDAS Improving Package Development and Its Application Methods], *Fujitsu* 39, 1, January 1988, p. 37.)

total customization and some systems containing more than 40 percent existing code from packages. Fujitsu found that it could more often meet the needs of small-systems users by packages, such as in the case of hospitals and newspaper companies. Overall, data suggested that SDAS-based applications packages, covering financial, manufacturing, distribution, government, newspaper, and medical applications, accounted for approximately 40 percent of applications systems Fujitsu delivered in 1988.[69]

Performance Improvement

Although project data Fujitsu released from the factory remained scant, selective (that is, probably reflecting particularly successful projects) and sometimes difficult to interpret information indicated improvements in productivity, quality, and reusability comparable to those Hitachi, Toshiba, and NEC had reported. In a 1981 article, for example, a team that worked on revising the SDEM standards claimed these brought roughly a 20 percent gain in productivity over projects not using the methodology. These gains came mainly from the "absence of rework," achieved through better scheduling and control, early discovery of problems, standardization of work and documentation, and use of formal planning and reviews to reduce discrepancies between user requirements and finished programs.[70] With SDEM in place, and tool development continuing at a rapid pace, in-house data later showed applications productivity doubling between 1980 and 1984 (measured as delivered lines of debugged code per month, normalized to 170-hour months) and increasing during 1984–1988 between 5 and 15 percent annually. Managers cited a combination of factors for these gains:

1. *Equipment*—investment in more time-sharing terminals, work stations, and other computer-center facilities in the software factory. (The Kamata factory maintained two terminals or work stations for every three employees, twice the level of its Japanese competitors.)
2. *Specialization*—accumulation of know-how by systems engineers and implementation groups in the software factory, subsidiaries, and subcontractors.
3. *Standardization*—introduction and enforcement of standards for documentation as well as for all phases of the development process, in addition to standardization that supported the linking of various tools.
4. *Tools*—greater application of computer-aided tools for design and testing, as well as reuse support.
5. *Reviews*—formalization of review procedures and checklists, as well as development of automated tools to assist in code reviews.
6. *Project Management*—introduction of productivity standards and revision of the quality-control process, including use of quality objectives and data collection.[71]

Among these factors, Fujitsu data suggested that most productivity gains after 1985 came from the greater use of computer-aided tools such as PARADIGM and from higher reuse levels, including the integration of packages into customized systems. Recycling designs, code, and whole programs reduced time needed for new program development as well as for debugging. In addition, Fujitsu claimed that PARADIGM and similar tools "enabled even inexperienced programmers to write high-quality programs" and "eliminated misunderstandings resulting from individual differences" by making design documents and code easier to read and maintain, reflecting the highly structured and standardized SDEM and SDAS methodology.[72] As a result, managers seemed able to deploy their skilled engineers more effectively.

PARADIGM's exact impact on productivity varied with the application, the phase of development, and the number of times a specific application reappeared, although a study Fujitsu published in 1982 estimated that two-thirds of business-applications programs seemed redundant and suitable for reuse technology or program generation. The 1982 data indicated that, in 80 percent of the business-applications programs developed with the tool, PARADIGM generated approximately 68 percent of the source code without new coding. PARADIGM thus tended to cut in half the time required for program design, construction, and debugging. Time spent in other aspects of integrated and system test, including test preparations, remained similar. Overall, Fujitsu projects using PARADIGM experienced a doubling of productivity, compared to similar projects done manually, with more time shifted from design and coding to testing. Projects also saved on manpower by generating up to 80 percent of design documents from the YACII diagrams.[73]

Fujitsu reported similar levels of improvement in quality with PARADIGM. From an average rate of approximately ten defects per 1,000 lines of code detected in module tests, programs written with the tool averaged two or three per 1,000 lines (again, prior to delivery) and between zero and one for particularly repetitive applications. Most of the errors introduced came not from reused PARADIGM components but from new software, suggesting that higher reuse had the potential to improve quality further.[74]

In using ACS to develop a conversational-mode data-entry system of approximately 10,000 lines of COBOL source code, Fujitsu reported a short-term decline in productivity in order to write reusable patterns but significant improvement over expected standard times for manual programming in COBOL, minus the reusable patterns, as well as a larger gain when producing another program that reused designs (Table 7.13). In Project 1, each developer using ACS averaged 1,219 lines of code per month versus the factory standard of 587 lines of code per month per person (the historical average for similar COBOL programs without special tool support). The numbers for the ACS project excluded twelve work-months required to write the 1,817 lines of code representing the reusable modules deposited in the ACS/PARADIGM library. If added, this work dropped the net-productivity rate for Project 1 to 495 lines per person per month—below the factory standard. In a larger project, however, which consisted of converting and extending a similar program using some ACS/PARADIGM patterns and subroutines, productivity jumped to 1,864 lines per work-month, since personnel reused and automatically generated 42 percent of the source lines.[75]

In applying BAGLES to banking programs of 2 to 3 million lines of COBOL source code, Fujitsu's experience as of 1987 indicated a 25 percent reduction in total work hours compared to manual development of similar programs without comparable tool support. As seen in Table 7.14, Fujitsu engineers claimed that BAGLES/CAD offered an even greater reduction, cutting development time by 40 percent. Both BAGLES and BAGLES/CAD also allowed developers to spend relatively more time in design and testing, which helped improve product functionality and quality, and less time in routine coding, compared to manual development in COBOL.[76] Furthermore, programs built with BAGLES have come out shorter than programs performing similar functions written without the tool—as much as one-fourteenth the size. Fujitsu engineers argued this was because BAGLES identified a large

Table 7.13 Application Control Support (ACS) PARADIGM Productivity Example

	Standard: Manual COBOL	Project 1: ACS Actual Times	Project 2: Extension & Conversion
System design (work-mo)	2.5	1.3	5.5
Program design, coding, integrated test (work-mo)	9	5.5	10.7
System and operations test (work-mo)	4	1.4	3
Subtotal work-mo	15.5	8.2	19.2
LOC	9,100	10,003	35,789
Productivity (LOC/work-mo)	587	1,219	1,864
Documentation (sheets)	170	160	50
Faults/1,000 lines (after operations test)	—	1	1.5
New/changed code (%)	—	12	58
Generated/reused code (%)	—	—	42
Paradigm definitions	—		
(lines of code)		1,817	
(work-mo)		12	
Total work-mo	—	20.2	
Net productivity (LOC/work-mo)	—	495	

LOC = lines of code; mo = month(s).
Source: Derived from Kometani Tadatoshi and Arakawa Yoshihiro, "Onrain shisutemu no kokateki kaihatsu e no kokoromi—ACS PARADIGM" [An attempt at efficient on-line system development ACS-PARADIGM], *Fujitsu* 35, 4, 1984, pp. 452–53.

number of repetitious functions that could be handled through subroutines. Users of the tool could cite these repeatedly in the program without rewriting the code.[77]

The combination of SDAS tools and packages again doubled productivity in the case of a major banking system, where Fujitsu had to replace

Table 7.14 COBOL, BAGLES, and BAGLES/CAD Productivity Comparison

	Design	Programming	Testing	Total
COBOL	30*	42	28	100
	(30)†	(42)	(28)	(100)
BAGLES	35	15	25	75
	(47)	(20)	(33)	(100)
BAGLES/CAD	20	18	22	55
	(33)	(30)	(37)	(100)

*Index of development time compared to COBOL standard; †nos. in parentheses = percentage of total times using each tool. Acronyms as in Table 7.12.
Source: Tsubuhari Yukio, "Tosha no kinyu shisutemu kaihatsu ni [Productivity improvement in the company's financial systems development], in Kindai Serususha (ed.), *Jitsurei konpyuta bankingu*, 13, Jan. 20, 1987, p. 231.

an old system consisting of 3.6 million lines of code. Packages had covered 30 percent of the old system, and work-months to complete the system had totaled 8,000. Therefore, the original system had a gross productivity rate of 450 lines of code per work-month. The replacement proved to be more than twice as large—8.3 million lines of code. Fujitsu obtained 79 percent of the code from SDAS packages for securities processing, customer control, cost accounting, international transactions, foreign-exchange dealings, regional information control, and database management, as well as for the outside network, branch operations, accounting, and operations. For the other 21 percent that Fujitsu had to develop from scratch, the factory used YPS and BAGLES to produce the designs and generate at least some code automatically. The resulting gross productivity came to 902 lines of code per work-month for the new system (Table 7.15 and Figure 7.8).[78]

Along with its Japanese competitors, Fujitsu encountered limits to reusability, depending on how much of a component developers had to modify. In applications programs, Fujitsu projects indicated a break-even point of approximately 60 percent for a given piece of software. If they had to rewrite more than 60 percent, then the impact on overall productivity of reusing the designs or code was slightly negative.[79] (More detailed data from Numazu was similar, showing a clear improvement in productivity as long as personnel reused 70 to 80 percent of a particular module or program part without significant changes. In a sample of forty-seven projects, median productivity, including manpower devoted to maintenance, was approximately 60 percent higher with 20 percent new code and an 80 percent reuse rate. In projects where there were attempts to reuse code but less than 70 percent was reusable without significant changes, the impact on productivity tended to be negative.[80])

Software CAD appeared to improve productivity without necessarily recycling existing code or designs, through partially automating the transformation of design specifications into code. While Fujitsu used the present tool only for a few tasks, results in limited trials were impressive. Software CAD cut the time needed to develop a tool to convert a set of

Table 7.15 Banking System Development Productivity

	Old System	New System
System length (LOC)	3,600,000	8,300,000
Reused code (LOC)	1,080,000 (30%)	6,550,00 (79%)
New code (LOC)	2,520,000	1,750,000
Total productivity (LOC/work-mo)	450	902

See Table 7.13 for abbreviations.
Source: Fukuta Zenichi, Yoshihara Tadao, and Maruyama Takeshi, "SDAS sogo kaihatsu shisutemo no teisho" [SDAS Systems Development Architecture and Support Facilities], *Fujitsu* 39, 1, January 1988, p. 11.

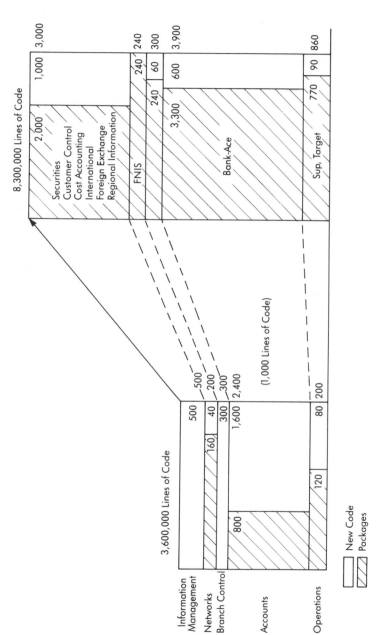

Figure 7.8 Banking System Productivity Comparison. FNIS = Foreign Network Information System. (*Source*: Fukuta Zenichi, Yoshihara Tadao, and Maruyama Takeshi, "SDAS sogo kaihatsu shisutemo no teisho" [SDAS Systems Development Architecture and Support Facilities], *Fujitsu* 39, 1, January 1988, p. 11.)

Table 7.16 Use of Software CAD for Tool Development

Task	Conventional	Software CAD	Development Time Improvement
Tool Development			
Tool for converting job-flow diagrams to job-control language (7.5 K-LOC in C)	9.3 wm/6 mo	0.5 wm/1 mo	6-fold
Tool for converting database structure diagrams to ADL (6.7 K-LOC in C)	8.4 wm/6 mo	0.5 wm/1 mo	6-fold
Program Development			
Software to convert screen format to definition language (100 screens)	2.3 wm	0.6 wm	4-fold
Software to implement screen transformation to programming language (10/screen)	8.0 wm	2.0 wm	4-fold
Software to implement database structure diagram to ADL	6.0 wh	2.0 wh	3-fold

K-LOC = 1,000 lines of code; wm = work-months; wh = work-hours; CAD = computer-aided design; mo = month; ADL = advanced development language.
Source: Kazuo Yabuta, Akihiro Yoshioka, and Noritoshi Murakami, "'Software CAD': A Generalized Environment for Graphical Software Development Techniques," *Proceedings of the International Computer Software and Applications Conference—COMPSAC '87* (IEEE Computer Society Press, 1987), p. 7.

job-control diagrams to job-control language from a normal 6 months to 1 month, and total manpower from a standard 9.3 work-months to 0.5 work-months. Engineers using Software CAD wrote a program to transform database logic-structure diagrams into a high-level programming language (ADL) in one-sixth the time (8.4 to 0.5 work-months) usually required for similar jobs. Other efforts showed comparable improvements, usually cutting development time one-fourth to one-third that of expected levels, with even larger gross productivity gains, compared to conventional design and programming (Table 7.16).[81]

Summary and Evaluation

Most notable in Fujitsu's approach to software development, as summarized in Table 7.17, proved to be management's early focus on and intermingling of process and quality control in basic software; establishment of a centralized laboratory for development and training in 1970; experimentation with a program-conversion factory during 1977–1978, followed by a factory for applications programming in 1979; gradual expansion of the factory's design responsibilities and capabilities; and

Table 7.17 Fujitsu Summary

Concept	Implementation
Process improvement	Commitment at division-level management in early and mid-1970s to improve process and quality control in basic software. Commitment to structure and standardize custom applications development from late 1970s and early 1980s.
Product-process focus & segmentation	Development sites, tools, methods, and standards divided among basic software and applications. Largest network of specialized, general, and regional subsidiaries among Japanese computer producers.
Process/quality analysis & control	Systematic data collection, document and product inspection and release procedures, standardization efforts, Development Planning and Report System, and BSMS database from mid-1970s in basic software. Similar standards in applications from late 1970s. Systematic quality data collection from the late 1970s, integrated with High-Reliability Program. Use of Taguchi methods to de-skill testing.
Tailored/centralized process R&D	Tools and methods distinct to product groups, with some transfers. Software tool and method development first centered in Numazu (basic software) during early 1970s. Kamata in late 1970s and 1980s developed methods and tools for applications, with assistance from a central research laboratory.
Skills standardization & leverage	Two to three months standard training for all software personnel, follwed by on-the-job training and short courses. Courses and career paths to promote advancement and specialization. Development of standardized tools and methods specifically to leverage knowledge of skilled personnel. Division of labor in the applications software factory between systems engineering and program construction, though gradual trend of doing more design in the factory.
Dynamic standardization	Performance standard times revised annually. Continual evolution of standardized methods and, especially, tools.
Systematic reusability	In applications, emphasis on reusable designs and packages incorporated in customized systems. Wide array of tools to support reuse, some dedicated to specific applications like banking. In basic software, emphasis on building common components for different products.
Computer-aided tools	Extensive investment in tools during the 1980s to facilitate transformation of designs into executable code or reuse of designs and code, such as PARADIGM, ACS-APG, CASET, YPS, BAGLES, and Software CAD. Other tools available since the 1970s, such as ADAMS and BSMS, to support project and library management, maintenance and testing.
Incremental product/ variety improvement	Emphasis in the 1970s on process and defect control, as well as evaluating products from customers' perspective (comparing performance with documentation). Recent emphasis in the 1980s on improving product functionality and ease of use, with quantified measures. Computer-aided tools useful in channeling more relative effort into design and less into coding. Overall, strong product positions in basic software, applications engineering, Japanese-language processing.

(*continued*)

Table 7.17 (*Continued*)

Assessment	
Strategic management & integration	Long-term effort first in basic software to improve the development process, directed by the Quality Assurance Department at Numazu. Similar effort in applications software directed by groups in Kamata, currently the SE Technical Support Center. Some efforts at company-wide and groupwide integration and technology transfer.
Scope economies	Building of unique and customized systems centralized in Numazu and Kamata, as well as in subsidiaries and software houses working under the direct control of Numazu and the Kamata Software Factory. Specific efforts directed at building and using common tools, methods, and software components.

BSMS = Basic Software Project Management Support System; other acronyms as in Tables 7.9 and 7.12.

extensive investment in computer-aided tools, especially to support design and programming for custom applications, with some dedicated to specific industries as well as nonexpert users. Fujitsu also developed numerous software packages, not so much to sell or lease on their own, but more to integrate into customized applications products—to reduce the need to write new code. In addition, Fujitsu maintained a huge network of subsidiaries, similar to those of Hitachi, Toshiba, and NEC but on a larger scale. Again similar to its major Japanese competitors but on a larger scale, Fujitsu used subcontractors (rather than subsidiaries) to provide most of the manpower for its applications software factory, eliminating the need to find and hire large numbers of permanent staff.

Fujitsu also offered what seemed to be a healthy mixture of strategic direction and adaptability, in the areas of technology and organization, as well as strategy. In hardware, engineers stayed too long with telephone relay circuits but then switched to transistors when these became the obvious components to use. Management pursued a foreign source of technology during the early 1960s, decided to develop computers independently when it could not find a good partner, and then found a partner after the death of its key designer in the early 1970s. In software, like SDC, Fujitsu experienced difficulty separating systems design from product construction in a software factory. But, rather than abandoning the goals of centralization and standardization—economies of scope as well as scale—management adopted different processes for different projects. Fujitsu brought, for example, more design operations into the factory for projects similar to previous work, and continued to invest in tools, methods, libraries, and training in order to increase the capability and capacity of its factory and other development facilities.

What the concept of a software factory meant in Fujitsu's context thus varied by the type of product, as at other Japanese firms, as well as over time. Both Numazu and Kamata pursued centralization of personnel, standardization of methods and tools, improvement in product reliability and productivity, reusability of designs and code, automation of development and management, and formalization of controls. Only Kamata, however, adopted the factory label, and only Kamata pursued a division of labor between systems design and program construction, before relaxing this policy gradually. In sum, though somewhat late in entering the industry as well as the business of establishing software factories, Fujitsu management clearly allocated the resources and attention to software necessary to become and maintain a position as Japan's leading manufacturer of computer hardware. The company also seemed superbly positioned for future competition centering on the continued refinement and utilization of computer-aided tools, especially for design support.

8

STANDARDIZATION
AND COOPERATIVE R&D

Hitachi, Toshiba, NEC, and Fujitsu all launched factory efforts between the late 1960s and late 1970s to promote internal process standardization and to diffuse good tools and techniques among in-house personnel as well as at subsidiaries and subcontractors. These companies also maintained R&D efforts in central and division laboratories, as well as in factory departments, to study or generate new capabilities, and improve their process technology incrementally. Software development, and the needs of Japanese customers, presented similar problems to Japanese producers; not surprisingly, they tended to adopt similar solutions, creating factory organizations that refined U.S. practices but, as in other industries, sought a tighter integration among product objectives and production management, in the broad sense—tools, techniques, controls, training, and product components.

It is fitting that this chapter looks beyond the level of software factories at individual companies to consider mechanisms for taking better advantage of current knowledge as well as for moving the state of the industry and the technology forward. Despite limited results, cooperative R&D projects since the late 1960s in Japan's computer industry provided a foundation for two major efforts in the 1980s sponsored by MITI and carried out mainly with personnel from private firms: Sigma (Software Industrialized Generator and Maintenance Aids), which tried to make the tools, techniques, standards, and reuse concepts refined in software factories more common throughout the industry, especially at smaller software houses; and the Fifth Generation Computer Project, which experimented with logic processing and parallel computing, areas of AI technology, and the required innovations in hardware and software architectures.

Comparisons with cooperative projects in the United States and Europe, as well as with efforts at two other Japanese producers not covered as separate cases, NTT and Mitsubishi Electric, support conclusions this book proposed in earlier chapters. The leading Japanese computer and software manufacturers, on their own and in joint arrangements, were exploring nearly all available technologies related to software development. Major projects would not reach all their goals, and much of the technology being disseminated in Japan remained a refinement of tools and techniques promoted in the United States during the late 1960s and 1970s, rather than constituting a radical leap forward. Nonetheless, the Japanese demonstrated the skill and commitment to stay close to the forefront, if not in the lead, in managing the process of large-scale software development. Nor did this position come easily, as a relatively long history of failures in joint research preceded the modest achievements of the late 1980s.

Projects Completed Prior to 1990

In computer hardware, several government-sponsored projects dating back to the FONTAC effort of the early 1960s contributed to advances in the skills of Japanese firms in areas such as processor design, architectural standardization, graphics processing, and various topics in basic research. In semiconductors especially, during the late 1970s, several Japanese firms joined together under MITI sponsorship to develop better capabilities in very large-scale integrated (VLSI) circuits fabrication and design. In software product and process technology, however, most cooperative efforts led to embarassing failures (Table 8.1).[1] Each attempt floundered for slightly different reasons, although common themes emerged: poor planning, disagreements on objectives, and poor results, all affected by the difficulties of dealing with still-evolving technologies and markets.

Japan Software Company (1966–1972)

MITI organized Japan's first cooperative effort in applied research not tied to hardware (as in the FONTAC) during 1966: the Japan Software Company, a joint venture of Hitachi, Fujitsu, NEC, and the Industrial Bank of Japan. The government provided a subsidy of 2 billion yen, recruited 200 software engineers, and charged them with producing a

Table 8.1 Japanese Cooperative R&D Projects in Software Technology

Period	Project/Organization (total yen funding)*	Objectives and Outcomes
1966–1972	Japan Software Company (2 billion)	Common development language and basic software for different architectures. Complete failure.
1970–1982	IPA Package Effort (10 billion)	70 packages developed. Very limited usage.
1971–1980	PIPS Project (22 billion)	Pattern-information (graphics) software, mainly for Japanese language processing. Several products commercialized. Links with Fifth Generation project.
1973–1976	Software Module Project (3 billion)	Applications development. Little coordination. Complete failure.
1976–1981	Software Production Technology Project (7.5 billion)	Automated and integrated factory tool set and modularization techniques for batch environment. 20 discrete tools finally developed by individual firms.
1981–1986	Software Maintenance Engineering Facility (SMEF) Project (5 billion)	Interactive, UNIX-based tool set for maintenance and development. Improved experience level of Japanese firms with UNIX.
1984–	TRON Project (company funds)	Development of a standardized architecture and operating system for multiple levels and types of computers. Some products announced. Promising idea despite competition from other standards.
1985–1989	Interoperable Database System Project (1.5 billion)	Network to link work stations using OSI protocols. Improvement of interface standards likely.
1985–1989	FASET Project (2.2 billion)	Development of CASE tools for automated code generation from formalized specifications. Promising goals but limited participation.
1985–1990	Sigma Project (25 billion)	Development of UNIX-based support tools as well as reusable code and packages, for a national network. Major dissemination of existing practical technology.
1982–1991	Fifth Generation Computer Project (50 billion)	Development of knowledge (logical-inference) processing and parallel computing hardware and software. Major long-term advances possible in Japanese AI capabilities. Short-term potential for software automation and reuse support. Limited commercial applications, however, and lukewarm support from major companies.

*In 1989 currency, approximately $7 million = 1 billion yen. AI = artificial intelligence; CASE = computer-aided software engineering tools; FASET = Formal Approach to Software Environment Technology; IPA = Information Processing Promotion Agency; OSI = Open Systems Interconnection; PIPS = Pattern Information Processing System; TRON = The Real-time Operating System Nucleus. *Source*: See notes in Chapter 8.

common development language that would allow firms to write basic software to operate on currently incompatible computers.

The effort to devise a common language failed completely. The architectures of Hitachi, Fujitsu, and NEC machines differed radically at this time, and the state of knowledge on portable computer languages remained primitive. Aside from these formidable technical hurdles, the members became distracted with different product strategies that, to a large degree, made a common language unnecessary. Hitachi and Fujitsu decided to adopt IBM-compatible architectures and thus use IBM as a standard (although Hitachi eventually varied its domestic architecture slightly). NEC, meanwhile, continued to support the incompatible architecture inherited from Honeywell. MITI dissolved the joint venture in 1972, after ending subsidies.[2]

IPA Package Effort (1970–1978)

Despite problems with the Japan Software Company, MITI established the Information Technology Promotion Agency (IPA) in 1970 to promote the software industry in several ways. It provided billions of yen in operating expenses and loan guarantees for fledgling software producers, funds for research in software engineering, and money, as well as an organization, to develop application packages for general use and register or buy existing packages for distribution. A major concern of the agency was to offset the growing, and labor-intensive, demand for custom programs. To alleviate this problem, the agency allocated 10 billion yen during 1970–1978 for package development and acquired seventy programs.

While software houses probably welcomed financial assistance in any form, neither the R&D work nor the package initiative proved useful. One problem was that IPA distributed funding over a large number of small firms that had insufficient expertise to develop general-purpose tools or programs. Several other factors severely limited the appeal of the packages: poor planning to insure that a program had more than one or two users, continued incompatibility in hardware architectures and operating systems, the strong preference among Japanese customers for tailored systems, and the insistence of many Japanese customers that computer manufacturers provide software free of charge. On the other hand, IPA itself survived into the 1980s and appeared to be a relatively useful agency, organizing a Software Technology Development Center in 1981 to conduct R&D in areas such as language compilers, CAD/CAM, database systems, and process methodologies and tools, and assisting in administering joint projects, including Sigma.[3]

PIPS Project (1971–1980)

Another MITI and IPA initiative during the 1970s had a more positive impact on the technical capabilities of individual firms, although not process technology specifically: the Pattern Information Processing System (PIPS) project, begun in 1971 with approximately 22 billion yen in funding over ten years. This focused on graphics technology needed for Japanese character (*kanji*) recognition—an important topic because of the difficulty involved in entering and processing Japanese characters on a computer.

Project members included the major computer manufacturers as well as MITI's Electrotechnical Laboratory, which integrated subsystems developed at individual firms. Although work done under the auspices of PIPS tended to merge with initiatives underway at individual firms, companies clearly utilized or built on some of the technology generated through the project funding. In particular, both Toshiba and Fujitsu introduced several products, including machines for the post office that read addresses automatically, and graphics displays with high resolutions. In addition, much of the experience IPA and member firms gained in managing and disseminating cooperative R&D, as well as some of the image-processing technology, they channeled into subsequent projects, especially Sigma and the Fifth Generation.

Software Module Project (1973–1976)

MITI in 1973 started a four-year effort known as the Software Module Project, channeling 3 billion yen in government funds to forty independent software houses organized into five groups to develop standardized modules for applications programming. The major manufacturers did not appear to participate at all, however, and this initiative met the same fate as the IPA Package Effort. The five groups produced little or no software that customers found appealing, reflecting poor planning and little coordination among participants regarding the content of the software developed, languages used, and portability strategies. On the other hand, this project seemed to generate interest in the concept of reusable modules as well as the need for standardization in products as well as tools and techniques. IPA quickly turned its attention to these issues and expressed them as part of a broader objective—the software factory.[4]

Software Production Technology Project (1976–1981)

MITI first directly promoted the concept of a software factory in its very next initiative, started in 1976—the Software Production Technology Project (also known as the Program Productivity Development System Project). In the first stage, seventeen Japanese firms, with 7.5 billion yen in funding over five years, came together to form the Joint System Development (JSD) Corporation and dedicated themselves to the creation of an "automated software factory system based on the concept of application software modularization." Initial objectives included the development of better languages to describe application systems and program components in a structured, modular fashion, as well as a module database. The members also hoped to build and disseminate general-purpose tools to support modular design, program generation, and testing. JSD itself built nothing but channeled R&D work to member firms through a series of projects.

Again, despite lofty goals, the project produced few concrete results. No group seemed to make progress during the first two years at all, prompting the directors of JSD to change course. Beginning in the third year, rather than working on centrally designed projects, JSD encouraged participants to use the government funding to devise support tools geared toward their specific needs, though still utilizing a base technology, such as a common programming language. Members completed approximately twenty tools, and individual firms used some in their facilities. Nevertheless, JSD failed to integrate the tools or disseminate them widely.

A major cause for this failure stemmed from technical judgments that, given changes in the technology and industry practices, proved unwise. First, especially during the initial two years, projects set out to devise tools that operated in a batch mode. By the late 1970s, however, more powerful hardware and basic software capabilities made interactive programming and debugging through on-line terminals or work stations (rather than writing a program and then running it later on) much more efficient and preferable for most applications. Batch-processing tools thus had limited usefulness by the end of the project.

Second, members chose to develop tools that supported programming in an uncommon language—PL/1. They selected this because it seemed more neutral than FORTRAN (heavily tailored for technical applications) or COBOL (dominant in business applications). In fact, PL/1 combined features of FORTRAN and COBOL as well as ALGOL, an "algorithmic" language for scientific computations developed in the early 1960s designed specifically to be independent of hardware architectures and to facilitate automatic code generation—important goals of the project.

PL/1 thus had many good features and was extremely rich functionally. It even gained temporary popularity in some segments of the industry (such as basic software groups in IBM), and Japanese mainframe producers continued to use it (or in-house variations) for operating-system development until the mid-1980s. But PL/1 never became accepted as a general programming language. It proved too time-consuming to learn and difficult to use (in essence, almost requiring knowledge of all the features of three very different languages). The difficulty and lack of acceptance for PL/1 in most applications limited the usefulness of the tools, most of which, in any case, supported batch processing. The project could have changed course with more flexible planning and foresight, but did not. Company teams carried out plans established in the early days of the project, so that Japan's cooperative software factory initiative consisted mainly of a few batch-processing tools for programming in PL/1.[5]

SMEF Project (1981–1986)

Japanese government planners and company engineers continued to learn from past mistakes and, in 1981, launched a follow-up initiative under the JSD Corporation with 5 billion yen more in funding, called the Software Maintenance Engineering Facility (SMEF) Project. Not only did this attempt to build a UNIX-based (Berkeley version) integrated environment for maintaining and developing software in an interactive (rather than batch-processing) mode, but project members spent more time in planning, coordination, and reflection, as well as achieved more freedom to determine what tools to build. While SMEF constructed ten maintenance environments and tool sets, including eight that relied on UNIX, this project failed to produce tools considered good enough for broad dissemination. Still, Japanese companies learned a lot about the UNIX environment and support tools. In this regard, SMEF proved to be a useful preparation for Sigma (which followed directly in 1985) as well as for individual company efforts aimed at utilizing UNIX.[6]

Interoperable Database System Project (1985–1989)

Once again under IPA sponsorship, the leading Japanese computer manufacturers, as well as Matsushita, Sharp, Oki, Sumitomo Electric, and several other firms, formed the Interoperable Database System Project in 1985. This five-year program, with a budget of 1.5 billion yen, adopted the internationally recognized OSI protocols in order to promote communications or data transfers among various types of hardware (computers and peripherals, office equipment) from different manufacturers.[7]

OSI clearly represented a positive development toward standardization on a limited but important dimension. As of early 1990, most of the major computer and peripherals producers in the United States and Europe, including IBM, had adopted the OSI standards along with Japanese firms, and several producers worldwide had introduced products utilizing these specifications. OSI thus promised to ease machine interconnections and simplify the building of networks, although these standards did not directly address issues such as software reusability or automation.[8]

FASET Project (1985–1989)

The JSD Corporation took another bold step in 1985 by launching the Formal Approach to Software Environment Technology (FASET) Project, with funding of 2.2 billion yen over five years, 80 percent provided from IPA and 20 percent from industry. JSD staff researchers, as well as personnel from several JSD member firms—Case Cachexia Engineering, Software Research Associates, Kanri Kogaku, Mitsubishi Research Institute, NEC Software, Japan Information Service Company, and INTEC—conducted the research.

As a first objective, FASET members evaluated existing specification tools and techniques prior to establishing a better methodology for generating executable code from formalized descriptions of system requirements. As a next step, they worked on creating a knowledge database of requirements or designs that developers could draw on in conjunction with tools to support specification of a software system. The last set of goals proved to be the most ambitious: to devise a practical but formalized (mathematical or algebraic) methodology for describing requirements, and then tools for optimization and transformation of the requirements into executable code (Figure 8.1). The FASET environment also assumed distributed development over a network of linked work

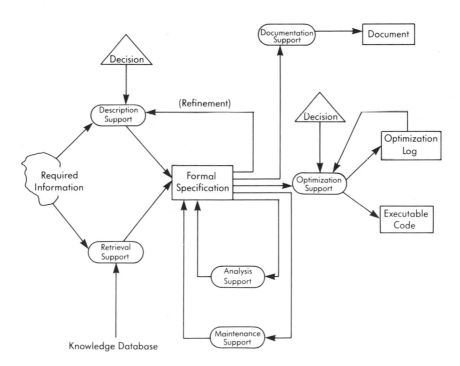

Figure 8.1 Formal Approach to Software Environments Technology (FASET) Project Development Environment. *Ovals* = tools; *Squares* = input/output of tools; *Triangles* = action of man/woman. (*Source*: Joint Software Development Corporation, "FASET—Formal Approach to Software Environments Technology—Overview of FASET Project," unpublished outline, January 1987, p. 3.)

stations and databases. The project schedule called for completion by 1989 of support tools for requirements analysis and description, database management, documentation generation, design retrieval, optimization, and maintenance. Other areas of research included tools and techniques to detect design errors, software standards, and methods for transferring specifications to different systems.

At the least, FASET brought more attention to the important goal of devising ways to generate computer programs from requirements—thus eliminating the need to write detailed system, program, and module designs, as well as code. Executable requirements also eliminated the need to worry about reusability, although recycling specifications still seemed a useful way to reduce time required for developing new systems. Yet the FASET Project appeared to have little impact. The objective remained technically difficult to achieve except for very restricted applications, which limited the usefulness of the tools. Furthermore, the major Japanese software producers—Fujitsu, Hitachi, NEC (except for a subsidiary), Toshiba, NTT, and Mitsubishi—did not directly participate, limiting the technical skills available to the FASET researchers. This lack of participation did not mean that the major Japanese computer producers saw no merit in FASET's agenda. In fact, as noted in the cases and later in this chapter, most of these companies had similar R&D efforts underway on their own, and probably saw no benefits to participating actively in this relatively small-scale project.[9]

The TRON Project (1984–1990s)

Although not a software-engineering effort in the sense of developing support tools and techniques, a cooperative effort in Japan of rising attention was the TRON Project, started in 1984.[10] Unlike prior projects, TRON started as and remained an independent initiative not sponsored by the Japanese government but conceived by a professor at the University of Tokyo, Ken Sakamura. Individual firms or researchers then agreed to carry out the work needed to meet Sakamura's objective: to construct an open family of computer architectures built around a thirty-two-bit microprocessor, with a high-performance operating system able to perform multitasking and real-time applications.

The unique feature of the architecture consisted of its design in well-planned layers, from the lowest level, the instruction-set processor, through the operating system and applications interfaces. Although developers had yet to complete all the components, standardized interfaces for each layer would make it possible for vendors to sell different types and sizes of computers as well as link them far more easily than most existing operating systems. The architecture would also greatly simplify communications and data transfer, as well as portability or reuse of software programs and tools. The ambitiousness of the effort can be seen in the subprojects, which targeted embedded industrial systems (ITRON), business-oriented work stations (BTRON), networking environments (CTRON), and interconnecting software objects (MTRON).

Despite MITI's support of UNIX through the Sigma Project, and TRON's origins as a private initiative, by 1988, scores of firms had joined the TRON association, including all the major Japanese computer and software manufacturers as well as foreign companies such as AT&T and IBM. The Japanese firms, led by Mitsubishi, Hitachi, Fujitsu, Matsushita, NEC, Toshiba, and NTT, had already introduced TRON VLSI processors and operating systems, as well as announced research results and concrete product plans. The Japanese Ministry of Education in 1987 provided a huge boost by adopting TRON as the operating system standard for at least some of the new computers introduced in Japanese schools, inspired in part by a useful feature of the standard TRON keyboard—an electronic pen and tablet that made it relatively simple for users to input Japanese characters. Some TRON work stations also ran more than one operating system (such as UNIX as well as TRON), and this seemed likely to improve the diffusion of the new standard and TRON hardware.

Nevertheless, and despite the technical excellence of the TRON architecture, this project faced major obstacles in the marketplace. Computer producers and, perhaps more importantly, computer users had enormous investments in existing hardware and software; to rewrite programs to work on TRON systems presented a daunting task few firms seemed likely to undertake without excellent reasons. In addition, most computer manufacturers were currently trying to link the interfaces among their incompatible machines, and making slow but steady progress. TRON presented a technically better but radically different solution that essentially involved discarding existing systems.

For new users, TRON offered potential benefits, although software producers still had to write programs to make the hardware and operating systems useful. Nevertheless, TRON seemed likely to grow in popularity. At the least, Japanese school children would become exposed to TRON hardware and basic software, and this generation might disseminate the standard more widely. As the 1990s unfolded, however, TRON seemed most likely to remain one of many standards, probably used mainly in Japanese schools and specific real-time applications in industry where benefits were obvious and users did not have major investments in other systems.

The Sigma Project (1985–1990)

The Sigma Project, begun in 1985 and slated for completion in 1990, had approximately 25 billion yen in funding from government and private sources.[11] In terms of key personnel and goals, it represented considerable continuity with previous JSD Corporation efforts, especially the Software Production Technology and the SMEF Projects. Also in common with previous cooperative efforts, Sigma faced organizational hurdles and competition from still-evolving standards or technologies. Yet it was likely to affect the industry positively because of modest goals. Sigma promised not to generate radically new tools or techniques, but to refine, standardize, and disseminate existing useful technology based on UNIX and closely resembling the tools used at Toshiba and other firms. Sigma thus supported a rising trend in that, while proprietary operating systems still dominated UNIX in market share, many Japanese firms were independently adopting this for their development environments and customers. One estimate held that UNIX would constitute approximately 25 percent of the world market for operating systems by 1990, including Japan.[12]

The center of activities for the Sigma Project, the Sigma Development Office, existed as part of the IPA structure. The staff, consisting of approximately 50 engineers on loan from 38 companies, took charge of planning, design, and management of the system. Private contractors building tools numbered at least 50 companies and 300 engineers. In total, as of 1989, 189 companies participated in the effort in some form. These included the major Japanese computer hardware and software manufacturers, producers of consumer electronics, and subsidiaries of U.S. computer makers operating in Japan (AT&T, Fuji Xerox, IBM Japan, NCR Japan, Nihon DEC, Nihon Sun Microsystems, Nihon Unisys, Nippon Data General, Olivetti of Japan, Yamatake Honeywell, and Yokogawa Hewlett-Packard).[13]

The director of Sigma's Planning Division, Noboru Akima, and a staff member, Fusatake Ooi, in stating their objectives in a 1989 article, made it clear that Sigma relied on concepts directly borrowed from previous factory efforts and other attempts to structure and automate software development: "Sigma . . . will industrialize the software-production process by using computerized development facilities and a nationwide communications network. . . . The ultimate goal of the project is to produce software through manufacturing instead of manual labor, moving the software industry from a labor-intensive to a knowledge intensive industry."[14] While Japanese companies pursued similar goals on their own, Sigma's potential contribution went beyond the individual firm: creation of a platform on which to integrate tools and hardware or reuse code from various vendors, and then make these tools and software available through an open network.

The project proceeded in two stages. In the first (1985–1987), researchers designed a prototype platform to evaluate user responses. This consisted of a hardware system, operating system specifications, software tools, and a network to share tools, computer programs, and other information. In the second phase (1987–1990), they enhanced and finished the prototype systems. Beginning in spring 1990, the Sigma hardware platform and software were to become commercially available from several vendors. Customers also had to pay a fee to operate the system and support R&D to improve the network as needed.

The system contained three major components: the Sigma Center, the network, and the user sites, expected to number approximately 10,000 (Figure 8.2). The Sigma Center, located in downtown Tokyo, assisted users who were building Sigma environments and then producing software. The center provided database services and demonstrations of tools, rather than time-sharing or remote job-entry services. The database services included information on existing software, such as applications and basic software packages (although few were available, because of limited funds), tools, and database management systems; software firms, such as what services companies offered; the Sigma system itself; available hardware; software standardization, such as technical articles, and Japanese as well as international practices; and other systems.

The network, the high-speed Digital Data Exchange-Pack Switching (DDX-PS) system leased from NTT, connected the Sigma Center to user sites and external networks as well as user sites to each other. It handled Japanese characters and functions for message communication (electronic mail, bulletin boards, conferences) and file transmission (data, programs, documents), and let users access computers from remote locations, allowing them to test how a new program ran on a particular machine.

User sites came with Sigma work stations, a local area network (LAN), and the Sigma Gateway, which facilitated communication and converted protocols between the system and different hardware. The work stations were thirty-two-bit machines with a high-resolution display, graphics support, and use of a mouse. While initial target prices came in at more than $20,000, inexpensive versions appeared by 1989 for the equivalent of approximately $12,000. These prices probably would decrease further since nearly a dozen firms (Fujitsu, Hitachi, Matsushita, Mitsubishi, NEC, Oki, Omron, Sharp, Sumitomo Electric, Toshiba, and Yokogawa) had agreed to make the work stations and operating systems, all according to common specifications so they could run the Sigma operating system and have the same communication protocols. Users, therefore, would be able to assemble equipment of varying capabilities and deploy the machines in different ways, but still be able to communicate with other Sigma sites and the Sigma Center, as well as exchange tools and programs.

The external specifications of the Sigma operating system, designed by the Development Office staff, combined the better features of two versions of UNIX—AT&T System V and Berkeley Software Distribution

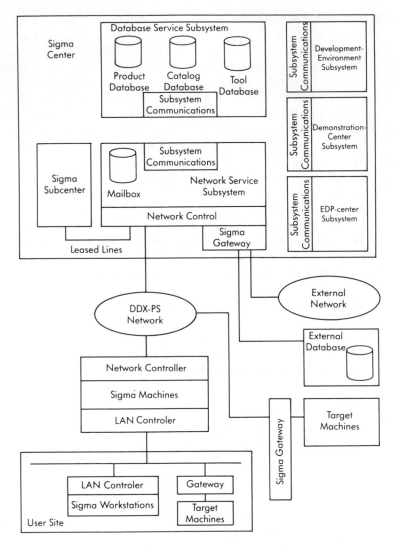

Figure 8.2 Sigma System Configuration. DDX-PS = Digital Data Exchange-Pack Switching System; EDP = Electronic Data Processing; LAN = local area network. (*Source*: Noboru Akima and Fusatake Ooi, "Industrializing Software Development: A Japanese Approach," *IEEE Software*, March 1989, p. 15. Copyright © 1989 IEEE. Reproduced with permission.)

Version 4.2—while adding capabilities for Japanese-language processing, graphics, multiple windows, and databases. Individual manufacturers had to write the internal designs and actual code to complete their specific version of the operating system, tailored to different hardware systems.

The Sigma network provided approximately thirty support tools for each development phase (Figure 8.3). The Sigma Development Office made and contracted for the tools, while member firms could put additional tools onto the network that met the interface specifications. Tools supported software development in COBOL, FORTRAN, and C, as well as assembly language. Several tools also specifically supported engineering applications.

As of early 1990, Sigma was completing its testing phase, with more than fifty companies assisting in the evaluation of tools. There remained gaps, such as the shortage of applications packages and good tools to support testing or designing the internal specifications of modules (which FASET was attempting); however, a few research groups were working on advanced tools for higher-level language processing and graphics-based prototyping. Future plans also called for Sigma to continue as a private company after 1990, jointly owned by the members, not only to maintain the system and the network but also to continue upgrading tools and network capabilities.

In addition to standardizing external specifications to facilitate tool portability, the open nature of the system allowed users to modify tools ordered through the Sigma office, again following the practice in Japanese software factories of tailoring tools to particular applications. To facilitate modification, when Sigma asked a vendor to develop a particular tool, rules called for the data architecture and source code that implemented the tool to be available to users. The original tools ordered by Sigma became the joint property of Sigma and the vendor, and if a user desired to modify the tool, then negotiations took place to determine royalties. Manufacturers of work stations who offered a tool might pay another firm to modify it to run on its work station or perform the modifications itself, paying only a licensing fee for the tool as determined by negotiations with the Sigma office. Firms that placed their proprietary tools on the Sigma network did not have to share source code.[15]

The objective of the tools and the overall support environment, again similar to factory approaches, was to provide support technology to reduce the need for highly skilled programmers, while still allowing users to tailor process technology, within limits that respected the network specifications and the rights of tool inventors. As Akima and Ooi asserted: "Sigma . . . supports all development phases and reduces the dependency of development efficiency on the skills and experience of each engineer. However, different software projects require different development environments. Furthermore, the development environment should keep growing and improving as advanced tools are introduced into the market. The Sigma system lets the development-environment designers customize the basic system to create an optimal development environment of their own."[16]

Another feature of Sigma, shown in Figure 8.3, was the integration of

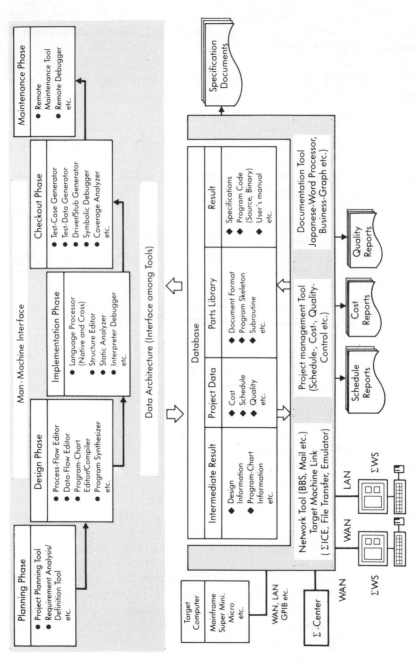

Figure 8.3 Sigma Software-Development Environment. (*Source*: Information Technology Promotion Agency, "Sigma Project," Tokyo, 1989, p. 18.)

a software parts library onto the network. Similar to the systems at Toshiba and other Japanese software factories, the library contained documentation, program skeletons, and executable subroutines. A program-composition tool also generated source code from the design skeletons. As in the case of Toshiba and other firms emphasizing reusability, however, the value of this library depended on how well its contents matched customer requirements, and how systematic management promoted development of code for reuse and construction of new programs from reusable modules.

Individual Japanese firms were modifying some in-house tools for the Sigma network. Hitachi, for example, created a version of SDL/PAD to run on UNIX so that it would qualify as a Sigma tool. Other manufacturers, ranging from computer firms already heavily in the tool-development business to consumer-electronics manufacturers just entering the computer or peripherals markets, found Sigma attractive as a way to sell or lease tools. NTT, Hitachi, Fujitsu, NEC, Data General, and Digital Equipment Corporation also benefitted by providing computer hardware and other systems for the Sigma Center. For many potentially useful tools already commercially available in Japan, however, Sigma provided no assistance. These included EAGLE, SEA/1, and an array of Fujitsu tools that ran on large computers incompatible with UNIX.

Sigma offered perhaps the most promise for small firms wishing to improve their level of support technology, although several issues remained unresolved for the government and tool developers. One obvious topic related to tool and code ownership, including network security. While the project set up an arbitration mechanism to settle disputes, tool modification and negotiated fees presented areas ripe for disagreements, especially if the open structure of the UNIX network allowed users to tap into databases and get access to tools and source code without the knowledge of the owners.[17]

Debates also continued in the United States and Europe regarding what versions of UNIX should become the international standard. This controversy positioned AT&T, which held the rights to UNIX and promoted Version V, against other firms that did not want AT&T to control the future of the system. While Japanese firms and Sigma might pursue an independent course, conflicts seemed likely over the evolution or international standardization of UNIX as well as over who owned the copyright to software based on the Sigma version of UNIX.[18]

Maintaining compatibility as well as harmony within Sigma presented another set of challenges, even putting aside the fact that member companies continued to support other versions of UNIX and many different operating systems for their individual product lines. Though they remained compatible with tools and programs on the network, Sigma in 1989 already had approximately a dozen firms creating different versions of the Sigma operating system. Most expressed dissatisfaction with aspects of the existing standards and tried to introduce improvements, thus keeping the Sigma staff constantly concerned with standardization and compatibility.[19]

A related dilemma was how competitive and popular the Sigma work stations would prove to be with Japanese users. The Japanese were accustomed to using time-sharing terminals and proprietary work stations connected to mainframes. They also had the option of buying many other types of less expensive hardware, including proprietary work stations from the major vendors as well as personal computers from NEC, IBM-compatible producers, and Apple, and even new machines running the TRON operating system. In software factories, managers or customers eliminated this issue of choice by determining what hardware developers would use. The Sigma staff, in contrast, had no control over customers, managers, or developers.

Every producer also faced a tradeoff between standardization and progress. While Sigma promised to disseminate practical tools and techniques, as in Japan's software factories, standardization constrained technological evolution. Producers of the Sigma operating system had already voiced objections to the common specifications because they saw better ways to design the system. In addition, Sigma had no choice but to evolve within the confines of UNIX, a product of the late 1960s with a variety of limitations. More radical product and process innovations, such as represented by TRON, the Fifth Generation Project, and numerous efforts in the United States and Europe, would be difficult for Sigma users to assimilate.

Nor did Sigma, in contrast to individual software factories, provide users with a management structure to accompany tools and further objectives such as effective project management or reusability. In its early phases, Sigma also suffered from weaknesses similar to preceding cooperative projects. A few eager government officials, managers, and academics took the lead without incorporating adequate input from sophisticated users and producers, such as organizations in Japan of software engineers, UNIX users, and university departments in information technology, although the project directors seem to have realized this and allowed their plans and objectives to evolve.

A final issue with regard to the value of Sigma tools and hardware remained: As in the case of SDC and other factories, tools always proved to be of limited value in software development. Individual firms and managers had to add the critical elements Sigma lacked—the management and training infrastructures needed to use tools effectively or produce reusable software and high-quality products systematically. There were no guarantees that small software houses would make the necessary investments in their organizations and people, although, based on the historical record established in other sectors, it seemed unwise to underestimate the determination and capabilities of Japanese companies in any industry.

Other Company Efforts: NTT and Mitsubishi

Japanese companies, other than those discussed in the previous chapters, also had underway important efforts in software support technology, some comparable to Sigma and others attempting to move beyond this to more advanced technologies. After Hitachi, Toshiba, NEC, and Fujitsu, the two most important players in terms of market shares and technical skills were NTT, the largest firm in the world measured by the value of outstanding shares and Japan's biggest systems integrator; and Mitsubishi Electric, a diversified electrical and electronics equipment producer that made commercial and industrial computers as well as software, primarily for the Japanese market.

Nippon Telegraph and Telephone

As noted in previous chapters, NTT had for years played an important role in promoting quality control and standardization among Japanese computer manufacturers through its procurement of hardware and software for telephone and data-processing systems. Of particular significance has been DIPS, begun in 1969 as Japan's domestic telephone switching network.[20] Although NTT produced some actual code in house or at newly formed subsidiaries, primarily for information systems it used internally, for much of the software it used, NTT personnel (approximately 6,000 were involved in software development during 1989) completed only requirement specifications and functional designs, and then transferred documentation to subcontractors (including Hitachi, NEC, Fujitsu, and others) to build the actual software. NTT followed the same process with hardware, issuing designs only and contracting out for manufacturing.[21]

Channeling programing tasks to several organizations required standardization of specifications, designs, coding, and documentation, as well as an excellent mechanism for quality control to assure comparability and compatibility. NTT thus cultivated various standards and controls since the 1960s, and these had an impact on the practices of its suppliers. For example, its encouragement of the use of structured flow charts for detailed design, which it called Hierarchical Compact (HCP) Charts, contributed to their acceptance at other Japanese firms during the 1970s.[22] NTT's rigorous quality standards also provided a model for other firms to improve their commercial operations.

As NEC, Fujitsu, and Hitachi became large-scale software producers during the 1970s and 1980s, they appeared to advance beyond NTT in technical skills and support technologies for program design and construction; however, along with becoming a private firm in 1985, NTT introduced several initiatives that promised to improve its capabilities in software. These included the establishment of a centralized Software Development Division (SDD) and a new subsidiary, NTT Software, which adopted factory organizational concepts and technologies similar to the Sigma system, as well as an extensive R&D network, much of it devoted to software tool and methodology development.

The SDD employed several hundred personnel at two main sites in Tokyo, with other groups linked through networks and on-line tools.[23] NTT had formerly dispersed these personnel throughout the Data Communications Sector and other groups developing basic software and videotext programs (Figure 8.4). Management assigned the new division four roles:

1. *Program Production Process Standardization*: standardize the way groups designed modules, module interfaces, and functional procedures, and did coding, in order to improve reusability of software across different projects. As in the other major Japanese firms, NTT relied heavily on structured design charts and code generators.
2. *Program Production*: implement specifications produced by industry-related or functional divisions in the Data Communications Sector utilizing a standardized process and tool set to serve as a software factory, focused on program construction rather than only design.
3. *Enhancement and Maintenance of Debugging System*: maintain the debugging system NTT had developed for use by most software developers within the company.
4. *Production Support System R&D*: conduct applied process R&D, including tools and techniques for automating program generation and reusability.[24]

The NTT Software Laboratories, part of the company's central R&D organization, conducted advanced R&D in language processing and design support, integrated software-development support and reuse systems, and systematization of production techniques and standards. The integrated production and reuse-support systems came in several versions, apparently for different product types, although they relied on NTT's communications network and the UNIX V operating system, as did Sigma.

NTT, for example, introduced a major tool set for switching systems software design during 1985–1988, called INSTEP. After noting a doubling of productivity over a large number of projects, NTT began moving much of its software design and in-house programming operations onto integrated support systems that provided a unified interface between the operating system and various tools.[25] Other versions of this concept included NTT Advanced Programming Support Environment (NAPSE) and Software Production and Circulation Environment (SPACE), which supported Ada, C, and COBOL.[26]

Most of the tools and techniques under development in NTT laborato-

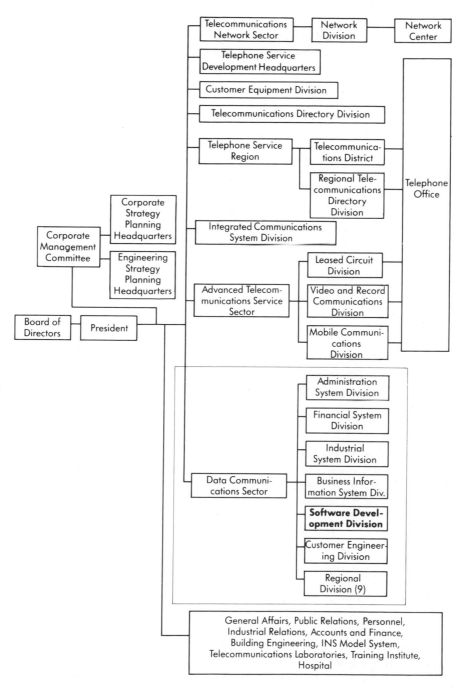

Figure 8.4 Nippon Telegraph and Telephone (NTT) Organizational Chart. (*Source*: Nippon Telegraph and Telephone Corporation, "Software Development Division Outline," July 1986, p. 4.)

ries had counterparts in other Japanese firms, although NTT's researchers demonstrated particularly broad interests. Projects ranged from an Ada compiler that operated on different computers and target machines, to an automatic remote-testing system that made it possible to test switching and communications software from dispersed locations and without direct human intervention.[27] In the design area, NTT offered several promising tools: HCP Design (HD), a prototype of a CAD system, helped users write designs in HCP charts, even if they did not understand all the HCP conventions, as well as reuse existing designs and automatically generate code.[28] SoftDA, another chart-based design system, supported reuse of designs and code as well as allowed users to execute and correct designs in a dynamic mode, among other functions. ADAM, a module management system, supported reuse of flow-chart designs, code, and specifications. Software Design Environment (SDE), another experimental tool, facilitated design and maintenance of communications software, with a specialized language that described communications functions and a subsystem that automatically translated specifications into executable code. The laboratories also worked on various AI and knowledge-processing technologies.[29]

Mitsubishi Electric

Mitsubishi had only a small market share in the Japanese data-processing industry (see Table 4.1) and many of its customers came from the Mitsubishi group. Among users of its hardware, however, the company scored well in various areas related to systems and applications programming (see Chapter 1 and Appendix C). Mitsubishi also experimented with a factory organizational approach as well as conducted advanced R&D on software tools and methodologies.

Mitsubishi's main center of software development, the Computer Works, located in Kamakura, nearby Tokyo, developed hardware as well as basic software and applications programs. In late 1987, it had approximately 700 personnel in applications and basic software serving 300 systems engineers (the latter remained organizationally outside the Computer Works). The structure introduced in 1987 separated systems engineering from applications development. Mitsubishi then combined applications with basic software, and systems engineering with computer sales, and operated each of these two groups as a set of independent profit centers by product (machine) line. Management did this to make both the systems-engineering and basic software groups more conscious of costs and profits, as well as to provide more opportunities for streamlining software production.[30]

The tools in use at the Computer Works and under development closely resembled those in the Sigma Project and other Japanese firms that utilized UNIX. Mitsubishi built an integrated UNIX workbench (also offered through Sigma) for technical or embedded engineering software, called Software Engineering Work Station (SEWS). This operated with Mitsubishi's Software Engineers Land-On Network (SOLON) for distributed development across multiple sites. The system supported NTT's HCP structured charts and automatic code generation in C and assembly language, as well as object-oriented interfaces among modules, high-speed graphics and text displays, and use of a mouse to point to objects on screens to reduce the need to input text or commands on a keyboard.[31]

Mitsubishi's Information Systems and Electronics Development Laboratory, located next to the Computer Works, also established an experimental software factory on one floor of its facility in 1985, to serve as a working area for software engineers in the laboratory and as a pilot model for an integrated software development environment. This included common facilities (review rooms, terminals), work stations linked by local area networks, standardized development and management procedures, and a formal system for program registration and reusability promotion.[32]

Reuse promotion also resembled the approaches of other Japanese firms as well as Sigma. Mitsubishi defined frequently reusable black-box parts, consisting of general-purpose executable subroutines, and specialized white-box parts, in the form of designs or executable code and intended for specific applications. Mitsubishi departed somewhat from other firms in its use of a separate group of "reuse engineers," for both

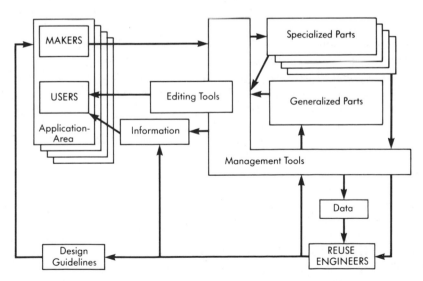

Figure 8.5 Mitsubishi's Software Reuse System. (*Source*: Mitsubishi Electric Corporation, "Software Reuse—Our Approach," Kamakura, Computer Works, 1986.)

basic and applications software, whose job consisted of reviewing existing designs and code as well as newly written software for potential reuse or modification for reuse (Figure 8.5). Other Japanese firms utilized reuse engineers probably as much or more than Mitsubishi, although none made this function quite so explicit. Other Japanese software factories tended to allocate engineering time either to building reusable packages, patterns, or subroutines, or to reviewing existing or newly written software for potential reuse, but without creating a special group for reengineering.[33]

The Fifth Generation Computer Project (1982–1991)

Although publicity waned after the initial years, Japan's Fifth Generation Computer Project had already made an important impact on the world's AI community by the late 1980s, stimulating research in Japan as well as in the United States and Europe.[34] Since the project architects hoped to develop a new type of hardware and software that would revolutionize the way people interacted with and used computers in the future, its broad goals made the Fifth Generation Computer Project both intriguing and unlikely to fulfill its more dramatic expectations. In addition to encouraging basic research in an important area of computer technology, the project settled on a few specific technical targets and promised limited but concrete results by the termination date in 1991. As of early 1990, however, Japan remained vague on plans to continue the venture, suggesting some dissatisfaction with the results so far.

MITI initiated the project in 1982, after two years of study, as a ten-year program starting with fifty researchers (ninety in 1989) and housed in the newly created Institute for New Generation Computer Technology (ICOT) near downtown Tokyo. The schedule called for three phases: study of existing knowledge in the fields of logic processing and parallel computing, and the development of prototype hardware and software systems (1982–1984); construction of small-scale subsystems for logic processing and parallel computing (1985–1988); and completion of a full-scale prototype (1989–1991).[35] The finished computer was expected to build both inference and knowledge-based functions into the hardware, thus facilitating extremely fast processing speeds, while the basic software controlled the hardware and provided a platform for a knowledge database-management program and applications.

The term *fifth generation* referred to the evolution of circuit components, although the major differeces with the new computer lay in its architecture—how it processed data, instructions, and other information. The first four generations consisted of computers built with vacuum tubes (1950s), transistors (1960s), integrated circuits (1970s), and then VLSI circuits (1980s), that processed data or instructions one at a time in a sequential fashion, following the design of the mathematician John von Neumann. The fifth generation would also use VLSI chips (of the latest variety) but deploy them in a different way.

The premise of the research held that von Neumann architectures limited the capabilities of computers and that significant progress in AI, expert systems, knowledge processing, automatic programming, and other advanced applications required moving away from conventional algebraic, sequential instructions and data sets. ICOT worked to perfect a machine that processed information in the form of "predicate logic" statements or inferences, and did this in a parallel rather than a sequential fashion (that is, parceling out pieces of a program to different processors that acted on the instructions or data simultaneously and then combined the results), much as the human brain functioned. Existing computers already used forms of parallel processing, but primarily with a small number of processors and with conventional data and instructions merely broken down into pieces. The new hardware would incorporate 1,000 parallel processors and process information at a calculation speed considerably faster than existing computers.

The software specifications called for several complementary functions: problem-solving capabilities, to perform deductive and inductive inferences; knowledge-base management technology, to express, collect, store, and retrieve various types of information required by the inference functions; intelligent interfaces, to allow people and the computer to converse in natural languages; and intelligent programming capabilities, to enable "persons without specialized knowledge to write programs easily" (Figure 8.6). Each of these objectives constituted a modular subsystem of the basic software. Working groups, organized under several larger laboratories, conducted research in each area (Table 8.2).

Pioneering such technology was expensive and, not surprisingly, the Fifth Generation had the largest budget among Japan's cooperative efforts in computer technology, with approximately 50 billion yen allocated over ten years, paid for entirely by the Japanese government. This amount constituted merely half MITI's original proposal, since MITI had anticipated (but did not receive) contributions from private firms. Hitachi President Katsushige Mita accepted the presidency of the venture and eight companies—Fujitsu, Hitachi, NEC, Toshiba, Mitsubishi, Oki, Matsushita, and Sharp—eventually agreed to send researchers to the project, at the government's expense. Companies declined to contribute financially, and only the company that agreed to build the hardware, Mitsubishi Electric, seemed to display much enthusiasm for the project.

The lack of enthusiasm reflected several factors. The risky and difficult nature of the research presented a major obstacle in that it seemed to have no immediate commercial applications. Another characteristic of

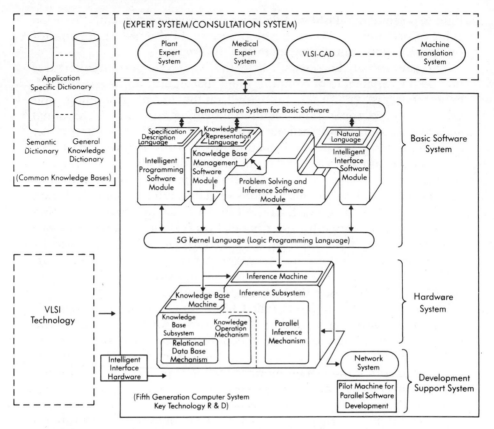

Figure 8.6 Fifth-Generation Computer System Configuration. CAD = computer-aided design; VSLI = very large-scale integration. (*Source*: Institute for New Generation Computer Technology, "Fifth Generation Computer Systems Project," Tokyo, unpublished manuscript, October 1986, p. 24.)

ICOT that probably made the effort uncomfortable for the participants was that, unlike in previous cooperative arrangements, which tended to have a small staff developing plans and then contracting work out to individual firms, the Fifth Generation called for most research to occur in common laboratories with personnel on full-time assignments. ICOT sponsored some important research at individual firms, but the structure required strict and common technical targets, and this made it difficult for any one firm to use funds to subsidize internal R&D or seize the advantage in capitalizing on research results, if any proved commercially viable.

In the initial phase during 1982–1984, ICOT researchers examined existing technologies on knowledge processing, synthesized the results,

Table 8.2 Fifth-Generation Project Working Groups

Parallel Software
Artificial Intelligence Foundations
Computer Games (Go, Shoji)
Natural Language Processing System
Japanese Generalized Phrase Structure Grammar
Speech Understanding System
Computer-Aided Proof
Term Rewriting System
Japanese Specification Language
Intelligent Programming System
Knowledge Base Machine
Parallel Inference Machine and Multi-PSI (Personal Sequential Inference) Machine
Knowledge System Shell
Knowledge Acquisition Support System

Source: Institute for New Generation Computer Technology, "Fifth Generation Computer Systems Project," Tokyo, unpublished manuscript, October 1986, p. 30.

and successfully built a Personal Sequential Inference (PSI) machine to serve as a tool and work station for research. This had approximately 100 processing elements, about one-tenth the number of the envisioned final system. They also experimented with a design for an operating system utilizing a logic language rather than a conventional computer language.

During 1985–1988, the researchers studied how to use and control groups of the PSI machines (Multi-PSI) for the actual goal: knowledge and inference processing in a parallel mode. This required creation of a parallel hardware architecture as well as extension of an existing logic language to make it suitable for programming in a parallel fashion. The researchers also began work on basic tools and techniques for building a Knowledge-Processing System (KIPS) and a knowledge-base subsystem (an advanced relational database called Delta) that took advantage of the parallel architecture.

The basic software consisted primarily of parallel control functions as well as logic or inference rules that allowed programs to act upon information stored in the relational database. To write the core software, ICOT initially chose PROLOG, a language developed in the early 1980s to support programming in mathematical logic. Writing a program in PROLOG requires constructing rules or hypotheses, as well as objectives or conditions, that a programmer wants to test, and providing data on which the rules can operate. It is a powerful language but proved difficult to learn and few programmers had experience with it.[36] In addition, the authors of PROLOG had designed it for sequential rather than parallel processing.

After some criticism and reflection, ICOT explored alternatives to

PROLOG and developed an extended low-level version specifically for parallel processing called Flat Guarded Horn Clauses (FGHC). This proved suitable for specifying the interface between the hardware and the software needed to process information in parallel. Using the computer then required the development of problem-solving inference programs and knowledge-base management software. ICOT employed a system description language developed in the first stage, Extended Self-Contained PROLOG (ESP), to create object-oriented modules and subroutines (macros) for applications that could run in a sequential mode. The relational database used predicate-logic inferences (rules) to perform particular functions or carry out specific instructions, rather than processing data sequentially or simply finding and matching identical words or pieces of data.

The pilot tool for software development consisted of a sequential inference machine that used a version of sequential instruction processing, as in von Neumann architectures, modified for parallel processing. As of late 1989, however, ICOT had made only limited progress toward building tools that assisted in intelligent programming or automating software development. Some advances came in methods for object-oriented modular programming using ESP and parallel-programming languages, and early experimental work on a software-development consultation system for parallel programming found some interest among developers of telephone switching systems. Yet most tool work centered on limited goals, such as theorem proving and mathematical verification techniques, including a computer-aided proof system. Still under development were Argus, a tool for program synthesis from high-level descriptions, as well as a software knowledge-management system to support library management, program and document generation, and other functions involved in developing logic programs. Work on intelligent interface software concentrated on studies of Japanese grammar and syntax, as well as semantic and contextual analysis, with most of this R&D located at a subsidiary project, the Japan Electronic Dictionary Research Center.

A few groups outside ICOT proper pursued applications. One potentially useful tool consisted of a programming support system produced at Fujitsu. This included an English-like specification language mechanically translated into predicate logic formulas, and a logic-based system to retrieve reusable software modules, stored by function, from a modules library. The library also stored specifications for each module, coded in PROLOG, which the tool compared with requirements to identify functionally equivalent modules reusable for particular parts of a new program. These capabilities resembled conventional reuse-support systems in use for several years but added superior retrieval and verification capabilities. Earlier reuse-support methods located modules by matching key words in the specifications or code, whereas the PROLOG system made it possible to identify modules with similar functions even if they did not match in a conventional search process. In addition, another capability of the tool, which supported reuse as well as maintenance, was an "explanation generator." This analyzed code and produced English-like explanations of the program logic by comparing the code with pre-existing templates (skeletons) of explanations stored in a separate database.[37]

Plans for ICOT's final stage of research during 1989–1991 remained vague, in part because work had not proceeded as quickly as desired. In particular, hardware development remained one or two years behind schedule, although researchers still expected to finish the hardware and the basic software by 1991, in addition to exploring techniques for knowledge processing, natural-language processing, and a few experimental applications, such as expert systems.

Unlike Sigma, ICOT did not distribute or license technology as commercial products. Rather, the Fifth Generation Project was in the business of basic research. Individual participants had to transfer technology to their parent organizations and pursue commercial applications. Some companies did introduce tools that processed or utilized PROLOG, as in Fujitsu's case, although their market remained unclear. In fact, many Japanese laboratories now contained PSI machines made by Mitsubishi Electric, although few researchers outside of ICOT projects appeared to utilize them. Perhaps the major benefits of ICOT would not exceed the stimulation of basic research, which the project's directors encouraged within and outside its membership by establishing an AI Center in 1986 to monitor activities of Japanese and foreign firms in the field and by organizing annual conferences to disseminate research results and promote information sharing.

American experts who examined the progress of ICOT through 1987 as part of the Japanese Technology Evaluation Program (JTECH), an effort supported by the U.S. National Science Foundation, made several observations regarding the project's objectives and achievements.[38] Most important, they concluded that the researchers had made significant progress in areas of AI such as speech and image processing, language translation, and expert systems, at least matching U.S. efforts in these areas and "even teaching us a lesson in the speed of development and smooth industrial coupling of these commercially-directed efforts." This seemed true even though many of the results required special hardware, Japanese did not use the machines widely, and many results remained far from commercial application without much more R&D.

The evaluation team expressed a concern that the reliance of the project on logic programming, even with the invention of a new version of PROLOG for parallel processing (FGHC), presented both benefits and limitations. On the one hand, this focus gave the project clear direction and made it likely to meet basic technical targets (even if society did not quickly advance to new uses of computers). On the other hand,

ICOT did not directly address promising areas of AI research, such as programming in LISP (a more common language than PROLOG that processes data and functions in the form of lists of symbolic expressions) or experimenting with neural networks (groups of many small-scale parallel processors that mimic more closely how the human brain processes information). While Japanese companies pursued these and other technologies in their own laboratories, the Fifth Generation represented a significant effort and potential diversion from more practical topics. The eventual value of ICOT thus depended heavily on how useful logic programming turned out to be, and this remained difficult to predict.

Nevertheless, and despite uncertainties over the future of logic programming, the U.S. experts appeared unanimous in their praise for the project's "superb software engineering design work." In the related area of supercomputer hardware and software development, the panel found the hardware to be "world-class" and "the software work competitive with, if not superior to, the best quality output in the United States," even though project planners dropped initial plans to develop new VLSI technology to go along with R&D in parallel architectures, programming, and AI.

Comparable U.S. and European Efforts

Comparisons with U.S. and European cooperative projects reinforce the conclusion that Japanese software producers and researchers were not only near the mainstream but also close to the forefront in research on standards as well as advanced technologies related to software development. In the United States, the most prominent example of a cooperative effort was the Microelectronics and Computer Corporation (MCC), founded in 1983 and located in Austin, Texas.[39] This R&D consortium had a staff of approximately 400 in 1989, an indeterminate lifespan, and a budget of $70 million per year. Membership (the shareholders) included leading U.S. producers of electronic equipment, components, and materials: 3M, Advanced Micro Devices, Bell Communications Research, Boeing, Control Data, Digital Equipment Corporation, Kodak, Harris, Hewlett-Packard, Hughes Aircraft, Lockheed, Motorola, National Semiconductor, NCR, General Electric, Rockwell, and Westinghouse. Research centered on four broad areas: (1) software technology (productivity and quality enhancement tools and methods); (2) semiconductor packaging and interconnection technologies (substrate materials, chip attachment, cooling and manufacturing methods); (3) VLSI/CAD systems (design support for very large integrated circuits); and (4) advanced computer architectures (divided among three laboratories—AI/ Knowledge-Based Systems, System Technology, and Human Interface).

In software production, the specific R&D topics resembled work in Sigma, ICOT, FASET, and other Japanese projects as well as the laboratories of NEC, Toshiba, Fujitsu, Hitachi, NTT, and Mitsubishi. All were trying to create tools, methods, and concepts to support an integrated design environment that covered a wide range of tasks, including reuse support and automatic code generation; but its combination of theoretical studies, such as on the design process, knowledge processing, and coordination among large teams, with empirical research on projects at member companies, distinguished MCC's research.

Much of the effort in software technologies at MCC concentrated on requirements specification, which usually required a great deal of time and expertise. Work on this theme included examining design decisions, rapid prototyping and simulation technologies, traceability of design steps, knowledge representation schemes (especially for "fuzzy" knowledge not easily expressible as, for example, zeros or ones), and reuse of designs. The reuse work included tools incorporating expert system techniques to analyze existing code and specifications in order to extract the underlying architecture, which could then be deposited in a database as design components for future reuse or maintenance. Other areas of research covered generic design representations, which could be compiled into different languages, as well as tool integration through platform standardization, and group coordination and management through highly integrated and automated project-management tools and databases. These appeared especially useful for building distributed, embedded systems (software encased in hardware, with the hardware spread in more than one location) in multiple teams.[40]

As with any cooperative effort, where members were likely to have disparities in skills, objectives, and resources, MCC encountered problems. Member companies disagreed on research agendas and thus supported different projects, with licensing rights to research results dependent on what work each funded. This structure restricted coordination and technical sharing, even in areas developing complementary technologies, such as VLSI and software.[41] Members were also supposed to provide many of the personnel but they did not always send their best researchers to the venture, leading MCC management to hire its own staff. In 1988, for example, only about 30 percent of the researchers came from member firms. The drawback was that MCC researchers had to market their organization to shareholders on a continual basis, while shareholders had to make extra efforts to transfer technology back to their organizations.

The U.S. Department of Defense had a longer history of promoting research on computer hardware and software. Many of the results have benefitted the world industry—the *Multics* time-sharing system, the Ada language, VLSI circuits, and various other applied tools and techniques, as well as basic research. In contrast to Japan and MCC, however, a common theme has been the focus of this research on military uses, thus limiting the total impact of cooperative ventures on the U.S. commercial sector. Nonetheless, in the 1980s, the U.S. Department of Defense seemed to shift somewhat and exhibited more interest in basic problems in software engineering and potentially general solutions, in response to the growing complexity and expense of software for modern weaponry and other defense as well as information systems.

For example, the Department of Defense in 1982 initiated STARS (Software Technology for Adaptable, Reliable Systems) as a multiyear industry, government, and university effort, with annual budgeting of roughly $60 million. This included the establishment of a Software Engineering Institute at Carnegie-Mellon University in 1985, where a staff of 250 researched new software tools and methods as well as evaluated factory concepts, much like the Sigma Project. In addition, the U.S. Department of Defense Advanced Research Projects Agency (DARPA) directly sponsored several projects that overlapped with the technical themes being explored in the Fifth Generation Project and FASET, as well as Japanese corporations, besides making grants to U.S. universities for research in every major area of computer hardware and software technology.

Of particular prominence among the DARPA projects was the Strategic Computing Initiative, a $600-million, five-year effort begun in 1983–1984. This brought together university, government, and industry researchers to study parallel architectures for symbolic computing, advanced microelectronics, and new hardware, with the objective, to an extent inspired by the Japanese Fifth Generation Project, of integrating vision, speech recognition and production, natural-language understanding, and expert systems, especially but not exclusively for military applications.[42] Compared to ICOT, however, progress in meeting research targets seemed slow, except for parallel-processing architectures.[43]

Major European electronics firms and governments had their equivalents of Sigma and the Fifth Generation, as well as the Strategic Computing Initiative and STARS. In all cases, similar to the Japanese and U.S. programs, the Europeans hoped to advance and diffuse basic knowledge in AI and other technologies, as well as make tools and methods available to a broad range of producers. In contrast to the recent Japanese initiatives, the European efforts seemed less focused, in part because the Europeans tended to fund efforts promoted by individual firms and give companies the right to commercialize the results of their R&D, rather than allowing firms to work, in effect, as subcontractors under a joint project.[44]

The European Strategic Program for Research and Development in Information Technologies (ESPRIT), begun in 1984, probably attracted the most attention in Europe, spending $1.5 billion on more than 200 projects. The research included forty-seven projects devoted to software technologies—knowledge-engineering and expert systems, advanced computer architectures, and improved user-machine interfaces, similar to the Fifth Generation, as well as applied tool and methodology development, similar to Sigma. Several groups worked on method and tool integration as well as reuse technology for a software-factory environment, with an analogue to the Sigma tool set, PCTE (Portable Common Tools Environment), based on UNIX V. The main firm behind this initiative, Bull of France, offered PCTE on its work stations. Other firms followed, including GEC and ICL in the United Kingdom, Nixdorf and Siemens in Germany, Olivetti in Italy, and Sun Microsystems in the United States.

Another cooperative program, the European Research Coordination Agency (EUREKA) Software Factory Project (ESF), worked on developing a tool set and integrated environment resembling PCTE but tailored for specific applications such as real-time software development and complex business programming. The development group consisted of Nixdorf, AEG, ICL, and several other firms in Germany, the United Kingdom, Norway, and Sweden. Individual countries had other efforts exploring similar tools and techniques, with perhaps the largest consisting of Britain's Alvey program, modeled after the Fifth Generation in objectives but resembling ESPRIT in organization, with 2,000 researchers from universities and companies working on 200 separate projects.[45]

Summary and Evaluation

In contrast to initiatives at individual firms, government direction and subsidies, including cooperative interfirm projects, played a very small role in promoting the factory approach and supporting technologies in Japan. This is not to say that the Japanese government did not try to do more. Various agencies sponsored cooperative efforts between the 1960s and early 1980s aimed at promoting tools, techniques, and concepts effectively used in factory environments, although none had much impact. By the mid-1980s, the situation had begun to change slightly. Old and new standards still competed for acceptance, and software continued to come in many sizes and shapes, maintaining a complex, fragmented industry of uncertain dimensions. Yet it seemed clearer what constituted good practice and where the key challenges in standardization or R&D remained. As a result, Japanese and other firms started to cooperate more actively and, as it seemed in the case of Sigma, more effectively.

Cooperation clearly proved necessary to further standardization. Japan especially exhibited a great need to spread good tools and techniques to the hundreds of small software houses that did programming work for larger software producers and other customers. Standardization and networks, such as with Sigma, helped make this possible. Even projects that failed to meet objectives at least familiarized companies with software-engineering concepts and tools, as well as with packages and operating systems such as UNIX. While Sigma appeared likely to be an effective environment for software development, firms still had to experiment with more advanced technologies, and cooperation seemed useful to complement efforts at individual firms. FASET, TRON, and the Fifth Generation, in addition to company laboratories, provided a mechanism to explore basic technologies as well as potential applications.

In the short term, standardization around UNIX and Sigma work stations promised to help small firms raise their level of tool support. At the same time, these or other standards would probably delay the Japanese from moving to newer technologies as they appeared. TRON provided a good example, since it offered a higher potential level of integration for different types of hardware and software. Japanese companies were introducing TRON products, particularly for industrial real-time settings and educational applications, but they maintained much larger commitments to UNIX, proprietary operating systems, or IBM compatibility.

In parallel computing and logic processing, Japanese government officials and researchers focused their efforts and created a fascinating project for a fifth-generation computer, but bet perhaps too heavily on a narrow aspect of AI technology and had difficulty maintaining the interest of major Japanese firms. FASET seemed more ambitious than Sigma technically and more practical than ICOT in pioneering a critical area—producing executable requirements—but lacked strong participation from key companies, who had their own R&D projects on the same theme.

One might also argue that the sheer variety of activity in Japan served as much to fragment precious engineering and financial resources as it helped push forward the state of computer technology and the capabilities of individual firms. Japanese managers appeared to recognize this, and companies tended to limit their participation in government-sponsored projects. In the long term, however, as international comparisons indicated, Japanese firms seemed well positioned for future competition, thoroughly exploring nearly all major areas of standardization as well as software-engineering tools, techniques, and advanced research.

CONCLUSION

9

SOFTWARE DEVELOPMENT: FROM CRAFT TO FACTORY PRACTICE

The quest for an absolute answer to whether software development is or should be managed more like an art or craft rather than like science, engineering, or manufacturing is probably moot. This is because the nature of software development, and the optimal process or organization, seem to depend on the specific tasks at hand. To the extent these tasks differ with product types, market segments, and competitive positioning, the appropriateness of managing software through a factory process or not becomes a strategic choice subject to management discretion. The most relevant concern for Japanese managers was not how to label their facilities but how to organize, control, and improve software development. For this latter task—improving the development *process*—Japan's factory efforts offered cause for reflection and presented a serious challenge to the belief that loosely structured craft or job-shop approaches constituted the most suitable way to organize all software development.

Evolutionary Phases

Moving beyond craft practices to a factory process, and systematically recycling reusable components, tools, methods, people, and other elements across a series of similar projects, required years of effort and passage through overlapping phases comparable to what firms in other

Table 9.1 Phases of Factory Structuring in Software

Phase I: (mid-1960s to early 1970s)	*Formalized Organization and Management Structure* Factory objectives established Product focus determined Process data collection and analysis begun Initial control systems introduced
Phase II: (early 1970s to early 1980s)	*Technology Tailoring and Standardization* Control systems and objectives expanded Standard methods adopted for design, coding, testing, documentation, maintenance On-line development through terminals Program libraries introduced Integrated methodology and tool development begun Employee training programs to standardize skills
Phase III: (late 1970s)	*Process Mechanization and Support* Introduction of tools supporting project control Introduction of tools to generate code, test cases, and documentation Integration of tools with on-line databases and engineering workbenches begun
Phase IV: (early 1980s)	*Process Refinement and Extension* Revisions of standards Introduction of new methods and tools Establishment of quality control and quality circle programs Transfer of methods and tools to subsidiaries, subcontractors, hardware customers
Phase V: (mid-1980s)	*Integrated and Flexible Automation* Increase in capabilities of existing tools Introduction of reuse-support tools Introduction of design-automation tools Introduction of requirements-analysis tools Further integration of tools through engineering workbenches
Phase VI: (late 1980s)	*Incremental Product/Variety Improvement* Process & reliability control, followed by: Better functionality & ease of use More types of products

industries encountered as they grew and formalized operations.[1] In software, however, the first step demanded almost a heretical conviction on the part of key engineers, division managers, and top executives that software was not an unmanageable technology. This led to the creation of formal organizations and control systems rather than continuing to treat software as a loosely organized service provided free to customers primarily to facilitate hardware sales. Imposing greater structure on the development process then required continual efforts to introduce and refine elements common in other manufacturing and engineering environments but not in software, at least not in the 1960s and early 1970s: a product focus narrower than simply "programming," to limit the range of problems managers and developers faced; standards, at least temporary ones and tailored to specific product families, that introduced solutions to recurring problems in the form of methods, procedures, and tools, as well as provided guidelines on expected worker performance to aid budgeting and scheduling; training of employees and managers, to standardize skills though without specifying all tasks for all situations; and development of mechanized or partially automated tools for design, testing, product control, reuse support, personnel and project management, and other functions, as well as continual refinements of these tools and methods as well as products (Table 9.1).

Japanese firms began their transition to a factory process a few years after IBM organized its basic software operations in the 1960s. Many other firms in the industry containing several hundreds or even thousands of programmers waited until the mid-1980s to move beyond project-centered, loosely structured organizations. Some relatively large firms, such as leading makers of packages for personal computers and high-end producers of apparently unique customized software, have yet to make this transition. Some may never find factory concepts appropriate, although any firm that needs to manage large-scale efforts and develop a series of similar products should benefit from the historical experiences and themes emphasized in Japanese software factories.

Common Elements Revisited

Strategic Management and Integration

Japanese software factories were strategic in that they resulted from long-term rather than just project-centered objectives, with managers systematically identifying productivity, quality, and performance goals, and introducing comprehensive measures to meet those goals. Implementation required leadership from high- and middle-level managers as well as senior engineers, and the allocation of enough resources to insure that organizational experimentation as well as process research and development continued.

Successful factory efforts were integrative in the sense that managers had to link their products and marketing strategies with organizational structures, production technology, control systems, training, and other elements so these operated not at cross purposes and supported management objectives as well as company traditions. While IBM, SDC, and other U.S. firms led the effort to manage software development through a more systematic or controlled process, few companies seemed to match the Japanese in coordination and effort. SDC, for example, despite being the only U.S. firm to adopt the factory analogy explicitly, appeared far less strategic and integrated in managing its factory initiative. Managers and R&D staff outlined by 1977 a factory strategy that seemed comprehensive and well planned. The resistance of project managers and an uneven work flow soon led to the end of the factory experiment, although the underlying failure proved to be insufficient analysis, planning, and control—concerns that remained the responsibility of executives above the level of project managers. In particular, the chief executive who first promoted the factory idea in SDC might have persuaded project managers to support and use the facility or at least anticipated resistance to a major process and organizational change. He did not.

Nor did SDC's top executives show much thought in how to end the factory or exploit its lessons. The effort started with the identification of a set of problems, a way to solve them, and the allocation of funds to implement a solution. The end came hardly through events one could call strategic. No one decided, officially, to dismantle the factory; it simply "devolved" out of existence, as project managers put no more jobs into it, and as corporate management allocated no more R&D resources. The end of a path-breaking experiment thus came, in the words of the factory's first manager, "not with a bang, but a whimper." Yet the factory's admirable performance in budget, quality, and schedule control suggests that, by not persisting, SDC wasted an opportunity to remain at the forefront of software production technology. In contrast, the Japanese established software factories as permanent facilities, serving as centers of divisional software development and handling huge volumes of work. Top executives accepted the need for time and resources, as well as trial and error, to refine the factory process.

When Hitachi centralized basic and applications software development in a single factory, managers clearly stated that they placed the highest priority on making products through a predictable factory process, even though they expressed doubts over what this meant precisely or how long it would take to perfect. The efforts at other Japanese firms resembled Hitachi's in technology and commitment, but differed in timing and scope. The Toshiba Software Factory was probably the most structured and complex facility, integrating focused products with long-term planning and funding decisions, tool and method development, training programs, and incentive systems, to maximize reusability in real-time industrial control software. Like Hitachi, the factory initiative came out of a single division and centered on one facility, where middle-level managers and researchers had a great deal of direct control over product and process development.

In contrast, NEC management took on a much grander task, attempting to promote standardization and quality control through all divisions of the firm simultaneously. Executives at the highest level of the corporation publicly stated in the early 1970s that they intended to move software production beyond the craft approaches commonly followed in the industry; they then allocated the resources, through a series of projects, committee activities, and a centralized research staff, to move toward this goal. Fujitsu managers seemed much more cautious and less in agreement about what to do with software, and were relatively slow to promote factory-type organizations. Nonetheless, by the late 1970s and early 1980s, Fujitsu had adopted approaches similar to those at Hitachi, Toshiba, and NEC, and had become a leader in automated tool development and usage.

The cases in Part II thus reflect a potential benefit of the factory approach that involves the very essence of strategic management: the identification of specific process and product objectives; establishment of plans and policies to meet those objectives; and allocation of the resources and time necessary for successful implementation.[2] Loosely organized groups with no central direction may or may not achieve the same ends. Japanese initiatives, on the other hand, served as managerial and organizational devices to mobilize large numbers of managers, engineers, and other employees, as well as financial resources, to insure steady progress toward an extraordinarily difficult goal: transforming software development from a craft activity or nonstandardized service into a structured design, engineering, and production process.

Planned Economies of Scope

Economies of scale proved possible in software with projects or facilities large enough to justify the expense of developing common tools or reusable modules, or investing in training programs.[3] On the other hand, traditional notions of scale economies through mass production did not readily apply to software development beyond large individual projects, since software consisted primarily of unique or customized design efforts, and replication was a simple electronic process. As a result, the most important economies appeared to be less in sheer scale of operations and more in scope—utilizing tools, methods, designs, people, and other elements across more than one project.

The Japanese software factories became sufficiently specialized over time to identify useful tools, methods, and components for multiple projects. Yet they remained broad enough to insure a steady flow of work for thousands of programmers, including personnel at subsidiaries and subcontractors. Fujitsu, Hitachi, and NEC also entered the business of leasing software-development tools to their hardware customers, which brought in additional revenues from process R&D while spreading tools and methods, and the programming burden, among more companies and projects. Scope economies came as well through the reuse of people on similar projects.

Calculating the optimal size for a software factory, however, seemed an uncertain task. Most started with just a few hundred programmers, although Toshiba had 1,200 in 1978, one year after opening; factories in 1989 included as many as 6,000 personnel in a Hitachi facility combining systems engineers and programmers as well as workers assigned from subsidiaries and subcontractors. Size appeared to depend on how much common work a firm generated. For the top Japanese computer manufacturers, these volumes appeared to be huge, especially in custom applications development.

On the other hand, SDC failed to sustain a factory of merely 200 programmers, excluding systems engineers. This reinforces a basic lesson of operations management: Any facility may be too large if managers do not manage capacity and work flows properly. In addition to controls over where product managers constructed products, more product focus on the division level or through integration among separate SDC facilities and divisions might have enabled SDC to generate enough similar work to justify continuation of the factory and centralized process R&D. Yet this was not how SDC managers structured and operated the company in the mid-1970s. Again, Japanese firms adopted another approach. Like SDC, most of their factories started as small facilities by current standards, but companies then expanded manpower levels gradually, as needed. This represented a compromise between the quest for greater efficiency and the continuing need for flexibility, and minimized initial risks in the factory investment while guaranteeing some improved potential for realizing scope if not scale economies.

Commitment to Process Improvement

Japanese firms that launched factory efforts in the 1960s and 1970s demonstrated a stubborn commitment, not always reinforced by initial results, to analyzing, standardizing, and then improving the process of software development. In retrospect, it seems especially important that Japanese companies organized factories as permanent institutions, rather than as temporary experiments dependent on the voluntary cooperation of project managers, because payoffs required years of effort. The cost of not persisting also seems evident in SDC's case, where loss of the factory, and the research, development, and thought behind it, left the company without a means of guaranteeing process improvements or scope economies across a series of projects and signaled a serious reduction in management's commitment to solving fundamental problems in software engineering.

Unlike SDC or other U.S. firms, however, the Japanese chose not to take the lead in product innovation, and this affected their priorities in managing software technology. While Japan's position changed slightly in the 1980s, as firms took more initiatives with projects such as the Fifth Generation and TRON, Japanese companies usually adopted or closely followed standards IBM, RCA, GE, and Honeywell established. In the 1960s, they even imported software directly (except for Fujitsu). Japanese firms undertook difficult applications projects, such as for on-line banking systems or plant automation, but even these they tried to pattern after existing U.S. systems. Hence, in software as in other industries, not pursuing a leadership role in product R&D freed Japanese companies to pour their scarce engineering resources into process improvement.

The focus on process, as well as the adoption of U.S. standards, did not mean that Japanese software producers ignored product improvement in the long term. In fact, process capabilities allowed firms to differentiate products or engineering services through a combination of functionality, reliability, and low prices. Factory infrastructures also helped Japanese firms develop large, complex software systems that might have exceeded the capabilities of less efficient producers. As discussed in the Toshiba case, during the late 1970s, factory tools and methods made it possible to complete real-time control programs running into millions of lines of code that automated power-plant operations to an extent never before achieved, at least not in Japan. Hitachi, NEC, and Fujitsu also delivered huge on-line applications programs and basic software at relatively low prices, while simultaneously upgrading levels of productivity, process control, and reliability.

Product-Process Focus and Segmentation

Focus remained essential to efficiency because software products, like conventionally engineered and manufactured products, served a variety of applications and often involved different design methods, control procedures, and tools. To complicate matters, many projects or customers had unique requirements, ranging from air forces requesting antiballistic missile systems of a scale and sophistication never before built, to simple business-applications packages designed once and then replicated for many customers. To develop too many different products thus demanded an enormous range of skills and made an efficient process relatively difficult to implement.

Japanese software factories exhibited a sufficient concentration of personnel to guarantee a steady flow of work into a single facility and even some economies of scale on large projects. They also focused on related product types—such as basic software (operating systems, database systems, or related systems software), general business-applications or data-processing software (usually written in COBOL), real-time process-control software, or telecommunications. This focus simplified development tasks, enabled personnel to accumulate functional skills in software engineering as well as applications expertise, and encouraged economies of scope across projects. In addition, Japanese firms segmented products and processes by channeling nonroutine work into less structured modes of production, such as independent projects, subsidiaries, or laboratories, and by negotiating requirements for cost, features, and reliability with customers (for applications projects).

In reviewing the SDC case, a lack of product, process, and market focus becomes immediately apparent. SDC's Santa Monica facility historically performed programming jobs for the U.S. Department of Defense, but increasingly took jobs from other government and private customers. Types and volumes of work fluctuated, making it difficult to accumulate applications expertise as well as achieve factory objectives such as tool and methodology standardization, smooth divisions of labor, mechanization and automation, or systematic reuse of designs and code. For at least some projects, SDC needed to continue operating as a job shop. Given more time, SDC might have found a more satisfactory way to manage work flows or mix functional and applied skills, although management did not allow the organization and its technology to evolve.

Japanese firms did not immediately arrive at optimal management systems or levels of focus either, but they proceeded while accumulating information and experience, through trial and error. Hitachi provides an illustrative example. Managers first viewed commercial software as a single product, and founded the Software Works in 1969 to handle both operating systems and business applications, with other hardware facilities taking over programming for telecommunications and real-time control systems. Only after realizing customized applications involved different practices and costs, compared to basic software, did Hitachi introduce different standard times for applications systems, develop another set of standardized methods and tools, and eventually found a separate applications factory as well as numerous specialized subsidiaries.

Process/Quality Analysis and Control

Creating performance standards, controls, tools, methods, reusable components, or specialized tasks requires a profound understanding of the software-development process. This understanding remains incomplete for new and especially complex systems. Too much uncertainty and variability in projects also creates confusing data, perhaps leading some observers to the erroneous conclusion that all software development remains beyond control all the time. To the contrary, the cases indicated that process or quality control was possible within similar families of familiar products. This control came not simply through focus or experience; it required extensive and continuous investments in data collection and analysis, and then process refinements.

SDC, along with IBM, actually pioneered process analysis and cost modeling for software development in the 1960s, and launched its factory effort as an attempt to standardize around the best tools and techniques known to the company. The problems SDC faced after 1975 lay more in organizational implementation, although variety in projects and uncontrolled work flows detracted significantly from the effectiveness of its factory approach.

Japanese firms not only persisted with their factories, but they relentlessly collected and analyzed project data, and embraced a view of process control that linked this inextricably to quality. These attitudes came from experiences in other industries. Hitachi executives, for example, long before the establishment of a software factory, created corporate standards for budgeting and quality for all engineering and manufacturing operations. When the computer division began producing large amounts of software in the 1960s, managers who moved from hardware development and inspection to software brought with them the corporate philosophy as well as control systems that inspired one of the most intensive data collection and analysis efforts in the industry. Hitachi thus began gathering project data in the mid-1960s, even before software development had become a major activity in the company. NEC, Fujitsu, and Toshiba followed, as they encountered larger and more complex projects in numbers that exceeded the supply of skilled engineers.

The mixture of process with quality control came in several forms and had far-reaching implications. First, better quality control had a potentially large impact on productivity, such as cutting the time required to fix defects during testing, or reducing maintenance requirements after delivery. Researchers in other industries have found similar relationships, such as the more time used to repair products, the lower overall productivity, as well as customer satisfaction, sales, and, ultimately, profitability.[4]

Japanese software facilities implemented this philosophy by collecting productivity, cost, and defect data simultaneously, and introducing independent reviews that checked the quality of designs, code, and tests as well as project progress and expenditures. In some firms, quality assurance or inspection departments even took the lead in introducing productivity-improvement measures that incorporated quality objectives. Standard procedures usually called for testing until finding all expected defects, adjusting tools and methods to prevent the recurrence of defects in future projects, automating error-prone tasks such as coding, and educating employees in quality control techniques, with ambitious objectives such as zero defects. Companywide efforts also helped Japanese managers coordinate quality control techniques with standards and training, including quality circle activities. Extending quality activities to examining designs and customer responses, as Fujitsu emphasized in the 1980s, also linked quality to all activities, from product design onward, rather than restricting quality to testing or final inspection.

Tailored and Centralized Process R&D

Centralized process R&D provided benefits and tradeoffs. On the positive side, centralization allowed software facilities to exploit scale and scope economies and systematically link process technology to products and training programs. Scale as well as scope remained important because elaborate tools and techniques usually required years to refine and might have extended beyond the ability of small facilities or individual projects to afford. Since factories brought together 1,000 or more personnel to work on similar products, R&D engineers could identify common process needs while managers could justify centralized, long-term research. Permanent organizations for process R&D then made this a continuous activity, rather than a function subject to the vicissitudes of individual projects and short-term budgets. Centralized process R&D also increased the likelihood that all projects would have access to relatively good tools and techniques, and this helped reduce the need for large numbers of highly expert personnel.

On the negative side, centrally developed tools and methods might not be appropriate for new or nonroutine projects, and this could create a myriad of problems: Projects might develop poor products, causing customers to rebel; the company might waste R&D effort, if the tools and methods proved difficult to use (as NEC experienced with the SDMS tool set); development engineers and even project managers might leave the firm, especially in U.S. and European cases where no lifetime obligations restricted mobility; an organization might rely so heavily on central R&D that personnel in product divisions gradually lose the ability to adapt to different product requirements or unique customer needs. There also exists evidence that standards proved easier to adopt than to change, indicating that centralization of process R&D might constrain the ability of the organization and individuals to evolve along with the technology.

Managers, engineers, and customers probably would add to this list of pluses and minuses, yet the important observation is that Japanese software factories, and software facilities in other firms, found ways to manage potential problems. It seemed that the more focused a facility, the more routine and common problems became, and the greater the likelihood that R&D introduced properly tailored methods, tools, or reuse libraries. Companies also used R&D teams that integrated laboratory researchers pursuing advanced technologies with engineers from production facilities familiar with current products, customers, and process issues. In addition, some Japanese producers combined division laboratories with corporate laboratories and these with engineering departments within factories, as well as relied on companywide programs to pursue various aspects of process or quality improvement and on corporate staff to help transfer good process technology among divisions and subsidiaries.

Skills Standardization and Leverage

While producers managed to standardize and even automate increasing aspects of software development, it proved impossible and unwise to standardize or automate all tasks. Individual projects usually required some adaptations of designs, methods, or tools, while computer technology and customer needs continued to evolve. Nonetheless, firms temporarily standardized tools, techniques, procedures, and reusable components, and then trained employees in their use—thus achieving a measure of process standardization through skills standardization, even without direct supervision or specification of each task in each phase of each project.

New company entrants in Japanese software factories underwent a minimum two or three months of classroom instruction and spent several months more in on-the-job training. They then took a sequence of short courses or workshops every year. This training differed from simply providing general education, which many large companies around the world offered their employees, because they taught a common set of methods and tools comprising the company standards, at least for a given product family. While this approach still might overly constrain creativity, it also increased the possibility of establishing a more predictable and repeatable process while raising average performance levels—thus leveraging whatever skills individuals, and the organization as a whole, possessed. Managers also claimed that training in a standard process facilitated communication among different groups, such as eliminating potential debates over which tools or methods to use, and made it possible to add personnel to late projects without making them later—a practice once thought impossible with software. One might further argue that encouraging young minds to value teamwork, product reliability, or reusability as much as individual creativity provided another way to insure that employees viewed their potential contributions from a larger perspective and adopted organizational rather than merely individual or project-centered goals.

Japanese producers, like the U.S. consulting firm discussed in Chapter Two, also tended to hire college graduates unskilled in software engineering and then educate them in their standardized process. This hiring practice lessened the possibility new employees would reject factory tools and methods, since nonexperts probably had no exposure to another approach. The Japanese also combined advanced training programs with career paths, providing a mechanism for management to create a pool of people skilled in a standardized process and to move them around as well as forward in the organization to become designers, systems engineers, tool and methodology developers, or managers. This provision for both continuing education and promotion appeared particularly important in software precisely because talented workers constituted the most important assets of the organization, and they might well be the least content to do relatively simple tasks such as coding for long periods of time.

Standardization of skills supported divisions of tasks and labor, a basic feature of conventional factories, although the cases suggest that firms observed limitations to this practice. Since much of software development involves design and testing around specific applications, it may be just as important for designers, and sometimes coders and testers, to be as familiar with a particular application as they are with programming languages or software-engineering tools and techniques. Managers in Japanese software factories recognized this and allowed systems engineers and some other personnel to specialize in applications areas. Furthermore, with products where no one customer or set of customers defined specifications precisely, such as operating systems or applications packages, factories did not organizationally separate design from program construction, but used integrated teams to complete all development phases. These teams probably facilitated experimentation and communication by reducing delays or errors in transforming specifications into executable code, though with the tradeoff of a potentially reduced ability for management to leverage the skills of its best engineers across many projects, except for the important area of package reuse.

Dynamic Standardization

Like flexibility and efficiency, or applications versus functional expertise, the terms *dynamic* and *standardization* usually had opposite connotations. While software factories experienced a constant tension between the need to standardize and the need to keep up with an evolving technology, they also managed this tension effectively.

Most important, Japanese managers viewed standards as dynamic. For example, led by Hitachi and NEC in the late 1960s, they introduced standard times for all activities and made these the basis of project management. These times soon became obsolete, with the appearance of new tools and methods, and increased knowledge about the development process. Rather than treat these measures as permanent, however, all institutionalized the practice of reviewing standard times annually. Nor did Japanese software factories stagnate technologically. Large R&D efforts insured a steady stream of new methods and tools as well as continual evaluations of how well existing technology performed.

It was true that, following the lead of U.S. firms in the 1970s, Japanese firms standardized around tools and techniques now considered outmoded by some software specialists. In fact, no Japanese factory used radically new process technology; all relied on conventional languages, though modified for use with code generators and diagramming tools, as well as life-cycle models of software development, structured design and programming, and flow charts for detailed program design. The Japanese did not strictly adhere to these concepts when better approaches seemed useful; for example, they did not always design in a top-down, structured manner, and frequently built programs around existing designs and code, as well as prototypes. Japanese factories were also gradually replacing structured diagrams or flow charts to write detailed program designs with other techniques, such as machine-readable pseudo-code, menus and templates, as well as graphical representations.

The Japanese factories and their suppliers not only introduced relatively advanced tools but used new and old tools wisely, refining and then exploiting proven technologies. In the case of flow charts, because Japanese programmers usually lacked fluency in English, the medium of most computer languages, it appeared easier for them to diagram program designs rather than writing computer code directly from specifications—possibly a faster approach for native English speakers or experienced software engineers. Standardized formats for flow charts, however, helped in quality control, maintenance, and productivity by making program structures easier to understand, debug, change, and reuse. In addition, Japanese as well as other firms eliminated error-prone coding by developing tools that read the diagrams and automatically generated code in different languages.

Systematic Reusability

Conventional factory production has been synonymous with standardized, interchangeable, mass-produced parts—a simple way to increase productivity while guaranteeing a particular level of product quality and cost. Since software developers divide large programs into modules, some parts should, in theory, be reusable. In practice, reuse faced strategic, technical, and organizational obstacles.

From the producer's perspective, reusability restricted the introduction of new features into products, because it emphasized building programs at least partially similar to existing ones. From the perspective of individual developers, requirements to reuse other people's code might involve compromises in design, if programmers felt they could make a better product. Customers might also object to reuse if this limited them to products ill suited to their individual needs or insufficiently differentiated from those available to competitors. Software packages offered the most efficient form of reuse, but could not completely replace customized programs, especially in the large computer segments of the industry, because most customers required some special features or tailoring of their programs and databases. This turned out to be particularly true in Japan, where package sales remained far below the United States (though increasing rapidly with the diffusion of smaller computers and better packages, including U.S. imports).

To overcome some of these problems, Japanese firms identified ways to promote reusability in relatively flexible ways; for example, they mixed packages with new code, thus giving customers the option of buying a *semicustomized* product rather than either a standardized package or a fully customized system. Japanese factories also emphasized the reuse of designs as much or more than executable code; this made it easier to modify features for different customers or reuse software across incompatible operating systems and hardware architectures. In addition, writing new designs and code for reusability, and depositing new parts in reuse libraries, created a continually expanding inventory of components. Raising reusability to the level of a factory policy also seemed to counteract objections by programmers to reusing other people's work and the reluctance of project managers to absorbing overhead costs associated with designing, documenting, and testing software for general usage rather than for a specific application.

SDC provides a useful comparison in several dimensions. The company included reusability among its factory goals and managers initially hoped to increase reuse simply through the standardization of what they considered to be good programming and documentation practices, including structured design and modular techniques. The SDC factory also created a core of people who could draw on their past experiences, and potentially employ code or designs from similar past projects when creating new systems; however, the decision to make code reuse a factory objective, in retrospect, proved impractical, given the variety in SDC projects and perhaps other factors, such as the tendency of structured programs to tie individual modules to higher and lower levels of modules in a hierarchical tree arrangement, thereby restricting reuse or modifications of components.[5]

SDC also lacked a formal strategy and system to promote whatever reusability might have been technically feasible across projects. This oversight, coupled with portability problems and machine diversity, meant that, even within the range of projects where the factory recycled designs or code, SDC primarily achieved reuse *accidentally*, that is, when applications and hardware turned out to be identical or very similar, and when people knew precisely what they or others had done in the past. In contrast, more product focus, larger scales of operation, and more compatible hardware helped Japanese software developers continually generate large amounts of similar and thus potentially reusable program components. Moreover, Japanese managers, as they gained experience and data, learned not to leave reuse only to chance; it became the focus of an integrated process consisting of tools and libraries, training in particular techniques, and incentives as well as controls for programmers and project managers.

Toshiba again provides an excellent counterexample, since management explicitly treated reusability as the central strategy for increasing productivity and product reliability while lowering costs. In fact, more than other Japanese facilities studied, Toshiba attempted to operate a true factory in the sense of separating high-level design and then building new programs by assembling components from an inventory of existing designs and code for specific product families. Other Japanese software facilities followed some of these practices, especially in business applications, but without the degree of strategic planning, organization, and control at Toshiba.

Nowhere else did management require personnel to register a certain number of modules for reuse each month (although management rewarded programmers who wrote frequently reused modules, rather than directly penalizing programmers who did not, suggesting that Toshiba used this control system in a positive manner). To facilitate reuse, Toshiba also had unique committees that decided what type of generic modules the factory needed and then allocated resources to develop these components for reuse libraries. Hitachi, NEC, and Fujitsu (as well as NTT and Mitsubishi), in contrast, generally screened newly written programs either for modules or whole programs that might be reusable, and then modified them if necessary.

One must not overestimate the extent and nature of reuse in Japanese firms. Like their counterparts elsewhere in the world, Japanese mainly confined the recycling of components to similar product families.[6] This suggests that more redundancy and opportunities for reuse existed across different types of products, perhaps through new design techniques or more advanced computer languages and architectures. Whatever the future, however, accumulations of practical experience, as well as research, and a steadfast commitment to exploiting reusability to improve both productivity and quality, suggested that the Japanese would probably remain among industry leaders in pursuing ways to improve reuse of software components even across seemingly dissimilar products.

Computer-Aided Tools and Integration

For several years, producers of textiles, machine tools, semiconductors, and specialty metal components have used automated tools that supported product customization by identifying redundancies in designs and helping engineers reconfigure standardized parts for new applications. Tools based on the same concept began appearing in software firms during the late 1970s and early 1980s to facilitate complex design and testing operations, reduce time spent in relatively routine tasks such as coding or documentation, help locate software components for reuse and maintenance, and ease project-data collection and analysis as well as control over budgets and schedules. In this sense, rather than investing in many highly skilled engineers and asking them to design new products from scratch for each customer, software producers, like firms in other industries, had the option of investing in tools that, in effect, captured the expertise of a few individuals and then disseminated this knowledge through preset or automated functions.

One family of tools, such as DECA, YPS, and PAD (with compilers), automated the transformation of design diagrams into executable programs in several languages. More advanced tools, such as SEA/1, EA-GLE, BAGLES, and PARADIGM, built programs, mainly in COBOL, through menus and databases of reusable program patterns and modules. These tools grew in capability continuously in the sense that their libraries of reusable parts expanded with each newly written program, although most did not generate code in more than one language. (Hitachi's EAGLE tool was an exception.) Toshiba relied heavily on design-support tools and semiautomated program generators to develop more complex real-time programs, mixing this approach with designs in specialized high-level languages that were also executable. Fujitsu's Software CAD and other tools represented yet another level of sophistication, turning graphical representations into designs and then code potentially in a variety of languages, and applying some basic concepts from the field of artificial intelligence. Producing entirely new programs from conversational requirements remained restricted to R&D, although Japanese as well as U.S. and European firms had numerous efforts in this area.

Yet, unlike in SDC's early planning of its factory, in no Japanese case did tools dominate the process. At Hitachi, not until the end of the 1970s (a decade after founding the Software Works) did management introduce standardized tools for project management and development support (CAPS and CASD) and require their use. Even Toshiba, which from 1977 centered its factory organization around the SWB, created simple tools first and then more sophisticated ones after 1980. Fujitsu also waited until the 1980s to start major tool-development efforts, except for project management, and this gave managers and researchers more time to decide what they would need and what would prove enduring.

In contrast, SDC managers and R&D engineers initially viewed a factory process as consisting mainly of tools or automation. They revised this view on learning that tools required a standardized methodology as well as an organizational structure to support their use. Subsequently, they discovered the difficulty of creating general-purpose tools for a wide variety of projects and hardware. In fact, SDC replaced nearly all the original factory tools through what managers termed a natural process of evolution, while the standardized methodology, codified in the *Software Development Manual*, turned out to be the most lasting element of its software factory.

A tighter product focus and customers that used a limited variety of hardware appeared to make it easier for Japanese firms to standardize tools. Nevertheless, Japanese firms usually spent years in process analysis and methods standardization before committing to major tool efforts, and they deliberately integrated tool development with standard methods and training. Nor did Japanese firms, with the possible exception of NEC, overly centralize tool or methodology R&D. In general, the evolution of Japanese factories supports the conclusion that, however important tools have become in software development, the process remains sufficiently dependent on human thought and experience that most problems continue to be managerial and organizational as much as or even more than technological in nature.

Tools also had a negative side. They restricted the degree of customization and innovation in products as well as development approaches. Product features and programmer skills could also evolve only along with or within the boundaries tools and other standards established. Highly creative employees might resent the control implicit in the use of any standards or automation. These and other potential problems made it imperative that firms tailor as well as centralize tool and methodology development, and make continual efforts to combine the insights of factory engineers with laboratory researchers in the pursuit of ever-more versatile and useful tools and methods.

Incremental Product and Variety Improvement

Few markets remain stagnant, and whatever their gains in process efficiency, Japanese software producers had to offer more and better products to survive, especially because U.S. firms began actively moving into the Japanese market in the late 1980s. Listings of Japanese weaknesses in software continued to cite the lack of product sophistication and the paucity of software packages. Nonetheless, the Japanese also had real strengths in productivity and product reliability. And while survey data of customer satisfaction also indicated that they trailed in basic software and office systems, Japanese producers generally surpassed U.S. firms operating in Japan in the largest segment of the Japanese market—customized applications systems. Furthermore, having made great strides in managing the process of software development, Japanese firms were now paying more attention to design and to improving product functionality, ease of use, and, to some degree, variety.

It also remained true in software, and no doubt in other industries as well, that an efficient process may be a prerequisite for firms to deliver complex products quickly and within specified levels of quality and cost. Toshiba, for example, relied on its factory infrastructure to produce huge real-time programs, first for a limited number of uses and gradually for more applications. Hitachi, NEC, and Fujitsu did not necessarily expand the product lines of their facilities as much as Toshiba, but they appeared to deliver large, reliable systems efficiently. They also had sufficient resources to extend the capabilities of their tools (which consisted of a type of software program) and place increasing emphasis on packages, either sold alone or integrated within customized systems, as an alternative available to customers in place of fully tailored software. In all cases, furthermore, the Japanese firms were actively establishing new subsidiaries to handle the increasing demand for more and different types of software in Japan.

Future Prospects

What future seemed likely for the software factory? In other industries, rigid automation and control, such as in the plant Ford used to produce the Model-T car, were revolutionary but temporary steps in a movement beyond the craft or job-shop stage. The current trends in engineering and manufacturing, led by Japanese firms such as Toyota, leaned toward more versatile machinery and production practices, and even relatively skilled workers. On the surface, these seemed like steps backward from the Model-T era and movements closer again to the higher variety, smaller production volumes, and higher skill requirements of craft or job-shop production. In reality, companies had come to recognize that combinations of efficiency and flexibility allowed them to meet various and changing customer needs more effectively than simply maximizing one dimension (Figure 9.1).

To a large extent, the Japanese merely continued efforts begun at IBM, SDC, and other U.S. firms in the 1960s and 1970s to bring software closer to the standards of industrial engineering and manufacturing practice—even though firms had to make unique products or modify designs for different customers, and engineers still did not fully understand why specifying requirements and transforming them into code usually proved harder than anticipated. Because the size and complexity of programs kept expanding along with dramatic increases in the capabilities of both large and small computers, countries continued to predict huge shortages of software engineers and backlogs for customized programs well into the future. (The Japanese alone, for example, estimated they would have a shortage of nearly 1 million systems engineers and programmers by the year 2000).[7] For these and other reasons, companies were likely to continue refining the concepts, tools, and techniques now used in Japanese software factories.

Current R&D efforts and technological trends both supported and contradicted factory approaches, depending on how firms chose to proceed; for example, operating systems such as UNIX, languages such as Ada and C, abstraction and object-oriented programming techniques, greater use of computer-aided design and program-generation tools, and increasing standardization of operating systems, hardware architectures, graphics, and various interface specifications—all could help both factories and nonfactories operate more smoothly and overcome shortages of skilled personnel. Tools, techniques, and products under development at cooperative or government-sponsored projects around the

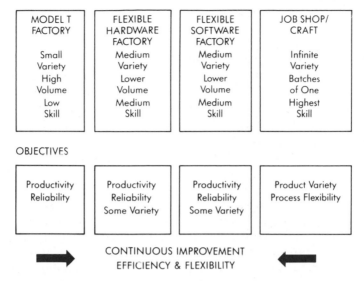

Figure 9.1 Production-Management Objectives.

world (such as Sigma, TRON, FASET, and even the Fifth Generation in Japan; various efforts sponsored by the Department of Defense as well as the Microelectronics and Computer Corporation in the United States; and the EUREKA and ESPRIT projects in Europe) also promised benefits, but no quick or magical solutions.

Another issue revolved around centralization and scale. Powerful desk-top computers or work stations, interconnected through local area networks, would continue to make distributed programming by small groups, rather than centralized development in large facilities, attractive for many software producers and users. Tools such as SEA/1, EAGLE, and BAGLES could also serve as portable software factories. It thus remained possible that distributed programming and electronic networks, as well as automation, would render large, centralized organizations of software developers, software factories, obsolete! Japanese firms even encouraged this trend to some degree. To ease the variety and capacity burdens on their in-house facilities, they actively supported distributed programming through subsidiaries and subcontractors, "satellite offices" (as at NEC), and leasing of tools to customers.

Although obsolescence constituted a possible future for software factories, the market for computer programs seemed sufficiently large and diversified for both centralized and distributed development approaches to coexist for different applications, just as job shops continued to serve customers along with larger engineering and production organizations in other industries. Physical centralization and the ability of project personnel to meet face to face also provided certain benefits, such as facilitating communication and problem solving—a critical concern for transforming software designs into code in general but especially for those instances, even in relatively routine projects, when developers encountered unusual or new requirements.[8]

The electronic nature of computer programming and support tools brings up another dimension that, while not the focus of this study, has become a major area of research in itself: Software factories represented a new type of large-scale production organization, where the "workers" differed from employees in conventional factories. There really were no true assembly lines, staffed by employees with minimal skills doing highly routinized tasks, such as making huge numbers of identical components and putting them together through a strictly controlled, sequential process. Software-factory employees remained relatively skilled and well educated, compared to factory workers in other industries; and most of their "work" consisted of meetings to coordinate tasks, individual and group planning and design (using thoughts, paper, and computer screens), product construction (mainly on computer screens), and testing as well as fixing and redesign (also mainly on computer screens).[9]

Accordingly, management in software factories also differed from conventional production facilities. The usual decision-making algorithms relying on economies of scale and learning curves to determine precisely the time and cost of different operations did not readily apply. In fact, some writers even lamented the appearance of diseconomies of scale: average productivity levels decreasing as the number of members in a project, or the size of a program, increased beyond a certain manageable level.[10] Diseconomies of scale suggested a potential limit to the size of software factories, although the real units of complexity were programs and projects, and at least Japanese managers found they could alter conventional wisdom through standardization of methods, tools, and training, as well as product focus and channeling nonroutine work to other sites. Be this as it may, most factories continued to rely on an iterative series of design and redesign operations, many highly dependent on the experience and skills of individuals, and most difficult and unwise to control precisely, especially when products had to be unique, customized, or even invented. What Japanese managers achieved in practice, therefore, consisted primarily of placing boundaries on unfamiliarity—in required inputs, the development process, and required outputs—and creating economies of scope across related but distinct projects.

The cases also suggest a need for software managers to adopt more of a strategic and contingency perspective as their counterparts in other industries have done for many years. The factory approach might not be appropriate for every market segment and competitive position. At the same time, this research supports another view that departs strongly from those who would insist software development forever remain an art or craft. Not only are more structured approaches possible to introduce, but, by not pursuing process refinements, managers may be wasting human and capital resources as well as the opportunity to improve the competitive capabilities of the firm.

It therefore seems a mistake to interpret the software factory as an overly rigid or outdated mode of organization operating within the wrong paradigm, or even as a facility requiring a certain size or centralization of operations. To understand the true origin and character of these facilities, it is useful to recall the comment of NEC's Yukio Mizuno that the software factory was essentially a *concept*, not a thing: a philosophy that at least some software could be produced in a manner more akin to engineering and manufacturing than craft or cottage-industry practices. While Hitachi, Toshiba, NEC, and Fujitsu did not reinvent product standards or even the fundamental process technology employed in their own factories, they put together the ideas, techniques, tools, and people—the technology and the organizations—that made the factory concept work, and work better than ad hoc approaches used earlier. The software factory thus reflected neither narrowness of mind nor lack of imagination, but a desire to affect history, to move forward the state of a new and complex technology.

Whether or not readers agree the factory metaphor is appropriate for developing computer programs, this author hopes they have come to share another conviction: that software provides a remarkably rich setting to explore the management of a new technology and the evolution of firms from a craft to factorylike process. Since the 1960s, managers of software development have struggled with measuring and improving efficiency in design as well as in product construction, testing, and customer service. They have dealt with product and process innovation as a fundamental strategic issue and practical constraint, with some realizing, as managers have in other industries, that the software market is not one but many, and that not all customers need or can afford the programming equivalent of a Rolls Royce car or a Michelangelo painting. They have faced questions such as when to maximize the autonomy of people to increase the likelihood of innovative products; and when to impose standardized procedures, methods, tools, designs, or training that may hinder a few but aid the performance of many.

Managers from every company interviewed during this research stated that improvements in software-process technology remained both necessary and possible. All believed that the critical problems were more managerial and organizational than technological, and that solving them required nothing less than a strategic, integrated approach such as described in this book and associated, at least metaphorically, with the term *factory*. Comparisons with U.S. firms suggest that, while the Japanese appeared more alike than different in their methods and tools, they had integrated and refined these to a considerable degree, and made remarkable progress in the development of all types of software, especially large-scale customized applications. At the very least, Japanese firms had built sufficient software capabilities to support their sales of extremely competitive hardware with program products that were high in reliability and low in price.

The historical methods used to pursue this topic appeared unusual to some participants in the study. To this author, however, determining how firms have evolved seemed a logical starting point to consider future prospects—an approach eloquently sanctioned in a recent report on the state of computer technology: "People built bridges that stayed up and airplanes that flew, long before scientists discovered the underlying mathematical principles and structures. If we want to make further progress in software, we must go back to study what can be done and what has been done, until we find out how to do it well. . . ."[11]

APPENDIXES

SURVEY OF MANAGER EMPHASES:
THE PROCESS SPECTRUM

The published descriptions and stated objectives for the SDC Software Factory provided a basis for drawing up eight criteria relating to inputs standardization (emphasis on reuse of software code), and tool and process standardization and control. The objective was to compare software managers on a few basic questions to examine a simple hypothesis: that not all software managers managed their facilities like job shops, but that there was a spectrum in the responses to these questions, with some reflecting practices resembling job shops and others factories (that is, a high emphasis on standardization and control as well as reusability).

The SDC Software Factory infrastructure consisted of a centralized program library to store modules, documentation, and completed programs; a central database to track production-management information; a uniform set of procedures for specification, design, coding, testing, and documentation; standardized project databases to guide individuals and groups constructing different parts of a program; and an on-line computerized interface linking various tools and databases. These five variables constituted the core process and tool questions in the survey. Since another factory characteristic was to produce standardized components and then to reuse them, rather than "reinventing the wheel" with every customer order, three questions were included about design for reuse, execution of reusability, and control (monitoring of reuse rates).

Major software producers in Japan and North America were identified through literature surveys and lists of software producers; further investigation led to the identification of senior managers either responsible for overall software-engineering management or with responsibilities over several projects and with sufficient experience to present an overview of practices_for an entire facility or product division. The intention was to study managers at the facility or product-division level, since software practices usually differed significantly among divisions in diversified or large firms, and some diversity seemed useful to meet different market or internal needs.

Managers who agreed to participate in the survey received a questionnaire containing the eight core questions plus more than a dozen other questions asking for supplementary data.[1] For the core questions, they had to rank their emphasis and impression of general policy at their facilities on a scale of 0 to 4, as well as to comment on each answer. Optional questions also requested performance measures such as actual rates of reused code in a recent sample year. The intent of the survey and meaning of questions was explained at least to the individuals in each firm handling distribution of the questionnaires. Japanese managers were sent questionnaires in English but asked to comment on each question either in Japanese or English.

The sample was limited to facilities or departments making products that usually require large amounts of people, time, and tools to develop, and that might therefore provide incentives for managers at least on the facility or division level to seek similarities and common components or tools across different projects: operating systems for mainframes or minicomputers ("systems" software), and various applications programs, such as for factory control or reservations systems ("applications" software). For data analysis, these were further broken down into telecommunications software (applications and systems were combined because of the smallness of the sample); commercial operating systems; industrial operating systems; real-time control applications; and general business applications.

All the Japanese firms contacted filled out the survey and approximately 75 percent of the other firms contacted completed the survey. To check answers, two managers at each firm or facility were asked to respond, although only about one-third of the companies returned two completed surveys for each type of facility. Among those, the answers were remarkably similar, differing by only a few percentage points, and therefore were averaged. Two-thirds of the answers, however, represented single responses.[2]

A factor analysis procedure with varimax rotation indicated that the eight questions constituted two approximately orthogonal factors, listed as the inputs and tool and process dimensions in Table A.1. Both factors had an eigenvalue rounding to approximately 1.0 or higher and together explained nearly 82 percent of the variance in the survey answers; the inputs dimension alone accounted for 62.3 percent of the variance (Ta-

Table A.1 Survey of Software Development Managers and Sample Outline (N − 52: 25 Japanese, 26 U.S., 1 Canadian)

Survey Questions

Answer Key:
4 = Capability or policy is fully used or enforced
3 = Capability or policy is frequently used or enforced
2 = Capability or policy is sometimes used or enforced
1 = Capability or policy is seldom used or enforced
0 = Capability or policy is not used

Dimension I: Inputs Standardization (max. score = 12)
1. Formal management promotion (beyond the discretion of individual project managers) that new code be written in modular form with the intention that modules (in addition to common subroutines) will then serve as reusable "units of production" in future projects.
2. Formal management promotion (beyond the discretion of individual project managers) that, if a module designed to perform a specific function (in addition to common subroutines) is in the program library system, rather than duplicating such a module, it should be reused.
3. Monitoring of how much code is being reused.

Dimension II: Tool and Process Standardization and Control (max. score = 20)
4. Project databases standardized for all groups working on the same product components, to support consistency in building of program modules, configuration management, documentation, maintenance, and potential reusability of code.
5. A system interface providing the capability to link support tools, project databases, the centralized production database and program libraries.
6. A centralized program library system to store modules and documentation.
7. A central production or development database connecting programming groups working on a single product family to track information on milestones, task completion, resources, and system components, to facilitate overall project control and to serve as a data source for statistics on programmer productivity, costs, scheduling accuracy, etc.
8. A uniform set of specification, design, coding, testing, and documentation procedures used among project groups within a centralized facility or across different sites working on the same product family to facilitate standardization of practices and/or division of labor for programming tasks and related activities.

Total for 8 Variables (max. score of 32 = 100%)

bles A.2 and A.3). For each dimension, the variables with a strong loading (minimum 0.4) were summed and used to test differences in the average Japanese and North American (United States plus one Canadian) scores, as well as to test if product type or country of origin of the facility were significantly correlated with the process and reuse scores.[3]

The data reported in Table A.4 reflects scores for each dimension. Table A.5 summarizes the average Japanese and North American responses to the inputs and process/tools dimensions. Table A.6 presents the results of analysis of variance tests to determine the effects of product types or country of origin on the scores reported for the two dimensions. Tables A.7 and A.8 compare reuse rates reported by the Japanese and North American facilities, and analyze correlations with type of

Table A.2 Eigenvalues and Percent of Variance

Factor	Eigenvalue	% of Variance	Cumulative %
1	2.67789	62.3	62.3
2	0.83910	19.5	81.9
3	0.55606	12.9	94.8
4	0.18915	4.4	99.2
5	0.03456	0.8	100.0

product and country of origin. Table A.9 is a regression analysis looking at the correlation between manager responses and reported reuse rates.

The results support the observation that there is a spectrum among managers in how they view aspects of software development reflected in the survey questions. Despite potential views of software development as largely a craft, art, or job-shop type of operation, some managers at facilities making similar types of products clearly placed more emphasis on control and standardization of inputs (reusable code) as well as basic tools and process questions. The analysis of variance tests confirmed that product types, at least defined generally, had no significant impact on where managers scored on either of the dimensions surveyed.

The data also suggest there are national differences in reusability emphasis. Japanese firms scored much higher on the inputs (8.7 to 5.9) dimension (significant at 0.0002), while there was no significant difference in Japanese and North American responses on the tools and process dimension. Reported actual reuse rates in Japan were also significantly higher than in North America (34.8 percent versus 15.4 percent), across all product types. This and other performance data are very tentative and subject to different methods of counting across firms. Nonethe-

Table A.3 Varimax Rotated Factor Matrix

Variables	Factors	1 Inputs	2 Tools/Process
Library		−0.06662	**0.63247**
Central database		0.26191	**0.55332**
Project database		0.32525	**0.65562**
Interface		0.34905	**0.59072**
Uniformity		0.12332	**0.41300**
Design for reuse		**0.79099**	0.27294
Reuse promotion		**0.75342**	0.02807
Monitoring reuse		**0.47341**	0.22997

Note: Bold numbers indicate those variables that loaded significantly on either Factor 1 or Factor 2. These were therefore included as the variables in the two factors for the factor analyses.

Table A.4 Summary and Ranking of Survey Scores (%)
(N = 52: 25 Japanese, 26 U.S., 1 Canadian)

Company/Facility	Inputs (max. score = 12)	Tools/Process (max. score = 20)
Telecommunications Software		
*NTT Applications	11	16
*Mitsubishi Electric	9	17
*Fujitsu Communications	9	15
*NEC Switching Systems	9	14
AT&T (Bell Labs Applications)	7	16
Bell Communications Research	6	15
*Hitachi Totsuka Works	6	13
*NTT Systems	6	12
Bell North Research	5	20
Commercial Operating Systems		
Digital VAX (layered products)	11	16
*NEC Software Ltd.	10	18
*NEC Fuchu Factory	9	18
IBM-Endicott	8	17
*†Hitachi Software Works	8	15
†Control Data	7	17.5
Digital VMS	7	16
*†Fujitsu Numazu Factory	7	16
*Mitsubishi Electric	7	12
†Unisys/Sperry	5.5	12
Data General	5	13.5
IBM-Raleigh	2	17
Real-Time Control Applications		
*Toshiba Software Factory	12	16
*NEC Industrial Systems	12	16
Unisys/SDC	11	14
*Hitachi Omika Works	10	15
TRW	9	20
†Unisys/Sperry	8	20
*Mitsubishi Electric	8	15
Hughes Aircraft	5.5	17
†Boeing	3	16
†Honeywell	2	10
†Draper Laboratories	1	6.5
Industrial Operating Systems		
*Toshiba Software Factory	12	16
†Boeing	3	15
Business Applications		
*Nippon Systemware	11	14
*Nippon Business Consultants	10	11
*†Fujitsu Kamata Software Factory	9.5	15
Martin Marietta/MD	9.5	13
*NEC Information Services	9	19
†Control Data	9	18
*Hitachi Omori Works	8	15
*NEC Mita	8	15
*†Hitachi Software Engineering	7.5	9
IBM (Office Products)	7	16
Arthur Anderson	7	20

(continued)

Table A.4 (*Continued*)

Company/Facility	Inputs (max. score = 12)	Tools/Process (max. score = 20)
†EDS/GM	6	12.5
Cullinet	6	13
*Nippon Electronics Development	6	7
*Mitsubishi Electric	4	10
Martin Marietta/Denver	3	14
†Computervision	3	6
Digital (Educational Products)	3	5

*Japanese facilities; †averaged responses.
Note: See Figure 1.1 for a graphical representation of this data.

less, the reuse data indicate that Japanese applications producers, who clearly are marketing customized products, as well as Japanese systems producers, who sell unique basic software, both tend to rely on reused code. The emphasis on reuse even in commercial operating systems is less easily explainable than for applications software, although the compatibility of a firm's hardware architectures and operating systems across different size machines, such as with Digital's VAX line, is an important factor facilitating reusability. As shown in Table A.9, it also appeared that manager emphases had some impact on process outcomes. There was a significant correlation between high emphases on reusability and high reported rates of actual reuse.

Most of the firms in the survey were producing either systems software (operating systems or telecommunications systems), which can be semi-customized depending on hardware considerations as well as design strategies; or custom applications software (real-time control or business applications). Some clearly appeared to be in the high-end of the market, such as Draper Laboratories and Honeywell, which designed unique command-control missile systems and other programs, largely for government use. They did not emphasize reuse of code across different projects and operated largely in project or job-shop modes of organization; however, some of their direct competitors—Unisys/SDC, TRW,

Table A.5 Comparison of Average Japanese and North American Survey Scores

Dimension	Japanese (n = 25)	North American (n = 27)	Sample Average (N = 52)
Inputs	8.7 (2.1)*	5.9 (2.7)	7.3 (2.4)
Tools/Process	14.4 (2.9)	15.0 (3.7)	14.7 (3.3)

*$p < 0.01$; standard deviations are in parentheses.

Table A.6 Effects of Country and Product Type: Analysis of Variance Test

	Variable	F-ratio	Sig. Level	Degrees of Freedom
Effects on Inputs	Country*	17.128	0.0002	1
Scores	Product type†	0.200	0.9367	4
Effects on Tools/	Country*	0.066	0.8013	1
Process Scores	Product type†	1.395	0.2522	4

*Coded as 0 = Japanese facility, 1 = North American facility; †coded as 1 = telecommunications software, 2 = commercial operating systems, 3 = industrial operating systems, 4 = real-time control applications, 5 = general applications.

and Unisys/Sperry—appeared to place more emphasis on reuse, as well as other measures of process control or tool standardization and integration that might be associated with a more factorylike approach.

The only firms in this sample that developed applications packages on a significant scale were IBM, Cullinet, and Computervision. They also showed a range in emphases, suggesting IBM placed relatively more emphasis on reuse, while Computervision appeared to operate more in a job shop or perhaps laboratory mode, with very little emphasis on the variables examined in the survey.

There are, of course, several caveats to this study. First, the survey represents no more than a sampling of the self-reported opinions of one or two middle-level managers from major software producing firms, rather than a comprehensive analysis of actual practices in projects done within a product group in a particular firm. Managers might be exaggerating or understating their emphases on the various questions, although the respondents were carefully selected and an attempt was made to examine the comments and other documents, such as technical articles, and to interview managers in person or by phone, and visit some actual sites, to see if answers corresponded to realities. Detailed interviews and/or site visits were conducted for NTT, Mitsubishi, Fujitsu, NEC, Hitachi, Digital Equipment Corporation, IBM, Data General, Unisys/SDC, Draper, Nippon Systemware, Hitachi, Hitachi Software Engineering, and Nippon Business Consultants.

Table A.7 Comparison of Reported Japanese and North American Reuse Rates

Japanese (n = 18)	North American (n = 18)	Sample Average (N = 36)
34.8% (18.3)*	15.4% (14.1)	25.1% (16.3)

*p < 0.01; standard deviations are in parentheses.

Table A.8 Effects of Country and Product Type on
Reuse Rates: Analysis of Variance Test (N = 36)

Variable	F-ratio	Sig. Level	Degrees of Freedom
Country*	12.728	0.0014	1
Product Type†	1.188	0.3395	4

*Coded as 0 = Japanese facility, 1 = North American facility; †coded
as 1 = telecommunications software, 2 = commercial operating systems, 3 = industrial operating systems, 4 = real-time control applications, 5 = general applications.

Another reservation regarding the survey is that, although managers
were asked to report on general practices in their areas, some companies
reported high levels of variability within product groups. This appeared
to be especially true in the cases of Digital and Hitachi Software Engineering. In Digital, while there were rigorous corporate guidelines, management placed more emphasis on the characteristics of final products
rather than the development process, and individual groups were allowed considerable autonomy, especially in applications. Thus, while
there was a management policy of stressing reusability, some project
managers, even within the VAX and VMS product areas, did not appear
to emphasize reuse at all.[4] In the case of Hitachi Software Engineering,
some groups worked directly within Hitachi's software factories, following the factory procedures and using the factory tools with the same
degree of conformance as Hitachi employees. Other groups worked on
independent projects where customers determined the standards. For
this reason, there was a large variation within Hitachi Software Engineering as a company and within product areas, and thus managers felt
compelled to score themselves on the low end of the spectrum, even
though they managed many projects using procedures identical to
Hitachi's.[5]

Furthermore, since the sample size is relatively small in absolute numbers, the results of this analysis must be considered as no more than

Table A.9 Reuse Emphasis and Reported Reuse Rates: Multiple Regression Test*

Ind. Variable	Coeff.	Standard Error	t Value	Sig. Level
Constant	3.234807	14.155589	0.2285	0.8207
Inputs	3.295832	1.036561	3.1796	0.0033
Tools	−1.080677	1.47857	−0.7309	0.4702
Process	0.450292	1.588475	0.2835	0.7786

*36 observations fitted, forecast(s) computed for 15 missing values of dependent variable.
R-Squared (Adjusted) = 0.1876; Standard Error of Estimate = 16.996120; Durbin-Watson Statistic =
2.020.

suggestive of managerial emphases existing at the participating software facilities. It should be noted, however, that the surveyed Japanese firms accounted for the vast majority of software written and sold in Japan, and the surveyed North American firms included most of the large producers of operating systems and applications software, and other basic software products such as databases.[6]

B

JAPANESE AND U.S. PROJECT PERFORMANCE

Another part of this research project collected data on software productivity, quality, reusability, and other measures to explore if there were observable differences between a comparable sample of projects from U.S. and Japanese companies. The details of this research and the statistical analyses, done jointly with Professor Chris F. Kemerer of the M.I.T. Sloan School of Management, are reported elsewhere.[1] This appendix summarizes the survey and findings.

The first task was to compile a list of major software producers in each country that also seemed comparable in terms of product or project size and applications. Names of firms came from annual lists of the largest software producers in U.S. and Japanese publications.[2] The next step identified project managers or their superiors in these firms willing to complete a standardized data-collection form. Managers at forty-three companies or sites in the United States agreed to complete the form; twenty-seven (58 percent) were returned, from eleven firms. Managers at twenty-six companies or sites in Japan agreed to complete the form; twenty (77 percent) were returned, from nine firms (Table B.1). After review of the returned forms, in several cases augmentation of some incomplete forms or clarification of some responses was attempted by telephone or letter. Overall, the response rate for returns was forty-eight (69 percent) out of seventy, and forty (83 percent) out of the forty-eight were usable for this research, although not every data-collection form

Table B.1 Participants in the Project Performance Study

U.S. Sites/Product Areas
Amdahl/Product Software
Amdahl/Engineering Software
AT&T Bell Laboratories/Switching & Communications (2 projects)
AT&T Bell Laboratories/Transaction Processing
Computervision/Computer-Aided Manufacturing
Computervision/Drafting
Computervision/Research & Development
Financial Planning Technologies/Planning Systems
Harris Corporation/Government Support Systems (3 projects)
Hewlett-Packard/Medical Division (2 projects)
Honeywell/Corporate Systems (3 projects)
Hughes Aircraft/Communications & Data Processing (3 projects)
International Business Machines/Basic Systems Software
International Business Machines/Systems Integration Division
Unisys/Computer Systems (3 projects)
Bell Communications Research/Applications
Bell Communications Research/Software Technology & Systems

Japanese Sites/Product Areas
Fujitsu/Communications Software
Fujitsu/Basic Software (2 projects)
Fujitsu/Applications Software
Hitachi/Basic Software
Hitachi/Applications Software
Hitachi/Switching Software
Hitachi Software Engineering/Financial Systems
Hitachi Software Engineering/Operating Systems
Kozo Keikaku/Communications Software
Mitsubishi Electric/Communications Software
Mitsubishi Electric/Systems Software
Mitsubishi Electric/Power & Industrial Systems Software
Nippon Business Consultant/System Software
Nippon Electronics Development/Communications Systems
Nippon Electronics Development/Information Service Systems
Nippon Systemware/System Software
Nippon Telegraph & Telephone/System Software
Nippon Telegraph & Telephone/Network Systems
Nippon Telegraph & Telephone/Applications

---

contained complete information on each question (for example, nine of the forty did not report quality data).

As shown in the summary data (Table B.2), the forty systems fell into the following product areas: data processing, scientific, systems (basic software), and telecommunications or embedded/real-time systems.[3] Although the mix of projects is not identical between the two samples,

Table B.2 Summary Data

	United States (%)	Japan (%)
Applications		
Data processing	8 (33)	2 (13)
Scientific	1 (4)	3 (19)
Systems	4 (17)	6 (38)
Telecommunications and Real-time	11 (46)	5 (31)
Total	24	16
Primary Language		
Assembler	5 (21)	2 (13)
C	3 (13)	3 (19)
COBOL	6 (25)	2 (13)
FORTRAN	3 (13)	2 (13)
PL/1	2 (8)	4 (25)
Other	5 (21)	3 (19)
Total	24	16
*Hardware Platform**		
Mainframe	11 (52)	7 (47)
Minicomputer	6 (29)	4 (27)
Microcomputer	4 (19)	4 (27)
Total	21	15

*Excludes systems with multiple platforms.

statistical analyses indicated that only data processing turned out to be a significant variable as a product type, and this tended to exaggerate the U.S. productivity averages because of their relative simplicity. Primary languages and hardware platforms were also similar across the two country samples.

To compare system sizes, the survey used noncomment source lines of code (SLOC) as the output size metric and work-years as the input size metric. The means and medians of these metrics, shown in Table B.3, indicate the U.S. and Japanese systems were roughly comparable on this dimension. To adjust for differences in languages used, the SLOC measures were converted to FORTRAN-equivalent statements, using the

Table B.3 Input and Output Metrics

Size	United States	Japan
Work-years	102 (22.5)*	47 (20.1)
SLOC	343K (124K)	433K (164K)
FORTRAN equivalent	288K (77K) (83.9% of SLOC)	389K (144K) (89.8% of SLOC)
Average FORTRAN conversion	0.90	0.94

*Expressed in means, with medians in parentheses. K = 1,000; SLOC = source lines of code.

Table B.4 Effort by Phase

	United States (%)	Japan (%)
Design	31	39
Coding	36	25
Testing	33	36

conversion factors proposed by Jones.[4] This conversion was performed on all of the SLOC data. The conversion produces FORTRAN-equivalent LOC that are slightly smaller than the raw SLOC data, reflecting the languages used. In addition, the relative numbers between the U.S. and Japanese companies do not change significantly. Data on life-cycle phases, shown in Table B.4, indicates that on average the Japanese spent significantly more time in the early life cycle phase and less in the coding phase. Their mean percentage in testing was also higher, although this difference was not statistically significant at usual levels.

Table B.5 presents the comparison of the U.S. and Japanese firms in several performance areas. In terms of productivity, defined as noncomment FORTRAN equivalent SLOC per work-year, both the mean and median for the Japanese firms appeared to be higher than (58 to 71 percent above) the U.S. numbers. The quality metric chosen for this research was the number of failures per thousand noncomment SLOC during the first twelve months of the system's service. Failures were defined as "basic service interruptions or basic service degradations of severity such that correction was not deferrable." Data available from twenty of the U.S. firms and eleven of the Japanese firms indicated that the Japanese firms showed mean and median numbers of failures lower than the U.S. firms (one-half to one-fourth). Reuse data also appeared to be higher for the Japanese firms. Although the sample proved to be too small and the variances too high for statistical analyses to show strongly significant results, the performance data presented in Table B.5 do clearly support the conclusion that, at the very least, Japanese projects

Table B.5 Performance Measures

	United States		Japan	
Mean productivity	7,290	(2,943)*	12,447	(4,663)
(FORTRAN-Equivalent SLOC/work-year)				
Failures/1,000 SLOC	4.44	(0.83)	1.96	(0.20)
during first 12 months after delivery	(N = 20)		(N = 11)	
Code reuse	9.71	(3)	18.25	(11)
(% of delivered lines)				

*Expressed in means, with medians in parentheses.

Table B.6 Quality Management Policies

	Mean Scores*	
	United States (N = 19)	Japan (N = 15)
Company QC	3.16	3.47
Top audit	1.68	2.60
QC training	3.21	3.47
Quality circles	2.16	3.13
Statistical methods	2.52	3.27

*Scale: 4 = very important, 3 = important, 2 = somewhat important, 1 = not important. QC = quality control.

studied were by no means behind their U.S. counterparts in LOC productivity, quality (defects), or reusability.

In addition to the time reporting and other behavioral data obtained, a separate effort was made to collect information on the attitudes of the managers completing the data collection forms toward quality control. They were asked to rate the following five approaches for their degree of importance in producing high-quality products:

> *Companywide Quality Control*: All departments and levels of personnel are engaged in systematic work guided by written quality policies from upper management.
>
> *Top Management Quality Control Audit*: A quality control audit team of executives visiting each department to uncover and eliminate any obstacles to the productivity and quality goals.
>
> *Quality Control Education and Training*: Education and training in quality control given to everybody in all departments at each level of the organization.
>
> *Quality Circles Activities*: A small group of people which meet voluntarily to perform quality control within their area of work.
>
> *Application of Statistical Methods*: Statistical methods for quality control such as Pareto analysis, cause and effect diagram, stratification, check sheet, histogram, scatter diagram.

The mean responses on a four-point scale are shown in Table B.6. The most striking result is that the Japanese means are higher than the U.S. means in all five categories. This difference is statistically significant for top audit, quality circles, and statistical methods.

C

MARKET SHARES AND CUSTOMER SATISFACTION IN JAPAN

This appendix contains tables referenced initially in Chapter 2 as supplementary information and relies on survey data from two issues of a leading Japanese industry journal, *Nikkei Computer*. The main survey, published on September 26, 1988, studied general-purpose mainframe users based on questionnaires sent to 14,407 sites in Japan excluding in-house departments of the computer manufacturers. Responses came from 5,422 sites, for a response rate of 37.6 percent. Excluding unclear answers, there were 5,226 effective responses.[1] A smaller specialized survey, published in the March 14, 1988 issue, focused on system-engineering (SE) services for general-purpose and office computers, provided mainly by the computer manufacturers but also by dealers, software houses, consultants, and other sources.[2] The *Nikkei* staff sent the later surveys to the information-systems departments of 6,000 large firms, including those listed in the first and second sections of the Tokyo Stock Exchange, and 448 nonlisted companies with annual sales of more than 50 billion yen. Responses came back from 1,589 companies, a rate of 26.5 percent. Including multiple responses from one company, there were 1,600 effective responses. Approximately 91 percent of the Japanese customers reported themselves as using machines from one vendor only in the categories in the survey, and only 5.6 percent claimed to be multivendor users. The remainder of the responses were unclear. Weighted averages that compare the average responses to the Japanese and U.S. services or products were calculated from the distribution of

Table C.1 Percentage of Manufacturer Placement Value Breakdown by Industry

Industry	F	I	H	N	S	B	R	M	Total*
Info. services	17	24	26	11	18	19	1	23	19
Finance	14	25	16	7	36	34	59	5	18
Government	19	2	14	22	5	0	0	13	13
Distribution	13	6	11	16	8	24	19	13	11
Machinery	5	10	9	7	4	2	9	10	7
Chemicals	6	7	6	5	9	2	2	2	6
Elec. machinery	6	9	3	6	4	1	1	11	6
Energy	3	4	6	4	8	0	1	2	4
Institutions	5	1	2	6	2	5	4	3	4
Construction	3	3	2	2	1	1	1	7	2
Foodstuffs	2	2	2	4	1	6	2	1	2
Services	1	1	1	3	1	3	1	2	1
Others	9	6	3	7	2	3	2	7	6
Company Total**	100	100	100	100	100	100	100	100	100

F = Fujitsu; I = IBM; H = Hitachi; N = NEC; S = Unisys/Sperry-Univac; B = Unisys/Burroughs; R = NCR; M = Mitsubishi.
*Industry segment as a percent of total placement value, based on user responses to the survey.
**Distribution of machine placements for each manufacturer by industry segment.
Source: *Nikkei Computer*, Sept. 26, 1988, p. 78.

Table C.2 System SE-Service Provided by Computer Makers: General-Purpose Computer Users

Questions*	1	2	3	4	5	6	7	8	9	10	11
Weighted Averages											
Total	5.9	7.1	7.3	6.1	5.5	5.1	6.9	5.9	4.8	7.2	6.5
Japan	5.9	7.1	7.3	6.0	5.5	5.1	6.9	5.9	4.7	7.1	6.4
U.S.	**6.2**	7.1	**7.4**	**6.3**	**5.6**	**5.3**	6.9	5.9	**4.9**	**7.4**	**6.6**
User Base											
Fujitsu	5.8	6.9	7.2	5.8	5.3	5.0	6.9	5.7	4.6	6.9	6.3
IBM	**6.4**	7.0	7.2	6.0	5.3	5.1	6.9	5.7	4.4	**7.4**	6.5
NEC	5.8	7.0	**7.3**	6.0	**5.7**	4.9	6.6	**6.0**	4.6	7.0	6.4
Hitachi	**6.2**	**7.5**	**7.5**	**6.2**	**5.7**	**5.5**	**7.3**	**6.0**	**5.0**	**7.5**	**6.6**
Unisys/Burroughs	5.6	6.9	7.2	**6.2**	**5.9**	**5.4**	6.6	5.7	**5.1**	**7.3**	**6.6**
Unisys/Sperry	**6.7**	**8.0**	**8.2**	**7.1**	**6.6**	**6.3**	**7.4**	**7.0**	**6.1**	**7.9**	**7.3**
NCR	5.1	6.6	7.0	**6.3**	4.9	4.6	6.2	5.3	4.7	7.1	6.1
Mitsubishi	4.3	6.9	**7.4**	**6.3**	5.0	4.3	6.8	5.7	4.6	7.1	6.3

*Questions = (1) explanation of new products; (2) system software version-up support; (3) new system configuration support; (4) proposals for solving problems related to improving system efficiency; (5) technical support for software development; (6) technical support for machine security; (7) promptness in responding to requests to fix defects; (8) technical support in communications areas; (9) offering of broad information from a neutral standpoint; (10) businessman-engineer morality; (11) total satisfaction. *Scale*: satisfied, 9–10 points; somewhat satisfied, 7–8; neither satisfied nor dissatisfied, 4–6; somewhat disatisfied, 2–3; dissatisfied, 0–1. Bold numbers = above average; SE = systems engineering. *Source*: *Nikkei Computer*, March 14, 1988, p. 72.

Table C.3 Applications SE-Service Provided by Computer Makers: General-Purpose Computer Users

Questions*	1	2	3	4	5	6	7	8	9	10
Weighted Averages										
Total	6.1	5.1	6.5	6.0	5.2	6.2	6.6	6.6	7.1	6.4
Japan	**6.2**	5.1	**6.6**	6.0	5.2	**6.3**	6.6	6.6	**7.2**	6.4
U.S.	6.0	5.1	6.1	6.1	5.2	6.2	6.6	**6.7**	7.1	**6.5**
User Base										
Fujitsu	**6.2**	**5.2**	6.5	5.9	5.2	6.1	6.5	6.5	7.0	6.4
IBM	5.8	4.8	6.2	6.0	4.7	6.1	6.4	6.5	6.9	6.4
NEC	**6.2**	5.1	**6.6**	**6.1**	5.1	**6.5**	6.6	**6.7**	7.1	6.4
Hitachi	**6.2**	4.9	**6.6**	6.0	**5.3**	**6.3**	6.6	**6.7**	**7.5**	6.4
Unisys/Burroughs	5.9	5.1	5.1	5.6	**5.4**	5.5	6.4	**6.7**	6.8	6.1
Unisys/Sperry	**6.5**	**5.9**	**6.7**	**6.6**	**6.0**	**7.0**	**7.2**	**7.3**	**7.8**	**7.1**
NCR	**6.8**	**5.4**	**6.7**	**6.4**	**5.6**	**6.3**	6.6	**6.8**	**7.2**	**6.7**
Mitsubishi	**6.4**	**5.8**	**7.4**	**6.8**	**6.2**	**8.0**	**7.8**	**7.4**	**7.8**	**7.0**

*Questions = (1) proposals for system planning and design; (2) understanding of business strategy; (3) knowledge regarding the application; (4) knowledge of industry trends; (5) ease of understanding product documentation; (6) communication ability; (7) application-system development methodology; (8) technical support in communications areas; (9) business-engineer morality; (10) total satisfaction. Scale and abbreviations as in Table C.2.
Source: *Nikkei Computer*, March 14, 1988, p. 72.

Table C.4 Average SE Charges by Industry (10,000 yen/work-month)

Industry	System Consulting	System Design	Programming	Operations	Training	System Audit
Average	94	77	58	43	52	84
	(114)*	(295)	(376)	(327)	(11)	(10)
Materials manu-	120	80	61	45	110	107
facturing	(8)	(31)	(36)	(24)	(2)	(3)
Machinery &	75	74	54	41	—	—
equipment	(10)	(18)	(33)	(30)		
Other manufac-	87	80	58	42	37	81
turing	(35)	(89)	(22)	(63)	(3)	(5)
Distribution	96	72	63	41	29	—
	(11)	(35)	(44)	(41)	(1)	
Finance	95	77	61	44	20	80
	(20)	(44)	(50)	(45)	(1)	(1)
Services	95	74	56	46	57	30
	(18)	(51)	(67)	(49)	(3)	(1)
Government/	100	70	62	54	20	—
Education	(1)	(1)	(3)	(4)	(1)	
Other	109	75	59	42	—	—
	(10)	(24)	(32)	(24)		

*Nos. in parentheses = number of responses. SE = system engineering.
Source: *Nikkei Computer*, March 14, 1988, p. 68.

survey responses as listed in Table 1.7 for the Sept. 26, 1988 survey and in Table C.7 for the March 14, 1988 survey. Tables C.1 and C.8 list the breakdown of user responses to the two surveys by industry.

In addition to the customer-satisfaction data summarized in Chapter 1, the *Nikkei Computer* surveys also provided considerable information on personnel and customer satisfaction with different types of vendors. For example, despite efforts made to train and support software personnel, more than 80 percent of the firms responding reported a shortage of software personnel in system design and programming. In system design, 37 percent of firms reported they were "extremely short" (Table C.9). As a result, users relied heavily on computer manufacturers for general system-engineering support, averaging nearly 88 percent for the U.S.-based firms' users, and 68 percent for the Japanese vendors' users. Customers of the Japanese vendors relied more heavily on dealers (18.5 percent compared to 7 percent) (Table C.10).

In applications development, between 25 and 50 percent of the users responding claimed that they relied on outside personnel, most notably for programming. In system planning, they relied mainly on the computer manufacturers. In other phases, from system design through maintenance, they relied most heavily on software houses, followed by the manufacturers and then dealers (Table C.11). Japanese customers were not, however, equally satisfied with the services of all vendors. The computer manufacturers, both U.S-based and Japanese, were rated con-

Table C.5 System SE-Service Provided by Computer Makers: Office-Computer Users

Questions*	1	2	3	4	5	6	7	8	9	10	11
Weighted Averages											
Total	5.5	6.4	6.7	5.5	5.0	4.9	6.8	5.4	4.6	7.3	6.2
Japan	5.1	5.6	6.3	4.9	4.6	4.4	6.2	4.9	4.2	6.9	5.8
U.S.	**6.0**	**7.3**	**7.0**	**6.2**	**5.5**	**5.4**	**7.3**	**6.0**	**5.1**	**7.9**	**6.8**
User Base											
Fujitsu	5.1	5.9	6.5	5.2	4.8	4.6	6.3	5.0	4.3	7.0	5.8
IBM	**6.1**	**7.4**	**7.1**	**6.3**	**5.5**	5.4	**7.4**	**6.1**	**5.1**	**8.0**	**6.9**
NEC	4.7	5.1	5.4	3.8	4.1	3.7	5.7	4.4	3.6	6.4	5.4
Hitachi	5.7	4.7	**6.9**	4.4	4.7	4.1	6.3	4.1	5.4	6.6	5.7
Unisys/Burroughs	5.7	**7.7**	**7.6**	**6.9**	**6.4**	**6.6**	**8.0**	**7.0**	**5.6**	**8.1**	**7.3**
Unisys/Sperry	4.8	6.0	6.2	4.8	4.7	4.5	6.3	3.4	**5.0**	6.5	5.3
NCR	5.2	6.2	6.2	**5.7**	4.3	4.2	6.2	5.0	**4.7**	6.5	5.8
Mitsubishi	5.1	5.7	**6.9**	5.4	4.5	4.9	6.3	5.0	4.4	7.0	**6.3**
Toshiba	**6.4**	6.3	**7.2**	5.9	**5.1**	4.4	**6.9**	**6.2**	4.3	7.3	**6.3**

*Questions, scale and abbreviations as in Table C.2.
Source: *Nikkei Computer*, March 14, 1988, p. 75.

Table C.6 Applications SE-Service Provided by Computer Makers: Office-Computer Users

Questions*	1	2	3	4	5	6	7	8	9	10
Weighted Averages										
Total	6.2	5.1	6.0	6.1	4.8	5.5	6.4	6.5	7.1	6.3
Japan	6.0	4.7	5.7	5.9	4.6	5.1	5.9	6.2	6.7	6.0
U.S.	**6.3**	**5.5**	**6.3**	**6.2**	**4.9**	**5.8**	**6.8**	**6.9**	**7.6**	**6.6**
User Base										
Fujitsu	6.1	4.8	5.6	5.8	4.4	5.4	6.0	6.2	6.8	6.0
IBM	6.2	**5.4**	**6.1**	6.1	4.7	**5.8**	**6.8**	6.8	7.7	**6.5**
NEC	6.0	4.5	6.0	6.1	**4.9**	5.0	5.9	6.3	6.4	6.1
Hitachi	**6.5**	**7.5**	**7.0**	6.0	**5.5**	4.0	5.0	4.5	5.0	5.5
Unisys/Burroughs	**7.0**	6.4	**7.8**	**7.2**	**6.4**	**6.8**	**7.6**	**7.8**	**8.0**	**7.4**
Unisys/Sperry	**7.0**	**7.0**	**8.0**	**7.0**	**6.0**	4.5	**7.0**	6.5	6.5	**7.0**
NCR	**6.8**	6.0	**6.8**	**7.0**	5.3	**6.8**	**6.8**	**7.3**	7.3	**6.8**
Mitsubishi	5.7	3.6	5.2	**6.6**	4.0	4.2	6.0	6.3	7.1	6.1
Toshiba	5.2	4.3	5.6	5.6	4.5	5.4	6.4	**6.6**	**7.8**	5.9

*Questions as in Table C.3; scale and abbreviations as in Table C.2.
Source: *Nikkei Computer*, March 14, 1988, p. 75.

siderably higher in software-related areas than dealers or software houses. This appears to reflect the severe shortage of skilled software personnel in Japan outside of the major computer companies and a few private consultants (Table C.12).

Table C.7 User Responses by Computer Make to Systems Engineering Survey

	Large Computers	Office Computers	Unclear	Total No. of Responses
Fujitsu	362	105	0	467
IBM	171	126	1	298
NEC	240	47	2	289
Hitachi	206	11	4	221
Unisys/Burroughs	69	7	0	76
Unisys/Sperry	61	6	0	67
NCR	32	7	0	39
Mitsubishi	12	17	0	29
Toshiba	2	13	0	15
Oki	0	4	0	4
Other Makers	6	15	1	22
Computer Centers	—	—	21	21
Unclear	32	13	7	52
Total	1,193	371	36	1,600

Source: *Nikkei Computer*, March 14, 1988, p. 85.

Table C.8 User Responses by Industry to Systems Engineering Survey

Materials Manufacturing	124
Machinery and Equipment Manufacturing	165
Other Manufacturing	490
Distribution	166
Finance	259
Service	258
Government and Education	14
Other	109
No Response	15
Total	1,600

Source: *Nikkei Computer*, March 14, 1988, p. 85.

Table C.9 Software Personnel Sufficiency(%)

	Surplus	Sufficient	Somewhat Short	Severe Shortage	No. of Responses
System planning	0.3	26.5	45.9	27.3	1,346
System design	0.2	15.7	47.2	36.9	1,393
Programming	1.0	17.5	53.2	28.3	1,400
Operations management	3.5	56.8	32.8	6.9	1,325
Training & education	—	20.0	42.4	37.6	800
System audit	—	17.1	25.9	57.0	627

Source: *Nikkei Computer*, March 14, 1988, p. 84.

Table C.10 System SE-Service Utilization Rates(%)

	Computer Makers	Dealers	Software Houses	Consulting Companies	Other	No Response
Weighted Averages						
Total	72.4	14.0	5.3	0.4	2.7	5.2
Japan	68.3	**18.5**	**5.5**	**0.6**	**2.9**	4.5
U.S.	**87.7**	7.0	4.4	1.0	0.8	3.6
Large computers	80.8	8.4	4.1	0.3	2.4	4.1
Office computers	48.1	32.3	9.4	0.5	3.2	6.5
User Base						
Fujitsu	56.7	29.6	5.4	—	3.2	5.1
IBM	83.9	7.0	4.0	1.0	0.6	3.4
Hitachi	85.1	5.0	2.3	0.9	3.6	3.2
NEC	77.2	8.3	7.3	0.3	2.0	4.8
Unisys/Burroughs	95.5	—	–	—	—	4.5
Unisys/Sperry	97.4	—	–	—	—	2.6
NCR	84.6	—	7.7	—	2.6	5.1
Mitsubishi	37.9	44.8	13.8	—	—	3.4

Bold numbers = above average; SE = systems engineering.
Source: *Nikkei Computer*, March 14, 1988, p. 75.

Table C.11 Use of Outside Service in Applications
(% of Service [work-months] Provided by Manufacturer)

	System Planning	System Design	Programming	Maintenance
% Using Outside Service				
Yes	25.5	39.8	50.8	28.3
No	68.6	55.1	44.6	65.5
No response	5.7	5.2	4.7	6.2
Major Source of Outside Service				
Computer makers	50.2	37.4	19.7	24.3
Software houses	21.1	41.8	57.3	46.1
Dealers	11.1	10.5	9.6	11.0
Consultants	7.8	2.0	0.5	0.2
Computer Centers	5.4	6.8	7.9	9.5
Other/No response	4.1	4.5	5.0	8.8

Source: *Nikkei Computer*, March 14, 1988, p. 73.

Table C.12 Applications SE Service Satisfaction by Source

Questions*	1	2	3	4	5	6	7	8	9	10
Average	6.5	5.4	6.6	6.3	5.3	6.2	6.6	6.8	7.2	6.6
Computer Makers	6.5	5.4	**6.7**	6.3	**5.4**	**6.4**	**6.7**	**6.9**	7.2	6.6
Dealers	5.9	4.4	6.2	6.2	4.6	5.4	6.3	6.2	6.8	6.0
Software Houses	5.9	4.7	5.8	6.0	4.8	6.2	6.5	6.6	7.0	6.3
Computing Centers	5.9	4.9	5.8	6.3	5.2	5.7	6.6	6.2	7.1	6.4
Consultants	**8.0**	**7.5**	**7.1**	**7.2**	**5.6**	**7.0**	**7.8**	**8.2**	**8.2**	**7.7**
Other	6.0	4.8	5.3	5.0	5.5	5.5	6.5	6.5	6.2	5.8

*Questions as in Table C.3; scale and abbreviations as in Table C.2. Bold numbers = above average.
Source: *Nikkei Computer*, March 14, 1988, p. 74.

NOTES

Introduction

1. See Horst Hunke (ed.), *Software Engineering Environments* (Amsterdam: North Holland, 1981), Introduction, pp. 1–9; and Werner L. Frank, *Critical Issues in Software* (New York: Wiley, 1983).
2. Bruce W. Arden (ed.), *What Can Be Automated?* (Cambridge, Mass.: MIT Press, 1980), p. 563.
3. For various data on software economics, productivity, and industry revenues, see U.S. Department of Commerce, International Trade Administration, *A Competitive Assessment of the U.S. Software Industry* (Washington, D.C.: U.S. Government Printing Office, 1984); and Robert Schware, *The World Software Industry and Software Engineering*, Technical Paper # 104, Washington, D.C., The World Bank, 1989.
4. The relevant literature on Japanese management and employee characteristics, as well as government and other structural elements affecting competition, is too voluminous to cite here in any depth. Some articles and books specifically discussing the generalizations noted here, usually including suggestions for the United States or other Western countries, are Ezra F. Vogel, *Japan as Number 1: Lessons for America* (Cambridge, Mass.: Harvard University Press, 1979); Robert E. Cole, *Work, Mobility, and Participation: A Comparative Study of American and Japanese Industry* (Berkeley and Los Angeles: University of California Press, 1979); William G. Ouchi, *Theory Z: How American Business Can Meet the Japanese Challenge* (Reading, Mass.: Addison-Wesley, 1981); Nina Hatvany and Vladimir Pucik, "An Integrated Management System: Lessons from the Japanese Experience," *Academy of Management Review*, July 1981, pp. 469–74; E. H. Schein, "Does Japanese Management Style Have a Message for U.S. Managers," *Sloan Management Review*, Fall 1981, pp. 55–68; Richard J. Schonberger, *Japanese Manufacturing Techniques* (New York: Free Press, 1982); Thomas Rohlen, *Japan's High Schools* (Berkeley and Los Angeles: University of California Press, 1983); James C. Abegglen and George Stalk, Jr., *Kaisha: The Japanese Corporation* (New York: Basic Books, 1985); Ronald P. Dore, *Flexible Rigidities: Industrial Policy and Structural Adjustment in the Japanese Economy, 1970–1980* (Stanford, Calif.: Stanford University Press, 1986); Michael A. Cusumano,

"Manufacturing Innovation: Lessons from the Japanese Auto Industry," *Sloan Management Review*, Fall 1988, pp. 29–30.

5. Discussions of the U.S. preeminence in software and decline in other industries can be found in numerous sources, such as U.S. Department of Commerce, *U.S. Software Industry*; Schware, *World Software Industry*; and Michael L. Dertouzos, Richard K. Lester, and Robert M. Solow, *Made in America: Regaining the Productive Edge* (Cambridge, Mass.: MIT Press, 1989).

6. See, for example, U.S. Department of Commerce; Laszlo A. Belady, "The Japanese and Software: Is It a Good Match?" *Computer*, June 1986, pp. 57–61; and Colin Johnson, "Software in Japan," *Electronic Engineering Times*, Feb. 11, 1985, p. 1.

7. For more formal definitions of economies of scope and discussion of applications, see John C. Panzar and Robert D. Willig, "Economies of Scope," *American Economic Review* 71, May 1981, pp. 268–72; William J. Baumol, John C. Panzer, and Robert D. Willig, *Contestable Markets and the Theory of Industry Structure* (New York: Harcourt Brace Johanovitch, 1982); Peter Lorange, Michael A. Scott Morton, and Sumantra Goshal, *Strategic Control Systems* (St. Paul, Minn.: West Publishing, 1984); and Robert S. Pindyck and Daniel L. Rubinfeld, *Microeconomics* (New York: MacMillan, 1989), esp. pp. 221–25.

Chapter 1

1. For useful descriptions of software products and producers, see U.S. Department of Commerce, International Trade Administration, *A Competitive Assessment of the U.S. Software Industry* (Washington, D.C.: U.S. Government Printing Office, 1984), esp. pp. 1–9; and Robert Schware, *The World Software Industry and Software Engineering*, Technical Paper # 104, Washington, D.C., The World Bank, 1989.

2. On bundling, see Franklin M. Fisher, James W. McKie, and Richard B. Mancke, *IBM and the U.S. Data Processing Industry: An Economic History* (New York: Praeger, 1983), pp. 175–79.

3. U.S. Department of Commerce, p. 10.

4. "The Free-for-All Has Begun," *Business Week*, May 11, 1987, pp. 148–59.

5. Whether or not software is a service continues to be a matter of debate, if not confusion. Various studies suggest that services are distinct from manufacturing in that they are intangible; involve a high degree of producer-consumer interaction; cannot be inventoried; cannot be transported; and do not involve the processing of materials into finished durable and nondurable goods. See W. Earl Sasser, "Match Supply and Demand in Service Industries," *Harvard Business Review*, November–December 1976; J. M. Juran (ed.), *Quality Control Handbook* (New York: McGraw-Hill, 1974), pp. 47–52. For example, the U.S. Office of Technology Assessment classified software as one of several information-technology services, along with telecommunications, data processing, and information services, but with the caveat that software had attributes both of a service ("computer programs have no necessarily fixed form") and a manufactured good ("programs can be reproduced, stored, and shipped"). See U.S. Congress, Office of Technology Assessment, *International Competition in Services* (Washington, D.C.: U.S. Government Printing Office, July 1987), pp. 36, 157.

6. For discussions of conventional production-process options, see Robert H. Hayes and Steven C. Wheelright, *Restoring Our Competitive Edge: Competing through Manufacturing* (New York: Wiley, 1984); Roger W. Schmenner, *Production/Operations Management: Concepts and Situations* (Chicago: Science Research Associates, 1984). For discussions of more flexible design and production systems, see Ramchandran Jaikumar, "Postindustrial Manufacturing," *Harvard Business Review*, September 1986, pp. 301–308, and "From Filing and Fitting to Flexible Manufacturing: A Study in the Evolution of Process Control," Boston, Harvard Business School, Working Paper, February 1988; and Paul S. Adler, "Managing Flexible Automation," *California Management Review*,

Spring 1988, pp. 34–56. A related study of flexibility and small firm specialization is Michael J. Piore and Charles F. Sabel, *The Second Industrial Divide: Possibilities for Prosperity* (New York: Basic Books, 1984).

7. See Nancy L. Hyer and Urban Wemmerloc, "Group Technology and Productivity," *Harvard Business Review*, July–August 1984, pp. 140–49.

8. A lengthier but similar typology was presented independently in Joseph Lampell and Henry Mintzberg, "Customizing Strategies . . . and Strategic Management," Working Paper, Montreal, McGill University, March 1987.

9. This list excludes a group of 200 people that did not produce software for sale but made up the System Development Department of Hallmark Cards, Inc., which produced programs for in-house use but is referred to by a former manager as a "software factory." See James R. Johnson, *The Software Factory: Managing Software Development and Maintenance* (Wellesley, Mass.: QED Information Sciences, 1989).

10. Capers Jones, *Programming Productivity* (New York: McGraw-Hill, 1986), p. 243.

11. On this debate, see Philip Kraft, *Programmers and Managers: The Routinization of Computer Programming in the United States* (New York: Springer-Verlag, 1977); Frederick P. Brooks, Jr., *The Mythical Man-Month: Essays on Software Engineering* (Reading, Mass.: Addison-Wesley, 1975); Oscar Hauptman, "Influence of Task Type on the Relationship Between Communication and Performance: The Case of Software Development," *R&D Management* 16, 1986, pp. 127–39; and Martin Schooman, *Software Engineering: Design, Reliability, and Management* (New York: McGraw-Hill, 1983). For a perspective on this debate as it fits into studies of the history of technology in general, see Michael S. Mahoney, "The History of Computing in the History of Technology," *Annals of the History of Computing* 10, 2, 1988, pp. 113–25.

12. See, in particular, Steven Levy, *Hackers: Heroes of the Computer Revolution* (New York: Anchor Press/Doubleday, 1984); Harry Braverman, *Labor and Monopoly Capital: The Degradation of Work in the Twentieth Century* (New York and London: Monthly View Press, 1974); and Kraft, *Programmers and Managers*.

13. R. W. Bemer, "Position Papers for Panel Discussion—The Economics of Program Production," *Information Processing 68* (Amsterdam: North-Holland, 1969), pp. 1626–27.

14. This section is based on M. D. McIlroy, "Mass Produced Software Components," in Peter Naur and Brian Randall (eds.), *Software Engineering: Report on a Conference Sponsored by the NATO Science Committee*, Brussels, Scientific Affairs Division, NATO, January 1969. The discussion of McIlroy's address is on pp. 151–55. See also Ellis Horowitz and John B. Munson, "An Expansive View of Reusable Software," *IEEE Transactions on Software Engineering* SE 10, 5, September 1984, p. 481.

15. William G. Griffin, "Software Engineering in GTE", *Computer*, November 1984, pp. 66–72.

16. Finn Borum, "Beyond Taylorism: The IT-Specialists and the Deskilling Hypothesis," Computer History (CHIPS) Working Paper, Copenhagen School of Economics, September 1987, pp. 8–9.

17. The development of this stream of thought is lengthy. Authors reviewed for this book in addition to Joan Woodward, Charles Perrow, Henry Mintzberg, and others listed in subsequent notes, include Paul R. Lawrence and Jay W. Lorsch, *Organization and Environment: Managing Differentiation and Integration* (Boston: Harvard Business School Press, 1967); Jay Galbreath, *Designing Complex Organizations* (Reading, Mass.: Addison-Wesley, 1973) and *Organization Design* (Reading, Mass.: Addison-Wesley, 1977); W. Richard Scott, *Organizations: Rational, Natural, and Open Systems* (Englewood Cliffs, N.J.: Prentice-Hall, 1981); and Stephen R. Barley, "Technology as an Occasion for Structuring: Evidence from Observations of CT Scanners and the Social Order of Radiology Departments," *Administrative Science Quarterly* 31, 1986, pp. 78–108.

18. Thoughts in this section were particularly influenced by works such as Joan Woodward, *Industrial Organization: Theory and Practice* (London: Oxford University Press, 1965); Alfred D. Chandler, Jr., *The Visible Hand: The Managerial Revolution in American*

Business (Cambridge, Mass.: Harvard University Press, 1977); William J. Abernathy, *The Productivity Dilemma: Roadblock to Innovation in the Automobile Industry* (Baltimore: Johns Hopkins University Press, 1978); William J. Abernathy and James Utterback, "Patterns of Industrial Innovation," in Michael L. Tushman and William L. Moore (eds.), *Readings in the Management of Innovation* (New York: Pitman, 1982); David A. Hounschell, *From the American System to Mass Production, 1800–1932* (Baltimore: Johns Hopkins University Press, 1984); Michael Porter, *Competitive Strategy: Techniques for Analyzing Industries and Competitors* (New York: Free Press, 1980), and *Competitive Advantage: Creating and Sustaining Superior Performance* (New York: Free Press, 1985); Piore and Sabel; and Jaikumar, 1988.

19. A classic example of the rigidities imposed by mass production is Ford's dramatic decline in market share during the mid-1920s, despite rising levels of productivity, when market demand and competitor offerings shifted to a greater variety of differentiated products. See William J. Abernathy and Kenneth Wayne, "Limits of the Learning Curve," *Harvard Business Review*, September–October 1974, pp. 109–19.

20. See Lawrence and Lorsch, *Organization and Environment*; Woodward, *Industrial Organization*; Charles Perrow, "A Framework for the Comparative Analysis of Organizations," *American Sociological Review*, April 1967, pp. 194–208; Peter M. Blau and Richard A. Schoenherr, *The Structure of Organizations* (New York: Basic Books, 1971); James G. March and Herbert A. Simon, *Organizations* (New York: Wiley, 1958); Jeffrey Pfeffer, *Power in Organizations* (Marshfield, Mass.: Pitman, 1981).

21. See Alfred D. Chandler, Jr., *Strategy and Structure: Chapters in the History of the Industrial Enterprise* (Cambridge, Mass.: MIT Press, 1962), and *The Visible Hand*; John Child, "Organization Structure, Environment, and Performance: The Role of Strategic Choice," *Sociology*, January 1972, pp. 1–22; and Raymond E. Miles and Charles C. Snow, *Organizational Strategy, Structure, and Process*, (New York: McGraw-Hill, 1978).

22. See Child, "Organization Structure, Environment, and Performance," as well as Derek S. Pugh, "The Management of Organization Structures: Does Context Determine Form?" *Organizational Dynamics*, Spring 1973, pp. 19–34, cited in Stephen P. Robbins, *Organization Theory: Structure, Design, and Applications* (Englewood Cliffs, N.J.: Prentice-Hall, 1987), p. 176.

23. Economists have explained economies of scale through a series of related concepts and phenomena. One involves "indivisibility." Many machines or facilities need to operate at particular volumes for a firm to be able to justify their cost. Some equipment or processes are designed with minimum and maximum operating ranges, so that they are not easily adapted to smaller volumes of a number of different products. Automated equipment especially can vastly improve both productivity and quality, but is usually expensive to introduce, thus requiring high utilization rates. Suppliers face these same constraints, and may not deliver materials to a firm unless there is a minimum size order, and offer their customers discounts for larger orders. They also argue it is to the advantage of a firm to spread fixed and variable costs related to equipment, land, research and product development, administration, and various "overhead" expenses among large numbers of identical products. This is another form of scale economy, although the notion of economies of scope—spreading costs or resources across different products—applies here as well as scale. Another reason for the drop in costs is specialization and division of labor. When production volumes for a particular product or component are high enough, it often becomes possible to divide a process into a series of tasks. Workers can specialize, and more quickly accumulate experience for their assigned tasks. For a general textbook discussion of the economics of production, including scale and scope economies, see Robert S. Pindyck and Daniel L. Rubinfeld, *Microeconomics* (New York: MacMillan, 1989).

24. Woodward, *Industrial Organization*, esp. pp. 35–50.

25. Henry Mintzberg, *The Structuring of Organizations* (Englewood Cliffs, N.J.: Prentice-Hall, 1979).

26. Arthur L. Stinchcombe, "Bureaucratic and Craft Administration of Production: A

Comparative Study," *Administrative Science Quarterly* 4, September 1959, pp. 168–87. My thanks to Professor Robert Thomas of the M.I.T. Sloan School of Management for this reference and other suggestions on this material.

27. See Mintzberg, *Structuring of Organizations*, pp. 431–67.

28. Ibid., pp. 299–480.

29. See Perrow, "A Framework for the Comparative Analysis of Organizations," as well as the discussion of Perrow in Robbins, *Organization Theory*, pp. 129–34.

30. The volume of literature on Japanese organizational styles and culture is enormous, and not monolithic in conclusions. Some works that argue in favor of a cultural or social orientation toward discipline, group activities, and consensus decision making include the following, in addition to those works cited in the Introduction: James C. Abegglen, *The Japanese Factory* (Glencoe, Ill.: Free Press, 1958); Michael Y. Yoshino, *Japan's Managerial System* (Cambridge, Mass.: MIT Press, 1968); Richard Pascale and Anthony Athos, *The Art of Japanese Management* (New York: Simon and Schuster, 1981). On the Japanese and software, see Laszlo A. Belady, "The Japanese and Software: Is It a Good Match?" *Computer*, June 1986, pp. 57–61.

31. Naur and Randell, *Software Engineering*, p. 84.

32. Denji Tajima and Tomoo Matsubara, "The Computer Software Industry in Japan," *Computer*, May 1981, pp. 89–96, and "Inside the Japanese Software Industry," *Computer*, March 1984, pp. 34–43.

33. K. H. Kim, "A Look at Japan's Development of Software Engineering Technology," *Computer*, May 1983, pp. 26–37.

34. Marvin V. Zelkowitz et al., "Software Engineering Practices in the US and Japan," *Computer*, June 1984, pp. 57–66.

35. Robert Haavind, "Tools for Compatability," *High Technology*, August 1986, pp. 34–42.

36. See, for example, Thomas A. Standish, "An Essay on Software Reuse," *IEEE Transactions on Software Engineering* SE-10, 5, September 1984, pp. 494–97; U.S. Office of Technology Assessment, *International Competition in Services*, pp. 160–66; Kouichi Kishida et al., "Quality-Assurance Technology in Japan," *IEEE Software*, September 1987, pp. 11–18; Will Tracz, "Software Reuse Myths," *Software Engineering Notes* 13, 1, January 1988, pp. 17–21; George Gamaota and Wendy Frieman, *Gaining Ground: Japan's Strides in Science and Technology* (Cambridge, Mass.: Ballinger, 1988); Michael A. Cusumano, "The Software Factory: A Historical Interpretation," *IEEE Software*, March 1989, pp. 23–30.

37. Toshio Sakai, "Software: The New Driving Force," *Business Week*, Feb. 27, 1984, pp. 96–97.

38. Bro Uttal, "Japan's Persistent Software Gap," *Fortune*, Oct. 15, 1984, pp. 151–60.

39. Glenn Rifkin and J. A. Savage, "Is U.S. Ready for Japan Software Push," *Computerworld*, May 8, 1989, p. 1.

40. Charles P. Lecht, "Japanese Software No Threat," *Computerworld*, May 8, 1989, p. 21.

41. U.S. Department of Commerce, p. 11.

42. U.S. Department of Commerce, pp. 61, 68.

43. Colin Johnson, "Software in Japan," *Electronic Engineering Times*, Feb. 11, 1985, p. 1.

44. This notion that generalizable differences in process approaches between Japanese and non-Japanese firms may stem from particular market conditions in Japan, along with or perhaps more than other factors, was not new and appeared to hold at least for one other major industry. An earlier study by this author, for example, indicated that specific characteristics of the Japanese automobile industry—the demand after World War II for a growing variety of products at extremely low volumes, compared to the United States—encouraged manufacturers such as Toyota to devise new techniques for manufacturing and personnel management that sought a combination of productivity and flexibility; that is, the ability to make a variety of models efficiently even at low volumes. See Michael A. Cusumano, *The Japanese Automobile Industry: Technology and Management at Nissan and Toyota* (Cambridge, Mass.: Council on East Asian Stud-

ies/Harvard University Press, 1985), and "Manufacturing Innovation: Lessons from the Japanese Auto Industry," *Sloan Management Review*, Fall 1988, pp. 29–39.

45. Michael A. Cusumano, "Diversity and Innovation in Japanese Technology Management," in Richard S. Rosenbloom (ed.), *Research on Technological Innovation, Management, and Policy* (Greenwich, Conn.: JAI Press, 1986), vol. 3, pp. 137–67.

46. Later chapters will discuss these linkages in more detail.

47. There are numerous discussions of the development of Japan's computer industry, including government policies. Discussions in English include William G. Ouchi, "Political and Economic Teamwork: The Development of the Microelectronics Industry of Japan," *California Management Review*, Summer 1984, pp. 8–33; Franklin B. Weinstein, Michiyuki Uenohara, and John Linvill, "Technological Resources," in Daniel Okimoto et al. (eds.), *Competitive Edge: The Semiconductor Industry in the U.S. and Japan* (Stanford, Calif.: Stanford University Press, 1984), pp. 35–77; Ezra F. Vogel, *Comeback: Case by Case—Building the Resurgence of American Business* (New York: Simon and Schuster, 1985), pp. 125–67; Thomas Pepper, Merit E. Janow, and Jimmy W. Wheeler, *The Competition: Dealing with Japan* (New York: Praeger, 1985), pp. 200–46; Marie Anchordoguy, "Mastering the Market: Japanese Government Targeting of the Computer Industry," *International Organization*, Summer 1988, pp. 509–43, and *Computers Inc.: Japan's Challenge to IBM* (Cambridge, Mass.: Council on East Asian Studies/Harvard University Press, 1989); and Kenneth Flamm, *Creating the Computer: Government, Industry, and High Technology* (Washington, D.C.: The Brookings Institution, 1988), pp. 172–202.

48. See Anchordoguy, "Mastering the Market," esp. pp. 513–30, as well as, *Computers Inc.*

49. International Data Corporation, *EDP Japan Report*, Feb. 1, 1988, p. 129.

50. International Data Corporation, "Japan Computer Industry: Review and Forecast, 1987–1992," Framingham, Mass., International Data Corporation, Inc., unpublished draft #3900, January 1989, pp. 2, 22.

51. See Anchordoguy, "Mastering the Market" p. 531.

52. U.S. Department of Commerce, pp. 40–42.

53. The specific sources for these figures are A. Zavala, *"Research on Factors that Influence the Productivity of Software Development Workers"* (Palo Alto, Calif.: SRI International, June 1985); H. Aiso, "Overview of Japanese National Projects in Information Technology" (Tokyo: International Symposium on Computer Architecture, lecture 1, June 1986).

54. The specific sources for this are U.S. Department of Commerce, p. 11, and Fumihiko Kamijo, "Information Technology Activities in the Japanese Software Industry," *Oxford Surveys in Information Technology* 3, 1986.

55. This research was conducted in conjunction with a faculty colleague at Massachussets Institute of Technology (M.I.T.), Professor Chris F. Kemerer. For a more detailed treatment than in Appendix B, see Michael A. Cusumano and Chris F. Kemerer, "A Quantitative Analysis of U.S. and Japanese Practice and Performance in Software Development," *Management Science*, November 1990.

56. See esp. Jones, *Programming Productivity*, pp. 5–40.

57. *Nikkei Computer*, Sept. 26, 1988, p. 67. These consisted mainly of the following lines:

Fujitsu	M Series, VP series
Japan IBM	43XX, 308X, 3090
Hitachi	M Series, H-8600, H-6700, S-800
NEC	ACOS Series, SX Series
Mitsubishi	COSMO Series, EX Series
NCR	V-8400-8600, I-9000, ITX/9000, NCR9800, NCRXL
Unisys	
Univac/Sperry	1100 Series, System 11, 2200 Series, 80 Series, 90 Series
Burroughs	B1800-7800, B1900-7900, A Series, V Series

58. Richard Thomas DeLamarter, *Big Blue: IBM's Use and Abuse of Power* (New York: Dodd, Mead, 1986), pp. 287–88.

59. Description of U.S.-owned firms in Japan is from International Data Corporation, "Japan Computer Industry," pp. 36–41; Takahashi Kenkichi et al., *Konpyuta gyokai* [The computer industry] (Tokyo: Kyoikusha, 1985); and Neal Doying et al., "IBM Japan," unpublished group project paper, subject 15.229, Cambridge, Mass., M.I.T. Sloan School of Management, Dec. 8, 1986.

Chapter 2

Note: Japanese names are given in the English style (given name preceding surname) in the text and for English publications; however, authors are listed in the Japanese style (surname preceding given name) for publications in Japanese.

1. See Bruce W. Arden (ed.), *What Can Be Automated?* (Cambridge, Mass.: MIT Press, 1980) for a useful review of computer software and hardware technology.

2. Similar versions of this life cycle, which has also been adopted by the U.S. Department of Defense, can be found in Peter Naur and Brian Randell (eds.), *Software Engineering: Report on a Conference Sponsored by the NATO Science Committee*, Brussels, Scientific Affairs Division, NATO, January 1969, pp. 20–21; Barry W. Boehm, "Software Engineering," *IEEE Transactions on Computers* C-25, 12, December 1976; and numerous other sources, with minor variations. The following discussion relies heavily on C. V. Ramamoorthy et al., "Software Engineering: Problems and Perspectives," *Computer*, October 1984, pp. 192–93.

3. Harvey Bratman and Terry Court, "The Software Factory," *Computer*, May 1975, pp. 28–29.

4. R. H. Thayer, "Modeling a Software Engineering Project Management System," Ph.D. dissertation, University of California at Santa Barbara, 1979, cited in Tarek Abdel-Hamid, "The Dynamics of Software Development Project Management: An Integrative Systems Dynamic Perspective," Ph.D. dissertation, M.I.T. Sloan School of Management, 1984, pp. 48–57.

5. Frederick P. Brooks, Jr., *The Mythical Man-Month: Essays on Software Engineering* (Reading, Mass.: Addison-Wesley, 1975), p. 4.

6. Arden, *What Can Be Automated?*, pp. 799–804.

7. Ibid., pp. 798–99.

8. Naur and Randell, *Software Engineering*, p. 123.

9. Interview with Tom Newman, project manager, Bell Communications Research, June 2, 1988.

10. Several interviews during 1987–1988 with Jan Norton, head, Technical Program Competitive Analysis Department, AT&T Bell Laboratories.

11. Barry W. Boehm, "Seven Basic Principles of Software Engineering," *Software Engineering Techniques—Invited Papers* (London: Nicholson House/Infotech International Ltd., 1977), p. 79.

12. Barry W. Boehm et al., "A Software Development Environment for Improving Productivity," *Computer*, June 1984, pp. 30–42.

13. See R. Goldberg, "Software Engineering: An Emerging Discipline," *IBM Systems Journal* 25, 3/4, 1986, pp. 334–53. A discussion of this shift in focus to environments can also be found in Horst Hunke (ed.), *Software Engineering Environments* (Amsterdam: North-Holland, 1981) and Philip Kraft, *Programmers and Managers: The Routinization of Computer Programming in the United States* (New York: Springer-Venlag, 1977).

14. Some date the origin of structured programming to the work of D.V. Schorre at UCLA in 1960, although the earliest publication on the subject seems to have been a 1965 conference paper by E. Dijkstra, who suggested that, since programmers were humans and thus had limited abilities, they were better off following a mathematically structured "divide and conquer" approach to programming rather than unsystematic meth-

ods. In a 1969 paper for a NATO Science Committee Conference, titled "Structured Programming," Dijkstra argued specifically that program logic "should be controlled by alternative, conditional, and repetitive clauses and procedure calls [IF-THEN-ELSE and DO-WHILE], rather than by statements transferring control to labelled points [GO-TO statements]." To suggest what is now called top-down design, he also used the analogy of a program constructed as "a string of ordered pearls, in which a larger pearl describes the entire program in terms of concepts or capabilities implemented in lower-level pearls." Most programming at the time was done in a "bottom-up" fashion, where program units were written and then integrated into subsystems that were in turn integrated at higher and higher levels into the final system. These and other articles from the *IBM Systems Journal* dealing with the development of structured programming can be found in Edward Nash Yourdon (ed.), *Classics in Software Engineering* (New York: Yourdon Press, 1979).

15. See F. T. Baker, "Chief Programmer Team Management of Production Programming," *IBM Systems Journal* 1, 1972, pp. 56–73; W. P. Stevens, G. J. Meyers, and L. L. Constantine, "Structured Design," *IBM Systems Journal* 2, 1974, pp. 115–139; Brooks, *The Mythical Man-Month*, pp. 32, 144.

16. See Stevens, Myers, and Constantine, "Structured Design," pp. 137–39. I am also indebted to Professor Joel Moses of M.I.T. for this observation about the negative effects of structured design on reusability. Some of his observations on this topic can be found in Joel Moses, "Organizing for Change: The Cultural Basis of Organizational Structures," unpublished manuscript, M.I.T. Dept. of Electrical Engineering and Computer Science, April 1988.

17. Boehm, "Software Engineering." This article is reproduced in Yourdon, *Classics in Software Engineering*; quotation from pp. 327–29.

18. Ibid. pp. 329–50.

19. The following elaboration on the table is based on Ramamoorthy et al., "Software Engineering."

20. For a more technical discussion of software errors and program reliability, see Martin Schooman, *Software Engineering: Design, Reliability, and Management* (New York: McGraw-Hill, 1983), pp. 296–407.

21. For an excellent discussion of productivity measurement and examples such as this, see Capers Jones, *Programming Productivity* (New York: McGraw-Hill, 1986). Also, as a general primer on software project management, see Barry W. Boehm, *Software Engineering Economics* (Englewood Cliffs, N.J.: Prentice-Hall, 1981).

22. Brooks, *The Mythical Man-Month*, p. 117.

23. According to the *IBM Systems Journal* index, an article by Rully titled "A Subroutine Package for FORTRAN" was published in 1968, no. 3, beginning on p. 248.

24. This section is based on M. D. McIlroy, "Mass Produced Software Components," in Naur and Randell, *Software Engineering*. The discussion of McIlroy's address is on pp. 151–55, as well as in Ellis Horowitz and John B. Munson, "An Expansive View of Reusable Software," *IEEE Transactions on Software Engineering* SE-10, 5, September 1984, p. 481.

25. Horowitz and Munson, "An Expansive View," pp. 477–78.

26. See Brian W. Kernighan, "The Unix System and Software Reusability," *IEEE Transactions on Software Engineering* SE-10, 5, September 1984, pp. 513–18.

27. See Robert G. Lanergan and Charles A. Grasso, "Software Engineering with Reusable Designs and Code," *IEEE Transactions on Software Engineering* SE-10, 5, September 1984, pp. 498–501; and Peter Freeman, *Tutorial: Software Reusability* (Washington, D.C.: IEEE Computer Society Press, 1987), pp. 2–7.

28. Lanergan and Grasso, "Software Engineering with Reusable Designs and Codes," pp. 500–501, and see Appendixes A and B.

29. T. Capers Jones, "Reusability in Programming: A Survey of the State of the Art," *IEEE Transactions on Software Engineering* SE-10, 5, September 1984, p. 488.

30. The following discussion is based on Jones, "Reusability in Programming," pp. 488–94.

31. For additional discussion of reusability along the same lines as presented here, see Lanergan and Grasso, "Software Engineering with Reusable Designs and Codes," pp. 498–501.

32. See Barbara Liskov and John Guttag, *Abstraction and Specification in Program Development* (Cambridge, Mass.: MIT Press, 1986), esp. pp. 3–10, 316–18; and John Savage, Susan Magidson, and Alex M. Stein, *The Mystical Machine: Issues and Ideas in Computing* (Reading, Mass.: Addison-Wesley, 1986), pp. 225–28.

33. Savage, Magidson, and Stein, *Mystical Machine*, pp. 238–41.

34. Lawrence M. Fisher, "A New Approach to Programming," *New York Times*, Sept. 7, 1988, p. D8.

35. For a framework to interpret and measure the effectiveness of different types of CASE tools, see John C. Henderson and Jay G. Cooprider, "Dimensions of I/S Planning and Design Technology," unpublished Working Paper, Cambridge, Mass., *M.I.T. Sloan School of Management*, 1988.

36. See W. D. Hagamen et al., "A Program Generator," *IBM Systems Journal* 2, 1975, p. 122.

37. David H. Freedman, "In Search of Productivity," *Infosystems*, November 1986, p. 12.

38. See Otis Porter et al., "The Software Trap: Automate—or Else," *Business Week*, May 9, 1988, pp. 142–54, as well as the Japanese cases in Part II of this book.

39. Leon G. Stucki et al., "Concepts and Prototypes of ARGUS," in Horst Hunke (ed.), *Software Engineering Environments* (Amsterdam: North Holland, 1981), pp. 61–79.

40. R. R. Willis, "AIDES: Computer Aided Design of Software Systems-II" in Hunke, *Software Engineering Environments*, pp. 27–48.

41. See the factory discussions, especially Chapter 7, for more detailed discussions of CASE tools and what steps in the development process they automate.

42. Neil Margolis, "CASE Fights to Beat 'All Talk, No Action' Image," *Computerworld*, Jan. 2, 1989, p. 46.

43. Barry W. Boehm and Thomas A. Standish, "Software Technology in the 1990's: Using an Evolutionary Paradigm," *Computer*, November 1983, pp. 30–37.

44. Software revenues are listed as "program products" and available in IBM's annual reports.

45. See, for example, Takeshita Toru (Programming Systems, IBM Japan), "Purogurramu seisaku-ue shinko kanri to hinshitsu kanri" [Progress control and quality control in program development], *Joho shori* 5, September 1965, pp. 260–65. This was the first article in this journal (the English title translates to "Information Processing"), which was launched in 1960, on software project management. Takeshita, who apparently took on the task of introducing U.S. practices to the Japanese, also published another article in 1971, "Sofutouea no hinshitsu to sono kanri" [Software quality and control], *Hinshitsu kanri* 22, 11, November 1971, pp. 19–23.

46. The general outlines of this discussion of IBM are based on an interview with James H. Frame, Oct. 13, 1988. Frame, a graduate of St. John's College in Maryland, initially worked as a systems engineer installing IBM computers and developing input/output software. During the early 1960s he was promoted to manager of the Endicott Programming Center, which developed software for the 1401 and 1410 models and laid out the specifications for OS 360 and DOS 360. In 1965 he moved to Raleigh to head its Programming Center, which concentrated on communications software. In 1973 he moved to California to set up IBM's Santa Teresa Laboratory. He served as director of programming before leaving IBM in 1978 to join ITT.

47. Norman Weizer, "A History of Operating Systems," *Datamation*, January 1981, pp. 119–26.

48. Franklin M. Fisher, James W. McKie, and Richard B. Mancke, *IBM and the U.S. Data Processing Industry: An Economic History* (New York: Praeger, 1983), pp. 118–19, 138–41.

49. Frame interview.

50. On the IBM Future System (FS) project, see also Richard Thomas DeLamarter, *Big Blue: IBM's Use and Abuse of Power* (New York: Dodd, Mead, 1986), pp. 215–20.

51. See Goldberg, "Software Engineering: An Emerging Discipline," and the description in Arden, *What Can Be Automated?*, pp. 3–31.

52. G. H. McCue, "IBM's Santa Teresa Laboratory: Architectural Design for Program Development," *IBM Systems Journal* 17, 1, 1978, p. 4.

53. Interviews with Frederick George, manager, Network Systems Design, IBM Corporation, Raleigh, N.C., Jan. 6, 1987; and Mark Harris, manager, Intermediate Processor Development, IBM Corporation, Endicott, N.Y., Dec. 12 and 16, 1986.

54. Glenn Bacon to Michael Cusumano, April 25, 1988.

55. Frame interview.

56. W. S. Humphrey, "The IBM Large-Systems Software Development Process: Objectives and Direction," *IBM Systems Journal* 24, 2, 1985, pp. 77–78.

57. This account of ITT is based on an unpublished paper provided by James H. Frame detailing his efforts in ITT between 1978 and 1985 and written by a former IBM colleague who moved with Mr. Frame to ITT. See Capers Jones, "A 10-Year Retrospective of Software Engineering within ITT," Cambridge, Mass., Software Productivity Research, Inc., May 15, 1988.

58. The center supplemented a few other software R&D organizations in the larger ITT companies in the U.S. and Europe, which totaled 235 researchers, giving Frame a worldwide software R&D staff of 385 in 1983.

59. Jones, "A Ten-Year Retrospective," p. 14.

60. Ibid., p. 13.

61. This discussion is based on Wanda J. Orlikowski, "Information Technology in Post-Industrial Organizations: An Exploration of the Computer-Mediation of Production Work," Ph.D. dissertation, Graduate School of Business, New York University, November 1988.

62. Robert Schware, *The World Software Industry and Software Engineering*, Technical Paper #104, Washington, D.C., The World Bank, 1989, p. 17.

63. Orlikowski, "Information Technology in Post-Industrial Organizations," p. 133.

64. Ibid., pp. 164–71.

65. Ibid., pp. 257, 345–46.

66. Ibid., p. 345.

67. Ibid., pp. 230–31, 260–61.

68. Ibid., pp. 260–61.

69. Ibid., p. 235.

70. Ibid., pp. 328, 342–43.

71. Ibid., pp. 327–35, 421–22.

72. Ibid., pp. 256, 433.

73. The following description of software operations at Digital is based primarily on an unpublished paper written by a former employee for my class at the M.I.T. Sloan School of Management, "Japanese Technology Management" (15.940): Cynthia Schuyler, "The Software Development Process: A Comparison—Toshiba vs. Digital Equipment," Dec. 11, 1987 as well as interviews with Wendy McKay, former manager, Educational Software, Digital Equipment Corporation, December 1986, and the Duncan and Harris report cited below.

74. Schuyler, "Software Development Process," pp. 16–17; McKay interview.

75. Anne Smith Duncan and Thomas J. Harris, "Software Productivity Measurement," Commercial Languages and Tools Group, Digital Equipment Corporation, 1988, p. 1.

76. Schuyler, "Software Development Process," pp. 17–18.

77. Ibid., pp. 19–20; McKay interview.

78. Interviews with J. Grady, engineering manager, Digital Equipment Corporation, April 1986.

79. Schuyler, "Software Development Process," pp. 27–28.

80. Duncan and Harris, "Software Productivity Measurements," p. 2.
81. Schuyler, "Software Development Process," pp. 26–27.
82. Ibid., p. 22.
83. Ibid., p. 23.
84. Ibid., pp. 24–25.
85. The remainder of this section is based on Duncan and Harris, "Software Productivity Measurements," pp. 1–9. Performance data cited is from pp. 6–8.

Chapter 3

1. I would like to thank David Finnell for his contributions to ideas expressed in this chapter through research done under my direction for a master's thesis at the M.I.T. Sloan School of Management, titled "Application of the Factory Model to Large-Scale Software Engineering," June 1987. The thesis work included the interviews with Ronald Atchley cited in the text.
2. SDC's official company history, written by an SDC employee, details the development of the firm from 1956 through 1981. See Claude Baum, *The System Builders: The Story of SDC* (Santa Monica, Calif.: System Development Corporation, 1981).
3. This background material is based on Baum, *System Builders*.
4. Ibid., p. 6.
5. Ibid., p. 168.
6. Ibid., pp. 166–67, 170.
7. Ibid., p. 246.
8. Ibid., pp. 219–20.
9. Ibid., p. 220.
10. Harvey Bratman and Terry Court, "The Software Factory," *Computer*, May 1975, pp. 28–37. This article describes the factory-tool set. A second article repeats the tool discussion but also describes the development of standards and procedures, as well as the division of labor between program offices and the central factory facility. See Bratman and Court, "Elements of the Software Factory: Standards, Procedures, and Tools," in Infotech International Ltd., *Software Engineering Techniques* (Berkshire, England: Infotech International Ltd., 1977), pp. 117–43.
11. In addition to their own experiences, Bratman and Court cited an influential 1974 study that had attempted, without success, to find such a correlation: R. W. Wolverton, "The Cost of Developing Large Scale Software," *IEEE Transactions on Computers* C-23, 6, June 1974, pp. 615–35.
12. Bratman and Court, "The Software Factory", pp. 28–29.
13. Ibid., p. 36.
14. Bratman and Court, "Elements of the Software Factory," p. 119.
15. Baum, *System Builders*, p. 221; interviews with John B. Munson, Oct. 4 and 5, 1987; interview with Terry Court, manager, Development Resources Laboratory, GM Hughes Electronics, June 22, 1989. Note: Quotations and other references in this chapter attributed to Court and Munson refer to these interviews.
16. Court interview.
17. Bratman and Court, "Elements of the Software Factory," p. 117.
18. Ibid., p. 120.
19. Baum, *System Builders*, p. 222.
20. Bratman and Court, "Elements of the Software Factory," p. 121.
21. This following discussion of the *SDM* procedures and the quotations are from Ibid., pp. 121–26.
22. Baum, *System Builders*, pp. 220–23.
23. Interviews with Ronald Atchley, March 27, 1987 and April 23, 1987. Note: Unreferenced quotes from Atchley refer to these interviews.
24. Bratman and Court, "Elements of the Software Factory," p. 127.

25. Ibid., p. 128.
26. This section's discussion and unreferenced quotations are from nearly identical descriptions of the tool set in Bratman and Court, "The Software Factory," pp. 30–36; and "Elements of the Software Factory," pp. 128–37.
27. In Bratman and Court's "Elements of the Software Factory," this tool is called the program analysis and test certification processor.
28. Ibid., p. 143 and Bratman and Court, "The Software Factory," p. 36.
29. Baum, *System Builders*, p. 205.
30. Ibid., pp. 200, 204–205, 217–19, 224 for references to these projects.
31. Ibid., pp. 205, 224.
32. Court interview.
33. Munson interview; and Baum, *System Builders*, p. 224.
34. Court and Munson interview.
35. Court interview.
36. Atchley interview.
37. Baum, *System Builders*, p. 222; Munson and Court interviews.
38. Interview with Clarence Starkey, manager, SDC, Oct. 3, 1986.
39. Atchley interview.
40. This discussion of problems 1, 2, and 3 is based primarily on the interviews with Munson and Atchley, as noted.
41. Interview with David Deaver, manager, SDC, Oct. 3, 1986.
42. Atchley interview.
43. Munson and Court interviews.
44. Bratman and Court, "Elements of the Software Factory," p. 137.
45. Munson interview.
46. Court interview.
47. Munson and Court interviews.
48. Atchley interview.
49. Deaver interview.
50. Munson and Atchley interviews.
51. Baum, *System Builders*, p. 43.
52. Court, Atchley, and Munson interviews.
53. Burroughs Corporation, *Annual Report 1984*, p. 15.
54. John Joss, "The Real Stuff," *Performance* (McLean, Va.: Unisys Defense Systems), no. 1, 1989, pp. 18–25.

Chapter 4

1. Actually, Hitachi used the Japanese term *kojo*, which translates as either "factory" or "works."
2. *Japan Economic Journal*, June 7, 1986, p. 14; and, for market share data, "Nihon no konpyuta setchi jokyo (The status of Japan's computer placements)," *Computer Report* [in Japanese], January 1985, p. 78.
3. Hitachi Ltd., "Introduction to Hitachi and Modern Japan" (Tokyo: Hitachi International Operations Group, 1983); Tadao Kagono et al., *Strategic vs. Evolutionary Management: A U.S.-Japan Comparison of Strategy and Organization* (Amsterdam: North-Holland, 1985), pp. 103–105.
4. RCA, Control Data, IBM, and NCR all delivered transistorized computers in 1958. See Franklin M. Fisher, James W. McKie, and Richard B. Mancke, *IBM and the U.S. Data Processing Industry: An Economic History* (New York: Praeger, 1983), pp. 50–51. For the Japanese story, see Shigeru Takahashi, "Early Transistor Computers in Japan," *Annals of the History of Computing* 8, 2, April 1986, pp. 144–54.
5. A useful book in Japanese on the details surrounding this incident is Nano Piko, *Nichi-Bei konpyuta senso: IBM sangyo supai jiken no teiryu* [The Japan-U.S. computer war:

underlying the IBM industrial spying incident] (Tokyo: Nihon Keizai Shimbunsha, 1982).

6. Dale F. Farmer, "IBM-Compatible Giants," *Datamation*, December 1981, pp. 96–97, 104.

7. "2 New Computers from IBM Rival," *New York Times*, March 12, 1985, p. D5; Y. Singh, G. King, and J. Anderson, "IBM 3090 Performance: A Balanced System Approach," *IBM Systems Journal* 25, 1, 1986, pp. 4–19; and Hitachi Seisakusho, "HITAC M-680H," company brochure. My thanks also to Steve Bello of the IBM Corporation for his unpublished paper for my course on Japanese Technology Management, titled "Design Competition in Mainframe Computer Hardware," Dec. 11, 1987.

8. These data and other information cited after on the Software Works primarily came from interviews with Kanji Shibata, manager, Engineering Department, Hitachi Software Works, conducted on Sept. 19, 1985; July 23, 1986; and Aug. 24, 1988. These data on the Systems Design Works primarily came from interviews with Michio Tsuda, senior engineer, Systems Technology Management Department, Systems Design Works, Hitachi, Ltd. and Ryoji Eguchi, engineer, Systems Technology Management Department, Systems Design Works, Hitachi, Ltd., Aug. 21, 1989.

9. Shibata interviews.

10. Usui Kenji, "HITAC kaihatsu shi (2)" [History of HITAC development], *Computopia*, July 1975, p. 30.

11. Hitachi Seisakusho, *Sofutouea Kojo 10 nen no ayumi* [A 10-year history of the Software Works] (Yokohama: Hitachi, Ltd., 1979), pp. 51–52.

12. Interviews with Dr. Shigeru Takahashi, former deputy general manager of Hitachi's Computer Division, Jan. 9 and 21, 1985 and Sept. 10, 1985. See also Hitachi, *Sofutouea Kojo*, tables on pp. 49–50.

13. Interview with Kazuyuki Sakata, managing director, Nippon Business Consultant, Ltd., and former deputy general manager of Hitachi Software Works, Sept. 10, 1985.

14. Shimada Shozo, "Hitachi no gijutsu (2): kaihatsu-ki (HITAC 5020)—sofutouea" [Hitachi technology (2): development period (HITAC 5020)-software] in HITAC Yuza Henshu Iinkai (ed.), *20 nen no ayumi* [A 20-year history] (Tokyo: Hitachi Computer Division, 1983), pp. 27–29. Also, Murata Kenro, "Hitachi no gijutsu: kaihatsu-ki (HITAC 5020, 8800)—hadouea" in HITAC, *20 nen no ayumi*, p. 22; and Minamisawa Noburo, *Nihon konpyuta hattatsu-shi* [A history of the development of Japanese computers] (Tokyo: Nihon Keizai Shimbun-sha, 1978).

15. Usui, "HITAC kaihatsu shi (2), p. 37.

16. Takahashi interviews; and Usui, "HITAC kaihatsu shi (2)," p. 37; Hitachi, *Sofutouea kojo*, p. 53.

17. Hitachi Seisakusho, *Kanagawa kojo 15 nen no ayumi* [A 15-year history of the Kanagawa Works] (Kanagawa: Hitachi, Ltd., 1978), p. 40. Since EDOS continued to build on the RCA operating system, the mainframes Hitachi has sold in Japan after 1970 are close to IBM but not compatible, although most machines Hitachi produces for export are modified to be IBM compatible.

18. Hitachi, *Sofutouea Kojo*, pp. 54–56.

19. Ibid., pp. 56, 130.

20. Hitachi Ltd. memorandum to Michael Cusumano, Aug. 21, 1985.

21. Takahashi interviews; and interviews with Yoichi Yokoyama, Engineering Department, Hitachi Software Works, Sept. 1, 1987 and Aug. 24, 1988.

22. Hitachi, *Sofutouea Kojo*, p. 19.

23. Hitachi Seisakusho, *Hitachi Seisakusho shi* [History of Hitachi Ltd.] (Tokyo: Hitachi Ltd., 1971), Vol. 3, pp. 55–56, 223–24; Usui, "HITAC kaihatsu shi (2)," pp. 36–38; Hitachi, *Kanagawa Kojo 15 nen no ayumi*, pp. 45–47.

24. Minamisawa, *Nihon konpyuta hattatsu-shi*, pp. 154, 163.

25. Usui, "HITAC kaihatsu shi (2)," p. 36; Sakata interview.

26. Sakata interview.

27. Usui, "HITAC kaihatsu shi (2)," pp. 36–37; Hitachi, *Sofutouea Kojo*, pp. 17, 129.

28. Hitachi, *Sofutouea Kojo*, p. 23.
29. Ibid., pp. 21–22; Hitachi, *Kanagawa Kojo 15 nen no ayumi*, pp. 18–22, 69. An analysis of the Odawara Works can be found in Hitachi Seisakusho, *Odawara Kojo 10 nen shi* [A 10-year history of the Odawara Works] (Kanagawa: Hitachi Ltd., 1977).
30. Hitachi, *Sofutouea Kojo*, pp. 4–5, 8; Yokoyama interview, Sept. 1, 1987.
31. Shibata interviews.
32. Sakata interviews.
33. Shibata interviews.
34. The next sections are based on Shibata interviews and Hitachi, *Sofutouea Kojo*, pp. 4–11, 118–19, 127–28, 160–65, 192–202.
35. Denji Tajima and Tomoo Matsubara, "Inside the Japanese Software Industry," *Computer*, March 1984, p. 40.
36. Hitachi, *Sofutouea Kojo*, p. 117.
37. Ibid., p. 5; Shibata interviews.
38. Hitachi, *Sofutouea Kojo*, pp. 114–15; interviews with Shibata and Yokoyama.
39. Sakata interview.
40. Hitachi, *Sofutouea Kojo*, pp. 117–18.
41. Kataoka Masanori, Domen Nobuyoshi, and Nogi Kenroku, "Sofutouea kozo sekkei giho" [Software Structure Specification Method], *Hitachi hyoron* 62, 12, December 1980, pp. 7–10.
42. The product-control system was started by the System Program Department in the Kanagawa Works, for both storing program source files and accompanying documentation for future reference, necessary either to correct defects or to add enhancements. In 1976, Hitachi started the practice of keeping copies of all programs in a separate location to guard against destruction from earthquakes or accidents. See Hitachi, *Sofutouea Kojo*, p. 115; Shibata interview, Sept. 19, 1985.
43. Hitachi, *Sofutouea Kojo*, pp. 113–14; undated Hitachi, Ltd. memorandum, "Table 1: History of Production Control at Hitachi's Software Works;" Sakata interview; Shibata interviews, Sept. 19, 1985 and July 23, 1986.
44. A recent book on the MI program at several Hitachi factories (although not including the Software Works) is Iwai Masakazu, *Hitachi-shiki keiei kakushin: MI undo no kenkyu* [Hitachi-style management innovation: a study of the MI program] (Tokyo: Daiyamondo-sha, 1983).
45. Hitachi, *Sofutouea Kojo*, pp. 118, 179–84. 198, 202. See also Nihon Noritsu Kyokai (Japan Management Association) (ed.), *Hitachi no seisan kakumei—MST seisan shisutemu no zenbo* [Hitachi's production revolution—the full story of the MST production system] (Tokyo, Nihon Noritsu Kyokai, 1982), p. 32. MST stands for minimum stocks/minimum standard time.
46. For a discussion of PERT applied to software projects see Martin L. Shooman, *Software Engineering: Design, Reliability, and Management* (New York: McGraw-Hill, 1983), pp. 457–60.
47. Sakata interview.
48. Frederick P. Brooks, Jr., *The Mythical Man-Month: Essays on Software Engineering* (Reading, Mass.: Addison-Wesley, 1975), pp. 16, 31.
49. This discussion is based primarily on interviews with Yoshiharu Matsumoto, R&D Department manager; Yoshizo Matsuzaki, Applications Software Department manager; and Tomoo Takahashi, Applications Software Department deputy manager, Hitachi Software Engineering, Sept. 3, 1987; and Shibata.
50. Sakata interview. Also see Sakata Kazuyuki, "Sofutouea no seisan kanri ni okeru yosoku giho no teishiki-ka—sei-teki na yosoku oyobi koshoritsu suii moderu" [Formulation for predictive methods in software production control—static prediction and failure rate transition model], pp. 277–83, and "Sofutouea no seisan kanri ni okeru yosoku giho no teishiki-ka—doteki na yosoku: sakidori hyoka giho" [Formulation for predictive methods in software production control—dynamic prediction: quality probe], in Denshi Tsushin Gakkai (ed.), *Denshi Tsushin Gakkai ronbun shi* [Transactions

of the Institute of Electrical and Communications Engineers] 57-D, 5, May 1974, pp. 284–91.

51. Shibata interviews; and Hitachi, *Sofutouea Kojo*, p. 115.

52. Shibata and Yokoyama interviews.

53. This discussion is based on Hashimoto Yaichiro et al. (Hitachi Software Works), "Sofutouea hinshitsu hyoka shisutemu 'SQE'" [Software quality estimation system 'SQE'], *Hitachi hyoron* 68, 5, May 1986, pp. 55–58.

54. Interviews with Yukio Mizuno (NEC) and Tadashi Yoshida (Fujitsu), cited in chapters 6 and 7.

55. Hitachi defined reused code as followed: The project reuse rate equaled the number of reused steps (lines) divided by reused steps plus new steps plus revised steps times 100. The cumulative reuse rate equaled the cumulative number of reused steps from version 1 divided by the number of steps in the current version times 100. Shibata memorandum to Cusumano, July 23, 1986.

56. Tajima and Matsubara, "Inside the Japanese Software Industry," pp. 36–39.

57. Interviews with Matsumoto, Matsuzaki, and T. Takahashi.

58. Hitachi, *Sofutouea Kojo*, p. 117; Yokoyama interviews.

59. Hitachi, *Sofutouea Kojo*, pp. 7–8. 124.

60. Hitachi, Ltd., "Computer Training System and Activities," Computer Division, Education and Training Division, unpublished internal document, May 1988; p. 56; and interview with Tsurayuki Kado, chief instructor, Systems Engineering Education and Training Department, Systems Design Works, Hitachi Ltd., July 21, 1989.

61. The following discussion, unless noted, is based on Hitachi Ltd., "Computer Training System and Activities," pp. 39–57, esp. pp. 43–46.

62. Sakata, Shibata, and Kado interviews.

63. Shibata interviews.

64. Regarding ICAS, see M. Kobayashi et al., "ICAS: An Integrated Computer Aided Software Engineering System," *IEEE Digest of Papers—Spring '83 COMPCON* (Washington, D.C.: IEEE Computer Society Press, 1983), pp. 238–44; and Kobayashi Masakazu and Aoyama Yoshihiko, "Sofutouea seisan gijutsu no saikin no koko" [Current topics in software engineering], *Hitachi hyoron* 68, 5, May 1986, pp. 1–6.

65. For HIPACE, see Miyazoe Hidehiko et al., "Apurikeshon shisutemu no koritsu-teki sekkei giho 'HIPACE'" [Software engineering methodology for development of application systems 'HIPACE'], *Hitachi hyoron* 62, 12, December 1980, pp. 15–20; for EAGLE, see Hagi Yoichi et al., "Shisutemu kaihatsu shien sofutouea 'EAGLE'" [Integrated software development and maintenance system 'EAGLE'], *Hitachi hyoron* 66, 3, March 1984, pp. 19–24.

66. This section is based on Kataoka Masanori, Hagi Yoichi, and Nogi Kenroku, "Sofutouea kaihatsu shien shisutemu (CASD shisutemu)" [Computer-aided software development system (CASD system)], *Hitachi hyoron* 62, 12, December 1980, pp. 33–36.

67. Unless noted, this section is based on Shibata Kanji and Yokoyama Yoichi (Hitachi Software Works), "Sogo sofutouea seisan kanri shisutemu 'CAPS'" [Computer-aided production control system for software 'CAPS'], *Hitachi hyoron* 62, 12, December 1980, pp. 37–42; and Shibata and Yokoyama interviews.

68. Hitachi Ltd. memorandum, "Table 1.2 Background and Conditions Affecting CAPS Development," ca. 1986.

69. Shibata and Yokoyama interviews; Hitachi Ltd. memorandum, "Software Development Project Diagnostics by Knowledge Engineering," 1988; and Sumida Naoichi et al. (Hitachi Software Works), "Sofutouea purojekuto shindan giho PDOCK" [Software project diagnostic method PDOCK] (Paper delivered at Japan's Information Processing Association [Joho Shori Gakkai] 37th National Conference, 1988).

70. The source of this discussion of ICAS and quotations, unless noted, is M. Kobayashi et al., "ICAS," pp. 241–43.

71. Miyazoe Hidehiko and Nakao Kazuo et al., "Shisutemu keikaku no tame no shisutemu

yokyu bunseki shuho 'PPDS' no kaihatsu" [System demand analysis procedures for system planning 'PPDS'], *Hitachi hyoron* 62, 12, December 1980, pp. 21–24.

72. Matsuzaki interview.

73. For a detailed description of PAD see Y. Futamura et al., "Development of Computer Programs by Problem Analysis Diagram (PAD)" (Paper delivered at the Fifth IEEE International Conference on Software Engineering, San Diego, Calif., March 1981), pp. 325–32.

74. This discussion of EAGLE, unless noted, is based on Hagi et al., "Shisutemu kaihatsu shien sofutouea 'EAGLE,'" pp. 19–24; and Hagi Yoichi et al., "Shisutemu kaihatsu shien sofutouea 'EAGLE'—EAGLE kakucho-han 'EAGLE 2'" [Integrated software development and maintenance system 'EAGLE'—the enhanced version of EAGLE, 'EAGLE 2'], *Hitachi hyoron* 68, 5, May 1986, pp. 29–34.

75. Interviews with Tsuda and Eguchi.

76. Matsuzaki interview.

77. Hitachi Seisakusho, "Omori Sofutouea Kojo annai" [Guide to Omori Software Works], pp. 10–15. For a discussion of the APP system, referred to previously as EAGLE/P (CANDO), see Ono Osamu, Matsumoto Hikozo, and Kotani Shingo, "EAGLE ni okeru shisutemu sekkei shien shisutemu no kaihatsu" [Development of system design aids for EAGLE], *Hitachi hyoron* 68, 5, May 1986, pp. 39–42.

78. Shibata, Yokoyama, and Matsumoto interviews.

79. This discussion is based on interviews with Dr. Sadamichi Mitsumori, chief researcher, Dr. Takeshi Chusho, senior researcher, and other researchers from the Systems Development Laboratory, Hitachi, Ltd., July 21, 1989; and Hitachi Ltd., "Systems Development Laboratory," undated company brochure.

80. Hitachi Ltd., "Production Engineering Department," undated company publication.

Chapter 5

1. See Table 4.1.

2. See *Datamation*, June 1, 1985, pp. 58–120, and June 15, 1987, p. 31; and Table 4.1.

3. Interviews with Dr. Yoshihiro Matsumoto, fellow scientist, Toshiba Corporation, Sept. 4, 1987 and Aug. 24, 1988; Shimoda Hirotsugu, *Sofutouea kojo* [Software factories] (Tokyo: Toyo Keizai Shimposha, 1986), pp. 100–101.

4. Matsumoto interviews; and Toshiba Corporation, "Trend of Application Software Size," transparency copy, received March 15, 1988.

5. Matsumoto interviews.

6. Yoshihiro Matsumoto, "A Software Factory: An Overall Approach to Software Production," in Peter Freeman (ed.), *Tutorial: Software Reusability* (Washington, D.C.: IEEE Computer Society Press, 1987), p. 155.

7. Yoshihiro Matsumoto, "Management of Industrial Software Production," *Computer*, February 1984, p. 70.

8. Yoshihiro Matsumoto and S. Yamamoto, "The SWB System Supports Industrial Software Production," *Proceedings of the International Workshop on Software Engineering Environments* (Beijing, China: China Academic Publishers, August 18–20, 1986), p. 74.

9. Matsumoto, "Management of Industrial Software Production," p. 70. See also Yoshihiro Matsumoto, "Software Education in an Industry," *Proceedings of the International Computer Software and Applications Conference—COMPSAC '82* (Los Angeles: IEEE Computer Society Press, November 8–12, 1982), p. 92.

10. This section is based on Yoshihiro Matsumoto et al., "SWB System. A Software Factory," in Horst Hunke (ed.), *Software Engineering Environments* (Amsterdam: North-Holland, 1981), pp. 305–309; and Matsumoto interviews.

11. Interview with Shinichi Kishi, senior specialist, Computer Application Systems Department, Fuchu Works, Toshiba Corporation, July 17, 1989.

12. Interview with Shuichi Yamamoto, senior specialist, Software Engineering Develop-

ment Group, Engineering Administration and Information Systems Department, Fuchu Works, Toshiba Corporation, July 17, 1989.

13. Shimoda, *Sofutouea kojo*, pp. 103–104.

14. Toshiba Corporation, "Toshiba Fuchu Works," Tokyo, 1987, p. 5.

15. This section is based on Matsumoto interviews and Shimoda, *Sofutouea kojo*, pp. 103–104.

16. This section is based on Matsumoto, "Management of Industrial Software Production," p. 59; Matsumoto, "The SWB System," p. 79; Matsumoto, "A Software Factory," p. 156; and Matsumoto interviews.

17. Interviews with Kishi, Yamamoto, and Yoshio Ebata, specialist, Electric Power Dispatch and Transmission Department, Computer Systems Designing Section, Fuchu Works, Toshiba Corporation, July 17, 1989.

18. This discussion is from Matsumoto, "Management of Industrial Software Production," pp. 61–64; Matsumoto, "A Software Factory," pp. 163–67; and Matsumoto interviews.

19. Matsumoto, "Management of Industrial Software Production," p. 63.

20. For a description of IBM practices, see T. C. Jones, "Measuring Programming Quality and Productivity," *IBM Systems Journal*, January 1978, pp. 39–63.

21. Kishi interview.

22. Matsumoto interviews. This last observation suggests there are practical limits to project sizes, depending on the degree to which design work could be divided up. It was another question whether there was an optimal size for a software factory as a whole, although there were probably limits to how much managers could effectively divide complex tasks that required interactions among team members, such as for detailed design, coding, and testing. For a treatment of this issue in a more general context, see Eric von Hippel, "Task Partitioning: An Innovation Process Variable," Working Paper #2030-88, Cambridge, Mass., M.I.T. Sloan School of Management, June 1988.

23. Matsumoto, "Management of Industrial Software Production," p. 69, and Matsumoto, "A Software Factory," p. 156.

24. Matsumoto interviews; Toshiba Corporation, "Programming Language," transparency copy, Sept. 1987; Matsumoto, "SWB System. A Software Factory," p. 316.

25. Matsumoto, "A Software Factory," p. 156.

26. Matsumoto cited Jones, "Measuring Programming," as justification for adopting the EASL method, but did not reveal the conversion coefficients Toshiba used. For a recent list of Jones' conversion factors from assembler to other higher-level languages, see Capers Jones, *Programming Productivity* (New York: McGraw-Hill, 1986), p. 49.

27. Matsumoto, "A Software Factory," pp. 163–66; interview with Yoshio Ikeda, program manager, Nuclear Power Generation Control Computer Systems Engineering Section, Power Generation Control Computer Systems Department, Fuchu Works, Toshiba Corporation, July 17, 1989.

28. Yamamoto, Ebata, and Kishi interviews.

29. Matsumoto, "A Software Factory," p. 159.

30. Matsumoto interviews.

31. This assumes a 1:3 conversion for the EASL data, a rate consistent with Jones' FORTRAN to assembler conversion. This seems a fair rate for the Toshiba data, given that 60 percent of Toshiba code was in FORTRAN; approximately 20 percent was in assembler or similar intermediate-level languages, requiring a lower conversion rate; and another 20 percent appeared in other languages.

32. Productivity numbers can be found in numerous sources, including Jones, *Programming Productivity*, pp. 92–114; S. D. Conte, H. E. Dunsmore, and V. Y. Shen, *Software Engineering Metrics and Models* (Menlo Park, Calif.: Benjaman/Cummings, 1986), pp. 251, 270; Martin Shooman, *Software Engineering: Design, Reliability, and Management* (New York: McGraw-Hill, 1983), pp. 438–45; Frederick P. Brooks, Jr., *The Mythical Man-Month: Essays on Software Engineering* (Reading, Mass.: Addison-Wesley, 1975), pp. 88–94; U.S. Department of Commerce, International Trade Administration, *A Com-*

petitive Assessment of the U.S. Software Industry (Washington, D.C.: U.S. Government Printing Office, 1984), p. 11.

33. This observation is based on analysis of the data and interviews with respondents for the survey discussed in Appendix B.

34. For a discussion of Japanese high school education, see Thomas Rohlen, *Japan's High Schools* (Berkeley, Calif.: University of California Press, 1983).

35. Matsumoto, "A Software Factory," pp. 172.

36. Matsumoto interviews.

37. Matsumoto, "A Software Factory," pp. 158–59.

38. Matsumoto, "SWB System. A Software Factory," pp. 307–308.

39. Matsumoto, "A Software Factory," p. 176.

40. Matsumoto interviews.

41. Yoshihiro Matsumoto response by letter to "Additional Information Questions" in Cusumano survey (discussed in Appendix A), Feb. 11, 1987.

42. Jones, *Programming Productivity*, pp. 168–69.

43. Matsumoto interviews. Depending on whether Toshiba conducted the tests in the factory or at the customers' plant sites, between 35 and 45 percent of the discovered faults were design errors, 10 to 20 percent programming errors, 20 to 30 percent data faults, and 15 to 25 percent hardware interface faults. See Matsumoto, "A Software Factory," pp. 159–63.

44. This next section is based on Matsumoto, "SWB System. A Software Factory," pp. 307, 315; and Matsumoto, "Management of Industrial Software Production," p. 70.

45. Matsumoto interviews.

46. Matsumoto, "A Software Factory," p. 163.

47. This discussion is based on interviews with Matsumoto and Ebata; Matsumoto, "A Software Factory," pp. 174, 176; and Matsumoto, "Software Education," pp. 92–94.

48. Matsumoto, "Software Education," p. 93; Matsumoto, "A Software Factory," p. 176.

49. Yamamoto, Ebata, Ikeda, and Kishi interviews.

50. Matsumoto, "SWB System. A Software Factory," p. 310; Matsumoto, "A Software Factory," p. 176; and Matsumoto interviews.

51. Y. Matsumoto et al., "SPS: A Software Production System for Mini-Computers and Micro-Computers," *Proceedings of the International Computer Software and Applications Conference—COMPSAC '78* (New York: IEEE Computer Society Press, November 1978), p. 396.

52. Matsumoto and Yamamoto, "The SWB System Supports Industrial Software Production," p. 78; and Matsumoto and Yamamoto interviews.

53. Matsumoto, "SPS," pp. 396–401; Matsumoto, "SWB System. A Software Factory," pp. 311–13.

54. This section is based on Matsumoto, "SWB System. A Software Factory," pp. 309–15; Matsumoto and Yamamoto, "The SWB System Supports Industrial Software Production," p. 77; Matsumoto, "A Software Factory," pp. 156, 166, 171; Matsumoto interviews; and Shimoda, *Sofutouea kojo*, p. 107.

55. Yoshihiro Matsumoto response to Cusumano's questionnaire, "Large-Scale Applications Software," Feb. 11, 1987.

56. Matsumoto and Yamamoto, "The SWB System etc.," p. 76; and Matsumoto, "A Software Factory," pp. 166, 171.

57. Yamamoto interview.

58. Matsumoto, "Management of Industrial Software Production," p. 70.

59. Ibid. pp. 65–68; Matsumoto, "SWB System. A Software Factory," p. 308.

60. Matsumoto response to survey questions; Matsumoto interviews.

61. Kazuo Matsumura et al., "Trend Toward Reusable Module Component: Design and Coding Technique 50SM," *Proceedings of the Eleventh Annual International Computer Software and Applications Conference—COMPSAC '87* (Washington, D.C.: IEEE Computer Society Press, October 7–9, 1987), p. 45.

62. Unless noted, this discussion is based on Matsumoto, "SWB System. A Software Factory," p. 314; Matsumoto, "Management of Industrial Software Production," pp. 60, 68–69; Matsumoto, "A Software Factory," pp. 171–74; Matsumoto response to survey questions; and Matsumoto interviews.
63. Interviews with Ikeda and Yamamoto; Matsumoto, "A Software Factory," pp. 171–74.
64. Ikeda interview.
65. Ebata interview.
66. Ikeda interview.
67. Ebata and Kishi interviews.
68. Matsumoto response to survey questions.
69. Matsumoto and Yamamoto, "The SWB System Supports etc.," pp. 76–77, and Matsumura et al., "Trend toward Reusable Module Component," pp. 45–52.
70. Kishi interview.
71. Ebata interview.
72. Shimoda, *Sofutouea kojo*, pp. 109–12.
73. Iizuka Matohi and Iwamoto Tadahiro, "OA-yo sofutouea kaihatsu shien shisutemu MYSTAR" [MYSTAR, software development support system for office automation], *Toshiba rebyu* 41, 8, 1986, pp. 689–92.
74. Matsumoto interviews.
75. Descriptions of these are contained in *Toshiba rebyu: tokushu—sofutouea seisan gijutsu* [Toshiba review: special issue on software production technology] 41, 8, 1986.
76. See Yutaka Ohfude, "Expected Changes in Software Development Using Engineering Work Station," *Proceedings of Fall Joint Computer Conference—FJCC '87* (Washington, D.C.: IEEE Computer Society Press, October 25–29, 1987), pp. 143–46.
77. Kaneko Shinichi, Yamashita Katsuhiko, and Yuki Hiroshi, "Sofutouea no buhin-ka—sairiyo shien gijutsu" [Technology for development and reuse of software parts], *Toshiba rebyu* 41, 8, 1986, p. 680.
78. Takahashi Ikumune and Ohfude Yutaka, "Sofutouea seisan kogyo-ka shisutemu IMAP" [Industrialized software production system IMAP], *Toshiba rebyu* 41, 8, 1986, p. 668.

Chapter 6

1. See Table 4.1 and NEC Corporation, *Annual Report 1987*.
2. *Japan Economic Journal*, Dec. 13, 1986, p. 22; interview with Dr. Hiromu Kaneda, former managing director and current corporate advisor, NEC Corporation, Sept. 26, 1985.
3. *Datamation*, June 15, 1987, pp. 30–32.
4. Interviews with Dr. Yukio Mizuno, senior vice-president, NEC Corporation, Sept. 26, 1985 and Aug. 25, 1988; and Usui Kenji, "NEAC kaihatsu shi (2)" [History of the development of the NEAC], *Computopia*, September 1975, p. 17.
5. Usui, "NEAC kaihatsu shi (2)," p. 21; Nippon Denki Kabushiki Kaisha, "Konpyuta sangyo no genjo to NEC" [The current state of the computer industry and NEC], NEC Information Processing Planning Office, July 1985. The initial ACOS models were designed in cooperation with Toshiba Corporation.
6. Usui, "NEAC kaihatsu shi (2)," pp. 22–23; Nippon Denki Kabushiki Kaisha, *Nippon Denki saikin 10 nen shi* [A history of the last 10 years of Nippon Denki] (Tokyo: NEC Corporation, 1980), p. 86.
7. Mizuno interviews.
8. Kaneda interviews.
9. Mizuno Yukio and Mitsugu Mamoru, "Sofutouea bijinesu no mirai" [Future of the software business], *Konpyuta*, April 1986, pp. 85–86.
10. Mizuno interviews.

11. Nippon Denki, *Nippon Denki saikin 10 nen shi*, pp. 230–31; NEC Corporation, *Annual Report 1976*.
12. Interviews with Dr. Kiichi Fujino, vice-president, NEC Corporation, July 28, 1986 and Sept. 8, 1987.
13. Koji Kobayashi, *Computers and Communications: A Vision of C&C* (Cambridge, Mass.: MIT Press, 1985), pp. 86–88.
14. Mizuno Yukio, "Sofutouea enjiniaringu no hitsuyosei" [The need for software engineering], *Joho shori* 16, 10, October 1975, pp. 836–37.
15. Ibid., pp. 838–39.
16. Mizuno and Mitsugi, "Sofutouea bijinesu," p. 92.
17. Kiichi Fujino, "Software Development for Computers and Communications at NEC," *Computer*, November 1984, p. 62.
18. Ibid., p. 57.
19. Fujino interviews.
20. Fujino, "Software Development for Computers," pp. 57, 62.
21. Fujino Kiichi, "Sofutouea seisan gijutsu no genjo" [The trends of software engineering], *NEC gijutsu* 40, 1, 1987, pp. 3–8. See also Sano Susumu, "Sofutouea bunsan kaihatsu kankyo" [Distributed software development environment], *NEC gijutsu* 40, 1, 1987, pp. 50–58.
22. Fujino interviews; and Fujino, "Sofutouea seisan gijutsu no genjo," pp. 2–9.
23. Interviews with Motoei Azuma, former manager of the Software Management Engineering Department in the Software Product Engineering Laboratory, NEC Corporation, July 28 and Oct. 1, 1986; Mizuno and Mitsugi, "Sofutouea bijinesu," p. 91.
24. Azuma Motoei et al., "Sofutouea kanri gijutsu" [Software management engineering], *NEC gijutsu* 40, 1, 1987, p. 67.
25. Katsumi Honda and Motoei Azuma, "Designing a Software Factory by Work Environment: Models, Methodology, and Case Study," *NEC Research and Development* 88, January 1988, p. 102.
26. Ibid., p. 103.
27. Interview with Yozo Hirai, manager of the Quality Assurance Department in the Basic Software Division, NEC Corporation, Sept. 8, 1987; also, Nobuyoshi Tsuchiya et al., "A Control and Management System for the C&C Satellite Office," *NEC Research and Development* 81, April 1986, pp. 19–23; and Sen Nakabayashi et al., "C&C Satellite Office and Networks," *NEC Research and Development* 81, April 1986, pp. 8–18.
28. Fujino Kiichi, *Sofutouea kaihatsu no saizensen* [The forefront of software development] (Tokyo: Nippon Denki Bunka Senta, 1983), p. 66.
29. Fujino and Mizuno interviews.
30. Azuma and Mizuno interviews.
31. Fujino, "Sofutouea seisan gijutsu no genjo," p. 3.
32. This next section is based on Fujino and Azuma interviews.
33. Azuma interviews.
34. Fujino interviews; Yukio Mizuno, "Software Quality Improvement," *Computer*, March 1983, p. 69.
35. Mizuno, "Software Quality Improvement," p. 69.
36. This next discussion is based on Mizuno, Fujino, and Azuma interviews.
37. Mizuno, "Software Quality Improvement," p. 69.
38. Ibid., pp. 69–71.
39. Mizuno interviews and Bro Uttal, "Japan's Persistent Software Gap," *Fortune*, Oct. 15, 1984, p. 154.
40. Kobayashi, *Computers and Communications*, p. 88.
41. Azuma interviews.
42. Mizuno, "Software Quality Improvement," p. 68.
43. Fujino and Azuma interviews.
44. Fujino interviews.

45. Interviews with Susumu Horie, Engineering Section manager, Basic Software Division, NEC Software Ltd., and Hiroshi Yamaguchi, general manager, Basic Software and Application Software Development Division, NEC Software Ltd., Sept. 2, 1987.

46. Ibid. and Akira Yamada, manager, Software Education Department, NEC Software Ltd., Sept. 2, 1987.

47. Azuma and Fujino interviews.

48. Honda Katsumi et al., "Designing a Software Factory by Environment Oriented Approach," *Proceedings of the Eleventh Annual International Computer Software and Applications Conference—COMPSAC '87* (Washington, D.C.: IEEE Computer Society Press, October 7–9, 1987), p. 9.

49. Ibid., pp. 3–8.

50. Mizuno interviews.

51. Fujino, "Software Development for Computers," p. 58.

52. This section is based on Motoei Azuma and Yukio Mizuno, "STEPS: Integrated Software Standards and Its Productivity Impact," *Proceedings of IEEE Computer Society Conference—COMPCON '81* (IEEE Computer Society Press, 1981), pp. 88–89.

53. Hirai interview.

54. Fumihiko Kamijo, "Information Activities in the Japanese Software Industry," *Oxford Surveys in Information Technology* 3, 1986, pp. 31–32.

55. Yukio Mizuno, "A Quantitative Approach to Software Quality and Productivity Improvement," NEC Corporation, ca. 1985, pp. 2–3, 5. See also Barry W. Boehm, *Software Engineering Economics* (Englewood Cliffs, N.J.: Prentice-Hall, 1981), and J. W. Bailey and V. R. Basili, "A Meta Model for Software Development Resource Expenditures," *Proceedings ICSE* (New York: IEEE Computer Society Press, March 1981), vol. 5, pp. 107–16.

56. Mizuno interviews.

57. Mizuno, "A Quantitative Approach," p. 6.

58. This discussion is based on Hirai and Fujino interviews.

59. Hirai interview.

60. NEC Corporation, "QA System in NEC: Scientific Control of Production and Quality in NEC—Basic Software," unpublished internal document, Sept. 8, 1987, pp. 10–12.

61. Fujino interviews.

62. Motoei Azuma et al., "SPD: A Humanized Documentation Technology," *Proceedings of the International Computer Software and Applications Conference—COMPSAC '83* (New York: IEEE Computer Society Press, November 7–11, 1983), p. 308; and Mikio Aoyama et al., "Design Specification in Japan: Tree-Structured Charts," *IEEE Software*, March 1989, pp. 31–37.

63. NEC Corporation, Software Product Engineering Laboratory, "SPD (Structured Programming Diagram)," unpublished and undated manuscript.

64. Hirai interview.

65. Ibid.

66. Mizuno interview; Software Product Engineering Laboratory, "Sofutouea kanrisha shien tsuru TOMATO" [Software managers' support tool, TOMATO], unpublished and undated manuscript.

67. Azuma et al., "Sofutouea kanri gijutsu," pp. 77–78.

68. This section is based on NEC Corporation, "QA System in NEC," pp. 14–25.

69. Fujino interviews.

70. Toshihiko Sunazuka, Motoei Azuma, and Noriko Yamagishi, "Software Quality Assessment Technology," *Proceedings ICSE* (New York: IEEE Computer Society Press, 1985), pp. 1–7.

71. Hirai interview.

72. Iwamoto Kanji and Okada Tadashi (NEC), "Purojekuto kanri tsuru" [Project control tools], *Joho shori* 20, 8, August 1979, pp. 719–24.

73. Uenohara Michiyuki (NEC) et al., "Development of Software Production and Mainte-

nance System," *Research and Development in Japan Awarded the Okochi Memorial Prize* (Tokyo, Okochi Memorial Foundation, 1984), pp. 26–32; and Shigo Osamu et al., "Tsushin-seigyo shisutemu-kei sofutouea seisan shisutemu" [Software production system for communication and control software], *NEC gijutsu* 40, 1, 1987, pp. 10–17.

74. Uenohara et al., "Development of Software Production," p. 32.

75. Hirai and Fujino interviews; Kanji Iwamoto (NEC) et al., "Early Experiences Regarding SDMS Introduction into Software Production Sites," *NEC Research and Development* 68, January 1983, p. 54.

76. Iwamoto et al., "Early Experiences Regarding SDMS," pp. 54–59.

77. Shigo, "Tsushin-seigyo shisutemu-kei," pp. 10–17.

78. This section and quotations are from Azuma and Mizuno, "STEPS," esp. pp. 87–88, 91.

79. Ibid., pp. 85–86.

80. Ibid., pp. 83, 86–88.

81. Hirai interview.

82. Fujino, "Software Development for Computers," p. 59.

83. Azuma and Mizuno, "STEPS," pp. 94–95.

84. Fujino, "Software Development for Computers," p. 59.

85. This general discussion of SEA/1 is based on Matsumoto Masao et al., "Joho shisutemu-kei sofutouea togo seisan shisutemu" [Integrated software life cycle system for information systems], *NEC gijutsu* 40, 1, 1987, pp. 19–24; Masao Matsumoto, "SEA/1 Application Software Productivity System," *IEEE SoftFair '83 Proceedings* (New York: IEEE Computer Society Press, 1983), pp. 376–78; and "NEC Probes CAD System for Software," *Electronic Engineering Times*, Feb. 11, 1985, p. 66.

86. Matsumoto Masao et al., "Joho shisutemu-kei sofutouea togo seisan shisutemu," p. 24.

87. This discussion is based on Hideo Yoshida, "Integrated Application Support System," *NEC Research and Development* 91, October 1988, pp. 116–29.

88. Iwamoto Kanji, Nishitani Yasuaki, and Wada Takashi, "Puroguramu jido seisei shisutemu" [Automatic program generation system], *NEC gijutsu* 40, 1, 1987, pp. 35–38.

89. Nakata Shuji, Yamazaki Go, and Ohishi Junko, "Deta besu oyo sotutouea seisei shisutemu" [Database oriented application software generation system], *NEC gijutsu* 40, 1, 1987, pp. 39–45.

90 Hiroyuki Kitagawa et al., "Form Document Management System SPECDOQ—Its Architecture and Implementation," *Proceedings of the Second Annual ACM-SIGOA Conference on Office Information Systems* (Toronto, June 1984); and Kitagawa Hiroyuki, "Shisutemu yokyu shiyo sakusei kanri shisutemu SPECDOQ/III" [SPECDOQ/III: system requirements specification/documentation system], *NEC gijutsu* 40, 1, 1987, pp. 28–34.

91. See, for example, the papers by Iwamoto et al., "Early Experiences Regarding SDMS Introduction into Software Production Sites," and Azuma and Mizuno, "STEPS."

Chapter 7

1. This reflects the introduction of Japanese-processing Extended Feature (JEF) in 1979, which, along with a successor version, quickly became the market leader in Japanese-language word-processing packages.

2. *Nikkei Computer*, Oct. 13, 1986, p. 75.

3. Fujitsu Ltd., "Numazu Kojo" [Numazu Works], undated company brochure.

4. Major sources for the corporate history are Usui Kenji, "FACOM kaihatsu shi" [History of FACOM development], *Computopia*, April 1975, pp. 14–24, and May 1975, pp. 16–26; Iwabuchi Akio, *Fujitsu no chosen* [Fujitsu's challenge] (Tokyo: Yamate shobo, 1984); Fujitsu Kabushiki Kaisha, *Fujitsu Kabushiki Kaisha shashi II* [History of Fujitsu Ltd., Vol. II], 1976, reprinted in Nihon Shashi Zenshu Kankokai, *Nihon shashi zenshu:*

Fujitsu shashi (Tokyo, Nihon Shashi Zenshu Kankokai 1977); Fujitsu Ltd., "FACOM no ayumi" [FACOM history], *FACOM janaru* 11, 1, pp. 20–47.

5. Minamisawa Noburo, *Nihon konpyuta hattatsu-shi* [History of the development of Japanese computers] (Tokyo: Nihon Keizai Shimbunsha, 1978), p. 145.

6. Iwabuchi, *Fujitsu no chosen*, pp. 34–42, 128–29, 198–202; Ogino Yuji et al., "Fujitsu-Hitachi no shin-konpyuta 'M shirizu' no senryaku o tettei kyumei" [A close look at the strategy of the new Fujitsu-Hitachi 'M-series' computers], *Computopia*, February 1975, pp. 17–18.

7. Dale F. Farmer, "IBM-Compatible Giants," *Datamation*, December 1981, pp. 96–97, 104; Usui, "FACOM kaihatsu shi," May 1975, pp. 17–18; *Japan Economic Journal*, Jan. 29, 1985, p. 10.

8. Iwabuchi, *Fujitsu no chosen*, p. 93; *Nikkei Computer*, Oct. 13, 1986, p. 81; "OS, Shimensu ni yushutsu" [OS, export to Siemens], *Yomiuri Shimbun*, Sept. 15, 1989, p. 7. See also Jeff Moad, "Special Report: Fujitsu Ltd.—Next Stop, World Markets," *Datamation*, Aug. 1, 1989, pp. 28–32.

9. Ogino et al., "Fujitsu-Hitachi," pp. 30–31.

10. See, for example, Franklin M. Fisher, James W. McKie, and Richard B. Mancke, *IBM and the U.S. Data Processing Industry: An Economic History* (New York: Praeger, 1983); Franklin M. Fisher, John J. McGowan, and Joel E. Greenwood, *Folded, Spindled, and Mutilated: Economic Analysis and U.S. v. IBM* (Cambridge, Mass.: MIT Press, 1983); Richard Thomas DeLamarter, *Big Blue: IBM's Use and Abuse of Power* (New York: Dodd, Mead, 1986).

11. See *Computerworld*, Dec. 5, 1988, pp. 1, 4; *New York Times*, Nov. 30, 1988, p. 1; *Business Week*, Dec. 19, 1988, pp. 100–102; and materials from the American Arbitration Association distributed at a May 25, 1989 press conference in Tokyo, available through Fujitsu Ltd., Department of Public Relations, Marunouchi 1-6-1, Tokyo, Japan.

12. Fujitsu Ltd., Information Processing Group, No. 1 Software Division, "Sofutouea kaihatsu: hinshitsu-seisansei kojo ni tsuite" [Software development: quality and productivity improvement], unpublished company document, received Sept. 24, 1985, pp. 40–41; and interviews with Tadashi Yoshida, general manager, Quality Assurance Department, Software Division (Numazu Works), Fujitsu Ltd., July 31, 1986, Sept. 7, 1987, and Aug. 22, 1989.

13. Fujitsu Kabushiki Kaisha, "Kaihatsu taisei: Densanki Jigyo Honbu, Sofutouea Jigyobu" [Organizational structure, Computer Group, Software Division], unpublished company document, 1986.

14. Yoshida interviews and written comments on a draft of this chapter, Dec. 8, 1988.

15. Shimoda Hirotsugu, *Sofutouea kojo* [Software factories] (Tokyo: Toyo Keizai Shimposha, 1986), p. 82; interview with Katsuro Yamaji, deputy general manager, Software Division, Fujitsu Ltd., July 31, 1986; interview with Mamoru Mitsugi, senior executive director and general manager, Systems Engineering Group, Fujitsu Ltd., Aug. 25, 1988.

16. Interviews with Hiroshi Narafu, section manager, Software Factory Department, Fujitsu Ltd., Aug. 23, 1988 and July 20, 1989, and written correspondence, Dec. 6, 1988.

17. Interviews with Noritoshi Murakami, manager, Systems Development Engineering Department, SE Technical Support Center, Systems Engineering Group, Fujitsu Ltd., Sept. 1, 1987, March 22, 1988, Aug. 23, 1988, and July 20, 1989.

18. Yoshida interviews.

19. This discussion is based on Kawaguchi Izawa, "Shoki no shisutemu sofutouea: FONTAC 8040 MONITOR no kaihatsu made o chushin to shite" [Early systems software: focus on period through the FONTAC 8040 MONITOR development], *Joho shori* 24, 3, March 1983, pp. 225–37; Usui, "FACOM kaihatsu shi," May 1975, pp. 20–21, 25; Fujitsu, *Fujitsu shashi II*, p. 104; Yamamoto Takuma, "Opereteingu shisutemu kaihatsu no omoide" [Recollections on operating system development], in Kyoto Daigaku Ogata Keisanki Senta (ed.), *Kyoto Daigaku Ogata Keisanki Senta 10 nen-shi* [A 10-year history of

the Kyoto University Ogata Computer Center] (Kyoto: Kyoto University, 1980), pp. 217–19; Uemura Mitsuo, "Sofutouea kaihatsu no omoide" [Recollections of software development], in *Kyoto Daigaku*, pp. 230–36; Okamoto Akira, "MONITOR-V shisutemu no omoide" [Recollections of the MONITOR-V system], in *Kyoto Daigaku*, pp. 224–29; and Iwabuchi, *Fujitsu no chosen*, pp. 44, 221–22.

20. Ogino et al., Fujitsu-Hitachi," pp. 30–31; Tabata Akira, "Kihon sofutouea no kaihatsu" [Basic software development], *FACOM janaru* 11, 1, 1985, p. 54; Shimoda, *Sofutouea kojo*, p. 73.

21. Mitsugi interview.

22. Quoted in Shimoda, *Sofutouea kojo*, pp. 73–76.

23. This discussion is based on Fujitsu Ltd. "Sofutouea kaihatsu," esp. pp. 7–10; Yoshida interviews; and Tadashi Yoshida, "Attaining Higher Quality in Software Development—Evaluation in Practice," *Fujitsu Scientific and Technical Journal* 21, 3, July 1985, p. 306.

24. Fujitsu Ltd., Computer Group, Software Division, "Sofutouea no hinshitsu kanri" [Software quality control], unpublished company document, Sept. 11, 1985, p. 6; and Fujitsu Ltd., "Sofutouea kaihatsu," p. 6.

25. Nihon Noritsu Kyokai (Japan Management Association), *Fujitsu no ko-shinraisei undo* [Fujitsu's high-reliability movement] (Tokyo: Nihon Noritsu Kyokai, 1985), esp. pp. 144–76.

26. This following discussion is based on Yoshida, "Attaining Higher Quality in Software Development," pp. 305, 308–309, 314–15.

27. Fujitsu Ltd. "Sofutouea kaihatsu," p. 15.

28. Keizo Tatsumi (Quality Assurance Department, Computer Software Development Group, Fujitsu Ltd.), "Test Case Design Support System" (Paper delivered at the International Conference on Quality Control, Tokyo, October 1987), pp. 1–2.

29. Also citing Taguchi's 1976 book in Japanese is a more detailed article on these methods used in Fujitsu. See Sato Shinobu and Shimokawa Haruki, "Jikken keikau-ho o mochiita sofutouea no tesuto komoku settei-ho" [Software test-case selection method based on experimental design methodology], Sofutouea Seisan ni okeru Hinshitsu Kanri Shinpojium [Symposium on quality control in software], no. 4, ca. 1983.

30. Murakami and Yoshida interviews.

31. Fujitsu, "FACOM M-shirizu OSIV/X8 FSP," undated customer product information, pp. 171–173.

32. "SDAS: Application Software Development Made Easy," *Electronics News from Fujitsu*, July 1987, p. 2; Yoshida interviews; Fujitsu Ltd., "Sofutouea no hinshitsu kanri," p. 16; and Yoshida's Feb. 8, 1987 written response to Jan. 20, 1987 Cusumano questionnaire on "Large-Scale Systems Software." Yoshida believed that a major reason U.S. firms have not refined flow-chart systems to this extent was because, for native speakers of English or similar languages, writing in a high-level computer language is close to their native language. For the Japanese, however, this was not the case, and YACII, PAD, or SPD diagrams could be written in Japanese, making them easier for Japanese programmers to use.

33. The literature on YACII and YPS, as well as other systems at other Japanese firms, is large and growing. The best summary available in English is Mikio Aoyama et al., "Design Specification in Japan: Tree-Structured Charts," *IEEE Software*, March 1989, pp. 31–37. Comments here are also based on papers on YACII Fujitsu engineers presented at Japan's Information Processing Association (Joho Shori Gakkai) annual conventions in 1983, 1985, 1986, and 1987.

34. Yoshida interviews.

35. Fujitsu Ltd., "Sofutouea kaihatsu," p. 29.

36. "Fujitsu," *Computopia*, June 1975, p. 92; *Fujitsu Kabushiki Kaisha shashi II*, pp. 102–103; *Nikkei Computer*, Oct. 13, 1986, p. 82; Usui, "FACOM kaihatsu shi," May 1975, pp. 25–26.

37. These comments that follow are based mainly on the interview with Narafu, Aug. 23, 1988, and his written comments to Cusumano, dated Dec. 6, 1988, that responded to a draft of this chapter; interview with Harukazu Onishi, manager, Software Factory Department, Aug. 23, 1988; and interviews with a former programmer in the factory who worked on distribution systems during 1981–1983, Hiromi Sakurai, May 4, 1988. Mr. Narafu has been employed in the factory since 1977; Mr. Onishi joined the factory in 1979. Also participating in these sessions with Narafu and Onishi were Noritoshi Murakami as well as Takashi Sano, deputy section manager, Software Factory Department, and two employees from the factory, Nobuhiko Sugizaki and Yasuhiro Yuma.

38. See Noritoshi Murakami, Isao Miyanari, and Kazuo Yabuta, "SDEM and SDSS: Overall Approach to Improvement of the Software Development Process," in Horst Hunke (ed.), *Software Engineering Environments* (Amsterdam: North-Holland, 1981), pp. 281–93.

39. Mitsugi interview.

40. Yoshiro Nakamura, Ryuzo Miyahara, and Hideshi Takeuchi, "Complementary Approach to the Effective Software Development," *Proceedings of the International Computer Software and Applications Conference—COMPSAC '78* (New York: IEEE Computer Society Press, November 1978), p. 236.

41. Ibid., pp. 235–36.

42. Murakami, Miyanari, and Yabuta, "SDEM and SDSS," pp. 286–87; Watanuki Hisashi, Hatta Makoto, and Okudaira Hajime, "Apurikeshon puroguramu kaihatsu toki no hinshitsu kanri" [Quality control for application program development], *Fujitsu* 34, 6, 1983, pp. 857–65; Fujitsu Ltd., "An Introduction to Software Factory Dept.," July 27, 1988, Systems Engineering Group, unpublished in-house document, pp. 9–10.

43. Fujitsu Ltd., "An Introduction to Software Factory Dept.," p. 11.

44. Narafu and Murakami interviews.

45. Murakami, Miyanari, and Yabuta, "SDEM and SDSS," pp. 284–86.

46. Murakami interviews and Fujitsu Ltd., "An Introduction to Software Factory Dept.," pp. 5–6.

47. Fujitsu Ltd., "An Introduction to Software Factory Dept.," pp. 5–6.

48. These comments again are based on Narafu and Murakami interviews as well as Narafu's written comments.

49. This section is based on interviews and correspondence with Murakami, Narafu, and Sakurai; Fujitsu Ltd., "Kyoiku jigyo no gaiyo" [Overview of education], in-house customer materials, August 1988 (this is the source of cited statistics on education); Murakami, Miyanari, and Yabuta, "SDEM and SDSS," p. 288.

50. *Nikkei Computer*, Oct. 13, 1986, pp. 80–81.

51. See Chapters 2 and 8 for additional discussions of CASE tools and AI applications.

52. Fujitsu Ltd., "SDAS: Application Software Development Made Easy," *Electronics News from Fujitsu*, July 1987, pp. 1–2.

53. Murakami, Miyanari, and Yabuta, "SDEM and SDSS," pp. 289–93.

54. Noritoshi Murakami and Tomio Takahashi, responses to Jan. 19, 1987 Cusumano surveys on "Large-Scale Applications Software" and "Software Facilities" (Sept. 1987); and Mikio Aoyama et al., "Design Specification in Japan: Tree-Structured Charts," *IEEE Software*, March 1989, pp. 31–37.

55. Uemura Takaki, "Gekihensuru sofutouea kaihatsu sutairu" [Rapidly-changing software-development styles], *Nikkei Computer*, Sept. 20, 1982, pp. 61–64.

56. Nagata Yuzuru, Mori Kuniaki, and Takahashi Tomio, "Shisutemu keikaku giho EPGII to C-NAPII" [System planning methodologies EPGII and NAPII], *Fujitsu* 39, 1, January 1988, pp. 13–20.

57. Fujitsu, "FACOM M-shirizu OSIV/X8 FSP," pp. 193–94; Fujitsu Ltd., "Sofutouea kaihatsu," p. 42; Sano and Onishi interviews.

58. Kometani Tadatoshi and Arakawa Yoshihiro, "Onrain shisutemu no kokateki kaihatsu

e no kokoromi—ACS PARADIGM" [An attempt at efficient on-line system development—ACS PARADIGM], *Fujitsu* 35, 4, 1984, pp. 445–53.

59. This discussion of BAGLES is based on Uemura, "Gekihensuru sofutouea kaihatsu sutairu," pp. 56–69; Wada Haruhiko, Fujisa Minoru, and Yanagisawa Minoru, "Kinyu onrain shisutemu kaihatsu shien tsuru—BAGLES" [Financial on-line systems development support tool—BAGLES], *Fujitsu* 34, 2, 1983, pp. 271–79; Fujitsu Financial Systems Engineering Development Department, "Kinyu onrain shisutemu kaihatsu shien tsuru—BAGLES' [Financial on-line systems development support tool—BAGLES], *FACOM janaru* 10, 12, 1984, pp. 146–55; Yokoyama Takeshi, Wada Haruhiko, and Ema Michiko, "Ronri sekkei gengo BAGLES ni okeru bubun-ka gijutsu" [Modularization technology in the BAGLES logic design language], Joho Shori Gakkai 'Puruguramu Sekkei-ho no Jitsuyo-ka to Hatten' Shinpojium [Information Processing Association Symposium on the application and development of program design methods], April 1984, pp. 77–86; Omori Noriyuki, "Ginko onrain shisutemu no koritsu-teki kochiku jitsurei" [An actual example of efficiently constructing an on-line banking system], *Data Management*, January 1987, pp. 66–73; Tsubuhari Yukio, "Tosha no kinyu shisutemu kaihatsu ni okeru seisansei kojo" [Productivity improvement in the company's financial systems development], in Kindai Serususha (ed.), *Jitsurei konpyuta bankingu*, 13, Jan. 20, 1987, pp. 226–31; Fujitsu Ltd., "BAGLES kaihatsu no keiro" [The process of BAGLES development], internal company document, March 20, 1986; and "BAGLES no gaiyo" [Outline of BAGLES], internal company documents, March 8, 1987 and July 3, 1987.

60. Ueki Sadahiro, Miyauchi Kazuto, and Nakada Haruyoshi, "Koseisansei tsuru CASET" [High-productivity tool CASET], *Fujitsu* 39, 1, January 1988, pp. 21–28.

61. See "Fujitsu Software: Banking to Realtime," *Electronic Engineering Times*, Feb. 11, 1985, pp. 63–64.

62. This discussion is based on Kazuo Yabuta, Akihiro Yoshioka, and Noritoshi Murakami, "'Software CAD': A Generalized Environment for Graphical Software Development Techniques," *Proceedings of the International Computer Software and Applications Conference—COMPSAC '87* (Washington, D.C.: IEEE Computer Society Press, 1987), pp. 1–8, and an interview with Murakami, July 20, 1989.

63. Fujii Norio, Ginbayashi Jun, and Murakami Noritoshi, "Kaiwa ni yoru konsarutesohn moderu kochiku tsuru" [Tool for construction of consultation models], *Fujitsu* 39, 3, 1986, pp. 223–28.

64. Fujitsu Ltd., "System for Supporting Software Development (for Switching Systems Software)," internal company document, 1977; Murakami interviews; Kato Hideki et al., "Chishiki besu o mochiita SDL shien shisutemu" [Intelligence-based SDL support system], Joho Shori Gakkai (Information Processing Association), 'Chishiki Kogaku to Jinko chino' Shipojium, May 8, 1984, pp. 1–8.

65. Matsuzaki Minoru and Yanagita Toshihiko, "SAA to SDAS/SIA de IBM to Fujitsu ga kisou" [IBM and Fujitsu compete with SAA and SDAS/SIA], *Nikkei Computer*, June 22, 1987, pp. 83–92.

66. "SDAS: Application Software Development Made Easy," p. 3.

67. Akiyama Masayuki and Nishimura Shuji, "SDAS ni okeru pakkeji kaihatsu to sono tekiyo gijutsu" [SDAS improving package development and its application needs], *Fujitsu* 39, 1, January 1988, pp. 36–41.

68. *Nikkei Computer*, Oct. 13, 1986, pp. 81–82.

69. Akiyama and Nishimura, "SDAS ni okeru pakkeji kaihatsu to sono tekiyo gijutsu," and "SDAS: Application Software Development Made Easy," p. 3.

70. Murakami, Miyanari, and Yabuta, "SDEM and SDSS," pp. 287–88.

71. Fujitsu Ltd., "An Introduction to the Software Factory Dept.," pp. 7–8.

72. Fujitsu, "FACOM M-shirizu OSIV/X8 FSP," pp. 193–94.

73. Murakami Noritoshi, Komoda Junichi, and Yabuta Kazuo, "Paradaimu ni yoru

sofutouea no seisansei kojo" [Productivity improvement through the use of PARA-DIGM], *Fujitsu* 33, 4, 1982, pp. 49, 53–55.

74. Fujitsu Ltd., "Paradigm," *FACOM janaru* 9, 3, 1983, pp. 136–37.

75. See Kometani and Arakawa, "ACS-PARADIGM," esp. pp. 452–53.

76. Tsubuhari, "Tosha no kinyu shisutemu kaihatsu ni okeru seisansei kojo," p. 231.

77. "Fujitsu Software: Banking to Realtime," pp. 63–64.

78. Fukuta Zenichi, Yoshihara Tadao, and Maruyama Takeshi, "SDAS sogo kaihatsu shisutemu no teisho" [SDAS systems development architecture and support facilities), *Fujitsu* 39, 1, January 1988, pp. 3–12.

79. Akiyama and Nishimura, "SDAS ni okeru pakkeji kaihatsu to sono tekiyo gijutsu," p. 38.

80. Yoshida Tadashi, "Sofutouea no keiryo-ka" [Quantifying software], *Joho shori* 26, 1, January 1985, pp. 48–51.

81. Yabuta, Yoshioka, and Murakami, "Software CAD," pp. 1–7.

Chapter 8

1. A comprehensive discussion of these various efforts, especially in hardware, is Marie Anchordoguy, *Computers Inc.: Japan's Challenge to IBM* (Cambridge, Mass.: Council on East Asian Studies/Harvard University Press 1989).

2. Ibid., pp. 19–58.

3. Robert Arfman, "The Japanese Software Industry: A Comparative Analysis of Software Development Strategy and Technology of Selected Corporations," Master's Thesis, Cambridge, Mass.: M.I.T. Management of Technology Program, May 1988, pp. 32–36.

4. Anchordoguy, *Computers Inc.*, pp. 131–34.

5. Kouichi Kishida, "Technology Transfer Aspects of Environment Construction," Tokyo, Software Research Associates, unpublished and undated manuscript, ca. 1986, pp. 4–6. See also Anchordoguy, *Computers Inc.*, pp. 148–49, 158.

6. Kishida, "Technology Transfer Aspects," pp. 6–9; Arfman, "The Japanese Software Industry," pp. 35–36, 60.

7. Arfman, "The Japanese Software Industry," p. 37.

8. See Joho Sabisu Sangyo Kyokai (ed.), *Joho sabisu sangyo hakusho 1987* [Information services industry white paper 1987] (Tokyo: Joho Sabisu Sangyo Kyokai, 1987), pp. 38, 283–84.

9. Thomas R. Howell et al., "Japanese Software: The Next Competitive Challenge" (Arlington, Va.: ADAPSO, the Computer Software and Services Industry Association, January 1989), p. 38; Joint Software Development Corporation, "FASET—Formal Approach to Software Environments Technology—Overview of FASET Project," unpublished outline, January 1987.

10. The best source of technical information on TRON, and the basis for the discussion in this section, is a special issue of *IEEE Micro*, April 1987, edited by Ken Sakamura. Particularly useful is the lead article, Ken Sakamura, "TRON," pp. 8–14. The April 1988 issue of *IEEE Micro* also contains two articles describing further technical progress. For general discussions of the TRON project, see Anchordoguy, *Computers Inc.*, pp. 160–62; Ken Sakamura, "Japan's New Strategy in Computer Software," *Electronic Business*, Nov. 15, 1986, pp. 82–84; Miyoko Sakurai, "Support Swells for TRON Realtime OS Project in Japan," *Electronic Engineering Times*, Dec. 1, 1986, p. 27.

11. This section is based primarily on Noboru Akima and Fusatake Ooi, "Industrializing Software Development: A Japanese Approach," *IEEE Software*, March 1989, pp. 13–21. Other sources include Arfman, "The Japanese Software Industry," pp. 43–61; Information Technology Promotion Agency, *Sigma News* 1, April 1986; and Anchordoguy, *Computers, Inc.*, pp. 158–160.

12. Arfman, "The Japanese Software Industry," pp. 60–61.

13. Information Technology Promotion Agency, "Sigma Project," Tokyo, 1989, p. 7.

14. Akima and Ooi, "Industrializing Software Development," p. 13.

15. Interview with Fusatake Ooi, senior engineer and director, Project Management Division, Sigma System Project, July 18, 1989.

16. Akima and Ooi, "Industrializing Software Development," pp. 17, 19.

17. Arfman, "The Japanese Software Industry," pp. 52–58.

18. Anchordoguy, *Computers Inc.*, pp. 158–59.

19. Ooi interview.

20. See Shimoda Hirotsugu, *Sofutouea kojo* [Software factories] (Tokyo: Toyo Keizai Shimposha, 1986), pp. 50–64.

21. Interviews with Rikio Onai, senior manager, and Ryoichi Hosoya, executive manager, NTT Software Laboratories, Nippon Telegraph and Telephone Corporation, July 17, 1989; and Kenshiro Toyosaki, department manager, Software Division, Nippon Telegraph and Telephone Corporation, Sept. 3, 1987.

22. Mikio Aoyama et al., "Design Specification in Japan: Tree-Structured Charts," *IEEE Software*, March 1989, pp. 31–37.

23. Toyosaki interview.

24. Nippon Telegraph and Telephone Corporation, "Software Development Division Outline," internal company document, July 1986.

25. Takenaka Ichiro et al., "Kokan sofutouea-yo sogo seisan shien shisutemu" [Integrated support system for switching systems software production], *Kenkyu jitsuyoka hokoku 36*, 6, 1987, pp. 799–809.

26. Shimoda, *Sofutouea kojo*, pp. 198–204; Nippon Telegraph and Telephone Corporation, "NTT Software Laboratories," Tokyo, 1989.

27. Nippon Telegraph and Telephone Corporation, "NTT Electrical Communications Laboratories," Tokyo, NTT Public Relations Group, 1987, pp. 18–19.

28. NTT Software Laboratories, "HD System," undated company document, received July 1989.

29. Nippon Telegraph and Telephone Corporation, "NTT Software Laboratories."

30. Interviews with Naoharu Miyakawa, manager, Software Engineering Strategy, Engineering Department, Mitsubishi Electric; and Kenzaburo Akechi, manager, Software Engineering Section, Production Administration Department, Computer Works, Mitsubishi Electric, Oct. 28, 1987.

31. Akira Takano et al., "A Software Development System: Solon," Kamakura, Information Systems and Electronics Development Laboratory, Mitsubishi Electric Corporation, July 1987.

32. Tsutomu Ohkawa and Naoharu Miyakawa, "Software Development Office Environment in Mitsubishi Electric Corp.," Mitsubishi Electric Corporation, 1987.

33. Mitsubishi Electric Corporation, "Software Reuse—Our Approach," Kamakura, Computer Works, 1986; and Miyakawa and Akechi interviews.

34. One of the first publications to bring wide attention to the project was Edward A. Feigenbaum and Pamela McCorduck, *The Fifth Generation: Artificial Intelligence and Japan's Computer Challenge to the World* (New York: Signet, 1983, 1984).

35. This discussion is based primarily on the following sources: Institute for New Generation Computer Technology, "Fifth Generation Computer Systems Project," Tokyo, unpublished manuscript, October 1986; Kazuhiro Fuchi, "Hop, Step, and Jump," *Fifth Generation Computer Systems Project: Report on ICOT's Research and Development in the Intermediate Stage* (Tokyo: Institute for New Generation Computer Technology, 1988), pp. 1–5; Takahashi Kurozumi, "Present Status and Plans for Research and Development," *Fifth Generation Computer Systems Project: Report on ICOT's Research and Development in the Intermediate Stage*, pp. 7–19; and interviews with Dr. Koichi Furukawa, deputy director, Research Center, and Dr. Kazunori Ueda, senior researcher, Institute for New Generation Computer Technology, July 19, 1989.

36. For a nontechnical but useful description of PROLOG and comparisons with LISP and

other languages, see John E. Savage, Susan Magidson, and Alex M. Stein, *The Mystical Machine: Issues and Ideas in Computing* (Reading, Mass.: Addison-Wesley, 1986), pp. 219–46.

37. Hideki Katoh, Hiroyuki Yoshida, and Masakatsu Sugimoto, "Logic-Based Retrieval and Reuse of Software Modules," Kawasaki, Fujitsu Ltd., unpublished and undated manuscript.

38. M. Denicoff et al., "Japanese Technology Evaluation Program: JTECH Panel Reporting on Advanced Computing in Japan," McLean, Va., Science Applications International Corporation, December 1987, pp. 3–5. The chairman of this panel, M. Denicoff, was on the board of directors of Thinking Machines Corporation, a leading AI firm. Other panel members included faculty and staff members from Massachussets Institute of Technology, SRI International, Stanford University, and New York University.

39. This discussion of MCC is based primarily on Janet Marie Kendrick, "Managing Cooperative Research for Fifth Generation Computer Development: A Comparison of Japan's M.I.T.I. and U.S. Microelectronics and Computer Technology Corporation Projects," Master's Thesis, Cambridge, Mass.: M.I.T. Management of Technology Program, May 1988. Other major sources on MCC include William H. Murphy, "The Micro-Electronics and Computer Technology Corporation," Doctoral dissertation, Boston, Mass., Harvard Graduate School of Business Administration, May 1987; and Merton J. Peck, "Joint R&D: The Case of Microelectronics and Computer Technology Corporation," *Research Policy* 15, May 1986, pp. 219–31.

40. This overview of MCC efforts in software is based on Microelectronics and Computer Technology Corporation, "Software Technology Program," Technical Paper # ILO-008-89, Spring 1989, Videocassettes 1–3. The presentations on which this discussion is based were by Les Belady (Software Technology Program—Research Overview), Ted Biggerstaff (Overview, Information Representation-Reuse/Recovery), and Bill Curtis (Process, Methods, Tools).

41. Karen Fitzgerald and Paul Wallach, "Next-Generation Race Bogs Down," *IEEE Spectrum*, June 1987, p. 32.

42. Kenneth Flamm, *Targeting the Computer: Government Support and International Competition* (Washington, D.C.: Brookings Institute, 1987), pp. 72–75; Feigenbaum and McCorduck, *Fifth Generation*, pp. 91–92, 271–76.

43. Fitzgerald and Wallach, "Next-Generation Race Bogs Down," p. 31.

44. This discussion is based on Gregory Michael Toole, "ESPRIT and European Software Capability: An Analysis of Cooperation in Software Technology R&D," Master's Thesis, Cambridge, Mass., M.I.T. Sloan School of Management, May 1989.

45. Fitzgerald and Wallach, "Next Generation Race Bogs Down," p. 33.

Conclusion

1. For a general discussion of organizational life cycles, see Stephen P. Robbins, *Organization Theory: Structure, Design, and Applications* (Englewood Cliffs, N.J.: Prentice-Hall, 1987), esp. pp. 16–19.

2. Many books and articles discuss the meaning of a strategic process. One treatment, complete with an extensive bibliography, is Arnoldo Hax and Nicolas Majluf, *Strategic Management: An Integrative Perspective* (Englewood Cliffs, N.J.: Prentice-Hall, 1984).

3. On the notion of scale economies in software, see Barry W. Boehm, *Software Engineering Economics* (Englewood Cliffs, N.J.: Prentice-Hall, 1981); and R. Banker and C. Kemerer, "Scale Economy in New Software Development," *IEEE Transactions on Software Engineering* 15, 10, October 1989, pp. 1199–205.

4. For discussions of why and how high productivity and quality may go together, see, for example, Philip B. Crosby, *Quality is Free* (New York: New American Library, 1979); William J. Abernathy, Kim B. Clark, and Alan M. Kantrow, *Industrial Renaissance* (New York: Basic Books, 1983), esp. pp. 57–67; David A. Garvin, *Managing Quality* (New

York: Free Press, 1988); and John F. Krafcik, "Triumph of the Lean Production System," *Sloan Management Review*, Fall 1988, pp. 41–51.

5. My thanks once again to Joel Moses of the Department of Electrical Engineering and Computer Science at M.I.T. for continuing to educate me and the software world in general on this point.

6. On this point, I must extend my thanks to Vice-President Robert Martin of Bell Communications Research for pushing me to clarify the extent of Japanese reusability, and for his suspicion that most reuse was not across vertical product lines.

7. See Information Technology Promotion Agency, *Sigma Project* (Tokyo: Information Technology Promotion Agency, 1989), p. 2.

8. There is much literature on this issue that argues physical proximity in engineering or R&D organizations usually contributes positively to communication and problem solving, especially in complex projects. See, for example, Thomas J. Allen, *Managing the Flow of Technology* (Cambridge, Mass.: MIT Press, 1977); and Michael L. Tushman, "Managing Communication Networks in R&D Laboratories," *Sloan Management Review*, Winter 1979, pp. 37–49, reprinted in M. L. Tushman and W. L. Moore, *Readings in the Management of Innovation* (Cambridge, Mass.: Ballinger, 1988).

9. An important topic in itself is the impact of computer-aided technologies on production activities in general as well as in software development. For discussions of both the positive and negative consequences of such technologies, see Larry Hirshhorn, *Beyond Mechanization: Work and Technology in a Postindustrial Age* (Cambridge, Mass.: MIT Press, 1984); Shoshana Zuboff, *In the Age of the Smart Machine: The Future of Work and Power* (New York: Basic Books, 1988); and Wanda J. Orlikowski, "Information Technology in Post-Industrial Organizations: An Exploration of the Computer-Mediation of Production Work," Ph.D. dissertation, Graduate School of Business, New York University, November 1988.

10. See, for example, Frederick P. Brooks, *The Mythical Man-Month* (Reading, Mass.: Addison-Wesley, 1975); Capers Jones, *Programming Productivity* (New York: McGraw-Hill, 1986); as well as Boehm, *Software Engineering Economics*, and Banker and Kemerer, "Scale Economy in New Software Development."

11. Bruce W. Arden, ed., *What Can Be Automated?* (Cambridge, Mass.: MIT Press, 1980), p. 797.

Appendix A

1. Additional questions were sent to survey participants, although comments from the respondees, site visits and interviews, as well as a partial correlation analysis, revealed that many of the noncore questions were not particularly useful for measuring "rationalization" along large-scale engineering and manufacturing lines. Three questions, for example, asked for emphasis on standardization of languages for high-level design, module description, and coding. It turned out that Japanese and English were mainly used for high-level design, and many managers did not know how to answer. The Japanese tended to develop specialized languages for module description because they were less comfortable than U.S. programmers in using English-based languages for this purpose, which made it unfair to U.S. firms to use this question; and coding languages were often determined by customers. A question about top-down design was discarded because emphasis on this tended to contrast with a more factory-type process of combining new and old code in layers. Similarly, questions about emphasis on high-level abstraction or layering were discarded because not everyone knew how to interpret these.

2. In the case of Toshiba, a single large facility (approximately 2,300 programmers) had different departments producing both systems and applications programs using similar procedures and tools, and the manager responsible for technical development, Dr. Yoshihiro Matsumoto, submitted one set of answers and asked that they be counted twice, under both systems and applications facilities.

3. This procedure is recommended as a simple data reduction technique by A. L. Comrey, *A First Course in Factor Analysis* (New York: Academic Press, 1973); and Barbara G. Tabachnick and Linda S. Fidell, *Using Multivariate Statistics* (New York: Harper and Row, 1983). Comrey suggested that loadings of 0.55 (explaining 30 percent of the variance) were "very good," and 0.63 (40 percent variance) or over were "excellent."

4. Interview with Anne Smith Duncan, software engineering manager, Software Development Technology, Digital Equipment Corporation (Nashua, N.H.), Feb. 10, 1988.

5. Interviews with Matsumoto Yoshiharu, R&D department manager; Matsuzaki Yoshizo, Applications Software Department manager; and Takahashi Tomoo, Applications Software Department deputy manager, Hitachi Software Engineering, Sept. 3, 1987.

6. The top three Japanese firms ranked by software sales in 1986 were NEC ($507 million), Fujitsu ($389 million), and Hitachi ($331 million). NEC ranked fourth in the world, behind IBM ($5,514 million), Unisys ($861 million), and Digital Equipment Corporation $560 million). The Japanese sales figures considerably understated actual software development, because Japanese firms included ("bundled") systems software with mainframe and minicomputer hardware prices, although the size of systems software operations corresponds roughly to hardware sales. The largest Japanese producers of mainframes by 1986 sales were Fujitsu ($2,470 million), NEC ($2,275 million), Hitachi ($1,371 million), and Mitsubishi ($185 million); the largest sellers of minicomputers were Toshiba ($766 million), Fujitsu ($620 million), and Mitsubishi ($475 million). On the U.S. side, IBM was by far the world's largest producer of hardware and software; three of its facilities are represented in the survey. Unisys, which ranked second in world software sales, had two facilities in the survey. In services, TRW ranked first and General Motors/EDS third; Control Data, Martin Marietta, and NTT sixth, seventh, and eighth, respectively; Boeing and IBM twelveth and thirteenth. See *Datamation*, June 15, 1987, pp. 28–32. Other large Japanese producers of software included in this survey were subsidiaries of Hitachi and NEC, including Nippon Business Consultants and Hitachi Software Engineering (Hitachi Ltd.), as well as NEC Software, NEC Information Systems, and Nippon Electronics Development (NEC Corporation). See Kiriu Hiroshi, *Sofutouea sangyo no jitsuzo* [The status of the software industry] (Tokyo: Nikkan Shobo, 1986).

Appendix B

1. Michael A. Cusumano and Chris F. Kemerer, "A Quantitative Analysis of U.S. and Japanese Practice and Performance in Software Development," *Management Science*, November 1990.

2. *Datamation*, June 1, 1985, pp. 58–120; Kiriu Hiroshi, *Sofutouea sangyo no jitsuzo* [The status of the software industry] (Tokyo: Nikkan Shobo, 1986).

3. These follow categories used in Capers Jones, *Programming Productivity* (New York: McGraw-Hill, 1986).

4. Ibid., p. 49, and T. Capers Jones, "A New Look at Languages," *Computerworld*, Nov. 7, 1988, pp. 97–103.

Appendix C

1. *Nikkei Computer*, Sept. 26, 1988, pp. 69–99.
2. Ibid., March 14, 1988, pp. 58–86.

INDEX